OFFICIAL PUBLICATION OF THE UNITED STATES OLYMPIC COMMITTEE

AMAZING AWAITS

TEAM USA AT THE GAMES OF THE XXIX OLYMPIAD

 COMMEMORATIVE PUBLICATIONS, LLC. | SALT LAKE CITY, UTAH

GOLD MEDALISTS KERRI WALSH AND MISTY MAY-TREANOR OF THE UNITED STATES CELEBRATE AFTER WINNING THE GOLD MEDAL MATCH AGAINST CHINA | *JAMIE SQUIRE/GETTY IMAGES*

JEREMY WARINER OF THE US CELEBRATES FOLLOWING THE MEN'S 400M FINAL | *OLIVIER MORIN/AFP/GETTY IMAGES*

FROM THE U.S. OLYMPIC COMMITTEE

Athletes from around the world came together in Beijing, China, to celebrate athleticism and the Olympic Ideals. The Olympic Movement is a unifying force that helps bring the world together in peace and to celebrate a common goal, and that was truly evident during the Beijing 2008 Olympic and Paralympic Games.

Over two months, the Beijing Organizing Committee for the Games of the XXIX Olympiad successfully staged the most competitive Olympic and Paralympic Games in history. A record 204 National Olympic Committees participated in the 2008 Olympic Games, and 87 countries won medals – the most ever. More than 40 World Records and 120 Olympic Records were set. The 2008 Paralympic Games welcomed athletes from 147 countries and saw 279 World Records.

Both on and off the field of play, the 2008 Olympic and Paralympic Games were spectacular. They have left a legacy for the city, the country and the worldwide Olympic Movement. We believe the Movement can be a catalyst for progress and change, which is exactly what we see happening in China today. The Games opened China to the world.

Throughout America, our athletes captured the attention of a nation. They not only displayed their outstanding athletic ability, but they were true ambassadors of everything the Olympic and Paralympic Movement stands for – excellence, friendship and respect. Their dedication and success transcends sport and demonstrates the everyday values of hard work, cooperation and fair play.

The Beijing Organizing Committee, the thousands of dedicated volunteers and the people of China did an extraordinary job as hosts. The U.S. Team was honored to participate in such a historic event.

Peter V. Ueberroth
U.S. Olympic Committee
Chairman, June 2004-October 2008

The performances of the 2008 U.S. Olympic and Paralympic Teams in Beijing, China, were among the greatest in American Olympic history. These teams represented our nation in exemplary fashion and found remarkable success on the field of play.

Team USA concluded the 2008 Olympic Games with 110 medals, leading the overall medal standings, and the U.S. Paralympic Team finished with 99 medals. In total, 810 athletes represented the United States in Beijing – 597 Olympians and 213 Paralympians – and 44 percent of them brought home medals.

The U.S. Olympic Committee takes great pride in the journey and performances of these athletes. Students and military veterans, single moms and a family of four, a 23-year-old wunderkind and NBA superstars, newcomers and five-time Olympians all came together in Beijing with the same desire and left with the experience of a lifetime. Their stories are the moments that will be forever imprinted in our memories, and we have captured them in this official commemorative book.

Through the pages of "Amazing Awaits," the images and stories of Team USA allow us to relive the spectacular moments in Beijing. This is the first book to include the reports from the Team Leaders of the U.S. Team since 1960. The Team Leaders worked side-by-side with the athletes and teams, coordinating with each sport and the U.S. Olympic Committee before, during and after the Olympic and Paralympic Games.

We are grateful for the support of partners, donors and fans who all contributed to the great success of the 2008 U.S. Olympic and Paralympic Teams. Together, we were inspired by Team USA. We hope these memories from Beijing will inspire millions of young people to pursue their dreams for years to come.

James E. Scherr
U.S. Olympic Committee
Chief Executive Officer

DAVID OLIVER OF USA WARMS UP BEFORE THE START OF THE MEN'S FIRST ROUND 110M HURDLES | *CHRISTOPHE SIMON/AFP/GETTY IMAGES*

AMAZING AWAITS

amazing awaits.

where we least expect it,
or after training for it all our lives.

it awaits in 200 meters,
in a hundredth of a second,
in our courageous first steps,
and with our every last breath.

it awaits on the shoulders of our teammates,
in the footsteps of our heroes,
when we shatter records,
and our spirits prove unbreakable.

amazing awaits
when a small-town playground takes us
to the world's stage,
and when that distance is measured in effort.
when hope makes us hopefuls,
and bravery carries us on her back.

it awaits when we cross finish lines,
and when the journey has just begun.
when we come from nothing, from nowhere,
over hurdles, over mountains.

amazing awaits in our Olympians.
in all Americans.
in the honor of victory
and the glory of pursuit.

it awaits when we work hard enough,
want badly enough,
and refuse to say we've had enough.

with a nation behind us,
with a world before us,
and within us all . . .

THE UNITED STATES TEAM CELEBRATES THEIR ROWING GOLD MEDAL IN THE WOMEN'S EIGHT | *JAMIE SQUIRE/GETTY IMAGES*

THE U.S. OLYMPIC TEAM ENTERS THE NATIONAL STADIUM BEHIND FLAG BEARER LOPEZ LOMONG AS PART OF THE OPENING CEREMONY | *CAMERON SPENCER/GETTY IMAGES*

THE US MEN'S BASKETBALL TEAM STANDS ON THE PODIUM DURING THE NATIONAL ANTHEM | *STREETER LECKA/GETTY IMAGES*

Because of the support of our sponsors, the Beijing Olympic
Games were amazing. From all 597 of us on Team USA,

THANK YOU!

Olympic Partners

Adecco, Amino Vital, Hershey's, Highmark, Kimberly-Clark, Maverick Ranch, Oroweat, Schenker, Polo Ralph Lauren, Staples, Aminco International, Asset Marketing, B. Dazzle, Bob Beamon Collection LLC, Build-A-Bear, China Sprout, Colonial Tag & Label Co. Inc., Commemorative Publications LLC, Concord, Dale of Norway, Direct Shopping Network, Extended Exposure, Fine Art Limited, Footlocker.com, Getty Images, Griffin Publishing, ISM, Jon Hair Studio, Jump Rope Tech, Museum Editions Ltd, The Northwest Group, OC Tanner, Omega, Panda America, Post No Bills, QVC, Ultimate Skate, WIN Enterprises LLC, Willey Publications, Wincraft, XP Apparel

Paralympic Partners

THE OFFICIAL PUBLICATION OF THE UNITED STATES OLYMPIC COMMITTEE
BEIJING 2008

LASHAWN MERRITT, ANGELO TAYLOR, JEREMY WARINER AND DAVID NEVILLE OF THE U.S. AFTER
WINNING GOLD IN THE MEN'S 4 X 400M RELAY | *JULIAN FINNEY/GETTY IMAGES*

PUBLISHER:
MIKKO LAITINEN
COMMEMORATIVE PUBLICATIONS, LLC.

CAPITAL PARTNER:
RICHARD SMITH

MANAGING EDITOR
MARK HUGO

CREATIVE DIRECTOR AND PHOTO EDITOR:
TRAVIS LOVELL

DESIGN TEAM:
DEVEN STEPHENS
NATALIE DAVIS
REEDING ROBERTS

EDITOR TEAM:
KURT KRAGTHORPE
SCOTT TAYLOR

SENIOR EDITOR:
PAUL RAWLINS

COPY EDITOR:
JESSICA LAITINEN

PRODUCTION ASSISTANTS:
GARREN LOFGREEN
SETH ALLING

CREATIVE TEAM:
JASON O. BUCK
MIKKO S. LAITINEN
KARI M. LAITINEN
MIKKO T. LAITINEN
RICHARD L. SMITH
JUDD L. PARR

PHOTOGRAPHY:
GETTY IMAGES
LONG PHOTOGRAPHY
MARK LOUIS WEINBERG PHOTOGRAPHY

PRINTER AND BINDER:
O'NEIL PRINTING, PHOENIX, AZ
ROSWELL BOOKBINDING, PHOENIX, AZ
Paper: Alfa 80# Coated Book
Ink: Toyo Ink

SPECIAL THANK YOU
Roxi Moss
Janey Marks
BYU Visual Arts &
  Graphic Design Department
Chris Schmutz
Eliisa Smith
David Eggertsen
Fred Buck
Lars Eggertsen
Lisa Albertson
Margaret Schaffer
Don Maeder
Tarja Laitinen
S. David Jackson
Rob Dodson
Tim Osborne
Lori Hugo
Allen Sohrab
David Zackrison
Preston Miller
Loretta Derrick
Christine Swann
Alice Carlson
Michelle Stephens
Jyll & Chloe Roberts
James & Linda Lovell
Blair & Susan Davis

SPECIAL EDITORIAL ASSISTANCE AND COVER DESIGN
PROVIDED BY UNITED STATES OLYMPIC COMMITTEE
CONTRIBUTING WRITERS:

Archery | Jason Mucher
Athletics | Jill Geer
Badminton | Cecil Bleiker
Baseball | Andrew Kitick
Basketball | Caroline Williams
Boxing | Julie Goldsticker
Canoe/Cayak | Bill McMillan
Cycling| Andy Lee
Diving | Jennifer Lowry
Equestrian | Joanie Morris

Fencing | Cecil Bleiker
Field Hockey | Jeff Gamza
Gymnastics | Leslie King
Judo | Nicole Jamantas
Modern Pentathlon | Cecil Bleiker
Rowing | Brett Johnson
Sailing | US Sailing
Shooting | Mary Beth Vorwerk
Soccer | Kate McMaster
Softball | Julie Bartel

Swimming | Karen Linhart
Synchronized Swimming | Taylor Payne
Table Tennis| Cecil Bleiker
Taekwondo| Bill Kellick
Tennis | USA Tennis
Triathlon | Jason Mucher
Volleyball | Bill Kauffman & B.J. Hoeptner Evans
Water Polo | USA Water Polo
Weightlifting | Cecil Bleiker
Wrestling | Gary Abbott

PUBLISHED UNDER LICENSE FROM THE U.S. OLYMPIC COMMITTEE BY:
COMMEMORATIVE PUBLICATIONS, LLC.
  P.O. BOX 711514
  SALT LAKE CITY, UT 84171
  801.706.2901
  (The Editorial Materials Contained In Amazing Awaits Are Produced By Commemorative Publications Exclusively And Are Not The Responsibility Of The U.S. Olympic Committee.)

ISBN: 0-918883-10-5

VOLUNTEERS DURING THE OLYMPIC TORCH CEREMONY ON THE GREAT WALL OF CHINA IN BADALING | *OLIVIER MORIN/AFP/GETTY IMAGES*

TABLE OF CONTENTS

14

A CONSTRUCTION WORKER TAKES PART IN THE CELEBRATIONS OF THE OPENING OF A NEW ROAD | *FENG LI/GETTY IMAGES*

北 京

奥 运

A CHINESE MAN HOLDS UP HIS BABY | *FENG LI/GETTY IMAGES*

A CLOSE UP OF A TABLE TENNIS PADDLE AND BALL | *ALEXANDER HASSENSTEIN/BONGARTS/GETTY IMAGES*

SCENERY ALONG THE YULONG RIVER | *CHINA PHOTOS/GETTY IMAGES*

MICHAEL PHELPS

MICHAEL PHELPS COMPETES IN THE 200-METER INDIVIDUAL MEDLEY | *CLIVE BRUNSKILL/GETTY IMAGES*

SWIMMING

Among the unfamiliar roles Michael Phelps was asked to play when he hosted the season premiere of Saturday Night Live a few weeks after the 2008 Olympic Games was that of a discouraged swimmer who was ready to quit. That certainly required some acting. In his nine days of Olympic competition—during which he swam 17 races, including all preliminaries and medal events—Phelps delivered a performance that can only be described as phenomenal. Well, there might be other words, such as consistent and determined. Winning eight gold medals was a triumph on many levels, but it was his ability to perform at the highest level, day after day, that truly set him apart. He had some help from his relay teammates and that final half-stroke during the 100-meter butterfly that gave him a fingertip victory, but the fact is, Michael Phelps lived up to expectations. And in this modern world of relentless promotion and endless hype, who does that anymore?

WHILE SLAPPING THE WATER, MICHAEL PHELPS PUNCTUATES GOLD MEDAL NO. 7, IN THE 100-METER BUTTERFLY | *PEDRO UGARTE/AFP/ GETTY IMAGES*

MICHAEL PHELPS GIVES A LITTLE KISS TO ONE OF HIS EIGHT GOLD MEDALS | *ADAM PRETTY/GETTY IMAGES*

BRYAN CLAY

DECATHLON

At the conclusion of the 10-event decathlon inside Beijing's Bird's Nest stadium, the "World's Greatest Athlete" was momentarily overshadowed by the "World's Fastest Athlete," as an exhausted Bryan Clay was ushered off the track after the 1,500-meter run to make way for Usain Bolt. Bolt was running for his third gold (and third world record), but Clay's winning effort in the two-day decathlon was just as impressive—and as dominant. Clay won by the largest point margin posted at the Olympic Games since 1972. In Athens, Clay netted the fourth-highest points total ever in the Games but had to settle for the silver. In Beijing, Clay left little doubt. He led the competition after the first of the decathlon's events, the 100 meters, and built up such a substantial cushion that his dead-tired, dead-last finish in the 1,500 was still good enough to guarantee gold.

BRYAN CLAY GETS A LEG UP IN THE HURDLES EVENT OF THE MEN'S DECATHLON | *OLIVIER MORIN/GETTY IMAGES*

MEMBERS OF CHINA'S CYCLING TEAM PASS BETWEEN TWO TOWERS OF THE GREAT WALL IN BADALING | *MARTIN BERNETTI/AFP/GETTY IMAGES*

MISTY MAY-TREANOR (L) AND KERRI WALSH CELEBRATE THEIR SECOND STRAIGHT GOLD MEDAL | *JAMIE SQUIRE/GETTY IMAGES*

KERRI WALSH &
MISTY MAY-TREANOR

MISTY MAY-TREANOR DIVES TO KEEP THE BALL ALIVE | *JEFF GROSS/GETTY IMAGES*

BEACH VOLLEYBALL

To call Kerri Walsh and Misty May-Treanor a dominant beach volleyball duo is an understatement. Some of the sport's insiders prefer labels like "sand supremacy" and "best ever" after the women notched back-to-back gold medals in Athens and Beijing to become the sport's first repeat Olympic champions. Just as they did four years earlier, the Walsh/May-Treanor side in Beijing not only won every match, they didn't even drop a set. At Chaoyang Park, the twosome had to overcome both the weather and their opponents. The "no day at the beach" gold-medal match took place in a driving rain that forced the postponement of the day's BMX cycling competition. The Americans faced China's Tian Jia and Wang Jie, the last side to defeat them in an international match, 15 months before. But in China Walsh/May-Treanor won 21–18, 21–18 to claim their 108th straight win and leave them both with triple-digit career tournament titles.

KERRI WALSH (C) SPLITS THE DEFENSE OF WANG JIE AND TIAN JIA IN THE
GOLD-MEDAL MATCH | *THOMAS COEX/AFP/GETTY IMAGES*

DARA TORRES

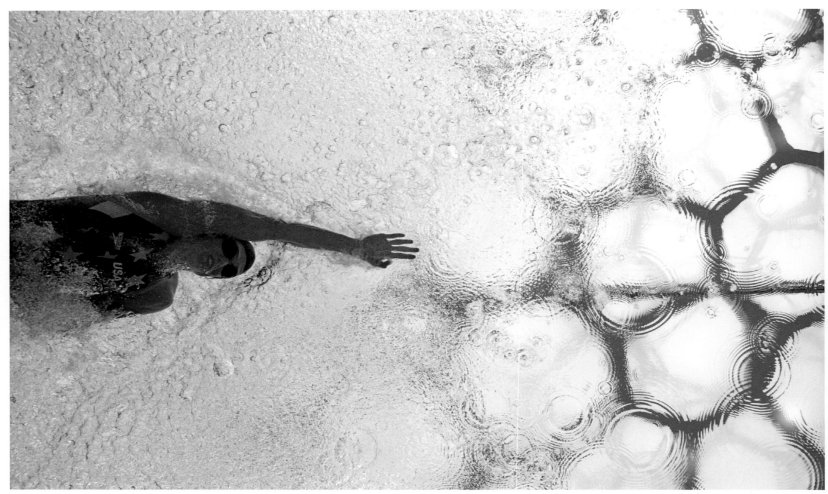

AN UNDERWATER PHOTO SHOWS DARA TORRES SPLITTING THE WATER WITH THE WATER CUBE ROOF ABOVE| *MARTIN BUREAU/AFP/GETTY IMAGES*

SWIMMING

Michael Phelps always called her "Mom" with just the right mixture of teasing and admiration and, well, because that's Dara Torres' title. One of them, anyway. Another is Olympic medalist—a title she has earned again and again. With three silver medals in Beijing, including a narrow miss at the gold in the 50-meter freestyle, Torres boosted her career total to 12, matching swimmer Jenny Thompson for the most won by an American female Olympian. Torres was happy to make the U.S. Team at age 41, but to say she was satisfied with merely competing in a fifth Olympic Games would sell her short. She wanted to win races, and she almost did in her individual event and two relays. Torres came close enough to "go home extremely thrilled," she said, while hoping she had inspired some "middle-aged" viewers to raise their own expectations for themselves. Undoubtedly, that's exactly what she accomplished.

DARA TORRES WAVES TO THE CROWD BEFORE HER SILVER-MEDAL SWIM IN THE
50-METER FREESTYLE | *CAMERON SPENCER/GETTY IMAGES*

DARA TORRES ENJOYS A PAUSE AFTER THE 50-METER FREESTYLE SEMIFINALS | *MICHAEL KAPPELER/AFP/GETTY IMAGES*

MICHAEL PHELPS OF THE USA GREETS HIS SISTERS WHITNEY AND HILARY AND MOTHER DEBBIE IN THE STANDS | *EZRA SHAW/GETTY IMAGES*

NATALIE WOOLFOLK OF THE UNITED STATES COMPETES IN WEIGHTLIFTING | *PAUL GILHAM/GETTY IMAGES*

TRACK CYCLISTS BOBBY LEE (R) AND MICHAEL FRIEDMAN OF THE U.S., COMPETE IN MEN'S MADISON FINAL | *MARTIN BERNETTI/AFP/GETTY IMAGES*

ALLYSON FELIX OF THE UNITED STATES COMPETES IN THE WOMEN'S 200M SEMIFINALS | *STU FORSTER/GETTY IMAGES*

THE U.S. WOMEN'S BASKETBALL TEAM CELEBRATE THEIR GOLD MEDALS | ANTONIO SCORZA/GETTY IMAGES

LISA LESLIE

LISA LESLIE LOOKS TO THE HOOP OVER RUSSIA'S MARIA STEPANOVA DURING THE USA-RUSSIA SEMIFINAL | *ANTONIO SCORZA/AFP/GETTY IMAGES*

BASKETBALL

The U.S. women's basketball team could have won the gold medal in Beijing without Lisa Leslie. The same could be said of any single player on a team that ruled over the competition and won eight games by an average of 37.6 points. But the experience would not have been the same without her, that's for sure. Although in her fourth Olympic Games, no one enjoyed this tournament more than Leslie, who eloquently reflected on her international career after the team's gold medal victory over Australia. "I've put on this uniform since I was in the 11th grade and had the opportunity to represent my country on a junior national team and then finally worked my way up," she said appreciatively. Her efforts did not go unnoticed by NBA commissioner David Stern and members of the U.S. men's team, who gave her a standing ovation when she, at age 36, left the floor after her final game. Leslie proudly chose the word "dominance" to describe her team's performance, and she was part of it from start to finish. In her final Olympic Games, Leslie averaged 10.1 points and 7.0 rebounds.

LISA LESLIE BATTLES RUSSIA'S IRINA SOKOLOVSKAYA FOR A REBOUND IN THEIR SEMIFINAL MATCH-UP | *PHIL WALTER/GETTY IMAGES*

HOPE SOLO

U.S. KEEPER HOPE SOLO KEEPS THE BALL AWAY FROM BRAZIL'S RENATA COSTA IN THE GOLD MEDAL MATCH | *HOANG DINH NAM/APF/GETTY IMAGES*

SOCCER

Goalkeeper Hope Solo's Olympic Games got off to an inauspicious start, as team lapses five minutes into the opening match against Norway resulted in a 2-0 deficit. However, Solo and the American women didn't allow a goal in the remaining 265 minutes of group play en route to the medal round. Once there, they doubled up both Canada (2-1) in overtime in the quarterfinals and Japan (4-2) in the semifinals to meet Brazil for the gold medal. The last time the two teams met on a global stage, Solo was pulled before the 2007 World Cup semifinals in favor of veteran keeper Briana Scurry. Brazil beat the top-ranked U.S. 4-0. Solo publically criticized the benching, and she was banished for the final match. Against Brazil in Beijing, Solo earned her keep, logging six saves in the 1-0 victory—her third shutout in the 2008 Games—while stifling the best shots from Brazilian superstars Cristiane and Marta.

HOPE SOLO KEEPS IN CONTACT WITH THE POST WHILE WATCHING ACTION
UPFIELD IN THE GOLD MEDAL MATCH | *MIKE HEWITT/GETTY IMAGES*

THE GREAT WALL OF CHINA WAS BUILT AS ONE OF FOUR MAJOR STRATEGIC STRONGHOLDS FOR DEFENSIVE PURPOSES | TEH ENG KOON/AFP/GETTY IMAGES

THE TEMPLE OF HEAVEN IN BEIJING | *JULIAN FINNEY/GETTY IMAGES*

PERFORMERS DEMONSTRATE MARTIAL ART PRACTICES IN TIANANMEN SQUARE TO HELP PROMOTE THE OLYMPIC GAMES | *GUANG NIU/GETTY IMAGES*

TAXI RIDERS COOL DOWN AS THEY WAIT FOR WORK IN THE HOUHAI DISTRICT IN BEIJING | *JULIAN FINNEY/GETTY IMAGES*

PINGYAO IS A WELL-PRESERVED ANCIENT CITY IN CHINA WITH A HISTORY OF OVER 2,700 YEARS | *CHINA PHOTOS/GETTY IMAGES*

MATTHEW MITCHAM

DIVING

Anyone researching the broad subject of "Australian divers" is likely to come across the story of Eric Nerhus, who once escaped from the jaws of a shark. In comparison, fellow Aussie Matthew Mitcham's feat was not death defying, but it was still a stunning recovery. He won a gold medal as an outsider, diving into a world ruled by the Chinese team. At the Water Cube, the Chinese divers were going into the water like Michael Phelps was going through it. The Chinese diving team was on the verge of going 8-for-8 in gold medals—until Mitcham performed his final dive. He entered the last round 34 points behind the leader, China's Zhou Luxin. With four perfect 10s from the judging panel, his 112.10 score in that final round was the highest in Olympic history for a single dive. He finished with 537.95 points total to Zhou's 533.15, an achievement he described as "absolutely surreal." Not quite like fighting off a shark attack, but close enough.

AUSTRALIA'S MATTHEW MITCHAM GETS EMOTIONAL AFTER HIS GOLD-GLEANING EFFORT OFF THE PLATFORM | *GREG WOOD/AFP/GETTY IMAGES*

MATTHEW MITCHAM TWISTS AND TURNS DURING HIS DIVE FROM THE 10-METER PLATORM | *MARTIN BUREAU/GETTY IMAGES*

USAIN BOLT IS SEVERAL STRIDES AHEAD OF THE FIELD IN THE 100 METERS | *NICOLAS ASFOURI/AFP/GETTY IMAGES*

TRACK AND FIELD

Never has an Olympian's name seemed more appropriate than Usain Bolt's—a flash of lightning, a sudden movement, to move or spring suddenly, to start suddenly and run away, or to break away from a group—that is Usain Bolt. The electrifying Jamaican sprinter captured the Beijing gold medals in the men's 100 and 200 meters in world-record style and then helped propel his country's 4x100 relay squad to the top of the podium, also in world-record time. The Bird's Nest crowd and viewers around the world knew they were witnessing history, as Bolt became the first human to run the 100 in under 9.7 seconds without a significant tailwind. He was the first man since Carl Lewis in the 1984 Olympic Games to sweep both the 100 and 200, and the first to snap Michael Johnson's 1992 world record in the 200.

JAMAICA'S USAIN BOLT CELEBRATES HIS 200-METER WIN, A SECOND STRAIGHT GOLD AND WORLD RECORD | WILLIAM WEST/AFP/GETTY IMAGES

SHAWN JOHNSON COMPETES IN THE WOMEN'S FLOOR FINAL, WINNING THE SILVER MEDAL IN THE EVENT | FRANCK FIFE/AFP/GETTY IMAGES

SHAWN JOHNSON

IN HIGH-FLYING FASHION, SHAWN JOHNSON TAKES A LEAP ON THE BEAM DURING THE TEAM EVENT | *FRANCK FIFE/AFP/GETTY IMAGES*

GYMNASTICS

The media were set to crown 16-year-old Shawn Johnson the next Olympic superstar. Not only was her U.S. women's gymnastics team the reigning world champion, but Johnson was the defending world champion in the individual all-around and the floor exercise. But at the Beijing Games, missteps left the U.S. with silver in the team competition behind host China, and then teammate Nastia Liukin edged out Johnson for the coveted all-around gold. Throw in a silver in the individual floor event, and Johnson had collected a trio of second-place finishes. Still, Johnson's good nature and nonstop smile never wavered. She was genuinely pleased with the honors and happy for Liukin, her good friend and Olympic Village roommate. But Johnson would soon have even more to smile about. On her final event, balance beam, she shook off a bad headache and seven flawed warm-up routines to blow away the field en route to the much-welcomed gold.

SHAWN JOHNSON IS ALL SMILES AFTER COMPLETING HER BALANCE BEAM
ROUTINE IN TEAM COMPETITION | *HARRY HOW/GETTY IMAGES*

ROMANIA'S CAMELIA ALINA POTEC COMPETES DURING THE WOMEN'S 800M FREESTYLE SWIMMING | *MARTIN BUREAU/AFP/GETTY IMAGES*

U.S. PRESIDENT GEORGE W. BUSH POSES FOR A PHOTO WITH MEMBERS OF THE U.S. OLYMPIC TEAM ON OPENING DAY | *JAMIE SQUIRE/GETTY IMAGES*

USA MEN'S INDOOR VOLLEYBALL HEAD COACH HUGH MCCUTCHEON CELEBRATES VICTORY IN THE GOLD MEDAL MATCH | *JONATHAN FERREY/GETTY IMAGES*

NOEMI BATKI & FRANCESCA DALLAPE' OF ITALY IN THE WOMEN'S SYNCHRONIZED 3M SPRINGBOARD | *ADAM PRETTY/GETTY IMAGES*

YAO MING

YAO MING IS SURROUNDED BY THE INTERNATIONAL PRESS, WITH AN ADORING CHINESE CROWD BEHIND | *KRISTIAN DOWLING/GETTY IMAGES*

BASKETBALL

Yao Ming was China's face for the 2008 Beijing Olympic Games even before Liu Xiang, whom China had been counting on for gold, limped off the track. The injury that kept Liu from running in the 110-meter hurdles was devastating to China and made the 7-foot-6 Yao an even more important symbol. While the Chinese basketball team did not win a medal, Yao's aura as an NBA star playing a home game helped burnish the country's new image as he carried China's flag in the Opening Ceremony. He delivered on the court as well, averaging 19.0 points and 8.2 rebounds. Yao desperately wanted to carry his team into the semifinals and "break the record for Chinese history." While China lost to Lithuania in the quarterfinals, the team still thrilled the fans in the Olympic Basketball Gymnasium—especially on the day China took eventual runner-up Spain into overtime.

YAO MING BACKS INTO ANGOLA'S JOAQUIM GOMES IN GROUP PLAY AT THE THE OLYMPIC BASKETBALL GYMNASIUM | *JEFF GROSS/GETTY IMAGES*

YAO MING GETS UP AND AROUND USA'S CARLOS BOOZER IN THEIR OPENING-ROUND MATCH-UP | *VLADIMIR RYS/BONGARTS/GETTY IMAGES*

FANS CHEER WITH MEMBERS OF THE UNITED STATES WATER POLO TEAM AFTER THEY DEFEATED SERBIA IN THE MEN'S SEMIFINAL | *STREETER LECKA/GETTY IMAGES*

AN ARCHER IS SILHOUETTED BY THE SETTING SUN AS HE PREPARES FOR THE THE MEN'S INDIVIDUAL RANKING ROUND | *PAUL GILHAM/GETTY IMAGES*

A TRADITIONAL JUNK BOAT SAILS THROUGH THE HARBOR OF HONG KONG | *MARK LOUIS WEINBERG PHOTOGRAPHY*

A BOAT SAILS ON THE TUOJIANG RIVER AT THE ANCIENT FENGHUANG TOWN IN JISHOU CITY | *CHINA PHOTOS/GETTY IMAGES*

PAVILION ON AN ISLAND IN THE WEST LAKE, HANGZHOU OF ZHEJIANG PROVINCE, EAST CHINA | *CHINA PHOTOS/GETTY IMAGES*

JASON LEZAK

JASON LEZAK COMPETES IN THE 100-METER FREESTYLE AT BEIJING'S WATER CUBE | *VLADIMIR RYS/BONGARTS/GETTY IMAGES*

SWIMMING

Nobody could beat Michael Phelps in the 2008 Beijing Olympic Games, but Jason Lezak did make him seem just a little more human. Lezak's remarkable comeback in the 400-meter freestyle relay brought out more emotion from his U.S. teammate than anyone had seen from Phelps in his five individual races combined. Phelps was thrilled when Lezak overtook French world record holder Alain Bernard on the final leg of the relay, and not merely because it kept alive his quest for eight gold medals, he just wanted his team to win that day, and Lezak came through. Bernard entered the pool with a body length's lead and, while Lezak gradually closed the gap, he was not optimistic at the halfway mark. "When I flipped at the wall," Lezak said, "I thought, 'There's no way.' Then in the next instant, I'm like, 'No, this is the Olympics. I'm not giving up'" He's glad he kept going—and so was Michael Phelps.

JASON LEZAK PAUSES IN PREPARATION FOR THE 100-METER FREESTYLE | *VLADIMIR RYS/BONGARTS/GETTY IMAGES*

NASTIA LIUKIN

NASTIA LIUKIN OF THE UNITED STATES COMPETES ON THE BALANCE BEAM DURING THE WOMEN'S ARTISTIC GYMNASTICS | *EZRA SHAW/GETTY IMAGES*

GYMNASTICS

The daughter of a multi-medalist Olympian and former world champion, Nastia Liukin enjoys a royal Russian gymnastic pedigree. Father Valeri Liukin starred for the Soviet gymnastics team at the 1988 Olympic Games, and mother Anna Kotchneva earned her world title in rhythmic gymnastics the year before. Still, Nastia broke into gymnastics only because her parents couldn't afford a babysitter, so their daughter tagged along to the gym and mimicked what she saw. In Beijing, the 18-year-old, whose routines are most often described as "elegant" managed to one-up her father on several counts. Her five medals—one gold, three silvers, and one bronze—gave her one more than the four he earned in Seoul. And Nastia earned her gold in the individual all-around by narrowly edging out teammate Shawn Johnson, while Valeri lost the men's all-around to a USSR peer by one-tenth of a point.

NASTIA LIUKIN REACTS AFTER HER LANDING DURING THE WOMEN'S UNEVEN BARS FINAL IN WHICH SHE WON SILVER | *KAZUHIRO NOGI/AFP/GETTY IMAGES*

NASTIA LIUKIN CAME HOME WELL DECORATED INCLUDING THE SILVER MEDAL WON HERE IN THE BALANCE BEAM
COMPETITION | *FRANCK FIFE/AFP/GETTY IMAGES*

LEBRON JAMES

LEBRON JAMES OUTREACHES FELIPE REYES FOR THE BALL IN THE GOLD-MEDAL GAME | *FILIPPO MONTEFORTE/AFP/GETTY IMAGES*

BASKETBALL

LeBron James's stats for the 2008 Beijing Olympic Games tell only part of the story. Coming off its disappointing performance in 2004, the U.S. team needed a number of things. Leadership from within was high on the list, and James provided it. He was basically an "extra" in Athens in 2004, but he became a star in Beijing. James played well, averaging 15.5 points and 5.4 rebounds, but that wasn't necessarily his greatest contribution. James's self-appointed role of leader, a status endorsed publicly by all the players, was critical in keeping everybody together and focused on team goals, not individual agendas. It worked. The players cared about one another, played unselfishly, and restored the U.S. men's basketball team to the top spot on the medals platform.

LEBRON JAMES RISES FOR THE SLAM DUNK IN A PRELIMINARY-ROUND VICTORY OVER GREECE | *NICOLAS ASFOURI/AFP/GETTY IMAGES*

A DRIVING LEBRON JAMES CAN'T BE STOPPED BY SPAIN'S PAU GASOL DURING THE GOLD-MEDAL GAME | *STREETER LECKA/GETTY IMAGES*

OPENING CEREMONY

BEIJING CHINA, 2008

Finally able to realize its dream of hosting the Olympic Games, the People's Republic of China showed what it could do with one National Stadium, hundreds of aerial wires, 15,000 performers, some 30,000 firework shells, and a supply of LED lights that seemed equal to the 2008 Beijing Olympic Games' estimated $40 billion budget.

But the real number to remember is eight, the luckiest number in Chinese culture. By design, Beijing's Opening Ceremony was scheduled for the eighth day of the eighth month of '08, with the start time slated for 8:08.08 p.m.

The world's best athletes shared a global stage and spotlight with China—and China delivered, wowing the crowd of 91,000 and an estimated television audience of 4 billion with a celebration that began with 2,008 pounding drummers and ended four hours later with a furious fireworks finale.

As with previous Olympic Games, the highlight was the lighting of the cauldron, done by gold-medal gymnast Li Ning. After receiving the flame, Li was carried by cables high above the National Stadium floor for a gravity-defying 90° angled run. Sprinting along the roof's inside edge, he followed a video-projected Chinese scroll as it unrolled before him to mark his route to the cauldron.

The ceremony opened with drummers each pounding a "fou," a Chinese percussion instrument dating back more than 3,000 years. While drumming, they also chanted a Confucian saying: "Friends have come from afar, how happy are we."

The program's first hour underscored China's heritage in pen, ink, paper, and movable type, followed by scenes highlighting Chinese opera, the nation's "Silk Road" routes via land and sea, and finally Chinese rites and music. Then came portions that symbolized starlight, nature, and modern China, with a huge illuminated globe rising from the stadium floor to serve as a stage for the 2008 Beijing Olympic Games theme song, "You and Me," sung by Britain's Sarah Brightman and China's Liu Huan.

FIREWORKS EXPLODE OVER THE NATIONAL STADIUM DURING THE OPENING CEREMONY | *CLIVE ROSE/GETTY IMAGES*

With some 11,000 athletes scheduled to compete, the parade of athletes took a little more than two hours. The team from Greece—home of the ancient Olympic Games—took its traditional spot at the front of the 204 national delegations. China, as the host country, took the final spot, entering the stadium to a thunderous welcome from the chanting, flag-waving crowd.

The flag-bearer for the 639-strong Chinese delegation was basketball idol Yao Ming, accompanied by nine-year-old schoolboy Lin Hao, a survivor of May's devastating earthquake in Sichuan Province.

Between the athletes' entrance and Li's aerial torch run, the program followed Games form: the presentation of the Olympic flag, the singing of the Olympic hymn, the offering of the athletes' and judges' oaths, and messages from Chinese and Olympic leaders. "For a long time, China has dreamed of opening its doors and inviting the world's athletes to Beijing for the Olympic Games," said International Olympic Committee president Jacques Rogge. "Tonight that dream comes true."

LOPEZ LOMONG OF THE UNITED STATES OLYMPIC MEN'S TRACK AND FIELD TEAM CARRIES HIS COUNTRY'S FLAG TO LEAD THE DELEGATION | *PAUL GILHAM/GETTY IMAGES*

CHINESE GYMNASTICS CHAMPION LI NING CARRIES THE TORCH BEFORE LIGHTING THE CAULDRON | *MICHAEL KAPPELER/AFP/GETTY IMAGES*

OPENING CEREMONY | *NICOLAS ASFOURI/AFP/GETTY IMAGES*

BASKETBALL PLAYER YAO MING IS ACCOMPANIED BY 9-YEAR-OLD SCHOOL BOY LIN HAO, A SURVIVOR OF MAY'S DEVASTATING EARTHQUAKE IN SICHUAN PROVINCE. | *MIKE HEWITT/GETTY IMAGES*

A POLICE GUARD WATCHES THE OPENING CEREMOY FROM OUTSIDE THE NATIONAL STADIUM | *FENG LI/GETTY IMAGES*

DANCERS PERFORM DURING THE OPENING CEREMONY | *ADAM PRETTY/GETTY IMAGES*

THE OLYMPIC FLAME IS LIT BY LI NING, FORMER OLYMPIC GYMNAST FOR CHINA | *CAMERON SPENCER/GETTY IMAGES*

SMOKE RISES OVER THE NATIONAL STADIUM (BIRD'S NEST) AFTER A FIREWORKS DISPLAY FOR THE OPENING CEREMONY | *JEWEL SAMAD/AFP/GETTY IMAGES*

DRUMMERS PERFORMANCE | *STREETER LECKA/GETTY IMAGES*

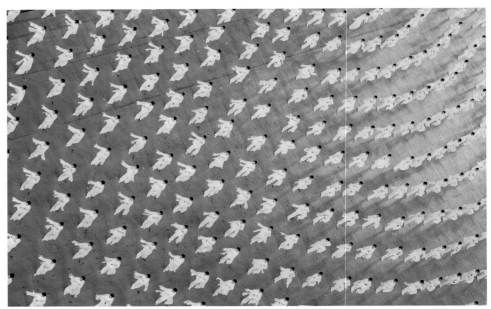

ENTERTAINERS PERFORMING TAIJIQUAN, THE MOST REPRESENTATIVE FORM OF SHADOW
BOXING IN CHINESE MARTIAL ARTS | *CHRISTOPHE SIMON/AFP/GETTY IMAGES*

AN ORCHESTRA PERFORMS DURING THE OPENING CEREMONY | *MIKE HEWITT/GETTY IMAGES*

OPENING CEREMONY | *VLADIMIR RYS/BONGARTS/GETTY IMAGES*

ARTISTS PERFORM AROUND THE ILLUMINATED GLOBE |
ALEXANDER HASSENSTEIN/BONGARTS/GETTY IMAGES

MORE THAN 15,000 PERFORMERS SHOWCASE THE NATION'S ANCIENT HISTORY AND ITS
RISE AS A MODERN POWER | *MANAN VATSYAYANA/AFP/GETTY IMAGES*

ARROWS AT HER SIDE, ZHANG JUAN JUAN OF CHINA WAITED IN THE RAIN IN ANTICIPATION OF HER GOLD MEDAL TRIUMPH ON THE OLYMPIC GREEN | *MICHAEL STEELE/GETTY IMAGES*

SIGHTING THE NEXT TARGET | THE 2008 ARCHERY COMPETITION WAS FILLED WITH EXCITEMENT ON THE OLYMPIC GREEN FIELD.

The men's and women's gold medal matches each went down to the final arrow, though no U.S. contestants had qualified for the final round. With a veteran team coached by Kisik Lee, the Americans had hoped for a stronger performance. However the American archers did compete well and now have their sights set on London in 2012.

Archer Khatuna Lorig, chosen to carry the U.S. flag in the Closing Ceremony, was competing in her first Olympic Games as an American citizen. She had previously competed in three Games, once for the Unified Team and twice for the Republic of Georgia. Lorig, who reached the quarterfinals, described her experience in Beijing as "absolutely excellent!" Three-time Olympian Vic Wunderle, the only American archer to make the top eight in both Sydney and Athens, also made it to the quarterfinals. "In our sport, you're lucky to make it to the top eight once, twice is pretty unheard of, so three times in a row, I feel very privileged," he said.

It was more thrilling for China's Zhang Juanjuan, who qualified as the 27th seed but went on to beat the three top-seeded South Korean women, including a 110-109 victory over defending champion Park Sunghyun in the finals. In the men's finals, Viktor Ruban of Ukraine defeated Park Kyung-mo 113-112.

South Korea defeated China 224-215 in the women's team event and edged Italy 227-225 in a men's match that was tied going into the last three arrows.

JENNIFER NICHOLS (L) AND KHATUNA LORIG KEPT THE U.S. TEAM MOVING TOWARD ITS TARGETS AS LORIG FINISHED FIFTH INDIVIDUALLY | *PAUL GILHAM/GETTY IMAGES*

BRADY ELLISON OF THE UNITED STATES KEPT HIS RINGS IN PLACE AND HIS EYES FOCUSED INTENTLY ON HIS GOALS DURING THE INDIVIDUAL COMPETITION | *FABRICE COFFRINI/AFP/GETTY IMAGES*

SAMUEL KAMAU WANSIRU OF KENYA CROSSES THE FINISH LINE INSIDE NATIONAL STADIUM TO WIN
THE MEN'S MARATHON ON THE FINAL DAY OF COMPETITION | *PHIL WALTER/GETTY IMAGES*

FASTER, STRONGER | *DO THESE NUMBERS FROM BEIJING IN THE SUMMER OF 2008 MEAN ANYTHING TO YOU—9.69, 19.30 AND 37.10? OR PERHAPS THESE NUMBERS – 100, 200*

and 4x100? One name and the images that accompanied it became permanent reminders of one of the most impressive individual performances at the 2008 Beijing Olympic Games.

Jamaican sprinter Usain Bolt electrified the world with not one, not two, but three breathtaking, world-record performances at the National Stadium. In a combined track time of a little more than 66 seconds total Bolt captured the men's 100 meters, the 200 meters, and shared in Jamaica's 4x100 relay—all at world- and Olympic-record speed. The mere mention of Bolt's name conjures up images from Beijing broadcast and photo coverage: the trademark "Lightning Bolt" celebration stance that was quickly mimicked across the globe, the great distances on the track between the gold-medal winner and his closest competitor as Bolt reached the finish line, and the sideways glances and chest-thumping.

The last two late-race gestures not only may have cost him the chance to shave even more off his already mind-boggling times but also split Olympic observers into a debate over whether he was showboating or merely exhibiting pure enthusiastic celebration.

Bolt became the first human to run the 100 in under 9.7 seconds without significant tailwind. Track aficionados say he may have been able to run somewhere between 9.55 and 9.6 seconds. On the eve of his 22nd birthday, Bolt shattered U.S. sprinter Michael Johnson's 12-year-old 200-meter record, outdistancing American silver medalist Shawn Crawford by four body lengths and nearly .7 seconds. And he became the first male Olympian sprinter to sweep both the 100 and 200 since Carl Lewis did it at the 1984 Los Angeles Games. Bolt's relay leg that contributed to a third gold and world record was pretty much expected after the two stellar individual performances. No wonder observers called the Beijing Games men's sprints an exercise of "Usain-ity."

While Bolt was using Beijing as a stage to cement his label as "world's fastest man," American Bryan Clay was doing the same en route to becoming "world's best athlete." He dominated the two-day, 10-event decathlon from start to finish, adding his name to the likes of Rafer Johnson, Bruce Jenner, Dan O'Brien, and other great U.S decathletes. The silver medalist in Athens, Clay never trailed after posting the best performance in the opening rain-drenched 100 meters event. From there, he went on to the long jump (first), shot put (second), high jump (tied for 12th), and 400 meters (10th). After just four hours of sleep, he continued as the overall points leader through the second day, with the 110-meter hurdles (second), then the discus (first), pole vault (tied for third), and javelin (third). In the final event, the 1,500, Clay finished dead last, 41 seconds off the race's winning pace, but with enough of a points cushion that he had 30 seconds more to spare. After his 8,791-point total (240 better than silver medalist Andrei Krauchanka of Belarus), Clay had one request: the traditional location of honor for top Olympic athletes. "I just want the Wheaties box," he said.

JAMAICA'S USAIN BOLT LOOKS SKYWARD BEFORE THE START OF THE 100 METERS | *MICHAEL KAPPELER/AFP/GETTY IMAGES*

The U.S. Olympic Track & Field Team collected 23 medals—seven gold, nine silver and seven bronze—leading all other nations in both gold and total medals. These included 11 of the 15 medals in the men's 100, 200, and 400 meters and the 110- and 400-meter hurdles. The American women posted their best Olympic showing in 16 years with nine medals. But the U.S. went 0-for-6 in gold medals in the men's and women's 100 and 200 and 4x100-meter relay for the first time ever with missed handoffs in the qualifying heats for both the men's and women's sprint relays. Americans missed the men's finals for the first time since 1988, only the second since 1912, and missed the women's finals for the first time since 1948.

Thank heavens for Team USA's "Fortune 400" Club, which combined for nine medals in the men's and women's 400 meters, 400-meter hurdles, and 4x400 relays. The wins included sweeps in the two men's individual events and double gold in the relays. LaShawn Merritt, Jeremy Wariner, and David Neville finished 1-2-3 in the men's 400, with Neville stretching out in a finish-line dive to claim the bronze. Meanwhile, Angelo Taylor claimed the 400 hurdles, repeating his gold from the 2000 Sydney Games and joining Edwin Moses as the only other man to win the event title twice eight years apart. The four medalists then joined forces in the men's 4x400 relay to turn in an Olympic-record time of 2:55.39 seconds, snapping a 16-year-old mark by .25 of a second.

Dawn Harper won the women's 110-meter hurdles when front-running U.S. teammate Lolo Jones clipped a hurdle and finished well out of contention. Allyson Felix in the 200- and Sheena Tosta in the 400-meter hurdles each added a silver to the total medal count. And Sanya Richards found a measure of redemption in the 4x400 after dehydration had prevented her from a late-race surge in the women's 400 where she settled for bronze. Teamed with Felix, Mary Winebert, and Monique Henderson, Richards trailed for three-quarters of her anchor lap before passing Russia's Anastasia Kapachinskaya, finding the homestretch burst she missed in her earlier individual race. The result was not only a gold medal but also the world's fastest 4x400 time in 15 years at 3:18.54.

U.S. discus thrower Stephanie Brown Trafton was an unlikely Beijing hero. A second-time Olympian, Trafton had never qualified for the world championships, had never won a major national championship, and had placed third at the U.S. Olympic Trials. In Beijing, however, Brown Trafton heaved her first attempt 64.74 meters, a mark that stood through six rounds to become the first American gold medalist in the event since 1932. In fact, the United States hadn't even been represented in the Olympic final round since 1984.

Other top U.S. performances included Shalane Flanagan breaking the national record in the women's 10,000 meters while winning the bronze, only the second American to medal in the 20-year history of the event; Hyleas Fountain claiming the silver in the women's heptathlon, also the second U.S. medalist in that event; and Jenny Barringer setting a U.S. record in the women's 3,000-meter steeplechase, which made its Olympic debut in Beijing.

Bolt's eye-popping sprint performances weren't the only Jamaican "cool runnings" in Beijing's sauna-like Bird's Nest. Jamaica swept the women's 100 meters with a gold by Shelly-Ann Fraser and two silvers when Sherone Simpson and Kerron Stewart tied. With Bolt and Fraser, the tiny Caribbean island

BETWEEN HER MULTIPLE EVENTS, U.S. HEPTATHLETE HYLEAS FOUNTAIN IS ENCIRCLED BY THE BIRD'S NEST | *ALEXANDER HASSENSTEIN/BONGARTS/GETTY IMAGES*

RUSSIA'S OXSANA UDMURTOVA KICKS UP SAND IN HER LANDING DURING THE WOMEN'S LONG JUMP
FINALS AT NATIONAL STADIUM | *GABRIEL BOUYS/AFP/GETTY IMAGES*

THE UNITED STATES' SANYA RICHARDS BEATS RUSSIA'S ANASTASIA KAPACHINSKAYA TO THE FINISH
OF THE WOMEN'S 4X400-METER RELAY | *ALEXANDER HASSENSTEIN/GETTY IMAGES*

of 2.8 million people was the first nation since 1912 to produce both the men's and women's 100 meters champions. The women's 1-2-2 outing in the 100 should not be surprising since the Fraser-Simpson-Stewart trio had outlegged the event's defending world champion and fellow Jamaican, Veronica Campbell-Brown, in their national trials earlier in the summer. Campbell-Brown, however, had her golden moment in Beijing when she successfully defended her Athens gold medal in the 200 meters.

Other successful Athens-to-Beijing gold medal repeat performances included Norway's Andreas Thorkildsen in men's javelin and Russia's Yelena Isinbayeva in the women's pole vault. Isinbayeva duplicated her Athens routine by easily outdistancing the vault competition en route to the top honor and then going solo to break the world record, this time to a new high of 5.05 meters. She then punctuated her performance with her trademark somersault on the landing mat.

The African nations maintained their stranglehold on the distance events, but national supremacy wasn't decided until the final event, the men's marathon, as Ethiopia and Kenya had captured four golds each in previous events. Ethiopia's four had come in a pair of grueling outings with Kenenisa Bekele claiming the men's 5,000 and 10,000 meters for the first Olympic distance double in 32 years and Tirunesh Dibaba duplicating the feat in the two women's races. It was the first-ever four-event, long-distance sweep for one nation in the history of the Games.

Meanwhile, Kenya earned its golds in the middle-distance events. Teenager Pamela Jelimo collected her country's first gold in the women's 800 meters, with other top medals going to Wilfred Bungei

U.S. HURDLER LOLO JONES COMPETES IN THE WOMEN'S 100-METER HURDLES HEATS | *FABRICE COFFRINI/AFP/GETTY IMAGES*

U.S. ATHLETE BRYAN CLAY TAKES PART IN THE JAVELIN EVENT OF THE MEN'S DECATHLON | *ADRIAN DENNIS/AFP/GETTY IMAGES*

in the men's 800 and Nancy Jebet Lagat in the women's 1,500. Brimin Kiprop Kipruto's triumph in the men's 3,000-meter steeplechase continued Kenya's lengthy nonstop string of gold-medal performances, which started at the 1984 Games.

Leading up to the 2008 Games, the marathon favorite was standout Ethiopian distance legend Haile Gebrselassie, a two-time gold medalist and world-record holder. Suffering from asthma and fearing Beijing's air pollution levels would aggravate his ailment, Gebrselassie withdrew from the race—a decision he later regretted when the event was contested on the final Sunday morning of the 2008 Games under blue skies and relatively clean air.

With the field of runners starting at Tiananmen Square and then circling around the Temple of Heaven before heading toward the Olympic Green and the Bird's Nest, Kenya's Samuel Wanjiru finally pulled away over the last few kilometers to win the 42.15K race in an Olympic-record time of 2:06.32, snapping a 24-year-old Games mark. Wanjiru broke the world half-marathon record twice in 2007 but had run only two full marathons prior to becoming Kenya's first gold medalist in the event, beating two-time world champion Jaouad Gharib of Morocco, who settled for the silver medal.

A FLAG-DRAPED SHALANE FLANAGAN CELEBRATES HER BRONZE-MEDAL FINISH IN THE WOMEN'S 10,000 METERS | *OLIVIER MORIN/AFP/GETTY IMAGES*

THE UNITED STATES' JENNIFER STUCZYNSKI IS SET TO LAND DURING QUALIFICATION COMPETITION OF THE WOMEN'S POLE VAULT AT NATIONAL STADIUM | *CHRISTOPHE SIMON /AFP /GETTY IMAGES*

70

SHARON DAY OF TEAM USA LOOKS TO GO UP AND OVER THE BAR IN WOMEN'S
HIGH JUMP QUALIFICATIONS | *STU FORSTER/GETTY IMAGES*

AN UNDERWATER CAMERA IN THE WATER TRAP CATCHES A UNIQUE VIEW OF THE MEN'S
STEEPLECHASE | *ALEXANDER HASSENSTEIN/BONGARTS/GETTY IMAGES*

LASHAWN MERRITT OF USA PASSES THE BATON TO ANGELO TAYLOR DURING THE MEN'S 4X400M
RELAY FINAL AT THE BIRD'S NEST | *OLIVIER MORIN/AFP/GETTY IMAGES*

ROMAN SEBRLE OF THE CZECH REPUBLIC HEAVES THE DISCUS DURING THE MEN'S DECATHLON COMPETITION | *JAMIE SQUIRE/GETTY IMAGES*

KIM KREINER OF THE UNITED STATES IS READY TO RELEASE THE JAVELIN IN THE WOMEN'S
QUALIFICATION ROUND | *MARK DADSWELL/GETTY IMAGES*

GREAT BRITAIN'S KELLY SOTHERTON IS SANDWICHED BETWEEN TWO HEPTATHLON COMPETITORS
IN THE 800-METER RUN | *STU FORSTER/GETTY IMAGES*

ERICA BARTOLINA OF THE UNITED STATES BENDS THE POLE ON HER WAY TO THE BAR IN WOMEN'S
POLE VAULT QUALIFICATIONS | *MARK DADSWELL/GETTY IMAGES*

SWEDEN'S MUSTAFA MOHAMED LEADS A TRIO OF AFRICAN COMPETITORS THROUGH THE WATER TRAP OF THE MEN'S 3,000-METER STEEPLECHASE FINALS | *HARRY HOW/GETTY IMAGES*

JAMAICA'S KERRON STEWART AND THE USA'S ALLYSON FELIX SPRINT TO THE WOMEN'S 200 FINISH
WHERE FELIX TOOK THE SILVER AND STEWART THE BRONZE | *OLIVIER MORIN/AFP/GETTY IMAGES*

REESE HOFFA IS SET TO UNLEASH A THROW IN THE MEN'S SHOT PUT FINALS AT
NATIONAL STADIUM | *STU FORSTER/GETTY IMAGES*

U.S. HURDLER DAVID OLIVER IS FOCUSED ON THE FINISH IN THE 110-METER EVENT | *MICHAEL STEELE/GETTY IMAGES*

SHELLY-ANN FRASER LETS LOOSE A SCREAM IN LEADING A TRIO OF JAMAICAN WOMEN TO A 1-2-2 FINISH IN THE 100 | *GABRIEL BOUYS/AFP/GETTY IMAGES*

JAMAICA'S USAIN BOLT IS THE RUNAWAY, RECORD-SETTING WINNER IN THE MEN'S 100 METERS, WELL AHEAD OF THE PACK | *GABRIEL BOUYS/AFP/GETTY IMAGES*

U.S. SPRINTER TYSON GAY BATTLES NIGERIA'S OLUSOJI FASUBA IN A
HEAT OF THE MEN'S 100 | *ADRIAN DENNIS/AFP/GETTY IMAGES*

TEAM USA'S WALTER DIX CELEBRATES HIS BRONZE-MEDAL FINISH IN THE
MEN'S 100 METERS | *JAMIE SQUIRE/GETTY IMAGES*

JEREMY WARINER OF THE UNITED STATES IS FAR AHEAD OF THE FIELD IN THE MEN'S
4X400-METER RELAY | *JEWEL SAMAD/AFP/GETTY IMAGES*

ETHIOPIA'S ZEMZEM AHMED DEKO WALKS AWAY FROM FALLEN COMPETITORS AT THE FINISH OF THE WOMEN'S STEEPLECHASE HEATS IN NATIONAL STADIUM | *MARK DADSWELL/GETTY IMAGES*

GRANADA'S PATRICIA SYLVESTER TAKES FLIGHT DURING WOMEN'S LONG JUMP COMPETITION AT THE BIRD'S NEST | *ADRIAN DENNIS/AFP/GETTY IMAGES*

ALLYSON FELIX, SANYA RICHARDS, MARY WINEBERG AND MONIQUE HENDERSON CELEBRATE THEIR GOLD-MEDAL EFFORT IN THE 4X400M RELAY | *OLIVIER MORIN/AFP/GETTY IMAGES*

PHOTOGRAPHERS GET AN UP-CLOSE VIEW OF RUNNERS SPLASHING IN THE WATER TRAP OF THE WOMEN'S STEEPELECHASE FINALS | *MICHAEL STEELE/GETTY IMAGES*

A MALE DECATHLETE CASTS A LONG SHADOW IN THE POLE VAULT COMPETITION | *JAMIE SQUIRE/GETTY IMAGES*

TEAM USA'S JACKIE JOHNSON ARCHES OVER THE HIGH JUMP BAR IN WOMEN'S HEPTATHLON COMPETITION | *STU FORSTER/GETTY IMAGES*

CHINESE SPECTATORS AT THE BIRD'S NEST ENTHUSIASTICALLY PERFORM 'THE WAVE' AROUND THE STADIUM | *FABRICE COFFRINI/AFP/GETTY IMAGES*

LASHAWN MERRITT OF THE UNITED STATES, LEADING AN AMERICAN SWEEP IN THE MEN'S 400, IS AWASH IN JOY WITH HIS GOLD-MEDAL RUN | *OLIVIER MORIN/AFP/GETTY IMAGES*

THE UNITED STATES' LAURYN WILLIAMS RACES TO SECOND IN HER 400-METER HEAT | *CHRISTOPHE SIMON/AFP/GETTY IMAGES*

MEN'S MARATHON COMPETITORS RAN THROUGHOUT BEIJING EN ROUTE TO NATIONAL STADIUM | *MATT DUNHAM-POOL/GETTY IMAGES*

CHINA'S LIN DAN CELEBRATES WITH THE HOME CROWD AFTER WINNING
THE MEN'S SINGLES GOLD | *CAMERON SPENCER/GETTY IMAGES*

ASIAN GAME | BADMINTON COMPETITION HAS
ALWAYS ENJOYED A STRONG ASIAN PRESENCE
SINCE BECOMING AN OLYMPIC SPORT IN 1992.

The competitions in Beijing drew the crowd to match, since badminton joins table tennis, soccer,
and basketball as China's favorite sports. Even the United States' most successful badminton
athletes in '08 were Asian by birth—Vietnam native Howard Bach and Khan "Bob" Malaythong of Laos.
The host team's players hardly needed the raucous home-crowd support, however, as China duplicated
the three-golds-in-five-events success in Beijing that it had achieved four years earlier in Athens.

Unlike 2004, where top-seeded Lin Dan suffered a first-round upset loss, the star dubbed "Super
Dan" didn't drop a set in his five matches. Sporting a gold pin of Chairman Mao Zedong on
his uniform, Lin celebrated his title-match victory over Malaysia's Lee Chong Wei by tossing his
shoes into the appreciative capacity crowd.

Lin's girlfriend was not quite as lucky—Xie Xingfang fell to countrywoman Zhang Ning in the women's singles finals. China's Du Jing and Yu Yang claimed the women's double gold, and South Korea's Lee Hyo-jung and Lee Yong-dae captured the mixed doubles' gold.

Bach and Malaythong made U.S. history by being the first Americans to reach an Olympic Games badminton quarterfinals, downing the South African brothers tandem of Chris and Roelof Dednam in their men's doubles opening-round match. Bach and Malaythong lost to eventual silver medalists Yu Cai and Fu Heifung of China, who in turn lost their bid for gold to Indonesia's Markis Kido and Hendra Setiawan.

Eva Lee was the busiest American player, competing in both women's singles and women's doubles. The United States boasted its largest Olympic badminton contingent since hosting the 1996 Games in Atlanta.

CHINA'S HE HANBIN AND YU YANG CELEBRATE THEIR BRONZE MEDAL IN MIXED DOUBLES | *CAMERON SPENCER/GETTY IMAGES*

THE UNITED STATES' EVA LEE RETURNS A FOREHAND IN WOMEN'S SINGLES PLAY | *NICK LAHAM/GETTY IMAGES*

CUBA'S EDUARDO PARET FOLLOWED THROUGH ALL THE WAY TO THE GOLD MEDAL GAME BEFORE
HIS TEAM FELL SHORT AGAINST SOUTH KOREA | *FREDERIC J. BROWN/AFP/GETTY IMAGES*

ONE LAST PITCH FOR A MEDAL | THE BACKDROP
OF THE 2008 BEIJING OLYMPIC BASEBALL TOUR-
NAMENT WAS THE ELIMINATION OF THE SPORT
from the 2012 program—and the hope of reinstatement for 2016.

But 2012 was not the most pressing issue for the '08 athletes, particularly the American players.
They were focused on winning a medal. With Major League Baseball players not available for the
Olympic Games, the minor leaguers (plus a collegiate star) who made up Team USA knew this was
their big shot—maybe their only shot—to shine on the international stage. Manager Davey Johnson's
team came through the balanced and competitive eight-team field with a bronze medal.

"Gold, silver, bronze, it doesn't matter," infielder Matt Brown said after an 8-4 win over Japan to take
the bronze. "The experience was well worth it, and it feels good to be taking home a medal." Among

the team highlights was the pitching of San Diego State's Stephen Strasburg. In a 7-0 victory over the Netherlands, the right-hander allowed one hit in seven innings while hurling 11 strikeouts.

The U.S. team went 5-2 in preliminary play, losing one-run decisions to Cuba and eventual champion South Korea. The loss to Cuba was tough to take and came via the Olympic tournament's unusual new format of beginning the 11th inning with runners at first and second bases. Cuba scored twice, and the Americans answered with only one run in a 5-4 defeat.

The U.S. team bounced right back with four consecutive wins, including a 5-4 victory over Canada on the strength of doubles by Brian Barden and Terry Tiffee. Two scoreless innings of relief pitching by Brian Duensing sealed the win.

That victory helped send the Americans into the semifinals against Cuba. The U.S. team trailed only 4-2 in the eighth inning before a pair of three-run homers made the final margin 10-2. That meant coming back the next morning to play for the bronze when the Americans responded by beating Japan for the medal.

Jason Donald batted .381 in the tournament, Tiffee hit .324, and Brown batted .281 with two homers and 10 RBIs. Among the pitchers, Jake Arrieta worked six scoreless innings against China in his only start, and relievers Mike Koplove, Kevin Jepsen, and Casey Weathers pitched a combined 14 innings without allowing an earned run.

TAYLOR TEAGARDEN (L) AND JASON DONALD RAISED THE U.S. OFFENSE AND CELEBRATE DONALDS 2-RUN HOME RUN IN A BRONZE MEDAL VICTORY OVER JAPAN | *JONATHAN FERREY/GETTY IMAGES*

SOME SOLITARY SWINGING HELPED YOUGMIN KO AND HIS SOUTH KOREAN TEAM-
MATES HIT THEIR WAY TO A GOLD MEDAL | *STREETER LECKA/GETTY IMAGES*

MATT LAPORTA NEEDED BOTH HANDS ON THE BAT TO HELP STEER THE U.S. TEAM TO A
PRELIMINARY VICTORY OVER HOST CHINA | *FREDERIC J. BROWN/AFP/GETTY IMAGES*

NATE SCHIERHOLTZ OF THE U.S. JOINED CHINESE CATCHER YANG YANG AT HOME PLATE IN SOME
NICE CHOREOGRAPHY WHILE ALSO SCORING A RUN | *FREDERIC J. BROWN/AFP/GETTY IMAGES*

THE USA'S JASON MCDONALD UNSUCCESSFULLY TRIED TO SLIDE INTO 2ND BASE BUT COULD NOT GET PAST CUBA'S YULIESKY GURRIEL | *FREDERIC J. BROWN/AFP/GETTY IMAGES*

THE MORE U.S. PITCHER TREVOR CAHILL GRIMACED, THE BETTER HE DELIVERED AGAINST JAPAN | *NICK LAHAM/GETTY IMAGES*

THE CLOUD OF POWDER SYMBOLIZED LEBRON JAMES' OWN OPENING CEREMONY AS HE TOOK THE
FLOOR FOR EACH OLYMPIC GAME | *ANTONIO SCORZA/AFP/GETTY IMAGES*

REDEEMING, ONLY WHEN NECESSARY | *IT ALL STARTED IN ATHENS—FOR THE MEN, ANYWAY. TEAM USA'S BRONZE MEDAL FINISH IN BASKETBALL IN 2004 OPENED* the door just wide enough to infuse the Beijing competition with a dash of curiosity, making the world wonder—could it happen again? Meanwhile, the American women's team, with no need to "redeem" itself, was simply intending to deliver more of the same.

Both teams came through in a fashion that left people wondering why there had been any doubt.

But redemption was unquestionably the theme of the men's team. The moniker "Redeem Team" was a play on the original "Dream Team" concept that began in 1992, when NBA players first appeared in the Olympic Games—and the Americans steamrolled the competition. But there was nothing dreamy about Team USA's performance in 2004, when the U.S. Olympic Team suffered three of its five losses in Olympic history and settled for a bronze medal in what forward Carmelo Anthony later described as "America's lowest point." American basketball gold was no longer guaranteed.

For the Beijing Games, USA Basketball officials took no chances. They assembled the best players, brought them together sooner, and worked to create an atmosphere where team members cared about one another, a trait that was starting to show in the team's summer preparation of practices and exhibition games.

"No one individual thinks they can do it without the next. So that makes it easy," said forward LeBron James.

The Americans opened the tournament with a 101-70 win over host China in a highly anticipated game that attracted viewers all around the world.

They also defeated Angola, Greece, Spain, and Germany in preliminary play to advance to the quarterfinals against Australia, where Kobe Bryant scored 25 points in a 116-85 victory. That earned the U.S. team a semifinal rematch with Argentina, the Athens champions. After NBA star Manu Ginobili injured his ankle early in the game, Argentina used a 27-12 scoring run to cut the lead to six points in the second quarter, but the scare was only temporary. The Americans rolled to a 101-81 victory.

Argentina then beat Lithuania for the bronze medal. Leading the way in Ginobili's absence was NBA player Luis Scola who finished the tournament with an 18.9-point average.

For the Americans, it was on to the finals against Spain, a team they had routed by 37 points in the preliminaries. This game was a different story. When Rudy Fernandez's three-pointer ripped the net, Spain was behind by only two points with eight minutes remaining.

The Americans responded. "It brought out the best in us," said U.S. coach Mike Krzyzewski. "They had to work for it," added Spain's Pau Gasol, who scored 20 points in the final and averaged a tournament-high 19.6 points.

After Fernandez's three-pointer, the USA answered with baskets on five straight possessions: Bryant's shot in the lane, Deron Williams' three-pointer from the left wing, Dwight Howard's inside shot, Bryant's three via a Williams assist, and James' rebound bucket. Defensive stops in between helped push the lead to 11. Not to be outdone, Dwyane Wade added a three-pointer to push the lead to 111-104 with 2:03 left. On a team of stars who played unselfishly, Wade stood out. He shot 67 percent from

AUSTRALIA'S ANDREW BOGUT PROVIDED AS MUCH RESISTANCE AS HE COULD TO KOBE BRYANT'S DRIVE TOWARD A GOLD MEDAL DURING A QUARTERFINAL GAME | *FILIPPO MONTEFORTE/AFP/GETTY IMAGES*

DERON WILLIAMS AND THE U.S. TEAM FENDED OFF A BIG CHALLENGE FROM PAU GASOL
AND SPAIN IN THE GOLD MEDAL GAME | *NICK LAHAM/GETTY IMAGES*

BECKY HAMMON (L) AND RUSSIA HOUNDED DIANA TAURASI AND THE AMERICANS BEFORE FADING
IN THE SECOND HALF OF A SEMIFINAL GAME | *FILIPPO MONTEFORTE/AFP/GETTY IMAGES*

MICHAEL REDD (8), DERON WILLIAMS AND CARLOS BOOZER (R) HELPED THE AMERICANS WRAP THEIR ARMS AROUND AN OLYMPIC CHAMPIONSHIP OVER SPAIN | *OMAR TORRES/AFP/GETTY IMAGES*

the field and averaged 16.0 points, part of a balanced lineup that also featured James (15.5), Bryant (15.0), Anthony (11.5), Howard (10.9), Chris Bosh (9.1), Williams (8.0), and Chris Paul (8.0). As further proof that this group bought into the team concept, starting guard Jason Kidd took only seven shots in eight games, making six. And during their time on and off the floor, Tayshaun Prince, Michael Redd and Carlos Boozer demonstrated what it meant to be true team players.

The women's team was similarly constructed and even more dominant, winning eight games by an average of 37.6 points. The triumph made Lisa Leslie the first U.S. basketball player to win four gold medals in succession.

Katie Smith earned her third straight gold medal; Sue Bird, Tamika Catchings, DeLisha Milton-Jones, Diana Taurasi, and Tina Thompson captured their second each. And Seimone Augustus, Sylvia Fowles, Kara Lawson, Candace Parker, and Cappie Pondexter brought home their first Olympic gold medals. Fowles averaged 13.4 points and 8.4 rebounds while shooting 64.3 percent from the field. Thompson (12.8) and Diana Taurasi (10.9) were also consistent scorers, and Parker shot 61.4 percent.

In preliminary play, the American women beat the Czech Republic, China, Mali, Spain, and New Zealand by an average of 43 points. Fowles posted 26 points and 14 rebounds in a 104-60 quarterfinal win over South Korea, and Taurasi scored 21 points (making an Olympic record five three-pointers) in a 67-52 semifinal victory over Russia (who went on to win the bronze medal with the help of U.S. native Becky Hammon).

In the third consecutive Olympic championship meeting with Australia, Kara Lawson's 15 points and Leslie's 14 points and seven rebounds keyed a 92-65 win for the American women—no redemption required.

RUSSIA'S IRINA OSIPOVA WATCHED IN AWE AS TEAM USA'S SYLVIA FOWLES DROVE TOWARD A FOURTH GOLD MEDAL | *FILIPPO MONTEFORTE/AFP/GETTY IMAGES*

RUSSIA'S ANDREI KIRILENKO FOUND A VICTORY OVER LINAS KLEIZA AND HIS LITHUANIAN TEAMMATES JUST OUT OF REACH IN A PRELIMINARY GAME | *FILIPPO MONTEFORTE/AFP/GETTY IMAGES*

DWYANE WADE AND HIS US TEAMMATES SOARED ABOVE ALL THE OLYMPIC COMPETITION IN A SPECTACULAR PERFORMANCE | *TIMOTHY A. CLARY/AFP/GETTY IMAGES*

CHRIS BOSH AND TEAM USA WERE READY TO HANDLE EVERYTHING FELIPE REYES AND HIS SPANISH
TEAMMATES BROUGHT INTO THE BATTLE FOR THE GOLD MEDAL | *STREETER LECKA/GETTY IMAGES*

KARA LAWSON AND HER U.S. TEAMMATES WERE EXTENDED BY THE RUSSIAN TEAM IN A SEMIFINAL
GAME BUT SURGED AHEAD IN THE SECOND HALF | *FILIPPO MONTEFORTE/AFP/GETTY IMAGES*

U.S. BOXER LUIS YANEZ (R) DELIVERED HIS BEST PUNCH AGAINST MONGOLIA'S SERDAMBA PUREVDORJ
BUT COULD NOT POUND OUT A 48 KG VICTORY | *JACQUES DEMARTHON/AFP/GETTY IMAGES*

CATCHING UP IN THE RING | CUBA LED THE OLYMPIC BOXING MEDAL COUNT AGAIN AT THE BEIJING OLYMPIC GAMES, BUT CONSIDERING CUBA'S HEAD START IN THE

sport, both the Chinese team and Deontay Wilder deserve a lot of credit for catching up.

Cuba took home eight boxing medals in 2008—but no gold. Remarkably, two of those gold medals went to China whose athletes were not allowed to pursue the sport until 1986 and did not participate in Olympic boxing competition until 1992. Despite being latecomers to the sport, China's boxers have made remarkable progress under coach Zhang Chuangling who incorporates martial arts skills in his boxers' training. China added a silver and a bronze to make four total medals—an amazing achievement for the new kids in the ring.

Another late bloomer who captured hearts along with his bronze medal in Beijing was Wilder, a heavyweight boxer for the U.S. Olympic Team.

A former high school football player and junior college basketball player in Alabama, Wilder took up boxing only three years ago in an effort to make a better life for his daughter, Naieya, who was diagnosed with spina bifida as an infant. Wilder held down two jobs, driving a delivery truck and working weekends at a restaurant, while he trained in pursuit of his new dream. The results speak for themselves.

With only 21 bouts of experience, he made the USA Team and earned a reputation for fourth-round comebacks. In his opening match in Beijing, Wilder outscored Abdelaziz Tulibini 6-0 over the final two minutes to win a 10-4 decision.

In the quarterfinals, Wilder pulled out a tiebreaker victory over Morocco's Mohammed Arajoui. Though the two were tied at 10-10 after four rounds, Wilder was awarded the win via a 23-22 "accepted score" edge.

His run culminated in the semifinals with a loss to Italy's Clemente Russo, after which Wilder was awarded a bronze medal. "To have a guy in his third year boxing and to enter the Olympics and then win a medal fighting all these guys who have double figures in years of experience over me is awesome," Wilder said.

Wilder's teammate Demetrius Andrade, a 2007 welterweight world champion, was the other American who came closest to a medal. Andrade had defeated Georgia's Kakhaber Jvania and Russia's Andrey Balanov before falling 11-9 to Korea's Jung Joo King despite a strong fourth round of his own in a quarterfinals bout.

ITALY'S CLEMENTE RUSSO (R) MANAGED TO DUCK U.S. BOXER DEONTAY WILDER'S BEST ATTEMPTS TO WIN A HEAVYWEIGHT SEMIFINAL MATCH | *JACQUES DEMARTHON/AFP/GETTY IMAGES*

HUNGARY'S NORBERT KALUCZA (L) FLEXED HIS MUSCLE AGAINST PUERTO RICO'S MCWILLIAMS ARROYO BUT COULD NOT CLAIM A FLYWEIGHT VICTORY | *JACQUES DEMARTHON/AFP/GETTY IMAGES*

THERE WAS NO LONGER ANYTHING FOR UKRAINE'S VASYL LOMACHENKO TO GUARD AGAINST AS HE EXULTED IN HIS GOLD MEDAL VICTORY OVER KHEDAFI DJELKHIR | *JOE KLAMAR/AFP/GETTY IMAGES*

A REFRESHING MOMENT IN THE CORNER DID NOT HELP YERKEBULAN SHYNALIYEV OF
KAZAKHSTAN WIN IN AN 81 KG QUARTERFINAL BOUT | *HARRY HOW/GETTY IMAGES*

VASYL LOMANCHENKO ENJOYED THE SPOTLIGHT OF WINNING A GOLD MEDAL MATCH WITH
KHEDAFI OF FRANCE IN THE 57 KG DIVISION | *NICK LAHAM/GETTY IMAGES*

CUBA'S EMILIO CORREA BAYEAUX (L) SWUNG AND MISSED IN HIS EFFORT TO BEAT GREAT BRITAIN'S
JAMES DEGALE FOR THE 75 KG GOLD MEDAL | *JACQUES DEMARTHON/AFP/GETTY IMAGES*

THE USA'S BENN FRAKER FOCUSES ON HIS SEMIFINAL RUN IN THE MEN'S
CANOE SINGLES | *ADAM PRETTY/GETTY IMAGES*

REPEAT PERFORMANCES | EXPERIENCE TENDED TO TRUMP YOUTH AS TIME AND AGAIN THE CANOE/KAYAK COMPETITION AT BEIJING'S SHUNYI

Olympic Canoeing-Rowing Park favored veterans who were defending prior gold medal performances. The United States fielded a relatively young team who had high aspirations. And while missed gates plagued some medal hopefuls—like Scott Parsons at the end of his final qualifying K-1 slalom run—strong showings by first-time Olympians like 19-year-old Benn Fraker (sixth in men's canoe) and Heather Corrie (eighth in women's kayak) bode well for Team USA's future on the water.

While many repeat gold medalists were defending titles from the 2004 Athens Olympic Games, one competitor, Slovakia's Michal Martikan, waited and worked for 12 years to claim his second gold. As a 17-year-old at the 1996 Atlanta Olympic Games, Martikan captured the men's single canoe slalom. He then took silvers in Sydney and Athens before finishing first in both the 2008 Beijing Olympic Games semifinal and final races to claim gold again—and his fourth Olympic medal.

Slovakia captured more repeat-gold performances in slalom, Elena Kaliska built up a 15-second cushion in the women's kayak singles to successfully defend her Games title from Athens. And twin brothers Pavol and Peter Hochschorner made it three straight golds in canoe doubles, having won the C-2 slalom in 2000 and 2004. In Beijing, though, they did it the hard way, finishing second in both the semifinals and final run but posting the best combined time overall to claim their third trip to the top of the podium.

Keeping Slovakia from a four-gold sweep in the slalom events was Alexander Grimm, a little-known 21-year-old German who posted a fast, penalty-free second run in the men's kayak singles to claim the gold.

Repeat performers in flatwater events included China's Meng Guanliang and Yang Wenjun in the men's 5,000-meter canoe doubles and Hungary's Katalin Kovacs and Natasa Janics in the women's 500-meter kayak doubles. But there were upsets here too, medal favorites Ronald Rauhe and Tim Wieskotter, the German men's 500-meters K-2 duo, were not only the Athens gold medalists but also world champions since 2001. In Beijing, they handed over top honors to Spain's Saul Craviotto and Carlos Perez.

One past medalist was mourned for his absence. Hungary's Gyorgy Kolonics, who captured gold in 1996 and 2000, died in his canoe while training a month before the Beijing Olympic Games. Hungarian paddlers wore black armbands during the Olympic events to pay tribute to Kolonics. In addition to the Kovacs-Janics gold, they earned three other medals: a second gold by Attila Sandor Vajda in the men's canoe singles 1,000 meters, a silver in the women's 500-meter kayak foursomes, and a bronze in the men's 100-meters canoe doubles.

Belarus picked up same-day golds in back-to-back fashion, beginning with brothers Andrei and Aliaksandr Bahdanovich in the men's 1,000-meter canoe doubles, followed by a Belarusian quartet taking the men's K-4 500 meters.

HEATHER CORRIE POSTS ONE OF THE UNITED STATES' TOP BEIJING PERFORMANCES |
JED JACOBSOHN/GETTY IMAGES

EVEN THE PADDLES OF KAYAKER RAMI ZUR, COMPETING IN THE MEN'S SINGLE 1000M SEMIFINALS
DISPLAY PATRIOTIC PRIDE | *FEZRA SHAW/GETTY IMAGES*

SLOVAKIA'S ELENA KALISKA COMPETES IN THE WOMEN'S KAYAK FINALS | *MIKE HEWITT/GETTY IMAGES*

TEAM USA'S HEATHER CORRIE LEANS INTO THE COURSE IN THE WOMEN'S SINGLES HEATS |
MANAN VATSYAYANA/AFP/GETTY IMAGES

WATER DRIPS OFF THE ARM AND FACE OF THE CZECH REPUBLIC'S VAVRINEC HRADILEK IN THE MEN'S KAYAK SINGLES | *ADRIAN DENNIS/AFP/GETTY IMAGES*

109

RICK POWELL AND CASEY EICHFELD OF THE U.S. COMPETE IN THE MENS C-2 SLALOM | *JED JACOBSOHN/GETTY IMAGES*

THE FIELD COMPETES IN THE MEN'S POINTS RACE AT THE LAOSHAN VELODROME | *STREETER LECKA/GETTY IMAGES*

PEDALS TO THE MEDALS | GREAT BRITAIN TOOK THE LAOSHAN VELODROME BY STORM, WINNING SEVEN OF THE 10 TRACK CYCLING GOLD MEDALS—THREE COLLECTED BY

Chris Hoy alone—and 12 medals total. Add Nicole Cooke's gold in the women's road race and teammate Emma Pooley's silver in the women's time trials, and the British were great indeed.

The United States posted its own impressive outing as BMX events made their debut at the 2008 Beijing Olympic Games. Americans won half of the six available medals in BMX, plus a pair in road events where cyclists spent much of their time circling in the shadows of the Badaling and Juyongguan sections of China's Great Wall. Team USA's five medals made for the best U.S. showing since 1984's nine-medal effort.

Three days after she crashed on a rain-soaked course in the 126-kilometer road race (which resulted in a 25th-place finish), Kristin Armstrong collected the sole U.S. cycling gold as she completed the 24-kilometer women's time trials in 34 minutes, 51.72 seconds. A former world-class triathlete who took up competitive cycling as therapy when she was diagnosed with osteoarthritis, Armstrong finished 24 seconds ahead of Britain's Pooley to become only the second U.S. female cyclist to capture Olympic gold. U.S. teammate Christine Thorburn was fifth, just three seconds away from the bronze.

Hearing "The Star-Spangled Banner" during Armstrong's medal ceremony while he prepared for the men's trials, U.S. cyclist Levi Leipheimer admitted to being inspired to improve on his 11th-place finish in the 102.6-kilometer road race. "Inspired" also describes Leipheimer's late-race trials surge, as he logged the second-fastest final lap to move up and take the bronze medal, behind Switzerland's Fabian Cancellara and Sweden's Gustav Larsson. Leipheimer's medal was the third men's trials bronze for the U.S. Olympic Team in as many Games. In fact, Americans have collected seven medals since the time trials were included in the Olympic Games in 1996, which is more than double the trials medals won by any other country.

In a cycling event tracing its roots to America four decades ago, BMX provided a stage for strong U.S. finishes, even if they didn't bring home the gold. Mike Day and Donny Robinson couldn't catch up with Latvia's Maris Strombergs, but took the men's BMX silver and bronze, respectively. And fellow Team USA rider Jill Kintner steered clear of a competitor's late-race tumble and surged to the women's bronze, behind the French duo of Anne-Caroline Chausson and Laetitia Le Corguille. A former world mountain-cross champion who returned to BMX just to vie for an Olympic medal, Kintner dedicated her effort to her late father, paying tribute to him with kisses to the "4 Dad" penned on her gloves.

Other noteworthy U.S. efforts included Sarah Hammer's fifth-place finish in the women's 3,000-meter individual pursuit; the debut of 18-year-old Taylor Phinney, son of American track medalists Connie Carpenter-Phinney and Davis Phinney; and the respective seventh- and eighth-place finishes by Mary McConneloug and Georgia Gould, the first pair of American top-10 finishes in Olympic mountain biking in 12 years.

DONNY ROBINSON OF THE U.S. RIDES HIS WAY TO THE BRONZE IN THE
MEN'S BMX EVENT | *JULIAN FINNEY/GETTY IMAGES*

CYCLISTS RIDE THROUGH A COOLING STATION'S WATER SPRAYS ALONG THE
MEN'S ROAD RACE COURSE | *JAMIE SQUIRE/GETTY IMAGES*

ITALY'S ERA CARRARA LEADS THE FIELD DURING THE WOMEN'S ROAD CYCLING EVENT | *PAUL GILHAM/GETTY IMAGES*

JOAN LLANERAS OF SPAIN EYES THE COMPETITION AS HE CLAIMED ANOTHER GOLD IN THE MEN'S POINTS RACE EVENT | *DANIEL GARCIA/AFP/GETTY IMAGES*

DENMARK'S CHRIS ANKER SOERENSEN RIDES IN THE SHADOW OF CHINA'S GREAT WALL IN THE MEN'S TIME TRIALS EVENT | *STU FORSTER/GETTY IMAGES*

SEVERAL RIDERS SOAR OVER THE MEN'S BMX COURSE | *ADAM PRETTY/GETTY IMAGES*

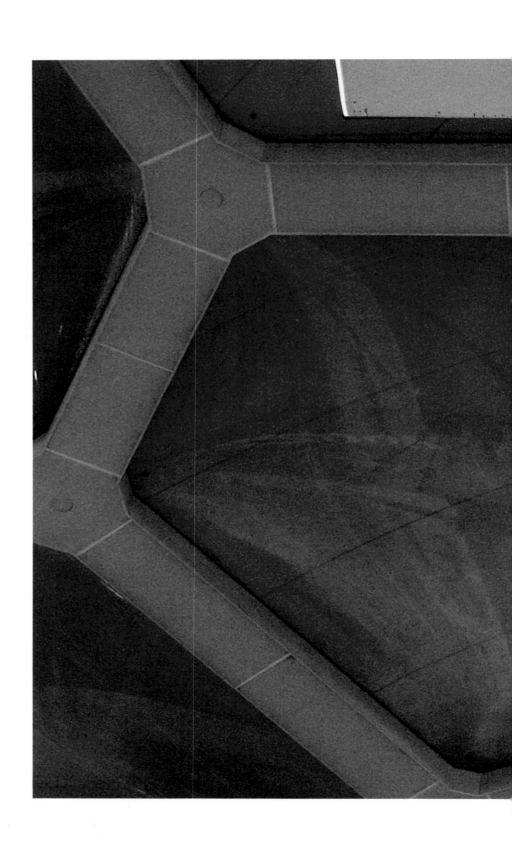

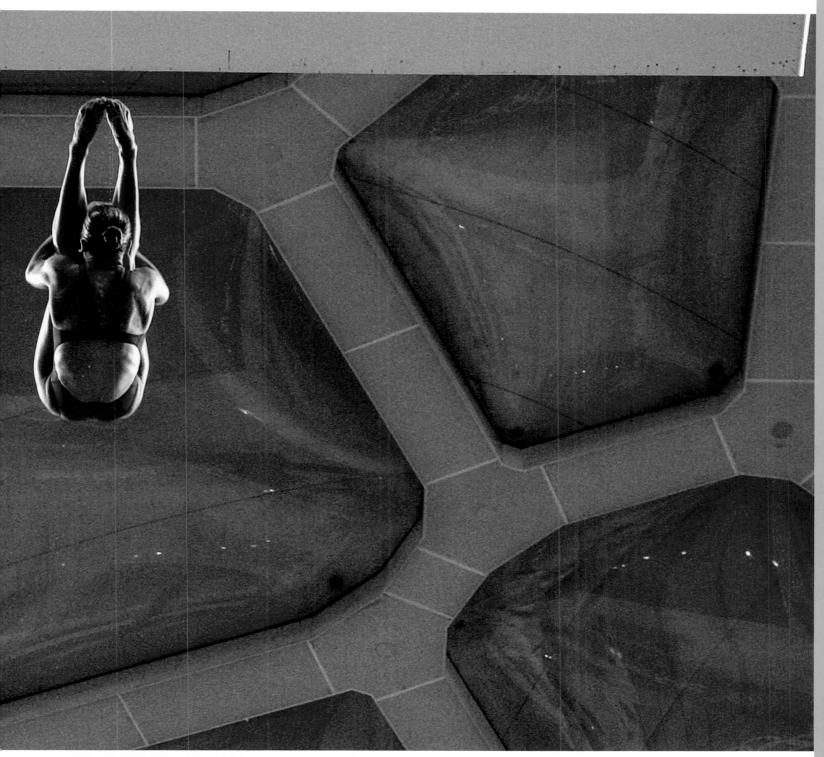

THE BEAUTIFUL WATER CUBE PROVIDED THE BACKDROP FOR DIVING. LAURA WILKINSON OF THE U.S. COMPETED IN THE
WOMEN'S 10M PLATFORM PRELIMINARY | *JONATHAN FERREY/GETTY IMAGES*

DIVING INTO THE DOMINATION | *NOBODY DOES DIVING LIKE THE CHINESE. SO IN AN OLYMPIC GAMES IN WHICH CHINA WON SEVEN OF EIGHT GOLD MEDALS, THERE ARE*

two obvious stories: what makes China so good, and who broke through the Chinese wall?

There's no question that China's diving dominance made Australian Matthew Mitcham's performance all the more impressive.

Competing in the same Water Cube where Michael Phelps had completed his Olympian feats, the Chinese divers thrilled the home crowd with another promise of perfection. Like Phelps, their team was poised to go 8-for-8 in gold medals—until Mitcham came along.

The Aussie entered the final round of dives 34 points behind the leader, China's Zhou Luxin. After completing his two-and-a-half somersault with two-and-a-half twists off the 10-meter platform, Mitcham looked at the scoreboard, discovered he had moved into first place and was thrilled, believing he had clinched a silver medal at that point. He ended up settling for the gold.

With four perfect 10s from the judging panel, his 112.10 score was the highest in Olympic history for a single dive. He finished with 537.95 points to Zhou's 533.15 total, becoming the first Australian male to win an Olympic diving title since 1924, an achievement he described as "absolutely surreal."

Mitcham's victory was a breakthrough for the rest of world in a meet that belonged to China, whose divers won seven gold, one silver, and three bronze medals. Russia captured five medals (three silver, two bronze); while Australia, Canada, and Germany won two medals each and Mexico and Ukraine each claimed one bronze.

While Team USA did not medal for a second consecutive Games, their performance pointed to an encouraging, and more competitive, future. "The Chinese didn't build a wall in four years. We'll be there in 2012," said diver David Boudia.

All eight divers who competed in an individual event made the semifinals, and seven advanced to the finals. In Athens, only four divers went beyond the preliminaries. All four U.S. synchronized diving teams finished in the top five, with three coming within five points of a medal.

"Obviously, we wanted medals," said team leader Bob Rydze. "You don't come here without wanting medals ... but the finishes we had here were much better. It's encouraging."

Laura Wilkinson, a 2000 gold medalist, completed her career with a ninth-place finish on the platform, but the Chinese divers resembled Wilkinson in her prime. Guo Jingjing won her fourth gold medal and sixth Olympic medal in all, becoming the most decorated Chinese diver in history. Her 415.35 score in the 3-meter competition was the highest ever in the event, and she finished well ahead of Russia's Julia Pakhalina. China's women have won six consecutive Olympic 3-meter golds.

Guo and partner Wu Minxia also successfully defended their title in the 3-meter synchronized event. On the women's platform, China's Chen Ruolin rallied in the final round to win.

HUO LIANG OF CHINA TWISTED AND TURNED HIS WAY THROUGH THE SEMIFINALS OF THE 10M PLATFORM EVENT
WITH NEARLY PERFECT FORM | *JAMIE SQUIRE/GETTY IMAGES*

KELCI BRYANT AND ARIEL RITTENHOUSE OF THE U.S. STAYED TOGETHER IN THE SYNCHRONIZED
DIVING 3M EVENT | *SHAUN BOTTERILL/GETTY IMAGES*

THOMAS FINCHUM OF THE U.S. KNEW A BIG CHALLENGE AWAITED HIM AMID THE STRONG
FIELD IN THE MEN'S 10M PLATFORM PRELIMINARIES | *MIKE HEWITT/GETTY IMAGES*

JAPAN'S KEN TERAUCHI WOULD NOT REST UNTIL EXECUTING HIS BEST DIVE DURING
THE 3M SPRINGBOARD COMPETITION | *MARTIN BUREAU/AFP/GETTY IMAGES*

MARYBETH DUNNICHAY AND HALEY ISHIMATSU OF THE U.S. KNEW THEY WERE PART OF A
BIGGER PICTURE DURING THEIR PRACTICE IN BEIJING | *HARRY HOW/GETTY IMAGES*

CHINA'S LIANG HUO LEFT AN IMPRESSIVE TRAIL IN THE 10M PLATFORM FINAL, BUT DID NOT COMPLETE
HIS COUNTRY'S SWEEP OF THE DIVING GOLD MEDALS | *MARTIN BUREAU/AFP/GETTY IMAGES*

USA'S REBECCA HOLDER OF USA LEADS 'COURAGEOUS COMET' IN THE
CROSS COUNTRY SECTION | *JULIAN HERBERT/GETTY IMAGES*

HORSE SENSE | EQUESTRIAN EVENTS WERE
CONTESTED 1,000 MILES SOUTH OF BEIJING IN
HONG KONG BECAUSE A LONG-ESTABLISHED
horse racing industry there provided existing stable sites and stricter quarantine measures. And
with Hong Kong even hotter and more humid in August than Beijing, the horses enjoyed some
Olympic firsts: airport transportation in air-conditioned vans, training in an air-conditioned indoor
arena, close monitoring for proper hydration, and show jumping moved from sweltering days to
cooler nights under the lights.

SWITZERLAND'S PIUS SCHWIZER AND 'NOBLESS M' SOAR IN TEAM JUMPING COMPETITION | *JULIAN HERBERT/GETTY IMAGES*

A HORSE CLEARS A FENCE IN EQUESTRIAN JUMPING COMPETITION |
DAVID HECKER/AFP/GETTY IMAGES

TIM LIPS AND 'ONCARLOS' OF THE NETHERLANDS SPLASH AFTER CLEARING A WATER JUMP |
JULIAN HERBERT/GETTY IMAGES

The United States claimed medals in two of three disciplines, with its two show jumping medals—a team gold and an individual bronze—both decided by jump-offs. With Beezie Madden (riding Authentic) and McLain Ward (Sapphire) back to lead the four-member show jumping team, the Americans successfully defended their '04 Athens gold, but needed a jump-off to break a tie with Canada after the two team rounds. Will Simpson (El Campeon's Carlsson vom Dach), Laura Kraut (Cedric), and Ward posted clean jumps to clinch the gold, so Madden did not need to ride.

But Madden faced her own jump-off to break a seven-way tie for the individual bronze. Ward had offered a tip to a course shortcut, and Madden directed Authentic over a decorative island of shrubbery and shaved enough time off her run to claim the bronze by .8 of a second. Canada's Eric Lamaze (Hickstead) also needed a jump-off to win the top individual medal over Sweden's Rolf-Goran Bengtsson (Ninja). For Lamaze, it was golden redemption after personal problems kept him off Canada's two previous Olympic Games equestrian teams.

Longtime dressage rivals Anky van Grunsven of the Netherlands and Isabell Werth of Germany squared off once again for the individual dressage gold. Werth had won the gold and van Grunsven the silver in '96, with the order flip-flopped in 2000, followed by van Grunsven riding Salinero for the gold in '04 in Athens. Van Grunsven and Salinero repeated their Athens win in Beijing by again edging Werth (Satchmo), though Werth and Satchmo returned the favor by helping the Germans win the team gold over the Dutch.

With a strong ride in the eventing discipline's final phase, the United States' Gina Miles (McKinlaigh) moved from fourth place to capture the individual silver. Germany won the individual gold—Hinrich Romeike riding Marius—and the team gold, winning a showdown with Australia that came down to each team's last rider and was separated by a single dropped jump rail.

GINA MILES OF THE U.S. GETS A HUG AFTER GUIDING 'MCKINLAIGH' TO THE SILVER IN INDIVIDUAL EVENTING COMPETITION | *DAVID HECKER/AFP/GETTY IMAGES*

SPECTATORS WATCH AN ITALIAN RIDER COMPETE | *DAVID HECKER/AFP/GETTY IMAGES*

BECCA WARD OF THE U.S. DESERVED A SALUTE AFTER WINNING A BRONZE MEDAL
MATCH IN THE SABRE COMPETITION | *JED JACOBSOHN/GETTY IMAGES*

LUNGE FOR GOLD | *WHILE IT IS TRUE THAT MARIEL ZAGUNIS REPEATED AS THE WOMEN'S FENCING GOLD MEDALIST, TO SAY THAT AMERICAN FENCERS*

do this every day would be a bit of an overstatement—and it sells Zagunis' achievement very short.

Zagunis' gold medal in 2004 was the Americans' first Olympic Games fencing victory in 100 years and their first medal of any kind in 20. In 2008, led by Zagunis, Sada Jacobson, and Becca Ward's sweep of the sabre competition, the U.S. men's and women's teams took home a record six medals, with 10 of the 13 U.S. Olympic Team members contributing to the unprecedented haul.

Accompanying the individual successes were team medals in women's foil (silver), men's sabre (silver), and women's sabre (bronze), all during the first few days of the Games.

The obvious highlight was the women's sabre sweep, with Zagunis defeating Jacobson 15-8 for the gold, and Ward, having lost to Zagunis in the semifinals, rallying to beat Russia's Sofiya Velikaya 15-14 for the bronze. No country had swept a women's individual event since Germany (women's foil) in 1988, and President Bush was there to congratulate the Americans.

"It was just one of those surreal Olympic experiences. When I met him, I was tearing up from the medal ceremony, and he handed me his handkerchief," said Jacobson, who joked that she should have kept it.

She would have to settle for taking home silver and bronze medals instead. The bronze came when the three sabre fencers teamed for a 45-38 win over France. The men's and women's team silvers came in more dramatic fashion, because each team was seeded seventh.

In the women's foil event, the Americans upset Poland 31-30 after trailing 22-15, then knocked off Hungary 35-33, before losing 28-11 to Russia in the finals. "We are usually the underdogs and sometimes the big guys fall asleep on us," said Erinn Smart, who teamed with Emily Cross and Hanna Thompson.

Smart's brother, Keeth, was the star of the men's sabre event. The team lost 45-37 to France in the finals, but was rewarded with a silver medal that teammate Tim Morehouse described as "the fruition" of nearly 20 years of work. The Americans had edged Hungary and Russia by identical 45-44 scores, with Keeth Smart delivering the comeback victories. According to Morehouse: "Keeth hit the equivalent of two grand slams in the bottom of the ninth."

127

CHINA'S XUE TAN (L) HAD UKRAINE'S OLENA KHOMROVA ON THE DEFENSIVE DURING THE WOMEN'S TEAM SABRE GOLD MEDAL MATCH | *JEWEL SAMAD/AFP/GETTY IMAGES*

GEREK MEINHARDT (R) OF THE U.S. NEEDED SOME FANCY FOOTWORK TO DEAL WITH HU JUN (L)
OF CHINA IN THE MEN'S FOIL EVENT | *VLADIMIR RYS/BONGARTS/GETTY IMAGES*

AZZA BESBES OF TUNISIA MADE SURE THE WORLD HEARD ABOUT HER VICTORY
IN THE SABRE ROUND OF 16 | *CLIVE BRUNSKILL/GETTY IMAGES*

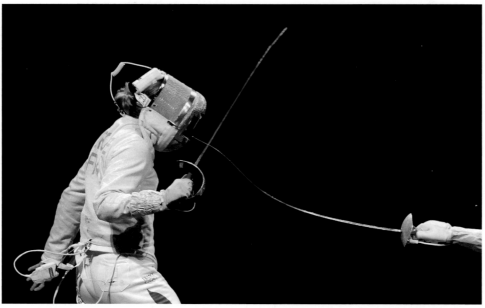

AS FRANCE'S LEONORE PERRUS (L) DISCOVERED, A BRONZE MEDAL WAS ALWAYS WITHIN REACH FOR
MARIEL ZAGUNIS OF USA IN THE WOMEN'S TEAM SABRE EVENT | *JEWEL SAMAD/AFP/GETTY IMAGES*

KEETH SMART OF THE U.S. SAVED ONE OF HIS BEST LUNGES FOR THE CELEBRATION OF A TEAM SABRE SEMIFINAL WIN OVER RUSSIA | *MIKE HEWITT/GETTY IMAGES*

MARIEL ZAGUNIS (R) OF THE U.S. MANAGED TO KEEP HER BALANCE AS SHE DUELED WITH CAROLE VERGNE OF FRANCE IN THE TEAM SABRE GOLD MEDAL MATCH | *SHAUN BOTTERILL/GETTY IMAGES*

KELI SMITH OF THE UNITED STATES GETS A BEAD ON THE BALL IN FRONT
OF SPAIN'S GEORGINA OLIVA | *QUINN ROONEY/GETTY IMAGES*

A GOLDEN REIGN | *FIELD HOCKEY'S REIGNING WORLD CHAMPIONS PLAYED WORTHY OF THEIR TOP RANKINGS IN BEIJING, AS GERMANY CAPTURED* the men's gold medal and the Netherlands took the women's top honors. And while the U.S. men did not compete, the American women qualified for the Olympic Games for the first time in two decades making their first appearance since playing hosts in Atlanta in 1996.

Entering the 12-team women's pool play with a number 11 world ranking, Team USA rested its hopes on a silver-medal finish at the 2007 Pan American Games. The Americans played equal to their opponents—a win over New Zealand, a loss to defending champion Germany, and draws against second-ranked Argentina, number 5 Japan, and Great Britain. It just wasn't quite enough to push the Americans into medal-round play. The U.S. finished in eighth place after a match with Spain.

In that match, America's Olympic Team enjoyed a 2-1 advantage on goals by Angie Loy and Dana Sensenig, but watched Spain score the equalizer late in regulation and then the winning golden goal off a penalty corner just 90 seconds before the end of sudden-death extra time. "For our first Olympics, I'm extremely proud of our performance," said Team USA captain Kate Barber. "I am proud to stand beside these fifteen girls."

The Netherlands shut out China 2-0 for the women's gold, though with the silver, the hosts claimed their first-ever field hockey medal. Argentina downed Germany for its second straight bronze. Germany won its first men's field hockey gold in 12 years, edging Spain 1-0, as the Spaniards settled for their third silver medal in three decades. In a repeat of the 2004 gold-medal match, Australia beat the Netherlands for the bronze.

TIFFANY SNOW (R) CELEBRATES WITH U.S. TEAMMATES AFTER SCORING
A GOAL AGAINST GERMANY | *ADAM PRETTY/GETTY IMAGES*

SPAIN'S DAVID ALEGRE AND A DIVING CHRISTOPHER ZELLER OF GERMANY COMPETE FOR
THE BALL IN THE MEN'S GOLD-MEDAL MATCH | *JED JACOBSOHN/GETTY IMAGES*

FRANCE'S LUC ABALO TAKES FLIGHT AND TAKES AIM AT CROATIA'S GOAL
IN MEN'S SEMIFINAL ACTION | *PHILIPPE DESMAZES/AFP/GETTY IMAGES*

EYES ON ICELAND | THE HANDBALL MEDALS AT THE BEIJING GAMES PROVED TO BE A SERIES OF FIRSTS. FRANCE CLAIMED ITS FIRST-EVER MEN'S gold. Norway won its first women's gold. And Iceland took home its first handball medal with the men's silver. Iceland also captured most of the global attention, as the tiny Nordic island nation of 300,000 celebrated its first silver medal in more than a half-century and just its fourth Olympic medal ever. The Icelandic medal count now sits at two silver and two bronze.

No wonder Iceland's streets were deserted, companies closed down, and the national stock market went on hiatus whenever the men's team was contesting medal-round matches. Iceland president Olafur Ragnar Grimsson was considering bestowing the Order of the Falcon, the country's highest honor, on the national team.

In winning the Beijing Olympic Games' final gold medal, France defeated Iceland 28-23 in the championship match. France relied on the play of goalkeeper Thierry Omeyer and leading scorer Nikola Karabatic, who netted eight goals.

Norway completed its full set of women's handball medals, adding the first gold to a pair of silver and a bronze, all claimed during the previous two decades. The final result never seemed in doubt, as Norway blitzed Russia with a 13-3 run in the finale's opening 15 minutes. Goalkeeper Katrine Lunde Haraldsen shined in the eventual 34-27 victory, and Norwegian teammate Linn-Kristin Riegelhuth scored nine goals against Russia.

Korea also completed its full-medal set in Beijing, returning to the handball podium after a dozen years. It added the women's bronze to the nation's two golds and two silvers, all won between 1984 and 1996. Spain beat Croatia for its third men's bronze medal in 12 years.

The United States has not competed in handball at the Olympic Games since America fielded host-nation squads at the 1996 Atlanta Games. The U.S. men haven't cracked the top eight since a sixth-place finish in 1936, while the women placed fourth at the 1984 Los Angeles Olympic Games.

Similar to basketball, soccer, and rugby and played on an indoor court with seven players on each side, team handball made its Olympic debut at the 1936 Olympic Games in Berlin, returning as a permanent program sport in 1972 at the Munich Olympic Games.

SPAIN'S GOALKEEPER DAVID BARRUFET TRIES TO BLOCK A SHOT BY CROATIA'S DOMAGOJ DUVNJAK IN THE MEN'S BRONZE MEDAL MATCH | *PHILIPPE DESMAZES/AFP/GETTY IMAGES*

MARIAMA SIGNATE OF FRANCE SHOOTS ON GOAL WITH ANGOLA DEFENDERS DRAPED ALL OVER HER | *ALEXANDER HASSENSTEIN/BONGARTS/GETTY IMAGES*

YANG WEI OF CHINA, THE MENS INDIVIDUAL ALL AROUND GOLD MEDAL WINNER COMPETES ON THE
PARALLEL BARS | *MIKE HEWITT/GETTY IMAGES*

THE NASTIA AND SHAWN SHOW | WHILE HOST CHINA GATHERED AN IMPRESSIVE 18 TOTAL MEDALS IN GYMNASTICS' THREE DISCIPLINES, THE UNITED STATES

enjoyed its best medal collection since 1984 and the most earned in a nonboycotted Games, 10 overall, and all coming in artistic gymnastics. In fact, the U.S. women won eight in that discipline—two better than their Chinese counterparts.

The women's team competition was expected to be an epic battle. The Team USA women entered as the reigning world champions, and host China not only finished a close second in 2007 but had captured the title the year before. The battle didn't quite materialize, as China ran away with the team gold by a margin of more than two points. But the USA Team gymnasts—Shawn Johnson, Nastia Liukin, Chellsie Memmel, Samantha Peszek, Alicia Sacramone, and Bridget Sloan—showed little disappointment with the silver, their second straight in as many Games for the best back-to-back Olympic showing in U.S. women's team history.

Then came the American onslaught of individual medals—or, the Nastia and Shawn Show. Nastia Liukin snagged the gold in the featured all-around competition, then added silvers in uneven bars and balance beam and closed with a bronze in the floor. Her achievements put her in rare company. Liukin joined 1984 star Mary Lou Retton and Athens Games standout Carly Patterson as the only U.S. women to claim the Olympic all-around title. With her five medals, she equaled Retton and the 1992 Games' Shannon Miller for the United States' best gymnastics medal total.

Meanwhile, Shawn Johnson, the 2007 world champion in all-around and floor, had to be wondering if and when her gold might come. She settled for silvers in all-around and floor, her two favored individual events, then had to shake off a bad headache before going on to the final individual event, the beam. It was here Johnson found her elusive gold and became only the second U.S. gold medalist in the event.

To top things off, the pair's Beijing blitz marked the first time U.S. gymnasts had ever finished 1-2 in the women's all-around.

The gymnasts' ages became a minor distraction during the women's artistic competition. International Gymnastics Federation (FIG) rules require that gymnasts be at least 16 at the year of the Olympiad, and the Chinese team in particular came under close scrutiny. After a five-plus-week investigation, the FIG cleared the ages of the Chinese women's gymnasts as meeting the minimum standard.

A feel-good story from the nine days of competition at the Beijing Indoor National Stadium came when five-time Olympian Oksana Chusovitina, who at 33 was nearly twice as old as most of her Beijing competitors, won the silver medal in the women's vault. Having represented the Soviet Union and Uzbekistan previously, Chusovitina was competing for the first time for Germany, where she had moved in 2002 so her son could be treated for leukemia. Chusovitina enjoyed celebrating her first-individual medal, happy to note her healthy son now competes himself as a 9-year-old aspiring gymnast.

As expected, China dominated the men's artistic events, taking the team title as well as six of the

THE UNITED STATES' NASTIA LIUKIN COMPETES ON THE BEAM DURING THE WOMEN'S TEAM FINAL OF THE ARTISTIC
GYMNASTICS EVENT | *LLUIS GENE/AFP/GETTY IMAGES*

seven individual events, with Yang Wei capturing the individual all-around gold and Zou Kai doubling up as the 2008 Olympic Games champion on the floor and horizontal bars. What wasn't expected, however, was Team USA winning the bronze medal in the team competition, especially because they were competing without Athens standouts, Paul and Morgan Hamm. The six Americans—Alexander Artemev, Raj Bhavsar, Joseph Hagerty, Jonathan Horton, Justin Spring, and Kevin Tan—held their own throughout the team rotations. In fact, Artemev, who less than a week before the Beijing Games had still been a team alternate, clinched the U.S. bronze with a strong pommel horse routine, his only performance of the final day. Horton punctuated the U.S. men's successes with a high bars individual silver using an energetic routine that he had upgraded in just the previous three days.

Gymnastics' other two disciplines—rhythmic gymnastics and trampoline—resulted in sweeps. China collected both trampoline golds, while Russia maintained its dominance in the team and individual rhythmic events.

RAJ BHAVSAR OF THE USA COMPETES ON THE RINGS DURING THE MEN'S TEAM FINAL | *KAZUHIRO NOGI/AFP/GETTY IMAGES*

UNITED STATES' ALEXANDER ARTEMEV COMPETES IN THE MEN'S POMMEL HORSE FINAL |
FRANCK FIFE/AFP/GETTY IMAGES

JONATHAN HORTON OF THE UNITED STATES PREPARES TO COMPETE ON THE POMMEL HORSE |
CAMERON SPENCER/GETTY IMAGES

VERONICA RUIZ OF SPAIN COMPETES IN THE INDIVIDUAL ALL-AROUND FINAL IN RYTHMIC GYMNASTICS | *HARRY HOW/GETTY IMAGES*

CHRIS ESTRADA PERFORMS DURING THE MEN'S QUALIFICATION ROUND IN TRAMPOLINE GYMNASTICS | *KAZUHIRO NOGI/AFP/GETTY IMAGES*

A DETAILED PICTURE OF A GYMNAST CHALKING HIS HANDS DURING THE MEN'S INDIVIDUAL ALL-AROUND ARTISTIC GYMNASTICS | *NICK LAHAM/GETTY IMAGES*

NASTIA LIUKIN OF THE UNITED STATES IS GIVEN A HUG BY TEAMMATE SAMANTHA PESZEK AS ALICIA SACRAMONE COMES TO CELEBRATE DURING THE TEAM EVENT | *HARRY HOW/GETTY IMAGES*

UNITED STATES' KEVIN TAN COMPETES ON THE RINGS DURING THE MEN'S TEAM FINAL | *KAZUHIRO NOGI/AFP/GETTY IMAGES*

CHINA'S WEI YANG COMPETES ON THE VAULT DURING THE MEN'S TEAM FINAL OF THE ARTISTIC GYMNASTICS EVENT | *LLUIS GENE/AFP/GETTY IMAGES*

144

RUSSIA'S ANNA PAVLOVA COMPETES IN THE WOMEN'S VAULT FINAL |
KAZUHIRO NOGI/AFP/GETTY IMAGES

EVGENIYA KANAEVA COMPETES IN THE INDIVIDUAL ALL-AROUND QUALIFICATION OF THE
RHYTHMIC GYMNASTICS | *FRANCK FIFE/AFP/GETTY IMAGES*

SHAWN JOHNSON OF THE UNITED STATES STANDS ON THE PODIUM WITH HER TEAMMATES AFTER
WINNING THE SILVER MEDAL IN THE TEAM EVENT | *HARRY HOW/GETTY IMAGES*

145

DAEEUN KIM OF SOUTH KOREA COMPETES ON THE FLOOR ELEMENT IN THE MEN'S TEAM FINAL |
JAMIE SQUIRE/GETTY IMAGES

CHINA'S YILIN YANG COMPETES ON THE UNEVEN BARS DURING THE WOMEN'S TEAM FINAL|
FRANCK FIFE/AFP/GETTY IMAGES

JONATHAN HORTON OF THE UNITED STATES COMPETES ON THE PARALLEL BARS | *CAMERON SPENCER/GETTY IMAGE*

RUSSIA'S SERGEY KHOROKHORDIN COMPETES ON THE RINGS DURING THE MEN'S INDIVIDUAL ALL-AROUND FINAL | *LLUIS GENE/AFP/GETTY IMAGE*

CHELLSIE MEMMEL OF THE UNITED STATES COMPETES IN THE UNEVEN BARS | *HARRY HOW/GETTY IMAGES*

MIKLOS UNGVARI (BLUE) OF HUNGARY AND WU RITUBILIGE OF CHINA WRAPPED THEMSELVES
UP IN A TIGHT COMPETITION IN A 66 KG BOUT | *NICK LAHAM/GETTY IMAGES*

FIGHTING FOR A NEW DISTINCTION | JAPAN, THE TRADITIONAL JUDO POWERHOUSE, WAS NOT ITS USUAL OVERWHELMING SELF AT THE BEIJING

Olympic Games. Instead, the medals podium was filled with new faces in the sport, from Mongolia's first gold medalist to a former American swimmer.

Ronda Rousey always knew she would be an Olympian, but before taking up judo at age 11, she figured her opportunity would come in swimming. She got bored "going back and forth, staring at a black line" in the pool, though, so Rousey switched to the sport in which her mother, AnnMaria DeMars, was a world champion in 1984.

It was a good choice. Rousey became the first American woman to win an Olympic medal in judo, which became a full medal sport for women in 1992.

Known internationally for the aggressive, ground-based style she used in Athens at age 17, Rousey broke through with a bronze medal in the 70k class. With a cat named Beijing and a tattoo of Olympic rings on her hip, Rousey valued everything that went into reaching this point of her career. "I already felt accomplished before today," she said. "It sounds corny, but a medal is just an inanimate object. It's really about the journey."

Rousey lost in the quarterfinals, but came back to earn her bronze-medal opportunity and defeated Annett Boehm of Germany, the bronze medalist in 2004. Typical of Rousey's confidence, she later said that before taking on Boehm, "I was making a list of all the things I was going to do after the match. I was going to look up in the stands at my mom. I think I even thought of what I was going to say to reporters, but I've forgotten those."

While other Americans fell short in their medal hopes, Adler Volmar still served as an inspirational story. Twelve years after his Olympic judo debut for Haiti, Volmar underwent knee surgery in February. His doctor gave him only a 1 percent chance of recovering in time for the U.S. Olympic Team Trials in June, but he succeeded.

So did athletes from many countries not necessarily accustomed to judo success. Japan won four gold medals, half its total from Athens. That left three golds for China's women, while Tuvshinbayar Naidan claimed Mongolia's first Olympic gold medal. Other new faces on the medals stand came from Tajikistan, Georgia, Italy, Romania, Germany, and Azerbaijan.

RONDA ROUSEY OF THE USA (BLUE) USED ALL HER LEVERAGE TO MAKE SURE ANNETT BOEHM OF GERMANY DID NOT COME OUT ON TOP IN A BRONZE MEDAL MATCH | *MIKE HEWITT/GETTY IMAGES*

VALERIA GOTAY OF THE USA (BLUE) AND GULZAT URALBAYEVA OF KAZAKHSTAN WENT
HEAD-TO-HEAD ON THE MAT IN BEIJING | *JED JACOBSOHN/GETTY IMAGES*

ANGE MERCIE JEAN BAPTISTE OF HAITI (L) AND YURISLEYDIS LUPETEY OF CUBA NEEDED A BREAK
FROM ONE ANOTHER AND ATTENTION FROM TRAINERS | *JED JACOBSOHN/GETTY IMAGES*

KONSTANTIN SEMENOV (WHITE) WAS WILLING TO STAND ON HIS HEAD IF IT MEANT BEATING AMAR
MERIDJA OF ALGERIA | *PAUL GILHAM/GETTY IMAGES*

CRAIG FALLON OF GREAT BRITAIN TASTED VICTORY IN A 60KG REPECHAGE BOUT WITH YOUNES AHMADI OF MOROCCO, BUT ONLY AFTER ABSORBING HIS SHARE OF PUNISHMENT | *JULIAN FINNEY/GETTY IMAGES*

ELI BREMER OF THE U.S. TAKES AIM IN THE MEN'S AIR PISTOL | *NICK LAHAM/GETTY IMAGES*

THREE-SPORT OLYMPIAN | *WHEN CASUAL OBSERVERS LOOK AT THE BEIJING OLYMPIC GAMES' MODERN PENTATHLON RESULTS, THEY* will see Germany's Lena Schoneborn winning the women's event and in a repeat performance from Athens 2004, Russian Andrey Moiseer claimed the gold in the men's event. But if they look further, they'll see a threesome—Sheila Taormina, United States, 19th; Zsuzsanna Voros, Hungary, 20th; Margaux Isaksen, United States, 21st—whose stories they may not know.

The 39-year-old Taormina and the 16-year-old Isaksen took up modern pentathlon in the four years since Voros won the women's gold at the Athens 2004 Games. For Isaksen to be a newcomer, at 16, is understandable but Taormina had been busy in earlier years—competing in previous Olympic Games. In fact, by qualifying for modern pentathlon in Beijing, she became the first person to compete in the Games in three different sports.

At the 1996 Atlanta Games, she was a member of the gold-winning, record-setting U.S. women's 4x200-meter freestyle relay team. At the Sydney 2000 Olympic Games, she participated in the Olympic debut of triathlon and finished sixth, adding a 23rd-place triathlon at the Athens 2004 Olympic Games.

Talk about Olympic diversity: Taormina went from a single swimming event in 1996 to triathlon's trio of swimming, cycling, and running in 2000 and 2004 to modern pentathlon's quintet of events in 2008—shooting, fencing, equestrian show jumping, swimming, and running.

In Beijing, she started the day struggling in two of her three new disciplines: she was 28th after the 20-shot pistol session, then dropped to last after beating just four of her 35 competitors in the one-touch epee fencing bouts. Almost ready to give up during the fencing segment, Taormina rebounded by setting a Games record in the swimming portion with a time of 2:8.86 in the 200-meter freestyle. She then logged a perfect ride on a randomly assigned horse, improving to 28th place. She made up another nine places, with a time of 10:25.05 in the grueling day's final event—the 3,000-meter run—giving her a total of 5,304 points.

Schoneborn's winning 5,729 points were 40 better than Great Britain's Heather Fell, who took the silver, with Ukraine's Victoria Tereshuk winning the women's bronze. The first repeat gold medalist since Sweden's Lars Hall in 1952 and 1956, Moiseev outlasted the Lithuania duo of Edvinas Krungolcas and Andrejus Zadneprovskis for the men's top honor. Sam Sacksen was the top U.S. male finisher at 18th.

ONE-TOUCH EPEE FENCING IS ONE OF THE SPORTS' FIVE SAME-DAY EVENTS |
NICK LAHAM/GETTY IMAGES

TEAM USA'S SHEILA TAORMINA, A MEDAL-WINNING SWIMMER IN 1992, COMPETES IN HER FAVORITE
EVENT OF THE MODERN PENTATHLON | *CLIVE ROSE/GETTY IMAGES*

SHEILA TAORMINA OF THE U.S. COMPETES IN THE EQUESTRIAN PORTION, POSTING ONE OF ONLY
THREE PERFECT RIDES IN THE WOMEN'S COMPETITION | *CLIVE ROSE/GETTY IMAGES*

FRANCE'S FOUR FELT THE SATISFACTION THAT COMES WITH A GOLD
MEDAL IN THE MEN'S QUADRUPLE SCULLS | *JAMIE SQUIRE/GETTY IMAGES*

EIGHT TIMES THE SATISFACTION | GOING INTO
THEIR OLYMPIC ROWING COMPETITION, THE
MEMBERS OF TEAM USA'S WOMEN'S EIGHT
enjoyed the confidence that came with being two-time world champions. But for extra incentive, they reached back into history.

Before leaving for China, the rowers gathered at USA Rowing headquarters in Princeton NJ and watched the videotape of the 1984 eight's Olympic victor.

At the halfway point of the team's 2,000-meter race at the Beijing Games, coxswain Mary Whipple reminded her rowers of the '84 team's achievement. "Then we just motored ahead," she said after the victory at the Shunyi Rowing-Canoeing Park on the northeast side of Beijing.

The U.S. Olympic Team finished ahead of the Netherlands and Romania—which was seeking a fourth consecutive gold medal in the event. The win was especially rewarding for Whipple and

Anna Cummins, both of whom had been on the silver medal winning team in 2004. They were joined this time by Erin Cafaro, Lindsay Shoop, Anna Goodale, Elle Logan, Susan Francia, Caroline Lind, and Caryn Davies, who all laughed and screamed as they crossed the finish line in slightly more than six minutes.

Equally inspirational was the performance of the U.S. men's eight. After finishing second in their heat, the U.S. rowers had to win the repecharge to make the final. They were in fourth place until they overtook the Netherlands in the third quarter of the race, finishing behind Canada and Great Britain to take the bronze.

"It's been pretty incredible," said Daniel Walsh. "We had a rough heat, but we came together as a team and that's the Olympic spirit. You persevere and you end up on the podium."

Joining Walsh were Beau Hoopman, Matt Schnobrich, Micah Boyd, Wyatt Allen, Steven Coppola, Josh Inman, Bryan Volpenhein, and coxswain Marcus McElhenney.

Michelle Guerette captured the first U.S. medal (silver) in single sculls since 1988. In 5th place at the halfway mark, Guerette told herself, "Keep it together. Don't let up." She must have listened. Guerette overtook two-time Olympic champion Ekaterina Karsten of Belarus for second, while finishing behind Rumyana Neykova of Bulgaria. Guerette described her effort as "better than my best race."

The team from Great Britain echoed that sentiment by winning two golds and six total medals, followed by Canada with four medals, and America and Australia with three each. Great Britain took a third consecutive gold in the men's four, while China's gold in the women's quadruple sculls was the country's first in the sport.

KEN JURKOWSKI OF THE U.S. WAS LOOKING FORWARD TO HIS CHANCE TO RACE IN THE SINGLE SCULLS QUARTERFINALS | *AL BELLO/GETTY IMAGES*

NOBODY WAS PAUSING TO SIZE UP THE COMPETITION IN THE MEN'S QUADRUPLE
SCULLS EVENT | *MICHAEL STEELE/GETTY IMAGES*

THE JOY WAS MAGNIFIED BY A FACTOR OF EIGHT WHEN THE U.S. TEAM FINISHED ITS GOLDEN
PERFORMANCE | *MUSTAFA OZER/AFP/GETTY IMAGES*

A SENSE OF HISTORY WAS AMONG THE BOATLOAD OF REASONS FOR THE U.S. WOMEN'S
EIGHT CONVINCING WIN | *JAMIE SQUIRE/GETTY IMAGES*

U.S. FOUR MEN'S ROWERS DAVID BANKS, PAUL TETI, GIUSEPPE LANZONE & BRETT NEWLIN BASK IN THE AFTERGLOW OF THEIR HEAT | *JONATHAN FERREY/GETTY IMAGES*

OLIVIA WHITLAM AND LOUISA REEVE OF GREAT BRITAIN WALKED TALL AT THE ROWING-CANOEING PARK | *SHAUN BOTTERILL/GETTY IMAGES*

COMPETITORS IN THE MEN'S 470 CLASS LINE UP IN QINGDAO'S FUSHAN
BAY IN PREPARATION FOR THE START | *CLIVE MASON/GETTY IMAGES*

ZACH RAILEY OF THE USA TAKES A GRAY DAY AND TURNS IT INTO A
SILVER-MEDAL DAY IN THE FINN CLASS | *PAUL GILHAM/GETTY IMAGES*

THE 'GREAT' BRITS | *A YELLOW SEA, BLUE-GREEN ALGAE AND RED-WHITE-AND-BLUE VICTORIES. THOSE WERE THE PREDOMINANT COLORS FOR*

the Beijing Games' sailing events, conducted 500 miles to the southeast in Qingdao, a major Chinese port city on the Yellow Sea coast. Earlier in the summer, a massive algae bloom blanketed Qingdao's Fushan Bay, hindering pre-Games practice sessions and nearly jeopardizing the 11 sailing events. In the end, the Games went on, with Great Britain (yes, that red-white-and-blue nation) demonstrating her mastery of the sea.

In duplicating its best sailing medal haul since 1908, Great Britain captured four golds, a silver, and a bronze for a Games-high six medals and top-boating-nation bragging rights for the third straight Olympic Games.

Australia picked up two golds and a silver for second place in the sailing medal tally, with the United States and Spain tying for third with one gold and one silver each.

The American medals came from a pair of twenty-somethings among the 14 first-time Team USA sailors. They were led by Anna Tunnicliffe, who captured gold in the women's Laser Radial class and who became the first American woman in 20 years to win a sailing medal. The top-ranked Tunnicliffe—born in England and jokingly claimed by the British as their own—battled varying wind conditions, choppy waves, and diminished visibility with persistent consistency. After falling to third midway in her multi-race event, Tunnicliffe rebounded to take the gold.

Zach Railey earned the first U.S. Finn medal since 1992 when he took the silver in the open Finn class, challenging Great Britain's heralded Ben Ainslie. Ranked No. 11 in the world, Railey found himself hot on the wake of Ainslie, who had already pocketed two golds and a silver from past Games.

Qingdao's quirky weather—this time, no wind—halted the medal race for a day, but Ainslie eventually took his third gold in as many Olympic Games.

However, no event was as thrilling as the open 49er skiff class, with Danish overall leaders Jonas Warrer and Martin Kirketerp suffering a broken mast just prior to the 10-boat final. They raced back to port, borrowed a boat from the eliminated Croatian team, and returned to the starting line with only seconds to spare. They finished high enough to maintain their lead and clinch the gold. Spain, which took the silver, and Italy, one spot behind bronze-medalist Germany, both protested Denmark's substituted boat. The race juries and the Court of Arbitration for Sport denied the protest, and the Danes kept the gold.

160

USA'S TIM WADLOW (L) AND CHRIS RAST (R) COMPETE IN DAY 2
OF THE 49ERS CLASS | *CLIVE MASON/GETTY IMAGES*

GREAT BRITAIN'S BEN AINSLIE CELEBRATES AFTER WINNING
THE FINN CLASS GOLD | *CLIVE MASON/GETTY IMAGES*

SAILBOARDERS LEAVE THE START OF THE MEN'S RS:X EVENT | *DON EMMERT/AFP/GETTY IMAGES*

161

NICO LUCA MARC DELLE KARTH AND NIKOLAUS RESCH OF AUSTRIA TAKE A WAVE TO
THE FACE IN THE 49ER CLASS COMPETITION | *CLIVE MASON/GETTY IMAGES*

THE BRAZILIAN DUO OF ANDRE FONSECA AND RODRIGO DUARTE TAKE A PEAK
AROUND THE SAIL IN THE 49ER CLASS RACE | *CLIVE MASON/GETTY IMAGES*

TEAM USA'S VINCENT HANCOCK REFLECTS DURING HIS GOLD-MEDAL
RUN IN MEN'S SKEET | *STREETER LECKA/GETTY IMAGES*

TAKING A SHOT AT HISTORY | *NO OLYMPIC SPORT IS QUITE AS DIVERSE AS SHOOTING. THE 2008 GAMES COMPETITION BROUGHT TOGETHER*

contestants from 65 countries in 15 events, with the U.S. Olympic Team featuring a 19-year-old gold medalist and a 56-year-old shooter, believed to be the oldest U.S. Olympic female athlete ever.

America's Olympic Team made its best showing in history, with two gold, two silver, and two bronze medals—plus another surprising ending for medalist Mark Emmons.

The gold medals highlighted Team USA's performance, with Vincent Hancock winning in men's skeet and Glenn Eller taking the men's double trap. Hancock, 19, needed a second shoot-off with Norway's Tore Brovold to emerge as the champion. "I like to deal with pressure, and now it's paid off," Hancock said.

Eller improved from finishes of 12th in Sydney in 2000 and 17th in Athens in 2004. "I was so happy after I won, but I didn't know whether to cry, smile or jump up and down," Eller said after the competition in the Beijing Shooting Range Hall, which was the first new venue completed for the 2008 Games.

Emmons experienced all of those emotions, which was nothing new. Famous for shooting at the wrong target and costing himself a medal in 2004—only to end up marrying a Czech Republic shooter who consoled him—Emmons was back for more in Beijing. He was "completely satisfied" with the silver in the men's 50-meter prone rifle event, but hit the trigger prematurely on his last shot in the 50-meter three-position rifle event and fell from first to fourth. "I don't know why I am not supposed to win this event," he said.

America's other medalists were Kim Rhode (silver) in women's skeet, Corey Cogdell (bronze) in women's trap, and Jason Turner (bronze) in the men's 10-meter air rifle event.

COREY COGDELL OF THE UNITED STATES GRINS AFTER WINNING THE WOMEN'S TRAP BRONZE MEDAL | *VLADIMIR RYS/BONGARTS/GETTY IMAGES*

MARIA GROZDEVA OF BULGARIA TAKES AIM IN THE 25M PISTOL EVENT | *QUINN ROONEY/GETTY IMAGES*

英式足球

SOCCER

BEIJING 2008

英式足球

BELGIUM'S KEEPER LOGAN BAILLY CAN'T STOP THIS SHOT FROM NIGERIA IN THE 4-1 MEN'S SEMIFINAL | *LIU JIN/AFP/GETTY IMAGES*

GOLDEN GIRLS | *THE UNITED STATES' SOCCER TEAMS STARTED THEIR RESPECTIVE BEIJING TOURNAMENTS IN OPPOSING FASHION. THE U.S. MEN OPENED WITH A SUR-*prising 1-0 victory over Japan. The American women—already without star Abby Wambach, sidelined with a broken leg—began their quest for gold with a gut-wrenching 2-0 loss to Norway, both goals coming on U.S. defensive lapses in the first four minutes. But the U.S. women proved it's not how you start but how you finish, as they rallied—with a little help from some preliminary-round friends—to reach the gold-medal match for the fourth straight Games. Meanwhile, the American men couldn't sustain their winning ways and were finally eliminated in group play.

After its opening loss, the U.S. women edged Japan 1-0 on Carli Lloyd's goal and then received help winning their group on goal differential. On the third and final day of preliminary matches, Japan upset previously unbeaten Norway 5-1 and the Americans blitzed winless New Zealand 4-0. Heather O'Reilly started the onslaught against New Zealand with the fastest goal in Olympic history, scoring 40 seconds in. In the quarterfinals, the U.S. weathered a 99-minute lightning delay and a late tying goal by Canada before Natasha Kai scored the game winner on a diving header in overtime. The Americans then faced the Japanese for the second time in 10 days. Angela Hucles scored twice in the rematch to help the U.S. turn an early 1-0 deficit into a 4-2 victory.

The gold-medal pairing pitted the U.S. and Brazil in a third major tournament match in four years—the United States having won the Athens gold, while Brazil shut out the top-ranked Americans in the 2007 Women's World Cup semis. In front of a Beijing Workers Stadium crowd of 51,612, the two powerhouses went scoreless in regulation. Lloyd finally scored in the 96th minute, and U.S. keeper Hope Solo stymied a flurry of shots on goal—including a point-blank shot by Brazilian star Marta—over the finale's last 24 minutes of overtime to clinch the 1-0 golden victory and the United States' 1,000th gold medal in over 100 years of participating in both the Olympic Games & the Olympic Winter Games.

The men on Team USA started out strong in their 1-0 Group B victory over Japan, with midfielder Stuart Holden accounting for the goal and keeper Brad Guzan registering the shutout. In their 2nd pool match, Goals by Sacha Kljestan and Iozy Altidore provided the USA team with a 2-1 lead over the Netherlands. But the Dutch scored a last minute free kick to draw the tie. Needing a win or a tie in the pool finale against Nigeria, the U.S. played a man down three minutes in and could muster only Kljestan's penalty-kick score in a 2-1, tournament-ending loss.

Argentina won its second consecutive men's gold, as Angel di Maria converted on Lionel Messi's through ball in the 58th minute of the championship match. The game was halted temporarily for a first-half water break because of excessive heat—107.6 degrees—inside a packed Beijing National Stadium.

NATASHA KAI CELEBRATES USA BEATING BRAZIL IN THE WOMEN'S GOLD-MEDAL MATCH | *DANIEL GARCIA/AFP/GETTY IMAGES*

USA'S SHANNON BOXX (R) IS HEAD AND SHOULDERS ABOVE CANADA'S EMILY ZURRER IN THE RAINY QUARTERFINAL WIN | *AFP/GETTY IMAGES*

DANNY SZETELA OF THE USA BEATS NIGERIA'S VICTOR OBINNA TO THE BALL IN A MATCH AT BEIJING WORKERS' STADIUM | *SHAUN BOTTERILL/GETTY IMAGES*

ARENTINA'S ANGEL DI MARIA (L) AND BRAZIL'S RAFIHNA BATTLE FOR POSSESSION IN ARGENTINA'S SEMIFINAL VICTORY | *MICHAEL KAPPELER/AFP/GETTY IMAGES*

USA'S HEATHER O'REILLY CHALLENGES JAPAN'S KARINA MARUYAMA FOR THE BALL IN THE UNITED STATES' 4-2 SEMIFINAL VICTORY | *QUINN ROONEY/GETTY IMAGES*

BRAZIL'S RONALDINHO HAS A LEG UP ON THE BALL AHEAD OF BELGIUM'S THOMAS VERMAELEN IN THE MEN'S BRONZE-MEDAL MATCH | *RODOLFO BUHRER/GETTY IMAGES*

CAT OSTERMAN AND HER U.S. TEAMMATES VIEWED THE TOURNAMENT THROUGH A WINDOW
OF HIGH EXPECTATIONS | *VLADIMIR RYS/BONGARTS/GETTY IMAGES*

NOT A FOUR-GONE CONCLUSION | *GOING INTO THE 2008 BEIJING OLYMPIC GAMES SOFTBALL TOURNAMENT, THE BIGGEST QUESTION WAS* whether the U.S. team would dominate the competition so thoroughly that it would harm efforts to have the sport reinstated to the Olympic program in 2016.

Yukiko Ueno, however, had her own ideas. She pitched Japan to a 3-1 victory in the championship game, spoiling the Americans' bid for a fourth consecutive gold medal since the sport was launched in 1996.

"There is some parity in the sport," said U.S. coach Mike Candrea, though the U.S. Olympic Team hardly supported that theory in their seven preliminary games, which they won by a total score of 53-1. The team also hit an Olympic-record 13 home runs, while pitchers Cat Osterman, Monica Abbott, and Jennie Finch held opponents to an .042 batting average.

"This is what the Olympics is about: having extraordinary performances," Abbott said.

The most extraordinary performer, though, might have been Ueno, who allowed only Crystl Bustos' solo homer in the gold medal game. It was a stunning ending for the members of a talented, cohesive U.S. team who had bonded over the 37,000 miles of pre-Olympic Games travel.

That emotional final game was the last USA Softball appearance for retiring players Tairia Flowers, Kelly Kretschman, Laura Berg, Lovieanne Jung, and Crystl Bustos, who left their cleats at home plate.

Bustos was the team's offensive star in Beijing, batting .500 with six homers and 10 RBIs in nine games. Other players who hit .300 or better while appearing in at least eight games included Caitlin Lowe, Kretschman, Jessica Mendoza, Jung, Natasha Watley, and Andrea Duran.

KELLY KRETSCHMAN OF THE U.S. RETIRED KNOWING SHE HAD LEFT IT ALL ON THE FIELD |
JONATHAN FERREY/GETTY IMAGES

CRYSTL BUSTOS ALWAYS KNEW A HOME RUN WOULD BE WELL RECEIVED
BY HER U.S. TEAMMATES | *CLIVE ROSE/GETTY IMAGES*

JENNIE FINCH HELPED RAISE THE BAR FOR THE DOMINANT U.S.
PITCHING STAFF | *AL BELLO/GETTY IMAGES*

SIMMONE MORROW OF AUSTRALIA WAS ON THE BALL AGAINST
HOST CHINA | *MARK DADSWELL/GETTY IMAGES*

PITCHER JOHANA ROSALYX GOMEZ SEQUERA OF VENEZUELA LIKED THIS DELIVERY AS SOON AS IT LEFT HER HAND | *JED JACOBSOHN/GETTY IMAGES*

BELINDA WRIGHT AND HER AUSTRALIAN TEAMMATES WERE SCRAMBLING TO STAY AHEAD OF JAPAN'S BEST EFFORTS | *OMAR TORRES/AFP/GETTY IMAGES*

MICHAEL PHELPS WAS TRANSCENDENT IN THE 100M BUTTERFLY | *FRANCOIS-XAVIER MARIT/AFP/GETTY IMAGES*

THE EIGHTH WONDER OF THE WORLD | *MAYBE BECAUSE HE WAS NOT A TEENAGE GIRL IN THE 1970S—AND SO HE DIDN'T HAVE THE POSTER ON HIS WALL—MICHAEL*

Phelps once wondered who this Mark Spitz was and why everybody was asking what he thought of him. He soon found out about Spitz.

In Beijing, the world found out about Michael Phelps, and now the two will be linked together. Forever. In 1972, Mark Spitz set an Olympic Record by winning seven gold medals in one Games. In 2008, Michael Phelps set a new Olympic Record by winning eight gold medals.

There is actually much more to tell about Team USA's performance in Beijing's Water Cube. The Americans broke 11 world records and won 31 medals, followed by Australia with 20, and Great Britain with six.

An American—Phelps—won five individual events and was a member of three winning relay teams in the most dominant individual performance in Olympic history. Natalie Coughlin followed up her "Golden Girl" performance of 2004 Games with six medals (one gold, two silver, and three bronze), the best showing ever for an American woman. Phelps' quest for perfection ended as a team victory, with America's win in the 4x100-meter medley relay, a race that contained some momentary tension. After the first half of Phelps' butterfly leg, the Americans were still behind. But then Phelps surged ahead, and Jason Lezak's freestyle lap finished off the win over Australia.

But the story has to start and end with Phelps. His races had everything: individual and team triumphs, convincing victories, dramatic finishes.

At last, he could acknowledge, "I literally wanted to do something that no one's ever done before in this sport." He did something that may never be done again. It may be that nobody even tries.

Phelps' achievement left everyone wondering how to quantify it on an Olympic level. Ranking it is tricky. How do you compare it with the track and field feats of Jesse Owens, Paavo Nurmi, Carl Lewis? Swimmers do have more opportunities to win medals, and there are few variables involved; it's just blocks, water, wall. Yet it is a sport of specialists, with a revolving cast for each new race, rested and ready to take on Phelps, on their day, in their event.

He took them all on, and he beat them all, sometimes easily, other times in close competition that further validated his prowess. In the 100-meter butterfly he needed great resolve and a lucky last stroke in his victory of one-hundredth of a second over Milorad Cavic. And, he needed the help of his teammates in the relays, especially that of Jason Lezak in the 4x100-meter freestlye relay. But no matter how you look at it, it all added up to eight golds, a number that's considered fortuitous in Chinese culture and a figure that will now be revered in American sports.

Those two close races deserve further review. Michael Phelps, Garrett Weber-Gale, Cullen Jones, and Jason Lezak destroyed the world record in the 400 free relay by four seconds, but only edged out France by eight-hundredths of a second to win in 3:08.24. Lezak and Alain Bernard were neck-and-neck at the finish, and with one last desperate reach, Lezak touched the wall first, turning in the fastest relay split in history at 46.06.

GARRETT WEBER-GALE (L) AND MICHAEL PHELPS ENTHUSIASTICALLY CHEERED TEAMMATE JASON LEZAK'S AMAZING FINISH IN THE 400 FREESTYLE RELAY | *CAMERON SPENCER/GETTY IMAGES*

In the 100 fly, Phelps was seventh after the first 50 meters and trailed Cavic by more than a half second. With just 15 meters to go Phelps pulled even with the California native, who swims for Serbia. As Cavic reached for the touchpad, Phelps took an extra half-stroke and somehow managed to get his hands on the wall first. No one in the Water Cube, including Phelps, knew he had won until the times flashed on the scoreboard.

"When I took that last half stroke, I thought I lost the race right there, but it turns out that was the difference," Phelps said.

Phelps arrived in Beijing with just the right blend of confidence and humility, of not fueling the focus on eight golds but not discouraging it ("My goals aren't published," he said), and of internal and external motivation. It worked beautifully.

Coughlin's performance also was outstanding. She took home a medal in each of her six events. She became the first woman to win consecutive Olympic gold medals in the 100 backstroke. She earned silver medals in the 400 free relay and 400 medley relay, and bronze medals in the 800 free relay, 400 free, and 200 individual medley.

Dara Torres also made history in Beijing by becoming the first American to swim in five Olympic Games. As the oldest female swimmer (at 41) to compete in the Olympic Games, Torres took home silver medals in the 50 free, 400 free relay, and 400 medley relay.

Margaret Hoelzer and Katie Hoff also won multiple medals. Hoelzer took the silver in the 200 back and a bronze in the 100 back. She also earned a silver medal by swimming in the preliminaries of the 400 medley relay. Hoff earned two silver medals; one in the 4x200-meter free relay and the other in the 400 free. She also captured a bronze in the 400 individual medley.

Even Olympic rookies Rebecca Soni and Christine Magnuson made big impacts. Soni left Beijing with three medals: a gold in the 200 breaststroke and silvers in the 100 breast and 400 medley relay.

In fact, Soni, who underwent minor heart surgery in 2006, broke a world record in the 200 breast, while dethroning Australian world-record holder Leisel Jones in 2:20.22. "It's been a long road to get here," Soni said. "I can't believe what just happened."

Magnuson won a silver medal in the 100 fly and added another silver in the 400 medley relay.

On the men's side, Ryan Lochte and Aaron Peirsol each turned in individual gold medal performances. Lochte earned four medals, two gold and two bronze. In fact, in the 200 back, Lochte finished ahead of Peirsol. Peirsol took home the gold in the 100 back with a world-record time of 52.54, and teammate Matt Grevers earned the silver medal.

Other men's individual medalists were Larsen Jensen, Peter Vanderkaay, and Lezak. Jensen won a bronze in the 400 free, while Vanderkaay earned a bronze in the 200 free. Lezak tied Brazil's Cesar Cielo for the bronze in the 100 free. US swimmers Mark Warkentin and Chloe Sutton participated in the Olympic Games inaugural 10k open water race. Overall, it was a great Olympic Games for American swimmers—it just happened to be the greatest of all for one of them.

DARA TORRES COMES OUT OF THE BLOCKS DURING A HEAT IN THE WOMEN'S 50M FREESTYLE. TORRES MISSED GOLD BY ONLY .01 OF A SECOND | *TIMOTHY CLARY/AFP/GETTY IMAGES*

IT WAS NOT ALL FUN AND GAMES FOR BRENDAN HANSEN (L) AND RYAN LOCHTE, BUT THE U.S.
SWIMMERS HAD GOOD TIMES | *NICK LAHAM/GETTY IMAGES*

AFTER BREAKING A WORLD RECORD IN WINNING THE 400 MEDLEY RELAY, THE U.S. TEAM ENJOYED
THE WALK OF CELEBRATION | *EZRA SHAW/GETTY IMAGES*

U.S. SWIMMER AARON PEIRSOL TRIED TO GET MIND AROUND A WORLD-RECORD PERFORMANCE IN
THE 100 BACKSTROKE | *MARTIN BUREAU/AFP/GETTY IMAGES*

THE START WAS SPECTACULAR, BUT THE FINISH WOULD BE EVEN MORE DRAMATIC FOR MILORAD CAVIC (L.) OF SERBIA AND MICHAEL PHELPS IN THE 100 BUTTERFLY | *ADAM PRETTY/GETTY IMAGES*

RYAN LOCHTE COMPETES IN THE MEN'S 200M INDIVIDUAL MEDLEY SEMI-FINAL | *CLIVE BRUNSKILL/GETTY IMAGES*

MARGARET HOELZER COMES OUT OF THE STARTING BLOCKS IN THE WOMEN'S 100M BACKSTROKE | *ADAM PRETTY/GETTY IMAGES*

CHRISTINE MAGNUSON IS SHOWN MID STROKE DURING THE WOMEN'S 100M BUTTERFLY SEMI-FINAL | *MARTIN BUREAU/AFP/GETTY IMAGES*

U.S. SWIMMER NATALIE COUGHLIN GAZED INTO THE RECORD BOOKS WITH HER PERFORMANCE IN BEIJING | *MARTIN BUREAU/AFP/GETTY IMAGES*

U.S. SWIMMER PETER VADERKAAY (L) WAS BUBBLING WITH CONCENTRATION DURING A 1,500 FREESTYLE HEAT | *JED JACOBSOHN/GETTY IMAGES*

EAMON SULLIVAN OF AUSTRALIA COMPETES IN THE MEN'S 50M FREESTYLE SEMIFINAL | *HARRY HOW/GETTY IMAGES*

RICKY BERENS WAS ANOTHER OF THE U.S. SWIMMERS WHO HELPED PRODUCE A BREATH-TAKING SHOWING IN BEIJING | *STU FORSTER/GETTY IMAGES*

U.S. SWIMMER KATIE HOFF REACHED BACK FOR A LITTLE EXTRA GOING INTO HER 200 FREE-STYLE SEMIFINAL RACE | *ALEXANDER HASSENSTEIN/BONGARTS/GETTY IMAGES*

U.S. SWIMMER MATT GREVERS (BOTTOM LANE) SURFACED QUICKLY AS A KEY FACTOR IN A HEAT OF THE 400 MEDLEY RELAY | *OLIVIER MORIN/AFP/GETTY IMAGES*

NATALIE COUGHLIN ENTERS THE WATER AT THE START OF THE 100M BACKSTROKE FINAL WHICH
SHE FINISHED BY EARNING A GOLD MEDAL | *AL BELLO/GETTY IMAGES*

BEN WILDMAN-TOBRINER PREPARES TO COMPETE IN THE MENS 50M FREESTLYE
SEMIFINAL | *HARRY HOW/GETTY IMAGES*

REBECCA SONI ON THE WAY TO WINNING THE GOLD MEDAL IN THE 200M BREASTSTROKE FINAL |
LARS BARON/GETTY IMAGES

RYAN LOCHTE CELEBRATES AFTER WINNING THE MEN'S 200M BACKSTROKE FINAL IN A WORLD RECORD TIME OF 1 MIN 53.94 SEC. | *MARTIN BUREAU/AFP/GETTY IMAGES*

(L-R) CAROLINE BURCKLE, KIM VANDERBERG AND CHRISTINE MARSHALL CHEER ON THEIR U.S. TEAMMATE JULIA SMITH DURING A RELAY HEAT | *NICK LAHAM/GETTY IMAGES*

CHINA'S JIAYING PANG (L), SLOVENIA'S SARA ISAKOVIC (C) AND KATHRYN HOFF OF THE U.S. DURING THE 200M FREESTYLE SEMIFINAL | *FRANCOIS-XAVIER MARIT/AFP/GETTY IMAGES*

REBECCA ADLINGTON OF GREAT BRITAIN SOAKED UP THE FULL OLYMPIC EXPERIENCE | *MICHAEL KAPPELER/AFP/GETTY IMAGES*

THE UNITED STATES' CHRISTINA JONES AND ANDREA NOTT COMPETE
IN THE DUET FREE ROUTINE | *JEFF GROSS/GETTY IMAGES*

REPEAT PERFORMANCES | *BESIDES SHARING A FIRST NAME, ANASTASIA DAYDOVA AND ANASTASIA ERMAKOVA ALSO SHARE THE SAME* same height, weight, age, and hometown. And the double delights don't end there for the Russian synchronized swimming duet. The two now have a pair of gold medals each after successfully defending their 2004 Athens Games title. The Anastasias' nearly flawless technical and free routines—half the scores for each being combined to arrive at a final score—received 99.8333 out of a possible 100 points. In similar dominant fashion the two also helped Russia claim its third consecutive gold medal in team competition scoring 99.500. The Russians unveiled a free routine shrouded in secrecy, since the team hadn't competed since the 2007 world championships.

And while Beijing's synchronized swimming venue was the Water Cube and not a courtroom, the theme for the United States' fortunes seemed to be "taking the fifth": fifth place in team competition and fifth for the U.S. duet combo of Christina Jones and Andrea Nott. Team USA was tied for fifth with Canada after its technical routine and finished tied for fifth with Japan after its innovative free routine, posting a 95.167 overall score. Reaching the finals after the original 24 pairs were whittled down to the top 12, Jones and Nott placed fifth with a 95.500 cumulative score.

Spain claimed the team silver and China the bronze, its first event medal. Spain's Gemma Mengual and Andrea Fuentes took silver, and Japan's Saho Harada and Emiko Suzuki won the bronze. Since the sport was added to the Olympic Games in 1984, Japan has won a medal in every Games, for a total of 12 medals.

ONE OF THE MEMBERS OF RUSSIA'S GOLD-WINNING TEAM RISES ABOVE THE WATER | *XAVIER MARIT/AFP/GETTY IMAGES*

EGYPT GOES HEELS OVER HEAD IN TEAM COMPETITION | *PHIL WALTER/GETTY IMAGES*

乒乓球

TABLE TENNIS
BEIJING 2008

COMPETING AGAINST CHINA'S CHUAN CHIH-YUAN (TOP) WAS ALL A BLUR FOR
GUSTAVO TSUBOI OF BRAZIL | *LARS BARON/BONGARTS/GETTY IMAGES*

JOINING THE TABLE OF GREATNESS | THERE IS APPARENTLY NO STOPPING CHINA'S DOMINATION OF OLYMPIC TABLE TENNIS, ALTHOUGH

the U.S. team is making major progress in the sport—thanks to some Chinese influence.

Beijing native Chen Wang delivered by far the best American performance ever by reaching the women's quarterfinals in the competition at Peking University.

After retiring from competition, Wang moved to New York in 2000 to be closer to her sister. She came out of retirement to compete for the U.S. and will take home memories of winning an epic seven-game match against Kim Kyung-ah of South Korea. She eventually lost to Li Jia Wei of Singapore in the quarterfinals.

"This was special because it was the first time the Olympics were in China and my first time in the Olympics," Wang said. "I was very emotional ... because it's been a long time and I've sacrificed a lot of things."

Wang's heritage was not unusual in this tournament. Of the 78 women's contestants, 35 (including the eight quarterfinalists and all three U.S. players) were born in China.

Not surprisingly, China easily won the men's and women's team competitions and swept both of the individual events. The silver medal for Singapore's women's team was the country's first Olympic medal since 1960. China's women swept the individual medals for the first time since 1988, with gold for Zhang Yining, silver for Wang Nan, and bronze for Guo Yue.

China's men beat Germany for the team title and Lin Ma (gold), Wang Hao (silver), and Wang Liq (bronze) took the individual medals. Defending champion Ryu Seung Min lost in the round of 32.

CHINA'S LIN MA FOUGHT OFF EVERYTHING KOREA'S OH SANG EUN SENT HIS
WAY IN A QUARTERFINAL MATCH | *PEDRO UGARTE/AFP/GETTY IMAGES*

POLAND'S NATALIA PARTYKA COULD NOT SMASH CHINA'S DYNASTY IN THE
TEAM EVENT | *LARS BARON/BONGARTS/GETTY IMAGES*

LI JIA WEI OF SINGAPORE DROPPED U.S. STAR CHEN WANG FROM MEDAL
CONTENTION | *TEH ENG KOON/AFP/GETTY IMAGES*

BEIJING NATIVE CHEN WANG MADE AN EMOTIONAL RETURN AS THE
TOP U.S. PLAYER | *ISSOUF SANOGO/AFP/GETTY IMAGES*

THE PLAYERS WERE CENTER STAGE IN THE PEKING UNIVERSITY GYMNASIUM FOR
ONE OF CHINA'S MARQUEE SPORTS | *CAMERON SPENCER/GETTY IMAGES*

CHINESE FLAGS WERE PROMIMENT THROUGHOUT THE TABLE TENNIS COMPETITION |
TEH ENG KOON/AFP/GETTY IMAGES

AKMAL IRGASHEV OF UZBEKISTAN (L) TOOK AN AERIAL APPROACH TO HIS BRONZE MEDAL
BOUT WITH CHIKA YAGAZIE CHUKWUMERIJE OF NIGERIA | *JUNG YEON-JE/AFP/GETTY IMAGES*

FIGHTING FAMILY SHINES | MERELY BECOMING
THE FIRST THREESOME OF SIBLINGS SINCE 1904
TO QUALIFY FOR THE U.S. OLYMPIC TEAM IN
the same year obviously was not enough for Mark, Steven, and Diana Lopez.

In Beijing, the Lopez siblings established a standard that may never be matched as a sister and
two brothers won medals for America in the same Olympic Games. Toss in the fact that their
coach is their older brother, Jean, and the family from Sugar Land, Texas, earns a distinct place
in U.S. Olympic history.

If there was any disappointment in their 2008 achievements, it was that welterweight Steven
Lopez lost for the first time in three Olympic tournaments, before earning a bronze medal. On the
other side of the equation, though, were Mark Lopez's silver medal after breaking his hand during
the first exchange of his opening match in the featherweight division. Diana Lopez's overtime victory
in the women's featherweight bronze medal match netted the family's third medal.

Two other stories vied for top billing: Afghanistan won its first Olympic medal when Rohullah

Nikpai took bronze in the men's 58kg class. And Valodia Matos received a lifetime ban from the sport for kicking a judge in the head after being disqualified from his bronze medal match. But neither story could overshadow the fighting Lopez family's showing at Beijing Science and Technology University.

After losing for the first time in six years at any level, Steven Lopez faced the unfamiliar challenge of rebounding from a defeat to Italy's Mauro Sarmiento in overtime in the quarterfinals. When Sarmiento advanced to the finals, Lopez was entered into the repechage to compete for one of two bronze medals. Lopez defeated Sebastien Konan from the Ivory Coast, then beat Azerbaijan's Rashad Ahmadov for the bronze.

"It's hard, but I'm happy with the bronze," Lopez said. "It encourages me to keep going. I love winning. I hate losing. And in no way does this discourage me from wanting to go to the 2012 Olympic Games."

Mark Lopez also had to deal with adversity, going on to win three matches after breaking his left hand in two places. In the finals, he finally lost 3-2 to Korea's Son Taejin, who scored the winning point in the final seconds of the third round.

Diana Lopez outlasted Italy's Veronica Calabrese for a bronze medal that made her "so happy, so emotional," she said. Her brother and coach had inspired her by saying that "her kids will brag about this medal and her grandkids will brag about this medal." Since taekwondo became an official Olympic sport in 2000, U.S. athletes have won six of 10 possible medals.

197

NESAR AHMAD BAHAVE (R) OF AFGHANISTAN BECAME ACQUAINTED WITH THE LOPEZ FAMILY, SPECIFICALLY MARK | *CLIVE ROSE/GETTY IMAGES*

THE ANGER OF CUBA'S VALODIA MATOS (L) WAS MISDIRECTED TOWARD REFEREE CHAKIR CHELBAT
AFTER MATOS LOST A BRONZE MEDAL CONTEST | *JUNG YEON-JE/AFP/GETTY IMAGES*

CHINA'S WU JINGYU RAISED THE HOST COUNTRY'S GOLD MEDAL TOTAL
WITH HER EMOTIONAL VICTORY | *JAMIE SQUIRE/GETTY IMAGES*

MARTINA ZUBCIC (R) OF CROATIA SERVED UP A KICK FOR AZIZE TANRIKULU
OF TURKEY TO CLOSELY CONSIDER | *JUNG YEON-JE/AFP/GETTY IMAGES*

AFTER A BRONZE MEDAL VICTORY, DIANA LOPEZ'S CLOSING MOVE WAS A LEAP INTO THE ARMS OF HER BROTHER AND COACH, JEAN LOPEZ | *BEHROUZ MEHRI/AFP/GETTY IMAGES*

FOR DIANA LOPEZ (L) AND HER BROTHERS, WINNING OLYMPIC MEDALS WAS QUITE A KICK | *BEHROUZ MEHRI/AFP/GETTY IMAGES*

THE WILLIAMS SISTERS, SERENA AND VENUS, DOUBLED THEIR FUN BY WINNING ANOTHER GOLD MEDAL | *CLIVE ROSE/GETTY IMAGES*

STARS COME OUT IN TENNIS STADIUM | *IF ANYONE EVER WONDERED HOW MUCH THE OLYMPIC GAMES MEANS TO A PROFESSIONAL TENNIS PLAYERS, ELENA DEMENTIEVA*

provided the answer. Players may travel around the world, competing in the prestigious Grand Slam events, but nothing hits home like playing for their own country.

After Dementieva came back to defeat fellow Russian Dinara Safina 3-6, 7-5, 6-3, she sank to her knees on the stadium court in the Olympic Green. She later described the victory as "the biggest achievement of my career."

Spain's Rafael Nadal made his own statement about the importance of the Games. Before 2008, no top-five player in the world rankings had ever won an Olympic men's singles title. Nadal changed that with his victory in Beijing.

The day before he officially became No. 1, Nadal beat Fernando Gonzalez of Chile 6-3, 7-6, 6-3 to become an Olympic champion during a remarkable year that included French Open and Wimbledon titles.

While no Americans medaled in singles play, James Blake delivered the perhaps the most memorable victory of the entire tournament. His 6-4, 7-6 quarterfinal win over Switzerland's Roger Federer, then still owning the No. 1 ranking, was the first of his career in nine meetings with Federer. "One day, I'll be able to tell my grandkids that I beat the best of all time," Blake said.

Blake lost to Gonzalez in the semifinals and finally fell to Novak Djokovic of Serbia in the bronze medal match.

Russia had never won a women's singles gold in the Olympic Games, but the country ruled the medals podium in Beijing.

Dementieva, who had won silver at the 2000 Olympic Games, joined Great Britain's Kathleen McKane, Germany's Steffi Graf, and Spain's Arantxa Sanchez Vicario as a winner of multiple Olympic singles medals. Russia's Vera Zvonareva won the bronze over China's Li Na, who had upset 2000 Games American gold medalist Venus Williams in the quarterfinals.

Williams bounced back in doubles play, as did Federer on the men's side. Williams and her sister, Serena, added another gold medal to their 2000 triumph with a 6-2, 6-0 win over Spain's Anabel Medina Garrigues and Virginia Ruano Pacual. Americans have won six of eight Olympic women's doubles titles.

Another pair of sisters, Ukraine's Alona and Kateryna Bondarenko, lost to China's Yan Zie and Zheng Jie in the bronze medal match.

American brothers Bob and Mike Bryan took the men's bronze medal, defeating France's Arnaud Clement and Michael Llodra 3-6, 6-3, 6-4. In the semifinals, the Frenchmen had lost 7-6, 4-6, 19-17 to Sweden's Simon Aspelin and Thomas Johansson in the longest set ever played in Olympic men's tennis.

The Swedes then lost 6-3, 6-4, 6-7, 6-3 to Switzerland's Federer and Stanislas Wawrinka in an exemplary effort for Federer, who had begun the Games by carrying Switzerland's flag in the Opening Ceremony.

AMERICA'S JAMES BLAKE SET HIS SIGHTS HIGH AFTER UPSETTING ROGER FEDERER, BUT LOST TO FERNANDO GONZALEZ IN THE SEMIFINALS | *NICK LAHAM/GETTY IMAGES*

IVETA BENESOVA AND HER CZECH REPUBLIC PARTNER WERE NOT LEFT STANDING IN THE DOUBLES
EVENT AFTER MEETING THE WILLIAMS SISTERS | *CLIVE BRUNSKILL/GETTY IMAGES*

ROGER FEDERER SERVED UP A DOUBLES GOLD MEDAL FOR SWITZERLAND WITH
PARTNER STANISLAS WAWRINKA | *BEHROUZ MEHRI/AFP/GETTY IMAGES*

ABOUT TO BECOME THE WORLD'S NO. 1-RANKED PLAYER, RAFAEL NADAL WAS ON TOP OF HIS GAME IN BEIJING | *PETER PARKS/AFP/GETTY IMAGES*

ROBBY GINEPRI IS AMONG THE YOUNG U.S. PLAYERS LOOKING AHEAD TO LONDON IN 2012 | *PHILIPPE HUGUEN/AFP/GETTY IMAGES*

A BRONZE MEDAL WAS WITHIN THE REACH OF U.S. BROTHERS BOB AND MIKE BRYAN (BOTTOM) IN A VICTORY OVER A FRENCH DUO | *JULIAN FINNEY/GETTY IMAGES*

COMPETITORS LINE UP AT THE START OF THE WOMEN'S TRIATHLON |
CLIVE ROSE/GETTY IMAGES

TRI FOR MEDALS | IN SPITE OF VERY DIFFERENT STARTS, GERMANY'S JAN FRODENO AND AUSTRALIA'S EMMA SNOWSILL ENDED THEIR 3-DISCIPLINE

competition by winning gold. Frodeno out-kicked the men's competition in a four-man sprint to the finish, while Snowsill eased into the women's winner circle with more than a minute's cushion. Beijing's setting for the triathlon—a 1.5-kilometer swim, 40-kilometer cycling segment, and 10K run—was the area around the Ming Tomb Reservoir, near the burial sites of 13 Ming Dynasty emperors.

The one American within grasp of a medal, Laura Bennett, placed fourth in the women's race, she led after the swim, but lost ground during the six-lap cycling portion. A late stomach cramp kept her from keeping up with the eventual medalists on the four-lap run.

U.S. teammate Sarah Haskins, silver medalist at the 2008 World Championships, placed 11th in Beijing. Three-time Olympian Hunter Kemper was the top American male, coming in 43 seconds off a medal pace. His seventh place finish was two spots better than his 2004 Games finish.

In capturing Australia's first triathlon gold, Snowsill logged a time of 1 hour, 58 minutes and 27.66 seconds, 67+ seconds ahead of silver medalist and 2007 world champion Vanessa Fernandes of Portugal. Australia's Emma Moffat claimed the bronze, 25 seconds ahead of Bennett.

With a time of 1:48:53.28, Frodeno earned his five-second winning margin by passing Canada's Simon Whitfield, the gold medalist at the inaugural 2000 Games triathlon, down the homestretch. New Zealand's Bevan Docherty, the Athens Games silver medalist, took the bronze over pre-race favorite Javier Gomez, the reigning world champ from Spain.

JAN FRODENO OF GERMANY SPRINTS TO THE FINISH TO WIN THE MEN'S TRIATHLON GOLD |
INDRANIL MUKHERJEE/GETTY IMAGES

TRIATHLETES ARE BUNCHED UP IN THE MEN'S CYCLING SEGMENT | *HARRY HOW/GETTY IMAGES*

SARAH HASKINS AND U.S. TEAMMATE LAURA BENNETT (R) FINISH THE WOMEN'S SWIMMING
SEGMENT AND HEAD OFF TO CYCLE | *CLIVE ROSE/GETTY IMAGES*

COMPETITORS RIDE IN A PACK ALONG THE CYCLING PORTION OF THE WOMEN'S TRIATHLON |
INDRANIL MUKHERJEE/AFP/GETTY IMAGES

FEMALE TRIATHLETES COMPLETE THE FINAL RUNNING SEGMENT |
CLIVE ROSE/GETTY IMAGES

ATHLETES CONVERGE DURING THE CYCLING PORTION OF THE MENS TRIATHALON |
PHILIPPE DESMAZES/AFP/GETTY IMAGES

TRIAHTLETES DIVE INTO THE MING TOMB RESERVOIR AT THE START OF THE WOMEN'S TRIATHLON |
BEHROUZ MEHRI/AFP/GETTY IMAGES

CHINA'S WANG JIE AND THE REST OF THE COMPETITORS SERVED UP EXCITING BEACH VOLLEYBALL ACTION |
HARRY HOW/GETTY IMAGES

TRAGEDY AND TRIUMPHS | *WHAT BEGAN UNDER THE PALL OF A MIND-NUMBING TRAGEDY ON THE OPENING DAY OF COMPETITION CONCLUDED ON THE BEIJING*

Games' final day with the United States claiming its fourth volleyball medal in as many events. In between, the U.S. became the first nation to win medals at the same Olympic Games in all four events: men's and women's indoor volleyball and men's and women's beach volleyball. And these weren't just any four medals; the U.S. Olympic Team laid claim to three golds and a silver, with the two indoor teams both ending 16-year medal droughts.

But Team USA's volleyball fortunes started in far from golden fashion, as the stabbings of two Americans in Beijing stunned both indoor teams. Todd Bachman was killed and Barbara Bachman seriously injured in an attack witnessed by their daughter Elisabeth, a member of the 2004 Olympic team and wife of Team USA men's head coach Hugh McCutcheon. With such close ties to the Bachman family, both teams played with heavy hearts and mixed emotions, the men's team struggling to win their first three matches without McCutcheon while he attended to his grieving wife and hospitalized mother-in-law.

With steeled resolve, the American men—ranked third in the world and coming off a 2008 World League title—finished preliminary pool play with a perfect 5-0 record. In medal-round play, they survived a pair of five-set thrillers after trailing both 2-1 after three sets: first against upset-minded Serbia in the quarterfinals and then against second-ranked Russia in the semis, a team they hadn't beaten in international play in four-plus years and who had defeated them for the 2004 bronze in Athens.

The men faced top-ranked Brazil in the title game, a team they had beaten in their previous three meetings. The Americans dropped the first set but then reeled off wins in the next three, setting off a Capital Indoor Stadium celebration from which McCutcheon excused himself momentarily to compose himself after his emotional two weeks. Clay Stanley was named tournament MVP, with fellow U.S. opposite Reid Priddy and middle blockers Ryan Millar and David Lee among the tournament statistical leaders.

In taking over as the new U.S. women's head coach, "Jenny" Lang Ping was hoping to relive her personal Games fortunes in reverse, having already helped her native China capture medals on American soil. She starred during a gold-medal run in 1984 in Los Angeles and then coached China to the silver in 1996 in Atlanta. Now, after another 12-year interval, she was leading the United States back to her homeland.

Ranked fourth internationally and reaching the medal round with a 4-1 pool record, the U.S. Olympic Team faced the toughest draw in its final three matches: No. 2 Italy, No. 3 Cuba, and No. 1 Brazil. The U.S. outlasted Italy in the quarterfinals with its third straight five-set victory when trailing after three sets. Then by avenging their previous loss by sweeping undefeated Cuba in the semifinals, the American women were guaranteed no worse than silver.

TODD ROGERS OF THE UNITED STATES DIVES FOR A DIG IN A PRELIMINARY MATCH
AGAINST ARGENTINA | *THOMAS COEZ/AFP/GETTY IMAGES*

In the final, the Americans handed the Brazilians their first set defeat in Beijing but still fell in four. Team USA had both exceeded expectations and matched the women's program's previous best finish, a silver in 1984. Logan Tom, who returned to the U.S. team after a three-year break to play pro beach volleyball, led the tournament in scoring. Teammates Tayyiba Haneef-Park and Nicole Davis finished among the top statistical leaders.

Meanwhile, the Chaoyang Park Beach Volleyball Ground was one of landlocked Beijing's most lively venues, no matter if matches were played in the sizzling sun or pouring rain, during the heat of the day or the cool of the night under stadium lights. And Chinese spectators, already fans of the indoor version of the sport, took to the pounding pop music riffs, bikini-clad dancers, and the nonstop action of the sand-tastic beach variety, with President George W. Bush, soccer legend Pelé, actor Vince Vaughn, and NBA basketball stars Kobe Bryant, LeBron James, and Jason Kidd also dropping by the high-octane venue.

Walsh and May-Treanor picked up where they left off in Athens, with gold medals hanging around their necks. The first Olympic side—men's or women's—to ever repeat as champions, the twosome never lost a set in Beijing, while extending their string of undefeated matches to 108. Their only setback was temporary: Walsh's wedding band flew off her finger in the opening match and was buried in the sand. A volunteer with a metal detector later dug it out and returned it.

Meanwhile, as she had done four years earlier in Athens, May-Treanor left a little something in the Beijing sand by spreading a smattering of the cremated remains of her late mother, who died from cancer in 2002. China, which had gone 2-11 in previous Olympic beach matches, boasted both the silver medalists (Tian Jia and Wang Jie) and the bronze medalists (19-year-old Xue Chen and 23-year-old Zhang Xi).

Favored in the men's tournament, the reigning world champions, Dalhausser and Rogers, were upset in their pool opener. The loss put them in the weaker medal round bracket, from which they won the title. They are the third U.S. men's side to win beach gold. Dalhauseer, nicknamed "The Thin Beast", produced four straight blocks to take a 5-1 lead to a 9-1 advantage.

Two other U.S. sides—Nicole Branagh-Elaine Youngs and Jake Gibb-Sean Rosenthal—went undefeated until being eliminated in quarterfinal matches, with both pairs finishing tied for fifth.

KERRI WALSH OF THE UNITED STATES BLOCKS AN ATTEMPT FROM BELGIUM'S LIESBETH MOUHA IN THEIR
ROUND OF 16 MATCH | *THOMAS COEX/AFP/GETTY IMAGES*

216

ZHOU SUHONG OF CHINA GETS THE BALL ABOVE THE OUTREACHED ARMS OF POLISH OPPONENTS | *NICOLAS ASFOURI/AFP/GETTY IMAGES*

FANS CHEER ON ACTION AT CHAOYANG PARK BEACH VOLLEYBALL GROUND, ONE OF BEIJING'S LIVELIEST VENUES DURING THE '08 GAMES | *JOE KLAMAR/AFP/GETTY IMAGES*

USA'S LOGAN TOM (R) BLASTS A KILL PAST BRAZIL'S FABIANA CLAUDINO IN THE WOMEN'S INDOOR GOLD-MEDAL MATCH | *MARK RALSTON/AFP/GETTY IMAGES*

REID PRIDDY OF THE U.S. RISES TO RETURN AGAINST BULGARIA'S ANDREY ZHEKOV IN MEN'S IN-DOOR PLAY | *ALEXANDER JOE/AFP/GETTY IMAGES*

LLOY BALL LETS OUT A SCREAM AFTER THE UNITED STATES DOWNED BRAZIL FOR THE MEN'S INDOOR GOLD | *MARK RALSTON/AFP/GETTY IMAGES*

HUNGARY'S TIBOR BENEDEK GETS SANDWICHED BY THE USA'S RYAN BAILEY FROM ABOVE
AND TONY AZEVEDO BELOW IN THE GOLD-MEDAL MATCH | *ADAM PRETTY/GETTY IMAGES*

SILVER LININGS | *THE UNITED STATES' WATER POLO FORTUNES IN BEIJING CAME WITH A PAIR OF SILVER LININGS. FOR THE AMERICAN* men, their silver-medal meant the first trip to the podium in 20 years—impressive for a team that began the Beijing Games with a No. 9 ranking and hadn't finished better than sixth in the previous three Games. As for the American women, their silver medal may have felt to be a notch below expectations for a team that entered the Yingdong Natatorium pool with the top international ranking. But looking at the proverbial big picture, the U.S. women have medaled in all three Olympic Games in which their event has been contested: a silver in Sydney, a bronze in Athens, and now a silver in Beijing. In all, the two '08 silvers made for the United States' best Olympic Games water polo success ever.

The U.S. men hadn't medaled since 1988, when current coach Terry Schroeder was team captain. The American men can claim only one Olympic gold—at the 1904 St. Louis Games, when the entire tournament field was comprised of just three teams, all from the host country.

In Beijing, the U.S. men won their six-team pool with a 4-1 record. Victories over top-ranked Croatia and powerhouse Germany afforded the Americans a quarterfinal bye. In the semifinals, they avenged their previous loss with a lopsided 10-5 defeat of Serbia, the first victory over that country in as long as anyone could remember. In the gold-medal match against Olympic buzz saw Hungary, the Americans were tied 9-all in the third period before giving up five uncontested goals in the 14-10 loss. Three-time Olympian Tony Azevedo logged four goals, but Hungary captured its third consecutive men's gold, the first country to achieve that feat since Britain in 1920.

In the eight-team women's tournament, the United States won its three preliminary-pool matches and also enjoyed a quarterfinal bye. In the semifinals, the U.S. met archrival Australia in a third pairing in as many Games. Brenda Villa tallied three goals—including the game winner with one minute remaining—in a costly 9-8 victory in which American Lauren Wenger broke her right hand. In the final against the Netherlands, Jessica Stephens scored two goals but there was no stopping Danielle de Bruijn, who racked seven goals in the Netherlands' 9-8 gold-medal victory.

IT'S AN ARMS RACE AS USA'S RYAN BAILEY (L) VIES WITH HUNGARY'S TAMAS MOLNAR (12) FOR THE BALL IN THEIR GOLD-MEDAL MATCH | *FRED DUFOUR/AFP/GETTY IMAGES*

JESSICA STEFFENS (L) TAKES A SHOT PAST SIMONE KOOT OF THE NETHERLANDS IN THE
GOLD-MEDAL MATCH | *MARK RALSTON/AFP/GETTY IMAGES*

LEGS ARE CONSTANTLY CHURNING IN THIS VIEW FROM THE BOTTOM OF THE POOL OF THE
USA-NETHERLANDS GOLD-MEDAL MATCH | *ADAM PRETTY/GETTY IMAGES*

AUSTRALIA'S GEMMA BEADSWORTH (L) SHOOTS PAST HUNGARY'S RITA DRAVUCZ (7) |
WILLIAM WEST/AFP/GETTY IMAGES

ITALY'S TANIA DI MARIO (TOP) LUNGES TO TACKLE RUSSIA'S OLGA BELYAEVA |
WILLIAM WEST/AFP/GETTY IMAGES

IT'S A REACH FOR CANADA GOALIE ROBIN RANDALL TO TRY AND STOP THIS SHOT FROM ITALY |
FRED DUFOUR/AFP/GETTY IMAGES

COLOMBIA'S CARLOS ANDICA PUNCTUATES HIS LIFT IN THE MEN'S 85 KG
EVENT WITH A SCREAM | *JUNG YEON-JE/AFP/GETTY IMAGES*

***LIFTED BY FAMILY | AFTER EARNING THE RIGHT
TO BE CALLED "THE WORLD'S STRONGEST MAN"
BY CAPTURING THE GOLD MEDAL IN THE SUPER-***
heavyweight division, Germany's Matthias Steiner shared a tender medal-ceremony moment at
Beijing University Gymnasium. After heaving a combined total of 461 kilograms—or 1,016.3
pounds—with a snatch of 203 kilograms and a stunning clean and jerk of 258,

Steiner held his gold medal in one hand and in the other a photo of his wife, Susann, who had
died in a car accident the previous year. "I thought of her before the competition," he said. "I
won this for her, for friends and family. But mostly for her."

Russia's Evgeni Chigishev—who claimed the silver in the same division over bronze medalist
Viktors Scerbaiths, the world champion from Latvia—had the super heavyweight's best snatch
at 210kg. (The snatch lift is taking the bar from the ground to above the head in one continuous
motion; the clean and jerk is a two-step lift: first to shoulder level and then overhead.)

Steiner wasn't the only lifter in Beijing with thoughts of family. Melanie Roach's thoughts did
not stem from loss, but from several additions. When women's weightlifting made its debut at
the 2000 Sydney Olympic Games, Roach was eyeing a spot on the U.S. squad—only to suffer a

herniated disk eight weeks out from the U.S. trials, from which she withdrew after a painful attempt to lift. Thinking her competitive career was over, she went on with life, having three children with her husband, their middle child a son with autism.

After a limited return to the sport in 2005 and 2006, and a return of the back woes, Roach had microdiscectomy surgery that relieved her pain for good in October 2006. In Beijing, amid cheers of "Go, Mom," Roach set an American record in the women's 53kg class with a total lift of 193 kilos—a snatch of 83 and a clean and jerk of 110. The day after her event Roach took her "Olympic Mom" label on the road by visiting a Beijing orphanage for special-needs children. Her sixth-place finish tied her for U.S.-best honors with three-time Olympian Cheryl Haworth, the 2000 bronze medalist, who totaled 259kg in the women's 75kg-plus division.

The top American male was Kendrick Farris in the 85kg class, who finished eighth while setting U.S. records with a 362kg total and a clean and jerk of 202. World champion Andrei Aramnau of Belarus collected three world records and the gold in the men's heavyweight class (105kg), while Chinese lifters hauled in eight gold and a silver.

USA'S CHERYL HAWORTH COMPLETES HER LIFT IN THE 75+KG WOMEN'S CLASS
| JED JACOBSOHN/GETTY IMAGES

IRAN'S ASGHAR EBRAHIMI IS DOUBLED OVER IN DISAPPOINTMENT AFTER FAILING
HIS LIFT IN THE MEN'S 94KG CLASS | JEFF GROSS/GETTY IMAGES

SA JAEHYOUK OF SOUTH KOREA APPLAUDS HIS GOLD-MEDAL WIN IN
THE MEN'S 77KG CLASS | *PHIL WALTER/GETTY IMAGES*

CHINA'S ZHANG XIANGXIANG CELEBRATES HIS MEN'S 62KG GOLD BY
HUGGING THE WEIGHTS | *STU FORSTER/GETTY IMAGES*

HUNGARY'S JANOS BARANYAI CRIES OUT IN PAIN AFTER DROPPING THE
WEIGHTS IN THE MEN'S 77KG CLASS | *PHIL WALTER/GETTY IMAGES*

USA'S MELANIE ROACH CELEBRATES SETTING AN AMERICAN RECORD IN
THE WOMEN'S 53KG CLASS | *HARRY HOW/GETTY IMAGES*

GERMANY'S MATTHIAS STEINER JUMPS FOR JOY AFTER WINNING THE GOLD MEDAL
IN THE MEN'S SUPER-HEAVYWEIGHT DIVISION | *JULIAN FINNEY/GETTY IMAGES*

摔跤

WRESTLING
BEIJING 2008

U.S. WRESTLER HENRY CEJUDO'S ARRIVAL AS AN OLYMPIC STAR COINCIDED WITH THE HEAD OF
JAPAN'S SHINGO MATSUMOTO HITTING THE MAT | *JED JACOBSOHN/GETTY IMAGES*

FUTURE ARRIVES AHEAD OF SCHEDULE | THANKS TO HIS PERFORMANCE IN BEIJING, WRESTLER HENRY CEJUDO FINISHED SECOND IN THE VOTING

for U.S. Olympic Male Athlete of the Month in August 2008. You may have heard of the guy who finished ahead of him…

Being measured against Michael Phelps' performance gives some context to what Cejudo achieved on the mat. Phelps may have gone 8-for-8 in the pool, but Cejudo was just as impressive in his own way, winning the only gold medal available to him and providing perhaps the most inspiring story among all the competitors at the China Agricultural University gym. That's where Russia won three Greco-Roman gold medals and 11 total medals in wrestling, while Japan captured six, and Georgia took two. Team USA's three medals each came with a unique story.

Officials always liked to describe him as "the future" of USA Wrestling, but Cejudo fast-forwarded the timetable in Beijing. "I'm no longer the future, I'm the present," he said in his celebratory news conference. "This yellow medal hanging around my neck is proof of that."

As a junior in high school, Cejudo left his Arizona home to live and wrestle at the U.S. Olympic Training Center in Colorado Springs. The following year, he became the first high school athlete to win a U.S. Senior National title since USA Wrestling became its governing body. But that still left a big jump to Olympic champion in the 55kg/121-pound class at age 21.

Yet Cejudo did exactly what he expected to do in China. His gold medal victory over Japan's Tomohiro Matsunaga touched off one of the most joyous, heartfelt celebrations of the Games, as Cejudo ran around the entire three-mat wrestling stage, carrying the American flag. Raised by his mother, an immigrant from Mexico, Cejudo said America is "a land of opportunity, and you choose your own path."

One of America's bronze medals came from Adam Wheeler in Greco-Roman wrestling at 96kg/211.5 pounds . Wheeler made the U.S. Olympic Team through a surprising defeat of former world bronze medalist Justin Ruiz. He ended his Olympic Games with a win over Han Tae-Young of Korea. Randi Miller took Team USA's second bronze in the women's freestyle division at 63kg/138.75 pounds. Miller defeated Martine Dugrenier of Canada in what U.S. coach Terry Steiner described as "almost a perfect match."

ADAM WHEELER (BLUE) OF THE U.S. HAD A GOOD GRIP ON A GRECO-ROMAN BRONZE MEDAL AFTER
DEFEATING HAN TAE-YOUNG OF SOUTH KOREA | *PETER PARKS/AFP/GETTY IMAGES*

ARA ABRAHAMIAN OF SWEDEN LEAVES HIS BRONZE MEDAL ON THE MAT TO PROTEST A RULING
THAT KEPT HIM OUT OF THE GOLD MEDAL MATCH | *PETER PARKS/AFP/GETTY IMAGES*

CANADA'S MARTINE DUGRENIER (BLUE) WAS PERSUADED THAT U.S. WRESTLER RANDI MILLER
DESERVED THE BRONZE MEDAL | *TOSHIFUMI KITAMURA/AFP/GETTY IMAGES*

NO OLYMPIC GOLD MEDAL CELEBRATION WAS MORE JOYOUS OR HEARTFELT THAN HENRY CEJUDO'S AFTER HIS WRESTLING TRIUMPH | *TOSHIFUMI KITAMURA/AFP/GETTY IMAGES*

CLOSING CEREMONY

BEIJING CHINA, 2008

"Truly exceptional Games!" The 2008 Beijing Olympic Games ended much like they started, with roaring pyrotechnics stretching from the Bird's Nest to Tiananmen Square, drummers, dancers, flying men, and center-stage towers. Serving as a fitting bookend to the awe-inspiring Opening Ceremony 16 nights earlier, the August 24 Closing Ceremony at National Stadium featured a few significant differences: a partylike atmosphere, "only" 7,000 performers (about half the number that opened the Games), and Olympians blanketing the stadium floor in a free-flowing international mix rather than being divided by nationality. During China's curtain-call event, an eight-minute segment showcased Great Britain's best-known icons—from red double-decker busses to soccer sensation David Beckham—in a visual appetizer for the 2012 London Olympic Games.

As Beijing Mayor Guo Jinlong transferred the Olympic flag to London Mayor Boris Johnson and the flame of the towering Olympic cauldron was extinguished, IOC President Jacques Rogge summarized the Beijing experience: "We have come to the end of 16 glorious days which we will cherish forever. ...

New stars were born. Stars from past Games amazed us again. We shared their joys and their tears, and we marveled at their ability. We will long remember the achievements we witnessed here..."

CLOSING CEREMONY, AUGUST 24, 2008 | *SHAUN BOTTERILL/GETTY IMAGES*

CLOSING CEREMONY PERFORMANCE | *SHAUN BOTTERILL/GETTY IMAGES*

LONDON DOUBLE DECKER BUS, 2012 OLYMPIC GAMES | *PAUL GILHAM/GETTY IMAGES*

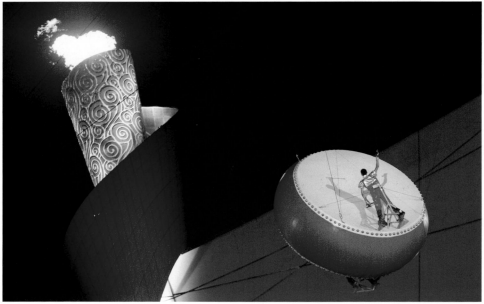

DRUMMER PERFORMANCE | *STU FORSTER/GETTY IMAGES*

LONDON MAYOR BORIS JOHNSON (L) WITH GUO JINLONG (R)
GIVES THE THUMBS UP | *CLIVE ROSE/GETTY IMAGES*

THE MAYOR OF LONDON BORIS JOHNSON (L) WAVES THE OLYMPIC FLAG DURING THE CLOSING
AND HAND-OVER CEREMONY | *CHRISTOPHE SIMON/AFP/GETTY IMAGES*

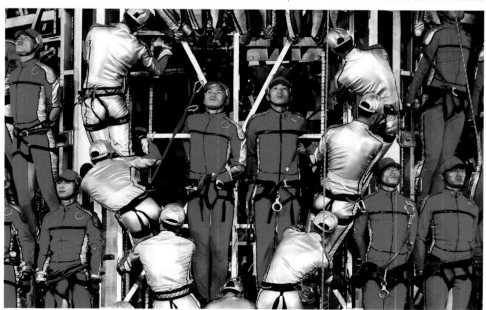

CLOSING CEREMONY PERFORMANCE | *JULIAN FINNEY/GETTY IMAGES*

FIREWORKS ERUPT NEAR THE "BIRD'S NEST" NATIONAL STADIUM DURING THE CLOSING CEREMONY
OF THE 2008 BEIJING OLYMPIC GAMES | *AXEL SCHMIDT/AFP/GETTY IMAGES*

NATALIE COUGHLIN POSES WITH HER 100M BACKSTROKE GOLD MEDAL |
AL BELLO/GETTY IMAGES

ARCHER KHATUNA LORIG OF THE UNITED STATES CARRIES THE FLAG INTO
THE CLOSING CEREMONY | *MICHAEL STEELE/GETTY IMAGE*

USA TEAM MEMBERS CELEBRATE WITH THEIR CHILDREN AFTER THE WOMEN'S SOCCER GOLD MEDAL MATCH | *MIKE HEWITT/GETTY IMAGE*

PARTICIPATING NATIONS

AFGHANISTAN | ARG
ALBANIA | ALB
ALGERIA | ALG
AMERICAN SAMOA | ASA
ANDORRA | AND
ANGOLA | ANG
ANTIGUA AND BARBUDA | ANT
ARGENTINA | ARG
ARMENIA | ARM
ARUBA | ARU
AUSTRALIA | AUS
AUSTRIA | AUT
AZERBAIJAN | AZE
BAHAMAS | BAH
BAHRAIN | BRN
BANGLADESH | BAN
BARBADOS | BAR
BELARUS | BLR
BELGIUM | BEL
BELIZE | BIZ
BENIN | BEN
BERMUDA | BER
BHUTAN | BHU
BOLIVIA | BOL
BOSNIA AND HERZEGOVINA | BIH
BOTSWANA | BOT
BRAZIL | BRA
BRITISH VIRGIN ISLANDS | IVB
BULGARIA | BUL
BURKINA FASO | BUR
BURUNDI | BDI
CAMBODIA | CAM
CAMEROON | CMR
CANADA | CAN
CAPE VERDE | CPV
CAYMAN ISLANDS | CAY
CENTRAL AFRICAN REPUBLIC | CAF
CHAD | CHA
CHILE | CHI
CHINA | CHN
CHINESE TAIPEI | TPE

COLOMBIA | COL
COMOROS | COM
DEMOCRATIC REPUBLIC OF THE CONGO |
CONGO | CGO
COOK ISLANDS ISLANDS | COK
COSTA RICA | CRC
CÔTE D'IVOIRE | CIV
CROATIA | CRO
CUBA | CUB
CYPRUS | CYP
CZECH REPUBLIC | CZE
DENMARK | DEN
DJIBOUTI | DJI
DOMINICA | DMA
DOMINICAN REPUBLIC | DOM
ECUADOR | ECU
EGYPT | EGY
EL SALVADOR | ESA
EQUATORIAL GUINEA | GEQ
ERITREA | ERI
ESTONIA | EST
ETHIOPIA | ETH
FIJI | FIJ
FINLAND | FIN
FRANCE | FRA
FEDERATED STATES OF MICRONESIA | FSM
FORMER YUGOSLAV REPUBLIC OF MACEDONIA | MKD
GABON | GAB
GAMBIA | GAM
GEORGIA | GEO
GERMANY | GER
GHANA | GHA
GREAT BRITAIN | GBR
GREECE | GRE
GRENADA | GRN
GUAM | GUM
GUATEMALA | GUA
GUINEA | GUI
GUINEA-BISSAU | GBS
GUYANA | GUY

HAITI | HAI
HONDURAS | HON
HONG KONG, CHINA | HKG
HUNGARY | HUN
ICELAND | ISL
INDIA | IND
INDONESIA | INA
IRAN | IRI
IRAQ | IRQ
IRELAND | IRL
ISRAEL | ISR
ITALY | ITA
JAMAICA | JAM
JAPAN | JPN
JORDAN | JOR
KAZAKHSTAN | KAZ
KENYA | KEN
KIRIBATI | KIR
NORTH KOREA | DPR
SOUTH KOREA | KOR
KUWAIT | KEW
KYRGYZSTAN | KGZ
LAOS | LAO
LATVIA | LAT
LEBANON | LIB
LESOTHO | LES
LIBERIA | LBR
LIBYA | LBA
LIECHTENSTEIN | LIE
LITHUANIA | LTU
LUXEMBOURG | LUX
MADAGASCAR | MAD
MALAWI | MAW
MALAYSIA | MAS
MALDIVES | MDV
MALI | MLI
MALTA | MLT
MARSHALL ISLANDS |
MAURITANIA | MTN
MAURITIUS | MRI
MEXICO | MEX
MOLDOVA | MDA

MONACO | MON
MONGOLIA | MGL
MONTENEGRO | MNE
MOROCCO | MAR
MOZAMBIQUE | MOZ
MYANMAR | MYA
NAMIBIA | NAM
NAURU | NRU
NEPAL | NEP
NETHERLANDS | NED
NETHERLANDS ANTILLES | AHO
NEW ZEALAND | NZL
NICARAGUA | NCA
NIGER | NIG
NIGERIA | NGR
NORWAY | NOR
OMAN | OMA
PAKISTAN | PAK
PALAU | PAW
PALESTINE | PLE
PANAMA | PAN
PAPUA NEW GUINEA | PNG
PARAGUAY | PAR
PERU | PER
PHILIPPINES | PHI
POLAND | POL
PORTUGAL | POR
PUERTO RICO | PUR
QATAR | QAT
ROMANIA | ROM
RUSSIA | RUS
RWANDA | RWA
SAINT KITTS AND NEVIS | SKN
SAINT LUCIA | LCA
SAINT VINCENT AND THE GRENADINES | VIN
SÃO TOMÉ AND PRÍNCIPE | STP
SAMOA | SAM
SAN MARINO | SMR
SAUDI ARABIA | KSA
SENEGAL | SEN
SERBIA | SRB

SEYCHELLES | SEY
SIERRA LEONE | SLE
SINGAPORE | SIN
SLOVAKIA | SVK
SLOVENIA | SLO
SOLOMON ISLANDS | SOL
SOMALIA | SOM
SOUTH AFRICA | RSA
SPAIN | ESP
SRI LANKA | SRI
SUDAN | SUD
SURINAME | SUR
SWAZILAND | SWZ
SWEDEN | SWE
SWITZERLAND | SUI
SYRIA | SYR
TAJIKISTAN | TJK
TANZANIA | TAN
THAILAND | THA
TIMOR-LESTE | TLS
TOGO | TOG
TONGA | TGA
TRINIDAD AND TOBAGO | TRI
TUNISIA | TUN
TURKEY | TUR
TURKMENISTAN | TKM
TUVALU | TUV
UGANDA | UGA
UKRAINE | UKR
UNITED ARAB EMIRATES | UAE
UNITED STATES | USA
URUGUAY | URU
UZBEKISTAN | UZB
VANUATU | VAN
VENEZUELA | VEN
VIETNAM | VIE
VIRGIN ISLANDS | ISV
YEMEN | YEM
ZAMBIA | ZAM
ZIMBABWE | ZIM

MEDAL COUNT

COUNTRY	GOLD	SILVER	BRONZE	TOTAL
UNITED STATES	36	38	36	110
CHINA	51	21	28	100
RUSSIA	23	21	28	72
GREAT BRITAIN	19	13	15	47
AUSTRALIA	14	15	17	46
GERMANY	16	10	15	41
FRANCE	7	16	17	40
KOREA	13	10	8	31
ITALY	8	10	10	28
UKRAINE	7	5	15	27
JAPAN	9	6	10	25
CUBA	2	11	11	24
BELARUS	4	5	10	19
CANADA	3	9	6	18
SPAIN	5	10	3	18
NETHERLANDS	7	5	4	16
BRAZIL	3	4	8	15
KENYA	5	5	4	14
KAZAKHSTAN	2	4	7	13
JAMAICA	6	3	2	11
HUNGARY	3	5	2	10
NORWAY	3	5	2	10
POLAND	3	6	1	10
NEW ZELAND	3	1	5	9
ROMANIA	4	1	3	8
TURKEY	1	4	3	8
AZERBAIJAN	1	2	4	7
DENMARK	2	2	3	7
ETHIOPIA	4	1	2	7
ARGENTINA	2	0	4	6
ARMENIA	0	0	6	6
CZECH REPUBLIC	3	3	0	6
DPR KOREA	2	1	3	6
GEORGIA	3	0	3	6
SLOVAKIA	3	2	1	6
SWITZERLAND	2	0	4	6
UZBEKISTAN	1	2	3	6
BULGARIA	1	1	3	5
CROATIA	0	2	3	5
INDONESIA	1	1	3	5
LITHUANIA	0	2	3	5
SLOVENIA	1	2	2	5
SWEDEN	0	4	1	5
CHINESE TAIPEI	0	0	4	4

COUNTRY	GOLD	SILVER	BRONZE	TOTAL
FINLAND	1	1	2	4
GREECE	0	2	2	4
MONGOLIA	2	2	0	4
NIGERIA	0	1	3	4
THAILAND	2	2	0	4
ZIMBABWE	1	3	0	4
AUSTRIA	0	1	2	3
INDIA	1	0	2	3
IRELAND	0	1	2	3
LATVIA	1	1	1	3
MEXICO	2	0	1	3
SERBIA	0	1	2	3
ALGERIA	0	1	1	2
BAHAMAS	0	1	1	2
BELGIUM	1	1	0	2
COLOMBIA	0	1	1	2
DOMINICAN REPUBLIC	1	1	0	2
ESTONIA	1	1	0	2
IRAN	1	0	1	2
KYRGYZSTAN	0	1	1	2
MOROCCO	0	1	1	2
PORTUGAL	1	1	0	2
TAJIKISTAN	0	1	1	2
TRINIDAD/ TOBAGO	0	2	0	2
AFGHANISTAN	0	0	1	1
BAHRAIN	1	0	0	1
CAMEROON	1	0	0	1
CHILE	0	1	0	1
ECUADOR	0	1	0	1
EGYPT	0	0	1	1
ICELAND	0	1	0	1
ISRAEL	0	0	1	1
MALAYSIA	0	1	0	1
MAURITIUS	0	0	1	1
PANAMA	1	0	0	1
REPUBLIC OF MOLDOVA	0	0	1	1
SINGAPORE	0	1	0	1
SOUTH AFRICA	0	1	0	1
SUDAN	0	1	0	1
TOGO	0	0	1	1
TUNISIA	1	0	0	1
VENEZUELA	0	0	1	1
VIETNAM	0	1	0	1

NAME, BIRTHDATE, HOMETOWN, EVENT

Khatuna Lorig 1/1/74, West Hollywood CA, Recurve
Jennifer Nichols 10/4/83, Cheyenne WY, Recurve
Brady Ellison 10/27/88, Glendale AZ, Recurve
Butch Johnson 8/30/55, Woodstock CT, Recurve

Vic Wunderle 3/4/76, Mason City IL, Recurve

STAFF
Kisik Lee Head Coach
Tom Parrish Team Leader
Don Rabska Asst Coach

ARCHERY RESULTS

WOMEN'S INDIVIDUAL

1	CHN	ZHANG, JUAJUAN
2	KOR	PARK, SUNG-HYUN
3	KOR	YUN, OK HEE
4	PRK	KWON, UN SIL
5	**USA**	**LORIG, KHATUNA**
6	JPN	HAYAKAWA, NAMI
7	KOR	JOO, HYUN JUNG
8	MEX	AVITIA, MARIANA
26	**USA**	**NICHOLS, JENNIFER**

MEN'S INDIVIDUAL

1	UKR	RUBAN, VIKTOR
2	KOR	PARK, KYUNG-MO
3	RUS	BADENOV, BAIR
4	MEX	SERRANO, JUANJO RENE
5	CUB	STEVENS, JUAN CARLOS
6	**USA**	**WUNDERLE, VICTOR**
6	JPN	MORIYA, RYUICHI
8	MAS	CHENG, CHU SIAN
27	**USA**	**ELLISON, BRADY**
28	**USA**	**JOHNSON, BUTCH**

WOMEN'S TEAM

1	KOR
2	CHN
3	FRA

NO **USA** TEAM

MEN'S TEAM

1	KOR	
2	ITA	
3	CHI	
9	**USA**	**WUNDERLE, VICTOR JOHNSON, BUTCH ELLISON, BRADY**

Abdi Abdirahman, 1/1/77, Tucson AZ, 10,000m
Amy Acuff 7/14/75, Corpus Christi TX, High Jump
Lindsey Anderson 5/23/85, Morgan UT, Steeplechase
Jennifer Barringer 8/23/86, Oviedo FL, Steeplechase

Erica Bartolina 5/15/80, Philomath OR, Pole Vault
Kenta Bell (NOT PICTURED) 3/16/77, Kilgore TX, Triple Jump
Magdalena Lewy Boulet 8/1/73, Oakland CA,, Marathon
Jillian Camarena 3/2/82, Woodland CA, Shot Put
Amber Campbell 6/5/81, Indianapolis IN, Hammer

Christian Cantwell 9/30/80, Eldon MO, Shot Put
Michelle Carter 10/12/85, Ovilla TX, Shot Put
Damu Cherry 11/29/77, Tampa FL, 100m Hurdles
Hazel Clark-Riley 10/3/77, South Orange, NJ, 800m

Bryan Clay 1/3/80, Glendora CA, Decathlon
Kerron Clement 10/31/85, Los Angeles CA, 400m Hurdles
Jessica Cosby 5/31/82, Mission Hills CA, Hammer
Shawn Crawford 1/14/78, Los Angeles CA, 200m

Rafeeq Curry 8/10/83, Tallahassee FL, Triple Jump
Sharon Day 6/9/85, Costa Mesa CA, High Jump
Walter Dix 1/31/86, Tallahassee FL, 200m, 100m
LeRoy Dixon 6/20/83, South Bend IN, 4x100m
Ian Dobson (NOT PICTURED) 2/6/82, Palo Alto CA, 5000m

Erin Donohue 5/8/83, Haddonfield NJ, 1500m
Joanne Dow 3/19/64, Manchester NH, 20k Race Walk
Philip Dunn 6/12/71, Portland OR, 50k Race Walk
Kevin Eastler 10/14/77, Farmington MA, 25km Walk
Torri Edwards (NOT PICTURED) 1/31/77, Los Angeles CA, 100m

Anthony Famiglietti 11/8/78, Medford NY, Steeplechase
Allyson Felix 11/18/85, Los Angeles CA, 200m
Shalane Flanagan 7/8/81, Marblehead MA, 5,000m, 10,000m
Ebonie Floyd 10/31/83, Fresno TX, 4x400 Relay

Hyleas Fountain 1/14/81, Dayton OH, Heptathlon
Tyson Gay (NOT PICTURED) 8/9/82, Fayetteville AR, 100m
Kara Goucher 7/9/78, Duluth MN, 5,000m, 10,000m
Breaux Greer 10/19/76, Monroe LA, Javelin
Ryan Hall 10/14/82, Big Bear Lake CA, Marathon

Trey Hardee 2/7/84, Vestavia Hills AL, Decathlon
Dawn Harper 5/13/84, East St. Louis IL, 100m Hurdles
Queen Quedith Harrison 9/10/88, Richmond VA, 400m Hurdles
Jeff Hartwig 9/25/67, Jonesboro AR, Pole Vault

240

Nastasha Hastings 7/23/86, Clermont FL, 4x400 Relay

Mike Hazle 3/22/79, Temple TX, Javelin

Kristin Heaston 11/23/75, Palo Alto CA, Shot Put

Monique Henderson 2/18/83, San Diego CA, 4x400 Relay

Reese Hoffa 10/8/77, Augusta GA, Shot Put

Marshevet Hooker (NOT PICTURED) 9/25/84, San Antonio TX, 200m

Chaunte Howard (NOT PICTURED) 1/12/84, Riverside CA, High Jump

Bershawn Jackson 5/8/83, Raleigh NC, 400m Hurdles

Funmi Jimoh 5/29/84, Houston TX, Long Jump

Brian Johnson 3/5/80, IA LA, Long Jump

Jackie Johnson 9/8/84, Yuma AZ, Heptathlon

Dustin Jonas 4/19/86, LaVernia TX, High Jump

LoLo Jones 8/5/82, Des Moines IA, 100m Hurdles

Deena Kastor 2/14/73, Mammoth Lakes CA, Marathon

Kim Kreiner 7/26/1077, Fresno CA, Javelin

Alfred Kruger 2/18/79, Sheldon IA, Hammer

Bernard Lagat (NOT PICTURED) 12/12/74, Tucson AZ, 1500m, 5000m

Muna Lee 10/30/81, Kansas City MO, 200m, 100m

Mechelle Lewis 9/20/80, Ft. Washington MD, 4x100m Relay

Lopez Lomong 1/1/85, Flagstaff AZ, 1500m

Casey Malone 4/6/77, Arvada CO, Discus

Andra Manson 4/30/84, Brenham TX, High Jump

Leonel Manzano 9/12/84, Austin TX, 1500m

Shani Marks 8/24/80, Apple Valley MN, Triple Jump

Rodney Martin (NOT PICTURED) 12/22/82, Las Vegas NV, 4x100m

Joshua McAdams 3/26/80, Broadview Heights OH, Steeplechase

Erica McLain 1/24/86, Plano TX, Triple Jump

LaShawn Merritt 6/27/86, Portsmouth VA, 400m

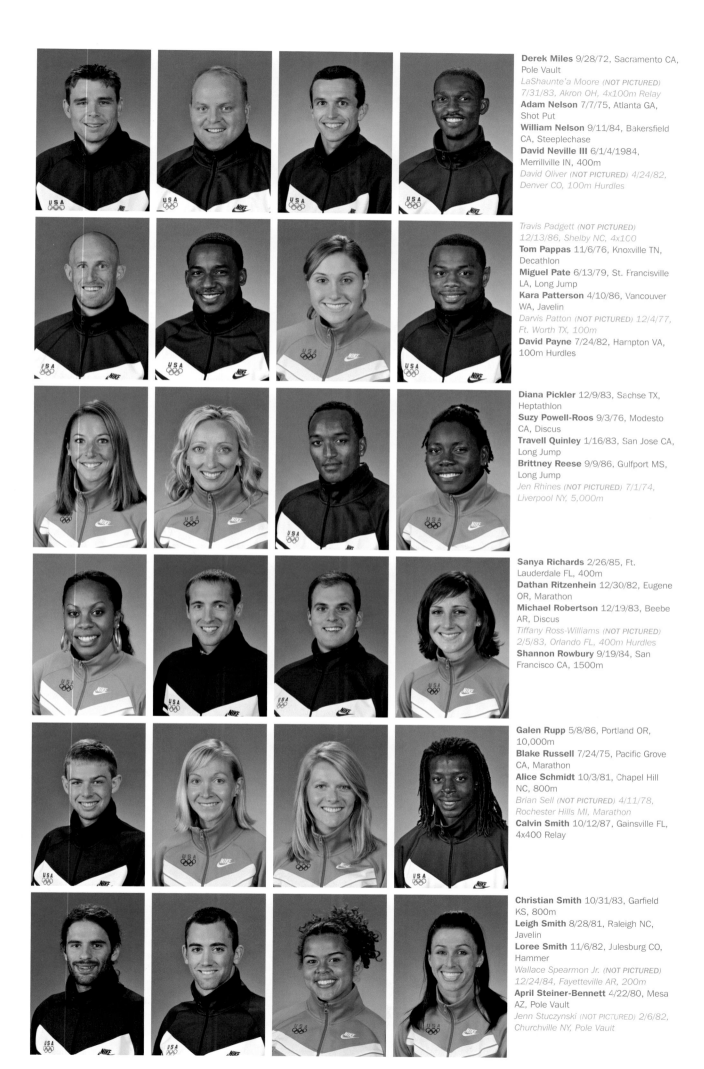

Derek Miles 9/28/72, Sacramento CA, Pole Vault

LaShaunte'a Moore (NOT PICTURED) 7/31/83, Akron OH, 4x100m Relay

Adam Nelson 7/7/75, Atlanta GA, Shot Put

William Nelson 9/11/84, Bakersfield CA, Steeplechase

David Neville III 6/1/4/1984, Merrillville IN, 400m

David Oliver (NOT PICTURED) 4/24/82, Denver CO, 100m Hurdles

Travis Padgett (NOT PICTURED) 12/13/86, Shelby NC, 4x100

Tom Pappas 11/6/76, Knoxville TN, Decathlon

Miguel Pate 6/13/79, St. Francisville LA, Long Jump

Kara Patterson 4/10/86, Vancouver WA, Javelin

Darvis Patton (NOT PICTURED) 12/4/77, Ft. Worth TX, 100m

David Payne 7/24/82, Hampton VA, 100m Hurdles

Diana Pickler 12/9/83, Sachse TX, Heptathlon

Suzy Powell-Roos 9/3/76, Modesto CA, Discus

Travell Quinley 1/16/83, San Jose CA, Long Jump

Brittney Reese 9/9/86, Gulfport MS, Long Jump

Jen Rhines (NOT PICTURED) 7/1/74, Liverpool NY, 5,000m

Sanya Richards 2/26/85, Ft. Lauderdale FL, 400m

Dathan Ritzenhein 12/30/82, Eugene OR, Marathon

Michael Robertson 12/19/83, Beebe AR, Discus

Tiffany Ross-Williams (NOT PICTURED) 2/5/83, Orlando FL, 400m Hurdles

Shannon Rowbury 9/19/84, San Francisco CA, 1500m

Galen Rupp 5/8/86, Portland OR, 10,000m

Blake Russell 7/24/75, Pacific Grove CA, Marathon

Alice Schmidt 10/3/81, Chapel Hill NC, 800m

Brian Sell (NOT PICTURED) 4/11/78, Rochester Hills MI, Marathon

Calvin Smith 10/12/87, Gainsville FL, 4x400 Relay

Christian Smith 10/31/83, Garfield KS, 800m

Leigh Smith 8/28/81, Raleigh NC, Javelin

Loree Smith 11/6/82, Julesburg CO, Hammer

Wallace Spearmon Jr. (NOT PICTURED) 12/24/84, Fayetteville AR, 200m

April Steiner-Bennett 4/22/80, Mesa AZ, Pole Vault

Jenn Stuczynski (NOT PICTURED) 2/6/82, Churchville NY, Pole Vault

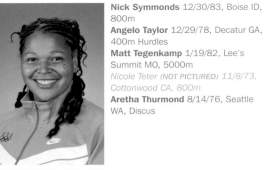

Nick Symmonds 12/30/83, Boise ID, 800m
Angelo Taylor 12/29/78, Decatur GA, 400m Hurdles
Matt Tegenkamp 1/19/82, Lee's Summit MO, 5000m
Nicole Teter (NOT PICTURED) 11/8/73, Cottonwood CA, 800m
Aretha Thurmond 8/14/76, Seattle WA, Discus

Jorge Torres 8/22/80, Wheeling, IL, 10,000m
Sheena Johnson Tosta 10/1/82, Los Angeles CA, 400m Hurdles
Stephanie Brown Trafton 12/1/79, Arroyo Grande CA, Discus
Terrence Trammell 11/23/78, Ellenwood GA, 100m Hurdles
Dee Dee Trotter (NOT PICTURED) 12/8/82, Cedar Grove GA, 400m

Grace Upshaw 9/25/75, Redwood City CA, Long Jump
Brad Walker 6/21/81, Spokane WA, Pole Vault
Ian Waltz 4/15/77, Chula Vista CA, Discus
Jeremy Wariner 1/31/84, Arlington TX, 400m

Andrew Wheating 11/21/87, Norwich VT, 800m
Anna Willard 3/31/84, Greenwood ME, Steeplechase
Angela Williams 1/30/80, Ontario CA, 4x100m Relay
Lauryn Williams 9/11/83, Miami FL, 100m

Jesse Williams 12/27/84, Raleigh NC, High Jump
Darold Williamson 2/19/83, Waco TX, 4x400 Relay
Aarik Wilson 10/25/82, Lawrence KS, Triple Jump
Mary Wineburg (Danner) 1/3/81, Cincinnati OH, 400m

Reggie Witherspoon 5/31/85, Marietta GA, 4x400 Relay
Christin Wurth-Thomas 7/11/80, Springdale AR, 1500m
Amy Yoder Begley 1/1/78, Beaverton OR, 10000m

STAFF

Randy Ballard Massage Therapist

STAFF

Hector Manuel Bautista Pool Manager
Melissa Beasley Doping Control Coordinator
Sharrieffa Barksdale Blair Pool Manager
Jeannette Bolden-Pickens Head Coach

Chandra Cheeseborough Asst Coach, Spr/Hur (W)
Joe (J.J.) Clark Asst Coach, Mid Dist (W)
Julie Endreson Massage Therapist
Harvey Glance Asst Coach, Spr/Hur (M)
Brooks Johnson (NOT PICTURED) Asst Coach, Relay (W)

Kim Keenan-Kirkpatrick Asst Coach, Long Dist (W)
James Li Head Manager (M)
Glenn Lowenberg DC Chiropractor
Ronald Mann Asst Coach, Mid/Long Dist (M)

Aron McGuire Asst Team Leader
Connie Price Smith Asst Coach, Throws (W)
Orin Richburg (NOT PICTURED) Asst Coach, Relay (M)
Irving (Boo) Schexnayder Asst Coach, Jumps/CE (M)
Sandra Snow Team Leader

Criss Somerlot Asst Coach, Throws (M)
Rita Somerlot Asst Coach, Jumps (W)
Charles (Bubba) Thornton Head Coach
Richard Torrellas Head Manager (W)

Benny Vaughn Massage Therapist
Joe Vigil Asst Coach, Long Dist (M)
Timothy Weaver Pool Manager

243

100 M MEN

1	JAM	BOLT, USAIN	09.69
2	TRI	THOMPSON, RICHARD	09.89
3	USA	DIX, WALTER	09.91
4	AHO	MARTINA, CHURANDY	09.93
5	JAM	POWELL, ASAFA	09.95
6	JAM	FRATER, MICHAEL	09.97
7	TRI	BURNS, MARC	10.01
8	USA	PATTON, DARVIS	10.03
9	USA	GAY, TYSON	10.05 ELIMS

200M MEN

1	JAM	BOLT, USAIN	19.30
2	USA	CRAWFORD, SHAWN	19.96
3	USA	DIX, WALTER	19.98
4	ZIM	DZINGAI, BRIAN	20.22
5	GBR	MALCOLM, CHRISTIAN	20.40
6	SKN	COLLINS, KIM	20.59
	USA	SPEARMON, WALLACE	DISQ
	AHO	MARTINA, CHURANDY	DISQ

400M MEN

1	USA	MERRITT, LASHAWN	43.75
2	USA	WARINER, JEREMY	44.74
3	USA	NEVILLE, DAVID	44.80
4	BAH	BROWN, CHRISTOPHER	44.84
5	FRA	DJHONE, LESLIE	45.11
6	GBR	ROONEY, MARTYN	45.12
7	TRI	QUOW, RENNY	45.22
8	SWE	WISSMAN, JOHAN	45.39

800M MEN

1	KEN	BUNGEI, WILFRED	01:44.65
2	SUD	ISMAIL, ISMAIL AHMED	01:44.70
3	KEN	YEGO, ALFRED KIRWA	01:44.82
4	CAN	REED, GARY	01:44.94
5	BHR	KAMEL, YOUSSEF SAAD	01:44.95
6	CUB	LOPEZ, YEIMER	01:45.88
7	ALG	MADI, NABIL	01:45.96
8	ALG	MANSEUR, NADJIM	01:47.19
17	USA	SYMMONDS, NICHOLAS	01:46.96 ELIMS
29	USA	WHEATING, ANDREW	01:47.05 ELIMH
41	USA	SMITH, CHRISTIAN	01:48.20 ELIMH

1500M MEN

1	BHR	RAMZI, RASHID	03:32.94
2	KEN	KIPROP, ASBEL	03:33.11
3	NZL	WILLIS, NICHOLAS	03:34.16
4	FRA	BAALA, MEDHI	03:34.21
5	ESP	HIGUERO, JUAN CARLOS	03:34.44
6	MAR	IGUIDER, ABDELATI	03:34.66
7	RSA	VANDEVENTER, JUAN	03:34.77
8	BHR	ALI, BELAL MANSOOR	03:35.23
13	USA	LAGAT, BERNARD	03:37.79 ELIMS
22	USA	LOMONG, LOPEZ	03:41.00 ELIMS
24	USA	MANZANO, LEONEL	03:50.33 ELIMS

5000M MEN

1	ETH	BEKELE, KENENISA	12:57.82
2	KEN	KIPCHOGE, ELIUD	13:02.80
3	KEN	SOI, EDWIN CHERUIYOT	13:06.22
4	UGA	KIPSIRO, MOSES NDIEMA	13:10.56
5	ETH	CHERKOS, ABRAHAM	13:16.46
6	ETH	BEKELE, TARIKU	13:19.06
7	MEX	BARRIOS, JUAN LUIS	13:19.79
8	QAT	C'KURUI, JAMES KWALIA	13:23.48
9	USA	LAGAT, BERNARD	13:26.89
13	USA	TEGENKAMP, MATT	13:33.13
32	USA	DOBSON, IAN	14:05.47 ELIMH

10,000M MEN

1	ETH	BEKELE, KENENISA	27:01.17
2	ETH	SIHINE, SILESHI	27:02.77
3	KEN	KOGO, MICAH	27:04.11
4	KEN	MASAI, MOSES NDIEMA	27:04.11
5	ERI	TADESSEE, ZERSENAY	27:05.11
6	ETH	GEBRSELASSIE, HAILE	27:06.68
7	KEN	MATHATI, MARTIN IRUNGU	27:08.25
8	QAT	HASSAN, ABDULLAH AHMAD	27:23.75
13	USA	RUPP, GALEN	27:36.99
15	USA	ABDIRAHMAN, ABDIHAKEM	27:52.53
25	USA	TORRES, JORGE	28:13.93

110MH MEN

1	CUB	ROBLES, DAYRON	12.93
2	USA	PAYNE, DAVID	13.17
3	USA	OLIVER, DAVID	13.18
4	FRA	DOUCOURE, LADJI	13.24
5	POL	NOGA, ARTUR	13.36
6	JAM	WIGNALL, MAURICE A	13.46
7	JAM	PHILLIPS, RICHARD	13.60
8	ESP	QUINONEZ, JACKSON	13.69
	USA	TRAMMELL, TERRENCE R.	DNF ELIMH

400MH MEN

1	USA	TAYLOR, ANGELO F.	47.25
2	USA	CLEMENT, KERRON	47.98
3	USA	JACKSON, BERSHAWN	48.06
4	JAM	MCFARLANE, DANNY	48.30
5	RSA	VANZYL, L.J.	48.42
6	POL	PLAWGO, MAREK	48.52
7	JAM	BUCKLEY, MARKINO	48.60
8	GRE	IAKOVAKIS, PERIKLIS	49.96

3000 M STEEPLECHASE MEN

1	KEN	KIPRUTO, BRIMIN	08:10.34
2	FRA	MEKHISSI-BENABBAD, MAHIEDINE	08:10.49
3	KEN	MATEELONG, RICHARD KIPKEMBOI	08:11.01
4	ETH	JARSO, YAKOB	08:13.47
5	FRA	TAHRI, BOUABDALLAH	08:14.79
6	AUS	ABDI, YOUCEF	08:16.36
7	KEN	KEMBOI, EZEKIEL	08:16.38
8	QAT	KAMAL, ABUBAKER ALI	08:16.59
13	USA	FAMIGLIETTI, ANTHONY	08:31.21
27	USA	MCADAMS, JOSHUA	08:33.26 ELIMH
30	USA	NELSON, WILLIAM	08:36.66 ELIMH

20K WALK MEN

1	RUS	BORCHIN, VALERIY	01:19:01.
2	ECU	PEREZ, JEFFERSON	01:19:15.
3	AUS	TALLENT, JARED	01:19:42.
4	CHN	WANG, HAO	01:19:47.
5	ITA	BRUGNETTI, IVANO	01:19:51.
6	AUS	ADAMS, LUKE	01:19:57.
7	ESP	FERNANDEZ, FRANCISCO JAVIER	01:20:32.
8	IRL	HEFFERNAN, ROBERT	01:20:36.
43	USA	EASTLER, KEVIN	01:28:44.

50K WALK MEN

1	ITA	SCHWAZER, ALEX	03:37:09.
2	AUS	TALLENT, JARED	03:39:27.
3	RUS	NIZHEGORODOV, DENIS	03:40:14.
4	ESP	GARCIA, JESUS ANGEL	03:44:08.
5	NOR	TYSSE, ERIK	03:45:08.
6	MEX	NAVA, HORACIO	03:45:21.
7	JPN	YAMAZAKI, YUKI	03:45:47.
8	POL	FEDACZYNSKI, RAFAL	03:46:51.
39	USA	DUNN, PHILIP MARTIN	04:08:32.

4X100M MEN

1	JAM		37.10
2	TRI		38.06
3	JPN		38.15
4	BRA		38.24
5	GER		38.58
6	CAN		38.66
	CHN		DISQ
	NED		DISQ ELIMH
	USA	PATTON, DARVIS	DNF
	USA	GAY, TYSON	
	USA	PADGETT, TRAVIS	
	USA	MARTIN, RODNEY	

4X400M MEN

1	USA	TAYLOR, ANGELO F.	02:55.39
	USA	WARINER, JEREMY	
	USA	MERRITT, LASHAWN	
	USA	WITHERSPOON, REGGIE	
	USA	CLEMENT, KERRON	
	USA	NEVILLE, DAVID	
2	BAH		02:58.03
3	RUS		02:58.06
4	GBR		02:58.81
5	BEL		02:59.37
6	AUS		03:00.02
7	POL		03:00.32
8	JAM		03:01.45

MARATHON MEN

1	KEN	WANJIRU, SAMUEL KAMAU	02:06:32.
2	MAR	GHARIB, JAOUAD	02:07:16.
3	ETH	KEBEDE, TSEGAY	02:10:00.
4	ETH	MERGA, DERIBA	02:10:21.
5	KEN	LEL, MARTIN	02:10:24.
6	SUI	ROTHLIN, VIKTOR	02:10:35.
7	ETH	ASFAW, GASHAW	02:10:52.
8	ERI	ASMEROM, YARED	02:11:11.
9	USA	RITZENHEIN, DATHAN	02:11:59.
10	USA	HALL, RYAN	02:12:33.
22	USA	SELL, BRIAN	02:16:07.

DISCUS MEN

1	EST	KANTER, GERD	68.82
2	POL	MALACHOWSKI, PIOTR	67.82
3	LTU	ALEKNA, VIRGILIJUS	67.79
4	GER	HARTING, ROBERT	67.09
5	ESP	CASANAS, YENNIFER FRANK	66.49
6	RUS	PISHCHALNIKOV, BOGDAN	65.88
7	NED	SMITH, RUTGER	65.39
8	HUN	FAZEKAS, ROBERT	63.43
16	USA	ROBERTSON, MICHAEL	61.64 ELMQ
19	USA	MALONE, CASEY	61.26 ELMQ
25	USA	WALTZ, IAN	60.02 ELMQ

JAVELIN MEN

1	NOR	THORKILDSEN, ANDREAS	90.57
2	LAT	KOVALS, AINARS	86.64
3	FIN	PITKAMAKI, TERO	86.16
4	FIN	JARVENPAA, TERO	83.95
5	FIN	WIRKKALA, TEEMU	83.46
6	AUS	BANNISTER, JARROD	83.45
7	RUS	KOROTKOV, ILYA	83.15
8	BLR	KAZLOU, ULADZIMIR	82.06
18	USA	SMITH, LEIGH	76.55 ELMQ
22	USA	GREER, BREAUX	73.68 ELMQ

| 24 | USA | HAZLE, MIKE | 72.75 ELMQ |

HAMMER THROW MEN

1	SLO	KOZMUS, PRIMOZ	82.02
2	BLR	DEVYATOVSKIY, VADIM	81.61
3	BLR	TSIKHAN, IVAN	81.51
4	HUN	PARS, KRISZTIAN	80.96
5	JPN	MOROFUSHI, KOJI	80.71
6	FIN	KARJALAINEN, OLLI-PEKKA	79.59
7	POL	ZIOLKOWSKI, SZYMON	79.22
8	SVK	CHARFREITAG, LIBOR	78.65
27	USA	KRUGER, A G	71.21 ELMQ

SHOT PUT MEN

1	POL	MAJEWSKI, TOMASZ	21.51
2	USA	CANTWELL, CHRISTIAN	21.09
3	BLR	MIKHNEVICH, ANDREI	21.05
4	CAN	ARMSTRONG, DYLAN	21.04
5	BLR	LYZHYN, PAVEL	20.98
6	UKR	BILONAH, YURIY	20.63
7	USA	HOFFA, RESSE	20.53
8	RUS	SOFIN, PAVEL	20.42
	USA	NELSON, ADAM	NM

HIGH JUMP MEN

1	RUS	SILNOV, ANDREY	2.36
2	GBR	MASON, GERMAINE	2.34
3	RUS	RYBAKOV, YAROSLAV	2.34
4	SWE	HOLM, STEFAN	2.32
5	GER	SPANK, RAUL	2.32
6	CZE	BABA, JAROSLAV	2.29
7	CZE	JANKU, TOMAS	2.29
8	GBR	PARSONS, TOM	2.25
13	USA	MANSON, ANDRA	2.25 ELMQ
18	USA	WILLIAMS, JESSE	2.25 ELMQ
25	USA	JONAS, DUSTIN	2.2 ELMQ

LONG JUMP MEN

1	PAN	SALADINO, IRVING	8.34
2	RSA	MOKOENA, GODFREY KHOTSO	8.24
3	CUB	CAMEJO, IBRAHIM	8.2
4	ZIM	MAKUSHA, NGONIDZASHE	8.19
5	CUB	MARTINEZ, WILFREDO	8.19
6	SEN	BADJI, NDISS KABA	8.16
7	ESP	MELIZ, LUIS FELIPE	8.07
8	CZE	NOVOTNY, ROMAN	8
19	USA	QUINLEY, TREVELL	7.87 ELMQ
22	USA	JOHNSON, BRIAN	7.79 ELMQ
38	USA	PATE, MIGUEL	7.34 ELMQ

POLE VAULT MEN

1	AUS	HOOKER, STEVEN	5.96
2	RUS	LUKYANENKO, UEVGENIY	5.85
3	UKR	YURCHENKO, DENYS	5.7
4	USA	MILES, DEREK	5.7
5	RUS	STARODUBTSEV, DMITRY	5.7
6	GER	ECKER, DANIEL	5.7
7	FRA	CLAVIER, JEROME	5.6
8	GER	HOLZDEPPE, RAPHAEL	5.6
20	USA	HARTWIG, JEFF	5.55 ELMQ
	USA	WALKER, BRAD	NM ELMQ

TRIPLE JUMP MEN

1	POR	EVORA, NELSON	17.67
2	GBR	IDOWU, PHILLIPS	17.62
3	BAH	SANDS, LEEVAN	17.59
4	CUB	GIRALT, DAVID	17.52
5	ROM	OPREA, MARIAN	17.22
6	BRA	GREGORIO, JADEL	17.2
7	GBR	ACHIKE, ONOCHIE	17.17
8	UKR	KUZNYETSOV, VIKTOR	16.87
20	USA	CURRY, RAFEEG	16.88 ELMQ
26	USA	BELL, KENTA	16.55 ELMQ
34	USA	WILSON, AARIK	15.97 ELMQ

DECATHLON MEN

1	USA	CLAY, BRYAN	8791
2	BLR	KRAUCHANKA, ANDREI	8551
3	CUB	SUAREZ, LEONEL	8527
4	RUS	POGORELOV, ALEKSANDR	8328
5	FRA	BARRAS, ROMAIN	8253
6	CZE	SEBRLE, ROMAN	8241
7	UKR	KASYANOV, OLEKSIY	8238
8	GER	NIKLAUS, ANDRE	8220
	USA	PAPPAS, TOM	DNF
	USA	HARDEE, TREY	DNF

100M WOMEN

1	JAM	FRASER, SHELLY-ANN	10.78
2	JAM	SIMPSON, SHERONE	10.98
3	JAM	STEWART, KERRON	10.98
4	USA	WILLIAMS, LAURYN	11.03
5	USA	LEE, MUNA	11.07
6	GBR	KWAKYE, JEANETTE	11.14
7	BAH	FERGUSON, DEBBIE	11.19
8	USA	EDWARDS, TORRI MECHELLE	11.20

200M WOMEN

1	JAM	CAMPBELL, VERONICA	21.74
2	USA	FELIX, ALLYSON	21.93
3	JAM	STEWART, KERRON	22.00
4	USA	LEE, MUNA	22.01
5	USA	HOOKER, MARSHEVET	22.34

6	JAM	SIMPSON, SHERONE	22.36
7	BAH	FERGUSON, DEBBIE	22.61
8	CAY	MOTHERSILL, CYDONIE	22.68

400M WOMEN

1	GBR	OHUROUGU, CHRISTINE	49.62	
2	JAM	WILLIAMS, SHERICKA	49.69	
3	USA	**RICHARDS, SANYA**	49.93	
4	RUS	GUSHCHINA, YULIYA	50.01	
5	RUS	KAPACHINSKAYA, ANASTASIYA	50.03	
6	RUS	FIROVA, TATYANA	50.11	
7	JAM	WHYTE, ROSEMARIE	50.68	
8	BOT	MONTSHO, AMANTLE	51.18	
11	USA	**WINEBERG, MARY**	51.13	*ELIMS*
17	USA	**TROTTER, DEEDEE**	51.87	*ELIMS*

800M WOMEN

1	KEN	JELIMO, PAMELA	01:54.87	
2	KEN	BUSIENEI, JANETH JEPKOSGEI	01:56.07	
3	MAR	BENHASSI, HASNA	01:56.73	
4	RUS	KLYUKA, SVETLANA	01:56.94	
5	MOZ	MUTOLA, MARIA DELURDES	01:57.68	
6	JAM	SINCLAIR, KENIA	01:58.24	
7	UKR	KREVSUN, YULIYA	01:58.73	
8	RUS	ANDRIANOVA, TATYANA	02:02.63	
25	USA	**CLARK, HAZEL**	02:01.59	*ELIMH*
30	USA	**SCHMIDT, ALICE**	02:02.33	*ELIMH*
	USA	**TETER, NICOLE**	DNF	*ELIMH*

1500M WOMEN

1	KEN	LANGAT, NANCY JEBET	04:00.23	
2	UKR	LISHCYNSKA, IRINA	04:01.63	
3	UKR	TOBIAS, NATALIYA	04:01.78	
4	GBR	DOBRISKEY, LISA	04:02.10	
5	BHR	JAMAL, MARYAM YUSUF	04:02.71	
6	ESP	RODRIGUEZ, NATALIA	04:03.19	
7	USA	**ROWBURY, SHANNON**	04:03.58	
8	ESP	FUENTES-PILA, IRIS	04:04.86	
20	USA	**WURTH-THOMAS, CHRISTIAN**	04:09.70	*ELIMH*
28	USA	**DONOHUE, ERIN**	04:16.05	*ELIMH*

5000M WOMEN

1	ETH	DIBABA, TIRUNESH	15:41.40
2	TUR	ABEYLEGESSE, ELVAN	15:42.74
3	ETH	DEFAR, MESERET	15:44.12
4	KEN	KIBET, SYLVIA JEBIWOTT	15:44.96
5	KEN	CHERUIYOT, VIVIAN	15:46.32
6	RUS	SHOBUKHOVA, LILIYA	15:46.62
7	TUR	BEKELE, ALEMITU	15:48.48
8	ETH	MELKAMU, MESELECH	15:49.03
9	USA	**GOUCHER, KARA**	15:49.39
10	USA	**FLANAGAN, SHALANE**	15:50.80

10,000M WOMEN

1	ETH	DIBABA, TIRUNESH	29:54.66
2	TUR	ABEYLEGESSE, ELVAN	29:56.34
3	USA	**FLANAGAN, SHALANE**	30:22.22
4	KEN	MASAI, LINET CHEPKWEMOI	30:26.50
5	RUS	KONOVALOVA, MARIYA	30:35.84
6	RUS	ABITOVA, INGA	30:37.33
7	KEN	WANGUI, LUCY	30:39.96
8	NED	KIPLAGAT, LORNA	30:40.27
10	USA	**GOUCHER, KARA**	30:55.16

100MH WOMEN

1	USA	**HARPER, DAWN**	12.54
2	AUS	MCLELLAN, SALLY	12.64
3	CAN	LOPES, PRISCILLA	12.64
4	USA	**CHERRY, DAMU**	12.65
5	JAM	ENNIS-LONDON, DELLOREEN	12.65
6	JAM	FOSTER-HYLTON, BRIGITTE	12.66
7	USA	**JONES, LO LO**	12.72
8	GBR	CLAXTON, SARAH	12.94

400MH WOMEN

1	JAM	WALKER, MELANIE	52.64
2	USA	**TOSTA, SHEENA**	53.70
3	GBR	DANVERS, NATASHA	53.84
4	UKR	RABCHENYUK, ANASTASIYA	53.96
5	POL	JESIEN, ANNA	54.29
6	RUS	BIKERT, YEKATERINA	54.96
7	CZE	HEJNOVA, ZUZANA	54.97
8	USA	**ROSS-WILLIAMS, TIFFANY**	57.55

20K WALK WOMEN

1	RUS	KANISKINA, OLGA	01:26:31.
2	NOR	PLAETZER, KJERSTI	01:27:07.
3	ITA	RIGAUDO, ELISA	01:27:12.
4	CHN	LIU, HONG	01:27:17.
5	ESP	VASCO, MARIA	01:27:25.
6	ESP	PASCUAL, BEATRIZ	01:27:44.
7	IRL	LOUGHNANE, OLIVE	01:27:45.
8	POR	CABECINHA, ANA	01:27:46.
31	USA	**DOW, JOANNE**	01:34:15.

4X100M WOMEN

1	RUS		42.31	
2	BEL		42.54	
3	NGR		43.04	
4	BRA		43.14	
5	GER		43.28	
	GMB		DNF	
	JAM		DNF	
	POL		DISQ	*ELIMH*
	USA	**WILLIAMS, ANGELA**	DISQ	*ELIMH*
	USA	**EDWARDS, TORRI MECHELLE**		
	USA	**LEWIS, MECHELLE**		
	USA	**WILLIAMS, LAURYN**		

4X400M WOMEN

1	USA	**HENDERSON, MONIQUE**	03:18.54
	USA	**FELIX, ALLYSON**	
	USA	**RICHARDS, SANYA**	
	USA	**WINEBERG, MARY**	
	USA	**HASTINGS, NATASHA**	
2	RUS		03:18.82
3	JAM		03:20.40
4	BLR		03:21.85
5	GBR		03:22.68
6	CUB		03:23.21
7	NGR		03:23.74
8	GER		03:28.45

3000 M STEEPLECHASE WOMEN

1	RUS	SAMITOVA, GULNARA	08:58.81	
2	KEN	JEPKORIR, EUNICE	09:07.41	
3	RUS	VOLKOVA, YEKATERINA	09:07.64	
4	RUS	PETROVA, TATYANA	09:12.33	
5	ROM	CASANDRA, CRISTINA	09:16.85	
6	KEN	NYANGAU, RUTH BISIBORI	09:17.35	
7	ETH	AHMED, ZEMZEM	09:17.85	
8	POL	FRANKIEWICZ, WIOLETTA	09:21.76	
9	USA	**BARRINGER, JENNIFER**	09:22.26	
10	USA	**WILLARD, ANNA**	09:25.63	
24	USA	**ANDERSON, LINDSEY**	09:36.81	*ELIMH*

MARATHON WOMEN

1	ROM	TOMESCU, CONSTANTINA	02:26:44.
2	KEN	NDEREBA, CATHERINE	02:27:06.
3	CHN	ZHOU, CHUNXIU	02:27:07.
4	CHN	ZHU, XIALON	02:27:16.
5	KEN	KOMU, MARTHA	02:27:23.
6	GBR	YAMAUCHI, MARA	02:27:29.
7	RUS	TIMOFEYEVA, IRINA	02:27:31.
8	ROM	SIMON, LIDIA	02:27:51.
27	USA	**RUSSELL, BLAKE**	02:33:1.
	USA	**KASTOR, DEENA**	DNF
	USA	**LEWY, MAGDALENA**	DNF

DISCUS WOMEN

1	USA	**BROWN, STEPHANIE**	64.74	
2	CUB	BARRIOS, YARELIS	63.64	
3	UKR	ANTONOVA, OLENA	62.59	
4	CHN	SONG, AIMIN	62.2	
5	CZE	CECHLOVA, VERA	61.75	
6	BLR	ZVEREVA, ELLINA	60.82	
7	CHN	LI, YANFENG	60.68	
8	FRA	ROBERT-MICHON, MELINA	60.66	
10	USA	**THURMOND, ARETHA**	59.8	
27	USA	**POWELL, SUZANNE N.**	58.02	*ELMQ*

JAVELIN WOMEN

1	CZE	SPOTAKOVA, BARBORA	71.42	
2	RUS	ABAKUMOVA, MARIYA	70.78	
3	GER	OBERGFOLL, CHRISTINA	66.13	
4	GBR	SAYERS, GOLDIE	65.75	
5	GER	NERIUS, STEFFI	65.29	
6	CUB	MENENDEZ, OSLEIDYS	63.35	
7	POL	MADEJCZYK, BARBARA	62.02	
8	GER	MOLITOR, KATHRINA	59.64	
39	USA	**KREINER, KIM**	55.13	*ELMQ*
42	USA	**PATTERSON, KARA**	54.39	*ELMQ*

HAMMER THROW WOMEN

1	BLR	MIANKOVA, AKSANA	76.34	
2	CUB	MORENO, YIPSI	75.2	
3	CHN	ZHANG, WENXIU	74.32	
4	BLR	PCHELNIK, DARYA	73.65	
5	FRA	MONTEBRUN, MANUELA	72.54	
6	POL	WLODARCZYK, ANITA	71.56	
7	ITA	CLARETTI, CLARISSA	71.33	
8	SVK	DANISOVA, MARTINA	71	
29	USA	**CAMPBELL, AMBER**	67.86	*ELMQ*
39	USA	**SMITH, LOREE**	63.6	*ELMQ*
	USA	**COSBY, JESSICA**	NO MARK	*ELMQ*

SHOT PUT WOMEN

1	NZL	VILI, VALERIE	20.56	
2	BLR	MIKHNEVICH, NATALLIA	20.28	
3	BLR	OSTAPCHUK, NADEZHDA	19.86	
4	CUB	GONZALEZ, MISLEIDIS	19.5	
5	CHN	GONG, LIJIAO	19.2	
6	RUS	OMAROVA, ANNA	19.08	
7	GER	KLEINERT-SCHMITT, NADINE	19.01	
8	CHN	LI, MEIJU	19	
12	USA	**CAMARENA, JILLIAN**	18.24	
15	USA	**CARTER, MICHELLE**	17.74	
23	USA	**HEASTON, KRISTIN L**	17.34	*ELMQ*

HIGH JUMP WOMEN

1	BEL	HELLEBAUT, TIA	2.05	
2	CRO	VLASIC, BLANKA	2.05	
3	RUS	CHICHEROVA, ANNA	2.03	
4	RUS	SLESARENKO, YELENA	2.01	
5	UKR	PALAMAR, VITA	1.99	
6	USA	**HOWARD, CHAUNTE**	1.99	
7	ESP	BEITIA, RUTH	1.96	
7	GER	FRIEDRICH, ARIANE	1.96	
19	USA	**ACUFF, AMY LYN**	1.89	*ELMQ*
25	USA	**DAY, SHARON**	1.85	*ELMQ*

LONG JUMP WOMEN

1	BRA	MAGGI, MAURREN HIGA	7.04
2	RUS	LEBEDEVA, TATYANA	7.03
3	NGR	AKAGBARE, BLESSING	6.91
4	JAM	HAMMOND, CHELSEA	6.79
5	USA	**REESE, BRITTNEY**	6.76
6	RUS	UDMURTOVA, OKSANA	6.7
7	GBR	JOHNSON, JADE	6.64
8	USA	**UPSHAW, GRACE**	6.58
12	USA	**JIMOH, FUNMI**	6.29

POLE VAULT WOMEN

1	RUS	ISINBAYEVA, YELENA	5.05	
2	USA	**STUCZYNSKI, JENNIFER**	4.8	
3	RUS	FEOFANOVA, SVETLANA	4.75	
4	RUS	GOLUBCHIKOVA, YULIYA	4.75	
5	POL	PYREK, MONIKA	4.7	
6	GER	HINGST, CAROLINE	4.65	
7	GER	SPIEGELBURG, SILKE	4.65	
8	USA	**STEINER, APRIL**	4.55	
	USA	**BARTOLINA, ERICA**	NM	*ELMQ*

TRIPLE JUMP WOMEN

1	CMR	MBANGO ETONE, FRANCOISE	15.39	
2	RUS	LEBEDEVA, TATYANA	15.32	
3	GRE	DEVETZI, HRYSOPIYI	15.23	
4	KAZ	RYPAKOVA, OLGA	15.11	
5	CUB	SAVIGNE, YANGELIS	15.05	
6	SLO	SESTAK, MARIJA	15.03	
7	RUS	GUROVA, VIKTORIYA	14.77	
8	RUS	PYATYKH, ANNA	14.73	
26	USA	**MCLAIN, ERICA**	13.52	*ELMQ*
28	USA	**MARKS, SHANI**	13.44	*ELMQ*

HEPTATHLON WOMEN

1	UKR	DOBRYNSKA, NATALIYA	6733
2	USA	**FOUNTAIN, HYLEAS**	6619
3	RUS	CHERNOVA, TATYANA	6591
4	GBR	SOTHERTON, KELLY	6517
5	CAN	ZELINKA, JESSICA	6490
6	RUS	BOGDANOVA, ANNA	6465
7	POL	TYMINSKA, KAROLINA	6428
	USA	**PICKLER, DIANA**	DNF
	USA	**JOHNSON, JACQUELYN**	DNF

Howard Bach 2/22/79, San Francisco CA, Doubles
Eva Lee 8/7/86, Orange CA, Singles/Doubles
Bob MALythong 4/10/81, Rockville MD, Doubles
Mesinee MangkALkiri 4/21/83, Garden Grove CA, Singles/Doubles

Raju Rai 2/3/83, Atlanta GA, Singles

STAFF

Cai, Zi Min Head Coach/Team Leader

BADMINTON RESULTS

SINGLES MEN
1	CHN	LIN, DAN
2	MAS	LEE, CHONG WEI
3	CHN	CHEN, JIN
4	KOR	LEE, HYUNIL
5	DEN	GADE, PETER
5	CHN	BAO, CHUNLAI
5	INA	KUNCORO, SONY DWI
5	TPE	HSIEH, YU HSING
	USA	RAI, RAJU *ELM 2ND ROUND*

DOUBLES MEN
1	INA	
2	CHN	
3	KOR	
4	DEN	
5	USA	BACH, HOWARD
	USA	MALAYTHONG, BOB
5	JPN	
5	POL	
5	MAS	

SINGLES WOMEN
1	CHN	ZHANG, NING
2	CHN	XIE, XINGFANG
3	INA	YULIANTI, MARIA
4	CHN	LU, LAN
5	FRA	PI, HONGYAN
5	GER	XU, HUAIWEN
5	IND	NEHWAL, SAINA
5	MAS	WONG, MEW CHOO
	USA	LEE, EVA *ELM 1ST ROUND*

DOUBLES WOMEN
1	CHN	
2	KOR	
3	CHN	
4	JPN	
5	TPE	
5	CHN	
5	JPN	
5	SIN	
	USA	LEE, EVA *ELM 1ST ROUND*
	USA	MANGKALAKIRI, MAY

MIXED DOUBLES
1	KOR
2	INA
3	CHN
4	INA
5	GBR
5	THA
5	POL
5	DEN

(NO **USA** MIXED DOUBLES TEAM)

Brett Anderson 2/1/88, Stillwater OK, Left-Handed Pitcher
Jake Arrieta 3/6/86, Farmington MO, Right-Handed Pitcher
Brian Barden 4/2/81, Templeton CA, Infield
Matthew Brown 8/8/82, Bellevue WA, Infield

Trevor Cahill 3/1/88, Oceanside CA, Right-Handed Pitcher
Jeremy Cummings 11/7/76, Charleston WV, Right-Handed Pitcher
Jason Donald 9/4/84, Fresno CA, Infield
Brian Duensing 2/22/83, Marysville KS, Left-Handed Pitcher

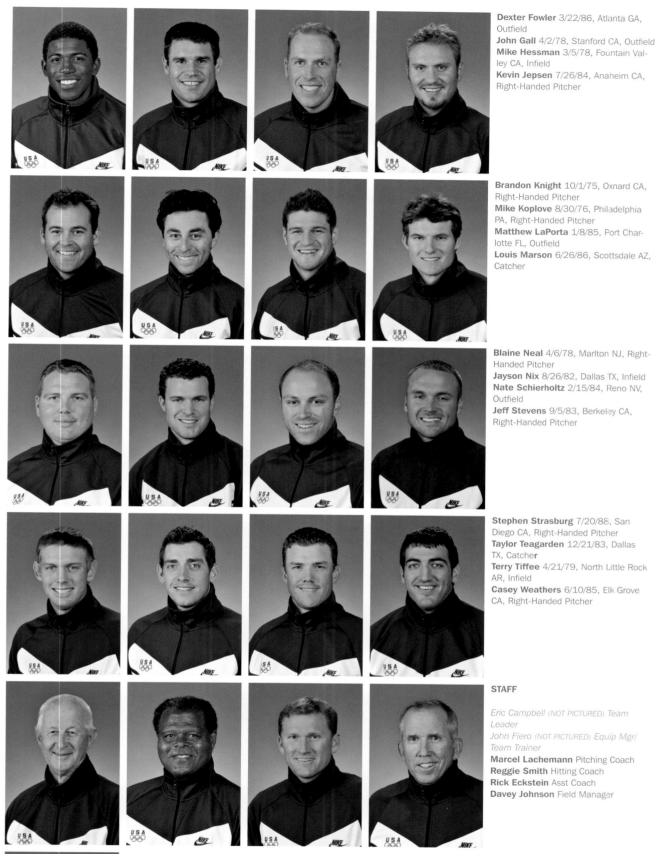

Dexter Fowler 3/22/86, Atlanta GA, Outfield
John Gall 4/2/78, Stanford CA, Outfield
Mike Hessman 3/5/78, Fountain Valley CA, Infield
Kevin Jepsen 7/26/84, Anaheim CA, Right-Handed Pitcher

Brandon Knight 10/1/75, Oxnard CA, Right-Handed Pitcher
Mike Koplove 8/30/76, Philadelphia PA, Right-Handed Pitcher
Matthew LaPorta 1/8/85, Port Charlotte FL, Outfield
Louis Marson 6/26/86, Scottsdale AZ, Catcher

Blaine Neal 4/6/78, Marlton NJ, Right-Handed Pitcher
Jayson Nix 8/26/82, Dallas TX, Infield
Nate Schierholtz 2/15/84, Reno NV, Outfield
Jeff Stevens 9/5/83, Berkeley CA, Right-Handed Pitcher

Stephen Strasburg 7/20/88, San Diego CA, Right-Handed Pitcher
Taylor Teagarden 12/21/83, Dallas TX, Catcher
Terry Tiffee 4/21/79, North Little Rock AR, Infield
Casey Weathers 6/10/85, Elk Grove CA, Right-Handed Pitcher

STAFF

Eric Campbell (NOT PICTURED) Team Leader
John Fiero (NOT PICTURED) Equip Mgr/ Team Trainer
Marcel Lachemann Pitching Coach
Reggie Smith Hitting Coach
Rick Eckstein Asst Coach
Davey Johnson Field Manager

Roly DeArmas Asst Coach

BASEBALL RESULTS

RANKINGS

1	KOR	3	*GOLD GAME SCORE*
2	CUB	2	
3	**USA**	8	*BRONZE GAME SCORE*
4	JPN	4	
5	TPE		
6	CAN		
7	NED		
8	CHN		

USA	vs	KOR	7-8
		NED	7-0
		CUB	4-5
		CAN	5-4
		CHN	9-1
		TPE	4-2
		JAP	4-2
		CUB	10-2
		JAP	8-4

BASKETBALL

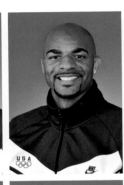  

Carmelo Anthony 5/29/84, Baltimore MD, Forward
Carlos Boozer 11/20/81, Juneau AK, Forward
Chris Bosh 3/24/84, Dallas TX, Forward
Kobe Bryant 8/23/78, Ardmore PA, Guard

 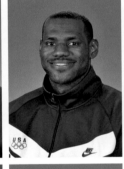  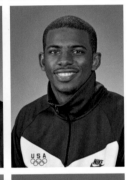

Dwight Howard 12/8/85, Atlanta CA, Forward/Center
LeBron James 12/30/84, Akron OH, Forward
Jason Kidd 3/23/73, Oakland CA, Guard
Chris Paul 5/6/85, Clemmons NC, Guard

 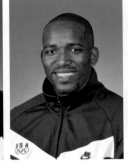  

Tayshaun Prince 2/28/80, Compton CA, Forward
Michael Redd 8/24/79, Columbus OH, Guard
Dwyane Wade 1/17/82, Robbins IL, Guard
Deron Williams 7/26/84, The Colony TX, Guard

Seimone Augustus 4/30/84, Baton Rouge LA, Forward
Sue Bird 10/16/80, Syosset NY, Guard
Tamika Catchings 7/21/79, Duncanville TX, Forward
Sylvia Fowles 10/6/85, Miami FL, Center

Kara Lawson 2/14/81, Alexandria VA, Guard
Lisa Leslie 7/7/72, Hawthorne CA, Center
DeLisha Milton-Jones 9/11/74, Riceboro GA, Forward
Candace Parker 4/19/86, Naperville IL, Forward/Center/Guard

Cappie Pondexter 1/7/83, Chicago IL, Guard
Katie Smith 6/4/74, Logan OH, Guard
Diana Taurasi 6/11/82, Chino CA, Guard/Forward
Tina Thompson 2/10/75, Los Angeles CA, Forward

  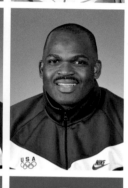 

STAFF

Ford Sean Team Leader (M)
Mike Krzyzewski Head Coach (M)
Jim Boeheim Asst Coach (M)
Nate McMillan Asst Coach (M)

Jerry Colangelo Managing Director (M)
Mike D'Antoni Asst Coach (M)
Carol Callan Team Leader (W)
Ann Donovan Head Coach (W)

Dawn Staley Asst Coach (W)
Mike Thibault Asst Coach (W)
Gail Goestenkors Asst Coach (W)
BJ (William) Johnson Team Manager (W)

BASKETBALL RESULTS

MEN

1	**USA**	118	*GOLD GAME SCORE*	**USA** GAME SCORES		
2	ESP	107		**USA** vs	CHN	101-70
3	ARG	87	*BRONZE GAME SCORE*		ANG	97-76
4	LTU	75			GRE	92-69
5	GRE				ESP	119-82
6	CRO				GER	106-57
7	AUS				AUS	116-85
8	CHN				ARG	101-81

WOMEN

1	**USA**	92	*GOLD GAME SCORE*	**USA** GAME SCORES		
2	AUS	65		**USA** vs	CZE	97-57
3	RUS	94	*BRONZE GAME SCORE*		CHN	108-63
4	CHN	81			MLI	97-41
5	ESP				ESP	93-55
6	BLR				NZL	96-60
7	TCH				KOR	104-60
8	KOR				RUS	67-52

   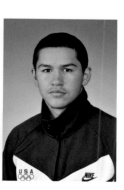

Sadam Ali 9/26/88, Brooklyn NY, Lightweight
Demetrius Andrade 2/26/88, Providence RI, Welterweight
Shawn Estrada 4/1/85, East Los Angeles CA, Middleweight
Javier Molina 1/2/90, Commerce CA, Light Welterweight

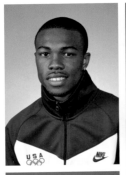

Gary Russell Jr. 6/5/88, Capitol Heights MD, Bantamweight
Rau'shee Warren 2/13/87, Cincinnati OH, Flyweight
Deontay Wilder 10/22/85, Tuscaloosa AL, Heavyweight
Raynell Williams 2/4/89, Cleveland OH, Featherweight

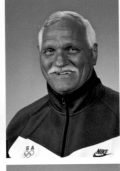

Luis Yanez 10/25/88, Duncanville TX, Light Flyweight

STAFF

Darryl "Joe" Smith Team Leader
Dan Campbell Head Coach
Willy Price Asst Coach, Defensive

Robert Martin Asst Coach, Offensive
Basheer Abdullah Technical Advisor

BOXING RESULTS

LT. FLYWEIGHT(106 LBS/48 KG) 106LBS

1	CHN	ZOU, SHIMING
2	MGL	PUREVDORJ, SERDAMBA
3	IRL	BARNES, PADDY
3	CUB	HERNANDEZ, YAMPIER
5	THA	RUENFROENG, AMNAT
5	BRA	CARVALHO, PAULO
5	POL	MASZCZYK, LUKASZ
5	KAZ	ZHAKYPOV, BIRZHAN
	USA	**YANEZ, LUIS** — *ELM- 2ND ROUND*

FLYWEIGHT (112.5 LBS/51 KG) 112LBS

1	THA	JONG JO HOR, SOMJIT
2	CUB	HERNANDEZ, ANDRY LAFITA
3	RUS	BALAKSHIN, GEORGY
3	ITA	PICARDI, VINCENZO
5	PUR	ARROYO ACEVEDO, MCWILLIAMS
5	TJK	YUNOSOV, ANVAR
5	TUN	CHERIF, WALID
5	IND	KUMAR, JITENDER
	USA	**WARREN, RAU'SHEE** — *ELM-1ST ROUND*

BANTAMWEIGHT(119.5 LBS/54 KG) 119LBS

1	MGL	ENKHBAT, BADAR-UUGAN
2	CUB	LEON ALARCON, YANKIEL
3	MDA	GOJAN, VEACESLAV
3	MRI	JULIE, BRUNO
5	THA	PETCHKOOM, WORAPOJ
5	VEN	MANZANILLA, HECTOR
5	BOT	IKGOPOLENG, KHUMISO
5	IND	KUMAR, AKHIL
	USA	**RUSSELL, GARY**

FEATHERWEIGHT (125 LBS/57 KG) 125LBS

1	UKR	LOMACHENKO, VASYL
2	FRA	DJELKHIR, KHEDAFI
3	TUR	KILIC, YAKUP
3	AZE	IMRANOV, SHAHIN
5	CHN	LI, YANG CHN
5	MEX	SANTOS REYES, ARTURO
5	CUB	TORRIENTE, IDEL
5	ALG	CHADI, ABDELKADER
	USA	**WILLIAMS, RAYNELL** — *ELM-MAIN RD 2*

LIGHTWEIGHT(132 LBS/60 KG) 132LBS

1	RUS	TISCHENKO, ALEXEY
2	FRA	SOW, DAOUDA
3	ARM	JAVAKHYAN, HRACHIK
3	CUB	UGAS, YORDENIS
5	KOR	BAIK, JONG-SUB
5	CHN	HU, QING
5	COL	PEREZ, DARLEY
5	ROM	POPESCU, GEORGIAN
	USA	**ALI, SADDAM** — *ELM-MAIN RD 1*

LT. WELTERWEIGHT(141 LBS/64 KG) 141LBS

1	DOM	DIAZ, FELIX
2	THA	BOONJUMNONG, MANUS
3	FRA	VASTINE, ALEXIS
3	CUB	IGLESIAS SOTOLONGO, RONIEL
5	RUS	KOVALEV, GENNADY
5	KAZ	SAPIYEV, SERIK
5	IRI	SEPAHVAND, MORTEZA
5	MGL	URANCHIMEG, MUNKH-ERDENE
	USA	**MOLINA, JAVIER** — *ELM-MAIN RD 1*

WELTERWEIGHT(152 LBS/69 KG) 152LBS

1	KAZ	SARSEKBAYEV, BAKHYT
2	CUB	BANTEAUX SUAREZ, CARLOS
3	KOR	KIM, JUNG JOO
3	CHN	HANATI, SILAMU
5	**USA**	**ANDRADE, DEMETRIUS**
5	UZB	MAHMUDOV, DILSHOD
5	BAH	JOHNSON, TOUREANO
5	EGY	ABDIN, HOSAM

MIDDLEWEIGHT (165.5 LBS/75 KG) 165LBS

1	GBR	DEGALE, JAMES
2	CUB	CORREA, EMILIO
3	IRL	SUTHERLAND, DARREN
3	IND	KUMAR, VIJENDER
5	KAZ	ARTAYEV, BAKHTIYAR
5	ECU	GONGORA, CARLOS
5	VEN	BLANCO, ALFONSO
5	UZB	RASULOV, ELSHOD
	USA	**ESTRADA, SHAWN** — *ELM-MAIN RD 2*

LT. HEAVYWEIGHT(178 LBS/81 KG) 178LBS

1	CHN	ZHANG, XIAOPING
2	IRL	EGAN, KENNETH
3	GBR	JEFFRIES, TONY
3	KAZ	SHYNALIYEV, YERKEBUIAN
5	BRA	SILVA, WASHINGTON
5	HUN	SZELLO, IMRE
5	ALG	BENCHABLA, ABDELHAFID
5	TJK	KURBANOV, DZHAKHON

HEAVYWEIGHT (201 LBS/91 KG) 201LBS

1	RUS	CHAKHKIEV, RAKHIM
2	ITA	RUSSO, CLEMENTE
3	**USA**	**WILDER, DEONTAY**
3	CUB	ACOSTA DUARTE, OSMAY
5	GRE	PAVLIDIS, ELIAS
5	FRA	MBUMBA, JOHN
5	MAR	ARJAOUI, MOHAMMED
5	UKR	USYK, OLEKSANDR

SUPER HEAVYWEIGHT(+201LB/91KG) 201LBS+

1	ITA	CAMMARELLE, ROBERTO
2	CHN	ZHANG, ZHI LEI
3	GBR	PRICE, DAVID
3	UKR	GLAZKOV, VYACHESLAV
5	LTU	JAKSTO, JAROSLAVAS
5	COL	RIVAS, OSCAR
5	KAZ	MYRSATAEV, RUSLAN
5	ALG	OUATAH, NEWFEL

Heather Corrie 7/25/71, Grandy MN, Whitewater Slalom K1W
Casey Eichfeld 11/15/89, Drums PA, Whitewater Slalom C2
Benn Fraker 2/23/89, Peachtree City GA, Whitewater Slalom C1
Carrie Johnson 1/16/84, San Diego CA, K-1-W 500m

Scott Parsons 3/27/79, Sylvania OH, Whitewater Slalom K1
Richard Powell 3/22/89, Parkesburg PA, Whitewater Slalom C2
Rami Zur 2/23/77, Costa Mesa CA, K-1 500m, 1000m

STAFF

CANOE/KAYAK Flatwater
Cliff Meidl Team Leader

Nathan Luce Head Coach
CANOE/KAYAK Slalom
Angela Lokken Team Leader
Silvan Poberaj Head Coach
Cathy Hearn Head Coach

CANOE/KAYAK RESULTS

C-1 CANOE SINGLE MEN - SLALOM (WHITEWATER)

1	SVK	MARTIKAN, MICHAL	176.65
2	GBR	FLORENCE, DAVID	178.61
3	AUS	BELL, ROBIN	180.59
4	ESP	ELOSEGUI, ANDER	182.12
5	CZE	JEZEK, STANISLAV	182.29
6	**USA**	**FRAKER, BENN**	183.14
7	GRE	TSAKMAKIS, CHRISTOS	186.67
8	POL	BIERYT, KRZYSZTOF	200.21

C-2 CANOE DOUBLE MEN - SLALOM (WHITEWATER)

1	SVK	190.82
2	CZE	192.89
3	RUS	197.37
4	FRA	198.19
5	ITA	204.12
6	GER	204.43
7	AUS	104.17
8	POL	105.32
11	**USA**	**POWELL, RICK** 253.34
	USA	**EICHFELD, CASEY**

K-1 KAYAK SINGLE MEN - SLALOM (WHITEWATER)

1	GER	GRIMM, ALEXANDER	171.7
2	FRA	LEFEVRE, FABIEN	173.3
3	TOG	BOUKPETI, BENJAMIN	173.45
4	IRL	RHEINISCH, EOIN	176.91
5	AUS	DRAPER, WARWICK	177.85
6	CAN	FORD, DAVID	178.35
7	AUT	OBLINGER, HELMUT	178.83
8	POL	POPIELA, DARIUSZ	179.68
20	**USA**	**PARSONS, SCOTT**	220.54

C-1 1000 METERS MEN - SPRINT (FLATWATER)

1	HUN	VAJDA, ATILLA	03:50.467
2	ESP	CAL, DAVID	03:52.751
3	CAN	HALL, TOM	03:53.653
4	UZB	MENKOV, VADIM	03:54.237
5	BLR	ZHUKOVSKII, ALIAKSANDR	03:55.645
6	ROM	MIRONCIC, FLORIN GEORGIAN	03:57.876
7	FRA	GOUBEL, BATHIEU	03:57.889
8	GER	DITTMER, ANDREAS	03:57.894

C-1 500 METERS MEN - SPRINT (FLATWATER)

1	RUS	OPALEV, MAXIM	01:47.140
2	ESP	CAL, DAVID	01:48.397
3	UKR	CHEBAN, IURII	01:48.766
4	FRA	GOUBEL, BATHIEU	01:49.056
5	BLR	ZHUKOVSKII, ALIAKSANDR	01:49.092
6	CHN	LI, QIANG	01:49.287
7	ROM	MIRONCIC, FLORIN GEORGIAN	01:49.861

C-2 1000 METERS MEN - SPRINT (FLATWATER)

1	BLR	03:36.365
2	GER	03:36.588
3	HUN	03:40.258
4	ROM	03:40.342
5	CHN	03:40.593
6	CAN	03:41.165
7	POL	03:42.845
8	RUS	03:44.669

C-2 500 METERS MEN - SPRINT (FLATWATER)

1	CHN	01:41.025
2	RUS	01:41.282
3	GER	01:41.964
4	BLR	01:41.996
5	CAN	01:42.450
6	ROM	01:43.195
7	BUL	01:43.971

K-1 1000 METERS MEN - SPRINT (FLATWATER)

1	GBR	BRABANTS, TIM	03:26.323
2	NOR	LARSEN, ERIK	03:27.342
3	AUS	WALLACE, KEN	03:27.485
4	NZL	FOUHY, BEN	03:29.193
5	GER	HOFF, MAX	03:29.391
6	SWE	OSCARSSON, MARKUS	03:30.198
7	CRO	JANIC, STJEPAN	03:30.495
8	CAN	VAN KOEVERDEN, ADAM	03:31.793
	USA	**ZUR, RAMI**	03:46.204

K-1 500 METERS MEN - SPRINT (FLATWATER)

1	AUS	WALLACE, KEN	01:37.252
2	CAN	VAN KOEVERDEN, ADAM	01:37.630
3	GBR	BRABANTS, TIM	01:37.671
4	NOR	LARSEN, ERIK	01:37.949
5	RUS	RYAKHOV, ANTON	01:38.187
6	HUN	VERECKEI, AKOS	01:38.318
7	SWE	GUSTAFSSON, ANDERS	01:38.447
8	NZL	FERGUSON, STEVEN	01:38.512
	USA	**ZUR, RAMI**	01:47.163

K-2 1000 METERS MEN - SPRINT (FLATWATER)

1	GER	03:11.809
2	DEN	03:13.580
3	ITA	03:14.750
4	POL	03:14.828
5	HUN	03:15.049
6	NZL	03:15.329
7	FRA	03:16.532

K-2 500 METERS MEN - SPRINT (FLATWATER)

1	ESP	01:28.736
2	GER	01:28.827
3	BLR	01:30.005

4	HUN	01:30.285
5	DEN	01:30.569
6	CAN	01:30.857
7	FRA	01:31.312

K-4 1000 METERS MEN - SPRINT (FLATWATER)

1	BLR	02:55.714
2	SVK	02:56.593
3	GER	02:56.676
4	ITA	02:57.626
5	HUN	02:59.009
6	POL	02:59.505
7	CHN	03:00.078
8	RUS	03:00.654

K-1 KAYAK SINGLE WOMEN - SLALOM (WHITEWATER)

1	SVK	KALISKA, ELENA	192.64
2	AUS	LAWRENCE, JACQUELINE	206.94
3	AUT	OBLINGER, P VIOLETTA	214.77
4	JPN	TAKESHITA, YURIKO	219.3
5	POL	STANUCH, AGNIESZKA	221.08
6	NED	HERDE, ARIANE	231.99
7	FRA	FER, EMILIE	251.96
8	**USA**	**CORRIE, HEATHER**	270.88

K-1 500 METERS WOMEN - SPRINT (FLATWATER)

1	UKR	OSYPENKO, INNA	01:50.673
2	ITA	IDEM, JOSEFA	01:50.677
3	GER	WAGNER, KATRIN	01:51.022
4	HUN	KOVACS, KATALIN	01:51.139
5	CHN	ZHONG, HONG YAN	01:52.220
6	SLO	PONOMARENKO, SPELA	01:52.363
7	GBR	WAINWRIGHT, LUCY	01:53.102
8	RSA	HODSON, JENNIFER	01:53.353
	USA	**JOHNSON, CARRIE**	01:53.721

K-2 500 METERS WOMEN - SPRINT (FLATWATER)

1	HUN	01:41.308
2	POL	01:42.092
3	FRA	01:42.128
4	GER	01:42.899
5	JPN	01:43.291
6	AUS	01:43.969
7	FIN	01:44.176

K-4 500 METERS WOMEN - SPRINT (FLATWATER)

1	GER	01:32.231
2	HUN	01:32.971
3	AUS	01:34.704
4	POL	01:34.752
5	ESP	01:35.366
6	JPN	01:36.465
7	RSA	01:36.724
8	ITA	01:36.770

Kristin Armstrong 8/11/73, Boise ID, Road, Time Trial
Kyle Bennett 9/25/79, Conroe TX, BMX
Michael Blatchford 1/29/86, Cypress CA, Track Team Sprint, Match Sprint
Adam Craig (NOT PICTURED) 8/15/81, Corinth ME, Mtn. Bike
Mike Day 10/9/84, Santa Clarita CA, BMX

Adam Duvendeck 10/28/71, Santa Barbara CA, Track Team Sprint
Michael Friedman 9/19/82, Pittsburgh PA, Track Madison
Georgia Gould (NOT PICTURED) 1/5/80, Baltimore MD, Mtn. Bike
Sarah Hammer 8/18/83, Temecula CA, Track Individual Pursuit, Points Race
George Hincapie (NOT PICTURED) 6/29/73, Greenville SC, Road
Jill Kintner 10/24/81, Seattle WA, BMX

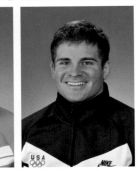

Bobby Lea 10/17/83, Topton PA, Track Points Race, Madison
Levi Leipheimer 10/24/73, Santa Rosa CA, Road, Time Trial
Giddeon Massie 8/27/81, Bethlehem PA, Track Team Sprint
Jason McCartney (NOT PICTURED) 9/3/73, Coralville IA, Road
Mary McConneloug 6/24/71, Fairfax CA, Mnt. Bike

Amber Neben 2/18/74, Irvine CA, Road
Taylor Phinney 6/27/90, Boulder CO, Track Individual Pursuit
Jennie Reed 4/20/78, Kirkland WA, Track Match Sprint
Donny Robinson 6/17/83, Napa CA, BMX

Christine Thorburn 9/17/69, Davenport IA, Road, Time Trial
Christian Vande Velde (NOT PICTURED) 5/22/76, Lemont IL, Road
Todd Wells (NOT PICTURED) 12/25/75, Kingston NY, Mtn. Bike
David Zabriskie 1/12/79, Salt Lake City UT, Road, Time Trial

STAFF

CYCLING BMX
Ken Whelpdale Team Leader
Mike King Head Coach

Nicholas Legan Mechanic
CYCLING MTB
Marc Gullickson Head Coach
CYCLING ROAD
Pat McDonough Team Leader
James Miller Coach, Road

252

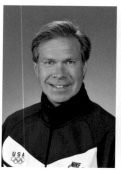

James Ochowicz Coach
Bernard Condeveaux *(NOT PICTURED)*
Soigneur #1
Brenda Phelps (NOT PICTURED) Soigneur #2
Vincent Gee (NOT PICTURED) Mechanic -#3
CYCLING TRACK
Ryan (Andy) Sparks Coach #1
Viggo Christensen Soigneur #3
Thomas J. (TJ) Grove Mechanic #2

CYCLING RESULTS

BIKE MOTO-CROSS MEN
1	LAT	STROMBERS, MARIS	36.190
2	**USA**	**DAY, MICHAEL**	36.606
3	**USA**	**ROBINSON, DONNY**	36.972
4	COL	JIMENEZ CAICEDO, A	39.137
5	NED	VAN DEN WILDENB, ROB	39.772
6	AUS	GRAVES, JARED	02:19.233
7	RSA	NHLAPO, SIFISO	DNF
10	**USA**	**BENNET, KYLE**	ELMS

MOUNTAIN BIKING CROSS-COUNTRY MEN
1	FRA	ABSALON, JULIEN	01:55:59.
2	FRA	PERAUD, JEAN-CHRISTOPHE	01:57:06.
3	SUI	SCHURTER, NINO	01:57:52.
4	SUI	SAUSER, CHRISTOPH	01:57:54.
5	ITA	FONTANA, MARCO AURELIO	01:59:59.
6	AUT	SOUKUP, CHRISTOPHER	02:00:11.
7	GBR	KILLEEN, LIAM	02:00:14.
29	**USA**	**CRAIG, ADAM**	1 LAP BACK
43	**USA**	**WELLS, TODD**	3 LAPS BACK

INDIVIDUAL ROAD RACE MEN
1	ESP	SANCHEZ GONZALEZ, SAMUEL	06:23:49.
2	ITA	REBELLIN, DAVIDE	06:23:49.
3	SUI	CANCELLARA, FABIAN	06:23:49.
4	RUS	KOLOBNEV, ALEXANDR	06:23:49.
5	LUX	SCHLECK, ANDY	06:23:49.
11	**USA**	**LEIPHEIMER, LEVI**	06:24:09.
17	**USA**	**VANDE VELDE, CHRISTIAN**	06:24:19.
40	**USA**	**HINCAPIE, GEORGE**	06:26:25.
	USA	**MCCARTNEY, JASON**	DNF
	USA	**ZABRISKIE, DAVID**	DNF

INDIVIDUAL TIME TRIAL MEN
1	SUI	CANCELLARA, FABIAN	01:02:11.43
2	SWE	LARSSON, GUSTAV ERIK	01:02:44.79
3	**USA**	**LEIPHEIMER, LEVI**	01:03:21.11
4	ESP	CONTADOR, ALBERTO	01:03:29.51
5	AUS	EVANS, CADEL	01:03:34.97
6	ESP	SANCHEZ GONZALEZ, SAMUEL	01:04:37.24
7	CAN	TUFT, SVEIN	01:04:39.44
12	**USA**	**ZABRISKIE, DAVID**	01:05:17.82

INDIVIDUAL PURSUIT MEN
1	GBR	WIGGINS, BRADLEY	04:16.977
2	NZL	ROULSTON, HAYDEN	04:19.611
3	GER	BURKE, STEVEN	04:20.947
4	RUS	MARKOV, ALEXEI	04:24.149
5	UKR	DYUDYA, VOLODYMYR	04:22.471 ELM 1 RD
6	ESP	TAULER LLUL, ANTONIO	04:24.974 ELM 1 RD
7	RUS	SEROV, ALEXANDER	04:25.391 ELM 1 RD
8	**USA**	**PHINNEY, TAYLOR**	04:26.644 ELM 1 RD

KEIRIN MEN
1	GBR	HOY, CHRIS	
2	GBR	EDGAR, ROSS	
3	JPN	NAGAI, KIYOFUMI	
4	AUS	KELLY, SHANE JOHN	
5	GER	BERGEMANN, CARSTEN	
6	FRA	TOURNANT, ARNAUD	
7	FRA	BAUGE, GREGORY	
8	AUS	BAYLEY, RYAN	
21	**USA**	**MASSIE, GIDDEON**	ELMP

MATCH SPRINT TEAM MEN
1	GBR		43.128
2	FRA		43.651
3	GER		44.014
4	AUS		44.022
5	NED		44.212
6	JPN		44.437
7	MAS		44.822
8	**USA**	**BLATCHFORD, MICHAEL**	45.423
	USA	**DUVENDECK, ADAM**	
	USA	**MASSIE, GIDDEON**	

SPRINT MEN
1	GBR	HOY, CHRIS	10.216
2	GBR	KENNY, JASON	
3	FRA	BOURGAIN, MICKAEL	10.560
4	GER	LEVY, MAXIMILIAN	10.666
5	FRA	SIREAU, KEVIN	10.719
6	NED	MULDER, TEUN	
7	NED	BOS, THEO	
15	**USA**	**BLATCHFORD, MICHAEL**	ELM IN REPECHAGE

TEAM PURSUIT MEN
1	GBR	03:53.314
2	DEN	04:00.040
3	NZL	03:57.776
4	AUS	03:59.006
5	NED	ELM 1 ROUND
6	RUS	ELM 1 ROUND
7	ESP	ELM 1 ROUND

MADISON MEN
1	ARG		8	
2	ESP		7	
3	RUS		6	
4	BEL		17	1 LAP BACK
5	GER		15	1 LAP BACK
6	DEN		14	1 LAP BACK
7	FRA		12	1 LAP BACK
16	**USA**	**LEA, BOBBY**	3	4 LAPS BACK
		FRIEDMAN, MICHAEL		

POINTS RACE MEN
1	ESP	LLANERAS ROSELLO, JOAN	60
2	GER	KLUGE, ROGER	58
3	GBR	NEWTON, CHRISTOPHER	56
4	AUS	MEYER, CAMERON	36
5	BLR	KIRYIENKA, VASIL	34
6	DEN	KREUTZFELD, DANIEL	29
7	CAN	BELL, ZACH	27
	USA	**LEA, BOBBY**	DNF

BIKE MOTO-CROSS WOMEN
1	FRA	CHAUSSON, ANNE-CAROLINE	35.976
2	FRA	LE CORGUILLE, LAETITIA	38.042
3	**USA**	**KINTNER, JILL**	38.674
4	NZL	WALKER, SARAH	38.805
5	ARG	DIAZ, MARIA GABRIELA	39.747
6	AUS	CALLISTO, NICOLE	01:19.609
7	CAN	COOLS, SAMANTHA	DNF
8	GBR	READE, SHANAZE	

MOUNTAIN BIKING CROSS-COUNTRY WOMEN
1	GER	SPITZ, SABINE	01:45:11.
2	POL	WLOSCZOWSKA, MAJA	01:45:52.
3	RUS	KALENTIEVA, IRINA	01:46:28.
4	CAN	PENDREL, CATHERINE	01:46:37.
5	CHN	REN, CHENGYUAN	01:47:40.
6	SUI	HENZI, PETRA	01:48:41.
7	**USA**	**MCCONNELOUG, MARY**	01:50:34.
8	**USA**	**GOULD, GEORGIA**	01:50:51.

INDIVIDUAL ROAD RACE WOMEN
1	GBR	COOKE, NICOLE	03:32:24.
2	SWE	JOHANSSON, EMMA	03:32:24.
3	ITA	GUDERZO, TATIANA	03:32:24.
4	AUT	SOEDER, CHRISTIANE	03:32:28.
5	DEN	SERUP, LINDA MELANIE	03:32:33.
6	NED	VOS, MARIANNE	03:32:45.
25	**USA**	**ARMSTRONG, KRISTIN**	03:33:07.
33	**USA**	**NEBEN, AMBER**	03:33:17.
52	**USA**	**THORBURN, CHRISTINE**	03:41:08.

INDIVIDUAL TIME TRIAL WOMEN
1	**USA**	**ARMSTRONG, KRISTIN**	00:34:51.72
2	GBR	POOLEY, EMMA	00:35:16.01
3	SUI	THURIG, KARIN	00:35:50.99
4	FRA	LONGO-CIPRELLI, JEANNIE	00:35:52.62
5	**USA**	**THORBURN, CHRISTINE**	00:35:54.16
6	GER	ARNDT, JUDITH	00:35:59.77
7	AUT	SOEDER, CHRISTIANE	00:36:20.75
8	SUI	DOPPMANN, PRISKA	00:36:27.79

INDIVIDUAL PURSUIT WOMEN
1	GBR	ROMERO, REBECCA	03:28.321
2	GBR	HOUVENHAGEL, WENDY	03:30.395
3	UKR	KALITOVSKA, LESYA	03:31.413
4	NZL	SHANKS, ALISON	03:34.156
5	**USA**	**HAMMER, SARAH**	03:34.237
6	LTU	SEREIKAITE, VILIJA	03:36.808
7	AUS	MACTIER, KATIE	03:37.296
8	CZE	KOZLIKOVA, LADA	DNF

SPRINT WOMEN
1	GBR	PENDLETON, VICTORIA	11.118
2	AUS	MEARES, ANNA	
3	CHN	GUO, SHUANG	11.617
4	NED	KANIS, WILLY	
5	FRA	SANCHEZ, CLARA	12.264
6	BLR	TSYLINSKAYA, NATALIA	
7	**USA**	**REED, JENNIE**	
8	LTU	KRUPECKAITE, SIMONA	

POINTS RACE WOMEN
1	NED	VOS, MARIANNE	30
2	CUB	GONZALEZ PEREZ, YOANKA	18
3	ESP	OLABERRIA, DORRONSORO LEIRE ESP	13
4	COL	CALLE, MARIA	13
5	UKR	KALITOVSKA, LESYA	10
6	AUS	BATES, KATHERINE	10
7	FRA	JEULAND, PASCALE	8
	USA	**HAMMER, SARAH**	DNF

David Boudia 4/24/89, Noblesville IN, 10m
Kelci Bryant 1/15/89, Chatham IL, Synchronized 3m
Chris Colwill 9/11/84, Brandon FL, 3m, Synchronized 3m
Troy Dumais 1/21/80, Ventura CA, 3m

DIVING

Mary Beth Dunnichay 2/25/93, Elwood IN, Synchronized 10m
Thomas Finchum 12/1/89, Indianapolis IN, 10m, Synchronized 10m
Nancilea Foster 9/14/83, Conroe TX, 3m
Haley Ishimatsu 9/10/92, Seal Beach CA, 10m, Synchronized 10m

Christina Loukas 12/19/85, Riverwoods IL, 3m
Ariel Rittenhouse 12/9/90, Santa Cruz CA, Synchronized 3m
Jevon Tarantino 1/30/84, Boca Raton FL, Synchronized 3m
Laura Wilkinson 11/17/77, Spring TX, 10m

STAFF

Robert Rydze Team Leader
John Wingfield Head Coach
Wenbo Chen Asst Coach
Christopher Carr (NOT PICTURED) Sport Psychologist
David Burgering Coach

Kenneth Armstrong Coach
Daniel Laak Coach
Jeffrey Huber Coach
Matthew Scoggin Coach

DIVING RESULTS

3 METER SPRINGBOARD MEN

1	CHN	HE, CHONG	572.9
2	CAN	DESPATIE, ALEXANDRE	536.65
3	CHN	QIN, KAI	530.1
4	RUS	SAUTIN, DMITRY	512.65
5	GER	ROZENBERG, PAVLO	485.6
6	**USA**	**DUMAIS, TROY**	472.5
7	MEX	CASTILLO, YAHEL	462.1
8	GER	HAUSDING, PATRICK	462.05
12	**USA**	**COLWILL, CHRIS**	425.9

PLATFORM (10 METER) MEN

1	AUS	MITCHAM, MATTHEW	537.95
2	CHN	ZHOU, LUXIN	533.15
3	RUS	GALPERIN, GLEB	525.8
4	CHN	HUO, LIANG	508.4
5	CUB	GUERRA, JOSE	507.15
6	AUS	HELM, MATHEW	467.7
7	GBR	DALEY, THOMAS	463.55
8	MEX	PACHECO MARRUFO, ROMMEL	460.2
10	**USA**	**BOUDIA, DAVID**	441.45
12	**USA**	**FINCHUM, THOMAS**	412.65

3 METER SYNCHRO SPRINGBOARD MEN

1	CHN		469.08
2	RUS		421.98
3	UKR		415.05
4	**USA**	**COLWILL, CHRIS**	410.73
	USA	**TARANTINO, JEVON**	
5	CAN		409.29
6	GER		402.84

7	GBR		402.36
8	AUS		393.6

10 METER SYNCHRO PLATFORM MEN

1	CHN		468.18
2	GER		450.42
3	RUS		445.26
4	AUS		444.84
5	**USA**	**FINCHUM, THOMAS**	440.64
	USA	**BOUDIA, DAVID**	
6	COL		423.66
7	CUB		409.38
8	GBR		408.48

3 METER SPRINGBOARD WOMEN

1	CHN	GUO, JINGJING	415.35
2	RUS	PAKHALINA, JULIA	398.6
3	CHN	WU, MINXIA	389.85
4	CAN	HARTLEY, BLYTHE	374.6
5	ITA	CAGNOTTO, TANIA	349.2
6	SWE	LINDBERG, ANNA	342.15
7	AUS	STRATTON, SHARLEEN	331
8	**USA**	**FOSTER, NANCILEA**	316.7
9	**USA**	**LOUKAS, CHRISTINA**	315.7

PLATFORM (10 METER) WOMEN

1	CHN	CHEN, RUOLIN	447.7
2	CAN	HEYMANS, EMILIE	437.05
3	CHN	WANG, XIN	429.9
4	MEX	ESPINOSA, PAOLA	380.95
5	MEX	ORTIZ, TATIANA	343.6
6	AUS	WU, MELISSA	338.15

7	CAN	MARLEAU, MARIE-EVE	332.1
8	GBR	COUCH, TONIA	328.7
9	**USA**	**WILKINSON, LAURA**	311.8
14	**USA**	**ISHIMATSU, HALEY**	292.95*ELMS*

3 METER SYNCHRO SPRINGBOARD WOMEN

1	CHN		343.5
2	RUS		323.61
3	GER		318.9
4	**USA**	**RITTENHOUSE, ARIEL**	314.4
	USA	**BRYANT, KELCI**	
5	AUS		311.34
6	ITA		296.7
7	UKR		293.1
8	GBR		278.25

10 METER SYNCHRO PLATFORM WOMEN

1	CHN		363.54
2	AUS		335.16
3	MEX		330.06
4	GER		310.29
5	**USA**	**DUNNICHAY, MARY BETH**	309.12
	USA	**ISHIMATSU, HALEY**	
6	PRK		308.1
7	CAN		305.91
8	GBR		303.48

254

Phillip Dutton 9/13/63, West Grove PA, Eventing/Connaught
Becky Holder 4/24/69, Mendota Heights MN, Eventing/Courageous Comet
Courtney King-Dye 11/20/77, Harbor Springs MI, Dressage
Laura Kraut 11/14/65, Wellington FL, Show Jumping

Beezie Madden 11/20/63, Cazenovia NY, Show Jumping
Deborah McDonald 8/27/54, Hailey ID, Dressage
Gina Miles 11/27/73, Davis CA, Eventing/McKinlaigh
Karen O'Connor 2/17/58, The Plains VA, Eventing/Mandiba

Steffen Peters 9/18/64, San Diego CA, Dressage
William Simpson 6/9/59, Thousand Oaks CA, Show Jumping
Amy Tryon 2/24/70, Duvall WA, Eventing/Poggio II
McLain Ward 10/17/75, Brewster NY, Show Jumping

STAFF

Gil Merrick (NOT PICTURED) Team Leader
Klaus Balkenhol (NOT PICTURED) Chef d' Equipe (Coach)
Rafael Hernandez Carrillo (NOT PICTURED) Groom (Ravel; Steffen Peters)
Ruben Palermo (NOT PICTURED) Groom (Brentina; Debbie McDonald)
Allana Marchand (NOT PICTURED) Groom (Mythilus; Courtney King-Dye)
Richard Mitchell (NOT PICTURED) Veterinarian
Todd Meister (NOT PICTURED) Farrier
Douglas Hannum (NOT PICTURED) Stable Manager
Sara Livingston Ike (NOT PICTURED) Team Leader
Captain Mark Phillips (NOT PICTURED) Chef d'Equipe (Coach)
Emma Ford (NOT PICTURED) Groom (Connaught; Phillip Dutton)
Aubrey Dunkerton (NOT PICTURED) Groom (Courageous Comet; Rebecca Holder)
Sara Williams (NOT PICTURED) Groom (McKinlaigh; Gina Miles)

Allyson Green (NOT PICTURED) Groom (Poggio II; Amy Tryon)
Marion (Max) Corcoran (NOT PICTURED) Groom (Mandiba; Karen O'Connor)
Wendy Furlong (NOT PICTURED) Veterinarian
Stephen Teichman (NOT PICTURED) Farrier
Brendan Furlong (NOT PICTURED) Veterinarian
James Wolf (NOT PICTURED) Chef d'Mission
Sara "Sally" Ike (NOT PICTURED) Lord Team Leader
George Morris (NOT PICTURED) Chef d'Equipe (Coach)
Clark Shipley (NOT PICTURED) Groom (Authentic; Beezie Madden)
Lee McKeever Groom (NOT PICTURED) (Sapphire; McClain Ward)
Roger Solis Groom (NOT PICTURED) (Carlsson Von Dach; Will Simpson)
Johanna Burtsoff (NOT PICTURED) Groom (Cedric; Laura Kraut)
Timothy Ober (NOT PICTURED) Veterinarian
Elizabeth Parker (NOT PICTURED) (Chesson) Asst Team Leader

EQUESTRIAN RESULTS

INDIVIDUAL DRESSAGE

1	NED	VAN GRUNSVEN, ANKY SALINERO	78.68
2	GER	WERTH, ISABELL SATCHMO	76.65
3	GER	KEMMER, HEIKE BONAPARTE	74.455
4	**USA**	**PETERS, STEFFEN** RAVEL	74.15
5	NED	MINDERHOUD, HANS PETER NADINE	73.035
6	RUS	KORELOVA, ALEXANDRA BALAGUR	72.625
7	GBR	HINDLE, EMMA LANCET	72.345
13	**USA**	**KING, COURTNEY** MYTHILUS	70.175
34	**USA**	**MCDONALD, DEBBIE** BRENTINA	63 ELM-MAIN ROUND 1

TEAM DRESSAGE

1	GER		72.917
2	NED		71.75
3	DEN		68.875
4	**USA**	**KING, COURTNEY** MYTHILUS	67.819
	USA	**PETERS, STEFFEN** RAVEL	
	USA	**MCDONALD, DEBBIE** BRENTINA	
5	SWE		67.347
6	GBR		66.806
7	FRA		65.403
8	AUS		64.625

INDIVIDUAL JUMPING

1	CAN	LAMAZE, ERIC HICKSTEAD	0
2	SWE	BENGTSSON, ROLF-GORAN NINJA	0
3	**USA**	**MADDEN, BEEZIE** AUTHENTIC	4

4	GER	MICHAELS-BEERBAUM, MEREDITH SHUTTERFLY	4
5	BRA	PESSOA, RODRIGO RUFUS	4
6	**USA**	**WARD, MCLAIN** SAPPHIRE	4
7	GER	BEERBAUM, LUDGER ALL INCLUSIVE	4
23	**USA**	**KRAUT, LAURA** CEDRIC	ELMF
39	**USA**	**SIMPSON, WILL** CARLSSON VOM DACH	ELMQ

TEAM JUMPING

1	**USA**	**SIMPSON, WILL** CARLSSON VOM DACH	20
	USA	**KRAUT, LAURA** CEDRIC	
	USA	**MADDEN, BEEZIE** AUTHENTIC	
	USA	**WARD, MCLAIN** SAPPHIRE	
2	CAN		20
3	NOR		27
4	SUI		30
5	GER		34
5	NED		34
7	GBR		37
8	SWE		38

INDIVIDUAL 3-DAY EVENT

1	GER	ROMEIKE, HINRICH MARIUS	54.2
2	**USA**	**MILES, GINA** MCKINLAIGH	56.1
3	GBR	COOK, KRISTINA MINERS FROLIC	57.4
4	AUS	JONES, MEGAN IRISH JESTER	59
5	GER	KLIMKE, INGRID ABRAXXAS	59.7
6	FRA	DHENNIN, DIDIER ISMENE DU TEMPLE	59.8

7	AUS	FREDERICKS, CLAYTON BEN ALONG TIME	61.4
8	GER	DIBOWSKI, ANDREAS BUTTS LEON	65.2
42	**USA**	**HOLDER, BECKY** COURAGEOUS COMET	125.7 ELM RD 3
44	**USA**	**O'CONNOR, KAREN** MANDIBA	131.7 ELM RD 3
0	**USA**	**DUTTON, PHILLIP** CONNAUGHT	DQ
0	**USA**	**TRYON, AMY** POGGIO II	ELM 1ST RD

TEAM 3-DAY EVENT

1	GER		166.1
2	AUS		171.2
3	GBR		185.7
4	SWE		230.5
5	NZL		240.9
6	ITA		246.4
7	**USA**	**DUTTON, PHILLIP** CONNAUGHT	250
	USA	**O'CONNOR, KAREN** MANDIBA	
	USA	**TRYON, AMY** POGGIO II	
	USA	**MILES, GINA** MCKINLAIGH	
	USA	**HOLDER, BECKY** COURAGEOUS COMET	
8	IRL		276.1

256

Emily Cross 10/15/86, New York NY, Foil
Kelley Hurley 9/30/90, San Antonio TX, Epee
Sada Jacobson 2/14/83, Donwoody GA, Sabre
Seth Kelsey 8/24/81, Brush Prairie WA, Epee

Gerek Meinhardt 7/27/90, San Francisco CA, Foil
Timothy Morehouse 7/29/78, Bronx NY, Sabre
Jason Rogers 4/14/83, Los Angeles CA, Sabre
Erinn Smart 1/12/80, Brooklyn NY, Foil

Keeth Smart 7/29/78, Brooklyn NY, Sabre
Hannah Thompson 11/1/83, Rochester NY, Foil
Rebecca Ward 2/7/90, Portland OR, Sabre
James Williams 9/22/85, Sacramento CA, Sabre

   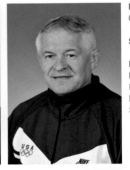

Mariel Zagunis 3/3/85, Beaverton OR, Sabre

STAFF

Robert Largman Team Leader
Michael Pederson Head Coach (W's Foil)
Edward Korfanty Head Coach (W's Sabre)

Yury Gelman Head Coach (M's Sabre)
Ron Herman Armorer
Arkady Burdan Coach (W's Sabre)
Jeffrey Bukantz Team Captain

Gregory Massialas Head Coach (M's Foil)

FENCING RESULTS

EPEE - INDIVIDUAL MEN

1	ITA	TAGLIARIOL, MATTEO
2	FRA	JEANNET, FABRICE
3	ESP	ABAJO, JOSE LUIS
4	HUN	BOCZKO, GABOR
5	KOR	JUNG, JIN SUN
6	POL	ZAWROTNIAK, RADOSLAW
7	ITA	CONFALONIERI, DIEGO
8	NED	VERWIJLEN, BAS
17	**USA**	**KELSEY, SETH**

EPEE - TEAM MEN

1	FRA	FRANCE
2	POL	POLAND
3	ITA	ITALY
4	CHN	CHINA
5	HUN	HUNGARY
6	VEN	VENEZUELA
7	UKR	UKRAINE
8	KOR	REPUBLIC OF KOREA

FOIL - INDIVIDUAL MEN

1	GER	KLEIBRINK, BENJAMIN
2	JPN	OTA, YUKI
3	ITA	SANZO, SALVATORE
4	CHN	ZHU, JUN
5	GER	JOPPICH, PETER
6	ITA	CASSARA, ANDREA
7	FRA	LEPECHOUX, ERWAN
8	CHN	LEI, SHENG
10	**USA**	**MEINHARDT, GEREK**

SABRE - INDIVIDUAL MEN

1	CHN	ZHONG, MAN
2	FRA	LOPEZ, NICOLAS
3	ROM	COVALIU, MIHAL
4	FRA	PILLET, JULIEN
5	ITA	TARANTINO, LUIGI
6	**USA**	**SMART, KEETH**

7	ESP	PINA, JORGE
8	BLR	BUIKEVICH, ALIAKSANDR
22	**USA**	**MOREHOUSE, TIMOTHY F**
28	**USA**	**ROGERS, JASON**

SABRE - TEAM MEN

1	FRA	FRANCE
2	**USA**	UNITED STATES OF AMERICA
	USA	**ROGERS, JASON**
	USA	**SMART, KEETH**
	USA	**MOREHOUSE, TIMOTHY F**
	USA	**WILLIAMS, JAMES L**
3	ITA	ITALY
4	RUS	RUSSIA
5	BLR	BELARUS

EPEE - INDIVIDUAL WOMEN

1	GER	HEIDEMANN, BRITTA
2	ROM	BRANZA, ANA
3	HUN	MINCZA, ILDIKO
4	CHN	LI, NA
5	GER	DUPLITZER, IMKE
6	RUS	SHUTOVA, LUBOV
7	FRA	FLESSEL-COLOVIC, LAURA
8	SWE	SAMUELSSON, EMMA
20	**USA**	**HURLEY, KELLEY**

FOIL - INDIVIDUAL WOMEN

1	ITA	VEZZALI, VALENTINA
2	KOR	NAM, HYUN-HEE
3	ITA	GRANBASSI, MARGHERITA
4	ITA	TRILLINI, GIOVANNA
5	HUN	KNAPEK, EDINA
6	RUS	LAMONOVA, EVGENIA
7	JPN	SUGAWARA, CHIEKO
17	**USA**	**CROSS, EMILY**
26	**USA**	**SMART, ERINN**
27	**USA**	**THOMPSON, HANNAH**

FOIL - TEAM WOMEN

1	RUS	RUSSIA
2	**USA**	UNITED STATES OF AMERICA
	USA	**SMART, ERINN**
	USA	**CROSS, EMILY**
	USA	**THOMPSON, HANNAH**
3	ITA	ITALY
4	HUN	HUNGARY
5	GER	GERMANY
6	CHN	CHINA
7	POL	POLAND

SABRE - INDIVIDUAL WOMEN

1	**USA**	**ZAGUNIS, MARIEL**
2	**USA**	**JACOBSON, SADA M.**
3	**USA**	**WARD, REBECCA**
4	RUS	VELIKAIA, SOFIA
5	CHN	TAN, XUE
6	CHN	BAO, YINGYING
7	TUN	BESBES, AZZA
8	UKR	KHOMROVA, OLENA

SABRE - TEAM WOMEN

1	UKR	UKRAINE
2	CHN	CHINA
3	**USA**	UNITED STATES OF AMERICA
	USA	**ZAGUNIS, MARIEL**
	USA	**JACOBSON, SADA M.**
	USA	**WARD, REBECCA**
4	FRA	FRANCE
5	RUS	RUSSIA
6	POL	POLAND

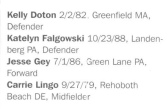

Kate Barber 11/22/76, West Chester PA, Midfielder
Kayla Bashore 2/20/83, Shoemakersville PA, Midfielder
Lauren Crandall 3/17/85, Doylestown PA, Defender
Rachel Dawson 8/2/85, Berlin NJ, Defender

Kelly Doton 2/2/82, Greenfield MA, Defender
Katelyn Falgowski 10/23/88, Landenberg PA, Defender
Jesse Gey 7/1/86, Green Lane PA, Forward
Carrie Lingo 9/27/79, Rehoboth Beach DE, Midfielder

Angela Loy 4/23/82, Loysville PA, Forward
Caroline Nichols 12/15/84, Virginia Beach VA, Defender
Lauren Powley 3/5/84, Moutaintop PA, Midfielder
Dina Rizzo 3/24/80, Walpole MA, Forward

Dana Sensenig 11/30/84, Denver PA, Midfielder
Keli Smith 1/25/79, Selinsgrove PA, Forward
Tiffany-Lynne Snow 12/2/81, Escondido CA, Forward
Amy Tran 10/2/80, Grantville PA, Goaltender

258

STAFF

Kate Reisinger Team Leader
Lee Bodimead Head Coach
Pam Bustin Asst Coach
Steve Jennings Asst Coach

Colleen Hacker Sport Psychologist
Shellie Onstead Video Technologist

FIELD HOCKEY RESULTS

FIELD HOCKEY - MEN			
1	GER	GERMANY	1	GOLD GAME SCORE
2	ESP	SPAIN	0	
3	AUS	AUSTRALIA	6	BRONZE GAME SCORE
4	NED	NETHERLANDS	4	
5	GBR	GREAT BRITAIN		
6	KOR	REPUBLIC OF KOREA		
7	NZL	NEW ZEALAND		
8	PAK	PAKISTAN		
		USA DID NOT QUALIFY		

FIELD HOCKEY - WOMEN			
1	NED	NETHERLANDS	2	GOLD GAME SCORE
2	CHN	CHINA	0	
3	ARG	ARGENTINA	3	BRONZE GAME SCORE
4	GER	GERMANY	1	
5	AUS	AUSTRALIA		
6	GBR	GREAT BRITAIN		
7	ESP	SPAIN		
8	**USA**	TEAM **USA**		

USA GAME SCORES		
USA VS.	ARG	2-1
	JPN	1-1
	GER	2-4
	NZL	4-1
	ESP	2-3

GYMNASTICS

Alex Artemev (NOT PICTURED) 8/29/85, Highlands Ranch CO, Artistic
Raj Bhavsar 9/7/80, Houston TX, Artistic
Erin Blanchard 11/20/89, Youngsville LA, Trampoline
Christopher Estrada 2/14/83, Lafayette LA, Trampoline
Joseph Hagerty 4/19/82, Rio Rancho NM, Artistic

Jonathan Horton 12/31/85, Houston TX, Artistic
Shawn Johnson 1/19/92, West Des Moines IA, Artistic
Nastia Liukin 10/30/89, Parker TX, Artistic
Chellsie Memmel 6/23/88, West Allis WI, Artistic

Samantha Peszek 12/14/91, Indianapolis IN, Artistic
Alicia Sacramone 12/3/87, Winchester MA, Artistic
Bridget Sloan 6/23/92, Pittsboro IN, Artistic
Justin Spring 3/11/84, Burke VA, Artistic

Kevin Tan 9/24/81, Fremont CA, Artistic

STAFF

GYMNASTICS ARTISTIC
Kathy Kelly Team Leader (+ Tramp) (W)
Martha Karolyi Coach (W)
Liang Qiao Head Coach (W)

Valeri Liukin Asst Coach (W)
Marvin Sharp Personal Coach (W)
Mihai Brestyan Personal Coach (W)
Andrew Memmel Personal Coach (W)

Xueyi Zhao Team Manager
Ron Brant Team Leader (M)
Kevin Mazeika Head Coch (M)
Dennis McIntyre Team Coordinator (M)

Keith Avery Miles Personal Coach (M)
Vitaly Marinitch Personal Coach (M)
Jon D. Valdez Personal Coach (M)
Mark W. Williams Personal Coach (M)

Randy L. Jepson Personal Coach (M)
GYMNASTICS TRAMPOLINE
Dzmitry Paliarush Head Coach/Team Leader
Ann Sims Team Administrator

259

GYMNASTICS RESULTS

ARTISTIC INDIVIDUAL ALL AROUND MEN

1	CHN	YANG, WEI	94.575
2	JPN	UCHIMURA, KOHEI	91.975
3	FRA	CARANOBE, BENOIT	91.925
4	JPN	TOMITA, HIROYUKI	91.75
5	RUS	KHOROKHORDIN, SERGEI	91.7
6	RUS	DEVIATOVSKI, MAXIM	91.7
7	GER	HAMBUCHEN, FABIAN	91.675
8	KOR	YANG, TAE YOUNG	91.6
9	USA	**HORTON, JONATHAN**	91.575
12	USA	**ARTEMEV, ALEXANDER**	90.675

ARTISTIC TEAM ALL AROUND MEN

1	CHN	TEAM CHINA	286.125
2	JPN	TEAM JAPAN	278.875
3	USA	TEAM USA	275.85
	USA	**BHAVSAR, RAJ**	275.85
	USA	**HAGERTY, JOSEPH**	275.85
	USA	**HORTON, JONATHAN**	275.85
	USA	**ARTEMEV, ALEXANDER**	275.85
	USA	**SPRING, JUSTIN**	275.85
	USA	**TAN, KAI WEN**	275.85
4	GER	GERMANY	274.6
5	KOR	REPUBLIC OF KOREA	274.375
6	RUS	RUSSIA	274.3
7	ROM	ROMANIA	274.175
8	FRA	FRANCE	272.875

FLOOR EXERCISE MEN

1	CHN	ZOU, KAI	16.05
2	ESP	DEFERR, GERVASIO	15.775
3	RUS	GOLOTSUTSKOV, ANTON	15.725
4	GER	HAMBUCHEN, FABIAN	15.65
5	JPN	UCHIMURA, KOHEI	15.575
6	BRA	HYPOLITO, DIEGO MATIAS	15.2
7	ROM	DRAGULESCU, MARIAN	14.85
8	ISR	SHATILOV, ALEXANDER	14.125

HORIZONTAL BAR MEN

1	CHN	ZOU, KAI	16.2
2	USA	**HORTON, JONATHAN**	16.175
3	GER	HAMBUCHEN, FABIAN	15.875
4	ITA	CASSINA, IGOR	15.675
5	JPN	NAKASE, TAKUYA	15.45
6	JPN	TOMITA, HIROYUKI	15.225
7	NED	ZONDERLAND, EPKE	15
8	FRA	CUCHERAT, YANN	14.825

PARALLEL BARS MEN

1	CHN	LI, XIAO-PENG	16.45
2	KOR	YOO, WON CHUL	16.25
3	UZB	FOKIN, ANTON	16.2
4	GER	HAMBUCHEN, FABIAN	15.975
5	SLO	PETKOVSEK, MITJA	15.725
6	CHN	HUANG, XU	15.7
7	KOR	YANG, TAE YOUNG	15.65
8	RUS	KRYUKOV, NOKOLAI	15.15

POMMEL HORSE MEN

1	CHN	XIAO, QIN	15.875
2	CRO	UDE, FILIP	15.725
3	GBR	SMITH, LOUIS	15.725
4	CHN	YANG, WEI	15.45
5	JPN	TOMITA, HIROYUKI	15.375
6	KOR	KIM, JIHOON	15.175
7	USA	**ARTEMEV, ALEXANDER**	14.975
8	VEN	FUENTES, JOSE	14.65

RINGS MEN

1	CHN	CHEN, YIBING	16.6
2	CHN	YANG, WEI	16.425
3	UKR	VOROBYOV, OLEXANDER	16.325
4	ITA	COPPOLINO, ANDREA	16.225
5	FRA	RODRIGUES, DANNY	16.225
6	ITA	MORANDI, MATTEO	16.2
7	ROM	STANESCU, ROBERT	15.825
8	BUL	IOVTCHEV, IORDAN	15.525

VAULT MEN

1	POL	BLANIK, LESZEK	16.537
2	FRA	BOUHAIL, THOMAS	16.537
3	RUS	GOLOTSUTSKOV, ANTON	16.475
4	ROM	DRAGULESCU, MARIAN	16.225
5	FRA	CARANOBE, BENOIT	16.062
6	BLR	KASPIAROVICH, DIMITRI	16.05
7	ROM	KOCZI, FLAVIUS	15.925
8	ESP	BOTELLA, ISAAC	15.737

TRAMPOLINE MEN

1	CHN	LU, CHUNLONG	41
2	CAN	BURNETT, JASON	40.7
3	CHN	DONG, DONG	40.6
4	JPN	SOTOMURA, TETSUYA	39.8
5	UKR	NIKITIN, YURIY	39.8
6	RUS	USHAKOV, DIMITRI	38.8
7	RUS	RUSAKOV, ALEXANDER	38.5
8	BLR	KAZAK, MIKALAI	38.1
15	USA	**ESTRADA, CHRIS**	65.9

ARTISTIC INDIVIDUAL ALL AROUND WOMEN

1	USA	**LIUKIN, NASTIA**	63.325
2	USA	**JOHNSON, SHAWN**	62.725
3	CHN	YANG, YILIN	62.65
4	RUS	SEMENOVA, KSENIA	61.925
5	ROM	NISTOR, STELIANA	61.05
6	CHN	JIANG, YUYAN	60.9
7	RUS	PAVLOVA, ANNA	60.825
8	ROM	IZBASA, SANDRA	60.75

ARTISTIC TEAM ALL AROUND WOMEN

1	CHN	TEAM CHINA	188.9
2	USA	TEAM USA	186.525
	USA	**LIUKIN, NASTIA**	186.525
	USA	**MEMMEL, CHELLSIE**	186.525
	USA	**SACRAMONE, ALICIA**	186.525
	USA	**PESZEK, SAMANTHA**	186.525
	USA	**JOHNSON, SHAWN**	186.525
	USA	**SLOAN, BRIDGET**	186.525
3	ROM	TEAM ROMANIA	181.525
4	RUS	RUSSIA	180.625
5	JPN	JAPAN	176.7
6	AUS	AUSTRALIA	176.525
7	FRA	FRANCE	175.275
8	BRA	BRAZIL	174.875

BALANCE BEAM WOMEN

1	USA	**JOHNSON, SHAWN**	16.225
2	USA	**LIUKIN, NASTIA**	16.025
3	CHN	CHENG, FEI	15.95
4	RUS	PAVLOVA, ANNA	15.9
5	ROM	DRAGOI, GABRIELA	15.625
6	CHN	LI, SHANSHAN	15.3
7	RUS	AFANASYEVA, KSENIA	14.825
8	JPN	TSURUMI, KOKO	14.45

FLOOR EXERCISE WOMEN

1	ROM	IZBASA, SANDRA	15.65
2	USA	**JOHNSON, SHAWN**	15.5
3	USA	**LIUKIN, NASTIA**	15.425
4	CHN	JIANG, YUYAN	15.35
5	RUS	KRAMARENKO, EKATERINA	15.025
6	BRA	SANTOS, DAIANE	14.975
7	CHN	CHENG, FEI	14.55
8	RUS	PAVLOVA, ANNA	14.125

UNEVEN BARS WOMEN

1	CHN	HE, KEXIN	16.725
2	USA	**LIUKIN, NASTIA**	16.725
3	CHN	YANG, YILIN	16.65
4	GBR	TWEDDLE, ELIZABETH	16.625
5	UKR	KOVAL, ANASTASIA	16.375
6	RUS	SEMENOVA, KSENIA	16.325
7	ROM	NISTOR, STELIANA	15.575
8	UKR	ZGOBA, DARIYA	14.875

VAULT WOMEN

1	PRK	HONG, UN JONG	15.65
2	GER	CHUSOVITINA, OKSANA	15.575
3	CHN	CHENG, FEI	15.562
4	USA	**SACRAMONE, ALICIA**	15.537
5	SUI	KASLIN, ARIELLA	15.05
6	ITA	GIOVANNINI, CARLOTTA	14.55
7	BRA	BARBOSA, JADE	14.487
8	RUS	PAVLOVA, ANNA	7.812

RHYTHMIC-INDIVIDUAL ALL AROUND WOMEN

1	RUS	KANAEVA, EVGENIYA	75.5
2	BLR	ZHUKOVA, INNA	71.925
3	UKR	BESSONOVA, ANNA	71.875
4	RUS	KAPRANOVA, OLGA	71.7
5	KAZ	YUSSUPOVA, ALIYA	69.8
6	AZE	GARAYEVA, ALIYA	69.675
7	UKR	GODUNKO, NATALIYA	68.85
8	ESP	CID, ALMUDENA	68.1

RHYTHMIC - GROUP ALL-AROUND WOMEN

1	RUS	RUSSIA	35.55
2	CHN	CHINA	35.225
3	BLR	BELARUS	34.9
4	ITA	ITALY	34.425
5	BUL	BULGARIA	33.55
6	ISR	ISREAL	32.1
7	AZE	AZERBAIJAN	31.575
8	UKR	UKRAINE	31.1

TRAMPOLINE WOMEN

1	CHN	HE, WENNA	37.8
2	CAN	COCKBURN, KAREN	37
3	UZB	KHILKO, EKATERINA	36.9
4	UKR	MOVCHAN, OLENA	36.6
5	RUS	KARAVAEVA, IRINA	36.2
6	GEO	GOLOVINA, LUBA	36.1
7	CAN	MACLENNAN, ROSANNAGH	35.5
8	GER	DOGONADZE, ANNA	18.9
14	USA	**BLANCHARD, ERIN**	27.1

HANDBALL RESULTS

MEN'S HANDBALL

1	FRA	28
2	ISL	23
3	ESP	35
4	CRO	29
5	POL	
5	RUS	
7	DEN	
8	KOR	
	USA	DNF

WOMEN'S HANDBALL

1	NOR	34
2	RUS	27
3	KOR	33
4	HUN	28
5	FRA	
6	CHN	
7	ROM	
8	SWE	
	USA	DNF

Valerie Gotay 11/5/73, Temecula CA, 57 kg
Sayaka Matsumoto 12/5/82, Richmond CA, 48 kg
Daniel McCormick 5/29/86, Arlington TX, 100+ kg
Brian Olson 3/6/73, Tallahassee FL, 90 kg

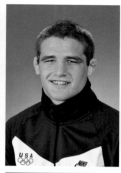

Ryan Reser 4/16/80, Dallas TX, 73 kg
Ronda Rousey 2/1/87, Santa Monica CA, 70 kg
Travis Stevens 2/28/86, Tacoma WA, 81 kg
Taylor Takata 4/6/82, Wahiawa HI, 66 kg

Adler Volmar 3/5/77, Miami FL, 100 kg
Taraje Williams-Murray 11/9/84, Bronx NY, 60 kg

STAFF

Leo White Team Leader (M)
Eddie Lidde Asst Coach

261

Jason Morris Coach (M)
Israel Hernandez Coach (W)

JUDO RESULTS

MEN'S 060KG

1	KOR	CHOI, MIN HO
2	AUT	PAISCHER, LUDWIG
3	NED	HOUKES, RUBEN
3	UZB	SOBIROV, RISHOD
5	ISR	YEKUTIEL, GAL
5	FRA	DRAGIN, DIMITRI
7	GBR	FALLON, CRAIG
7	CAN	WILL, FRAZER
	USA	**WILLIAMS-MURRAY, TARAJE** *ELM-MAIN ROUND 3*

MEN'S 066KG

1	JPN	UCHISHIBA, MASATO
2	FRA	DARBELET, BENJAMIN
3	CUB	ARENCIBIA, YORDANIS
3	PRK	PAK, CHOL MIN
5	RUS	GADANOV, ALIM
5	UZB	SHARIPOV, MIRALI
7	ITA	CASALE, GIOVANNI
7	EGY	ELHADY, AMIN
9	**USA**	**TAKATA, TAYLOR** *ELM REPECHAGE ROUND 3*

MEN'S 073KG

1	AZE	MAMMADLI, ELNUR
2	KOR	WANG, KI CHUN
3	BRA	GUILHEIRO, LEANDRO
3	TJK	BOQUIEV, RASUL
5	BEL	VANTICHELT, DIRK
5	IRI	MALOMAT, ALI
7	JPN	KANAMARU, YUSUKE
7	UKR	BILODID, GENNADIY
	USA	**RESER, RYAN** *ELM-MAIN ROUND 1*

MEN'S 081KG

1	GER	BISCHOF, OLE
2	KOR	KIM, JAE-BUM
3	BRA	CAMILO, TIAGO
3	UKR	GONTYUK, ROMAN
5	NED	ELMONT, GUILLAUME
5	MGL	DAMDINSUREN, NYAMKHUU
7	GBR	BURTON, EUAN
7	POL	KRAWCYK, ROBERT
9	**USA**	**STEVENS, TRAVIS** *ELM REPECHAGE ROUND 3*

MEN'S 090KG

1	GEO	TSIREKIDZE, IRAKLI
2	ALG	BENIKHLEF, AMAR
3	SUI	ASCHWANDER, SERGEI
3	EGY	MESBAH, HESHAM
5	FRA	DAFREVILLE, MATHIEU

5	RUS	PERSHIN, IVAN
7	BLR	KAZUSIONAK, ANDREI
7	BRA	SANTOS, EDUARDO
	USA	**OLSON, BRIAN** *ELM-MAIN ROUND 1*

MEN'S 100KG

1	MGL	NAIDAN, TUVSHINBAYAR
2	KAZ	ZHITKEYEV, ASKHAT
3	AZE	MIRALIYEV, MOVLUD
3	NED	GROL, HENK
5	POL	MATYASZEK, PRZEMYSLAW
5	GEO	ZHORZHOLIANI, LEVAN
7	KOR	JANG, SUNG-HO
7	HUN	HADFI, DANIEL
	USA	**VOLMAR, ADLER** *ELM-MAIN ROUND 1*

MEN'S 100KG+

1	JPN	ISHII, SATOSHI
2	UZB	TANGRIEV, ABDULLO
3	FRA	RINER, TEDDY
3	CUB	BRAYSON, OSCAR
5	GEO	GUJEJIANI, LASHA
5	IRI	RODAKI, MOHAMMAD
7	RUS	TMENOV, TAMERLAN
7	BRA	SCHLITTLER, JOAO GABRIEL
9	**USA**	**MCCORMICK, DANIEL** *ELM REPECHAGE ROUND 3*

WOMEN'S 048KG

1	ROM	DUMITRU, ALINA
2	CUB	BERMOY, YANET
3	JPN	TANI, RYOKO
3	ARG	PARETO, PAULA
5	RUS	BOGDANOVA, LIUDMILA
5	PRK	PAK, OK SONG
7	POR	HORMIGO, ANA
7	HUN	CSERNOVICZKI, EVA
	USA	**MATSUMOTO, SAYAKA** *ELM REPECHAGE ROUND 1*

WOMEN'S 052KG

1	CHN	XIAN, DONGMEI
2	PRK	AN, KUM AE
3	ALG	HADDAD, SORAYA
3	JPN	NAKAMURA, MISATO
5	KOR	KIM, KYUNG OK
5	KAZ	KALIYEVA, SHOLPAN
7	ESP	CARRASCOSA, ANA
7	BEL	HEYLEN, ILSE

WOMEN'S 057KG

1	ITA	QUINTAVALLE, GIULIA
2	NED	GRAVENSTIJN, DEBORAH

3	CHN	XU, YAN
3	BRA	QUADROS, KETLEYN
5	AUS	PEKLI, MARIA
5	FRA	HAREL, BARBARA
7	JPN	SATO, AIKO
7	HUN	BACZKO, BERNADETT
	USA	**GOTAY, VALERIE** *ELM-MAIN ROUND 2*

WOMEN'S 063KG

1	JPN	TANIMOTO, AYUMI
2	FRA	DECOSSE, LUCIE
3	NED	WILLEBOORDSE, ELISABETH
3	PRK	WON, OK IM
5	CUB	GONZALES, DRIULIS
5	AUT	HEILL, CLAUDIA
7	SLO	ZOLNIR, URSKA
7	VEN	BARRETO, ISIS

WOMEN'S 070KG

1	JPN	UENO, MASAE
2	CUB	HERNANDEZ, ANAISIS
3	**USA**	**ROUSEY, RONDA**
3	NED	BOSCH, EDITH
5	GER	BOEHM, ANNETT
5	ESP	IGLESIAS, LEIRE
7	HUN	MESZAROS, ANETT
7	COL	ALVEAR, YURI

WOMEN'S 078KG

1	CHN	YANG, XIULI
2	CUB	CASTILLO, YELENNIS
3	FRA	POSSAMAI, STEPHANIE
3	KOR	JEONG, GYEONG MI
5	BRA	SILVA, EDINANCI
5	ESP	SANMIGUEL, ESTHER
5	GER	WOLLERT, HEIDE
7	MGL	PUREVJARGAL, LKHANDEGD

WOMEN'S 078KG+

1	CHN	TONG, WEN
2	JPN	TSUKADA, MAKI
3	SLO	POLAVDER, LUCIJA
3	CUB	ORTIZ BOUCURT, IDALIS
5	KOR	KIM, NA YOUNG
5	MGL	DORJGOTOV, TSERENKHAND
7	FRA	MONDIERE, ANNE SOPHIE
7	EGY	RAMADAN, SAMAH

Eli Bremer 5/31/78, Monument CO, Pentathlon
Margaux Isaksen 10/7/91, Fayetteville AR, Pentathlon
Sam Sacksen 3/1/86, Somerset PA, Pentathlon
Sheila Taormina 3/18/69, Livonia MI, Pentathlon

STAFF

Scott Novack Team Leader
Janusz Peciak Head Coach
Michael Cintas Riding Coach

PENTATHLON RESULTS

MODERN PENTATHLON - MEN

			TOTAL POINTS	SHOOTING	FENCING	SWIMMING	RIDING	RUNNING
1	RUS	MOISEEV, ANDREI	5632	1168	1024	1332	1060	1048
2	LTU	KRUNGOLCAS, EDVINAS	5548	1156	904	1272	1144	1072
3	LTU	ZADNEPROVSKIS, ANDREJUS	5524	1120	760	1336	1168	1140
4	CHN	QIAN, ZHENZUA	5516	1204	1024	1272	1032	984
5	GER	GEBHARDT, STEFFEN	5480	1132	832	1280	1128	1108
6	CZE	MICHALIK, MICHAL	5460	1192	784	1260	1172	1052
7	UKR	TYMOSHCHENKO, PAVLO	5436	1156	908	1252	1048	1072
8	MEX	SOTO, OSCAR	5420	988	880	1236	1160	1156
18	USA	SACKSEN, SAM	5272	1072	736	1256	1104	1104
22	USA	BREMER, ELI	5172	916	736	1328	1060	1132

MODERN PENTATHLON - WOMEN

			TOTAL POINTS	SHOOTING	FENCING	SWIMMING	RIDING	RUNNING
1	GER	SCHONEBORN, LENA	5792	1060	1072	1280	1172	1208
2	GBR	FELL, HEATHER	5752	1156	880	1328	1144	1244
3	UKR	TERESHUK, VICTORIA	5672	1072	928	1316	1088	1268
4	BLR	SAMUSEVICH, ANASTASIA	5640	1180	856	1128	1172	1304
5	CHN	CHEN, QIAN	5612	1060	880	1260	1200	1212
6	POL	BOENISZ, PAULINA	5564	1132	904	1192	1096	1240
7	GBR	LIVINGSTON, KATIE	5548	1072	808	1292	1172	1204
8	EGY	MEDANY, AYA	5544	1144	928	1292	1004	1176
19	USA	TAORMINA, SHEILA	5304	1012	496	1376	1200	1220
21	USA	ISAKSEN, MARGAUX	5292	988	760	1240	1144	1160

Wyatt Allen 1/11/79, Portland ME, Men's Eight
Michael Altman 8/21/75, Marin County CA, Men's Lightweight Four
David Banks 8/30/83, Potomac MD, Men's Four
Micah Boyd 4/6/82, St. Paul MN, Men's Eight

Erin Cafaro 6/9/83, Modesto CA, Women's Eight
Steven Coppola 5/22/84, Buffalo NY, Men's Eight
Anna Cummins 3/21/80, Bellevue WA, Women's Pair/Women's Eight
Will Daly 8/2/83, Vail CO, Men's Lightweight Four

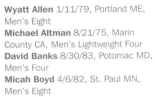

Caryn Davies 4/14/82, Ithaca NY, Women's Eight

Susan Francia 11/8/82, Abington PA, Women's Eight

Scott Gault 1/31/83, Piedmont CA, Men's Quad Sculls

Jennifer Goldsack 7/12/82, Princeton NJ, Lightweight Double Sculls

Anna Goodale 3/18/83, Camden ME, Women's Eight

Michelle Guerette 10/6/80, Bristol CT, Single Sculls

Beau Hoopman 10/1/80, Sheboygan WI, Men's Eight

Elliot Hovey 2/17/83, Manchester MA, Men's Double Sculls

Matthew Hughes 10/2/81, Ludington MI, Men's Quad Sculls

Renee Hykel 5/31/79, Haverford PA, Women's Lightweight Double Sculls

Joshua Inman 3/13/80, Hillsboro OR, Men's Eight

Kenneth Jurkowski 9/2/81, New Fairfield CT, Men's Single Sculls

Jennifer Kaido 3/14/81, West Leyden NY, Women's Quad

Megan Kalmoe 8/21/83, St. Croix Falls WI, Double Sculls

Giuseppe Lanzone 10/12/82, Annandale VA, Men's Four

Caroline Lind 10/11/82, Greensboro NC, Women's Eight

Eleanor Logan 12/27/87, Boothbay Harbor ME, Women's Eight

Marcus McElhenney 7/27/81, Philadelphia PA, Men's Eight

Portia McGee 3/9/79, Seattle WA, Women's Two

Lindsay Meyer 9/23/88, Seattle WA, Women's Quad

Brett Newlin 3/24/82, Riverton WY, Men's Four

Thomas Paradiso 12/7/79, Blue Bell PA, Men's Lightweight Four

Lia Pernell 8/16/81, Seattle WA, Women's Quad

Wes Piermarini 11/19/82, West Brookfield MA, Men's Double Sculls

263

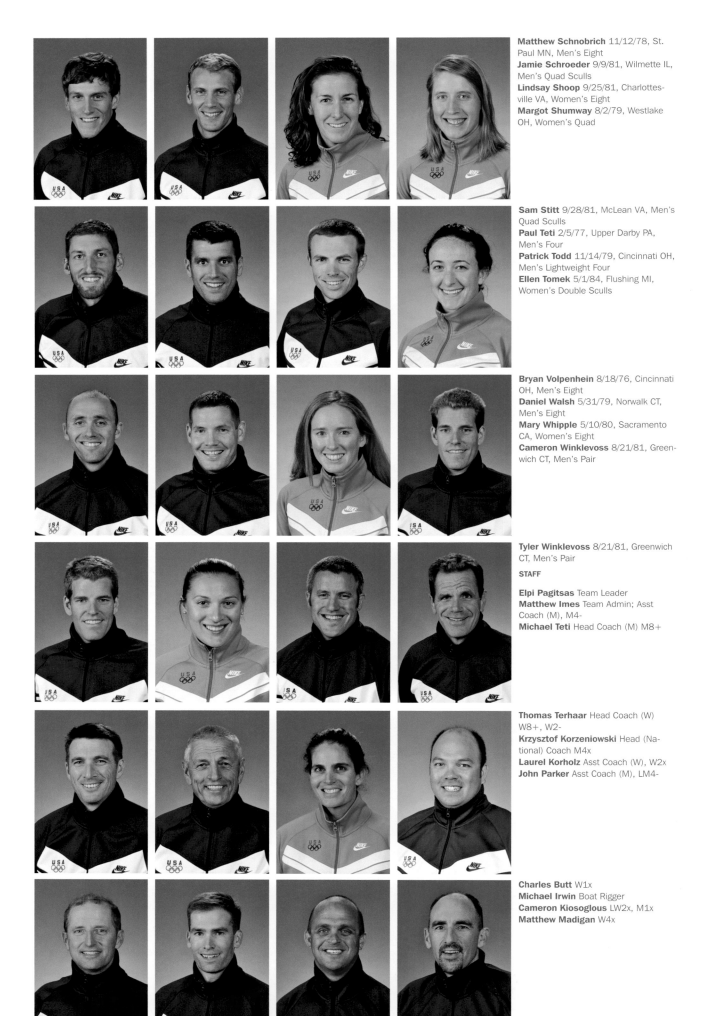

Matthew Schnobrich 11/12/78, St. Paul MN, Men's Eight
Jamie Schroeder 9/9/81, Wilmette IL, Men's Quad Sculls
Lindsay Shoop 9/25/81, Charlottesville VA, Women's Eight
Margot Shumway 8/2/79, Westlake OH, Women's Quad

Sam Stitt 9/28/81, McLean VA, Men's Quad Sculls
Paul Teti 2/5/77, Upper Darby PA, Men's Four
Patrick Todd 11/14/79, Cincinnati OH, Men's Lightweight Four
Ellen Tomek 5/1/84, Flushing MI, Women's Double Sculls

Bryan Volpenhein 8/18/76, Cincinnati OH, Men's Eight
Daniel Walsh 5/31/79, Norwalk CT, Men's Eight
Mary Whipple 5/10/80, Sacramento CA, Women's Eight
Cameron Winklevoss 8/21/81, Greenwich CT, Men's Pair

Tyler Winklevoss 8/21/81, Greenwich CT, Men's Pair

STAFF

Elpi Pagitsas Team Leader
Matthew Imes Team Admin; Asst Coach (M), M4-
Michael Teti Head Coach (M) M8+

Thomas Terhaar Head Coach (W) W8+, W2-
Krzysztof Korzeniowski Head (National) Coach M4x
Laurel Korholz Asst Coach (W), W2x
John Parker Asst Coach (M), LM4-

Charles Butt W1x
Michael Irwin Boat Rigger
Cameron Kiosoglous LW2x, M1x
Matthew Madigan W4x

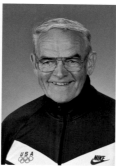

Timothy McLaren M2x
Theodore Nash M2-

ROWING RESULTS

DOUBLE SCULLS MEN'S

1	AUS		06:27.77
2	EST		06:29.05
3	GBR		06:29.10
4	NZL		06:30.79
5	FRA		06:33.36
6	SLO		06:33.96
7	BLR		06:34.39
8	BEL		06:35.55
12	USA	HOVEY, ELLIOT	06:33.15
		PIERMARINI, WES	

EIGHT WITH COXSWAIN MEN'S

1	CAN		05:23.89
2	GBR		05:25.11
3	USA	SCHNOBRICH, MATTHEW	05:25.34
	USA	VOLPENHEIN, BRYAN	
	USA	WALSH, DANIEL	
	USA	ALLEN, WYATT	
	USA	HOOPMAN, BEAU	
	USA	BOYD, MICAH	
	USA	MCELHENNEY, MARCUS	
	USA	INMAN, JOSH	
	USA	COPPOLA, STEVE	
4	NED		05:29.26
5	POL		05:31.42
6	AUS		05:35.10
7	CHN		05:34.59
8	GER		05:36.89

FOURS W/O COXSWAIN MEN'S

1	GBR		06:06.57
2	AUS		06:07.85
3	FRA		06:09.31
4	SLO		06:11.62
5	CZE		06:16.56
6	GER		06:19.63
7	NZL		06:06.30
8	NED		06:06.37
9	USA	BANKS, DAVID	06:07.17
	USA	TETI, PAUL	
	USA	LANZONE, GIUSEIPPE	
	USA	NEWLIN, BRETT	

LIGHTWEIGHT DOUBLE SCULLS MEN'S

1	GBR		06:10.99
2	GRE		06:11.72
3	DEN		06:12.45
4	ITA		06:16.15
5	CHN		06:16.69
6	CUB		06:19.96
7	NZL		06:27.14
8	POR		06:28.47

LIGHTWEIGHT FOUR W/O COXSWAIN MEN'S

1	DEN		05:47.76
2	POL		05:49.39
3	CAN		05:50.09
4	FRA		05:51.22
5	GBR		05:52.12

11	USA	DALY, WILL	06:07.79
	USA	ALTMAN, MIKE	
	USA	TODD, PATRICK	
	USA	PARADISO, TOM	

PAIRS W/O COXSWAIN MEN'S

1	AUS		06:37.44
2	CAN		06:39.55
3	NZL		06:44.19
4	GER		06:47.40
5	RSA		06:47.83
6	USA	WINKLEVOSS, TYLER	07:05.58
	USA	WINKLEVOSS, CAMERON	
7	SRB		06:49.12
8	CZE		06:52.57

QUADRUPLE SCULLS MEN'S

1	POL		05:41.33
2	ITA		05:43.57
3	FRA		05:44.34
4	AUS		05:44.68
5	USA	HUGHES, MATT	05:47.64
	USA	SCHROEDER, JAMIE	
	USA	GAULT, SCOTT	
	USA	STITT, SAM	
6	GER		05:50.96
7	RUS		05:46.17

SINGLE SCULLS MEN'S

1	NOR	TUFTE, OLAF	06:59.83
2	CZE	SYNEK, ONDREJ	07:00.63
3	NZL	DRYSDALE, MAHE	07:01.56
4	BEL	MAEYENS, TIM	07:03.40
5	GBR	CAMPBELL, ALAN	07:04.47
6	SWE	KARONEN, LASSI	07:07.64
7	GER	HACKER, MARCEL	07:07.82
8	LTU	GRISKONIS, MINDAUGAS	07:09.23
11	USA	JURKOWSKI, KEN	07:22.75

DOUBLE SCULLS WOMEN'S

1	NZL		07:07.32
2	GER		07:07.33
3	GBR		07:07.55
4	CHN		07:15.85
5	USA	TOMEK, ELLEN	07:17.53
	USA	KALMOE, MEGAN	
6	CZE		07:25.09
7	UKR		07:17.82
8	AUS		07:19.73

EIGHT WITH COXSWAIN WOMEN'S

1	USA	CAFARO, ERIN	06:05.34
	USA	DAVIES, CARYN	
	USA	WHIPPLE, MARY	
	USA	CUMMINS, ANNA	
	USA	LIND, CAROLINE	
	USA	LOGAN, ELLIE	
	USA	FRANCIA, SUSAN	
	USA	SHOOP, LINDSAY	
	USA	GOODALE, ANNA	
2	NED		06:07.22

3	ROM		06:07.25
4	CAN		06:08.04
5	GBR		06:13.74
6	AUS		06:14.22
7	GER		06:14.45

LIGHTWEIGHT DOUBLE SCULLS WOMEN'S

1	NED		06:54.74
2	FIN		06:56.03
3	CAN		06:56.68
4	GER		06:56.72
5	CHN		07:01.90
6	GRE		07:04.61
7	DEN		07:06.94
8	AUS		07:07.17
10	USA	GOLDSACK, JENNIFER	07:09.02
	USA	HYKEL, RENEE	

PAIRS W/O COXSWAIN WOMEN'S

1	ROM		07:20.60
2	CHN		07:22.28
3	BLR		07:22.91
4	GER		07:25.73
5	NZL		07:28.80
6	GBR		07:33.61
7	USA	CUMMINS, ANNA	07:33.17
	USA	MCGEE, PORTIA	
8	FRA		07:36.25

QUADRUPLE SCULLS WOMEN'S

1	CHN		06:16.06
2	GBR		06:17.37
3	GER		06:19.56
4	UKR		06:20.02
5	USA	MEYER, LINDSAY	06:25.86
	USA	PERNELL, LIA	
	USA	SHUMWAY, MARGOT	
	USA	KAIDO, JENNIFER	
6	AUS		06:30.05
7	RUS		06:28.10

SINGLE SCULLS WOMEN'S

1	BUL	NEYKOVA, RUMYANA	07:22.34
2	USA	GUERETTE, MICHELLE	07:22.78
3	BLR	KARSTEN, EKATERINA	07:23.98
4	CHN	ZHANG, XIUYUN	07:25.48
5	CZE	KNAPKOVA, MIROSLAVA	07:35.52
6	POL	MICHALSKA, JULIA	07:43.44
7	SWE	SVENSSON, FRIDA	07:48.19
8	ITA	BASCELLI, GABRIELLA	07:48.91

265

Benjamin Barger 12/24/83, St. Petersburg FL, RS:X
Sally Barkow 7/10/80, Chenequa WI, Yngling
Graham Biehl 8/31/86, San Diego CA, 470
Andrew Campbell 2/3/84, San Diego CA, Laser

SAILING

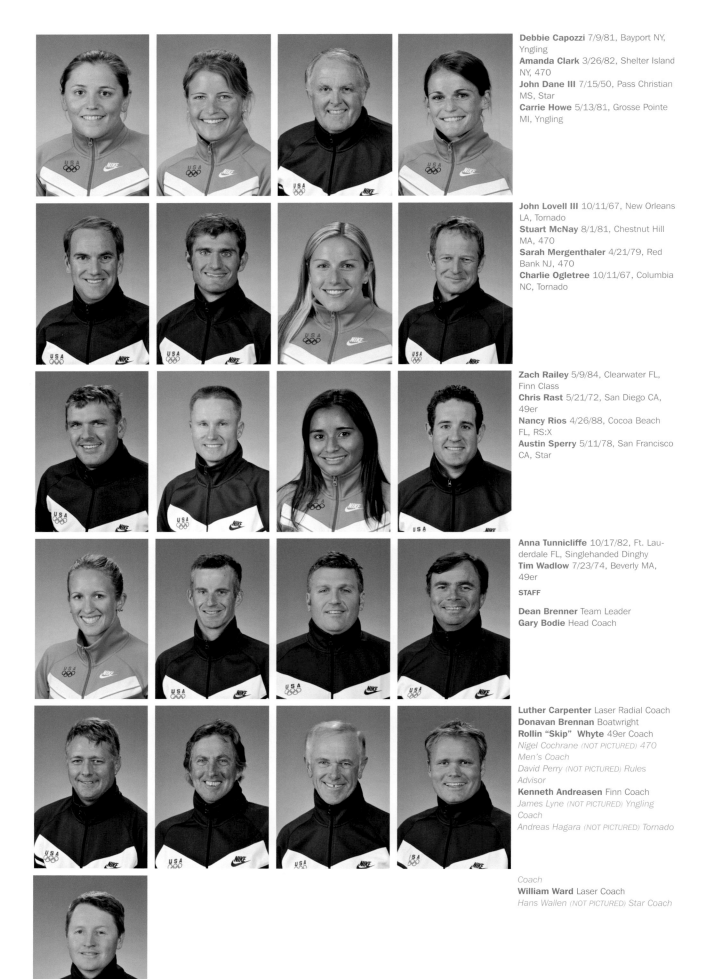

Debbie Capozzi 7/9/81, Bayport NY, Yngling
Amanda Clark 3/26/82, Shelter Island NY, 470
John Dane III 7/15/50, Pass Christian MS, Star
Carrie Howe 5/13/81, Grosse Pointe MI, Yngling

John Lovell III 10/11/67, New Orleans LA, Tornado
Stuart McNay 8/1/81, Chestnut Hill MA, 470
Sarah Mergenthaler 4/21/79, Red Bank NJ, 470
Charlie Ogletree 10/11/67, Columbia NC, Tornado

Zach Railey 5/9/84, Clearwater FL, Finn Class
Chris Rast 5/21/72, San Diego CA, 49er
Nancy Rios 4/26/88, Cocoa Beach FL, RS:X
Austin Sperry 5/11/78, San Francisco CA, Star

Anna Tunnicliffe 10/17/82, Ft. Lauderdale FL, Singlehanded Dinghy
Tim Wadlow 7/23/74, Beverly MA, 49er

STAFF

Dean Brenner Team Leader
Gary Bodie Head Coach

Luther Carpenter Laser Radial Coach
Donavan Brennan Boatwright
Rollin "Skip" Whyte 49er Coach
Nigel Cochrane (NOT PICTURED) 470 Men's Coach
David Perry (NOT PICTURED) Rules Advisor
Kenneth Andreasen Finn Coach
James Lyne (NOT PICTURED) Yngling Coach
Andreas Hagara (NOT PICTURED) Tornado Coach
William Ward Laser Coach
Hans Wallen (NOT PICTURED) Star Coach

SAILING RESULTS

470 (DOUBLE-HANDED DINGHY) MEN'S

1	AUS		44
2	GBR		75
3	FRA		78
4	NED		78
5	ESP		87
6	ITA		91
7	JPN		97
8	POR		102
13	USA	BIEHL, GRAHAM	105
	USA	MCNAY, STUART	105

FINN (SINGLE-HANDED DINGHY) MEN'S

1	GBR	AINSLIE, BEN	23
2	USA	RAILEY, ZACH	45
3	FRA	FLORENT, GUILLAUME	58
4	SWE	BIRGMARK, DANIEL	58
5	CAN	COOK, CHRIS	67
6	DEN	HOEGH-CHRISTENSEN, JONAS	70
7	SLO	VINCEC, GASPER	72
8	CRO	KLJAKOVIC GASPIC, IVAN	76

NEIL PRYDE RS:X MEN'S

1	NZL	ASHLEY, TOM	52
2	FRA	BONTEMPS, JULIEN	53
3	ISR	ZUBARI, SHAHAR	58
4	GBR	DEMPSEY, NICK	60
5	BRA	SANTOS, RICARDO	77
6	HKG	CHAN, KING-YIN	84
7	CHN	WANG, AICHEN	95
8	GRE	KAKLAMANAKIS, NIKOLAS	97
26	USA	BARGER, BEN	217

STAR(TWO-PERSON KEELBOAT OPEN) MEN'S

1	GBR		45
2	BRA		53
3	SWE		53
4	POL		59
5	SUI		59
6	FRA		69
7	GER		70
8	POR		72

11	USA	SPERRY, AUSTIN	86
	USA	DANE, JOHN	86

49ER (HIGH PERF DINGHY OPEN) MIXED

1	DEN		61
2	ESP		64
3	GER		66
4	ITA		66
5	AUS		73
6	USA	WADLOW, TIM	89
	USA	RAST, CHRIS	89
7	BRA		99
8	AUT		99

LASER MIXED

1	GBR	GOODISON, PAUL	63
2	SLO	ZBOGAR, VASILIJ	71
3	ITA	ROMERO, DIEGO	75
4	POR	LIMA, GUSTAVO	76
5	NZL	MURDOCH, ANDREW	81
6	SWE	MYRGREN, RASMUS	83
7	ARG	ALSOGARAY, JULIO	92
8	FRA	BAPTISTE BERNAZ, JEAN	104
25	USA	CAMPBELL, ANDREW	174

TORNADO (MULTIHULL OPEN) MIXED

1	ESP		44
2	AUS		49
3	ARG		56
4	CAN		61
5	NED		64
6	GBR		68
7	ITA		74
8	GER		74
15	USA	LOVELL, JOHN	114
	USA	OGLETREE, CHARLIE	114

470 (DOUBLE-HANDED DINGHY) WOMEN'S

1	AUS		43
2	NED		53
3	BRA		60
4	ISR		66
5	ITA		75

6	GBR		82
7	CZE		83
8	AUT		84
12	USA	CLARK, AMANDA	89
	USA	MERGENTHALER, SARAH	89

LASER RADIAL WOMEN'S

1	USA	TUNNICLIFFE, ANNA	37
2	LTU	VOLUNGEVICIUTE, GINTARE	42
3	CHN	XU, LIJIA	50
4	AUS	BLANCK, SARAH	62
5	FRA	STEAYERT, SARAH	77
6	SUI	BRUGGER, NATHALIE	90
7	NZL	ALEH, JO	90
8	BEL	VAN ACKER, EVI	91

NEIL PRYDE RS:X WOMEN'S

1	CHN	YIN, JIAN	39
2	ITA	SENSINI, ALESSANDRA	40
3	GBR	SHAW, BRYONY	45
4	ESP	ALABAU NEIRA, MARINA	54
5	AUS	CRISP, JESSICA	66
6	NZL	KENDALL, BARBARA	75
7	POL	KLEPACKA, ZOFIA	82
8	UKR	MASLIVETS, OLGA	83
26	USA	RIOS, NANCY	224

YNGLING WOMEN'S

1	GBR		24
2	NED		31
3	GRE		48
4	GER		56
5	FRA		56
6	RUS		56
7	USA	HOWE, CARRIE	61
	USA	BARKOW, SALLY	
	USA	CAPOZZI, DEBBIE	
8	CHN	CHINA	63

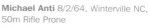

Michael Anti 8/2/64, Winterville NC, 50m Rifle Prone
Brian Beaman 5/16/84, Selby SD, 10m Air Pistol
Jamie Beyerle 5/26/84, Lebanon PA, 50m 3-position Rifle
Libby Callahan 2/25/52, Columbia SC, Sport Pistol

Emily Caruso 6/4/77, Fairfield CT, 10m Air Rifle
Corey Cogdell 9/2/86, Eagle River AK, Trap
Glenn Eller 1/6/82, Katy TX, Double Trap
Matt Emmons 4/5/81, Browns Mills NJ, 50m Rifle 3 positions, 50m Rifle Prone

Bret Erickson 9/26/60, Bennington NE, Trap
Sandra Fong 4/15/90, New York NY, 50m 3-position Rifle
Dominic Grazioli 2/4/64, San Antonio TX, Trap
Vincent Hancock 3/19/89, Eatonton GA, Skeet

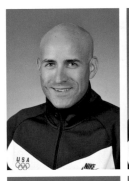   

Jeffrey Holguin 10/24/78, Yorba Linda CA, Double Trap
Sean McLelland 9/17/85, Mission TX, Skeet
Jason Parker 6/27/74, Omaha NE, 10m Air Rifle
Kimberly Rhode 7/16/79, El Monte CA, Skeet

Keith Sanderson 2/2/75, San Antonio TX, Rapid Fire Pistol
Stephen Scherer 2/22/89, Billerica MA, 10m Air Rifle
Brenda Shinn 1/1/62, Riverside CA, 10m Air Pistol
Beki Snyder 7/15/76, Colorado Springs CO, 10m Air Pistol

Daryl Szarenski 3/14/68, Saginaw MI, Free Pistol
Jason Turner 1/31/75, Rochester NY, 10m Air Pistol

STAFF

Duane Weger Team Leader
Sergey Luzov Pistol Coach

 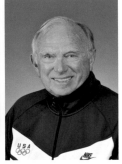

David A. Johnson Rifle Coach
Lloyd Woodhouse *Shotgun Coach*
Nick Potter (NOT PICTURED) Physiotherapist

268

SHOOTING RESULTS

AIR PISTOL MEN'S
1	CHN PANG, WEI	688.2
2	KOR JIN, JONG OH	684.5
3	**USA TURNER, JASON**	682
4	**USA BEAMAN, BRIAN**	682
5	RUS EKIMOV, LEONID	680.5
6	FRA LAPEYRE, WALTER	680.3
7	THA PANICHPATIKUM, JAKKRIT	679

PISTOL, INDIVIDUAL, 50 METERS MEN'S
1	KOR JIN, JONG OH	660.4
2	CHN TAN, ZONGLIANG	659.5
3	RUS ISAKOV, VLADIMIR	658.9
4	UKR OMELCHUK, OLEG	658.9
5	SVK KOPP, PAVEL	657.6
6	BUL KIRIAKOV, TANIOU	656.8
7	SRB MIKEC, DAMIR	655.8
13	**USA SZARENSKI, DARYL LEE**	
20	**USA TURNER, JASON**	

RAPID FIRE PISTOL MEN'S
1	UKR PETRIV, OLEKSANDR	780.2
2	GER SCHUMANN, RALF	779.5
3	GER REITZ, CHRISTIAN	779.3
4	RUS EKIMOV, LEONID	778.2
5	**USA SANDERSON, KEITH**	776.6
6	UKR BONDARUK, ROMAN	774.7

AIR RIFLE MEN'S
1	IND BINDRA, ABHINAV	700.5
2	CHN ZHU, QINAN	699.7
3	FIN HAKKINEN, HENRI	699.4
4	ROM MOLDOVEANU, ALIN	698.9
5	RUS PRIKHODTCHENKO, KONSTANTIN	698.4
6	HUN SIDI, PETER	698.4
7	SRB PLETIKOSIC, STEVAN	697.7
8	RUS KRUGLOV, SERGUEI	697
23	**USA PARKER, JASON ALAN**	
27	**USA SCHERER, STEPHEN**	

50 METER RIFLE - PRONE MEN'S
1	UKR AYVAZIYAN, ARTUR	702.7
2	**USA EMMONS, MATTHEW**	701.7
3	AUS POTENT, WARREN	700.5
4	NOR BERG, VEBJOERN	699.1
5	RUS PRIKHODTCHENKO, KONSTANTIN	699
6	FRA SAUVEPLANE, VALERIAN	698.8
7	FIN HIRVI, JUHA	698.5
8	BLR MARTYNOV, SERGEI	698.3
9	**USA ANTI, MICHAEL E**	

50 METER RIFLE - 3 POSITIONS MEN'S
1	CHN QIU, JIAN	1272.5
2	UKR SUKHORUKOV, JURY	1272.4
3	SLO DEBEVEC, RAJMOND	1271.7
4	**USA EMMONS, MATTHEW**	1270.3
5	AUT FARNIK, THOMAS	1268.9
6	AUT KNOEGLER, MARIO	1268.4
7	FRA SAUVEPLANE, VALERIAN	1267.1
8	NOR BERG, VEBJOERN	1266.5
22	**USA PARKER, JASON ALAN**	

DOUBLE TRAP MEN'S
1	**USA ELLER, WALTON GLENN**	190
2	ITA DANIELLO, FRANCESCO	187
3	CHN HU, BINYUAN	184
4	**USA HOLGUIN, JEFFREY**	182
5	AUS MARK, RUSSELL	181
6	GBR FAULDS, RICHARD	180

SKEET MEN'S
1	**USA HANCOCK, VINCENT**	145
2	NOR BROVOLD, TORRE	145
3	FRA TERRAS, ANTHONY	144
4	CYP NIKOLAIDIS, ANTONIS	144
5	CYP ACHILLEOS, GEORGE	143
6	CHN QU, RIDONG	142
11	**USA MCLELLAND, RANDALL**	

TRAP (CLAY PIGEON) MEN'S
1	CZE KOSTELECKY, DAVID	146
2	ITA PELLIELO, GIOVANNI	143
3	RUS ALIPOV, ALEXEI	142
4	AUS DIAMOND, MICHAEL	142
5	CRO GLASNOVIC, ANTON	140
6	ITA FRASCA, ERMINIO	140
22	**USA ERICKSON, BRET**	
23	**USA GRAZIOLI, DOMINIC**	

AIR PISTOL WOMEN'S
1	CHN GUO, WENJUN	492.3
2	RUS PADERINA, NATALIA	489.1
3	GEO SALUKVADZE, NINO	487.4
4	BLR CHAIKA, VICKTORIA	482
5	POL SAGUN, MIROSLAWA	481.3
6	SRB SEKARIC, JASNA	480.9
7	FIN NEVANSUU, MIRA	480.5

2	RUS	GALKINA, LIOUBOV		502.1	8	MGL	TSOGBADRAH, MUNKZUL	479.6	8	CHN	WU, LIUXI	685.9
3	CRO	PEJCIC, SNJEZANA		500.9	37	USA	**SHINN, BRENDA**		21	USA	**FONG, SANDRA**	

50 METER RIFLE - 3 POSITIONS WOMEN'S (left); **PISTOL, 25M WOMEN'S** (center); **SKEET WOMEN'S** (right)

4	**USA**	**BEYERLE, JAMIE**	499.8	41	USA	**SNYDER, BEKI (REBECCA)**		
5	CHN	DU, LI	499.6			**PISTOL, 25M WOMEN'S**		
6	KAZ	DOVGUN, OLGA	498.1	1	CHN	CHEN, YING	793.4	
7	FRA	GIGON, MARIE LAURE	497.3	2	MGL	OTRYAD, GUNDEGMAA	792.2	
8	POL	BOGACKA, SYLWIA	495.7	3	GER	DORJSUREN, MUNKHBAYAR	789.2	
15	**USA**	**CARUSO, EMILY**		4	CHN	FEI, FENGJI	787.9	

50 METER RIFLE - 3 POSITIONS WOMEN'S

1	CHN	DU, LI	690.3	5	BUL	GROZDEVA, MARIA	786.6	
2	CZE	EMMONS, KATERINA	687.7	6	PRK	JO, YONG SUK	783.4	
3	CUB	CRUZ, EGLIS YAIMA	687.6	7	THA	PRUCKSAKORN, TANYAPORN	777.7	
4	RUS	GALKINA, LIOUBOV	687.4	8	ESA	MAIDA, LUISA	774	
5	**USA**	**BEYERLE, JAMIE**	686.9	25	USA	**CALLAHAN, ELIZABETH**		
6	KAZ	DOVGUN, OLGA	686.3	28	USA	**SNYDER, BEKI (REBECCA)**		
7	SRB	MIHAJLOVIC, LIDIJA	686			**AIR RIFLE WOMEN'S**		
				1	CZE	EMMONS, KATERINA	503.5	

SKEET WOMEN'S

1	ITA	CAINERO, CHIARA	93
2	**USA**	**RHODE, KIMBERLY SUSAN**	93
3	GER	BRINKER, CHRISTINE	93
4	SWE	LARSSON. NATHALIE	92
5	THA	JIEWCHALOEMMIT, SUTIYA	92
6	CHN	WEI, NING	91

TRAP (CLAY PIGEON) WOMEN'S

1	FIN	MAKELA-NUMMELA, SATU	91
2	SVK	STEFECEKOVA, ZUZANA	89
3	**USA**	**COGDELL, COREY**	86
4	JPN	NAKAYAMA, YUKIE	86
5	LTU	GUDZINEVICIUTE, DAINA	86
6	KAZ	STRUCHAEVA, ELENA	86

Freddy Adu 6/2/89, Potomac MD, Forward/midfielder

Jozy Altidore 11/6/89, Boca Raton FL, Forward

Nicole Barnhart 10/10/81, Gilbertsville PA, Goalkeeper

Shannon Boxx 6/29/77, Redondo Beach CA, Midfielder

Michael Bradley 7/31/87, Manhattan Beach CA, Midfielder

Rachel Buelhler 8/26/85, Del Mar CA, Defender

Lori Chalupny 1/29/84, St. Louis MO, Defender

Lauren Cheney 9/30/87, Indianapolis IN, Forward

Stephanie Cox 4/3/86, Elk Grove CA, Defender

Charlie Davies 6/25/86, Manchester NH, Forward

Maurice Edu 4/18/86, Fontana CA, Defensive Midfielder

Benny Feilhaber 1/19/85, Irvine CA, Midfielder

Brad Guzan 9/9/84, Homer Glen IL, Goalkeeper

Tobin Heath 5/29/88, Basking Ridge NJ, Midfielder

Stuart Holden 8/1/85, Houston TX, Midfielder

Angela Hucles 7/5/78, Virginia Beach VA, Midfielder

Patrick Ianni 6/15/85, Lodi CA, Defender

Natasha Kai 5/22/83, Kahuku HI, Forward

Sacha Kljestan 9/9/85, Huntington Beach CA, Midfielder

Carli Lloyd 7/16/82, Delran NJ, Midfielder

Kate Markgraf 8/23/76, Bloomfield Hills MI, Defender
Brian McBride 6/19/72, Arlington Heights IL, Forward
Michael McCarty 4/30/87, Maitland FL, NA
Heather Mitts 6/9/78, Cincinnati OH, Defender

Heather O'Reilly 1/2/85, East Brunswick NJ, Midfielder
Michael Orozco 2/7/86, Orange CA, Defender
Michael Parkhurst 1/24/84, Providence RI, Defender
Christine Rampone 6/24/75, Point Pleasant NJ, Defender

Amy Rodriguez 2/17/87, Lake Forest CA, Forward
Robbie Rogers 5/12/87, Huntington Beach CA, Midfielder/Forward
Chris Seitz 3/12/87, San Luis Obispo CA, Goalkeeper
Hope Solo 7/30/81, Richland WA, Goalkeeper

Danny Szetela 6/17/87, Clifton NJ, Midfielder
Lindsay Tarpley 9/22/83, KALmazoo MI, Midfielder
Aly Wagner 8/10/80, San Jose CA, Midfielder
Marvell Wynne II 5/8/86, Poway CA, Defender

STAFF

Alfonso Cerda III Team Leader (M)
Piotr Nowak Head Coach (M)
Lubos Kubik Ass Coach (M)
Timothy Mulqueen Asst Coach (M)

Randall Rocha Asst Coach (M)
Gabriel Vogler (NOT PICTURED) Equipment Manager (M)
Cheryl Bailey Team Leader (W)
Pia Sundhage Head Coach (W)
Philip Wheddon Asst Coach (W)

270

Helena Andersson Massage Therapist (W)
Erica Walsh Asst Coach (W)
Jillian Ellis Asst Coach (W)
Michele Gould (NOT PICTURED)ATC (W)
Andrew Dessert Equipment Manager (W)

SOCCER RESULTS

SOCCER - MEN

1	ARG	1	*GOLD GAME SCORE*
2	NGR	0	
3	BRA	3	*BRONZE GAME SCORE*
4	BEL	0	
5	ITA		
6	CIV		
7	NED		
8	CMR		
9	**USA**		

SOCCER - WOMEN

1	**USA**	1	*GOLD GAME SCORE*
2	BRA	0	
3	GER	2	*BRONZE GAME SCORE*
4	JPN	0	
5	CHN		
6	SWE		
7	NOR		
8	CAN		

MEN GAME SCORES

USA	vs	JPN	1-0
		NED	2-2
		NGR	1-2

WOMEN GAME SCORES

USA	vs	NOR	2-0
		JPN	1-0
		NZL	4-0
		CA	2-1
		JPN	4-2
		BRA	1-0

SOFTBALL

Monica Abbott 7/28/85, Salinas CA, Left-handed Picher
Laura Berg 1/6/75, Santa Fe Springs CA, Outfield
Crystl Bustos 9/8/77, Canyon Country CA, Designated Player
Andrea Duran 4/12/84, Selma CA, Third Base

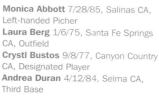

Jennie Finch 9/3/80, La Mirada CA, Right-handed Pitcher
Tairia Flowers 1/9/81, Tucson AZ, First Base
Vicky Galindo 12/22/83, Union City CA, Utility
Lovieanne Jung 1/11/80, Orange County CA, Second Base

Kelly Kretschman 8/26/79, Indian Harbor Beach FL, Outfield
Lauren Lappin 6/26/84, Anaheim CA, Utility
Caitlin Lowe 2/6/85, Tustin CA, Outfield
Jessica Mendoza 11/11/80, Camarillo CA, Outfield

   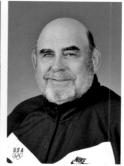

Stacey Nuveman 4/26/78, La Verne CA, Catcher
Cat Osterman 4/16/33, Houston TX, Left-handed Pitcher
Natasha Watley 11/27/81, Irvine CA, Shortstop

STAFF

Ronnie Isham Team Leader

Michael Candrea Head Coach
John Rittman Richard Asst Coach
Karen Johns Asst Coach Pitching
Charles D'Arcy Asst Coach

Brandon Michael Marcello Strength &
Conditioning Coach

272

SOCCER RESULTS

WOMEN'S SOFTBALL

1	JPN	3	*GOLD GAME*
2	**USA**	1	
3	AUS	5	*BRONZE GAME*
4	CAN	3	
5	TPE		
6	CHN		
7	VEN		
8	NED		

SOFTBALL GAME SCORES

USA	vs	VEN	11-0
		AUS	3-0
		JPN	7-0
		CAN	8-1
		TPE	7-0
		NED	8-0
		CHN	9-0
		JPN	4-1
		JPN	1-3

SWIMMING

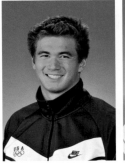

Nathan Adrian 12/7/88, Bremerton
WA, 4x100m Free Relay
Amanda Beard 10/29/81, Irvine CA,
200m Breast
Elizabeth Beisel 8/18/92, Saunder-
stown RI, 200m Back, 400m IM
Ricky Berens 4/21/88, Charlotte NC,
4x200m Free Relay

Elaine Breeden 11/18/88, Lexington
KY, 100m Fly, 200m Fly
Caroline Burckle 6/24/86, Louisville
KY, 4x200m Free Relay
Natalie Coughlin 3/23/82, Lafayette
CA, Back, 100m Free, 200m IM,
4x100m Free Relay
Ian Crocker 8/31/82, Portland ME,
100m Fly

Mark Gangloff 6/8/82, Stow OH,
100m Breast
Matt Grevers 3/26/85, Lake Forest IL,
100m Back, 4x100m Free Relay
Brendan Hansen 8/15/81, Havertown
PA, 100m Breast
Kathleen Hersey 2/21/90, Atlanta GA,
200m Fly

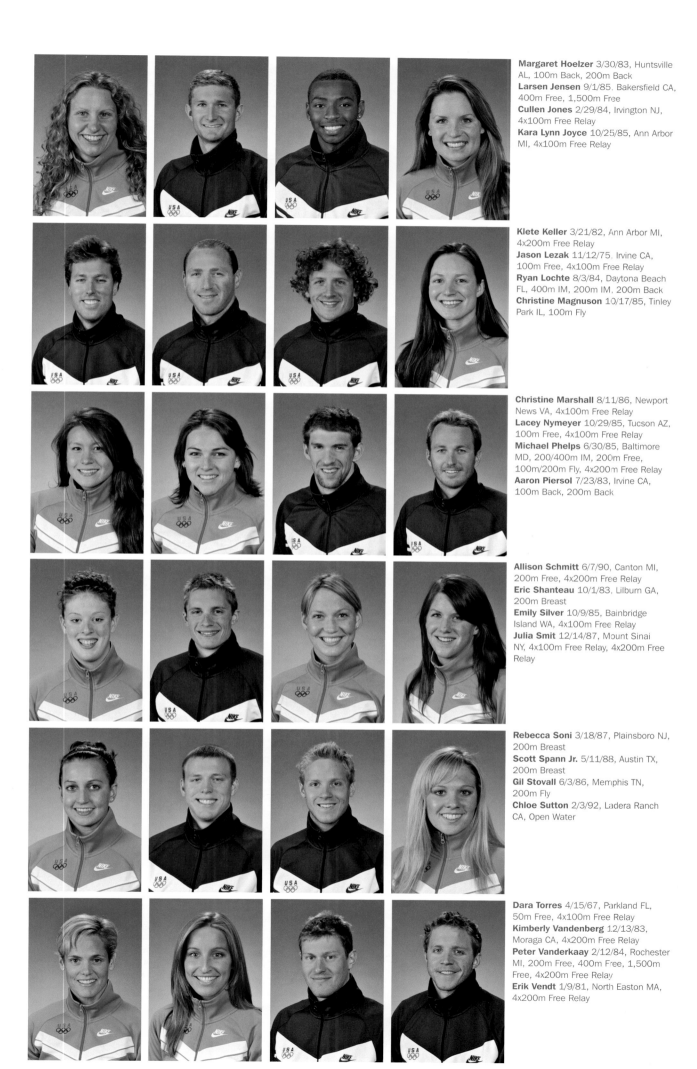

Margaret Hoelzer 3/30/83, Huntsville AL, 100m Back, 200m Back
Larsen Jensen 9/1/85. Bakersfield CA, 400m Free, 1,500m Free
Cullen Jones 2/29/84, Irvington NJ, 4x100m Free Relay
Kara Lynn Joyce 10/25/85, Ann Arbor MI, 4x100m Free Relay

Klete Keller 3/21/82, Ann Arbor MI, 4x200m Free Relay
Jason Lezak 11/12/75. Irvine CA, 100m Free, 4x100m Free Relay
Ryan Lochte 8/3/84, Daytona Beach FL, 400m IM, 200m IM, 200m Back
Christine Magnuson 10/17/85, Tinley Park IL, 100m Fly

Christine Marshall 8/11/86, Newport News VA, 4x100m Free Relay
Lacey Nymeyer 10/29/85, Tucson AZ, 100m Free, 4x100m Free Relay
Michael Phelps 6/30/85, Baltimore MD, 200/400m IM, 200m Free, 100m/200m Fly, 4x200m Free Relay
Aaron Piersol 7/23/83, Irvine CA, 100m Back, 200m Back

Allison Schmitt 6/7/90, Canton MI, 200m Free, 4x200m Free Relay
Eric Shanteau 10/1/83. Lilburn GA, 200m Breast
Emily Silver 10/9/85, Bainbridge Island WA, 4x100m Free Relay
Julia Smit 12/14/87, Mount Sinai NY, 4x100m Free Relay, 4x200m Free Relay

Rebecca Soni 3/18/87, Plainsboro NJ, 200m Breast
Scott Spann Jr. 5/11/88, Austin TX, 200m Breast
Gil Stovall 6/3/86, Memphis TN, 200m Fly
Chloe Sutton 2/3/92, Ladera Ranch CA, Open Water

Dara Torres 4/15/67, Parkland FL, 50m Free, 4x100m Free Relay
Kimberly Vandenberg 12/13/83, Moraga CA, 4x200m Free Relay
Peter Vanderkaay 2/12/84, Rochester MI, 200m Free, 400m Free, 1,500m Free, 4x200m Free Relay
Erik Vendt 1/9/81, North Easton MA, 4x200m Free Relay

David Walters 9/27/87, Yorktown VA, 4x200m Free Relay
Mark Warkentin 11/14/79, Santa Barbara CA, Open Water
Ben Wildman-Tobriner 9/21/84, San Francisco CA, 50m Free, 4x100m Free Relay
Katie Ziegler 6/27/88, Great Falls VA, 400m Free, 800m Free

Katie Hoff 6/3/89, Towson MD, 200m/400m IM, 200m/400m/800m Free, 4x200m Free Relay
Megan Jendrick 1/15/84, Tacoma WA, 100m Breast
Garrett Weber-Gale 8/6/85, Milwaukee WI, 50m Free, 100m Free, 4x100m Free Relay

STAFF

Lindsay Mintenko Head Team Leader

   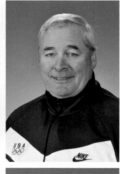

Joke Schubert Asst. Team Leader
Ted Knapp Men's Team Leader
Edward Sinnott Women's Team Leader
Mark Schubert Nat'l Team Head Coach

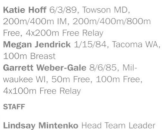   

Jack Bauerle Head Coach (W)
Eddie Reese Head Coach (M)
William Rose (NOT PICTURED) Head Coach (OW)
Gregg Troy Asst Coach (M)
Robert Bowman Asst Coach (M)

Theresa McKeever Asst Coach (W)
Paul Yetter Asst Coach (W)
Frank Busch Asst Coach (M)
Sean Hutchison (NOT PICTURED) Asst Coach (W)
Jon Urbanchek NT Special Assist Pool
Paul Asmuth (NOT PICTURED) NT Special Assist OW

John Dussiliere (NOT PICTURED) Assist Coach (OW)
Brian Campbell (NOT PICTURED) Massage Therapist
Wade Alberts Massage Therapist

SWIMMING RESULTS

50 METER FREESTYLE MEN'S

1	BRA	CIELO, CESAR	21.30
2	FRA	LEVEAUX, AMAURY	21.45
3	FRA	BERNARD, ALAIN	21.49
4	AUS	CALLUS, ASHLEY	21.62
5	USA	WILDMAN-TOBRINER, BEN	21.64
6	AUS	SULLIVAN, EAMON	21.65
7	RSA	SCHOEMAN, ROLAND	21.67
8	SWE	NYSTRAND, STEFAN	21.72
	USA	WEBER-GALE, GARRETT	22.08 ELMS

100 METER BACKSTROKE MEN'S

1	USA	PEIRSOL, AARON	52.54
2	USA	GREVERS, MATT	53.11
3	RUS	VYATCHANIN, ARKADY	53.18
3	AUS	STOECKEL, HAYDEN	53.18
5	AUS	DELANEY, ASHLEY	53.31
6	GBR	TANCOCK, LIAM	53.39
7	ESP	WILDEBOER, ASCHWIN	53.51
8	JPN	MIYASHITA, JUNICHI	53.99

100 METER BREASTSTROKE MEN'S

1	JPN	KITAJIMA, KOSUKE	58.91
2	NOR	OEN, ALEXANDER DALE	59.20
3	FRA	DUBOSCQ, HUGUES	59.37
4	USA	HANSEN, BRENDAN	59.57
5	AUS	RICKARD, BRENTON	59.74
6	RUS	SLUDNOV, ROMAN	59.87
7	UKR	BORYSIK, IGOR	01:00.20
8	USA	GANGLOFF, MARK	01:00.24

100 METER BUTTERFLY MEN'S

1	USA	PHELPS, MICHAEL	50.58
2	SRB	CAVIC, MILORAD	50.59
3	AUS	LAUTERSTEIN, ANDREW	51.12
4	USA	CROCKER, IAN	51.13
5	KEN	DUNFORD, JASON	51.47
6	JPN	FUJII, TAKURO	51.50
7	UKR	SERDINOV, ANDRIY	51.59
8	PNG	PINI, RYAN	51.86

100 METER FREESTYLE MEN'S

1	FRA	BERNARD, ALAIN	47.21
2	AUS	SULLIVAN, EAMON	47.32
3	USA	LEZAK, JASON	47.67
3	BRA	CIELO, CESAR	47.67
5	NED	VAN DEN HOOGENBAND, PIETER	47.75
6	RSA	FERNS, LYNDON	48.04
7	AUS	TARGETT, MATT	48.20
8	SWE	NYSTRAND, STEFAN	48.33
	USA	WEBER-GALE, GARRETT	48.12 ELMS

10K OPEN WATER MEN'S

1	NED	VAN DER WEIJDEN, MAARTEN	01:51:51.6
2	GBR	DAVIES, DAVID	01:51:53.1
3	GER	LURZ, THOMAS	01:51:53.6
4	ITA	CLERI, VALERIO	01:52:07.5
5	RUS	DRATSEV, EVGENY	01:52:08.9
6	BUL	STOYCHEV, PETAR	01:52:09.1
7	BEL	RYCKEMAN, BRIAN	01:52:10.7
8	USA	WARKENTIN, MARK	01:52:13.0

1500 METER FREESTYLE MEN'S

1	TUN	MELLOULI, OUSSAMA	14:40.84
2	AUS	HACKETT, GRANT	14:41.53
3	CAN	COCHRANE, RYAN	14:42.69
4	RUS	PRILUKOV, YURI	14:43.21
5	USA	JENSEN, LARSEN A	14:48.16
6	GBR	DAVIES, DAVID	14:52.11
7	CHN	ZHANG, LIN	14:55.20
8	CHN	SUN, YANG	15:05.12
	USA	VANDERKAAY, PETER	14:52.11 ELMH

200 METER BACKSTROKE MEN'S

1	USA	LOCHTE, RYAN	01:53.94
2	USA	PEIRSOL, AARON	01:54.33
3	RUS	VYATCHANIN, ARKADY	01:54.93
4	AUT	ROGAN, MARKUS	01:55.49
5	JPN	IRIE, RYOSUKE	01:55.72
6	AUS	STOECKEL, HAYDEN	01:56.39
7	ROM	FLOREA, RAZVAN	01:56.52
8	GBR	TAIT, GREGOR	01:57.00

200 METER BREASTSTROKE MEN'S

1	JPN	KITAJIMA, KOSUKE	02:07.64
2	AUS	RICKARD, BRENTON	02:08.88
3	FRA	DUBOSCQ, HUGUES	02:08.94
4	CAN	BROWN, MICHAEL	02:09.03
5	HUN	GYURTA, DANIEL	02:09.22
6	USA	SPANN, SCOTT	02:09.76
7	ITA	FACCI, LORIS	02:10.57
8	ITA	BOSSINI, PAOLO	02:11.48
	USA	SHANTEAU, ERIC	02:10.10 ELMS

200 METER BUTTERFLY MEN'S

1	USA	PHELPS, MICHAEL	01:52.03
2	HUN	CSEH, LASZLO	01:52.70
3	JPN	MATSUDA, TAKESHI	01:52.97
4	CHN	WU, PENG	01:54.35
4	NZL	BURMESTER, MOSS	01:54.35
6	POL	KORZENIOWSKI, PAWEL	01:54.60
7	BRA	ALMEIDA, KAIO	01:54.71
8	RUS	SKVORTSOV, NIKOLAY	01:55.14
	USA	STOVALL, GIL	01:55.36 ELMS

200 METER FREESTYLE MEN'S

1	USA	PHELPS, MICHAEL	01:42.96
2	KOR	PARK, TAE HWAN	01:44.85
3	USA	VANDERKAAY, PETER	01:45.14
4	RSA	BASSON, JEAN	01:45.97
5	GER	BIEDERMANN, PAUL	01:46.00
6	SUI	MEICHTRY, DOMINIK	01:46.95
7	JPN	OKUMURA, YOSHIHIRO	01:47.14
8	GBR	RENWICK, ROBBI	01:47.47

200 METER INDIVIDUAL MEDLEY MEN'S

1	USA	PHELPS, MICHAEL	01:54.23
2	HUN	CSEH, LASZLO	01:56.52
3	USA	LOCHTE, RYAN	01:56.53
4	BRA	PEREIRA, THIAGO	01:58.14
5	JPN	TAKAKUWA, KEN	01:58.22
6	GBR	GODDARD, JAMES	01:59.24
7	CAN	BEAVERS, KEITH	01:59.43
8	GBR	TANCOCK, LIAM	02:00.76

4X100 METER FREESTYLE RELAY MEN'S

1	USA	ADRIAN, NATHAN	03:08.24
	USA	LEZAK, JASON	
	USA	PHELPS, MICHAEL	
	USA	GREVERS, MATT	
	USA	WEBER-GALE, GARRETT	
	USA	WILDMAN-TOBRINER, BEN	
	USA	JONES, CULLEN	
2	FRA		03:08.32
3	AUS		03:09.91
4	ITA		03:11.48
5	SWE		03:11.92
6	CAN		03:12.26
7	RSA		03:12.66
8	GBR		03:12.87

400 METER FREESTYLE MEN'S

1	KOR	PARK, TAE HWAN	03:41.86
2	CHN	ZHANG, LIN	03:42.44
3	USA	JENSEN, LARSEN A	03:42.78
4	USA	VANDERKAAY, PETER	03:43.11
5	TUN	MELLOULI, OUSSAMA	03:43.45
6	AUS	HACKETT, GRANT	03:43.84
7	RUS	PRILUKOV, YURI	03:43.97
8	RUS	LOBINTSEV, NIKITA	03:48.29

400 METER INDIVIDUAL MEDLEY MEN'S

1	USA	PHELPS, MICHAEL	04:03.84
2	HUN	CSEH, LASZLO	04:06.16
3	USA	LOCHTE, RYAN	04:08.09
4	ITA	BOGGIATTO, ALESSIO	04:12.16
5	ITA	MARIN, LUCA	04:12.47
6	HUN	KIS, GERGO	04:12.84
7	CAN	JOHNS, BRIAN	04:13.38
8	BRA	PEREIRA, THIAGO	04:15.40

4X100 METER MEDLEY RELAY MEN'S

1	USA	WEBER-GALE, GARRETT	03:29.34
	USA	GANGLOFF, MARK	
	USA	HANSEN, BRENDAN	
	USA	LEZAK, JASON	
	USA	CROCKER, IAN	
	USA	PEIRSOL, AARON	
	USA	PHELPS, MICHAEL	
	USA	GREVERS, MATT	
2	AUS		03:30.04
3	JPN		03:31.18
4	RUS		03:31.92
5	NZL		03:33.39
6	GBR		03:33.69
7	RSA		03:33.70
	ITA		DSQ

4X200 METER FREESTYLE RELAY MEN'S

1	USA	WALTERS, DAVID	06:58.56
	USA	VENDT, ERIK	
	USA	KELLER, KLETE	
	USA	PHELPS, MICHAEL	
	USA	LOCHTE, RYAN	
	USA	VANDERKAAY, PETER	
	USA	BERENS, RICHARD	
2	RUS		07:03.70
3	AUS		07:04.98
4	ITA		07:05.35
5	CAN		07:05.77
6	GBR		07:05.92
7	JPN		07:10.31
8	RSA		07:13.02

50 METER FREESTYLE WOMEN'S

1	GER	STEFFEN, BRITTA	24.06
2	USA	TORRES, DARA	24.07
3	AUS	CAMPBELL, CATE	24.17
4	AUS	TRICKETT, LISBETH	24.25
5	NED	VELDHUIS, MARLEEN	24.26
6	USA	JOYCE, KARALYNN	24.63
7	NED	SCHREUDER, HINKELIEN	24.65
8	BLR	GERASIMENYA, ALEKSANDRA	24.77

100 METER BACKSTROKE WOMEN'S

1	USA	COUGHLIN, NATALIE	58.96
2	ZIM	COVENTRY, KRISTY	59.19
3	USA	HOELZER, MARGARET	59.34
4	GBR	SPOFFORTH, GEMMA	59.38
5	RUS	ZUEVA, ANASTASIA	59.40
6	JPN	NAKAMURA, REIKO	59.72
7	FRA	MANAUDOU, LAURE	01:00.10
8	JPN	ITO, HANAE	01:00.18

100 METER BREASTSTROKE WOMEN'S

1	AUS	JONES, LEISEL	01:05.17
2	USA	SONI, REBECCA I	01:06.73
3	AUT	JUKIC, MIRNA	01:07.34
4	RUS	EFIMOVA, YULIYA	01:07.43
5	USA	JENDRICK, MEGAN	01:07.62
6	AUS	WHITE, TARNEE	01:07.63
7	CHN	SUN, YE	01:08.08
8	JPN	KITAGAWA, ASAMI	01:08.43

100 METER BUTTERFLY WOMEN'S

1	AUS	TRICKETT, LISBETH	56.73
2	USA	MAGNUSON, CHRISTINE	57.10
3	AUS	SCHIPPER, JESSICAH	57.25
4	CHN	ZHOU, YAFEI	57.84
5	SIN	TAO, LI	57.99
6	GBR	LOWE, JEMMA	58.06
7	BRA	SILVA, GABRIELLA	58.10
8	NED	DEKKER, INGE	58.54
	USA	BREEDEN, ELAINE	58.55 ELMS

100 METER FREESTYLE WOMEN'S

1	GER	STEFFEN, BRITTA	53.12
2	AUS	TRICKETT, LISBETH	53.16
3	USA	COUGHLIN, NATALIE	53.39
4	FIN	SEPPALA, HANNA MARIA	53.97
5	DEN	OTTESEN, JEANETTE	54.06
6	CHN	ZHU, YINGWEN	54.21
6	NED	VELDHUIS, MARLEEN	54.21
8	GBR	HALSALL, FRANCESCA	54.29
	USA	NYMEYER, LACEY P	54.74 ELMS

10K OPEN WATER WOMEN'S

1	RUS	ILCHENKO, LARISA	01:59:27.7
2	GBR	PAYNE, KERI-ANNE	01:59:29.2
3	GBR	PATTEN, CASSANDRA	01:59:31.0
4	GER	MAURER, ANGELA	01:59:31.9
5	BRA	CUNHA, ANA MARCELA	01:59:36.8
6	SUI	OBERSON, SWANN	01:59:36.9
7	BRA	OKIMOTO, POLIANA	01:59:37.4
8	CZE	PECHANOVA, JANA	01:59:39.7
22	USA	SUTTON, CHLOE	02:02:13.6

200 METER BACKSTROKE WOMEN'S

1	ZIM	COVENTRY, KRISTY	02:05.24
2	USA	HOELZER, MARGARET	02:06.23
3	JPN	NAKAMURA, REIKO	02:07.13
4	RUS	ZUEVA, ANASTASIA	02:07.88
5	USA	BEISEL, ELIZABETH	02:08.23
6	GBR	SIMMONDS, ELIZABETH	02:08.51
7	AUS	NAY, MEGAN	02:08.84
8	AUS	HOCKING, BELINDA	02:10.12

200 METER BREASTSTROKE WOMEN'S

1	USA	SONI, REBECCA I	02:20.22
2	AUS	JONES, LEISEL	02:22.05
3	NOR	NORDENSTAM, SARA	02:23.02
4	AUT	JUKIC, MIRNA	02:23.24
5	RUS	EFIMOVA, YULIYA	02:23.76
6	CAN	PIERSE, ANNAMAY	02:23.77
7	JPN	KANETO, RIE	02:25.14
8	JPN	TANEDA, MEGUMI	02:25.23
	USA	BEARD, AMANDA	02:27.70 ELMH

200 METER BUTTERFLY WOMEN'S

1	CHN	LIU, ZIGE	02:04.18
2	CHN	JIAO, LIU-YANG	02:04.72
3	AUS	SCHIPPER, JESSICAH	02:06.26
4	POL	JEDRZEJCZAK, OTYLIA	02:07.02
5	JPN	NAKANISHI, YUKO	02:07.32
6	FRA	MONGEL, AURORE	02:07.36
7	USA	BREEDEN, ELAINE	02:07.57
8	USA	HERSEY, KATHLEEN	02:08.23

200 METER FREESTYLE WOMEN'S

1	ITA	PELLEGRINI, FREDERICA	01:54.82
2	SLO	ISAKOVIC, SARA	01:54.97
3	CHN	PANG, JIAYING	01:55.05
4	USA	HOFF, KATIE	01:55.78
5	ROM	POTEC, CAMELIA ALINA	01:56.87
6	GBR	MCCLATCHEY, CAITLIN	01:57.65
7	AUS	BARRATT, BRONTE	01:57.83
7	FRA	ETIENNE, OPHELIE	01:57.83
	USA	SCHMITT, ALLISON	01:58.01 ELMS

200 METER INDIVIDUAL MEDLEY WOMEN'S

1	AUS	RICE, STEPHANIE	02:08.45
2	ZIM	COVENTRY, KRISTY	02:08.59
3	USA	COUGHLIN, NATALIE	02:10.34
4	USA	HOFF, KATIE	02:10.68
5	AUS	COUTTS, ALICIA	02:11.43
6	JPN	KITAGAWA, ASAMI	02:11.56
7	CAN	WILKINSON, JULIA	02:12.43
8	POL	BARANOWSKA, KATARZYNA	02:13.36

4X100 METER FREESTYLE RELAY WOMEN'S

1	NED		03:33.76
2	USA	SMIT, JULIA E	03:34.33
	USA	TORRES, DARA	
	USA	COUGHLIN, NATALIE	
	USA	SILVER, EMILY	
	USA	JOYCE, KARALYNN	
	USA	NYMEYER, LACEY P	
3	AUS		03:35.05
4	CHN		03:35.64
5	GER		03:36.85
6	FRA		03:37.68
7	GBR		03:38.18
8	CAN		03:38.32

400 METER FREESTYLE WOMEN'S

1	GBR	ADLINGTON, REBECCA	04:03.22
2	USA	HOFF, KATIE	04:03.29
3	GBR	JACKSON, JOANNE	04:03.52
4	FRA	BALMY, CORALIE	04:03.60
5	ITA	PELLEGRINI, FREDERICA	04:04.56
6	ROM	POTEC, CAMELIA ALINA	04:04.66
7	AUS	BARRATT, BRONTE	04:05.05
8	FRA	MANAUDOU, LAURE	04:11.26
	USA	ZIEGLER, KATE	04:09.59 ELMH

400 METER INDIVIDUAL MEDLEY WOMEN'S

1	AUS	RICE, STEPHANIE	04:29.45
2	ZIM	COVENTRY, KRISTY	04:29.89
3	USA	HOFF, KATIE	04:31.71
4	USA	BEISEL, ELIZABETH	04:34.24
5	ITA	FILIPPI, ALESSIA	04:34.34
6	GBR	MILEY, HANNAH	04:39.44
7	RUS	MARTYNOVA, YANA	04:40.04
8	CHN	LI, XUANXU	04:42.13

4X100 METER MEDLEY RELAY WOMEN'S

1	AUS		03:52.69
2	USA	MAGNUSON, CHRISTINE	03:53.30
	USA	TORRES, DARA	
	USA	COUGHLIN, NATALIE	
	USA	JENDRICK, MEGAN	
	USA	HOELZER, MARGARET	
	USA	JOYCE, KARALYNN	
	USA	SONI, REBECCA I	
	USA	BREEDEN, ELAINE	
3	CHN		03:56.11
4	GBR		03:57.50
5	RUS		03:57.84
6	JPN		03:59.54
7	CAN		04:01.35
	SWE	SWEDEN	DSQ

4X200 METER FREESTYLE RELAY WOMEN'S

1	AUS		07:44.31
2	CHN		07:45.93
3	USA	SCHMITT, ALLISON	07:46.33
	USA	COUGHLIN, NATALIE	
	USA	VANDENBERG, KIM	
	USA	MARSHALL, CHRISTINE	
	USA	BURCKLE, CAROLINE	
	USA	SMIT, JULIA E	
	USA	HOFF, KATIE	
4	ITA		07:49.76
5	FRA		07:50.66
6	HUN		07:55.53
7	JPN		07:57.56
8	SWE		07:59.83

800 METER FREESTYLE WOMEN'S

1	GBR	ADLINGTON, REBECCA	08:14.10
2	ITA	FILIPPI, ALESSIA	08:20.23
3	DEN	FRIIS, LOTTE	08:23.03
4	ROM	POTEC, CAMELIA ALINA	08:23.11
5	CHN	LI, XUANXU	08:26.34
6	AUS	PALMER, KYLIE	08:26.39
7	RUS	SOKOLOVA, ELENA	08:29.79
	USA	ZIEGLER, KATE	08:26.98 ELM IN HEATS
	USA	HOFF, KATIE	08:27.78 ELM IN HEATS

276

Brooke Abel 2/15/88, Fallbrook CA, Team
Janet Culp 2/24/82, Centennial CO, Team
Kate Hooven 1/3/85, Pleasanton CA, Team
Christina Jones 9/17/87, Fremont CA, Team/Duet

Becky Kim 2/28/85, Walnut Creek CA, Team
Andrea Nott 4/15/82, San Jose CA, Team/Duet
Annabelle Orme 3/9/87, Walnut Creek CA, Team
Jillian Penner 11/14/87, Seattle WA, Team

Kim Probst 3/6/81, Troy NY, Team

STAFF

Laura LaCurisa Team Leader
Tammy McGregor Head Coach
Stephan Miermont Head Choreographer
Gail Emery (NOT PICTURED) Designated Routine Coach
Denise Shively (NOT PICTURED) Asst Team Leader

SYNCHRONIZED SWIMMING RESULTS

DUET

1	RUS		99.251
2	ESP		98.334
3	JPN		97.167
4	CHN		96.334
5	USA	JONES, CHRISTINA	95.5
		NOTT, ANDREA	
6	CAN		95.084
7	ITA		93.751
8	UKR		92.668

TEAM

1	RUS		99.5
2	ESP		98.251
3	CHN		97.334
4	CAN		95.668
5	JPN		95.334
5	USA	ABEL, BROOKE	95.334
	USA	NOTT, ANDREA	
	USA	CULP, JANET	
	USA	HOOVEN, KATE	
	USA	KIM, BECKY	
	USA	PROBST, KIM	
	USA	JONES, CHRISTINA	
	USA	ORME, ANNABELLE	
	USA	PENNER, JILLIAN	
7	AUS		82.167
8	EGY		80.833

Jun Gao 1/25/69, Gaithersburg MD
Crystal Huang 7/8/79, San Gabriel CA
Chen Wang 1/17/74, New York NY
David Zhuang 9/1/63, West Windsor NJ, Singles

STAFF

Robert Fox Team Leader
Teodor Gheorghe Head Coach (W)

TABLE TENNIS RESULTS

MEN'S SINGLES

1	CHN	MA, LIN
2	CHN	WANG, HAO
3	CHN	WANG, LIQIN
4	SWE	PERSSON, JORGEN
5	CRO	PRIMORAC, ZORAN
5	KOR	OH, SANG-EUN
5	HKG	KO, LAI CHAK
5	CRO	TAN, RUIWU
	USA	**ZHUANG, DAVID**	ELM PRELIM

MEN'S TEAM

1	CHN	
2	GER	
3	KOR	

4	AUT	
5	HKG	
5	JPN	

WOMEN'S SINGLES

1	CHN	ZHANG, YINING
2	CHN	WANG, NAN
3	CHN	GUO, YUE
4	SIN	LI, JIA WEI
5	**USA**	**WANG, CHEN**
5	HKG	TIE, YANA
5	DOM	WU, XUE
5	SIN	FENG, TIANWEI
	USA	**GAO, JUN**	ELM 4TH ROUND
	USA	**HUANG, CRYSTAL**	ELM PRELIM

WOMEN'S TEAM

1	CHN	
2	SIN	
3	KOR	
4	JPN	
5	**USA**	**HUANG, CRYSTAL**
5	**USA**	**GAO, JUN**
5	**USA**	**WANG, CHEN**
5	HKG	
7	AUT	
7	ROM	

Charlotte Craig 2/2/91, Murrieta CA, Flyweight (-49kg)
Diana Lopez 1/7/84, Sugar Land TX, Bantum-Featherweight (-57kg)
Mark Lopez 4/25/82, Sugar Land TX, Bantum-Featherweight (-68kg)
Steven Lopez 11/9/78, Sugar Land TX, Light-welterweight (-80kg)

STAFF

Meredith Miller Team Leader
Jean Lopez Head Coach
Juan Moreno Asst Coach
Herbert Perez Tech Specialist

TAEKWONDO RESULTS

MEN'S 58KG

1	MEX	PEREZ, GUILLERMO
2	DOM	MERCEDES, YULIS
3	TPE	CHU, MU YEN
3	AFG	NIKPAI, ROHULLAH
5	ESP	RAMOS, JUAN ANTONIO
5	THA	KHAWLAOR, CHUTCHAWAL
7	GBR	HARVEY, MICHAEL
7	POR	POVOA, PEDRO

MEN'S 68KG

1	KOR	SON, TAJIN
2	**USA**	**LOPEZ, MARK**
3	TPE	SUNG, YU-CHI

3	TUR	TAZEGUL, SERVET
5	GER	MANZ, DANIEL
5	CAN	LOPEZ, PETER
7	NED	BEKKERS, DENNIS
7	AFG	BEHAVE, NESAR AHMAD

MEN'S 80KG

1	IRI	SAEI, HADI
2	ITA	SARMIENTO, MAURO
3	**USA**	**LOPEZ, STEVEN**
3	CHN	ZHU, GUO
5	AZE	AHMADOV, RASHAD
5	GBR	COOK, AARON
7	NEP	BISTA, DEEPAK
7	CIV	KONAN, N'GUESSAN SEBASTIEN

MEN'S 80KG+

1	KOR	CHA, DONGMIN
2	GRE	NIKOLAIDIS, ALEXANDROS
3	KAZ	CHILMANOV, ARMAN
3	NGR	CHUKWUMERIJE, CHIKA YAGAZIE
5	UZB	IRGASHEV, AKMAL
7	MAR	ZROURI, ABDELKADER
7	CRC	MOITLAND, KRISTOPHER

WOMEN'S 49KG

1	CHN	WU, JINGYU
2	THA	PUEDPONG, BUTTREE
3	VEN	CONTRERAS, DALIA
3	CUB	MONTEJO, DAYNELLI
5	TPE	YANG, SHU CHUN

TENNIS

James Blake 12/28/79, Yonkers NY, Doubles
Bob Bryan 4/29/78, Camarillo CA, Doubles
Mike Bryan 4/29/78, Camarillo CA, Doubles
Jill Craybas 7/4/74, East Greenwich RI, Singles

Lindsay Davenport 6/8/76, Palos Verdes CA, Singles/Doubles
Robby Ginepri 10/7/82, Kennesaw GA, Singles
Liezel Huber 8/21/76, Cypress TX, Doubles
Sam Querrey 10/7/87, Thousand Oaks CA, Singles/Doubles

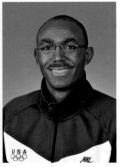

Serena Williams 9/26/81, Lynwood CA, Singles/Doubles
Venus Williams 6/17/80, Lynwood CA, Singles/Doubles

STAFF

Jeff Ryan Team Leader
Rodney Harmon Head Coach (Men)

Zina Garrison Head Coach (Women)
Elke Juul Team Administrator
Lori McNeil Asst Coach (W)
Jay Berger Asst Coach (M)

TENNIS RESULTS

MEN'S SINGLES

1	ESP	NADAL, RAFAEL	
2	CHI	GONZALEZ, FERNANDO	
3	SRB	DJOKOVIC, NOVAK	
4	**USA**	**BLAKE, JAMES**	
5	SUI	FEDERER, ROGER	
5	FRA	MATHIEU, PAUL-HENRI	
5	AUT	MELZER, JURGEN	
5	FRA	MONFILS, GAEL	
	USA	**GINEPRI, ROBBIE**	*ELM 1ST ROUND*
	USA	**QUERREY, SAM**	*ELM 1ST ROUND*

MEN'S DOUBLES

1	SUI		
2	SWE		
3	**USA**	**BRYAN, BOB**	
	USA	**BRYAN, MIKE**	
4	FRA		
5	IND		
5	RUS		
5	POL		
	USA	**BLAKE, JAMES**	*ELM 1ST ROUND*
	USA	**QUERREY, SAM**	

WOMEN'S SINGLES

1	RUS	DEMENTIEVA, ELENA
2	RUS	SAFINA, DINARA
3	RUS	ZVONAREVA, VERA
4	CHN	LI, NAI
5	USA	**WILLIAMS, SERENA**
5	USA	**WILLIAMS, VENUS**
5	AUT	BAMMER, SYBILLE
5	SRB	JANKOVIC, JELENA
	USA	**CRYBAS, JILL** *ELIM 1ST ROUND*

WOMEN'S DOUBLES

1	USA	**WILLIAMS, SERENA**
	USA	**WILLIAMS, VENUS**
2	ESP	
3	CHN	
4	UKR	
5	USA	**DAVENPORT, LINDSAY**
	USA	**HUBER, LIEZEL**
5	RUS	
5	ITA	
5	RUS	

Laura Bennett 4/25/75, North Palm Beach FL
Sarah Haskins Korteum 3/13/81, St. Louis MO
Hunter Kemper 5/4/76, Longwood FL
Matt Reed 11/8/75, Boulder CO

Jarrod Shoemaker 7/17/82, Sudbury MA
Julie Swail Ertel 12/27/72, Placentia CA

STAFF

Scott Schnitzspahn Team Leader
Sharon Donnelly Head Coach

Andrew Schmitz Asst Coach
Jeffrey Donaldson (NOT PICTURED) Mechanic
Alex Keith (NOT PICTURED) Chiropractor

TRIATHLON RESULTS

MEN'S TRIATHLON

1	GER	FRODENO, JAN	01:48:53.28
2	CAN	WHITFIELD, SIMON	01:48:58.47
3	NZL	DOCHERTY, BEVAN	01:49:05.59
4	ESP	GOMEZ, JAVIER	01:49:13.92
5	ESP	RANA, IVAN	01:49:22.03
6	GER	UNGER, DANIEL	01:49:43.78
7	USA	**KEMPER, HUNTER**	01:49:48.75
8	DEN	HENNING, RASMUS	01:49:57.47
18	USA	**SHOEMAKER, JARROD**	01:50:46.39
32	USA	**REED, MATTHEW**	01:52:30.44

WOMEN'S TRIATHLON

1	AUS	SNOWSILL, EMMA	01:58:27.66
2	POR	FERNANDES, VANESSA	01:59:34.63
3	AUS	MOFFAT, EMMA	01:59:55.84
4	USA	**BENNETT, LAURA**	02:00:21.54
5	JPN	IDE, JURI	02:00:23.77
6	SUI	SPIRIG, NICOLA	02:00:30.48
7	SUI	RYF, DANIELA	02:00:40.20
8	NZL	HEWITT, ANDREA	02:00:45.99
11	USA	**HASKINS, SARAH**	02:01:22.57
19	USA	**SWAIL, JULIE**	02:02:39.22

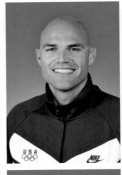   

Robyn Ah Mow-Santos 9/15/75, Honolulu HI, Indoor, Setter
Lloy Ball 2/17/72, Ft. Wayne IN, Indoor, Setter
Lindsey Berg 7/16/80, Honolulu HI, Indoor, Setter
Heather Bown 11/29/78, Yorba Linda CA, Indoor, Middle Blocker

Nicole Branagh 1/31/79, Orinda CA, Beach
Phil Dalhausser 1/26/80, Ormond Beach FL, Beach
Nicole Davis 4/24/82, Stockton CA, Indoor, Libero
Gabe Gardner March, 1976, San Clemente CA, Indoor, Opposite

Jacob Gibb 2/6/76, Bountiful UT, Beach
Kimberly Glass 8/18/84, Lancaster PA, Indoor, Outside Hitter
Tayyiba Haneef-Park 3/23/79, Laguna Hills CA, Indoor, Opposite hitter
Kevin Hansen 3/19/82, Newport Beach CA, Indoor, Setter

  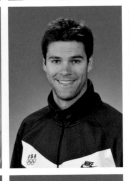 

Tom Hoff 6/9/73, Park Ridge, IL, Indoor Middle Blocker
Jennifer Joines 11/23/82, Milpitas CA, Indoor, Middle Blocker
Richard Lambourne 5/6/75, Tustin CA, Indoor, Libero
David Lee 3/8/82, Alpine, CA, Indoor Middle Blocker

Misty May-Treanor 7/30/77, Costa Mesa CA, Beach
Ryan Millar 1/22/78, Palmdale CA, Indoor, Middle Blocker
Ogonna Nnamani 7/29/82, Bloomington IL, Indoor, Outside Hitter
William "Reid" Priddy 10/1/77, Richmond VA, Indoor, Outside Hitter

Todd Rogers 9/30/73, Santa Barbara CA, Beach
Sean Rooney 11/13/82, Wheaton IL, Indoor, Outside Hitter
Sean Rosenthal 6/19/80, Redondo Beach CA, Beach
Riley Salmon 2/7/76, Houston TX, Indoor, Outside Hitter

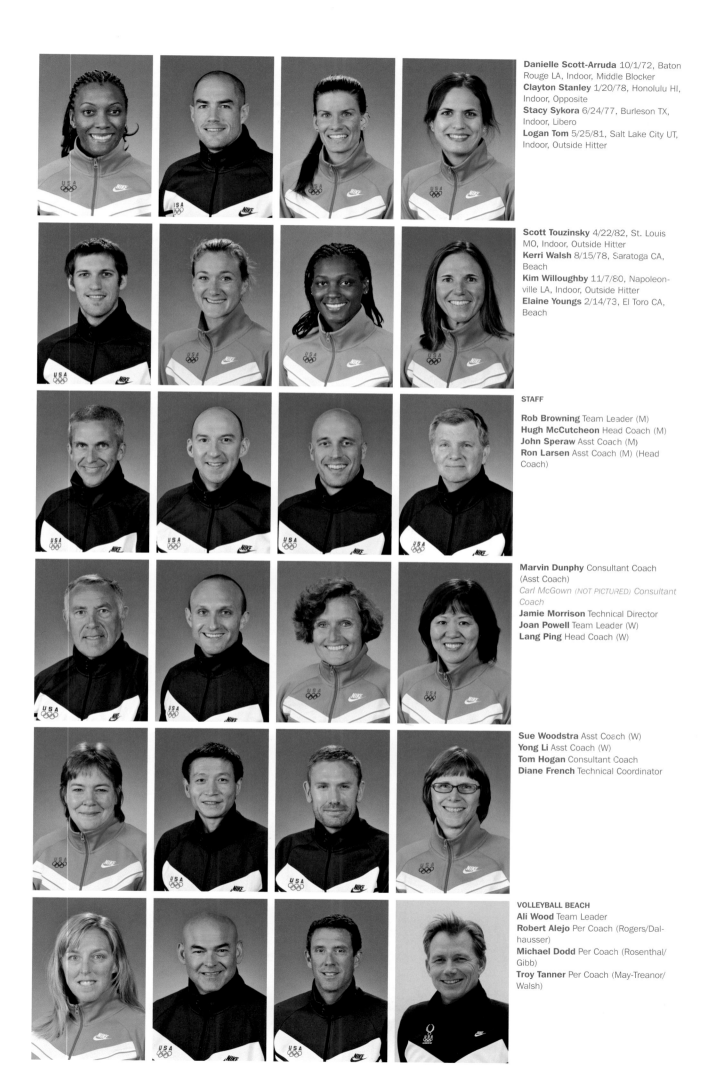

Danielle Scott-Arruda 10/1/72, Baton Rouge LA, Indoor, Middle Blocker
Clayton Stanley 1/20/78, Honolulu HI, Indoor, Opposite
Stacy Sykora 6/24/77, Burleson TX, Indoor, Libero
Logan Tom 5/25/81, Salt Lake City UT, Indoor, Outside Hitter

Scott Touzinsky 4/22/82, St. Louis MO, Indoor, Outside Hitter
Kerri Walsh 8/15/78, Saratoga CA, Beach
Kim Willoughby 11/7/80, Napoleonville LA, Indoor, Outside Hitter
Elaine Youngs 2/14/73, El Toro CA, Beach

281

STAFF

Rob Browning Team Leader (M)
Hugh McCutcheon Head Coach (M)
John Speraw Asst Coach (M)
Ron Larsen Asst Coach (M) (Head Coach)

Marvin Dunphy Consultant Coach (Asst Coach)
Carl McGown (NOT PICTURED) Consultant Coach
Jamie Morrison Technical Director
Joan Powell Team Leader (W)
Lang Ping Head Coach (W)

Sue Woodstra Asst Coach (W)
Yong Li Asst Coach (W)
Tom Hogan Consultant Coach
Diane French Technical Coordinator

VOLLEYBALL BEACH
Ali Wood Team Leader
Robert Alejo Per Coach (Rogers/Dalhausser)
Michael Dodd Per Coach (Rosenthal/Gibb)
Troy Tanner Per Coach (May-Treanor/Walsh)

Liz Maskayan Per Coach (Branagy/Youngs)
Al Lau Team Leader

VOLLEYBALL RESULTS

MEN'S INDOOR

1	**USA**	3
2	BRA	1
3	RUS	3
4	ITA	0
5	BGR	
6	CHN	
7	POL	
8	SRB	

GOLD METAL SCORES

BRONZE METAL SCORES

WOMEN'S INDOOR

1	BRA	3
2	**USA**	1
3	CHN	3
4	CUB	1
5	ITA	
6	JPN	
7	RUS	
8	SRB	

MEN'S INDOOR SET SCORES

USA vs	VEN	3-2
	ITA	3-1
	BUL	3-1
	CHN	3-0
	JPN	3-0
	SRB	3-2
	RUS	3-2
	BRA	3-1

WOMEN'S INDOOR SET SCORES

USA vs	JPN	3-1
	CUB	0-3
	VEN	3-1
	CHN	3-2
	POL	3-2
	ITA	3-2
	CUB	3-0
	BRA	1-3

MEN'S BEACH

1	USA	ROGERS, TODD
	USA	DALHAUSSER, PHILLIP
2	BRA	
3	BRA	
4	GEO	
5	USA	GIBB, JAKE
	USA	ROSENTHAL, SEAN
5	GER	
5	NED	
5	AUT	

WOMEN'S BEACH

1	USA	MAY, MISTY
	USA	WALSH, KERRI
2	CHN	
3	CHN	
4	BRA	
5	USA	YOUNGS, ELAINE
	USA	BRANAGH, NICOLE
5	AUS	
5	AUT	
5	BRA	

282

WATER POLO

Betsey Armstrong 1/31/83, Ann Arbor MI, Goalkeeper
Tony Azevedo 11/21/81, Long Beach CA, Attacker
Ryan Bailey 8/28/75, Long Beach CA, Center
Layne Beaubien 7/4/76, Coronado CA, Defender

Brandon Brooks 4/29/81, Honolulu HI, Goalkeeper
Patty Cardenas 8/19/84, Commerce CA, Attacker
Kami Craig 7/21/87, Santa Barbara CA, Center
Natalie Golda 12/28/81, Fullerton CA, Defender

Alison Gregorka 6/29/85, Ann Arbor MI, Defender
Brittany Hayes 2/5/85, Santa Ana CA, Left-Handed Attacker
Jaime Hipp 9/1/81, Fresno CA, Goalkeeper
Peter Hudnut 2/16/80, Encino CA, Defender

Tim Hutten 6/4/85, Seal Beach CA, 2-Meter Defense
JW Krumpholz 9/22/87, Santa Ana CA, Center
Rick Merlo 8/5/82, Fresno CA, 2-Meter Defense
Merril Moses 8/13/77, Rancho Palos Verdes CA, Goalkeeper

Heather Petri 6/13/78, Orinda CA, Attacker
Jeff Powers 1/21/80, San Luis Obispo CA, Defender
Jesse Smith 4/27/83, Coronado CA, Defender
Jessica Steffens 4/7/87, Danville CA, Defender

Moriah van Norman 5/30/84, San Diego CA, Center
Peter Varellas 10/2/84, Moraga CA, Attacker
Brenda Villa 4/18/80, Commerce CA, Attacker
Lauren Wenger 3/11/84, Long Beach CA, Defender

Elsie Windes 6/17/85, Portland OR, Defender
Adam Wright 5/4/7, Seal Beach CA, Attacker

STAFF

Richard McKee Team Leader (M)
Terry Schroeder Head Coach (M)

Robert Lynn Asst Coach (M)
Ryan Brown Asst Coach (M)
James Brumm Video Scout Coach (M)
Nikki Jost Team Administrator (M&W)

Bernice Orwig Team Leader (W)
Guy Baker Head Coach (W)
Kyle Kopp Asst Coach (W)
Heather Moody Asst Coach (W)

283

Kyle Utsumi Video Scout Coach (W)

WATERPOLO RESULTS

MEN

1	HUN	14	GOLD GAME SCORE
2	**USA**	10	
3	SRB	6	BRONZE GAME SCORE
4	MNE	4	
5	ESP		
6	CRO		
7	GRE		
8	AUS		

WOMEN

1	NED	9	GOLD GAME SCORE
2	**USA**	8	
3	AUS	12	BRONZE GAME SCORE
4	HUN	11	
5	CHN		
6	ITA		
7	RUS		
8	GRE		

MEN'S GAME SCORES

USA VS	CRO	7-5
	SRB	2-4
	GER	8-7
	ITA	12-11
	CHN	8-4
	SBR	10-5
	HUN	10-14

WOMEN'S GAME SCORES

USA VS	ITA	9-9
	CHN	12-11
	RUS	12-7
	AUS	9-8
	NED	8-9

WEIGHTLIFTING

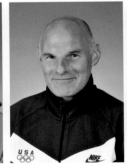
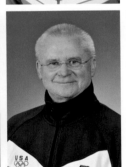

Kendrick Farris 7/2/86, Shreveport LA, 85kg
Carissa Gump 8/24/83, Essex VT, 63kg
Cheryl Haworth 4/19/83, Savannah GA, 75+kg
Melanie Roach 12/15/74, Bonney Lake WA, 53kg

Chad Vaughn 3/11/80, Konawa OK, 77kg
Natalie Woolfolk 11/7/83, Arnold MD, 63kg

STAFF

Frank Eksten Team Leader
Roger Nielsen Head Coach (M)

Dennis Snethen Head Coach (W)
Bob Morris Asst Coach (W)

WEIGHTLIFTING RESULTS

MEN'S 056KG

			SNATCH	CLN/JRK	TOTAL
1	CHN	LONG, QINGQUAN	132	160	292
2	VIE	HOANGANH, TUAN	130	160	290
3	INA	IRAWAN, EKO YULI	130	158	288
4	TPE	YANG, CHIN-YI	128	157	285
5	PRK	CHA, KUM CHOL	128	155	283
6	CUB	ALVAREZ, SERGIO	120	152	272
7	TPE	WANG, SHIN-YUAN	115	150	265
8	MAS	IBRAHIM, AMIRUL HAMIZAN	121	144	265

MEN'S 062KG

			SNATCH	CLN/JRK	TOTAL
1	CHN	ZHANG, XIANGXIANG	143	176	319
2	COL	SALAZAR, DIEGO	138	167	305
3	INA	TRIYATNO,	135	163	298
4	ROM	BUCI, ANTONIU	130	165	295
5	THA	HANSAWONG, PHAISAN	132	162	294
6	CUB	RUIZ, LAZARO	132	162	294
7	TKM	HUDAYBERGENOV, TOLKUNBEK	126	162	288
8	EGY	ABD ELBAKI, MOHAMED	120	159	288

MEN'S 069KG

1	CHN	LIAO, HUI	158	190	348
2	FRA	DABAYA, VENCELAS	151	187	338
3	ARM	MARTIROSYAN, TIGRAN	153	185	338
4	CUB	BORRERO, YORDANIS	148	180	328
5	AZE	MIRZAYEV, TURAN	146	181	327
6	PRK	KIM, CHOL JIN	146	180	326
7	AZE	BAYRAMOV, AFGAN	145	175	320
8	THA	SUPHALAK, SITTHISAK	147	171	318

MEN'S 077KG

1	KOR	SA, JAE-HYOUK	163	203	366
2	CHN	LI, HONGLI	168	198	366
3	ARM	DAVTYAN, GEVORG	165	195	360
4	KOR	KIM, KWANG-HOON	155	200	355
5	RUS	PEREPETCHECNOV, OLEG	162	192	354
6	CUB	CAMBAR, RODRIGEZ IVAN	157	196	353
7	ARM	KHACHATRYAN, ARA	162	191	353
8	POL	SZRAMIAK, KRZYSZTOF	161	191	352
24	**USA**	**VAUGHN, CHAD**	147		DNF

MEN'S 085KG

1	CHN	LU, YONG	180	214	394
2	BLR	RYBAKOU, ANDREI	185	209	394
3	ARM	MARTIROSYAN, TIGRAN	177	203	380
4	KAZ	SEDOV, VLADIMIR	180	200	380
5	CUB	VALLADARES, JADIER	169	203	372
6	FRA	HENNEQUIN, BENJAMIN	162	205	367
7	UZB	CHASHEMOV, MANSURBEK	165	202	367
8	USA	**FARRIS, KENDRICK**	160	202	362

MEN'S 094KG

1	KAZ	ILIN, ILYA	180	226	406
2	POL	KOLECKI, SZYMON	179	224	403
3	RUS	AKKAEV, KHADZHIMURAT	185	217	402
4	GEO	KASABIER, ARSEN	176	223	399
5	AZE	PASHAYEV, NIZAMI	181	215	396
6	CUB	HERNANDEZ, YOHANDRYS	178	215	393
7	IRI	EBRAHIMI, ASGHAR	180	212	392
8	RUS	KONSTANTINOV, ROMAN	175	212	387

MEN'S 105KG

1	BLR	ARAMNAU, ANDREI	200	236	436
2	RUS	KLOKOV, DMITRIY	193	230	423
3	RUS	LAPIKOV, DMITRI	190	230	420
4	POL	DOLEGA, MARCIN	195	225	420
5	KAZ	AKHMETOV, BAKHYT	190	225	415
6	GEO	KUZILOV, ALBERT	182	227	409
7	KAZ	ISTOMIN, SERGEY	181	225	406
8	POL	DOLEGA, ROBERT	184	221	405

MEN'S 105KG+

1	AUT	STEINER, MATTHIAS	203	258	461
2	RUS	CHIGISHEV, EVGENY	210	250	460
3	LAT	SCERBATIHS, VIKTORS	206	242	448
4	UKR	UDACHIN, ARTEM	207	235	442
5	UKR	SHYMECHKO, IHOR	201	232	433
6	IRI	SHARIFI, SADEH RASHID	196	230	426
7	POL	KLESZCZ, GRZEGORZ	185	234	419
8	GER	VELAGIC, ALMIR	188	225	413

WOMEN'S 048KG

1	CHN	CHEN, XIEXIA	95	117	212
2	TUR	OZKAN, SIBEL	88	111	199
3	TPE	CHEN, WEI-LING	84	112	196
4	KOR	IM, JUNG-HWA	86	110	196
5	THA	LAOSIRIKUL, PENSIRI	85	110	195
6	JPN	MIYAKE, HIROMI	80	105	185
7	FRA	NOEL, MELANIE	80	97	177
8	JPN	OSHIRO, MISAKI	80	92	172

WOMEN'S 053KG

1	THA	JAROENRATTANATARAKOON, P	95	126	221
2	KOR	YOON, JIN-HEE	94	119	213
3	BLR	NOVIKAVA, NATASSIA	95	118	213
4	INA	RUMBEWAS, RAEMA LISA	91	115	206
5	DOM	MARIDALIN, YUDELQUIS	93	111	204
6	USA	**ROACH, MELANIE**	83	110	193
7	GER	ROHDE, JULIA	82	103	185
8	PNG	TOUA, DIKA	80	104	184

WOMEN'S 058KG

1	CHN	CHEN, YANQING	106	138	244
2	RUS	SHAINOVA, MARINA	98	129	227
3	PRK	O JONG, AE	95	131	226
4	THA	KAMEAIM, WANDEE	98	128	226
5	ECU	ESCOBAR, ALEXANDRA	99	124	223
6	ALB	BEGAJ, ROMELA	98	118	216
7	POL	KLEJNOWSKA, ALEKSANDRA	95	120	215
8	ROM	COCOS, ROXANA	89	115	204

WOMEN'S 063KG

1	PRK	PAK, HYON SUK	106	135	241
2	KAZ	NEKRASSOVA, IRINA	110	130	240
3	TPE	LU, YING-CHI	104	127	231
4	CAN	GIRARD, CHRISTINE	102	126	228
5	VIE	NGUYEN, THI THIET	100	125	225
6	KOR	KIM, SOOKYUNG	98	127	225
7	NOR	KASIRYE, RUTH	103	121	224

12	USA	**WOOLFOLK, NATALIE**	97	114	211
14	USA	**GUMP, CARISSA**	88	116	204

WOMEN'S 069KG

			SNATCH	CLN/JRK	TOTAL
1	CHN	LIU, CHUNHONG	128	158	286
2	RUS	SLIVENKO, OXANA	115	140	255
3	UKR	DAVYDOVA, NATALYA	115	135	250
4	COL	SOLIS, LEIDY YESSENIA	105	135	240
5	EGY	KHALIL, ABIR	105	133	238
6	COL	MEDINA, TULIA	106	124	230
7	BLR	BATSIUSHKA, HANNA	105	120	225
8	JPN	SAITO, RIKA	87	122	209

WOMEN'S 075KG

			SNATCH	CLN/JRK	TOTAL
1	CHN	CAO, LEI	128	154	282
2	KAZ	VAZHENINA, ALLA	119	147	266
3	RUS	EVSTJUKHINA, NADEZHDA	117	147	264
4	BLR	KULESHA, IRYNA	118	137	255
5	ESP	VALENTIN, LIDIA	115	135	250
6	MEX	AGUIRRE, DAMARIS	109	136	245
7	COL	VALOYES, UBALDINA	110	134	244
8	CAN	LASSEN, JEANE	105	135	240

WOMEN'S 075KG+

1	KOR	JANG, MI-RAN	140	186	326
2	UKR	KOROBKA, OLHA	124	153	377
3	KAZ	GRABOVETSKAYA, MARIYA	120	150	270
4	SAM	OPELOGE, ELE	119	150	269
5	NIG	USMAN, MARIAM	115	150	265
6	USA	**HAWORTH, CHERYL**	115	144	259
7	UKR	DOVHAL, YULIYA	118	140	258
8	AUS	LOVELY, DEBORAH	113	135	248

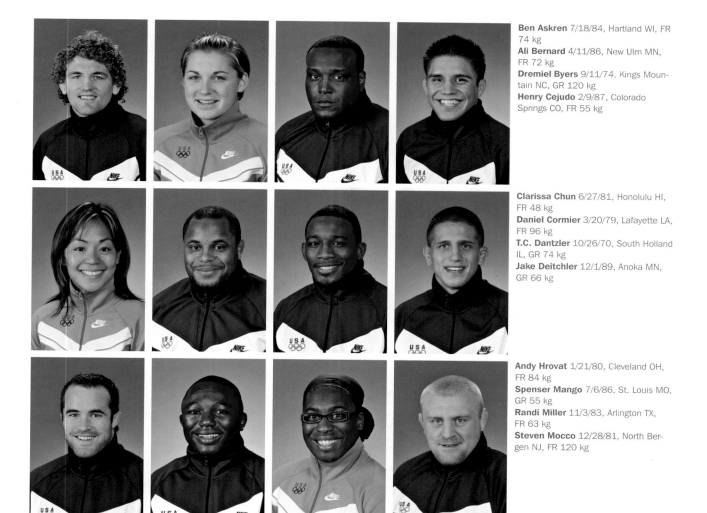

Ben Askren 7/18/84, Hartland WI, FR 74 kg

Ali Bernard 4/11/86, New Ulm MN, FR 72 kg

Dremiel Byers 9/11/74, Kings Mountain NC, GR 120 kg

Henry Cejudo 2/9/87, Colorado Springs CO, FR 55 kg

Clarissa Chun 6/27/81, Honolulu HI, FR 48 kg

Daniel Cormier 3/20/79, Lafayette LA, FR 96 kg

T.C. Dantzler 10/26/70, South Holland IL, GR 74 kg

Jake Deitchler 12/1/89, Anoka MN, GR 66 kg

Andy Hrovat 1/21/80, Cleveland OH, FR 84 kg

Spenser Mango 7/6/86, St. Louis MO, GR 55 kg

Randi Miller 11/3/83, Arlington TX, FR 63 kg

Steven Mocco 12/28/81, North Bergen NJ, FR 120 kg

WRESTLING

Douglas Schwab 8/3/77, Osage IA, FR 66 kg
Marcie Van Dusen 6/25/82, Lake Arrowhead CA, FR 55 kg
Brad Vering 8/21/77, Howells NE, GR 84 kg
Adam Wheeler 3/24/81, Lancaster CA, GR 96 kg

Michael Zadick (NOT PICTURED) 7/12/78, FR 60kg

STAFF

John Bardis Team Leader
Steve Fraser Head Coach
Jay Antonelli Asst Coach
Rich Estrella Asst Coach

WRESTLING FREESTYLE
Steve Silver Team Leader (M)
Mitch Hull (NOT PICTURED) Asst Team Leader/Team Mgr
Kevin Jackson Head Coach (M)
Kerry McCoy Asst Coach (M)
Lee Kemp Asst Coach (M)

Stan Zeamer Team Leader (W)
Terry Steiner Head Coach (W)
Tadaaki Hatta Asst Coach (W)

WRESTLING RESULTS

MEN'S FREESTYLE 120 KG

1	UZB	TAIMAZOV, ARTUR	120KGF
2	RUS	AKHMEDOV, BAKHTIYAR	120KGF
3	KAZ	MUTALIMOV, MAZID	120KGF
3	SVK	MUSULBES, DAVID	120KGF
5	IRI	MASOUMI VALADI, FARDIN	120KGF
5	CUB	RODRIGUES, DISNEY	120KGF
7	**USA**	**MOCCO, STEPHEN**	120KGF
8	HUN	AUBELI, OTTO	120KGF

MEN'S FREESTYLE 55 KG

1	**USA**	**CEJUDO, HENRY**	055KGF
2	JPN	MATSUNAGA, TOMIHIRO	055KGF
3	BUL	VELIKOV MARINOV, RADOSLAV	055KGF
3	RUS	KUDUKHOV, BESIK	055KGF
5	UZB	MANSUROV, DILSHOD	055KGF
5	AZE	SEVDIMOV, NAMIG	055KGF
7	BLR	GADSHIEV, RIZVAN	055KGF
8	GEO	GOCHASHVILI, BESARION	055KGF

MEN'S FREESTYLE 60 KG

1	RUS	BATIROV, MAVLET	060KGF
2	UKR	FEDORISHIN, VASIL	060KGF
3	JPN	YUMOTO, KENICHI	060KGF
3	IRI	MOHAMMADI PAHNEKALAEI, SEYED MOURAD	060KGF
5	KGZ	BAZAGURUEV, BAZAR	060KGF
5	AZE	GUSSEINOV, ZELIMKHAN	060KGF
7	MKD	RAMAZANOV, MURAT	060KGF
8	CUB	QUINTANA, YANDRO	060KGF
19	**USA**	**ZADICK, MIKE**	060KGF

MEN'S FREESTYLE 66 KG

1	TUR	SHAHIN, RAMAZAN	066KGF
2	UKR	STADNIK, ANDREY	066KGF
3	GEO	TUSHISHVILI, OTAR	066KGF
3	IND	KUMAR, SUSHIL	066KGF
5	CUB	GARZON CABALLERO, GEANDRY	066KGF
5	KAZ	SPIRIDONOV, LEONID	066KGF
7	RUS	FARNIEV, IRBEK	066KGF
8	MGL	BUYANJAV, BATZORIG	066KGF
14	**USA**	**SCHWAB, DOUG**	066KGF

MEN'S FREESTYLE 74 KG

1	RUS	SAITIEV, BOUVAISSA	074KGF
2	UZB	TIGIEV, SOSLAN	074KGF
3	BLR	GAIDAROV, MOURAD	074KGF
3	BUL	TERZIEV, KIRIL	074KGF
5	CUB	FUNDORA ZALDIVAR, IVAN	074KGF
5	ROM	GHEORGHITA, STEFAN	074KGF
7	**USA**	**ASKREN, BEN**	074KGF
8	KGZ	GITINOV, ARSEN	074KGF

MEN'S FREESTYLE 84 KG

1	GEO	MINDORASHVILI, REVAZ	084KGF
2	TJK	ABDUSALAMOV, YUSUP	084KGF
3	UKR	DANKO, TARAS	084KGF
3	RUS	KETOEV, GEORGI	084KGF
5	TUR	BALCI, SERHAT	084KGF
5	GER	BICHINASHVILI, DAVID	084KGF
7	AZE	TEMREZOV, NAURUZ	084KGF
8	ARM	YENOKYAN, HARUTYUN	084KGF
12	**USA**	**HROVAT, ANDY**	084KGF

MEN'S FREESTYLE 96 KG

1	RUS	MURADOV, SHIRVANI	096KGF
2	KAZ	TIGIEV, TAIMURAZ	096KGF
3	AZE	GAZUMOV, KHETAG	096KGF
3	GEO	GOGSHELIDZE, GEORJI	096KGF
5	RUS	TIBILOV, GEORGI	096KGF
5	CUB	BATISTA MARTINEZ, MICHEL	096KGF
7	UZB	KURBANOV, KURBAN	096KGF
8	HUN	KISS, GERGELY	096KGF
19	**USA**	**CORMIER, DANIEL**	096KGF

MEN'S GRECO-ROMAN 120 KG

1	CUB	LOPEZ, MIJAIN	120KGGR
2	RUS	BAROEV, KHASSAN	120KGGR
3	LTU	MIZGAITIS, MINDAUGAS	120KGGR
3	ARM	PATRIKEEV, YURI	120KGGR
5	FRA	SZCZEPANIAK, YANNICK	120KGGR
5	SWE	SJOEBERG, JALMAR	120KGGR
7	**USA**	**BYERS, DREMIEL**	120KGGR
8	HUN	DEAK-BARDOS, MIHALY	120KGGR

MEN'S GRECO-ROMAN 55 KG

1	RUS	MANKIEV, NAZIR	055KGGR
2	AZE	BAYRAMOV, ROVSHAN	055KGGR
3	KOR	PARK, EUN-CHUL	055KGGR
3	ARM	AMOYAN, ROMAN	055KGGR
5	CUB	HERNANDEZ, JAGNIEL	055KGGR
5	IRI	SORYAN REIHANPOUR, HAMID	055KGGR
7	SRB	FRIS, KRISTIJAN	055KGGR
8	BUL	VENKOV, VENELIN	055KGGR
9	**USA**	**MANGO, SPENSER**	055KGGR

GRECO-ROMAN 60 KG

1	RUS	ALBIEV, ISLAMBEK	060KGGR
2	AZE	RAHIMOV, VITALY	060KGGR
3	KAZ	TENGIZBAYEV, NURBAKYT	060KGGR
3	KGZ	TUMENBAYEV, RUSLAN	060KGGR
5	CUB	MONZON, ROBERTO	060KGGR
5	CHN	SHENG, JIANG	060KGGR
7	BUL	NAZARIAN, ARMEN	060KGGR
8	ROM	DIACONU, EUSEBIO	060KGGR

MEN'S GRECO-ROMAN 66 KG

1	FRA	GUENOT, STEVE	066KGGR
2	KGZ	BEGALIEV, KANATBEK	066KGGR
3	UKR	VARDANYAN, ARMEN	066KGGR
3	BLR	SEMENOV, MIKHAIL	066KGGR
5	BUL	GERGOV, NIKOLAY	066KGGR
5	KAZ	BAYAKHMETOV, DARKHAN	066KGGR
7	RUS	KOVALENKO, SERGEY	066KGGR
8	HUN	LOERINCZ, TAMAS	066KGGR
12	**USA**	**DEITCHLER, JAKE**	066KGGR

MEN'S GRECO-ROMAN 74 KG

1	GEO	KVIRKELIA, MANUCHAR	074KGGR
2	CHN	CHANG, YOUNGXIANG	074KGGR
3	FRA	GUENOT, CHRISTOPHE	074KGGR
3	BUL	YANAKIEV, YAVOR	074KGGR
5	HUN	BACSI, PETER	074KGGR
5	BLR	MIKHALOVICH, OLEG	074KGGR
7	RUS	SAMOURGACHEV, VARTERES	074KGGR
8	KAZ	MELYOSHIN, ROMAN	074KGGR
16	**USA**	**DANTZLER, T.C.**	074KGGR

MEN'S GRECO-ROMAN 84 KG

1	ITA	MINGUZZI, ANDREA	084KGGR
2	HUN	FODOR, ZOLTAN	084KGGR
3	TUR	AVLUCA, NAZMI	084KGGR
5	FRA	NOUMONVI, MELONIN	084KGGR
5	CHN	MA, SANYI	084KGGR
7	ARM	FOROV, DENNIS	084KGGR
12	**USA**	**VERING, BRAD**	084KGGR

MEN'S GRECO-ROMAN 96 KG

1	RUS	KHUSHTOV, ASLANBEK	096KGGR
2	GER	ENGLICH, MIRKO	096KGGR
3	**USA**	**WHEELER, ADAM**	096KGGR
3	KAZ	MAMBETOV, ASSET	096KGGR
5	CZE	SVEC, MAREK	096KGGR
5	KOR	HAN, TAE-YOUNG	096KGGR
7	LTU	EZERSKIS, MINDAUGAS	096KGGR
8	ALB	GURI, ELIS	096KGGR

WOMEN'S FREESTYLE 48 KG

1	CAN	HUYNH, CAROL	048KGF
2	JPN	ICHO, CHIHARU	048KGF
3	UKR	MELNIK, IRINA	048KGF
3	AZE	STADNIK, MARIYA	048KGF
5	**USA**	**CHUN, CLARISSA**	048KGF
5	KAZ	BAKATYUK, TATYANA	048KGF
7	FRA	BOUBRYEMM, VANESSA	048KGF
8	KOR	KIM, HYUNG-JOO	048KGF

WOMEN'S FREESTYLE 55 KG

1	JPN	YOSHIDA, SAORI	055KGF
2	CHN	XU, LI	055KGF
3	CAN	VERBEEK, TONYA	055KGF
3	COL	RENTERIA, JACKELINE	055KGF
5	ROM	PAVAL, ANA MARIA	055KGF
5	SWE	NERELL, IDA-THERES	055KGF
7	KAZ	SMIRNOVA, OLGA	055KGF
8	RUS	GOLTS, NATALYA	055KGF
9	**USA**	**VANDUSEN, MARCIE**	055KGF

WOMEN'S FREESTYLE 63 KG

1	JPN	ICHO, KAORI	063KGF
2	RUS	KARTASHOVA, ALENA	063KGF
3	**USA**	**MILLER, RANDI**	063KGF
3	KAZ	SHALYGINA, YELENA	063KGF
5	FRA	GOLLIOT, LISE	063KGF
5	CAN	DUGRENIER, MARTINE	063KGF
7	BUL	VASEVA, ELINA	063KGF
8	POL	MICHALIK, MONIKA	063KGF

WOMEN'S FREESTYLE 72 KG

1	CHN	WANG, JIAO	072KGF
2	BUL	ZLATEVA, STANKA	072KGF
3	JPN	HAMAGUCHI, KYOKO	072KGF
3	POL	WIESZCZEK, AGNIESKA	072KGF
5	**USA**	**BERNARD, ALI**	072KGF
5	ESP	UNDA, MAIDER	072KGF
7	GER	SCHAETZLE, ANITA	072KGF
8	BRA	CONCEICAO, ROSANGELA	072KGF

USOC BOARD OF DIRECTORS

Peter V. Ueberroth
USOC Chairman of the Board

Bob Bowlsby
USOC Board Member

Robert Ctvrtlik
USOC Board Member;
IOC Member;
First Vice President,
International

Error B. Davis
USOC Board Member

Anita L. DeFrantz
USOC Board Member;
IOC Member

James L. Easton
USOC Board Member;
IOC Member

John S. Hendricks
USOC Board Member

Jair K. Lynch
USOC Board Member

Mary McCagg
USOC Board Member

Michael P. Plant
USOC Board Member

Stephanie A. Streeter
USOC Board Member

Christopher DuPlanty
Board Liaison

PARALYMPIC GAMES

BEIJING 2008

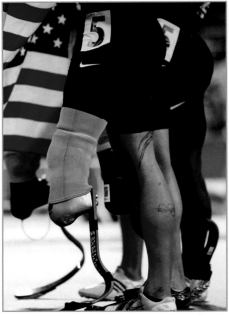

CHINA PHOTOS/GETTY IMAGES

PARALYMPIC GAMES | TABLE OF CONTENTS

INTRODUCTION TO THE PARALYMPIC GAMES

From a village in the middle of England, a simple idea has grown into a sporting event recognized the world over as the Paralympic Games. The Paralympic Games have come a long way in 60 years, evolving to a point where "Olympic Games" and "Paralympic Games" resonate much the same way with athletes, host cities, and spectators.

As U.S. wheelchair basketball player Matt Scott observed, "Some may think a kid growing up with a physical disability should find a new dream." The Paralympic Games have left that kind of thinking outdated.

It all started in 1948 in Stoke Mandeville, England. Sir Ludwig Guttmann could not have known where his efforts would someday lead when he organized a series of sporting events for World War II veterans with spinal cord injuries. He simply believed sports could serve as therapy for patients at Stoke Mandeville Hospital. Yet when competitors from the Netherlands joined them four years later, the international aspect of Guttmann's games took hold.

By 1960, when a complete program of Olympic-style games was staged in Rome, 400 athletes from 23 countries participated. And that was just the start. Beginning in 1988, in Seoul, in the summer and 1992, in Albertville, in the winter, Olympic and Paralympic athletes have performed in the same venues. By 2001, that arrangement was formalized as part of the bid process to host the Olympic Games. As of 2008 in Beijing, the Paralympic Games had grown to include more than 4,000 athletes from 140 countries.

The practice of staging the Paralympic Games in the same city as the Olympic Games has both raised the profile of the competition and helped validate the participants' status as world-class athletes.

One of the guiding principles of the Paralympic Games is "quality." The International Paralympic Committee (IPC) has designed the Paralympic Games to be elite, exciting, inspirational, and to promote fair play. They feature high-level competition by athletes dedicated to their sports.

Paralympic Games organizers always emphasize achievements rather than disabilities, which was the focus again when the Paralympic Hall of Fame inducted its first members in 2006. "We can only make progress if we emphasize that the athletes are at the center of everything we do," said IPC president Sir Phillip Craven. The Class of 2008 included Connie Hansen of Denmark (athletics), Claudia Hengst of Germany (swimming), Peter Homann of Australia (cycling), André Viger of Canada (athletics), and coach Kevin McIntosh of Australia (cycling).

Besides following the examples of these stars, Paralympic athletes now benefit from a scientific approach to their pursuits. In 1993, the IPC formed a sports science committee to research further development of sports for people with disabilities. The work covers physiology, psychology, biomechanics, performance analysis, nutrition, and sports technology.

And to help spread the word, a Paralympian Ambassadors Program was launched in February 2008, featuring 11 medalists from around the world, including U.S. stars Cheri Blauwet, Muffy Davis, and Chris Waddell.

Sixty years later, Sir Ludwig Guttmann would probably not recognize the Paralympic Games. Yet it all started with him, and some amazing athletes will be forever thankful.

FENG LI/GETTY IMAGES

ERIN POPOVICH

SWIMMING

Team USA swimmer Erin Popovich says she loves the Paralympic Games because they prove that appearances are misleading. She's not speaking of herself necessarily, but she is proof that being short and being fast in the pool are not mutually exclusive. Popovich won four more gold medals in Beijing in 2008, bringing her career total to 14. She's still only 23 years old, having first competed when she was 15. Popovich may not have gone seven-for-seven in gold medals in Beijing the way she did in Athens in 2004, but she still broke world records in the 200-meter individual medley and the 100 breaststroke, while earning four golds and two silvers. Because of a genetic disorder that restricted her growth, Popovich stands 4-foot-5, but she's a big figure in Paralympic swimming. While attending Colorado State, where she earned a degree in health and exercise science in 2007, Popovich practiced six days a week with the university swim team. It was an investment that paid off handsomely in Beijing.

CHANTAL PETITCLERC

CHANTAL PETITCLERC OF CANADA CROSSES THE FINISH LINE FIRST DURING THE WOMEN'S 800M -T54 FINAL | *ANDREW WONG/GETTY IMAGES*

ATHLETICS

Five-time Paralympian Chantal Petitclerc punctuated the end of her illustrious wheelchair-racing career by collecting five gold medals for the second straight Paralympic Games with victories in the 100, 200, 400, 800 and 1,500 meters in the T54-class events. With the five-gold repeat of her Athens Games performance in 2004, the 38-year-old—who said 2008 would be her final Paralympic Games—turned a two-bronze start at the 1992 Barcelona Paralympic Games into an overall haul of 21 medals, including 14 gold. Not bad for a woman who at age 18 used a homemade wheelchair in her inaugural race—and finished dead last. But love of the sport and the competition took hold. And in her final race in Beijing—the 1,500 meters—Petitclerc broke away from the pack with 300 meters remaining to triumph easily. Afterwards, she told the Canadian press: "I felt like it was a gift to finish it all alone. It was great."

CHANTAL PETITCLERC OF CANADA CELEBRATES AFTER WINNING THE FINAL OF THE WOMEN'S 800 METRE T54 | *NICOLAS ASFOURI/AFP/GETTY IMAGES*

JONAS JACOBSSON

JONAS JACOBSSON OF SWEDEN COMPETES IN THE MIXED R6-50M FREE RIFLE PRONE-SH1 FINAL | *CHINA PHOTOS/GETTY IMAGES*

SHOOTING

He's still relatively young at age 43, but Jonas Jacobsson is considering retiring from competitive shooting, which raises this question: Could they really stage the Paralympic Games without him? That's hard to imagine at the shooting venue, where the Beijing competition marked Jacobsson's eighth Paralympic Games. He started when he was 15, having been born in Sweden with a leg disability and grown up as the son of a shooting coach. The gold medals have flowed his way nonstop ever since. Three more golds in Beijing increased his career total to 16, among his 25 medals in all. Once a soccer goalkeeper and a table tennis expert as a child, the left-handed shooter eventually found his true niche on the range. He now works for the Swedish Association of Sports for the Disabled. The bachelor was recently asked if he plans to marry anytime soon and he admitted to having "a target." An interesting choice of words.

JONAS JACOBSSON OF SWEDEN WAITS FOR HIS TURN IN THE MIXED R6-50M FREE RIFLE PRONE SH1 QUALIFICATION ROUND | *CHINA PHOTOS/GETTY IMAGES*

NATALIE DU TOIT

NATALIE DU TOIT OF SOUTH AFRICA ON HER WAY TO GOLD IN THE 200M MEDLEY SM9 FINAL | *DUIF DU TOIT/GALLO IMAGES/GETTY IMAGES*

SWIMMING

Natalie du Toit had already made history in Beijing in August as a Paralympic athlete competing in the Olympic Games, but she didn't stop there. She came back for more in September and went five-for-five in her attempts at gold medals. Having finished 16th among 25 contestants in the Olympic Games women's 10K open-water swim, du Toit enjoyed the relative comfort of the Water Cube a few weeks later. She won gold in three free-style races (50, 100, and 400 meters), plus the 200 individual medley and the 100 butterfly. She carried South Africa's flag in the Opening Ceremony of both the Olympic and the Paralympic Games and lived up to her inspirational story, seven years after being struck by a car and having her left leg amputated below the knee. The year before her accident, she had barely missed qualifying for the Olympic Games. Now, du Toit just keeps coming back, with full intentions of competing in both sets of Games in London in 2012.

NATALIE DU TOIT OF SOUTH AFRICA PREPARES HERSELF MENTALLY BEFORE ONE OF HER RACES | *DUIF DU TOIT /GALLO IMAGES/GETTY IMAGES*

OSCAR PISTORIUS

OSCAR PISTORIUS OF SOUTH AFRICA BREAKS AWAY FROM THE PACK TO WIN ONE OF HIS THREE GOLD MEDALS IN THE MEN'S 200M -T44 | *GALLO IMAGES/GETTY IMAGES*

ATHLETICS

Dubbed "Blade Runner" and billed as "the fastest man on no legs," South Africa sprinter Oscar Pistorius is the Paralympic Games equivalent to Olympic Games counterpart Usain Bolt. In fact, Pistorius had plans to share the Jamaican's stage. Running on carbon-fiber artificial legs called "Cheetah Flex-Foot," Pistorius hoped to run in the Beijing Olympic Games, but he missed the qualifying times and a slot as a relay-squad member. Instead, he ran in the Paralympic Games and did his best Bolt imitation, setting a Paralympic record in the 100 meters with a time of 11.16 seconds in a heat en route to the gold. He then won the 200 with another Paralympic-best time of 21.67, and broke the world record, while earning a third gold with a 47.49 time in the 400. After undergoing double amputation at 11 months, Pistorius grew up competing in rugby, water polo, tennis, and wrestling before turning to running. The 21-year-old still has his eyes focused on the Olympic Games and hopes to qualify for the 2012 Games in London.

OSCAR PISTORIUS OF SOUTH AFRICA CELEBRATES HIS GOLD MEDAL AND WORLD RECORD IN THE 400M T44 | *DUIF DU TOIT/GALLO IMAGES/GETTY IMAGES*

TEAM USA RUGBY

JOEL WILMOTH AND HIS TEAMMATES SING THE NATIONAL ANTHEM AFTER DEFEATING AUSTRALIA IN THE FINAL OF WHEELCHAIR RUGBY | *JAMIE MCDONALD/GETTY IMAGES*

WHEELCHAIR RUGBY

After a powerhouse United States team suffered a semifinal loss four years ago, in Athens, and ended up with a bronze medal, they resolved to seek redemption in Beijing in 2008. No, we're not talking about the men's basketball team. This was Team USA's wheelchair rugby squad. The Americans had never lost a Paralympic Games contest before falling to Canada in the 2004 Athens semifinals. In Beijing, Team USA returned to dominance, winning all five games. Their run included avenging the '04 loss by beating Canada in group play, edging Great Britain in the semis, and downing Australia 53-44 in the gold-medal championship. "We have trained and prepared for this since the day we left Athens four years ago," said Andy Cohn, one of the six returnees on the 11-man roster. "Everyone on this team is so close and we did this together, as a group." Redemption accomplished.

BRYAN KIRKLAND FIGHTS OFF A DEFENDER DURINGA WHEELCHAIR RUGBY MATCH AGAINST JAPAN | *CHINA PHOTOS/GETTY IMAGES*

DANCERS PERFORM AMONG A SEA OF FOG AND LIGHT | *GUANG NIU/GETTY IMAGEST*

OPENING CEREMONY

Thousands of performers and millions of lights, athletes and nations, flags and fireworks, oaths and anthems, all in a sold-out National Stadium—the parallels between the September 6 Beijing Paralympic Games Opening Ceremony and its Olympic Games counterpart from a month earlier were obvious. But there was one noticeable difference: Unlike the Olympians, whose entrance comes toward the end of the program, more than 4,200 Paralympians representing 148 nations entered soon after the start of the performance, allowing the athletes to be part of their own festivities and watch the Opening Ceremony. Following the Paralympic Games theme of "Transcendence, Equality, and Integration," the Opening Ceremony underscored the harmony between humankind and nature. They began with a sunbird—an important icon in Chinese culture—descending from, appropriately enough, a stadium called the Bird's Nest and inspiring a visually impaired man to break out into song. More than 2,000 children, between the ages of 8 and 12, dressed as frogs, ducks, seagulls, and other wildlife characters wowed the audience and the athletes, as did the 320 hearing-impaired young women dancing in the "Hello, Stars" segment, who moved not to the beat of audible sounds but the instructions of 49 sign-language teachers. Another touching moment came when a troupe of ballerinas surrounded an 11-year-old Chinese girl and Szechuan earthquake victim whose own dreams of becoming a ballet dancer were derailed when her left leg was amputated.

Similar to the Opening Ceremony of a few weeks before, the cauldron above National Stadium was ignited by a Chinese athlete rising to great heights. This time, the torch's flame was carried by wheelchair-bound Hou Bin, who with strength and grace, slowly pulled himself up a rope to do the evening's final honors.

USA ATHLETES PARADE DURING THE OPENING CEREMONY OF THE 2008 BEIJING PARALYMPIC GAMES | *FREDERIC J. BROWN/AFP/GETTY IMAGES*

DANCERS SURROUND 11-YEAR-OLD CHINESE GIRL AND SZECHUAN EARTHQUAKE VICTIM |
CHINA PHOTOS/GETTY IMAGES

CHINESE SWIMMER WU YUNHU CARRIES THE TORCH IN THE NATIONAL STADIUM |
PETER PARKS/AFP/GETTY IMAGES

PERFORMERS DURING THE OPENING CEREMONY SHARE THE UNDERLYING MESSAGE THAT ALL LIFE
HAS VALUE AND DIGNITY | *LIU JIN/AFP/GETTY IMAGES*

LINDSEY CARMICHAEL OF THE U.S. RELEASES AN ARROW ON HER WAY TO WINNING THE BRONZE
MEDAL OF THE WOMEN'S INDIVIDUAL RECURVE - STANDING | *ANDREW WONG/GETTY IMAGES*

SIGHTING THE NEXT TARGET | *JEFF FABRY DID
NOT HAVE MUCH TIME TO DWELL ON A CLOSE
SEMIFINAL LOSS IN THE ARCHERY COMPETI-*
tion at the Paralympic Games. Apparently, that was a good thing. Only five minutes after missing his opportunity for a gold medal, the American archer was summoned to his bronze medal
match, where he defeated Osmo Kinnunen of Finland 111-101. "The gold will have to wait four
more years," Fabry said. "I am overwhelmed by it all, but I am happy to have won the bronze."

Archery events in the Paralympic Games include divisions for both standing contestants and
wheelchair users. Fabry competed in the men's individual compound bow event's W1 category
for wheelchair users with upper-limb limitations. He broke a Paralympic Games record with a
score of 113 in the first round.

U.S. archer Lindsay Carmichael also started impressively and finished well. She defeated reigning gold medalist Wang Yangshong of China in the first round and reached the semifinals before losing to top-ranked Lee Hwa-Sook of Korea. Carmichael came back with a bronze medal victory over Malgorzata Olejnik of Poland in the women's recurve bow competition for standing contestants.

Overall, China won the majority of archery medals, with seven to Korea's three. China's 19-year-old Cheng Changjie was among the stars, winning the men's individual recurve W2 event.

A big breakthrough came from Baatarjav Dambadondog in the men's individual recurve standing event. He became the first athlete from Mongolia to win a Paralympic gold medal, claiming the gold with a 94-90 victory over Fabrice Meunier of France.

ERIC BENNETT OF THE UNITED STATES COMPETES IN THE MEN'S INDIVIDUAL COMPOUND-OPEN ARCHERY EVENT | *CHINA PHOTOS/GETTY IMAGES*

JEFF FABRY OF USA USES HIS MOUTH TO LAUNCH HIS SHOT PRIOR TO WINNING THE BRONZE MEDAL IN THE MEN'S INDIVIDUAL COMPOUND ARCHERY EVENT | *STR/AFP/GETTY IMAGES*

LEX GILLETTE OF THE UNITED STATES AND HIS GUIDE COMPETE IN THE
MEN'S 200M T11 DIVISION | *MARK KOLBE/GETTY IMAGES*

RIGHT ON TRACK | *OSCAR PISTORIUS DID HIS
BEST USAIN BOLT IMPRESSION ON THE SAME
NATIONAL STADIUM TRACK, WINNING THREE*
golds in the 100-, 200-, and 400-meter events, while setting Paralympic Games records in
each and breaking his own world record in the 400. But other athletes can boast successes
equally impressive, including wheelchair racer Chantal Petitclerc of Canada, with her second
consecutive five-gold Games, and Team USA's Jeremy Campbell, who posted a world-record
performance in the grueling five-event pentathlon.

International competition for disabled athletes dates back to 1952 when returning WWII veterans began racing in wheelchairs. Athletics has been on the program of the Paralympic Games
since its 1960 inception. It continues to be a marquee event. In Beijing, there were 1041
athletes, a quarter of all 2008 Paralympic athletes, competing in 160 events.

China collected a Paralympic Games-best 77 medals, including 31 gold. Team USA garnered
28 total, with nine gold—two medals better than 2004.

Classifications for athletic events are designated by a letter and a number: T for track, F for field, and P for pentathlon. The number represents disability type and extent: 11–13 for the visually impaired, 32–38 for those with cerebral palsy, 42–46 for amputees, and 51–58 for spinal cord disabilities.

Dubbed "Blade Runner" and billed as "the fastest man on no legs" (he competes on carbon-fiber artificial legs called "Cheetah Flex-Foot"), the 21-year-old Pistorius had hopes of running in the Beijing Olympic Games (he's now eyeing 2012). Competing instead in the Paralympic Games' T44 class, he ran the 100 in 11.17 seconds (his record 11.16 came in qualifying), the 200 in 21.67, and the 400 in 47.49. He edged out two Americans in his races—Jerome Singleton was just .03 seconds behind in the 100 and settled for the silver, while Jim Bob Bizzell, who had lost a leg in a motorcycle accident just 17 months earlier, placed second in the 200 and 400 and was credited with T44 world-record times, since Pistorius' actual designation is T43.

Several athletes duplicated Pistorius' three-gold efforts, but Petitclerc—who lost the use of her legs in an accident at age 13—nearly doubled his total, with five T54 golds in the 100 through 1,500 distances. Beginning with a pair of 1992 Barcelona bronzes, the 38-year-old concluded her storied Paralympic Games career in Beijing with 21 total Olympic medals, 14 of which are gold.

Leading a one, two U.S. finish with teammate Jeff Skiba over three-time pentathlon champion Urs Kolly of Switzerland, Campbell cruised through the five events—long jump, shot put, 100 meters, discus, 400 meters—to the P44 gold and the world record. He later claimed the F44 discus gold for good measure. Skiba added a gold and upped his previous world mark to 2.11 meters in the F44/46 high jump. Also, Josiah Jamison captured the T12 100 gold, and Josh George added a gold and a silver in the T53 100 and 800 meters, respectively. Bizzell and Singleton joined bronze medalists Brian Frasure and Casey Tibbs to win the T42–46 4x100 relay.

Jessica Galli led the Team USA women with a gold and three silvers in the T53 sprint and mid-distance races and, with Tatyana McFadden, Amanda McGrory, and Anjali Forber-Pratt took bronze in the T53-54 4x100 relay. The 19-year-old McFadden added three silvers in T54, while McGrory collected a bronze in the 800m, a marathon silver, and a 5K gold. She won the gold on a re-race after a multi-chair crash scuttled the original results. Also, April Holmes rallied, after a fall and five stitches, to win the gold in the 100m.

TATYANA MCFADDEN OF THE UNITED STATES COMPETES IN THE WOMEN'S 100M
T54 ROUND | *CHINA PHOTOS/GETTY IMAGES*

SCOT SEVERN OF THE USA LAUNCHES THE SHOT PUT IN THE F53/54 DIVISION |
JAMIE MCDONALD/GETTY IMAGES

**MEN'S PENTATHLON SILVER AND GOLD MEDALISTS JEFF SKIBA AND JEREMY CAMPBELL OF THE US
POSE WITH BRONZE MEDALIST URS KOLLY OF SWITZERLAND |** *CHRIS HYDE/GETTY IMAGES*

APRIL HOLMES OF THE UNITED STATES (C) CROSSES THE FINISH LINE AHEAD OF ANDREA SCHERNEY OF AUSTRIA (L) AND KATRIN GREEN OF GERMANY (R) TO WIN THE FINAL OF THE WOMEN'S 100M -T44 | *ANDREW WONG/GETTY IMAGES*

JEREMY CAMPBELL OF THE UNITED STATES COMES IN FOR A LANDING IN THE LONG JUMP OF THE MEN'S PENTATHLON P44 | *MARK KOLBE/GETTY IMAGES*

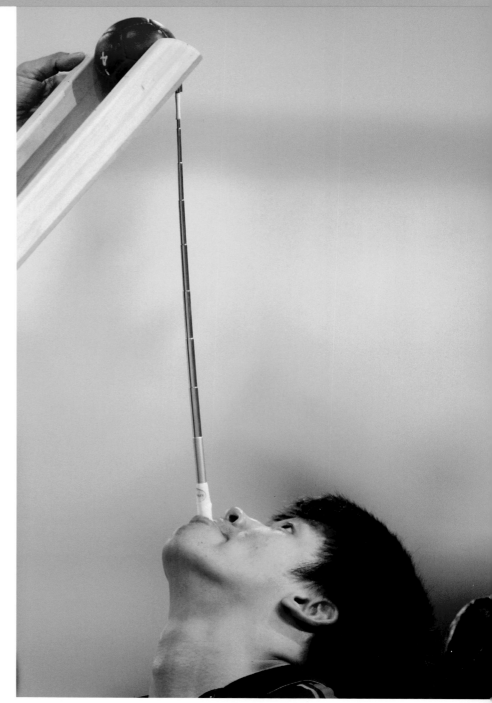

HO-WON JEONG OF KOREA COMPETES IN THE BRONZE MEDAL BC3 BOCCIA MATCH AGAINST
MARIO PEIXOTO OF POLAND | *MARK KOLBE/GETTY IMAGES*

SIGHTING THE NEXT TARGET | *WINNING
A MEDAL IS NOT THE ONLY WAY TO GAUGE
ACHIEVEMENT IN THE PARALYMPIC GAMES.*
Sometimes, it is simply a matter of winning a point. In the boccia competition in Beijing, Team
USA contestant Timothy "T J" Hawker lost 9-1 to Francisco Javier Beltran of Spain in the third
round. However, Hawker did succeed in becoming the first opponent to score a point against
Beltran, showing a desire to compete that has characterized his life.

Paralympic boccia, stemming from an ancient sport, is for athletes with cerebral palsy or related
neurological conditions. On a long, narrow court, they throw or bowl balls in an attempt to land
them close to the target ball, or "jack."

When he first started playing as a youngster, Hawker could barely hold the ball. Yet he reached the Paralympic Games level in a sport the IPC describes as a "test of muscle control and accuracy, requiring high focus and concentration."

Great Britain's Nigel Murray, Dan Bentley, and David Smith demonstrated those traits in an 8-4 win over Portugal for the team gold medal in the highlight of the mixed-gender competition staged in the Fencing Hall on the Olympic Green. With their win, they kept Portugal's Joao Paulo Fernandes from claiming both the individual and team gold for the second time. Fernandes had defeated teammate Antonio Marques for the individual title.

AN ATHLETE FOLLOWS HIS SHOT DURING A TRAINING SESSION FOR BOCCIA AT THE FENCING HALL OF THE NATIONAL INDOOR STADIUM | *FREDERIC J. BROWN/AFP/GETTY IMAGES*

NIGEL MURRAY OF GREAT BRITAIN COMPETES IN THE MIXED TEAM - BC1-2 SEMIFINAL 1 BOCCIA MATCH BETWEEN CHINA AND GREAT BRITAIN | *CHINA PHOTOS/GETTY IMAGES*

OZ SANCHEZ OF USA (FRONT) COMPETES IN THE MEN'S ROAD RACE (HC C) ON
HIS WAY TO ONE OF HIS TWO MEDALS | *FENG LI/GETTY IMAGES*

NIFTY 50S | ONE COULD CALL THE DOUBLE-GOLD
EFFORTS OF SWITZERLAND'S HEINZ FRIE AND
TEAM USA'S BARBARA BUCHAN "VINTAGE
performances," since both have passed the 50-year mark. Yet, each out-pedaled younger competitors
to win a pair of Paralympic titles apiece. Frie claimed the men's HC B road time trial and road
race events, and Buchan captured the gold medals in the women's LC 3-4/CP 3 track time trial
and LC 1-2/CP 4 track pursuit. Buchan led a strong USA Team that ranked second in cycling's
medal count with five golds and 14 medals overall.

Cycling has been part of the Paralympic Games for two decades, with road cycling debuting in
1988 and track added eight years later. Beijing's 44 events were broken down by gender and
classifications, including HC for hand cycles, CP for cerebral palsy, LC for locomotor disabilities,

and B&VI for the blind and visually impaired. The track events were contested at the Laoshan Velodrome, while the road events were held in the Ming Tombs area, where the triathlon's cycling events had taken place a few weeks earlier in the Olympic Games.

Great Britain set the pace with 16 golds and 20 total medals, including 12 titles in the 21 track events. Several Brits enjoyed double dipping in the gold-medal well, with Darren Kenny alone accounting for a quarter of his country's golds in LC classes of the road race, track pursuit, track time trial, and track team sprint.

American multiple medalists included Oz Sanchez with a gold and a bronze and Alejandro Albor with a silver and a bronze in the two HC C road events. Karissa Whitsell and pilot Mackenzie Woodring won a full set—gold, silver, and bronze—of B&VI medals. Jennifer Schuble took a gold and two silver in LC/CP road and track events.

KARISSA WHITSELL AND MACKENZIE WOODRING OF USA WINS THE SILVER IN THE ROAD CYCLING WOMEN'S ROAD RACE | *FENG LI/GETTY IMAGES*

ALLISON JONES (L) AND BARBARA BUCHAN (R) OF USA POSE WITH THEIR SILVER AND GOLD MEDALS FROM THE WOMEN'S TIME TRIAL (LC 3/LC 4/CP 3) | *FENG LI/GETTY IMAGES*

LYNN SEIDEMANN OF THE UNITED STATES COMPETES WITH HORSE
RHETT IN THE TEAM TEST | *GETTY IMAGES*

MULTI-MEDAL WINNERS | *A NUMBER OF MEDALISTS IN THE 11 EQUESTRIAN EVENTS CONTESTED AT THE HONG KONG EQUESTRIAN CENTER MADE* many happy returns to the podium, with eight riders claiming two medals each and another half dozen winning three medals each. Leading them was Great Britain's Lee Pearson, whose magic number was "three" for the "third straight" Paralympic Games.

The Paralympic Games feature individual championship and freestyle dressage events in five disability classifications, as well as a team overall event. Visually impaired riders are allowed "callers" positioned around the arena, with the most experienced riders needing only one.

For the third time in as many Paralympic Games, Pearson collected three golds: the Ib class individual championship, the freestyle and the team event, the latter being the fourth straight team gold for Great Britain. In leading Great Britain's 10-medal haul, Pearson—who suffers from arthrogryposis, a rare disorder affecting muscles and joints—achieved his nine career golds on three different horses, riding "Gentleman" in Beijing, the first Paralympic Games that didn't require riders to use host-city mounts.

Other double-gold individual winners included Germany's Hannelore Brenner on "Women of the World" in the III class and South Africa's Philippa Johnson on "Benedict" in the IV. Brenner picked up a third medal by helping Germany to the team silver.

Of the three Team USA riders, Lynn Seidemann's ninth-place finish in Ib class was an American best in Beijing. She rode "Rhett" after just two months training together. The mother of two, who was left a paraplegic after a skiing accident, had won two Paralympic silver medals previously—in wheelchair tennis doubles in 1992 and in equestrian in Athens in 2004.

GERMANY'S BETTINA EISTEL ON FABULEUX 5 COMPETES IN THE INDIVIDUAL
FREESTYLE TEST GRADE III | *MIKE CLARKE/AFP/GETTY IMAGES*

GOLDEN GOALS | *TEAM USA'S GOALBALL GOLD-MEDAL DROUGHT HAD GONE LONG ENOUGH, NEARLY A QUARTER-CENTURY HAD PASSED SINCE* the Americans swept the men's and women's gold at the Los Angeles 1984 Paralympic Games. The women on Team USA decided that was long enough, bringing an end to the drought with a 6-5 victory over host China in the gold-medal match at the Beijing Institute of Technology Gymnasium.

Invented in 1946 to help blind World War II veterans with physical and social rehabilitation, goalball was added to the Paralympic Games program in 1976. In goalball, a game for visually impaired athletes (the partially sighted wear blindfolds to ensure equality), two teams of three players attempt to throw the ball over the goal line at the opposite end of the court. Throwing rules include that the ball must touch the floor on one's own half of the court, the ball must be thrown or passed within eight seconds of possession, and no player can attempt more than two consecutive throws.

With a preliminary-pool record of four wins, one loss, and two draws, Team USA's women downed Denmark 4-3 in the medal round semifinals and looked to avenge their sole loss to China in the gold-medal match. With the lead changing five times, Asya Miller scored Team USA's game-winning goal with a devastating crosscourt throw with just 49 seconds remaining.

After winning two of five preliminary group games, Team USA's men advanced to the medal round seeded sixth and promptly upset third-seeded Slovenia 6-3. But the USA Team fell 4-0 to host China in the semifinals and 5-2 to Sweden in the bronze-medal match to finish just shy of a medal.

TYLER MERREN TAKES A SHOT AGAINST BRAZIL IN GOALBALL | *CHINA PHOTOS/GETTY IMAGES*

GOALBALL PLAYERS OF THE UNITED STATES BLOCK A SHOT BY CHINA | *CHINA PHOTOS/GETTY IMAGES*

JORDAN MOUTON OF THE USA (BLUE) COMPETES IN A JUDO -70KG MATCH AGAINST NIKO-
LETT SZABO OF HUNGARY | *JAMIE MCDONALD/GETTY IMAGES*

GOING FOURTH | THE PARALYMPIC GAMES JUDO COMPETITION FEATURED TWO ATHLETES TRYING FOR THEIR FOURTH CONSECUTIVE GOLD MEDALS

Brazil's Antonio Tenorio Silva succeeded, while Japan's Fujimoto Satoshi fell short.

Judo, in the Paralympic Games, is for visually impaired athletes, who grapple with recognized moves and holds. The only differences from the Olympic Games version are that athletes are allowed to have contact with their opponent before the match begins, and the mats have different textures to indicate competition areas and zones. The sport tests strength, balance, touch, sensitivity, and instinct.

Silva defeated Karim Sardarov of Azerbaijan for his fourth gold in the men's –100kg event. Algeria's Sidali Lamri prevented Satoshi from collecting his fourth gold in the –66kg event. Women first competed in judo in the Athens Paralympic Games in 2004, and Carmen Herrera of Spain repeated her title in the –70kg division.

Team USA's most inspiring story came from a newcomer. Greg De Wall had less than three years of competitive experience when he arrived in Beijing, but a series of comebacks earned him a bronze medal. He secured the medal opportunity by going through the repechage after losing to eventual silver medalist Song Wang of China. De Wall trailed in the bronze-medal match against Jung Min-Park of Korea but took the victory in the end.

ANDRE WATSON OF THE USA (BLUE) COMPETES IN A JUDO -90KG MATCH AGAINST
MESSAOUD NINE OF ALGERIA | *JAMIE MCDONALD/GETTY IMAGES*

JORDAN MOUTON OF THE USA (BLUE) COMPETES IN A JUDO -70KG MATCH AGAINST MARIA DEL CAR-
MEN HERRERA OF SPAIN | *JAMIE MCDONALD/GETTY IMAGES*

KENJI OGA OF JAPAN (WHITE) AND SCOTT JONES OF THE UNITED STATES COMPETE IN A MEN'S -81KG
PRELIMINARY JUDO MATCH | *ANDREW WONG/GETTY IMAGES*

RUEL ISHAKU OF NIGERIA CELEBRATES AFTER BREAKING A PARALYMPIC AND WORLD RECORD
BY LIFTING 169KG IN THE MEN'S 48KG DIVISION | *CHIEN-MIN CHUNG/GETTY IMAGES*

BROKEN RECORDS | POWERLIFTING COMPETITION SOARED SKY HIGH AT THE BEIJING UNIVERSITY OF AERONAUTICS & ASTRONAUTICS GYMNASIUM amid a flurry of world and Paralympic records—some being repeatedly broken by competitors in the same weight class or by individuals in successive lifts.

Dating back to 1964 in Tokyo at the second Paralympic Games, the sport was originally called "weightlifting" and involved only participants with spinal cord injuries. Since then, the sport has been renamed and opened to any disabled athlete.

Extended on a specially designed bench, powerlifters keep their head, trunk, buttocks, legs, and both heels in contact with the bench, with spotters allowed to help lower the weight bar to the chest. After holding the bar motionless momentarily, the lifter bar presses the bar up and away to full extension.

Team USA fielded two lifters among the 300 total in the 10 weight classes per gender: Anderson Wise in the men's 67.5 kilogram class and Mary Stack in the women's 82.5 kg division.

Host China collected 14 medals overall, including nine gold, while Egypt was second in the medal haul with four gold and 10 total medals. Highlights included China's Qi Dong and Nigeria's Obioma Daleth Aligekwe breaking world and Paralympic marks back and forth in the men's 100kg class before Qi topped out at 247.5kg to claim the gold. Also, 31-year-old Kazem Rajabi Golojeh—the youngest lifter in the men's +100 kg class—set new standards with a lift of 265kg. Egypt's Heba Said Ahmed improved the world record by 12 kilograms and the Paralympic Games mark by an astounding 20 kilograms with her best lift of 155 in the women's 82.5 kg class. Not to be outdone, Egypt's Sherif Othman hefted nearly four times his weight with a record-breaking lift of 202.5 in the men's 56kg class.

RAE MORSHEDI OF EGYPT COMPLETES IN THE POWERLIFTING WOMEN'S - 67.50 KG FINAL | *FENG LI/GETTY IMAGES*

KEUM-JONG JUNG OF KOREA EXERTS ALL HIS STRENGTH TO WIN THE BRONZE MEDAL IN THE MEN'S -56 KG DIVISION | *JAMIE MCDONALD/GETTY IMAGES*

ROWERS FROM TEAM USA RELAX IN THE BOAT HOUSE | *JAMIE MCDONALD/GETTY IMAGES*

ALL IN A ROW | *ROWING WAS NEW TO THE PARALYMPIC GAMES IN 2008, AND THE ATHLETES WERE EAGER TO HIT THE WATER AT SHUNYI*

Park. That was especially true for Team USA rower Laura Schwanger, who was determined to set an example as a breast cancer survivor making a comeback in more ways than one.

While dealing with multiple sclerosis, Schwanger became a three-time Paralympic Games star by winning 11 medals, including four golds, in athletics before retiring in 1996. Or so she thought. Twelve years later, nearing age 50, Schwanger was back in the Paralympic Games in the women's single sculls race.

A strong finish produced her 12th Paralympic medal (bronze), as Schwanger went from fifth to third in the last 200 meters—though nobody could catch Great Britain's Helene Raynsford, who won the gold by 12 seconds. "The competition was incredibly tough. I am just happy to win a medal," Schwanger said.

Team USA's mixed four with coxswain team was made up of Simona Chin, Jamie Dean, Jesse Karmazin, Tracy Tackett, and Emma Preuschl—who was determined to finish first. "I expected to win gold, but it's hard to get there," said Preuschl, promising to return for London in 2012. Her team almost got there in Beijing, overtaking Great Britain down the stretch, but finishing behind Italy to take the silver medal.

Overall, it was a good showing for Team USA and a nice Paralympic Games debut for a sport that has come a long way since 1975, when adaptive rowing was initiated in several countries.

LAURA SCHWANGER OF USA REACHES THE FINISH LINE IN THE ROWING
WOMEN'S SINGLE SCULLS FINAL | *FENG LI/GETTY IMAGES*

SCOTT BROWN AND ANGELA MADSEN OF USA CELEBRATE AFTER WINNING THE ROWING MIXED
DOUBLE SCULLS - TA FINA B | *FENG LI/GETTY IMAGES*

EMMA PREUSCHL, TRACY TACKETT, JESSE KARMAZIN, JAMIE DEAN AND SIMONA CHIN OF USA CEL-
EBRATE THEIR SILVER MEDAL IN THE ROWING MIXED COXED FOUR - LTA | *FENG LI/GETTY IMAGES*

NICK SCANDONE AND MAUREEN MCKINNON-TUCKER OF THE UNITED STATES COMPETE IN THE
2P KEELBOAT SAILING EVENT | *CHIEN-MIN CHUNG/GETTY IMAGES*

U.S. FIRSTS | THE UNITED STATES TANDEM OF NICK SCANDONE AND MAUREEN MCKINNON-TUCKER ENJOYED A COUPLE OF AMERICAN firsts after swamping the two-person keelboat competition. The two are the first U.S. sailors to ever claim Paralympic gold, and McKinnon-Tucker is the first woman to medal in the history of the Paralympic Sailing Regatta. And it all came in the Paralympic Games debut of SKUD 18 competition.

Sailing and the Paralympic Games first appeared together in 1992 in Spain, when the World Disabled Championships were conducted simultaneously with – but not part of – the Barcelona Paralympic Games. Sailing was an exhibition sport in 1996 and was added as a medal event in 2000. In China, the two-person keelboat (SKUD 18) event joined the single-person (2.4mR) and three-person (Sonar) keelboat events, with all three competitions hampered by the light and shifty winds along Qingdao's Fushan Bay.

A sailor since childhood with Olympic aspirations, Scandone – who is in the advanced stages of Lou Gehrig's disease – teamed with McKinnon-Tucker, who cut her Paralympic teeth four years earlier as part of the U.S. Sonar trio. The twosome placed first in five of the races, clinching SKUD18 gold with two races still remaining.

First-time Paralympian John Ruf claimed the bronze in the tight 2.4mR class, behind training partner and gold medalist Paul Tingley of Canada. 2004 gold medalist Damien Sequin, of France, settled for the silver. The event's top seven finishers all finished within single-digit points of each other.

The German crew of Jens Kroker, Robert Prem and Seigmund Mainka won the three-person keelboat gold after points leader France failed to finish the final race – its boat's jib ripped on the forestay – and settled for the silver.

THE AMERICAN TEAM OF RICK DOERR, TIM ANGLE AND BILL DONOHUE COMPETES
IN THE 3P KEELBOAT SAILING | *CHIEN-MIN CHUNG/GETTY IMAGES*

MAUREEN MCKINNON-TUCKER AND NICK SCANDONE OF USA ACCEPT THEIR GOLD MEDAL IN THE
SKUD18 SAILING EVENT | *CHIEN-MIN CHUNG/GETTY IMAGES*

JOHN RUF OF THE UNITED STATES COMPETES IN THE 2.4MR SAILING EVENT AT QINGDAO
OLYMPIC SAILING CENTRE | *GETTY IMAGES*

VALERIY PONOMARENKO OF RUSSIA COMPETES IN THE MIXED P4-50M FREE PISTOL-SH1
FINAL SHOOTING COMPETITION | *CHINA PHOTOS/GETTY IMAGES*

FIRING AHEAD | *MIKE DICKEY FOUND OUT JUST HOW DEMANDING THE SHOOTING COMPETITION IN THE PARALYMPIC GAMES CAN BE. THE ONLY*
Team USA men's shooter in Beijing, Dickey failed to advance to the afternoon session of the men's R3 10-meter air rifle prone event in his first Paralympic Games. "I'll use this performance as motivation for the future," said Dickey, who had to take some consolation in knowing the level of competition was so high that not even the legendary Jonas Jacobsson of Sweden advanced in that division.

Otherwise, Jacobsson performed at his usual level in the Beijing Shooting Range Hall. In his eighth Paralympic Games at age 43, Jacobsson won three more gold medals, giving him 16 in his career. He competes in the SH1 classification for athletes who can support the weight of the firearm; SH2 contestants use a shooting stand.

Another legendary figure in the sport narrowly missed another medal. Australia's Libby Kosmala, 66, first competed in the Paralympic Games in 1968. In Beijing, she finished fourth in her air rifle event.

Overall, Korea ruled the shooting venue by winning nine medals, including four golds. China's seven medals included one gold, and Russia's six medals included two golds. Korea's star was Lee Ji-Seok, who won two gold medals in men's air rifle events in the SH2 classification. Zhang Cuiping led China's effort by winning two golds in her first Paralympic Games.

Isabel Newstead was missed in Beijing. She died in 2007 at age 51, amid preparation for her eighth Paralympic Games. Having competed in athletics, shooting, and swimming, she had won her ninth career gold medal in the 2004 Paralympic Games air pistol event.

MARTELLA ANTONIO (L) OF ITALY AND SERGEY MALYSHEV OF RUSSIA COMPETE IN THE MIXED P3-25M SPORT PISTOL-SH1 FINAL | *CHINA PHOTOS/GETTY IMAGES*

DANIELLE FONG OF THE US COMPETES IN THE WOMEN'S R2-10M AIR RIFLE STANDING SH1 QUALIFICATION | *ANDREW WONG/GETTY IMAGES*

SABAHUDIN DELALIC (#11) OF BOSNIA & HERZEGOVINA SETS THE BALL FOR HIS TEAMMATE
DURING A MATCH WITH IRAN | *GUANG NIU/GETTY IMAGES*

SITTING PRETTY | EXPECTED TO COMPETE FOR THE BEIJING PARALYMPICS GAMES SITTING VOLLEYBALL BRONZE AT BEST, TEAM USA'S women decided to set their sights on a more precious medal. The American women kept their eyes on that prize, logging a rare upset against the Netherlands in the semifinals to advance to the gold-medal match against defending champion China. They took silver—the team's best-ever finish since the sport made it on the Paralympic Games program in 1980.

The women of Team USA went 2-1 in preliminary group play—their only loss being to China—and advanced to the four-team semifinals to face the Netherlands in a repeat pairing from the Athens Games semis. In a back-and-forth, five-set match that lasted a minute shy of two hours in the China Agricultural University Gymnasium, the Americans prevailed to make a first-ever trip to the gold-medal championship. "I have been playing for five years, and we have never beat them [the Dutch] in an official competition," said USA Team captain Brenda Maymon. "We could never get the job done, but we finally did it!"

The Americans couldn't unseat the Chinese, who swept Team USA in straight sets and claimed their second straight Paralympic gold. "Playing the defending gold-medal team in their home country—that is a once-in-a-lifetime opportunity," said Team USA assistant coach Denise Van De Walle. "We have improved a lot and we've come so far, but we were simply outplayed today."

The Netherlands downed Slovenia for the women's bronze, while the Iranian men's team improved on its Athens Games silver by not dropping a set en route to its fifth Paralympic sitting volleyball gold. Bosnia and Herzegovina took the silver and Russia the bronze.

GINA MCWILLIAMS AND NICHOLE MILLAGE OF THE USA TRY AND BLOCK A SPIKE DURING THE GOLD MEDAL MATCH AGAINST CHINA | *ADAM PRETTY/GETTY IMAGES*

KATIE HOLLOWAY OF THE UNITED STATES PASSES THE BALL DURING THE GOLD MEDAL MATCH AGAINST CHINA | *ADAM PRETTY/GETTY IMAGES*

DAVID CLARKE (L) OF GREAT BRITAIN AND CHINA'S CHEN SHANYONG (#3) FIGHT FOR
A BALL IN A FIVE-A-SIDE SOCCER MATCH | *GUANG NIU/GETTY IMAGES*

GOLDEN DEFENSES | *"FAMILIAR FACES, FAMILIAR PLACES" SERVED AS THE THEME FOR THE TWO BEIJING PARALYMPICS GAMES SOCCER* tournaments as Ukraine successfully defended its 2004 Games gold medal in the 7-a-side event, and Brazil returned to the medal podium's top spot in the 5-a-side competition.

The United States did not field a squad in either the six-team 5-a-side tournament or the eight team 7-a-side event, both of which were men's competitions contested at the Olympic Green Hockey Field.

Part of the Paralympic Games program since 1984, the 7-a-side soccer event is for athletes with cerebral palsy. The sport has a few rules that are different from traditional soccer, including no offside calls and athletes may do one-handed throw-ins and roll-ins.

Ukrainian captain Volodymyr Antonyuk scored twice in added time in the 2-1 gold-medal victory over Russia, which came to Beijing having won the silver in Atlanta, the gold in Sydney, and the bronze in Athens. Behind tournament scoring leader Abdolreza Karimzadeh, Iran beat Brazil 4-0 for the bronze, its first-ever medal in the event.

New to the Paralympic Games in 2004, the 5-a-side sport involves two teams of four blind athletes each, who wear blindfolds or masks to guarantee equality, and one sighted or visually impaired goalkeeper per side. Each team is allowed a guide behind the opponent's goal to direct players. The walled field negates the need for throw-ins.

Brazil repeated with a 2-1 gold-medal-match victory against host China, with the game winner being a last-minute strike by Marcos Felipe. Argentina captured the bronze over Spain in a match decided by penalty kicks, with defender Diego Cerega the only player to score in the shootout.

BRAZIL'S RICARDO ALVES (L) FALLS AFTER A COLLISION DURING A MEN'S 5-A-SIDE SOCCER MATCH | *FREDERIC J. BROWN/AFP/GETTY IMAGES*

TARAS DUTKO (L), VITALIY TRUSHEV (R) OF UKRAINE AND IVAN POTEKHIN OF RUSSIA COMPETE IN THE SEVEN-A-SIDE SOCCER FINAL | *GUANG NIU/GETTY IMAGES*

RUDY GARCIA TOLSON OF THE US DIVES IN AT THE START OF THE MEN'S
200M INDIVIDUAL MEDLEY SM7 FINAL | *LIU JIN/AFP/GETTY IMAGES*

POOL RECORDS CUBED | *COMPETING IN THE SAME ICONIC VENUE WHERE MICHAEL PHELPS BECAME A STAR OF THE OLYMPIC GAMES A FEW WEEKS*

before, it was inevitable that Paralympians would evoke some comparisons to his performance in the Water Cube. Let's just say there were a lot of Phelpsian efforts to come.

The list of stars in the pool was long and distinguished, and more than 100 world records fell during the competition. While South Africa's Natalie du Toit , who went right from the Olympic Games into the Paralympic Games, went five-for-five in gold medals, she was hardly the only high achiever. Among those winning four gold medals was Brazil's Daniel Dias, who also claimed four silvers and a bronze.

Great Britain's David Roberts' four golds pushed his career total to 11, while the up-and-coming generation was represented by Great Britain's 13-year-old Eleanor Simmonds, who won two gold medals.

As for America's Olympic Team, it was simply their best showing ever. Team USA topped the swimming medal count for the first time with 44 medals, including 17 golds. "As a team, we have taken leaps and bounds since Athens," said coach Julie O'Neill.

The medals came from a powerful mix of veterans and newcomers. Erin Popovich's four golds (plus two silvers) gave her 14 career medals. Jessica Long also won four golds, and Lantz Lamback shined for the Team USA men with a gold and three silvers—while breaking two world records.

"We have a really young team and we're going to be around for a while," said swimmer Anna Eames.

JESSICA LONG OF THE UNITED STATES COMPETES IN THE WOMEN'S 400M
FREESTYLE S8 DIVISION | *MARK KOLBE/GETTY IMAGES*

MIRANDA UHL OF USA CELEBRATES WINNING GOLD IN THE WOMEN'S
200M IND MEDLEY - SM6 | *JAMIE MCDONALD/GETTY IMAGES*

ROY PERKINS OF THE USA COMPETES IN THE MEN'S 50M BUTTERFLY - S5 |
CHINA PHOTOS/GETTY IMAGES

JARRETT PERRY OF USA COMES OUT OF THE BLOCKS IN THE 100M BACKSTROKE S9 |
ADAM PRETTY/GETTY IMAGES

CHANTAL BOONACKER OF NETHERLANDS AND ERIN POPOVITCH OF THE USA IN ACTION
DURING THE 50M FREESTYLE S7 | *ADAM PRETTY/GETTY IMAGES*

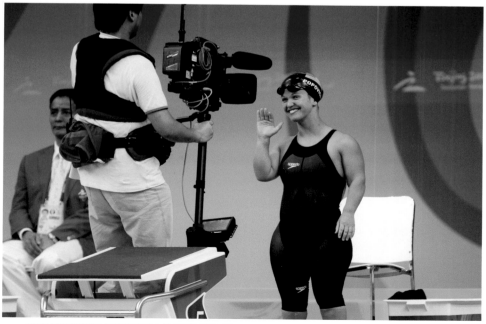

ERIN POPOVICH OF THE USA SMILES AND WAVES AT A TELEVISION CAMERA BEFORE COMPETING
IN THE WOMEN'S 50M BUTTERFLY S7 FINAL | *NATALIE BEHRING/GETTY IMAGES*

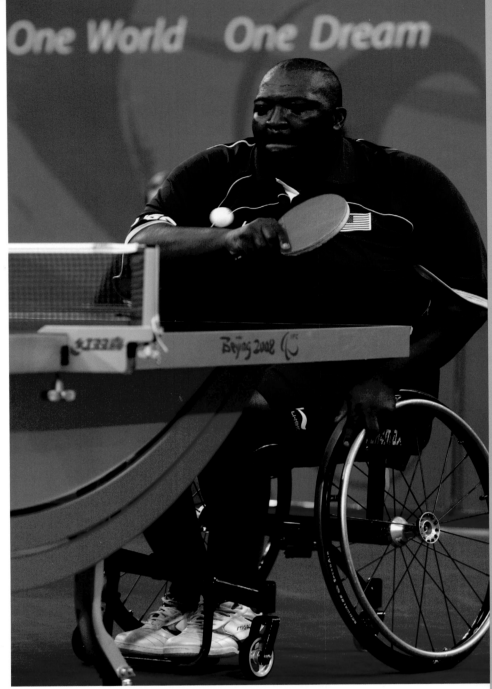

SCOTT ANDRE OF THE USA RETURNS VOLLEY AGAINST KOBER DIETMAR OF GERMANY DURING A MEN'S INDIVIDUAL CLASS 4/5 | *CHINA PHOTOS/GETTY IMAGES*

SETTING THE TABLE | *ANYONE FAMILIAR WITH TABLE TENNIS KNOWS THAT CHINA RULES THE SPORT AT ALL LEVELS, SO IT WAS NATURAL TO* expect that the competition in the Beijing Paralympic Games might yield a familiar outcome.

And that's exactly what happened. France did make a strong showing with five gold medals, but the big story was China, who won 13. "The results are even better than what we expected," China coach Lin Xiubing said after the tournaments in the Peking University Gymnasium.

In 2004, China claimed seven of 28 gold medals in table tennis at the Athens Paralympic Games. At the Beijing Paralympic Games, China fielded a 26-member team, with 14 first-time contestants accounting for nine gold medals.

The 11 classes in table tennis at the Paralympic Games are based on range of movement, ability to handle the paddle, and, for those who use a wheelchair, balance.

Standing players were first included in table tennis in 1976; athletes with cerebral palsy joined the competition in 1980.

Three-time Paralympian Mitch Seidenfeld was the top American contestant, reaching the bronze-medal match before being defeated by Spain's Alvaro Valera. "There were opportunities to take the match to a fifth game, but I'm proud of the way he played," said Team USA coach Sean O'Neill.

ANDREA ZIMMERER OF GERMANY LUNGES FOR THE BALL DURING THE WOMEN'S TEAM - CLASS 4/5 TABLE TENNIS MATCH AGAINST GU GAI OF CHINA | *CHINA PHOTOS/GETTY IMAGES*

MITCHELL SEIDENFELD OF THE UNITED STATES RETURNS THE BALL AGAINST YE CHAOQUN OF CHINA DURING THE MIC7 SEMI-FINALS | *ANDREW WONG/GETTY IMAGES*

JOE CHAMBERS OF THE UNITED STATES ATTEMPTS A LAYUP DURING A GAME BE-
TWEEN THE UNITED STATES AND ISRAEL | *CHINA PHOTOS/GETTY IMAGES*

DIGGING DEEP | *AFTER WINNING A SECOND CONSECUTIVE PARALYMPIC GAMES GOLD MEDAL IN WOMEN'S WHEELCHAIR BASKETBALL, TEAM USA*

captain Patty Cisneros described the repeat performance as more difficult because opponents were targeting her team in Beijing. Fortunately, she had a lot of help.

Team USA was remarkably deep with talent and simply overwhelmed opponents with waves of players coming off the bench. In winning seven games by an average of 21 points, the Americans used 12 players for an average of at least 10 minutes each, with only one player averaging double-figures scoring for the tournament. That great balance carried the American Paralymmpic Team to a 50-38 win over Germany for the gold.

Christina Ripp led the Americans with 16 points in the championship game, and the team's aggressive defensive strategy resulted in 19 turnovers by Germany.

"This experience has been so incredible," said Cisneros, who joined Ripp, Carlee Hoffman, Emily Hoskins, Stephanie Wheeler, and Jennifer Ruddell as repeat gold medalists.

The Team USA men improved considerably after a seventh-place finish in the Athens Paralympic Games in 2004, barely missing a medal. The Americans lost 69-62 to Canada in an epic, double-overtime semifinal game after leading by 16 points at halftime. Physically and emotionally drained, they fell 85-77 to Great Britain in the bronze-medal match, despite Joe Chambers' 25 points.

"Our guys put our hearts on the line," said USA Team co-captain Jeremy Lude. "We tried to fight back as well as we could."

Canada left the semifinals similarly worn down, which left the door open for Australia to take the gold in a 72-60 win in the finals.

CHRISTINA RIPP OF THE US (#12) LOOKS TO PASS UNDER PRESSURE FROM GERMANY'S ANNETTE KAHL | *FREDERIC J. BROWN/AFP/GETTY IMAGES*

CARLEE HOFFMAN OF THE UNITED STATES SHOOTS WHILE MEMBERS OF
GERMANY'S TEAM LOOK ON | *ADAM PRETTY/GETTY IMAGES*

MIKEY PAYE OF THE UNITED STATES PASSES THE BALL OVER HIS SHOULDER DURING
THE BRONZE MEDAL GAME | *ADAM PRETTY/GETTY IMAGES*

NATALIE SCHNEIDER (3R) AND CARLEE HOFFMAN (2R) HUG AS US PLAYERS CELEBRATE VICTORY OVER GERMANY IN THE GOLD MEDAL GAME | *FREDERIC J. BROWN/AFP/GETTY IMAGES*

JEREMY LADE (C) OF THE USA LOOKS TO PASS UNDER STRONG PRESSURE FROM THE AUSTRALIA'S TEAM | *FREDERIC J. BROWN/AFP/GETTY IMAGES*

MAREN BUTTERBRODT (12#) OF GERMANY DIVES FOR THE BALL WHILE SARAH CASTLE (11#) OF THE USA WATCHES ON | *FENG LI/GETTY IMAGES*

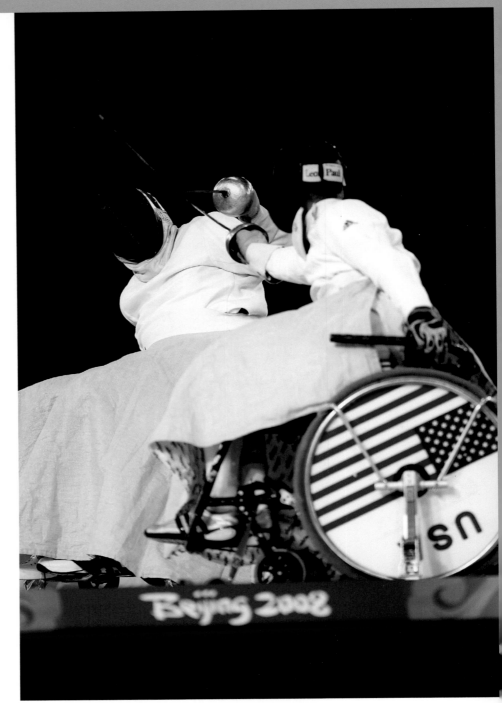

BENJY WILLIAMS OF THE UNITED STATES (L) AND TEAMMATE SCOTT RODGERS COMPETE IN THE
MEN'S IND. EPEE - CAT. B | *ANDREW WONG/GETTY IMAGES*

PERFECTLY BALANCED | *IN THE PARALYMPIC*
GAMES, THE WHEELCHAIRS OF THE FENCING
CONTESTANTS ARE FIXED IN PLACE BY METAL
frames. The sport still requires great balance, which was China's hallmark in the Beijing Paralympic Games.

The Chinese team was deep and talented in both the men's and women's divisions. In 2004,
China sent only three male fencers to Athens. In Beijing, the home team was fully staffed—a
fact that was amply evident on the medals podium. China's men won five of the gold medals,
and the host country was also represented in all four women's finals. In all, China claimed six
golds, six silvers, and one bronze in the Fencing Hall on the Olympic Green.

The only Europeans appearing in the men's gold-medal matches were Laurent Francois of France and Mikalai Bezyazychny of Belarus. Each lost to China's Hu Daoliang, who swept the foil and epee titles in Category B, one of three divisions in fencing, each based on disability.

Team USA fencer Scott Rodgers competed very well in Category B, reaching the quarterfinals and holding a four-touch lead over Hu at one stage before losing. "I thought I had it," Rodgers said, "but I ran out of gas at the end."

China's Ye Ruyi won the foil and sabre golds in Category A.

In the women's tournament, Hong Kong took three of the four golds and combined with China to claim 11 of the 12 medals overall. The only fencer to break up the domination was Sayasunee Jana of Thailand, who won a bronze. Hong Kong's Chan Yui-chong was the women's star with golds in foil and epee in Category B.

YE RUYI OF CHINA (L) FIGHTS HIS COMPATRIOT TIAN JIANQUAN (R) IN THE MEN'S INDIVIDUAL SABRE A FINAL | *PETER PARKS/AFP/GETTY IMAGES*

RADOSLAW STANCZUK OF POLAND (R) FIGHTS WONG TAT-TAT OF HONG KONG (L) IN THE MEN'S INDIVIDUAL EPEE A | *PETER PARKS/AFP/GETTY IMAGES*

轮椅橄
榄球

WHEELCHAIR RUGBY
BEIJING 2008

PLAYERS OF THE UNITED STATES (L) AND AUSTRALIA SHAKE HANDS AFTER THE
FINAL MATCH OF WHEELCHAIR RUGBY | *ANDREW WONG/GETTY IMAGES*

HOT WHEELS | *IT'S A STORYLINE SHARED WITH A U.S. OLYMPIC TEAM: GAMES DOMINATION INTERRUPTED BY A 2004 ATHENS SEMIFINAL* upset loss, a disappointing bronze medal, then gold-medal redemption in 2008 in Beijing.

Team USA's 2008 Olympic Games gold-medal basketball squad was led by names that are household familiar: LeBron, Kobe, Carmelo, and D-Wade. The second "redeem team" was the 11-member United States Paralympic wheelchair rugby team, led by names like Norm Lyduch, Bryan Kirkland, Will Grouix, Nick Springer, and Joel Wilmoth.

Combining elements of basketball, handball, and ice hockey, wheelchair rugby features four athletes of mixed functional ability on the court, passing the ball at least every 10 seconds and trying to carry it across the opposing team's goal line. Originating in Canada in 1977, wheelchair rugby was originally called "murder ball" and is also known as "quad rugby." A demonstration sport at the 1996 Atlanta Paralympic Games, it became a full medal sport four years later in Sydney.

Focused on returning to the top of the medals podium at the Beijing Science and Technology University Gymnasium, Team USA went 5-0 in its matches, including a tight victory over Great Britain in the semifinals. In the gold medal final, the U.S. won 53-44 over Australia, with Kirkland and Grouix combining for 29 goals and 15 assists and Andy Cohn adding another 10 goals. Meanwhile, Springer and Wilmoth helped slow down Australian scoring machine Ryley Batt, who still finished with 23 goals and 12 assists.

"We have trained and prepared for this since the day we left Athens four years ago," said Cohn, one of six returnees from the 2004 team. "Everyone on this team is so close, and we did this together, as a group."

NICK SPRINGER (#9) OF THE UNITED STATES CELEBRATES AFTER THE VICTORY OVER JAPAN
| *CHINA PHOTOS/GETTY IMAGES*

SETH MCBRIDE (R) OF THE US HEADS TO SCORE AFTER A MOVE BY BRIAN KIRKLAND (C)
TO BLOCK CHINA'S XIA JUNFENG | *FREDERIC J. BROWN/AFP/GETTY IMAGES*

CHEN JUN (R) OF CHINA WATCHES WILL GROULX (L) OF THE USA GET THE BALL |
GUANG NIU/GETTY IMAGES

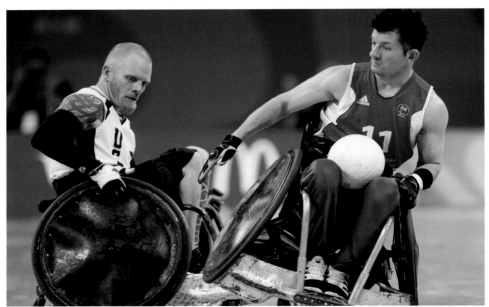

MARK ZURPAN OF THE UNITED STATES (L) RAMS INTO ALAN ASH OF GREAT BRITAIN (R)
AS THEY GO FOR THE WIN | *NATALIE BEHRING/GETTY IMAGES*

CHINA'S HAN GUIFEI (C#2) LOOKS TO PASS UNDER PRESSURE FROM SCOTT HOGSETT OF THE UNITED
STATES (R/#8) IN THEIR MIXED WHEELCHAIR RUGBY GAME | *FREDERIC J. BROWN/AFP/GETTY IMAGES*

SETH MCBRIDE OF THE UNITED STATES WATCHES THE BALL IN A MATCH BETWEEN THE USA AND GREAT BRITAIN | *NATALIE BEHRING/GETTY IMAGES*

CHINA'S CHENG SHUANGMIAO (R) CHASES CHANCE SUMNER OF THE U.S. (L) IN THEIR MIXED WHEELCHAIR RUGBY GAME | *FREDERIC J. BROWN/AFP/GETTY IMAGES*

KAITLYN VERFUERTH OF THE UNITED STATES SERVES IN A MATCH AGAINST
KGOSTO MONTJANE OF SOUTH AFRICA | *CHINA PHOTOS/GETTY IMAGES*

WINNING FRIENDS| *AMERICAN WHEELCHAIR TENNIS PLAYERS NICK TAYLOR AND DAVID WAGNER ARE CLOSE FRIENDS, WHICH MADE* their bronze-medal match at the Beijing Paralympic Games a little unusual. It also made their second gold medal in doubles even more meaningful.

Competing in the quad division for athletes with disability in three or more limbs, Taylor and Wagner defeated Israel's Boaz Kramer and Shraga Weinberg in three sets to take the gold medal. "This win was more dramatic than Athens because it was three sets, but the feeling is the same," Taylor said.

The singles match between the doubles teammates also went to a spirited third set before Wagner prevailed in a high-level competition in the tennis stadium on the Olympic Green. The only concession to these athletes is the ball being allowed to bounce twice before being returned.

The Dutch dominated the women's open divisions, although there was an intrasquad upset. Since teaming up in 2004, Esther Vergeer and Jiske Griffioen of the Netherlands had not lost a doubles match in 39 tournaments, but they fell to Korie Homan and Sharon Walraven in three sets. Vergeer had defeated Homan for the singles title, extending her personal streak to 349 matches. Vergeer cites excellent accommodation, facilities, and encouragement of players with disabilities for her country's tennis success.

But the Netherlands' strength did not extend through the men's singles final. Top seed Shingo Kunieda of Japan needed less than an hour to overcome Athens Paralympic Games champion Robin Ammerlaan, winning 6-3, 6-0.

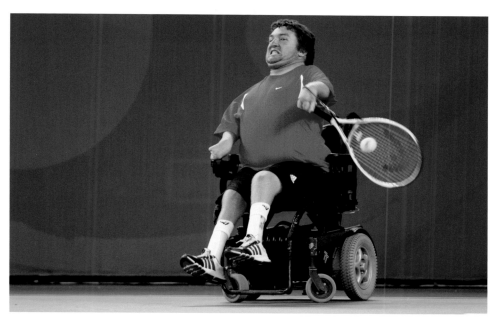

A LOSS TO PETER NORFOLK LED TO A BRONZE MEDAL MATCH BETWEEN FRIENDS NICK TAYLOR (ABOVE) AND DAVID WAGNER | *NATALIE BEHRING/GETTY IMAGES*

LEE HINSON OF THE UNITED STATES RETURNS A VOLLEY IN A MATCH AGAINST MAURICIO POMME | *CHINA PHOTOS/GETTY IMAGES*

DAVID WAGNER OF THE UNITED STATES REACHES FOR THE BALL IN A WHEELCHAIR TENNIS SINGLES MATCH | *NATALIE BEHRING/GETTY IMAGES*

PERFORMERS DANCE AS PEDALS FROM BEIJING'S FRAGRANT HILL ARE SHOWERED OVER THEM | *GUANG NIU/GETTY IMAGES*

CLOSING CEREMONY

BEIJING, '08

Twelve days, 1,432 medals, 279 world records, and 339 Paralympic Games records later, the September 17 Closing Ceremony at the Bird's Nest served not only as a curtain call for more than 4,200 Paralympians but also a fond farewell for the entire five-plus weeks of the Beijing 2008 Olympic Games and Paralympic Games.

The common thread from start to finish was the theme "A Letter to the Future," culminating with an invitation for the National Stadium audience to write well-wishes on provided postcards. Later, more than 100 "postmen" dropped petals from the stadium roof onto athletes and the crowd, while another 100-plus flew from the stadium floor upward, symbolically carrying postcards to spread throughout the world.

Also dropped from above were 600,000 red leaves gathered from Beijing's Fragrant Hill, with performers subsequently pretending to sow seeds, water them, and then celebrate the harvest.

Helping to extinguish the flame in the Olympic cauldron towering above the Bird's Nest were a "thousand-arm goddess" and 10-year-old Wang Yimei, who lost her hearing after suffering a high fever as a baby. "Sacred flame, you are burning in my heart. Are you hearing me? I'm singing for you," gestured young Yimei in sign language, as the flame went out for the final time in Beijing.

POSTMEN TRAVEL SKYWARD TO SYMBOLICALLY DELIVER POSTCARDS TO THE WORLD | *CHINA PHOTOS/GETTY IMAGES*

A SCENE FROM THE 'RED LEAVES OF FRAGRANT HILL' | *JAMIE MCDONALD/GETTY IMAGES*

FIREWORKS EXPLODE OVER THE NATIONAL STADIUM DURING
THE CLOSING CEREMONY | *FENG LI/GETTY IMAGES*

PERFORMERS PRODUCE A 'LETTER TO THE FUTURE' | *CHINA PHOTOS/GETTY IMAGES*

SPORT CLASSIFICATIONS

SPORT	AMPUTEE/ LES AUTRES	BLIND/ VISUALLY IMPAIRED	SPINAL CORD INJURY	TRAUMATIC BRAIN INJURY/ CEREBRAL PALSY/STROKE
ARCHERY	X		X	X
ATHLETICS	X	X	X	X
BOCCIA				X
CYCLING	X	X	X	X
EQUESTRIAN	X	X	X	X
GOALBALL		X		
JUDO		X		
POWERLIFTING	X		X	X
ROWING	X	X	X	X
SAILING	X	X	X	X
SHOOTING			X	X
SOCCER		X		X
SWIMMING	X	X	X	X
TABLE TENNIS				
VOLLEYBALL	X			
WHEELCHAIR BASKETBALL	X		X	
WHEELCHAIR FENCING	X		X	X
WHEELCHAIR RUGBY			X	
WHEELCHAIR TENNIS	X		X	

MARY ALLISON MILFORD AND ALANA NICHOLLS OF THE UNITED STATES CELEBRATE WINNING THE GOLD MEDAL FOLLOWING THE WOMEN'S GOLD MEDAL WHEELCHAIR BASKETBALL GAME | *ADAM PRETTY/GETTY IMAGES*

PARTICIPATING NATIONS

AFGHANISTAN | AFG
ALGERIA | ALG
ANGOLA | ANG
ARGENTINA | ARG
ARMENIA | ARM
AUSTRALIA | AUS
AUSTRIA | AUT
AZERBAIJAN | AZE
BAHRAIN | BRN
BANGLADESH | BAN
BARBADOS | BAR
BELARUS | BLR
BELGIUM | BEL
BENIN | BEN
BERMUDA | BER
BOSNIA AND HERZEGOVINA | BIH
BOTSWANA | BOT
BRAZIL | BRA
BULGARIA | BUL
BURKINA FASO | BUR
BURUNDI | BDI
CAMBODIA | CAM
CANADA | CAN
CAPE VERDE | CPV
CENTRAL AFRICAN REPUBLIC | CAF
CHILE | CHI
CHINA | CHN
COLOMBIA | COL
COSTA RICA | CRC
CÔTE D'IVOIRE | CIV
CROATIA | CRO
CUBA | CUB
CYPRUS | CYP
CZECH REPUBLIC | CZE
DENMARK | DEN
DOMINICAN REPUBLIC | DOM
ECUADOR | ECU
EGYPT | EGY
EL SALVADOR | ESA
ESTONIA | EST
ETHIOPIA | ETH
FAROE ISLANDS | FRO

FIJI | FIJ
FINLAND | FIN
FYR MACEDONIA | MKD
FRANCE | FRA
GABON | GAB
GEORGIA | GEO
GERMANY | GER
GHANA | GHA
GREAT BRITAIN | GBR
GREECE | GRE
GUATEMALA | GUA
GUINEA | GUI
HAITI | HAI
HONDURAS | HON
HONG KONG, CHINA | HKG
HUNGARY | HUN
ICELAND | ISL
INDIA | IND
INDONESIA | INA
IRAN | IRI
IRAQ | IRQ
IRELAND | IRE
ISRAEL | ISR
ITALY | ITA
JAMAICA | JAM
JAPAN | JPN
JORDAN | JOR
KAZAKHSTAN | KAZ
KENYA | KEN
KUWAIT | KUW
KYRGYZSTAN | KGZ
LAOS | LAO
LATVIA | LAT
LEBANON | LIB
LESOTHO | LES
LITHUANIA | LTU
LUXEMBOURG | LUX
LIBYA | LBA
MACAU | MAC
MADAGASCAR | MAD
MALAYSIA | MAS
MALI | MLI

MALTA | MLT
MAURITIUS | MRI
MEXICO | MEX
MOLDOVA | MDA
MONGOLIA | MGL
MONTENEGRO | MNE
MOROCCO | MAR
MYANMAR | MYA
NAMIBIA | NAM
NEPAL | NEP
NETHERLANDS | NED
NEW ZEALAND | NZL
NIGER | NIG
NIGERIA | NGR
NORWAY | NOR
OMAN | OMA
PAKISTAN | PAK
PALESTINE | PLE
PANAMA | PAN
PAPUA NEW GUINEA | PNG
PERU | PER
PHILIPPINES | PHI
POLAND | POL
PORTUGAL | POR
PUERTO RICO | PUR
QATAR | QAT
ROMANIA | ROM
RUSSIA | RUS
RWANDA | RWA
SAMOA | SAM
SAUDI ARABIA | KSA
SENEGAL | SEN
SERBIA | SRB
SINGAPORE | SIN
SLOVAKIA | SVK
SLOVENIA | SLO
SOUTH AFRICA | RSA
SOUTH KOREA | KOR
SPAIN | ESP
SRI LANKA | SRI
SURINAME | SUR
SWEDEN | SWE

SWITZERLAND | SUI
SYRIA | SYR
CHINESE TAIPEI | TPE
TAJIKISTAN | TJK
TANZANIA | TAN
THAILAND | THA
TIMOR-LESTE | TLS
TONGA | TGA
TUNISIA | TUN
TURKEY | TUR
TURKMENISTAN | TKM
UGANDA | UGA
UKRAINE | UKR
UNITED ARAB EMIRATES | UAE
UNITED STATES | USA
URUGUAY | URU
UZBEKISTAN | UZB
VANUATU | VAN
VENEZUELA | VEN
VIETNAM | VIE
ZAMBIA | ZAM
ZIMBABWE | ZIM

MEDAL COUNT

COUNTRY	GOLD	SILVER	BRONZE	TOTAL
CHINA	89	70	52	211
GREAT BRITAIN	42	29	31	102
UNITED STATES	36	35	28	99
AUSTRALIA	23	29	27	79
UKRAINE	24	18	32	74
RUSSIA	18	23	22	63
GERMANY	14	25	20	59
SPAIN	15	21	22	58
FRANCE	12	21	19	52
CANADA	19	10	21	50
BRAZIL	16	14	17	47
SOUTH KOREA	10	8	13	31
SOUTH AFRICA	21	3	6	30
POLAND	5	12	13	30
CZECH REPUBLIC	6	6	3	27
JAPAN	5	14	8	27
GREECE	5	9	10	24
NETHERLANDS	5	10	7	22
TUNISIA	9	9	3	21
MEXICO	10	3	7	20
ITALY	4	7	7	18
ALGERIA	4	3	8	15
IRAN	5	6	3	14
CUBA	5	3	6	14
BELARUS	5	7	1	13
THAILAND	1	5	7	13
NEW ZEALAND	5	3	4	12
SWEDEN	5	3	4	12
EGYPT	4	4	4	12
HONG KONG	5	3	3	11
SWITZERLAND	3	2	6	11
AZERBAIJAN	2	3	5	10
KENYA	5	3	1	9
NIGERIA	4	4	1	9
DENMARK	3	2	4	9
MOROCCO	4	1	2	7
PORTUGAL	1	4	2	7
NORWAY	1	3	3	7
AUSTRIA	4	1	1	6
SLOVAKIA	2	3	1	6
FINLAND	2	2	2	6
HUNGARY	1	0	5	6
ISRAEL	0	5	1	6
ARGENTINA	0	1	5	6

COUNTRY	GOLD	SILVER	BRONZE	TOTAL
IRELAND	3	1	1	5
CROATIA	3	1	0	4
CYPRUS	1	2	1	4
SINGAPORE	1	1	2	4
VENEZUELA	1	1	2	4
JORDAN	0	2	2	4
LATVIA	1	2	0	3
ANGOLA	0	3	0	3
SLOVENIA	0	1	2	3
SAUDI ARABIA	1	1	0	2
CHINESE TAIPEI	1	0	1	2
TURKEY	1	0	1	2
LITHUANIA	0	2	0	2
SERVIA	0	2	0	2
BULGARIA	0	1	1	2
IRAQ	0	1	1	2
COLOMBIA	0	1	1	2
LEBANON	0	0	2	2
MONGOLIA	1	0	0	1
BOSNIA & HERZEGOVINA	0	1	0	1
PAKISTAN	0	1	0	1
PAPUA NEW GUINEA	0	1	1	1
ROMANIA	0	1	0	1
UNITED ARAB EMIRATES	0	1	0	1
BELGIUM	0	0	1	1
ESTONIA	0	0	1	1
JAMAICA	0	0	1	1
LAOS	0	0	1	1
MALAYSIA	0	0	1	1
NAMIBIA	0	0	1	1
PUERTO RICO	0	0	1	1
SYRIA	0	0	1	1

ARCHERY

348

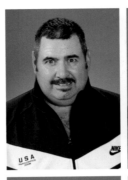

NAME, BIRTHDATE, HOMETOWN

Joe Bailey 5/27/1961, Flushing, MI
Eric Bennett 11/4/1973, Surprise, AZ
Lindsey Carmichael, 7/22/1985, Lago Vista, TX
Jeff Fabry 4/14/1973, Tulare, CA

Chuck Lear 6/30/1946, Lee's Summit, MO
T.J. Pemberton 5/29/1968, Guthrie, OK
Kevin Stone, 3/31/1961, Kodak, TN
Russell Wolfe, 11/31/1968, Williamsburg, VA

STAFF

Randi Smith Head Coach
Paul Miller Asst Head Coach

ARCHERY RESULTS

INDIVIDUAL COMPOUND OPEN MEN
1	GBR	STUBBS, JOHN	
2	ITA	SIMONELLI, ALBERTO	
3	SUI	HORNER, PHILIPPE	
4	**USA**	**PEMBERTON, TJ**	
	USA	**BAILEY, JOE**	*ELIMQ*
	USA	**BENNETT, ERIC**	*ELIM1/8*

INDIVIDUAL COMPOUND W1 MEN
1	CZE	DRAHONINSKY, DAVID	
2	GBR	CAVANAGH, JOHN	
3	**USA**	**FABRY, JEFF**	
4	FIN	KINNUNEN, OSMO	
	USA	**LEAR, CHUCK**	*ELIM1/8*

INDIVIDUAL RECURVE STANDING MEN
1	MGL	DAMBADONDOG, BAA-TARJAV	
2	FRA	MEUNIER, FABRICE	
3	CHN	CHEN, YEGANG	
4	ITA	ESPOSITO, MARIO	

INDIVIDUAL RECURVE W1/W2 MEN
1	CHN	CHENG, CHANGJIE	
2	ITA	VITALE, MARCO	
3	TPE	TSENG, LUNG HUI	
4	TUR	OZEN, OZGUR	
	USA	**STONE, KEVIN**	*ELIM1/8*
	USA	**WOLFE, RUSSELL**	*ELIM1/16*

TEAM RECURVE OPEN MEN
1	KOR	KOREA
2	CHN	CHINA
3	ITA	ITALY
4	JPN	JAPAN

INDIVIDUAL COMPOUND OPEN WOMEN
1	GBR	BROWN, DANIELLE
2	JPN	KAMIYA, CHIEKO
3	GBR	CLARKE, MEL
4	TUR	SU, GULBIN

INDIVIDUAL RECURVE STANDING WOMEN
1	KOR	LEE, HWA SOOK
2	CHN	GAO, FANGXIA
3	**USA**	**CARMICHAEL, LINDSEY**
4	POL	OLEJNIK, MALGORZATA

INDIVIDUAL RECURVE W1/W2 WOMEN
1	TUR	GIRISMEN, GIZEM
2	CHN	FU, HONGZHI
3	CHN	XIAO, YANHONG
4	JPN	NAKANISHI, AYA

TEAM RECURVE OPEN WOMEN
1	CHN	CHINA
2	KOR	KOREA
3	CZE	CZECH REPUBLIC
4	POL	POLAND

ATHLETICS

Danny Andrews 8/13/1981, Tucson, AZ/Miami, FL
Jerome Avery 12/22/1978, Chula Vista, CA/Lamoore, CA
Mallerie Badgett 2/25/1989, Oxford, AL
Jim Bob Bizzell 11/22/1985, Abilene, TX

Cheri Blauwet 5/15/1980, Palo Alto, CA/Larchwood IA
Adam Bleakney 8/27/1975, Champaign, IL
Matt Brown 11/24/1976, Idalou, TX
Tyler Byers 5/7/1982, Washington, D.C./Spokane, WA

Jeremy Campbell 8/19/1987, Chula Vista, Calif./Perryton, TX
Edwin Cockrell 5/19/1959, New Athens, IL
Julie Crisp 4/27/1966, Portland, OR
Scott Danberg 7/28/1962, Cooper City, FL

Anjali Forber-Pratt 6/22/1984, Champaign, IL/Natick, Mass
Brian Frasure 2/2/1973, Apex, NC
Jessica Galli 12/1/1983, Savoy, IL/Hillsborough, NJ
Joshua George 3/18/1984, Champaign, IL/Fairfax, VA

Elexis Gillette 10/19/1984, Chula Vista, CA/Raleigh, NC
Jennifer Goeckel 2/19/1982, Seattle, WA
Peter Gottwald 7/23/1984, West Chester, PA
Sabra Hawkes 2/2/1988, Rockport, MA

Erik Hightower 4/6/1986, Glendale, AZ
April Holmes 3/11/1973, Chula Vista, Calif./Somerdale, NJ
Tony Iniguez 9/5/1980, Aurora, IL
Josiah Jamison 8/18/1982, Chula Vista, CA/Vance, SC

Jill Kennedy 2/2/1971, Charlottesville, Va./Zalmo, MO
Cheryl Leitner 4/4/1983, Myrtle Beach, S.C./Toms River, NJ
Carlos Leon 11/1/1984, Birmingham, AL/N. Lauderdale, FL
Chelsea McClammer 3/1/1994, Benton, WA

349

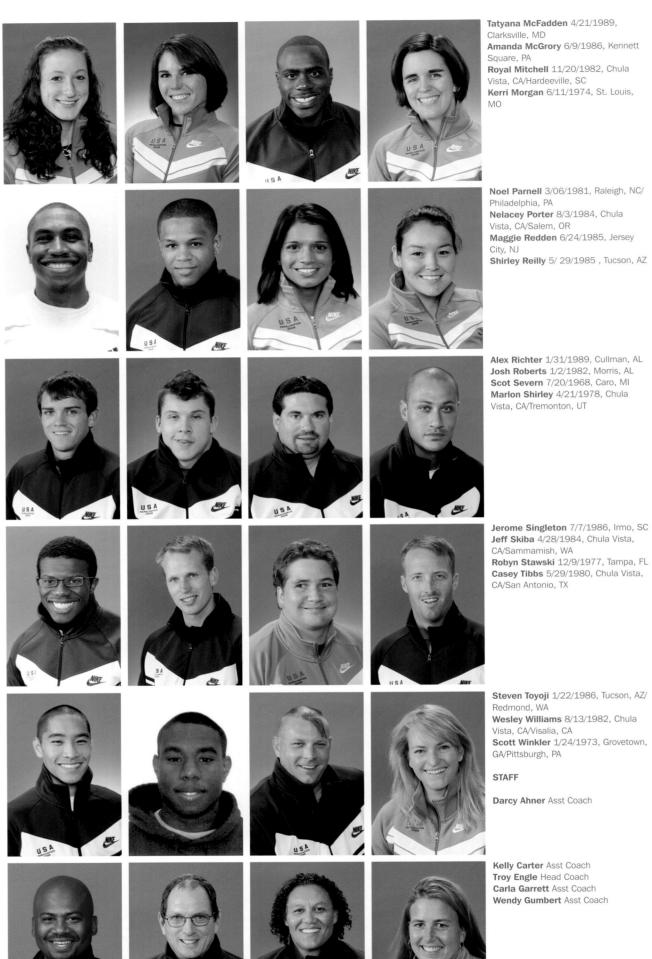

Tatyana McFadden 4/21/1989, Clarksville, MD
Amanda McGrory 6/9/1986, Kennett Square, PA
Royal Mitchell 11/20/1982, Chula Vista, CA/Hardeeville, SC
Kerri Morgan 6/11/1974, St. Louis, MO

Noel Parnell 3/06/1981, Raleigh, NC/ Philadelphia, PA
Nelacey Porter 8/3/1984, Chula Vista, CA/Salem, OR
Maggie Redden 6/24/1985, Jersey City, NJ
Shirley Reilly 5/ 29/1985 , Tucson, AZ

Alex Richter 1/31/1989, Cullman, AL
Josh Roberts 1/2/1982, Morris, AL
Scot Severn 7/20/1968, Caro, MI
Marlon Shirley 4/21/1978, Chula Vista, CA/Tremonton, UT

Jerome Singleton 7/7/1986, Irmo, SC
Jeff Skiba 4/28/1984, Chula Vista, CA/Sammamish, WA
Robyn Stawski 12/9/1977, Tampa, FL
Casey Tibbs 5/29/1980, Chula Vista, CA/San Antonio, TX

Steven Toyoji 1/22/1986, Tucson, AZ/ Redmond, WA
Wesley Williams 8/13/1982, Chula Vista, CA/Visalia, CA
Scott Winkler 1/24/1973, Grovetown, GA/Pittsburgh, PA

STAFF

Darcy Ahner Asst Coach

Kelly Carter Asst Coach
Troy Engle Head Coach
Carla Garrett Asst Coach
Wendy Gumbert Asst Coach

350

Chad James Asst Coach
Tobias Lemon Asst Coach
Kevin Orr Asst Coach
Teresa Skinner Asst Coach

ATHLETICS RESULTS

1,500 M T11 MEN

1	CHN	ZHANG, ZHEN	4:10.05
2	KEN	KIMANI, SAMWEL MUSHAI	4:11.76
3	CAN	DUNKERLEY, JASON	4:12.53
4	DEN	ANDERSEN, MIKAEL	4:13.90
5	BRA	SILVA, CARLOS BARTO	4:14.80
6	AUS	GOSENS, GERRARD	4:24.65

1,500 M T13 MEN

1	KEN	KIRWA, HENRY KIONO	4:06.11
2	CUB	RASCHID AGUILAR, LAZARO	4:06.40
3	ESP	AVILA, IGNACIO	4:07.00
4	MAR	BENIBRAHIM, YOUSSEF	4:08.97
5	NZL	ENDERGAST, TIM	4:09.09
6	MAR	MAME, ABDELILLAH	4:09.12
7	MAR	ZALZOULI, TARIK	4:09.56
8	ESP	AVILA, ABEL	4:10.22
9	VEN	SANCHEZ, LUIS	4:10.44
10	USA	GOTTWALD, PETER	4:16.59

1,500 M T46 MEN

1	KEN	TARBEI, ABRAHAM CHERUIYOT	3:52.50
2	ESP	AIT KHAMOUCH, ABDERRAHMAN	3:53.46
3	ALG	NOUIOUA, SAMIR	3:53.63
4	POL	AWIZEN, MARCIN	3:54.24
5	ETH	KEBEDE, TESFALEM GEBRU	3:55.41
6	KEN	MUSYOKI, STEPHEN WAMBUA	3:57.21
7	CHN	QIN, NING	3:58.23
8	AUS	ROEGER, MICHAEL	3:59.21
9	MAR	TOUMI, SAID	4:08.29
10	ETH	HIBU, FEREJ MOHAMMED	4:16.74
11	UKR	LESHCHYSHYN, OLEH	4:17.96
12	TUN	FOUZAI, MOHAMED	4:41.87

1,500 M T54 MEN

1	GBR	WEIR, DAVID	3:10.34
2	THA	WAHORAM, AWAT	3:10.68
3	AUS	FEARNLEY, KURT	3:14.28
4	ARG	MALDONADO, ALEJANDRO	3:14.92
5	FRA	LEMEUNIER, DENIS	3:16.43
6	POL	HAMERLAK, TOMASZ	3:17.60
	FRA	CASOLI, JULIEN	DNF
	SUI	HUG, MARCEL	DNF
	USA	BYERS, TYLER	*ELIMS*
	USA	GEORGE, JOSH	*ELIMS*
	USA	INIGUEZ, TONY	*ELIMS*

10,000 M T12 MEN

1	KEN	KIRWA, HENRY KIONO	31:42.97
2	TUN	ZHIOU, ABDERRAHIM	31:43.15
3	BRA	SANTOS, ODAIR	31:57.91
4	COL	SERNA, ELKIN	32:39.24
5	KEN	KARANJA, FRANCIS THUO	33:03.51
6	MEX	BERISTAIN, MOISES	33:17.07
7	BRA.	MENDONCA, ALEX	33:48.45
8	IRI	ELAHI, ALI	34:38.75

100 M T11 MEN

1	BRA	ADO, LUCAS	11.03
2	ANG	ARMANDO, JOSE	11.35
3	FRA	MAKUNDA, TRESOR	11.46
4	BRA	SILVA, DANIEL	11.56
5	CHN	LIU, XIANGKUN	11.57
6	NGR	ROTAWO, OLUSEGUN FRANCIS	11.60
7	ANG	DOS SANTOS, OCTAVIO	11.64
8	BRA	GOMES, FELIPE	11.72
	USA	GILLETTE, LEX	*ELIM1*
	USA	PORTER, NELACEY	*ELIM1*

100 M T12 MEN

1	USA	JAMISON, JOSIAH	10.89
2	NGR	ADESOJI, ADEKUNLE	10.95
3	CHN	YANG, YUQING	10.96
4	CHN	LI, QIANG	11.02
5	RUS	TRIKOLICH, FEDOR	11.18
6	AZE	MURADOV, ELCHIN	11.19
7	GER	SCHRODER, MATTHIAS	11.23
8	CUB	ROQUE, JULIO	30.91

100 M T13 MEN

1	IRL	SMYTH, JASON	10.62
2	RUS	LABZIN, ALEXEY	10.88
3	CUB	GUTIERREZ, LUIS FELIPE	10.98
4	AZE	MEHDIYEV, VUGAR	11.01
5	RSA	NTUTU, JONATHAN	11.06
6	BUL	ZLATANOV, RADOSLAV	11.11

7	USA	MITCHELL, ROYAL	11.17
8	BRA	ANDRADE, ANDRE LUIZ	11.18

100 M T35 MEN

1	CHN	YANG, SEN	12.29
2	CHN	FU, XINHAN	12.55
3	RSA	MOKGALAGADI, TEBOHO	12.82
4	UKR	SLYNKO, SERGII	12.83
5	ISL	HALLDORSSON, JON ODDUR	13.40
6	ALG	BOUKHALFA, ALLEL	13.59
7	GER	STEIN, NIELS	13.70
8	FRA	QUIATOL, HUGUES	14.12

100 M T36 MEN

1	UKR	PAVLYK, ROMAN	12.25
2	GBR	RUSHGROVE, BEN	12.35
3	HKG	SO, WA WAI	12.38
4	CHN	XU, RAN	12.40
5	POL	MIELCZAREK, MARCIN	12.42
6	CHN	CHE, MIAN	12.46
7	MAS	EMEARI, MOHD RADUAN	12.64
8	GBR	BALLARD, GRAEME	12.65

100 M T37 MEN

1	RSA	VAN DER MERWE, FANIE	11.83
2	CHN	MA, YUXI	11.90
3	ALG	HAMDI, SOFIANE	12.01
4	NZL	SLADE, MATT	12.46
5	RUS	KHOLOSTYAKOV, ANDREY	12.49
6	GER	SCHRAMM, RENE	12.50
7	AUS	THRUPP, DARREN	12.59
8	GBR	CHURM, MICHAEL	12.60

100 M T38 MEN

1	AUS	O'HANLON, EVAN	10.96
2	CHN	ZHOU, WENJUN	11.14
3	UKR	SENYK, MYKYTA	11.18
4	BRA	PINHEIRO, EDSON	11.30
5	TUN	CHIDA, FARHAT	11.39
6	UKR	ONUFRIYENKO, ANDRIY	11.70
7	AUS	SULLIVAN, TIMOTHY	11.91
8	GRE	MARINOS, ARISTOTELIS	11.93

100 M T42 MEN

1	CAN	CONNOR, EARLE	12.32
2	GER	POPOW, HEINRICH	12.98
3	GBR	MCFALL, JOHN	13.08
4	ITA	LIPPI, STEFANO	13.50
5	JPN	YAMAMOTO, ATSUSHI	13.68
	FRA	KAYITARE, CLAVEL	DISQ

100 M T44 MEN

1	RSA	PISTORIUS, OSCAR	11.17
2	USA	SINGLETON, JEROME	11.20
3	USA	FRASURE, BRIAN	11.50
4	RSA	FOURIE, ARNU	11.65
5	AUS	WILSON, STEPHEN	11.78
6	SUI	BAUSCH, CHRISTOPH	12.03
7	ITA	MARAI, HEROS	12.25
8	USA	SHIRLEY, MARLON	34.43

100 M T46 MEN

1	AUS	FRANCIS, HEATH	11.05
2	PNG	KOMPAON, FRANCIS	11.10
3	BRA	NASCIMENTO, YOHANSSON	11.25
4	CHN	ZHAO, XU	11.26
5	FRA	ASSOUMANI, ARNAUD	11.34
6	KSA	ALKHALDI, SAEED	11.36
7	NGR	MBAKARA, GODWIN JOSEPH	11.37
8	CUB	CALDERON, ETTIAM	11.57

100 M T52 MEN

1	CAN	BERGERON, DEAN	17.47
2	SUI	BOSCH, BEAT	17.51
3	CAN	BEAUDOIN, ANDRE	17.77
4	MEX	HERNANDEZ, SALVADOR	17.89
5	VEN	CASTILLO, MARCOS	18.23
6	THA	RUNGSRI, PETH	18.87
7	USA	ROBERTS, JOSH	19.88

100 M T53 MEN

1	USA	GEORGE, JOSH	14.79
2	GBR	BUSHELL, MICKEY	14.86
3	CHN	YU, SHIRAN	15.09
4	THA	INTASEN, SOPA	15.20
5	THA	KRUNGGET, PICHET	15.20
6	CAN	LAKATOS, BRENT	15.21
7	KUW	ALADWANI, HAMAD	15.36
8	BRA	SILVA, ARIOSVALDO	15.40

100 M T54 MEN

1	FIN	TAHTI, LEO-PEKKA	13.81
2	THA	KONJEN, SAICHON	14.04
3	THA	KOYSUB, SUPACHAI	14.22
4	CHN	ZONG, KAI	14.27
5	NED	VAN WEEGHEL, KENNY	14.47
6	CHN	LI, JUN	14.58
7	UAE	VAHDANI, MOHAMMAD	14.58
8	TUN	AOUADI, AHMED	14.72
	USA	HIGHTOWER, ERIK	*ELIM1*

200 M T11 MEN

1	BRA	ADO, LUCAS	22.48
2	ANG	ARMANDO, JOSE	22.70
3	CUB	IZNAGA, ARIAN	22.79
4	BRA	SILVA, DANIEL	23.38
5	ANG	DOS SANTOS, OCTAVIO	23.78
6	POR	BAPTISTA, FIRMINO	24.13
7	FRA	MAKUNDA, TRESOR	25.55
8	UKR	IVANIUKHIN, OLEKSANDR	27.93
	USA	GILLETTE, LEX	*ELIM1*

200 M T12 MEN

1	RSA	LANGENHOVEN, HILTON	21.94
2	CHN	LI, YANSONG	22.21
3	CHN	YANG, YUQING	22.39
4	NGR	ADESOJI, ADEKUNLE	22.48
5	CHN	LI, QIANG	22.64
6	GER	SCHRODER, MATTHIAS	22.71
7	POL	MICHALSKI, MATEUSZ (AT)	22.75
	USA	JAMISON, JOSIAH	DNS

200 M T13 MEN

1	IRL	SMYTH, JASON	21.43
2	RUS	LABZIN, ALEXEY	21.87
3	AZE	MEHDIYEV, VUGAR	22.00
4	CUB	GALANO, LUIS MANUEL	22.00
5	CUB	GUTIERREZ, LUIS FELIPE	22.31
6	CUB	DURRUTHY, FREDDY	22.51
7	GRE	OTOS, IOANNIS	22.74
8	RSA	NTUTU, JONATHAN	22.85
	USA	MITCHELL, ROYAL	*ELIM1*

200 M T36 MEN

1	HKG	SO, WA WAI	24.65
2	UKR	PAVLYK, ROMAN	25.05
3	CHN	CHE, MIAN	25.34
4	POL	MIELCZAREK, MARCIN	25.46
5	CHN	XU, RAN	25.54
6	GBR	BALLARD, GRAEME	25.69
7	BLR	DANILIUK, ALIAKSANDR	26.61
8	ALG	BOULESNAM, MOHAMED	27.55

200 M T37 MEN

1	RSA	VAN DER MERWE, FANIE	23.84
2	ALG	HAMDI, SOFIANE	24.10
3	CHN	MA, YUXI	24.48
4	AUS	SCOTT, BRAD	25.09
5	GBR	CHURM, MICHAEL	25.36
6	GER	SCHRAMM, RENE	25.37
7	RUS	KHOLOSTYAKOV, ANDREY	25.70
8	TUN	CHARMI, MOHAMED	53.24

200 M T38 MEN

1	AUS	O'HANLON, EVAN	21.98
2	CHN	ZHOU, WENJUN	22.38
3	UKR	SENYK, MYKYTA	22.52
4	TUN	CHIDA, FARHAT	22.60
5	CHN	YANG, CHEN	22.99
6	BRA	PINHEIRO, EDSON	23.46
7	AUS	SULLIVAN, TIMOTHY	23.62
8	RSA	STANDER, MARIUS	24.23

200 M T44 MEN

1	RSA	PISTORIUS, OSCAR	21.67
2	USA	BIZZELL, JIM BOB	22.62
3	GBR	JONES, IAN	23.00
4	USA	TIBBS, CASEY	23.40
5	USA	ANDREWS, DANNY	23.54
6	RSA	FOURIE, ARNU	23.87
7	BRA	OLIVEIRA, ALAN	24.21
8	SUI	BAUSCH, CHRISTOPH	24.61

200 M T46 MEN

1	AUS	FRANCIS, HEATH	21.74
2	CYP	ARESTI, ANTONIS	22.15
3	CUB	CALDERON, ETTIAM	22.42
4	RUS	NOSULENKO, YURY	22.48

ATHLETICS

ATHLETICS RESULTS

5	BRA	NASCIMENTO, YOHANSSON	22.53
6	FRA	ASSOUMANI, ARNAUD	22.56
7	AUT	MATZINGER, GUENTHER	23.12
8	ZIM	MUJAJI, ELLIOT	50.75

200 M T52 MEN

1	CAN	BERGERON, DEAN	30.81
2	SUI	BOSCH, BEAT	31.41
3	THA	RUNGSRI, PETH	32.07
4	CAN	BEAUDOIN, ANDRE	32.07
5	AUT	GEIERSPICHLER, THOMAS	32.31
6	JPN	UEYONABARU, HIROKAZU	32.46
7	MEX	HERNANDEZ, SALVADOR	33.34
8	VEN	CASTILLO, MARCOS	33.38
9	**USA**	**ROBERTS, JOSH**	36.82

200 M T53 MEN

1	CHN	YU, SHIRAN	26.64
2	AUS	COLMAN, RICHARD	26.71
3	KOR	HONG, SUK MAN	26.87
4	**USA**	**GEORGE, JOSH**	26.98
5	CAN	LAKATOS, BRENT	27.44
6	KUW	ALADWANI, HAMAD	27.67
7	VEN	AGUILAR, JESUS	27.86
8	FRA	FAIRBANK, PIERRE	27.94

200 M T54 MEN

1	CHN	ZHANG, LIXIN	24.34
2	THA	KONJEN, SAICHON	25.15
3	FIN	TAHTI, LEO-PEKKA	25.17
4	NED	VAN WEEGHEL, KENNY	25.28
5	CHN	LI, JUN	25.86
6	UAE	VAHDANI, MOHAMMAD	26.10
7	MEX	VALDOVINOS, GONZALO	26.31
	CHN	ZONG, KAI	DISQ
	USA	**HIGHTOWER, ERIK**	*ELIM1*

400 M T11 MEN

1	BRA	ADO, LUCAS	50.27
2	ANG	ARMANDO, JOSE	50.44
3	UKR	IVANIUKHIN, OLEKSANDR	50.82
4	BRA	SILVA, DANIEL	52.05

400 M T12 MEN

1	GER	SCHRODER, MATTHIAS	49.45
2	POR	GONCALVES, LUIS	50.15
3	AZE	OSMANOV, REZA	50.20
	CHN	LI, YANSONG	DISQ
	USA	**JAMISON, JOSIAH**	*ELIM1*

400 M T13 MEN

1	CUB	GALANO, LUIS MANUEL	49.12
2	CUB	DURRUTHY, FREDDY	49.52
3	GRE	OTOS, IOANNIS	49.99
4	MAR	MAME, ABDELILLAH	50.01
5	RUS	ZVEREV, ALEXANDER	50.05
6	ALG	SEKHRI, ZINE EDDINE	50.24
7	KEN	AUMA, ANDREW ADIMO	50.70
8	**USA**	**MITCHELL, ROYAL**	51.23

400 M T36 MEN

1	UKR	PAVLYK, ROMAN	54.13
2	RUS	AREFYEV, ARTEM	55.59
3	CHN	CHE, MIAN	55.70
4	RUS	KHARAGEZOV, PAVEL	57.51
5	CHN	HE, CHENGEN	58.29
6	HKG	SO, WA WAI	58.44
7	UKR	SAKOVSKYY, SERHIY	59.00
8	GBR	BALLARD, GRAEME	59.22

400 M T38 MEN

1	TUN	CHIDA, FARHAT	51.14
2	TUN	SAIDI, ABBES	51.97
3	UKR	ONUFRIYENKO, ANDRIY	52.45
4	RSA	STANDER, MARIUS	52.56
5	GBR	PAYTON, STEPHEN	54.02
6	AUS	MULLINS, CHRISTOPHER	54.59
7	CHN	ZHOU, WENJUN	01:27.97

400 M T44 MEN

1	RSA	PISTORIUS, OSCAR	47.49
2	**USA**	**BIZZELL, JIM BOB**	50.98
3	GBR	JONES, IAN	51.69
4	**USA**	**ANDREWS, DANNY**	53.15
5	AUS	WILSON, STEPHEN	55.49
6	AUT	LINHART, MICHAEL	55.76
	USA	**TIBBS, CASEY**	DNS

400 M T46 MEN

1	AUS	FRANCIS, HEATH	47.69
2	CYP	ARESTI, ANTONIS	48.87
3	VEN	COLMENARES, SAMUEL	49.51
4	BRA	SOUZA, EMICARLO	49.54
5	AUT	MATZINGER, GUENTHER	49.56
6	RUS	NOSULENKO, YURY	49.66
7	KEN	WAMBUGU, SIMON	53.32

400 M T52 MEN

1	JPN	ITO, TOMOYA	57.25
2	JPN	TAKADA, TOSHIHIRO	01:00.3
3	CAN	BERGERON, DEAN	01:00.4
4	AUT	GEIERSPICHLER, THOMAS	01:01.0
5	THA	RUNGSRI, PETH	01:02.1
6	JPN	UEYONABARU, HIROKAZU	01:02.8
7	**USA**	**TOYOJI, STEVEN**	01:05.4
8	CAN	BEAUDOIN, ANDRE	01:05.6
	USA	**ROBERTS, JOSH**	*ELIM1*

400 M T53 MEN

1	KOR	HONG, SUK MAN	47.67
2	CHN	LI, HUZHAO	48.43
3	AUS	COLMAN, RICHARD	48.92
4	KOR	YOO, BYUNG HOON	49.84
5	CAN	LAKATOS, BRENT	50.40
6	FRA	FAIRBANK, PIERRE	50.84
7	KUW	ALADWANI, HAMAD	51.03
8	JPN	HIROMICHI, JUN	51.54
	USA	**BLEAKNEY, ADAM**	*ELIM1*
	USA	**GEORGE, JOSH**	*ELIM1*

400 M T54 MEN

1	CHN	ZHANG, LIXIN	45.07
2	GBR	WEIR, DAVID	46.02
3	THA	KONJEN, SAICHON	46.86
4	FRA	CASOLI, JULIEN	47.64
5	SUI	HUG, MARCEL	47.67
6	THA	KOYSUB, SUPACHAI	48.39
7	NED	VAN WEEGHEL, KENNY	48.52
8	UAE	VAHDANI, MOHAMMAD	49.20
	USA	**HIGHTOWER, ERIK**	*ELIMS*

4X100 M T11-13 MEN

1	CHN		42.75
2	VEN		43.55
3	FRA		44.49
4	ANG		45.4
	USA		*ELIM1*
		PORTER, NELACEY	
		GILLETTE, LEX	
		MITCHELL, ROYAL	
		JAMISON, JOSIAH	

4X100 M T35-38 MEN

1	AUS		44.81
2	CHN		45.00
3	TUN		47.81
	UKR		DNF
	ALG		DISQ

4X100 M T42-46 MEN

1	**USA**		42.75
		BIZZELL, JIM BOB	
		TIBBS, CASEY	
		FRASURE, BRIAN	
		SINGLETON, JEROME	
2	BRA		45.25
3	AUS		45.8
4	FRA		46.68
	JPN		DISQ

4X100 M T53/54 MEN

1	CHN		49.9
2	THA		51.93
3	KOR		53.52
	AUS		DISQ

4X400 M T53/54 MEN

1	CHN		03:05.7
2	THA		03:11.6
3	FRA		03:17.9
	KOR		DISQ
	USA		*ELIM1*
		(NAMES NOT RECORDED)	

5,000 M T11 MEN

1	CHN	ZHANG, ZHEN	15:27.35
2	KEN	KARANJA, FRANCIS THUO	15:32.28
3	KEN	WANYOIKE, HENRY	15:47.17
4	MEX	ANGELES, CONSTANTINO	16:31.88
5	POR	VALE, RICARDO	16:32.49
6	BRA	FARIAS, CHRISTIANO	16:38.15

5,000 M T13 MEN

1	KEN	KIRWA, HENRY KIONO	14:24.02
2	MAR	BENIBRAHIM, YOUSSEF	14:50.32
3	BRA	SANTOS, ODAIR	14:53.35
4	NZL	ENDERGAST, TIM	15:13.60
5	GER	BERGMANN, MAX	15:28.06
6	CRO	LOZANOV, VEDRAN	15:41.36

5,000 M T46 MEN

1	KEN	TARBEI, ABRAHAM CHERUIYOT	14:20.88
2	TUN	FOUZAI, MOHAMED	14:38.96
3	MEX	SANTILLAN, MARIO	14:43.78
4	ETH	KEBEDE, TESFALEM GEBRU	14:59.41
5	BDI	NIKOBIMEZE, REMY	15:07.95
6	MEX	MEZA, PEDRO	15:25.26
7	SUI	SOMMER, CHRISTOPH	15:28.19
8	TUN	CHAABANI, SAMIR	15:28.30

5,000 M T54 MEN

1	THA	WAHORAM, AWAT	10:22.38
2	AUS	FEARNLEY, KURT	10:22.97
3	GBR	WEIR, DAVID	10:23.03
4	SUI	HUG, MARCEL	10:23.20
5	JPN	HOKINOUE, KOTA	10:23.70
6	MEX	MENDOZA, SAUL	10:25.48
7	MEX	GORDIAN, AARON	10:25.49
8	POL	HAMERLAK, TOMASZ	10:25.67
	USA	**BLEAKNEY, ADAM**	*ELIM1*
	USA	**BYERS, TYLER**	*ELIM1*
	USA	**INIGUEZ, TONY**	*ELIM1*

800 M T12 MEN

1	TUN	ZHIOU, ABDERRAHIM	01:52.13
2	CUB	RASCHID AGUILAR, LAZARO	01:52.40
3	BRA	SANTOS, ODAIR	01:53.73
4	ESP	AVILA, IGNACIO	01:55.17

800 M T13 MEN

1	MAR	MAME, ABDELILLAH	01:54.78
2	**USA**	**GOTTWALD, PETER**	01:55.49
3	ALG	SEKHRI, ZINE EDDINE	01:55.90
4	MAR	AIT MALA, RACHID	01:55.90
5	VEN	SANCHEZ, LUIS	01:55.98
6	NZL	ENDERGAST, TIM	01:56.28
7	BRA	PEREIRA, NELSON NED	02:02.81
8	SUI	BEELER, MANUEL	02:03.08

800 M T36 MEN

1	RUS	AREFYEV, ARTEM	02:08.83
2	CHN	HE, CHENGEN	02:14.76
3	RUS	KHARAGEZOV, PAVEL	02:14.80
4	ESP	GONZALEZ, JOSE MANUEL	02:15.26
5	UKR	SAKOVSKYY, SERHIY	02:15.84
6	ESP	PAMPANO, JOSE MARIA	02:18.01
7	POL	REGA, JAKUB	02:23.70
8	POL	PLICHTA, ROBERT	02:27.89

800 M T37 MEN

1	IRL	MCKILLOP, MICHAEL	01:59.39
2	AUS	SCOTT, BRAD	02:02.71
3	FRA	MASTOURI, DJAMEL	02:03.04
4	TUN	CHARMI, MOHAMED	02:03.91
5	CHN	LU, JIANMING	02:10.26
6	TUN	OTHMANI, FAYCAL	02:12.42
7	POL	TUBIELEWICZ, MARIUSZ	02:15.45
8	ALG	HANANI, KHALED	02:16.03

800 M T46 MEN

1	POL	AWIZEN, MARCIN	01:52.36
2	ALG	NOUIOUA, SAMIR	01:52.97
3	ESP	AIT KHAMOUCH, ABDERRAHMAN	01:53.68
4	TUN	FOUZAI, MOHAMED	01:53.75
5	KEN	MUSYOKI, STEPHEN WAMBUA	01:54.63
6	KEN	WAMBUGU, SIMON	01:57.86
7	RUS	YALCHIK, ALEXANDER	01:58.04
8	MAR	FERHAT, AHMED	02:01.86

800 M T52 MEN

1	JPN	ITO, TOMOYA	01:53.42
2	JPN	TAKADA, TOSHIHIRO	01:53.67
3	AUT	GEIERSPICHLER, THOMAS	01:56.26
4	JPN	UEYONABARU, HIROKAZU	02:00.65
5	ESP	SANZ, SANTIAGO JOSE	02:00.89
6	CAN	BERGERON, DEAN	02:02.01
7	CAN	BEAUDOIN, ANDRE	02:08.54
8	THA	RUNGSRI, PETH	02:10.83
	USA	**ROBERTS, JOSH**	*ELIM1*
	USA	**TOYOJI, STEVEN**	*ELIM1*

800 M T53 MEN

1	CHN	LI, HUZHAO	01:36.30
2	**USA**	**GEORGE, JOSH**	01:37.09
3	KOR	HONG, SUK MAN	01:37.45
4	AUS	COLMAN, RICHARD	01:37.49
5	ESP	PUIGBO, ROGER	01:37.50
6	SUI	FREI, HEINZ	01:37.68
7	KOR	YOO, BYUNG HOON	01:37.80
8	JPN	HIROMICHI, JUN	01:37.86
	USA	**BLEAKNEY, ADAM**	*ELIM1*

800 M T54 MEN

1	GBR	WEIR, DAVID	01:36.61
2	AUS	FEARNLEY, KURT	01:36.76
3	THA	WAHORAM, AWAT	01:37.12
4	CHN	CUI, YANFENG	01:37.41
5	SUI	HUG, MARCEL	01:37.51
6	FRA	CASOLI, JULIEN	01:37.56
7	MEX	MENDOZA, SAUL	01:38.61
8	THA	THAMSOPHON, KHACHONSAK	01:38.73
	USA	**BYERS, TYLER**	*ELIMS*
	USA	**INIGUEZ, TONY**	*ELIMS*

CLUB THROW F32/51 MEN

1	TUN	IDOUDI, MOURAD	35.77
2	GBR	MILLER, STEPHEN	34.37
3	CZE	VANEK, JAN	25.59
4	CZE	BELES, RADIM	25.43
5	CZE	ZVOLANEK, MARTIN	25.07
6	ALG	BETINA, KARIM	31.36
7	GBR	MURPHY, KIERON	29.03
8	CRO	MATIC, MIROSLAV	21.46

DISCUS F11/12 MEN

1	UKR	LISHCHYNSKYI, VASYL	40.59
2	ARG	BALDASSARRI, SEBASTIAN	40.43
3	UKR	IASYNOVYI, OLEKSANDR	49.52
4	RUS	ANDRYUSHCHENKO, VLADIMIR	49.49
5	ESP	CASINOS, DAVID	38.85
6	AUT	MARINKOVIC, BIL	37.24
7	LTU	URBONAS, ROLANDAS	44.41
8	BLR	BUCHKOU, YURY	43.43

DISCUS F32/51 MEN

1	TUN	IDOUDI, MOURAD	19.72
2	SLO	FLERE, JOZE	10.99
3	CZE	ZVOLANEK, MARTIN	10.78
4	ALG	BETINA, KARIM	19.04
5	CZE	BELES, RADIM	9.92

6	GRE	KALOGEROS, PANTELIS	9.78
7	CZE	SERBUS, FRANTISEK	17.05
8	GBR	SCHABEL, RICHARD	9.55

DISCUS F33/34/52 MEN

1	LAT	APINIS, AIGARS	20.47
2	GBR	MARTIN, CHRIS	28.37
3	CZE	MUSIL, ROMAN	27.11
4	TUN	KRID, MOHAMED	38.09
5	IRL	CULLITON, GARRETT	17.79
6	GBR	WEST, DANIEL	37.38
7	JOR	YASEEN, MOHAMMAD	17.05
8	UAE	BIN DABBAS ALMEHAIRI, MOHAMMAD	33.36

DISCUS F35/36 MEN

1	CHN	GUO, WEI	54.13
2	CHN	WANG, WENBO	38.98
3	NAM	BENADE, REGINALD	37.57
4	RSA	STRYDOM, DUANE	36.47
5	LAT	BERGS, EDGARS	47.02
6	BRA	SOUZA, PAULO	34.10
7	NED	NOORDUIN, WILLEM	32.60
8	POL	PIOTROWSKI, PAWEL	31.75

DISCUS F37/38 MEN

1	IRI	HARDANI, JAVAD	45.62
2	UKR	ZHABNYAK, MYKOLA	52.00
3	CHN	XIA, DONG	51.65
4	PAK	ALI, HAIDER	43.95
5	POL	BLATKIEWICZ, TOMASZ	49.72
6	EGY	RAMADAN, MOHAMED MOHAMED	49.60
7	TUN	WARFILI, HAMDI	39.47
8	GER	LOOSCH, THOMAS	39.40

DISCUS F42 MEN

1	RSA	LOMBARD, FANIE	46.75
2	IRI	KARAM ZADEH, MEHRDAD	44.74
3	CHN	WANG, LEZHENG	42.95
4	**USA**	**BROWN, MATT**	42.25
5	BEL	DE KEERSMAEKER, GINO	41.84
6	GRE	FYLACHTOS, MARINOS	41.16
7	BUL	OVCHAROV, DECHKO	39.25
8	BLR	KHILMONCHYK, VIKTAR	38.89

DISCUS F44 MEN

1	**USA**	**CAMPBELL, JEREMY**	55.08
2	DEN	CHRISTIANSEN, JACKIE	53.69
3	GBR	GREAVES, DANIEL	53.04
4	IRI	SEPAHVAND, FARZAD	51.23
5	AUS	RAISON, PAUL	49.77
6	**USA**	**SKIBA, JEFF**	48.72
7	GRE	PAPPAS, GEORGIOS	44.84
8	CHN	HA, SILAO	42.80

F53/54 MEN

1	CHN	FAN, LIANG	31.08
2	SRB	MITROVIC, DRAZENKO	29.09
3	JPN	OI, TOSHIE	26.21
4	JAM	CUNNINGHAM, ALPHANSO	25.90
5	GRE	KALARAS, EFTHYMIOS	27.98
6	ITA	BERNARDI, GERMANO	25.78
7	**USA**	**SEVERN, SCOT**	23.71
8	SRB	BRKIC, JOVICA	24.57

DISCUS F55/56 MEN

1	CUB	DIAZ, LEONARDO	40.87
2	IRI	MOHAMMAD YARI, ALI	39.39
3	JAM	CAMPBELL, TANTO	39.31
4	CZE	NEMEC, MARTIN	37.48
5	CZE	SPERK, MIROSLAV	36.64
6	BUL	YUSEINOV, MUSTAFA	35.73
7	CZE	STIAK, JOSEF	36.12
8	EGY	ABDELSEMIA, MAHMOUD	35.24

DISCUS F57/58 MEN

1	RUS	ASHAPATOV, ALEXEY	57.61
2	CHN	ZHENG, WEIHAI	49.09
3	CZE	POHLMANN, ROSTISLAV	45.48
4	GER	GHARDOONI, ALI	44.69
5	FRA	TAFILAGI, PASILIONE	50.93
6	EGY	ELATTAR, MAHMOUD RAMADAN	50.74
7	BRA	AMANCIO, LEONARDO	50.54
8	NGR	EZEIKPE, CHINEDU SILVER	50.42

HIGH JUMP F44/46 MEN

1	**USA**	**SKIBA, JEFF**	2.11
2	AUS	CHATMAN, AARON	2.02
3	CHN	CHEN, HONGJIE	1.96
4	CHN	DU, JUN	1.93
5	JPN	SUZUKI, TORU	1.93
6	GER	BOTZEL, REINHOLD	1.87
7	CHN	WU, YANCONG	1.84
8	RSA	ROOS, DAVID	1.84

JAVELIN F11/12 MEN

1	CHN	ZHU, PENGKAI	63.07
2	CRO	BUDETIC, BRANIMIR	57.11
3	POL	PYCH, MIROSLAW	56.01
4	AUT	MARINKOVIC, BIL	46.44
5	BLR	TRYPUTS, ALIAKSANDR	52.40
6	JPN	OZAKI, MINEHO	44.46
7	GER	HEGEHOLZ, SIEGMUND	43.18
8	SRB	GRLICA, MILOS	49.19

JAVELIN F33/34/52 MEN

1	TUN	RZIG, FAOUZI	34.81
2	TUN	KRID, MOHAMED	31.26
3	FRA	TALATINI, JEAN-PIERRE	31.19
4	CZE	MUSIL, ROMAN	25.05
5	UAE	BIN DABBAS ALMEHAIRI, MOHAMMAD	28.72
6	AUS	FARR, ROD	17.55
7	AUS	BOWEN, DAMIEN	26.52
8	GRE	KARAMINAS, GEORGIOS	16.45

JAVELIN F35/36 MEN

1	CHN	GUO, WEI	56.07
2	POL	PIOTROWSKI, PAWEL	42.88
3	RSA	NEWMAN, NICHOLAS	42.48
4	BRA	SOUZA, PAULO	39.72
5	IRI	KAEIDI, MOHSEN	42.61
6	CHN	WANG, WENBO	32.49

JAVELIN F37/38 MEN

1	CHN	XIA, DONG	57.81
2	CHN	ZHANG, XUELONG	50.24
3	IRI	HARDANI, JAVAD	47.65
4	AUS	MCMAHON, WADE	46.71
5	BRN	MESHAIMA, AHMED	46.22
6	GBR	CHURCHILL, KENNY	45.30
7	UKR	ZHABNYAK, MYKOLA	44.57
8	CZE	VRATIL, PETR	44.66

JAVELIN F42/44 MEN

1	CHN	GAO, MINGJIE	57.60
2	RUS	GUDKOV, EVGENY	55.50
3	CHN	GAO, CHANGLONG	55.30
4	NED	HERTOG, RONALD	51.69
5	**USA**	**SKIBA, JEFF**	51.46
6	CHN	HA, SILAO	50.73
7	BUL	OVCHAROV, DECHKO	45.54
8	POL	KALUZIAK, LUKASZ	49.57

JAVELIN F53/54 MEN

1	FIN	NIINIMAKI, MARKKU	29.33
2	IRI	JOKAR, ABDOLREZA	22.08
3	MEX	ZEPEDA, FELIX	28.67
4	SRB	MITROVIC, DRAZENKO	27.42
5	MEX	MAXIMO, MAURO	20.39
6	RUS	KUZNETSOV, ALEXEY	26.78
7	CHN	FAN, LIANG	26.06
8	MEX	PAZ, ADRIAN	19.55

JAVELIN F55/56 MEN

1	NED	GRUIJTERS, PIETER	42.27
2	CHN	ZHANG, YINGBIN	32.70
3	EGY	ELSAYED, YASER ABDELAZIZ	30.54
4	CZE	STIAK, JOSEF	31.88
5	CUB	DIAZ, LEONARDO	30.70
6	POL	KOZUN, KAROL	26.69

JAVELIN F57/58 MEN

1	IRI	MIRZAEI JABERI, MOHAMMADREZA	40.84
2	EGY	ELATTAR, MAHMOUD RAMADAN	48.80
3	CZE	POHLMANN, ROSTISLAV	39.85
4	GBR	STEPHENS, NATHAN	38.56
5	NGR	EZEIKPE, CHINEDU SILVER	45.86
6	SYR	MOHAMAD, MOHAMAD	37.66
7	CHN	XU, CHONGYAO	45.62
8	SVK	HUTKA, JULIUS	35.98

LONG JUMP F11 MEN

1	CHN	LI, DUAN	6.61
2	**USA**	**GILLETTE, LEX**	6.46
3	GRE	BARAKAS, ATHANASIOS	6.17
4	ESP	PORRAS, JAVIER	5.96
5	JPN	TAKADA, KOICHI	5.74
6	THA	PUNTHONG, JAKKRIT	5.66
7	SUI	HENDRY, LUKAS	5.54
8	BLR	ZHUKOUSKY, VIKTAR	5.41

LONG JUMP F12 MEN

1	RSA	LANGENHOVEN, HILTON	7.31
2	KSA	ALSHANQITI, OSAMAH	7.06
3	AZE	PANYUTIN, OLEG	7.06
4	AZE	ZAYETS, VLADIMIR	6.81
5	BLR	BURDUKOU, SIARHEI	6.75
6	FRA	PALLIER, RONAN	6.66
7	FRA	BOZZOLO, STEPHANE	6.53
8	UKR	KATYSHEV, RUSLAN	6.38

LONG JUMP F37/38 MEN

1	TUN	CHIDA, FARHAT	6.44
2	PAK	ALI, HAIDER	6.44
3	CHN	MA, YUXI	6.19
4	GRE	MARINOS, ARISTOTELIS	5.95
5	AUS	THRUPP, DARREN	5.82
6	TUN	HAMDI, FARES	5.77
7	ISL	BALDURSSON, BALDUR	5.42
8	POL	LABUCH, LUKASZ	5.42

LONG JUMP F42/44 MEN

1	GER	CZYZ, WOJTEK	6.50
2	JPN	YAMAMOTO, ATSUSHI	5.84
3	**USA**	**TIBBS, CASEY**	6.39
4	**USA**	**CAMPBELL, JEREMY**	6.36
5	SUI	KOLLY, URS	6.36
6	CHN	WANG, QIUHONG	6.31
7	BRA	OLIVEIRA, ANDRE LUIZ	6.19
8	ITA	LA BARBERA, ROBERTO	6.14

LONG JUMP F46 MEN

1	FRA	ASSOUMANI, ARNAUD	7.23
2	RSA	ROOS, DAVID	6.64
3	CHN	LI, KANGYONG	6.61
4	CUB	CALDERON, ETTIAM	6.48
5	BLR	SUBOTA, ALIAKSANDR	6.46
6	CHN	WU, YANCONG	6.42
7	IND	SINGH, JAGSEER	6.40
8	ESP	BRAVO, DAVID	6.05

MARATHON T12 MEN

1	CHN	QI, SHUN	2:30:32
2	COL	SERNA, ELKIN	2:31:16
3	RUS	POMYKALOV, ILDAR	2:33:27
4	TUN	ZHIOU, ABDERRAHIM	2:35:26
5	ITA	COCCHI, FABRIZIO	2:35:27
6	ESP	GARNICA, MANUEL	2:36:02
7	ITA	CIONNA, ANDREA	2:36:43
8	MEX	BERISTAIN, MOISES	2:38:17

MARATHON T46 MEN

1	MEX	SANTILLAN, MARIO	2:27.04
2	BRA	SENA, TITO	2:30.49
3	ITA	ENDRIZZI, WALTER	2:32.51
4	CHN	HAN, GUIMING	2:33.57
5	BRA	BONFIM, OZIVAN	2:35.31
6	TUN	CHAABANI, SAMIR	2:35.54
7	BEL	VAN DEN HEEDE, FREDERIC	2:37.03
8	MEX	MEZA, PEDRO	2:38.57

MARATHON T52 MEN

1	AUT	GEIERSPICHLER, THOMAS	1:40.07
2	JPN	UEYONABARU, HIROKAZU	1:40.10
3	JPN	TAKADA, TOSHIHIRO	1:40.20
4	ESP	SANZ, SANTIAGO JOSE	1:42.05
5	**USA**	**TOYOJI, STEVEN**	1:58.37
6	CAN	GEREIN, CLAYTON	2:08.04
7	TUN	ZIDI, OMAR	2:09.04

MARATHON T54 MEN

1	AUS	FEARNLEY, KURT	1:23.17
2	JPN	SASAHARA, HIROKI	1:23.17
3	RSA	VAN DYK, ERNST	1:23.18
4	MEX	GORDIAN, AARON	1:23.20
5	JPN	HOKINOUE, KOTA	1:23.22
6	JPN	YAMAMOTO, HIROYUKI	1:23.22
7	JPN	HIROMICHI, JUN	1:23.23
8	ESP	MADERA, JORGE	1:23.26
15	**USA**	**INIGUEZ, TONY**	1:26.04
17	**USA**	**GEORGE, JOSH**	1:30.29
23	**USA**	**BLEAKNEY, ADAM**	1:30.36
24	**USA**	**BYERS, TYLER**	1:32.33

PENTATHLON P12 MEN

1	RSA	LANGENHOVEN, HILTON	3403
2	GER	ULBRICHT, THOMAS	3178
3	TUN	KHALDI, MAHMOUD	3149
4	FRA	BOZZOLO, STEPHANE	3111
5	CRO	BUDETIC, BRANIMIR	3102
6	TUN	ZHIOU, ABDERRAHIM	3050
7	UKR	KATYSHEV, RUSLAN	3027
8	BEL	VANRAEFELGHEM, KURT	2997

MEN'S PENTATHLON P44 MEN

1	**USA**	**CAMPBELL, JEREMY**	4662
2	**USA**	**SKIBA, JEFF**	4274
3	SUI	KOLLY, URS	4118
	USA	**TIBBS, CASEY**	2713-DNF
	ITA	LA BARBERA, ROBERTO	DNF

SHOT PUT F11/12 MEN

1	ESP	CASINOS, DAVID	14.50
2	RUS	ANDRYUSHCHENKO, VLADIMIR	16.46
3	UKR	LISHCHYNSKYI, VASYL	13.59
4	BLR	HRYBANAU, SIARHEI	15.35
5	BLR	BUCHKOU, YURY	14.98
6	AUS	SHORT, RUSSELL	14.79
7	LTU	URBONAS, ROLANDAS	14.72
8	ARG	BALDASSARRI, SEBASTIAN	11.11

SHOT PUT F32 MEN

1	ALG	BETINA, KARIM	10.65
2	TUN	IDOUDI, MOURAD	10.40
3	ALG	BAKIRI, MOUNIR	9.37
4	GRE	ZISIDIS, DIMITRIOS	8.69
5	KOR	PARK, SE HO	6.93
6	CZE	SERBUS, FRANTISEK	6.55
7	IRL	CLEARE, EOIN THOMAS	6.11

SHOT PUT F33/34/52 MEN

1	ALG	KARDJENA, KAMEL	11.54
2	LAT	APINIS, AIGARS	10.02
3	CAN	PETTEY, KYLE	11.04
4	FRA	TALATINI, JEAN-PIERRE	11.01
5	AUS	HIBBERD, GREG	10.83
6	AUS	MACDONALD, HAMISH	10.82
7	CZE	MUSIL, ROMAN	10.37
8	GBR	WEST, DANIEL	10.39

SHOT PUT F35/36 MEN

1	CHN	GUO, WEI	16.22
2	LAT	BERGS, EDGARS	15.54
3	POL	PIOTROWSKI, PAWEL	13.03
4	CHN	WANG, WENBO	12.13
5	FRA	CIBONE, THIERRY	14.03
6	NAM	BENADE, REGINALD	11.59
7	NED	NOORDUIN, WILLEM	11.27
8	CHN	FU, XINHAN	12.20

SHOT PUT F37/38 MEN

1	CHN	XIA, DONG	16.60
2	POL	BLATKIEWICZ, TOMASZ	14.74
3	GER	LOOSCH, THOMAS	14.44
4	POL	CHYRA, ROBERT	13.01
5	GBR	CRUTCHLEY, MARTIN	12.72
6	BRN	MESHAIMA, AHMED	12.80

7	UKR	ZHABNYAK, MYKOLA	12.73
8	TUN	WARFILI, HAMDI	12.56

SHOT PUT F40 MEN

1	GRE	STATHELAKOS, PASCHALIS	11.75
2	GER	MESTER, MATHIAS	11.16
3	ALG	GHERZOULI, HOCINE	11.08
4	GRE	KONSTANTINIDIS, ALEXANDROS MICHAIL	10.58
5	BRA	SANTOS, JONATHAN	10.53
6	SVK	MARGOC, MAREK	9.90
7	CRO	SLUNJSKI, DENIS	9.83
8	**USA**	**DANBERG, SCOTT**	9.79

SHOT PUT F42 MEN

1	CRO	KRALJ, DARKO	14.43
2	RUS	NAROZHNYY, MAXIM	13.92
3	RSA	LOMBARD, FANIE	13.87
4	CHN	WANG, LEZHENG	13.63
5	IRI	KARAM ZADEH, MEHRDAD	13.58
6	CRO	TOMIC, MLADEN	12.78
7	IRI	ASGHARI, MAHDI	12.50
8	**USA**	**BROWN, MATT**	12.46

SHOT PUT F44 MEN

1	DEN	CHRISTIANSEN, JACKIE	17.89
2	AUS	RAISON, PAUL	15.83
3	CUB	FONSECA, GERDAN	15.65
4	GRE	PAPPAS, GEORGIOS	15.03
5	CRO	SLIVAR, JOSIP	14.67
6	**USA**	**COCHRELL, ED**	14.16
7	GER	FRISCHMANN, JORG	13.75
8	FRA	FALELAVAKI, TONY	12.47

SHOT PUT F53/54 MEN

1	MEX	MAXIMO, MAURO	8.72
2	FIN	NIINIMAKI, MARKKU	9.92
3	GRE	FERNANDES, CHE JON	8.29
4	CZE	KISY, ALES	8.25
5	AUT	GRATT, ANDREAS	9.62
6	AUT	TISCHLER, GEORG	9.61
7	ITA	BERNARDI, GERMANO	9.46
8	PLE	AZZAM, HUSAM F. A.	7.89

SHOT PUT F55/56 MEN

1	AZE	MUSAYEV, OLOKHAN	13.49
2	POL	SMORSZCZEWSKI, KRZYSZTOF	11.95
3	CZE	NEMEC, MARTIN	11.55
4	RUS	IVANOV, ALEXEY	11.75
5	**USA**	**WINKLER, SCOTT**	11.27
6	EGY	BESHTA, MOHAMED ROSHDY	11.35
7	NED	GRUIJTERS, PIETER	11.33
8	GRE	NALMPANTIS, ILIAS	10.99

SHOT PUT F57/58 MEN

1	RUS	ASHAPATOV, ALEXEY	16.03
2	JOR	ELSHEBLI, JAMIL	14.28
3	GRE	TSIOU, ANASTASIOS	13.72
4	POL	ROKICKI, JANUSZ	15.29
5	RSA	LOUENS, MICHAEL	13.64
6	IRI	MORADI, MEHDI	13.44
7	GRE	CHARAKOPOULOS, MINAS	12.84
8	GBR	STEPHENS, NATHAN	12.57

TRIPLE JUMP F11 MEN

1	CHN	LI, DUAN	13.71
2	AZE	BILALOV, ZEYNIDIN	12.80
3	ESP	PORRAS, JAVIER	12.71
4	RUS	KOPTEV, ANDREY	12.44
5	**USA**	**GILLETTE, LEX**	12.19
6	RUS	SEVOSTYANOV, SERGEY	11.92
7	GRE	BARAKAS, ATHANASIOS	11.89
8	BLR	ZHUKOUSKY, VIKTAR	11.53

TRIPLE JUMP F12 MEN

1	KSA	ALSHANQITI, OSAMAH	15.37
2	UKR	KYTSENKO, IVAN	15.24
3	AZE	ZAYETS, VLADIMIR	15.00
4	BLR	KOUZMICHOU, ALIAKSANDR	14.28
5	BLR	SIVITSKI, RUSLAN	13.91
6	BLR	BURDUKOU, SIARHEI	13.30
7	RUS	KEGELEV, EVGENY	12.97

1,500 M T13 WOMEN

1	TUN	BOUSAID, SOMAYA	4:14.00
2	FRA	EL HANNOUNI, ASSIA	4:19.20
3	RUS	PAUTOVA, ELENA	4:32.91
4	RUS	BATALOVA, RIMA	4:44.21
5	CZE	SEDLACKOVA, MIROSLAVA	4:53.78
6	ESP	CONGOST, ELENA	4:54.50
7	KEN	MUNIALO, NELLY NASIMIYU	4:56.88
8	POR	FIUZA, ODETE	5:03.51

1,500 M T54 WOMEN

1	CAN	PETITCLERC, CHANTAL	3:39.88
2	GBR	WOODS, SHELLY	3:40.99
3	SUI	HUNKELER, EDITH	3:41.03
4	**USA**	**GALLI, JESSICA**	3:41.68
5	**USA**	**MCGRORY, AMANDA**	3:42.17
6	SUI	GRAF, SANDRA	3:42.26
7	**USA**	**REILLY, SHIRLEY**	3:43.54
8	CAN	ROY, DIANE	3:43.66

100 M T11 WOMEN

1	CHN	WU, CHUNMIAO	12.31
2	BRA	GUILHERMINA, TEREZINHA	12.40
3	BRA	SANTOS, ADRIA	12.99

4	BRA	SANTOS, ADRIA	13.07
5	VEN	TORRES, ALBERLIS	13.08
6	GBR	HINTON, TRACEY	13.18
7	GRE	KANTZA, PARASKEVI	13.20
8	VEN	SUAREZ, IRENE	13.21

100 M T12 WOMEN

1	UKR	BOTURCHUK, OXANA	12.38
2	GBR	CLEGG, LIBBY	12.51
3	ESP	NGUI, EVA	12.58
4	BLR	ZINKEVICH, VOLHA	12.71
5	SVK	KOLNIKOVA, HANA	12.87
6	BRA	GUILHERMINO, SIRLENE	12.95
7	VEN	DE TOVAR TATIANA, TATIANA DEL CARMEN	12.99
8	CUB	MIJAN, DAINERIS	13.05

100 M T13 WOMEN

1	MAR	BENHAMA, SANAA	12.28
2	RSA	HAYES, ILSE	12.45
3	GRE	DIMOGLOU, ALEXANDRA	12.56
4	FRA	KEITA, NANTENIN	12.57
5	UKR	CHYSHKO, MARYNA	12.58
6	CUB	DURAND, OMARA	12.59
7	GRE	KARAGIANNI, ANTHI	12.81
8	GER	MULLER-ROTTGARDT, KATRIN	12.85

100 M T36 WOMEN

1	CHN	WANG, FANG	13.82
2	GER	NICOLEITZIK, CLAUDIA	15.00
3	GBR	SIMPSON, HAZEL	15.40
4	JPN	KATO, YUKI	15.42
5	HKG	YU, CHUN LAI	15.66
6	KOR	JEON, MIN JAE	15.67
7	RUS	SAKHIBZADAEVA, AYGYUL	15.74
8	RUS	LINEVICH, YULIA	16.10

100 M T37 WOMEN

1	AUS	MCINTOSH, LISA	14.14
2	UKR	KRAVCHENKO, VIKTORIYA	14.21
3	GER	SEIFERT, MARIA	14.28
4	GER	FOERDER, ISABELLE	14.54
5	POL	LANGNER, MARTA	14.94
6	UKR	KRECHUNYAK, OKSANA	15.09
7	GBR	HART, KATRINA	15.12
8	RUS	SERGEEVA, SVETLANA	15.24
	USA	**HAWKES, SABRA**	ELIM1

100 M T38 WOMEN

1	UKR	DYACHENKO, INNA	13.43
2	TUN	MANSOUR, SONIA	13.66
3	RUS	KOPTILOVA, MARGARITA	13.97
4	BRA	SANTOS, JENIFER	14.31
5	GER	SLABY, TAMIRA	14.75
6	BLR	KIRUSHCHANKA, KATSIARYNA	14.79
7	CZE	VEJRAZKOVA, ANEZKA	14.81

100 M T42 WOMEN

1	MEX	BUSTAMANTE, PERLA	16.32
2	NED	ROOZEN, ANNETTE	17.13
3	AUS	WOLF, CHRISTINE	17.49
4	POL	ZIELINSKA, EWA	17.89
5	NED	SMITS, MARIJE	18.27
6	AUS	CARTIGHT, KELLY	18.36
7	GER	BIENE, CLAUDIA	18.92

100 M T44 WOMEN

1	**USA**	**HOLMES, AIL**	13.72
2	FRA	LE FUR, MARIE-AMELIE	13.73
3	CHN	WANG, JUAN	13.73
4	GER	GREEN, KATRIN	13.74
5	NZL	HORAN, KATE	14.01
6	JPN	NAKANISHI, MAYA	14.24
7	GER	HOFTE, ASTRID	14.47
8	AUT	SCHERNEY, ANDREA	14.48

100 M T46 WOMEN

1	POL	FIODOROW, ALICJA	12.60
2	AUS	SMITH, JULIE	12.65
3	RUS	RODOMAKINA, NIKOL	12.79
4	UKR	RUDKIVS'KA, TETYANA	12.83
5	BLR	LEANTSIUK, IRYNA	12.91
6	RUS	MOGUCHAYA, ALEXANDRA	13.04
7	NED	METTES, MARIJKE	13.30
8	BRA	FINDER, SHEILA	13.32

100 M T52 WOMEN

1	CAN	STILWELL, MICHELLE	19.97
2	JPN	YAMAKI, TOMOMI	21.00
3	JPN	TANAKA, TERUYO	21.33
4	SUI	SCHMID, PIA	21.53
5	**USA**	**MORGAN, KERRI**	21.56
6	**USA**	**BADGETT, MALLERIE**	24.01
7	**USA**	**LEITNER, CHERYL**	24.40
8	AUS	BUCHHOLZ, GEMMA	24.64

100 M T53 WOMEN

1	CHN	HUANG, LISHA	16.22
2	**USA**	**GALLI, JESSICA**	16.88
3	CAN	DUFF, ILANA	17.69
4	ITA	PORCELLATO, FRANCESCA	17.86
5	AUS	BALLARD, ANGIE	17.89
6	**USA**	**FORBER ATT, ANJALI**	17.99
7	SWE	NORDLUND, MADELENE	18.40
8	MEX	ENCISO, EVELYN	18.43
	USA	**REDDEN, MAGGIE**	ELIM1

100 M T54 WOMEN

1	CAN	PETITCLERC, CHANTAL	16.15
2	CHN	LIU, WENJUN	16.20
3	CHN	DONG, HONGJIAO	16.24
4	SUI	SCHAR, MANUELA	16.35
5	CHN	ZHANG, TING	16.61
6	**USA**	**MCFADDEN, TATYANA**	16.62
7	GER	SEHMISCH, YVONNE	17.08
8	AUS	DE ROZARIO, MADISON	17.21

200 M T11 WOMEN

1	BRA	GUILHERMINA, TEREZINHA	25.14
2	CHN	WU, CHUNMIAO	25.40
3	BRA	SANTOS, JERUSA	26.09
4	GBR	HINTON, TRACEY	26.68
5	GRE	KANTZA, PARASKEVI	26.87
6	VEN	SUAREZ, IRENE	27.61
7	RUS	FROLOVA, ELENA	27.69
8	BRA	SANTOS, ADRIA	28.15

200 M T12 WOMEN

1	FRA	EL HANNOUNI, ASSIA	24.84
2	UKR	BOTURCHUK, OXANA	25.03
3	FRA	EL HANNOUNI, ASSIA	25.27
4	ESP	NGUI, EVA	25.70
5	ANG	ALEXANDRE, EVALINA	25.72
6	ESP	NGUI, EVA	25.87
7	GBR	CLEGG, LIBBY	26.16
	ANG	ALEXANDRE, EVALINA	DISQ

200 M T13 WOMEN

1	MAR	BENHAMA, SANAA	24.89
2	FRA	KEITA, NANTENIN	25.51
3	GRE	DIMOGLOU, ALEXANDRA	25.59
4	CUB	DURAND, OMARA	25.67
5	RSA	HAYES, ILSE	26.22
6	UKR	CHYSHKO, MARYNA	26.50
7	BRA	SILVA, JOANA	26.85
8	UKR	SMYRNOVA, TETIANA	26.93

200 M T36 WOMEN

1	CHN	WANG, FANG	29.57
2	GER	NICOLEITZIK, CLAUDIA	31.48
3	GBR	SIMPSON, HAZEL	32.43
4	KOR	JEON, MIN JAE	32.62
5	JPN	KATO, YUKI	33.53
6	HKG	YU, CHUN LAI	33.55
7	RUS	SAKHIBZADAEVA, AYGYUL	33.91

200 M T37 WOMEN

1	AUS	MCINTOSH, LISA	29.28
2	UKR	KRAVCHENKO, VIKTORIYA	29.60
3	GER	SEIFERT, MARIA	29.99
4	GER	FOERDER, ISABELLE	30.70
5	RUS	TRUSHNIKOVA, EVGENIA	31.06
6	UKR	KRECHUNYAK, OKSANA	31.17
7	POL	LANGNER, MARTA	31.25
	USA	**HAWKES, SABRA**	ELIM1

200 M T38 WOMEN

1	UKR	DYACHENKO, INNA	27.81
2	TUN	MANSOUR, SONIA	28.07
3	RUS	KOPTILOVA, MARGARITA	28.62
4	GER	SLABY, TAMIRA	30.02
5	AUS	PARRISH, KATY	30.46
6	CZE	VEJRAZKOVA, ANEZKA	30.61
7	BLR	KIRUSHCHANKA, KATSIARYNA	31.00
8	POR	FERNANDES, MARIA	31.38

200 M T44 WOMEN

1	GER	GREEN, KATRIN	28.02
2	NZL	HORAN, KATE	28.36
3	CAN	REID, STEFANIE	28.85
4	JPN	NAKANISHI, MAYA	28.98
5	GER	HOFTE, ASTRID	29.33
6	ITA	GARGANO, GIUSEPPINA	30.17
7	RSA	MARAIS, SARISA	30.41
8	FRA	LE FUR, MARIE-AMELIE	31.09
	USA	**HOLMES, AIL**	DISQ

200 M T46 WOMEN

1	CUB	CASTILLO, YUNIDIS	24.72
2	POL	FIODOROW, ALICJA	25.96
3	AUS	SMITH, JULIE	26.03
4	UKR	RUDKIVS'KA, TETYANA	26.05
5	RUS	CHISTILINA, ELENA	26.15
6	POL	MAYER, ANNA	26.48
7	RUS	RODOMAKINA, NIKOL	26.52
8	BLR	LEANTSIUK, IRYNA	27.11

200 M T52 WOMEN

1	CAN	STILWELL, MICHELLE	36.18
2	JPN	YAMAKI, TOMOMI	37.44
3	SUI	SCHMID, PIA	39.95
4	JPN	TANAKA, TERUYO	40.36
5	**USA**	**MORGAN, KERRI**	40.82
6	**USA**	**LEITNER, CHERYL**	41.01
7	**USA**	**BADGETT, MALLERIE**	43.42
8	AUS	BUCHHOLZ, GEMMA	44.57

200 M T53 WOMEN

1	CHN	HUANG, LISHA	29.17
2	**USA**	**GALLI, JESSICA**	29.68
3	CHN	ZHOU, HONGZHUAN	30.15
4	**USA**	**FORBER ATT, ANJALI**	30.99
5	CAN	DUFF, ILANA	31.47

	ITA	PORCELLATO, FRANCESCA	31.61
6	ITA	PORCELLATO, FRANCESCA	31.61
7	AUS	BALLARD, ANGIE	31.81
8	SWE	NORDLUND, MADELENE	32.31
	USA	REDDEN, MAGGIE	ELIM1

200 M T54 WOMEN

1	CAN	PETITCLERC, CHANTAL	27.52
2	USA	MCFADDEN, TATYANA	28.43
3	SUI	SCHAR, MANUELA	28.84
4	CHN	ZHANG, TING	29.00
5	CAN	MATASSA, JESSICA	30.14
6	GER	SEHMISCH, YVONNE	30.49
7	MEX	BATAZ, YAZMITH	31.05
8	CAN	FERGUSON, TRACEY	31.66
	USA	GOECKEL, JENNIFER	ELIM1

400 M T12 WOMEN

1	FRA	EL HANNOUNI, ASSIA	55.06
2	UKR	BOTURCHUK, OXANA	55.88
3	BRA	GUILHERMINA, TEREZINHA	57.02
4	ANG	ALEXANDRE, EVALINA	1:00.46
5	CHN	SUN, XIN	1:02.46

400 M T13 WOMEN

1	MAR	BENHAMA, SANAA	55.56
2	GRE	DIMOGLOU, ALEXANDRA	56.09
3	FRA	KEITA, NANTENIN	56.28
4	TUN	BOUSAID, SOMAYA	56.72
5	UKR	SMYRNOVA, TETIANA	0.00
6	GER	MULLER-ROTTGARDT, KATRIN	0.00
7	BRA	SILVA, JOANA	0.00
	CUB	DURAND, OMARA	DNF

400 M T53 WOMEN

1	USA	GALLI, JESSICA	54.88
2	CHN	ZHOU, HONGZHUAN	55.28
3	USA	FORBER ATT, ANJALI	56.79
4	USA	BLAUWET, CHERI	57.07
5	ITA	PORCELLATO, FRANCESCA	58.83
6	CAN	DUFF, ILANA	58.93
7	AUS	BALLARD, ANGIE	59.82
8	MEX	ENCISO, EVELYN	1:01.89

400 M T54 WOMEN

1	CAN	PETITCLERC, CHANTAL	52.02
2	USA	MCFADDEN, TATYANA	53.49
3	CAN	ROY, DIANE	54.72
4	SUI	HUNKELER, EDITH	55.25
5	CHN	DONG, HONGJIAO	55.83
6	SUI	SCHAR, MANUELA	56.24
7	CAN	MATASSA, JESSICA	57.02
8	SWE	WALLENGREN, GUNILLA	58.20
	USA	GOECKEL, JENNIFER	ELIM1

4X100 M T53/54 WOMEN

1	CHN		57.61
2	AUS		1:01.9
3	USA		1:02.2
		MCFADDEN, TATYANA	
		FORBER ATT, ANJALI	
		GALLI, JESSICA	
		MCGRORY, AMANDA	
	MEX		DISQ

5,000 M T54 WOMEN

1	USA	MCGRORY, AMANDA	12:29.07
2	CAN	ROY, DIANE	12:29.08
3	GBR	WOODS, SHELLY	12:29.32
4	USA	BLAUWET, CHERI	12:29.43
5	SUI	GRAF, SANDRA	12:30.55
6	AUS	DAWES, CHRISTIE	12:31.66
7	CAN	FERGUSON, TRACEY	12:31.77
8	USA	REILLY, SHIRLEY	12:32.19

800 M T12/13 WOMEN

1	TUN	BOUSAID, SOMAYA	2:03.21
2	FRA	EL HANNOUNI, ASSIA	2:04.96
3	RUS	PAUTOVA, ELENA	2:15.70
4	RUS	BATALOVA, RIMA	2:20.94

800 M T53 WOMEN

1	CHN	ZHOU, HONGZHUAN	1:57.25
2	USA	GALLI, JESSICA	1:57.25
3	USA	MCGRORY, AMANDA	1:57.31
4	USA	BLAUWET, CHERI	1:58.38
5	ITA	PORCELLATO, FRANCESCA	2:01.99
6	AUS	BALLARD, ANGIE	2:02.56
7	MEX	ENCISO, EVELYN	2:02.99

800 M T54 WOMEN

1	CAN	PETITCLERC, CHANTAL	1:45.19
2	USA	MCFADDEN, TATYANA	1:46.95
3	CAN	ROY, DIANE	1:48.07
4	SUI	HUNKELER, EDITH	1:49.11
5	GBR	WOODS, SHELLY	1:50.03
6	SWE	WALLENGREN, GUNILLA	1:50.09
7	CHN	LIU, WENJUN	1:51.85
8	USA	MCCLAMMER, CHELSEA	1:51.88

DISCUS F12/13 WOMEN

1	BLR	SIVAKOVA, TAMARA	41.29
2	CHN	ZHANG, LIANGMIN	40.35
3	ARG	ALMADA, ELIZABETH	38.03
4	GER	CHRISTEN, SIENA	36.60
5	GBR	WILLIAMS, CLAIRE	35.01
6	CHN	TANG, HONGXIA	33.88
7	ESP	CASTELLANO, JESSICA	32.72
8	ESP	MARTINEZ, MARIA	32.14
9	CRO	IVEKOVIC, MARIJA	31.76

DISCUS F32-34/51-53 WOMEN

1	UKR	YAKYBCHUK, TETYANA	17.05
2	GER	HERRMANN, FRANCES	21.19
3	TUN	BEN JEMAA, YOUSRA	21.00
4	GER	POHL, BIRGIT	20.54
5	AUS	MOORE, BRYDEE	16.02
6	IRL	WAYLAND, CATHERINE	6.13
7	NZL	HAMILL, JESSICA	19.27
8	GBR	ESCOTT, GEMMA	11.01
15	USA	STAWSKI, ROBYN	11.24

DISCUS F35/36 WOMEN

1	CHN	WU, QING	25.80
2	AUS	OUDFOOT, KATH	23.91
3	UKR	MALCHYK, ALLA	22.15
4	POL	CHILEWSKA, RENATA	23.81
5	CHN	BAI, XUHONG	23.42
6	RSA	VAN ZYL, CHENELLE	22.16
7	CAN	VRIEND, KRIS	17.46
8	ARG	MUNOZ, PERLA	17.74

DISCUS F37/38 WOMEN

1	CHN	MI, NA	33.67
2	AUS	FRASER, AMANDA	29.73
3	CHN	LI, CHUNHUA	27.95
4	CZE	VRATILOVA, DANIELA	28.13
5	CHN	JIA, QIANQIAN	27.40
6	LAT	IEDE, INGRIDA	27.64
7	GBR	JONES, BEVERLEY	27.27
8	LTU	GRIGALIUNIENE, ALDONA	26.73

DISCUS F40 WOMEN

1	CHN	MENGGEN, JIMISU	28.04
2	TUN	TLILI, RAOUA	27.61
3	MAR	EL GARAA, NAJAT	26.86
4	MAR	EL GARAA, LAILA	23.44
5	GBR	HANCOCK, SOPHIE	21.53
6	USA	KENNEDY, JILL	20.89
7	GER	HOMMEN, PETRA	20.29
8	FRA	MARQUIS, PATRICIA	17.84

DISCUS F42-46 WOMEN

1	CHN	WANG, JUN	36.99
2	CHN	YANG, YUE	42.38
3	CHN	ZHENG, BAOZHU	33.19
4	GER	FLOETH, MICHAELA	38.87
5	GER	BIENE, CLAUDIA	28.55
6	AUT	SCHERNEY, ANDREA	32.29
7	CRO	VUKOVIC, JELENA	24.90
8	CPV	SEQUEIRA, ARTIMIZA	17.83

DISCUS F54-56 WOMEN

1	GER	BUGGENHAGEN, MARIANNE	27.80
2	CHN	WANG, TING	17.04
3	CZE	FESSLOVA, JANA	24.82
4	CHN	DONG, FEIXIA	24.59
5	CHN	CHEN, LIPING	15.82
6	GER	WILLING, MARTINA MONIKA	23.36
7	SLO	MAJCEN LJUBIC, TATJANA	14.78
8	BRA	GUIMARAES, SUELY	21.98

DISCUS F57/58 WOMEN

1	NGR	IYIAZI, EUCHARIA NJIDEKA	35.21
2	BUL	ENEVA, STELA	34.58
3	ALG	MEDJEMEDJ, NADIA	28.74
4	ALG	SAIFI, NASSIMA	34.09
5	IRL	BARRY, ORLA	27.08
6	TUN	SOUDANI, MARIEM	30.78
7	BRA	SANTOS, ROSEANE MONTAZERI	30.51
8	IRI	GHAHJAVERESTANI, FATEMEH	28.20

LONG JUMP F12 WOMEN

1	UKR	ZUBKOVSKA, OKSANA	6.28
2	BLR	ZINKEVICH, VOLHA	5.81
3	CHN	LIU, MIAOMIAO	5.74
4	CUB	MIJAN, DAINERIS	5.71
5	BLR	KANIOUK, ANNA	5.56
6	CRO	IVEKOVIC, MARIJA	5.54
7	ESP	LAZARO, ROSALIA	5.52
8	UKR	BOTURCHUK, OXANA	5.28

LONG JUMP F13 WOMEN

1	RSA	HAYES, ILSE	5.68
2	GRE	KARAGIANNI, ANTHI	5.63
3	UKR	GORBENKO, SVITLANA	5.62
4	FRA	KEITA, NANTENIN	5.49
5	GER	MULLER-ROTTGARDT, KATRIN	5.24
6	BLR	SIVITSKAYA, AKSANA	5.22
7	MAR	BENHAMA, SANAA	5.05
8	UKR	KORUNCHAK, YULIYA	5.04

LONG JUMP F42 WOMEN

1	AUS	WOLF, CHRISTINE	3.73
2	NED	ROOZEN, ANNETTE	3.63
3	POL	ZIELINSKA, EWA	3.62
4	MEX	BUSTAMANTE, PERLA	3.51
5	CHN	ZHANG, HAIYUAN	3.44
6	NED	SMITS, MARIJE	3.39
7	NOR	HOLEN, ELIN	3.38
8	GER	BIENE, CLAUDIA	2.78

LONG JUMP F44 WOMEN

1	AUT	SCHERNEY, ANDREA	4.82
2	FRA	LE FUR, MARIE-AMELIE	4.71
3	GER	HOFTE, ASTRID	4.67
4	CHN	WANG, JUAN	4.61
5	CAN	REID, STEFANIE	4.61
6	JPN	SATO, MAMI	4.28
	USA	HOLMES, AIL	DNS

MARATHON T54 WOMEN

1	SUI	HUNKELER, EDITH	1:39:59
2	USA	MCGRORY, AMANDA	1:40:00
3	SUI	GRAF, SANDRA	1:40:01
4	GBR	WOODS, SHELLY	1:40:03
5	USA	BLAUWET, CHERI	1:40:04
6	CHN	LIU, WENJUN	1:40:12
7	USA	REILLY, SHIRLEY	1:40:26
8	CAN	ROY, DIANE	1:40:37
9	ITA	PORCELLATO, FRANCESCA	1:54:27
10	TUN	SIFFI, MASOUDA	1:57:19

SHOT PUT F12/13 WOMEN

1	CHN	TANG, HONGXIA	12.69
2	BLR	SIVAKOVA, TAMARA	12.13
3	AUS	WILLIS-ROBERTS, JODI	11.21
4	CHN	ZHANG, LIANGMIN	10.91
5	ESP	CASTELLANO, JESSICA	10.89
6	ARG	ALMADA, ELIZABETH	10.74
7	GER	CHRISTEN, SIENA	10.49
8	LTU	SKERIENE, DANGUTE	10.17

SHOT PUT F32-34/52/53 WOMEN

1	CRO	BALEK, ANTONIA	5.69
2	GER	POHL, BIRGIT	8.46
3	GRE	STAMATOULA, MARIA	5.64
4	UKR	YAKYBCHUK, TETYANA	6.48
5	AUS	MOORE, BRYDEE	6.38
6	AUS	ELLERY, LOUISE	5.07
7	GBR	ESCOTT, GEMMA	4.77
8	RUS	BURDYKINA, ELENA	7.05
13	USA	STAWSKI, ROBYN	5.56

SHOT PUT F35/36 WOMEN

1	UKR	MALCHYK, ALLA	9.33
2	CHN	WU, QING	9.13
3	POL	CHILEWSKA, RENATA	9.26
4	AUS	OUDFOOT, KATH	8.35
5	RSA	VAN ZYL, CHENELLE	7.42
6	CAN	VRIEND, KRIS	7.05
7	BRA	HERRERA, ROSENEI	6.94
8	ARG	MUNOZ, PERLA	7.13

SHOT PUT F37/38 WOMEN

1	CHN	MI, NA	11.58
2	LTU	GRIGALIUNIENE, ALDONA	12.58
3	CZE	BERNA, EVA	10.84
4	AUS	FRASER, AMANDA	10.52
5	GBR	JONES, BEVERLEY	10.35
6	CHN	XU, QIUPING	10.21
7	CHN	JIA, QIANQIAN	10.11
8	BRA	COELHO, SHIRLENE	10.09

SHOT PUT F40 WOMEN

1	TUN	TLILI, RAOUA	8.95
2	CHN	MENGGEN, JIMISU	8.48
3	MAR	EL GARAA, LAILA	8.44
4	MAR	EL GARAA, NAJAT	7.75
5	GBR	HANCOCK, SOPHIE	7.48
6	GER	HOMMEN, PETRA	7.28
7	GBR	MINETT, KIM	6.92
8	USA	KENNEDY, JILL	6.39

SHOT PUT F42-46 WOMEN

1	CHN	ZHENG, BAOZHU	10.06
2	CHN	ZHONG, YONGYUAN	9.80
3	GER	FLOETH, MICHAELA	12.58
4	CHN	JIN, YAJUAN	12.14
5	GER	SCHMIDT, JANA	9.01
6	MEX	BUSTAMANTE, PERLA	8.70
7	CRO	VUKOVIC, JELENA	8.31
8	GRE	PAVLIDOU, NIKOLETTA	9.79

SHOT PUT F54-56 WOMEN

1	CZE	KACANU, EVA	6.73
2	GER	WILLING, MARTINA MONIKA	8.61
3	GER	BUGGENHAGEN, MARIANNE	8.54
4	TUN	AIDI, HANIA	6.31
5	SLO	MAJCEN LJUBIC, TATJANA	6.27
6	LTU	PERMINIENE, IRENA	5.97
7	CHN	YANG, LIWAN	7.94
8	AUS	BRYCE, JENNI	7.85

SHOT PUT F57/58 WOMEN

1	NGR	IYIAZI, EUCHARIA NJIDEKA	10.96
2	MEX	ORTIZ, ANGELES	10.94
3	ALG	MEDJEMEDJ, NADIA	10.93
4	BUL	ENEVA, STELA	10.28
5	MEX	ROSALES, CATALINA	9.51
6	BUL	KOLEVA, IVANKA	9.44
7	BRA	SANTOS, ROSEANE MONTAZERI	9.06
8	IRI	GHAHJAVERESTANI, FATEMEH	9.01

Timothy Hawker 5/8/1980, Holland, OH

STAFF

Mark McMillan Head Coach

BOCCIA RESULTS

INDIVIDUAL BC1

1	POR	FERNANDES, JOAO PAULO
2	POR	MARQUES, ANTONIO
3	IRL	SHELLY, GABRIEL
4	CHN	WANG, YI
	USA	HAWKER, TJ *ELIMP*

INDIVIDUAL BC2

1	HKG	KWOK, HOI YING KAREN
2	GBR	MURRAY, NIGEL
3	ESP	MARTIN, MANUEL ANGEL
4	ARG	CORTEZ, PABLO

INDIVIDUAL BC3

1	KOR	PARK, KEON WOO
2	GRE	POLYCHRONIDIS, GRIGORIOS
3	KOR	JEONG, HO WON
4	POR	PEIXOTO, MARIO

INDIVIDUAL BC4

1	BRA	PINTO, DIRCEU
2	HKG	LEUNG, YUK WING
3	BRA	SANTOS, ELISEU
4	ESP	DUESO, JOSE MARIA

PAIRS BC3

1	KOR

2	ESP
3	POR
4	THA

PAIRS BC4

1	BRA
2	POR
3	CZE
4	ESP

PAIRS BC1-BC2

1	GBR
2	POR
3	ESP
4	CHN

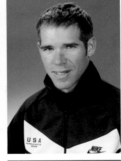

Alejandro Albor 1/13/1964, Elk Grove, CA
Barbara Buchan 9/4/1956, Bend, OR
Michael Farrell 12/11/1977, Colorado Springs, CO
Allison Jones 5/12/1984, Colorado Springs, CO

David Lee 5/5/1969, Cardiff-by-the-Sea, CA
Greta Neimanas 5/4/1988, Colorado Springs, CO/Chicago, IL
Oscar Sanchez 12/2/1975, San Diego, CA
Jennifer Schuble 7/8/1976, Homewood, AL

Karissa Whitsell 6/15/1981, Colorado Springs, CO/Eugene, OR
Ron Williams 11/20/1973, Hoover, AL
Mackenzie Woodring (Pilot) 2/16/1979, Grand Rapids, MI
Matthew Updike 9/24/1971, Denver, CO

Anthony Zahn 10/14/1974, Riverside, CA

STAFF

Craig Griffin Head Coach
Jim Lehman Asst Coach

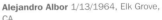

INDIVIDUAL ROAD RACE B VI 1-3 MEN

1	POL		2:14:44
2	FIN		2:14:45
3	FRA		2:14:49
4	SVK		2:16:54
5	POL		2:17:53
6	CAN		2:17:53
7	CAN		2:18:04
8	ESP		2:18:06

INDIVIDUAL ROAD RACE HC B MEN

1	SUI	FREI, HEINZ	1:28:25
2	GER	WEBER, MAX	1:28:26
3	LIB	MAALOUF, EDWARD	1:28:26
4	AUT	PUTZ, MANFRED	1:28:31
5	ITA	PODESTA, VITTORIO	1:28:41
6	GER	KNECHT, TOBIAS	1:30:24
7	SUI	WEBER, LUKAS	1:30:24
8	CZE	CIVIS, RADOVAN	1:31:56
10	**USA**	**UPDIKE, MATT**	1:32:17
14	**USA**	**LEE, DAVID**	1:38:09

INDIVIDUAL ROAD RACE HC C MEN

1	RSA	VAN DYK, ERNST	1:21:40
2	**USA**	**ALBOR, ALEJANDRO**	1:21:41
3	**USA**	**SANCHEZ, OZ**	1:21:41
4	ESP	ARZO, JOSE VICENTE	1:26:11
5	AUT	STERNATH, ELMAR	1:27:35
6	GER	MOSANDL, NORBERT	1:29:31
7	NED	VAN DER LINDEN, DON	1:31:48
8	SUI	NIETLISPACH, FRANZ	1:33:49

INDIVIDUAL ROAD RACE LC1-2/CP4 MEN

1	ITA	TRIBOLI, FABIO	1:46:03
2	FRA	MERCIER, DAVID	1:46:03
3	AUS	GALLAGHER, MICHAEL	1:46:03
4	BEL	BOYEN, JAN	1:46:03
5	CZE	BOUSKA, JIRI	1:46:13
6	BRA	GOHR, SOELITO	1:46:13
7	AUT	EIBECK, WOLFGANG	1:46:13
8	ESP	ALCAIDE, ROBERTO	1:46:13
25	**USA**	**WILLIAMS, RON**	2:01:44
28	**USA**	**FARRELL, MICHAEL**	2:01:58

INDIVIDUAL TIME TRIAL B VI 1-3 MEN

1	ESP		32:01.12
2	NED		32:28.15
3	POL		32:50.31
4	SVK		32:57.06
5	AUS		33:03.24
6	ESP		33:09.09
7	FRA		33:26.83
8	BLR		33:30.42

INDIVIDUAL TIME TRIAL CP3 MEN

1	ESP	OCHOA, JAVIER	37:26.47
2	GBR	KENNY, DARREN	37:38.42
3	KOR	JIN, YONG SIK	38:45.83
4	ESP	ECKHARD, MAURICE FAR	38:47.82
5	CAN	QUEVILLON, JEAN	41:52.97
6	CZE	KVASNICKA, TOMAS	42:36.23
7	POR	PEREIRA, AUGUSTO	43:43.02
8	ARG	LOPEZ, RODRIGO	43:56.42

INDIVIDUAL TIME TRIAL CP4 MEN

1	ESP	NEIRA, CESAR	35:53.98
2	AUS	SCOTT, CHRISTOPHER	35:55.99
3	JPN	ISHII, MASASHI	36:10.20
4	CZE	BOUSKA, JIRI	36:18.49
5	GER	LUNGERSHAUSEN, KLAUS	36:52.33
6	CZE	JIRKA, LUBOS	37:25.57
7	**USA**	**FARRELL, MICHAEL**	38:14.76
8	RSA	PLEKKER, JANOS	38:43.17

INDIVIDUAL TIME TRIAL HC A MEN

1	AUT	SCHATTAUER, WOLFGANG	29:57.77
2	SVK	TURECEK, RASTISLAV	30:53.09
3	FRA	QUITTET, ALAIN	31:17.72
4	GER	BROER, TORBEN	35:02.87
5	FRA	BUCHMANN, YVON	37:51.29
6	AUT	ETZLSTORFER, CHRISTOPH	40:40.36
7	MEX	NAVARRO, EDGAR	46:16.11

INDIVIDUAL TIME TRIAL HC B MEN

1	SUI	FREI, HEINZ	22:06.23
2	ITA	PODESTA, VITTORIO	22:12.06
3	LIB	MAALOUF, EDWARD	22:12.91
4	GER	BAUMANN, STEFAN	22:44.21
5	AUT	PUTZ, MANFRED	22:44.88
6	SUI	WEBER, LUKAS	22:50.12
7	GER	WEBER, MAX	23:08.88
8	GER	KNECHT, TOBIAS	23:08.91
13	**USA**	**UPDIKE, MATT**	24:39.59
14	**USA**	**LEE, DAVID**	25:04.99

INDIVIDUAL TIME TRIAL HC C MEN

1	**USA**	**SANCHEZ, OZ**	20:16.52
2	ESP	ARZO, JOSE VICENTE	20:36.91
3	**USA**	**ALBOR, ALEJANDRO**	20:59.49
4	RSA	VAN DYK, ERNST	21:01.59
5	GER	MOSANDL, NORBERT	21:33.09
6	SUI	NIETLISPACH, FRANZ	21:53.12
7	GER	KOCH, NORBERT	21:59.90
8	NED	VAN DER LINDEN, DON	22:31.28

INDIVIDUAL TIME TRIAL LC1 MEN

1	GER	SACHER, WOLFGANG	34:41.62
2	AUT	EIBECK, WOLFGANG	34:52.20
3	ITA	TRIBOLI, FABIO	35:23.70
4	SUI	RENGGLI, IVAN	35:25.66
5	AUS	GALLAGHER, MICHAEL	35:29.74
6	BRA	GOHR, SOELITO	35:50.02
7	FRA	MERCIER, DAVID	36:13.31
8	AUT	GATTRINGER, MANFRED	36:26.50

INDIVIDUAL TIME TRIAL LC2 MEN

1	CZE	JEZEK, JIRI	33:36.70
2	ROU	NOVAK, CAROL EDUARD	34:04.60
3	ESP	ALCAIDE, ROBERTO	34:18.86
4	BEL	BOYEN, JAN	35:39.55
5	**USA**	**WILLIAMS, RON**	36:12.84
6	COL	CHACON, LUIS	36:56.74
7	NOR	JAHR, MORTEN	37:53.80
8	CHN	ZHENG, YUANCHAO	38:30.72

INDIVIDUAL TIME TRIAL LC3 MEN

1	FRA	THIRIONET, LAURENT	38:00.31
2	GBR	RICHARDSON, SIMON	38:23.73
3	JPN	FUJITA, MASAKI	38:38.96
4	ESP	GARCIA, ANTONIO	38:48.66
5	GER	GRAF, TOBIAS	38:55.25
6	FRA	BAHIER, STEPHANE	39:13.55
7	ITA	MACCHI, FABRIZIO	39:38.98
8	VEN	MOLINA, CIRIO	40:02.48

INDIVIDUAL TIME TRIAL LC4 MEN

1	GER	TEUBER, MICHAEL	38:46.79
2	ESP	MENDEZ, JUAN JOSE	39:54.68
3	**USA**	**ZAHN, ANTHONY**	41:08.21
4	AUT	HOHLRIEDER, ALEXANDER	41:20.07
5	GER	WINKLER, ERICH	42:42.91
6	GER	SENSKA, PIERRE	44:18.16
7	AUT	DABERNIG, WOLFGANG	47:57.44
	ITA	VIGANO, PAOLO	DNF

1KM TIME TRIAL B VI 1-3 MEN

1	GBR		1:02.864
2	AUS		1:03.718
3	AUS		1:04.053
4	RSA		1:04.130
5	JPN		1:04.593
6	AUS		1:04.792
7	CAN		1:06.371
8	ESP		1:07.721

1KM TIME TRIAL CP3 MEN

1	GBR	KENNY, DARREN	1:08.668
2	GBR	WADDON, RIK	1:11.161
3	CZE	KVASNICKA, TOMAS	1:17.670
4	ESP	OCHOA, JAVIER	1:18.523
5	ARG	LOPEZ, RODRIGO	1:20.572
6	CAN	QUEVILLON, JEAN	1:21.348
7	CAN	MCDOUGALL, BRAYDEN	1:22.780
8	ESP	ECKHARD, MAURICE FAR	1:27.449

1KM TIME TRIAL CP4 MEN

1	JPN	ISHII, MASASHI	1:08.771
2	CZE	BOUSKA, JIRI	1:11.189
3	AUS	SCOTT, CHRISTOPHER	1:12.229
4	ESP	NEIRA, CESAR	1:15.390
5	RSA	PLEKKER, JANOS	1:15.547
6	CZE	JIRKA, LUBOS	1:16.013
7	IRL	SMYTH, ENDA	1:16.074
8	**USA**	**FARRELL, MICHAEL**	1:17.594

1KM TIME TRIAL LC1 MEN

1	GBR	BRISTOW, MARK	1:08.873
2	CHN	ZHANG, KUIDONG	1:10.475
3	GER	SACHER, WOLFGANG	1:10.812
4	AUS	GALLAGHER, MICHAEL	1:11.008
5	AUT	EIBECK, WOLFGANG	1:11.238
6	GER	HAMMER, MARIO	1:11.335
7	IRL	MILLER, CATHAL GUSTAVUS	1:11.824
8	AUT	GATTRINGER, MANFRED	1:12.173

1KM TIME TRIAL LC2 MEN

1	GBR	CUNDY, JODY	1:05.466
2	CZE	JEZEK, JIRI	1:11.182
3	CHN	ZHENG, YUANCHAO	1:11.198
4	ROU	NOVAK, CAROL EDUARD	1:12.739
5	ESP	GRANADO, AMADOR	1:12.760
6	CAN	BOURGAULT, ERIC	1:14.387
7	BEL	BOYEN, JAN	1:14.881
8	ESP	ALCAIDE, ROBERTO	1:16.062

INDIVIDUAL PURSUIT B VI 1-3 MEN

1	AUS		4:18.166
2	ESP		OVL
3	AUS		4:26.626
4	CAN		4:28.171

INDIVIDUAL PURSUIT CP3 MEN

1	GBR	KENNY, DARREN	
2	KOR	JIN, YONG SIK	OVL
3	CAN	QUEVILLON, JEAN	4:03.277
4	ESP	ECKHARD, MAURICE FAR	4:08.430

INDIVIDUAL PURSUIT CP4 MEN

1	AUS	SCOTT, CHRISTOPHER	3:40.144
2	JPN	ISHII, MASASHI	3:40.157
3	ESP	NEIRA, CESAR	3:45.753
4	CZE	BOUSKA, JIRI	3:48.912
	USA	**FARRELL, MICHAEL**	ELIMQ

INDIVIDUAL PURSUIT LC1 MEN

1	AUS	GALLAGHER, MICHAEL	4:43.279
2	GER	SACHER, WOLFGANG	4:46.788
3	ITA	TRIBOLI, FABIO	4:45.677
4	BRA	GOHR, SOELITO	4:53.407

INDIVIDUAL PURSUIT LC2 MEN

1	CZE	JEZEK, JIRI	4:46.999
2	ESP	ALCAIDE, ROBERTO	4:50.318
3	BEL	BOYEN, JAN	4:56.630
4	ROU	NOVAK, CAROL EDUARD	4:59.078

INDIVIDUAL PURSUIT LC3 MEN

1	GBR	RICHARDSON, SIMON	3:57.510
2	JPN	FUJITA, MASAKI	3:59.020
3	GER	GRAF, TOBIAS	3:49.214
4	FRA	THIRIONET, LAURENT	3:55.535

INDIVIDUAL PURSUIT LC4 MEN

1	ESP	MENDEZ, JUAN JOSE	4:14.984
2	GER	WINKLER, ERICH	4:21.550
3	ITA	VIGANO, PAOLO	4:02.782
4	GER	TEUBER, MICHAEL	4:10.113
	USA	**ZAHN, ANTHONY**	ELIMQ

SPRINT B VI 1-3 MEN

1	GBR	
2	AUS	
3	RSA	
4	JPN	
5	IRL	
6	CAN	
7	COL	
8	ARG	

TEAM SPRINT LC1-4 CP3/4 MEN

1	GBR	49.323
2	CHN	50.480
3	CZE	52.379
4	AUS	54.239

INDIVIDUAL ROAD RACE B VI 1-3 WOMEN

1	BLR		1:55:35
2	**USA**		1:58:35
		WHITSELL, KARISSA	
		WOODRING, MACKENZIE	
3	CAN		2:01:17
4	AUS		2:01:17
5	POL		2:01:20
6	BLR		2:01:20
7	ESP		2:01:24
8	NZL		2:01:27

INDIVIDUAL ROAD RACE HC A-C WOMEN

1	GER	ESKAU, ANDREA	1:13:00
2	NED	VAN DER VORST, MONIQUE	1:13:00
3	GER	VIETH, DOROTHEE	1:13:27
4	CAN	WHITE, SHAUNA	1:17:10
5	NED	DE VAAN, LAURA	1:17:12
6	GBR	MORRIS, RACHEL	1:17:12
7	FRA	MARTIN, CATHERINE	1:17:14
8	AUS	LECKIE, MEL	1:31:14

INDIVIDUAL TIME TRIAL B VI 1-3 WOMEN

1	**USA**		36:14.87
		WHITSELL, KARISSA	
		WOODRING, MACKENZIE	
2	BLR		36:58.98
3	NZL		38:40.40
4	AUS		39:01.62
5	ESP		39:11.65
6	ITA		39:36.06
7	IRL		40:09.67
8	BLR		40:19.02

1KM TIME TRIAL B VI 1-3 WOMEN

1	GBR		1:09.066
2	AUS		1:10.465
3	AUS		1:12.463
4	**USA**		1:12.787
		WHITSELL, KARISSA	
		WOODRING, MACKENZIE	
5	NZL		1:14.048
6	CAN		1:15.639
7	IRL		1:16.208
8	ESP		1:19.712

INDIVIDUAL PURSUIT B VI 1-3 WOMEN

1	AUS		3:39.809
2	GBR		3:41.494
3	**USA**		3:41.521
		WHITSELL, KARISSA	
		WOODRING, MACKENZIE	
4	NZL		3:47.900

INDIVIDUAL ROAD RACE CP1-2 WOMEN

1	GBR	STONE, DAVID	45:05
2	RSA	NEL, RIAAN	48:32
3	ITA	FARRONI, GIORGIO	48:34
4	JPN	OGAWA, MUTSUHIKO	49:47
5	AUT	WINTERLEITNER, HELMUT	49:47
6	GRE	KOTZIAS, STAMATIOS	50:09
7	CZE	WINKLER, JOSEF	52:56
8	GER	WEISE, BARBARA	57:15

CYCLING RESULTS

1KM TIME TRIAL LC3-4 MEN

				FACTOR%	CALCULATED TIME
1	GBR	RICHARDSON, SIMON	1:14.936	100.000	01:14.936
2	JPN	FUJITA, MASAKI	1:17.314	100.000	01:17.314
3	AUS	BALL, GREG	1:21.157	95.718	01:17.681
4	ITA	VIGANO, PAOLO	1:21.172	95.718	01:17.696
5	GER	GRAF, TOBIAS	1:18.515	100.000	01:18.515
6	CHN	ZHANG, LU	1:18.603	100.000	01:18.603
7	GER	TEUBER, MICHAEL	1:22.473	95.718	01:18.941
8	FRA	THIRIONET, LAURENT	1:20.561	100.000	01:20.561
20	**USA**	**ZAHN, ANTHONY**	1:33.275	95.718	01:29.280

INDIVIDUAL TIME TRIAL HC A-C WOMEN

1	GBR	MORRIS, RACHEL	25:39.22	81.671	20:57.09
2	NED	VAN DER VORST, MONIQUE	23:40.64	100.000	23:40.64
3	GER	VIETH, DOROTHEE	23:41.95	100.000	23:41.95
4	SUI	SCHWALLER, URSULA	29:29.66	81.671	24:05.29
5	GER	ESKAU, ANDREA	24:06.03	100.000	24:06.03
6	AUS	LECKIE, MEL	30:32.61	81.671	24:56.71
7	NED	DE VAAN, LAURA	25:15.15	100.000	25:15.15
8	NZL	DONALDSON, ANNEMARIE	32:13.21	81.671	26:18.87

INDIVIDUAL TIME TRIAL LC1-2/CP4 WOMEN

1	GBR	STOREY, SARAH	37:16.65	100.000	37:16.65
2	**USA**	**SCHUBLE, JENNIFER**	40:42.28	94.950	38:38.94
3	CHN	ZHOU, JUFANG	39:30.84	100.000	39:30.84
4	**USA**	**NEIMANAS, GRETA**	40:26.09	100.000	40:26.09
5	CHN	YE, YAPING	43:58.22	93.336	41:02.40
6	CHN	DONG, JINGPING	44:08.71	93.336	41:12.19
7	NZL	SOUTHORN, FIONA	43:02.78	100.000	43:02.78
8	ITA	VINCI, SILVANA	47:28.24	94.950	45:04.40

INDIVIDUAL TIME TRIAL LC3-4/CP3 WOMEN

1	**USA**	**BUCHAN, BARBARA**	44:45.17	94.919	42:28.73
2	**USA**	**JONES, ALLISON**	44:42.88	100.000	44:42.88
3	NZL	TESORIERO, PAULA	45:00.92	100.000	45:00.92
4	GER	SIMANOWSKI, NATALIE	45:38.23	100.000	45:38.23
5	CHN	TANG, QI	47:23.63	100.000	47:23.63
6	ESP	ACINAS, RAQUEL	47:30.48	100.000	47:30.48
7	CHN	NIU, ZHIFENG	48:45.64	100.000	48:45.64
8	AUS	PARIS, JAYME	52:51.82	94.919	50:10.65

500M TIME TRIAL LC1-2/CP4 WOMEN

1	**USA**	**SCHUBLE, JENNIFER**	40.278	85.236	34.331
2	CHN	YE, YAPING	41.133	87.825	36.125
3	CHN	DONG, JINGPING	41.996	87.825	36.882
4	CHN	ZHOU, JUFANG	36.937	100.000	36.937
5	GBR	STOREY, SARAH	38.356	100.000	38.356
6	RSA	BURNS, ROXY	45.617	85.236	38.882
7	ITA	VINCI, SILVANA	46.871	85.236	39.950
8	**USA**	**NEIMANAS, GRETA**	40.265	100.000	40.265

500M TIME TRIAL LC3-4/CP3 WOMEN

1	NZL	TESORIERO, PAULA	43.281	100.000	43.281
2	GER	SIMANOWSKI, NATALIE	43.800	100.000	43.800
3	AUS	PARIS, JAYME	46.427	95.829	44.490
4	AUS	ARMSTRONG, JANE	45.402	100.000	45.402
5	CHN	TANG, QI	45.869	100.000	45.869
6	**USA**	**JONES, ALLISON**	46.397	100.000	46.397
7	RSA	VAN STADEN, SUSAN	47.038	100.000	47.038
8	**USA**	**BUCHAN, BARBARA**	49.156	95.829	47.105

INDIVIDUAL PURSUIT LC1-2/CP4 WOMEN

1	GBR	STOREY, SARAH	3:36.637	100.000	3:36.637
2	**USA**	**SCHUBLE, JENNIFER**	4:02.758	89.335	3:36.867
3	CHN	DONG, JINGPING	4:14.103	90.418	3:49.754
4	CHN	YE, YAPING	4:19.711	90.418	3:54.825

INDIVIDUAL PURSUIT LC3-4/CP3 WOMEN

1	**USA**	**BUCHAN, BARBARA**	4:33.459	93.560	4:15.848
2	GER	SIMANOWSKI, NATALIE	4:19.396	100.000	4:19.396
3	NZL	TESORIERO, PAULA	4:26.080	100.000	4:26.080
4	AUS	PARIS, JAYME	4:44.938	93.560	4:26.587

TIME TRIAL CP1-2 WOMEN

1	GBR	STONE, DAVID	22:14.86	100.000	22:14.86
2	GER	WEISE, BARBARA	28:52.76	81.277	23:28.33
3	CZE	MACKOVA, MARKETA	29:10.38	81.277	23:42.65
4	NED	HOMAN, MARK	31:17.43	76.768	24:01.26
5	RSA	NEL, RIAAN	24:23.26	100.000	24:23.26
6	ITA	FARRONI, GIORGIO	24:26.57	100.000	24:26.57
7	ESP	OROZA, AITOR	31:58.01	76.768	24:32.41
8	JPN	OGAWA, MUTSUHIKO	25:35.80	100.000	25:35.80

Robin Brueckmann (NOT PICTURED)
1/4/1958, Summerfield, NC
Barbara Grassmyer 5/7/1972, Placerville, CA
Rebecca Hart 10/26/1984, Erie, PA
Keith Newerla 2/3/1983, King of Prussia, PA
Lynn Seidemann 10/19/1963, Coppell, TX

STAFF

Missy Ransehousen Head Coach
Sharon Schneidman Asst Coach

EQUESTRIAN RESULTS

DRESSAGE - CHAMPIONSHIP GRADE IA

1	GBR	DUNHAM, ANNE	73.1
2	GBR	CHRISTIANSEN, SOPHIE	72.8
3	SIN	TAN, LAURENTIA	68.8
4	ITA	VIGON, ANDREA	63.8
5	CRO	HUDINA, SLAVEN	63.7
6	CRO	SRSIC, IVAN	61.5
7	SVK	JOBBAGYOVA, KATARINA	61.3
8	BRA	OLIVA, SERGIO	60.9

DRESSAGE - CHAMPIONSHIP GRADE IB

1	GBR	PEARSON, LEE	73.238

2	NOR	DOKKAN, JENS	68.857
3	BRA	ALVES, MARCOS	67.714
4	FIN	KARJALAINEN, KATJA	65.714
5	GBR	BALSHAW, RICKY	64.953
6	**USA**	**SEIDEMANN, LYNN**	63.905
7	CAN	GOWANLOCK, ASHLEY	63.714
8	BEL	LORQUET, JOSE	63.619
12	**USA**	**NEWERLA, KEITH**	58.571

DRESSAGE - CHAMPIONSHIP GRADE II

1	GER	NAEPEL, BRITTA	71.909
2	CAN	BARWICK, LAUREN	68.454

3	DEN	NIELSEN, CAROLINE	68.182
4	NED	VAN DE SANDE, PETRA	66.909
5	GER	ZEIBIG, STEFFEN	66.097
6	GBR	COULTHARD, FELICITY	65.546
7	SWE	RUTBERG, CAROLIN	65.182
8	GER	TRABERT, ANGELIKA	64.909
12	**USA**	**HART, REBECCA**	62.545

DRESSAGE - CHAMPIONSHIP GRADE III

1	GER	BRENNER, HANNELORE	71.44
2	DEN	LYKKE DALSKOV, ANNIKA	71.04
3	GER	EISTEL, BETTINA	70.88

EQUESTRIAN

4	AUS	JARVIS, SHARON	69.2
5	GBR	CRIDDLE, DEBORAH	68.16
6	ITA	VERATTI, SILVIA	64.56
7	BEL	VERMEIR, BERT	64
8	GBR	LAURENS, SIMON	62.88
10	USA	**GRASSMYER, BARBARA**	57.12

DRESSAGE - CHAMPIONSHIP GRADE IV

1	RSA	JOHNSON, PHILIPPA	69.29
2	NOR	LUBBE, ANN CATHRIN	68.516
3	AUS	BRUCE, GEORGIA	68.258
4	NED	VERMEULEN, SJERSTIN	66.452
5	FRA	BIZET, NATHALIE	66.387
6	SWE	ARONSSON, LOTTEN	64.839
7	NED	DE GROOT, INEKE	63.161
8	NED	PETERS, SABINE	62.516
14	USA	**BRUECKMANN, ROBIN**	56.387

DRESSAGE - FREESTYLE GRADE IA

1	GBR	CHRISTIANSEN, SOPHIE	76.166
2	GBR	DUNHAM, ANNE	73.333
3	SIN	TAN, LAURENTIA	70.167
4	ITA	VIGON, ANDREA	69.667
5	CRO	HUDINA, SLAVEN	66.889
6	CRO	SRSIC, IVAN	65.998
7	AUS	PIKE, JAN	65.555
8	BRA	OLIVA, SERGIO	63.556

DRESSAGE - FREESTYLE GRADE IB

1	GBR	PEARSON, LEE	77.057
2	GBR	BALSHAW, RICKY	70.444
3	BRA	ALVES, MARCOS	67.333
4	AUS	KULLEN, NICOLE	66.11
5	NOR	DOKKAN, JENS	65.555
6	BEL	LORQUET, JOSE	65.333

7	FIN	KARJALAINEN, KATJA	64.999
8	CAN	GOWANLOCK, ASHLEY	64.221
9	USA	**SEIDEMANN, LYNN**	64.221
14	USA	**NEWERLA, KEITH**	60.5

DRESSAGE - FREESTYLE GRADE II

1	CAN	BARWICK, LAUREN	72.776
2	GBR	COULTHARD, FELICITY	71.056
3	GER	NAEPEL, BRITTA	70.277
4	USA	**HART, REBECCA**	68.11
5	POR	DUARTE, SARA	66.336
6	CHN	PENG, YULIAN	66.279
7	BRA	MELARANCI, ELISA	66.277
8	IRL	BYRNE, EILISH	65.833

DRESSAGE - FREESTYLE GRADE III

1	GER	BRENNER, HANNELORE	74.223
2	GBR	LAURENS, SIMON	73.499
3	DEN	LYKKE DALSKOV, ANNIKA	73.222
4	GBR	CRIDDLE, DEBORAH	73.11
5	ITA	VERATTI, SILVIA	69.834
6	GER	EISTEL, BETTINA	69.612
7	AUS	JARVIS, SHARON	69.446
8	BEL	VERMEIR, BERT	67.389
10	USA	**GRASSMYER, BARBARA**	63.389

DRESSAGE - FREESTYLE GRADE IV

1	RSA	JOHNSON, PHILIPPA	77.272
2	NOR	LUBBE, ANN CATHRIN	75.046
3	AUS	BRUCE, GEORGIA	74.319
4	NOR	RUI, SIGRID	69.498
5	FRA	BIZET, NATHALIE	68.453
6	SWE	ARONSSON, LOTTEN	68.362
7	NED	VERMEULEN, SJERSTIN	67.908
8	DEN	THORNING JOERGENSEN, LINE	66.045

Steve Denuyl 9/30/1986, Kalamazoo, MI
Chris Dodds 9/22/1983, Logan, UT
Tyler Merren 5/29/1984, Kalamazoo, MI
Donte' Mickens 10/19/1980, Tallahassee, FL

Eddie Munro 4/12/1975, St Augustine, FL
Daryl Walker 12/29/1981, Jacksonville, FL
Jen Armbruster 2/12/1975, Birmingham, AL/Colorado Springs, CO
Lisa Banta 5/29/1979, Tucson, AZ

Jaclyn Barnes 11/29/1986, Wadsworth , Ill.
Jessica Lorenz 11/22/1987, Oakland, Calif.; 2004
Asya Miller 10/16/1979, Colorado Springs, CO/Lapeer, MI
Robyn Theryoung 11/11/1978, Colorado Springs, CO

STAFF

Thomas Parrigin Head Coach (M)
Michael Lege' Asst Coach (M)
Ken Armbruster Head Coach (W)
Sharon Gunderman Asst Coach (W)

GOALBALL RESULTS

GOALBALL MEN

1	CHN	CHINA
2	LTU	LITHUANIA
3	SWE	SWEDEN
4	**USA**	**TEAM USA**
5	CAN	CANADA
6	DEN	DENMARK
7	SLO	SLOVENIA
8	FIN	FINLAND
9	IRI	IRAN
10	BEL	BELGIUM
11	BRA	BRAZIL
12	ESP	SPAIN

GOALBALL WOMEN

1	**USA**	**TEAM USA**
2	CHN	CHINA
3	DEN	DENMARK
4	SWE	SWEDEN

Greg Dewall 2/10/1979, Chico, CA
Scott Jones, 5/23/1974, Little Rock, AR
Myles Porter, 11/22/1985, Colorado Springs, CO
Andre Watson, 11/7/1976, Upper Darby, PA

Jordan Mouton, 7/26/1989, Houston, TX

STAFF

Raul Tamayo (NOT PICTURED) Head Coach
Scott Moore Asst Coach

JUDO RESULTS

OVER 100 KG MEN

1	AZE	ZAKIYEV, ILHAM
2	CHN	WANG, SONG
3	FRA	TAURINES, JULIEN
3	**USA**	**DEWALL, GREG**

UP TO 100 KG MEN

1	BRA	SILVA, ANTONIO TENORIO
2	AZE	SARDAROV, KARIM
3	UKR	LYIVYTSKYI, MYKOLA
3	CUB	CORTADA, JUAN CARLOS
	USA	**PORTER, MYLES** *ELIM REPECHAGE FINAL*

UP TO 60 KG MEN

1	ALG	NOURA, MOULOUD
2	IRI	RAHMATI, SAEED
3	CHN	LI, XIAODONG
3	AZE	IBRAHIMOV, RAMIN

UP TO 66 KG MEN

1	ALG	LAMRI, SIDALI
2	JPN	FUJIMOTO, SATOSHI
3	CUB	SANCHEZ, VICTOR
3	FIN	KALLUNKI, JANI

UP TO 73 KG MEN

1	MEX	AVILA, EDUARDO
2	CHN	XU, ZHILIN
3	UKR	SYDORENKO, SERGII
3	ARG	RAMIREZ, FABIAN

UP TO 81 KG MEN

1	CUB	CRUZ, ISAO
2	FRA	JONARD, CYRIL
3	VEN	CARVALLO, REINALDO
3	ARG	LENCINA, JORGE
	USA	**JONES, SCOTT** *ELIM MAIN 1/8*

UP TO 90 KG MEN

1	RUS	KRETSUL, OLEG
2	AZE	MAMMADOV, TOFIG
3	GBR	INGRAM, SAMUEL
3	FRA	CUGNON DE SEVRICOURT, OLIVIER
	USA	**WATSON, ANDRE** *ELIM REPECHAGE QUARTER*

OVER 70 KG WOMEN

1	CHN	YUAN, YANPING
2	BRA	SILVA, DEANNE
3	ALG	BOUAZOUG, ZOUBIDA
3	RUS	KALYANOVA, IRINA

UP TO 48 KG WOMEN

1	CHN	GUO, HUAPING
2	BRA	CARDOSO, KARLA
3	GER	BRUSSIG, CARMEN
3	RUS	POTAPOVA, VICTORIA

UP TO 52 KG WOMEN

1	CHI	CUI, NA
2	FRA	AURIERES-MARTINET, SANDRINE
3	BRA	FERREIRA, MICHELLE
3	RUS	STEPANYUK, ALESYA

UP TO 57 KG WOMEN

1	CHN	WANG, LIJING
2	GER	BRUSSIG, RAMONA
3	BRA	SILVA, DANIELE
3	ESP	MERENCIANO, MARIA MONICA

UP TO 63 KG WOMEN

1	VEN	SOAZO, NAOMI
2	ESP	ARCE, MARTA
3	FRA	QUESSANDIER, ANGELIQUE
3	RUS	KAZAKOVA, MADINA

UP TO 70 KG WOMEN

1	ESP	HERRERA, MARIA DEL CARMEN
2	MEX	RUVALCABA, LENIA
3	NED	VERMEULEN, SANNEKE
3	RUS	SAVOSTYANOVA, TATIANA
	USA	**MOUTON, JORDAN** *ELIM REPECHAGE SEMI*

Mary Stack 4/3/1974, Ann Arbor, MI
Anderson Wise 3/14/1983, Needham, MA

STAFF

Mary Hodge Head Coach

POWERLIFTING RESULTS

OVER 100 KG MEN

1	IRI	RAJABIGOLOJEH, KAZEM	265
2	AUS	GARDINER, DARREN	230
3	CHN	LI, BING	225
4	TPE	HUANG, KUO TAI	225
5	GER	HOCHBERG, MARIO	210
6	RUS	MARFIN, NIKOLAY	207.5
7	AZE	ALIYEV, MAHARRAM	205

UP TO 100 KG MEN

1	CHN	QI, DONG	247.5
2	NGR	ALIGEKWE, OBIOMA DALETH	245
3	IRI	SADEGHZADEH SALMANI, ALI	230
4	EGY	FARAG, ABD ELMONEM SALAH	222.5
5	POL	KULIG, DAMIAN	222.5
6	GRE	ANATOLITIS, DIMITRIOS	215
7	HUN	SAS, SANDOR	195
8	AZE	RAMAZANZADE, MEHMAN	190

UP TO 48 KG MEN

1	NGR	ISHAKU, RUEL	169
2	JOR	QARADA, OMAR	162.5
3	LAO	SIMAY, EAY	157.5
4	IND	BASHA, FARMAN	155
5	THA	SUKJARERN, CHOOCHAT	155
6	POL	ROCH, RAFAL	150
7	CIV	DIAMOUTENE, ALIDOU	142
8	SRI	BATAPOLA MUDALIGE, SANDUN	135

UP TO 52 KG MEN

1	CHN	WU, GUOJING	175
2	EGY	ELSERNGAWY, OSAMA	167.5
3	THA	KASANUN, NARONG	167.5
4	IRQ	JUBOORI, HUSSEIN	165
5	RUS	BEDDERDINOV, ILDAR	157.5
6	POL	SZYMANSKI, SLAWOMIR	150
7	SYR	ABOU MUGHDEB, YAHYA	137.5
8	MAS	CHEOK, KON FATT	137.5

UP TO 56 KG MEN

1	EGY	OTHMAN, SHERIF OTHMAN	202.5
2	IRQ	MOHSIN, RASOOL	185
3	KOR	JUNG, KEUM JONG	180
4	THA	MARASRI, THONGSA	180
5	CHN	WANG, JIAN	180
6	GBR	IRVING, JASON	177.5
7	IRI	CHALTOUKKAR, GHOLAMHOSSEIN	172.5
8	KEN	OKUTTO, SAMSON	165

UP TO 60 KG MEN

1	IRI	MOHAMMADI, HAMZEH	202.5
2	RUS	ZAKIEV, AYRAT	200
3	EGY	IBRAHIM, SHABAN YEHIA	195
4	POL	TOMCZYK, MARIUSZ	170
5	IND	SINGH, RAJINDER	170
6	COL	CANTILLO, JAINER	160
7	THA	THONGDEE, PRASIT	160
8	INA	MAKAL, BILLY ZETH	157.5

UP TO 67.5 KG MEN

1	EGY	MATHNA, METWALY IBRAHIM	217.5
2	IRI	HOSSEINI, ALI	215
3	CHN	WU, MAOSHUN	200
4	RUS	SYCHEV, SERGEY	190
5	GRE	MOYSIADIS, GKREMISLAV	187.5
6	MAR	EL AMMARI, ABDERRAHIM	182.5
7	CUB	PEREA, LUIS	180
8	MAS	PERUMAL, MARIAPPAN	180
11	**USA**	**WISE, ANDY**	150

UP TO 75 KG MEN

1	CHN	LIU, LEI	225
2	IRI	FARZIN, MAJID	212.5
3	JOR	ALJUNEIDI, MUTAZ	210
4	EGY	ELELFAT, MOHAMED SOBHY	205
5	MEX	ARREDONDO, PORFIRIO	197.5
6	KSA	ALNOWESER, HUSSAIN	195
7	GRE	GKOUNTANIS, NIKOLAOS	190
8	JPN	ODO, HIDEKI	187.5

UP TO 82.5 KG MEN

1	CHN	ZHANG, HAIDONG	230
2	GRE	MAMALOS, PAVLOS	225
3	IRQ	AL-ALI, THAER	222.5
4	EGY	ABD ELHADY, HANY MOHSEN	220
5	RUS	RAKITIN, VADIM	200
6	SYR	SHEKH AHMAD, AMMAR	192.5
7	TKM	ORJIYEV, OVEZGELDI	190
8	FIN	PIIPPONEN, JANNE	172.5

UP TO 90 KG MEN

1	CHN	CAI, HUICHAO	235
2	UAE	KHALAF, MOHAMMED KHAMISS	227.5
3	POL	ROGALA, RYSZARD	215
4	MEX	CASTILLO, JESUS	200
5	AZE	HUSEYNOV, ELSHAN	190
6	FRA	CASTEL, CHARLY	190
7	VEN	CHIRINOS, JOSE	175
8	GEO	GORGODZE, IAGO	140

OVER 82.5 KG WOMEN

1	CHN	LI, RUIFANG	165
2	NGR	ANOZIE, GRACE EBERE	165
3	EGY	ALI, NADIA MOHAMED	150
4	AUS	MCINTYRE, DEAHNNE	127.5
5	UKR	FROLOVA, TETYANA	120
6	POL	RUSIELEWICZ, KAMILLA	115
7	ROU	CUSTURA, CORINA VIORICA	95

UP TO 40 KG WOMEN

1	UKR	SOLOVYOVA, LIDIYA	105.5
2	CHN	CUI, ZHE	95
3	MEX	CERERO, LAURA	92.5
4	TUR	MUSLU, NAZMIYE	90
5	ECU	MARTINEZ, NANCY	80
6	MAR	MATAR, MALIKA	77.5
7	POL	LIPOWSKA, EMILIA	70
8	HKG	LAM, YIM HUNG	62.5

UP TO 44 KG WOMEN

1	CHN	XIAO, CUIJUAN	100
2	POL	KOZDRYK, JUSTYNA	92.5
3	EGY	OTEIFY, ZEINAB SAYED	92.5
4	UKR	TOPORKOVA, RAYISA	85
5	BRA	OLIVEIRA, MARIA	82.5
6	THA	CHAREONYING, PHIKUL	75
	VEN	HERNANDEZ, NAIROBYS	NMR

UP TO 48 KG WOMEN

1	NGR	EJIKE, LUCY OGECHUKWU	130
2	RUS	LAFINA, OLESYA	115
3	FRA	GHAZOUANI, SOUHAD	112.5
4	VIE	CHAU, HOANG TUYET LOAN	100
5	CHN	SHI, SHANSHAN	97.5
6	GBR	BLAKE, NATALIE	97.5
7	ESP	ZABALA, LOIDA	80

UP TO 52 KG WOMEN

1	MEX	PEREZ, AMALIA	127.5
2	RUS	PODPALNAYA, TAMARA	125
3	THA	ANON, SAMKHOUN	95
4	VIE	DINH, THI NGA	92.5
5	UKR	VOITKO, OLENA	87.5
6	SYR	ELIAS, NATALI	87.5
7	JOR	ALLAWI, FATAMA	80
8	RSA	GROBBELAAR, MOEKIE	80

UP TO 56 KG WOMEN

1	EGY	OMAR, FATMA OMAR	141.5
2	RUS	KAZANTSEVA, IRINA	97.5
3	MAS	SIOW, LEE CHAN	95
4	UKR	SHYROKOLAVA, TETYANA	92.5
5	IRQ	SALEEM, DHIKRA	90
6	TPE	LIN, YA HSUAN	82.5
7	TKM	PEKIYEVA, MAYAGOZEL	82.5
8	SVK	BARTOSOVA, MARIA	70

UP TO 60 KG WOMEN

1	CHN	BIAN, JIANXIN	135
2	EGY	OSMAN, AMAL MAHMOUD	117.5
3	NGR	IGBITI, PATIENCE AGHIMILE	110
4	MAR	ACEM, KHADIJA	110
5	THA	BOOTPO, ARAWAN	100
6	POL	LAZARZ, MARZENA	82.5
7	KOR	YUN, JIN KYOUNG	72.5

UP TO 67.5 KG WOMEN

1	CHN	FU, TAOYING	145.5
2	NGR	NNEJI, AMOGE VICTORIA	132.5
3	SYR	ALSHIKH, RASHA	117.5
4	EGY	MORSHEDI, RANIA ALAA ELDIN	115
5	BRA	FERREIRA, JOSILENE	100
6	UKR	HEDIAN, SVITLANA	95
7	GRE	KAZANTZIDOU, ANASTASIA	87.5
8	MDA	MARINENCOV, LARISA	77.5

UP TO 75 KG WOMEN

1	TPE	LIN, TZU HUI	137.5
2	EGY	MOHAMED, RANDA TAGELDIN	135
3	CHN	ZHANG, LIPING	132.5
4	MEX	DIAZ, CATALINA	115
5	RUS	KISELEVA, OLGA	100
6	TKM	SIMAKOVA, VALENTINA	97.5
7	KAZ	SALIMZHANOVA, LYAZAT	80

UP TO 82.5 KG WOMEN

1	EGY	AHMED, HEBA SAID	155
2	CHN	ZUO, JUE	137.5
3	MEX	BARCENAS, PERLA PATRICIA	130
4	NGR	OGUNBAMOWO, ADEDEJI KIKE	127.5
5	FRA	BURGY, CARINE	127.5
6	MAS	SYED AKIL, SHARIFAH RAUDZAH	117.5
7	LBA	EL GNEMI, SAHAR MOSTAFA	95
	USA	**STACK, MARY**	NMR

Scott Brown 4/7/1967, Collingdale, PA
Simona Chin 6/27/1980, Houston, TX
James Dean 5/31/1982, Pickerington, OH
Ronald Harvey 7/15/1971, Long Beach, CA

Jesse Karmazin 9/30/1984, Palm Beach Gardens, FL
Angela Madsen 5/10/1960, Long Beach, CA
Emma Preuschl 10/13/1984, Indianapolis, IN
Laura Schwanger 11/15/1958, Harrisburg, PA

ROWING

Tracy Tackett 5/6/1970, Phoenixville, PA

STAFF

Karen Lewis Head Coach
Frank Biller Asst Coach

SAILING

ROWING RESULTS

SINGLE SCULLS AM1X MEN

1	GBR	AGGAR, TOM	05:22.1
2	UKR	PETRENKO, OLEKSANDR	05:26.0
3	ISR	NAWI, ELI	05:39.1
4	CHN	TAN, YETENG	05:42.3
5	FRA	LAUREAU, PATRICK	05:44.3
6	ITA	MIRAMONTI, SIMONE	05:45.9
7	**USA**	**HARVEY, RONALD**	05:46.3
8	BRA	BONFIM, ANTONY	05:52.2

SINGLE SCULLS AW1X WOMEN

1	GBR	RAYNSFORD, HELENE	06:12.9
2	BLR	VAUCHOK, LIUDMILA	06:25.4
3	**USA**	**SCHWANGER, LAURA**	06:35.1

4	UKR	KUPRIIANOVA, SVITLANA	06:40.0
5	CHN	ZHANG, JINHONG	06:40.8
6	BRA	SANTOS, CLAUDIA	06:54.8
7	ITA	MORO, AGNESE	07:01.2
8	ISR	BERCOVITCH, PASCAL	07:02.4
	NED		05:29.26

COXED FOUR LTAMIX4

1	ITA		03:33.1
2	**USA**		03:37.6
		PREUSCHL, EMMA	
		TACKETT, TRACY	
		KARMAZIN, JESSE	
		DEAN, JAMIE	
		CHIN, SIMONA	
3	GBR		03:38.4

4	GER		03:41.7
5	CHN		03:44.2
6	CAN		03:45.7
7	BRA		03:50.4
8	RSA		03:51.9

DOUBLE SCULLS TAMIX2X

1	CHN		04:20.7
2	AUS		04:21.6
3	BRA		04:28.4
4	**USA**		04:30.3
		MADSEN, ANGELA	
		BROWN, WILLIAM	
5	ITA		04:32.3
6	GBR		04:32.5
7	POL		04:35.1
8	UKR		04:37.8

Tim Angle 5/24/1952, Marblehead, MA
Rick Doerr 11/21/1960, Clifton, NJ
Bill Donahue 5/24/1952 Brick, NJ
Maureen Mckinnon-Tucker 2/25/1965, Marblehead, MA

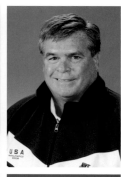

John Ruf 3/4/1968, Pewaukee, WI
Nick Scandone 3/4/1966, Fountain Valley, CA

STAFF

Betsy Alison Head Coach
Marko Dahlberg 2.4mR Coach

Mike Pinckney SKUD 18 Coach

ROWING RESULTS

SINGLE PERSON 2.4MR

1	CAN	TINGLEY, PAUL	21
2	FRA	SEGUIN, DAMIEN	25
3	**USA**	**RUF, JOHN**	28
4	GER	KROGER, HEIKO	28
5	NED	SCHMITTER, THIERRY	32
6	DEN	ALS ANDERSEN, JENS	39
7	GBR	LUCAS, HELENA	41
8	NOR	ERIKSTAD, BJORNAR	64

THREE PERSON SONAR

1	GER		35
2	FRA		36
3	AUS		36
4	NOR		37
5	ISR		38
6	GBR		41
7	GRE		41
8	**USA**		47
		DONOHUE, BILL	
		ANGLE, TIM	
		DOERR, NICK	

TWO PERSON SKUD18

1	**USA**		11
		SCANDONE, NICK	
		MCKINNON TUCKER, MAUREEN	
2	AUS		18
3	CAN		21
4	CHN		35
5	GBR		37
6	MAS		39
7	SWE		45
8	SIN		49

Michael Dickey 9/26/1957, Trafford, AL
Danielle Fong 8/3/1991, New York, NY

STAFF

Dan Durben Head Coach

SHOOTING RESULTS

AIR PISTOL SH1 MEN
1	RUS	PONOMARENKO, VALERIY	672.4
2	RUS	MALYSHEV, SERGEY	556.8
3	KOR	LEE, JU HEE	664.6
4	RUS	LEBEDINSKY, ANDREY	663.7
5	CHN	RU, DECHENG	662.8
6	CHN	LI, JIANFEI	662.2
7	KOR	PARK, SEA KYUN	660.9
8	TUR	YAMAC, KORHAN	658.4

AIR RIFLE STANDING SH1 MEN
1	SWE	JACOBSSON, JONAS	700.5
2	GER	GAU, NORBERT	693.7
3	SLO	PINTER, FRANC	693.2
4	AUS	ADAMS, ASHLEY	693
5	GER	NEUMAIER, JOSEF JOHANN	692
6	CHN	GOU, DINGCHAO	691.5
7	FRA	FRIGGERI, CEDRIC	689.6
8	GBR	MILGATE, NATHAN	686.9

FREE RIFLE 3X40 SH1 MEN
1	SWE	JACOBSSON, JONAS	1264.3
2	ISR	SHAZIRI, DORON	1259.9
3	CHN	DONG, CHAO	1253.5
4	SLO	PINTER, FRANC	1243.6
5	KOR	SIM, JAE YONG	1242.1
6	KOR	JANG, SUNG WON	1240.6
7	GER	NEUMAIER, JOSEF JOHANN	1238.9
8	CHN	GOU, DINGCHAO	1237.1
	USA	DICKEY, MICHAEL	ELIMP

AIR PISTOL SH1 WOMEN
1	CHN	LIN, HAIYAN	467.7
2	KOR	MOON, AEE KYUNG	463.2
3	RUS	DALEKOVA, NATALIA	462.6
4	RUS	PANTELEEVA, ANASTASIA	462.5
5	MKD	NAKOVSKA-BIKOVA, OLIVERA	462.1
6	AZE	TARANOVA, YELENA	460.1
7	TUR	OZGAN, AYSEL	456.2 TIE
8	KOR	BAE, YOUNG EE	456.2 TIE

AIR RIFLE STANDING SH1 WOMEN
1	SVK	VADOVICOVA, VERONIKA	494.8
2	GER	SCHMERMUND, MANUELA	490.2
3	PUR	GOMEZ LOPEZ, NILDA	489.2
4	AUS	KOSMALA, LIBBY	489.1
5	NOR	LILLEHAGEN, MONICA	488.3
6	SWE	HELSINGER, LOTTA	487.2
7	KOR	KIM, IM YEON	486.3
8	FRA	AMIEL, MICHELE	483.8
	USA	FONG, DANIELLE	ELIMP

SPORT RIFLE 3X20 SH1 WOMEN
1	KOR	LEE, YUN RI	676.9
2	KOR	KIM, IM YEON	671
3	CHN	ZHANG, CUIPING	668.6
4	SVK	VADOVICOVA, VERONIKA	667.8
5	KOR	LEE, YOO JEONG	666.1
6	GER	SCHMERMUND, MANUELA	663.2
7	SWE	HELSINGER, LOTTA	659.9
8	CHN	ZHANG, NAN	655.3
	USA	FONG, DANIELLE	ELIMP

AIR RIFLE PRONE SH1 OPEN
1	GBR	SKELHON, MATT	704.9
2	CHN	ZHANG, CUIPING	704.4
3	KOR	SIM, JAE YONG	703.8 TIE
4	CAN	TRIFONIDIS, CHRISTOS	703.8 TIE
5	SVK	MALENOVSKY, RADOSLAV	703.8 TIE
6	SVK	VADOVICOVA, VERONIKA	703.7
7	RUS	NOCHEVNOY, SERGEY	703
8	JPN	TAGUCHI, AKI	702

AIR RIFLE PRONE SH2 OPEN
1	KOR	LEE, JI SEOK	705.3
2	FRA	VOLTZ, RAPHAEL	705.1
3	SWE	WEDIN, VIKTORIA	704.1 TIE
4	KOR	YOU, HO GYOUNG	704.1 TIE
5	SLO	PAVLIN, DAMJAN	704
6	AUS	MARONEY, JASON	703.9
7	DEN	ANDERSEN, JOHNNY	703.8
8	CHN	LIU, JIE	702.9

AIR RIFLE STANDING SH2 OPEN
1	KOR	LEE, JI SEOK	704.3
2	FRA	VOLTZ, RAPHAEL	703.5
3	NZL	JOHNSON, MICHAEL	701.2 TIE
4	KOR	YOU, HO GYOUNG	701.2 TIE
5	AUS	MARONEY, JASON	700.6
6	GER	BRENGMANN, MICHAEL	700.4
7	FRA	DE LA FOREST, TANGUY	699.7
8	CHN	LIU, JIE	698.6

FREE PISTOL SH1 OPEN
1	KOR	PARK, SEA KYUN	644.9
2	KOR	LEE, JU HEE	630.1
3	RUS	PONOMARENKO, VALERIY	627.8
4	CHN	RU, DECHENG	627
5	RUS	MALYSHEV, SERGEY	623.8
6	IRI	KARIMI, BAHMAN	622.7 TIE
7	TUR	YAMAC, KORHAN	622.7 TIE
8	CHN	HUANG, WEI	621.5

FREE RIFLE PRONE SH1 OPEN
1	SWE	JACOBSSON, JONAS	695.8
2	CHN	ZHANG, CUIPING	692.9
3	CHN	DONG, CHAO	689.3
4	AUS	ADAMS, ASHLEY	688.5
5	IND	SHARMA, NARESH	688.2
6	RUS	NOCHEVNOY, SERGEY	687.8 TIE
7	KOR	LEE, YOO JEONG	687.8 TIE
8	SVK	VADOVICOVA, VERONIKA	687.4

SPORT PISTOL SH1 OPEN
1	RUS	LEBEDINSKY, ANDREY	774.7
2	CHN	LI, JIANFEI	774.3
3	RUS	PONOMARENKO, VALERIY	768.9
4	KOR	LEE, JU HEE	766.4
5	CHN	HUANG, WEI	764.5
6	RUS	MALYSHEV, SERGEY	762.9
7	ITA	MARTELLA, ANTONIO	762
8	AUT	AUFSCHNAITER, HUBERT	761.8

SOCCER RESULTS

5-A-SIDE MEN
1	CHN	CHINA
2	BRA	BRAZIL
3	ARG	ARGENTINA
4	ESP	SPAIN
5	GBR	GREAT BRITAIN
6	KOR	KOREA

7-A-SIDE MEN
1	UKR	UKRAIN
2	RUS	RUSSIA
3	IRI	IRAN
4	BRA	BRAZIL
5	NED	NETHERLANDS
6	IRL	IRELAND
7	GBR	GREAT BRITAIN
8	CHN	CHINA

Cheryl Angelelli-Kornoelje 8/1/1968, Clinton Township, MI
Kelley Becherer 7/3/1990, Sheboygan, WI
Aimee Bruder 8/3/1974, Birmingham, AL
Anna Eames 10/1/1990, Golden Valley, MN

Amanda Everlove 3/26/1990, Colorado Springs, CO/Wichita, KS
Deb Gruen 10/23/1987, Hamden, CT
Casey Johnson 1/12/1990, Cypress, CA
Cortney Jordan 6/24/1991, Henderson, NV

April Kerley 6/29/1978, Loveland, OH
Beth Kolbe 4/9/1986, Tiffin, OH
Jessica Long 2/29/1992, Baltimore, MD
Marin Morrison 6/19/1990, Sammamish, WA

Ashley Owens 10/2/1989, Stockbridge, GA
Erin Popovich 6/29/1985, Ft. Collins, CO/Silverbow, MT
Susan Beth Scott 5/27/1992, Colorado Springs, Colol/Cape Girardeau, MO
Melissa Stockwell 1/31/1980, Colorado Springs, CO/Minneapolis, MN

Elizabeth Stone 6/11/1990, Grand Rapids, MI
Miranda Uhl 10/15/1992, Alachua, FL
Kendall Bailey 1/12/1989, San Diego, CA
Mark Barr 8/24/1986, Davis, CA

Cody Bureau 6/4/1988, Colorado Springs, CO/Latrobe, PA
Michael DeMarco 3/19/1969, San Diego, CA
Dave Denniston 9/29/1978, Longmont, CO
Alex Dionne 12/2/1990, Mequon, WI

Tucker Dupree 5/11/1989, Raleigh, NC
Grover Evans 3/6/1952, Little Rock, AR
Rudy Garcia-Tolson 9/14/1988, Colorado Springs, CO/Bloomington, CA
Lantz Lamback 6/30/1986, Colorado Springs, CO/Augusta, GA

Curtis Lovejoy 5/13/1957, Atlanta, GA
Joe McCarthy 8/31/1979, San Diego, CA
Tom Miazga 3/31/1991, Cedarburg, WI
Aaron Paulson 4/4/1977, Portland, OR

Roy Perkins 5/9/1990, Del Mar, CA
Jarrett Perry 11/19/1986, Colorado Springs, CO/Wichita, KS
Michael Prout 2/18/1986, West Springfield, MA
Philip Scholz 4/12/1988, Mt. Sinai, NY

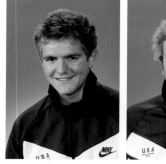

Joe Wise 5/22/1993, Menlo Park, CA
Justin Zook 10/16/1985, Plymouth, MN

STAFF

Julie O'Neil (NOT PICTURED) Head Coach
Andrew Barranco Asst Coach
Peggy Ewald Asst Coach

Tom Franke Asst Coach
Dave Thomas Asst Coach
Kiko Kimura Van Zandt Asst Coach

SWIMMING RESULTS

100 M BACKSTROKE S10 MEN
1	USA	ZOOK, JUSTIN	01:01.3
2	AUS	ANDERSON, MICHAEL	01:01.5
3	EST	PLOOMIPUU, KARDO	01:03.4
4	BRA	BRASIL, ANDRE	01:03.6
5	CAN	HUOT, BENOIT	01:03.8
6	GER	TOBIS, ROY	01:03.9
7	AUS	PASTERFIELD, ANDREW	01:04.2
8	AUS	TIDY, JEREMY	01:05.3

100 M BACKSTROKE S11 MEN
1	CHN	YANG, BOZUN	01:07.7
2	POL	PIETRASIK, DAMIAN	01:08.8
3	UKR	SMYRNOV, VIKTOR	01:09.4
4	JPN	KAWAI, JUNICHI	01:09.5
5	CAN	TILDESLEY, DONOVAN	01:11.9
6	UKR	MASHCHENKO, OLEKSANDR	01:15.1
7	ARG	ZAYAS, SERGIO	01:16.1
8	ESP	ENHAMED, ENHAMED	01:16.9
	USA	SCHOLZ, PHILIP	*ELIM1*

100 M BACKSTROKE S12 MEN
1	RUS	NEVOLIN-SVETOV, ALEXANDER	59.37
2	UKR	KLIPPERT, SERGII	01:00.3
3	UKR	VERAKSA, MAKSYM	01:02.1
4	BLR	MAKARAU, RAMAN	01:02.8
5	USA	DUPREE, TUCKER	01:04.1
6	ARG	GONZALEZ, IGNACIO	01:06.0
7	AUS	MCCLURE, JEREMY	01:06.3
8	ESP	GELIS, ALBERT	01:06.7

100 M BACKSTROKE S13 MEN
1	GRE	TAIGANIDIS, CHARALAMPOS	59.85
2	UKR	FEDYNA, OLEKSII	01:02.9
3	UKR	ALEKSYEYEV, DMYTRO	01:03.4
4	RSA	BOUWER, CHARL	01:03.9
5	CAN	HILL, BRIAN	01:05.5
6	GER	CLAUSNER, DANIEL	01:06.8
7	FIN	LATIKKA, ANTTI	01:08.1
8	CAN	GOTELL, DEVIN	01:08.2

100 M BACKSTROKE S6 MEN
1	RUS	PLOTNIKOV, IGOR	01:14.4
2	CHN	YANG, YUANRUN	01:16.4
3	CHN	TANG, YUAN	01:17.1
4	POL	MICHALSKI, MATEUSZ	01:21.7
5	UKR	SEMENENKO, IAROSLAV	01:23.1
6	GER	MICHAELIS, SWEN	01:23.8
7	ARG	PASTORE, DIEGO	01:24.5
8	IRL	CUMMINGS, JOHNNY	01:29.3
	CAN	ROY, DIANE	3:43.66

100 M BACKSTROKE S7 MEN
1	USA	LAMBACK, LANTZ	01:12.1
2	GBR	FOX, JON	01:14.3
3	ARG	MARRO, GUILLERMO	01:15.2
4	GBR	LINDSAY, ANDREW	01:16.0
5	JPN	EJIMA, DAISUKE	01:16.4
6	CHN	GAO, NAN	01:17.3
7	CHN	MA, FEI	01:18.0
8	SLO	FABCIC, DEJAN	01:18.4

100 M BACKSTROKE S8 MEN
1	RUS	LISENKOV, KONSTANTIN	01:06.3
2	AUS	LEEK, PETER	01:07.3
3	GBR	FRASER, SEAN	01:11.3
4	RUS	FOMENKOV, ALEXEY	01:12.3
5	AUS	MOFFATTI, RICARDO	01:12.6
6	UKR	POLTAVSKYI, IEVGEN	01:13.4
7	CRO	SPANJA, MIHOVIL	01:14.2
8	CAN	CHRISTENSEN, DREW	01:15.5
	USA	MIAZGA, TOM	*ELIM1*

100 M BACKSTROKE S9 MEN
1	AUS	COWDREY, MATTHEW	01:03.3
2	CHN	GUO, ZHI	01:03.6
3	USA	PERRY, JARRETT	01:03.7
4	ESP	COLLADO, JESUS	01:05.4
5	USA	BUREAU, CODY	01:05.5
6	UKR	SIROVATCHENKO, ANDRIY	01:06.8
7	CHN	WANG, RENJIE	01:07.5
8	USA	PROUT, MICHAEL	01:08.1

100 M BREASTSTROKE SB11 MEN
1	UKR	MASHCHENKO, OLEKSANDR	01:12.4
2	CHN	YANG, BOZUN	01:12.9
3	UKR	SMYRNOV, VIKTOR	01:14.7
4	DEN	BUNDGAARD, CHRISTIAN	01:16.4
5	JPN	KIMURA, KEIICHI	01:17.3
6	CHN	DENG, SANBO	01:18.8
7	THA	LAGSANAPRIM, PANOM	01:21.1
8	CUB	LEON, ADONIS	01:22.7

100 M BREASTSTROKE SB12 MEN

1	UKR	VERAKSA, MAKSYM	01:07.5	
2	BLR	PUNKO, SERGEI	01:09.7	
3	UKR	KLIPPERT, SERGII	01:09.8	
4	ESP	FLORIANO, ENRIQUE	01:12.3	
5	ESP	OLIVER, ISRAEL	01:13.3	
6	BLR	RUDZENOK, YURY	01:15.2	
7	POL	MUSIORSKI, ROBERT	01:15.4	

100 M BREASTSTROKE SB13 MEN

1	UKR	FEDYNA, OLEKSII	01:04.6	
2	NZL	SHARP, DANIEL	01:08.7	
3	BLR	IZOTAU, ULADZIMIR	01:08.9	
4	RUS	ZIMIN, MIKHAIL	01:09.1	
5	UKR	ZAVODNYY, MAKSYM	01:09.2	
6	GER	CLAUSNER, DANIEL	01:09.5	
7	GBR	ELLIS, DAVE	01:09.8	
8	ITA	PALANTRANI, ANDREA	01:12.8	

100 M BREASTSTROKE SB4 MEN

1	ESP	TEN, RICARDO	01:36.6	
2	BRA	DIAS, DANIEL	01:40.4	
3	COL	FUENTES, MOISES	01:42.0	
4	HUN	KOVACS, ERVIN	01:44.1	
5	ESP	CIMADEVILA, PABLO	01:46.1	
6	BRA	VASCONCELOS, IVANILDO	01:47.9	
7	CHN	ZENG, HUABIN	01:52.7	
8	KOR	LEE, KWON SIK	02:13.4	
	USA	**DENNISTON, DAVE**		ELIM1

366

100 M BREASTSTROKE SB5 MEN

1	MEX	RANGEL, PEDRO	01:34.7	
2	GER	GRIMM, THOMAS	01:35.4	
3	RSA	SLATTERY, TADHG	01:36.1	
4	GER	GRUNENBERG, NIELS	01:36.7	
5	KOR	LIM, WOO GEUN	01:39.0	
6	SWE	OLSSON, ANDERS	01:40.5	
7	**USA**	**PAULSON, AARON**	01:42.4	
8	ISR	AMAR, LIOZ	01:42.5	

100 M BREASTSTROKE SB6 MEN

1	RUS	FOMENKOV, ALEXEY	01:27.2	
2	GBR	DUKE, GARETH	01:28.2	
3	GBR	WHORWOOD, MATT	01:30.0	
4	RUS	SOKOLOV, KIRILL	01:33.8	
5	JPN	KIMURA, JUMPEI	01:35.9	
6	SLO	FABCIC, DEJAN	01:36.2	
7	BRA	SANTOS, DANIELSON	01:36.5	
8	RUS	ZAKHAROV, ARTEM	01:39.6	

100 M BREASTSTROKE SB7 MEN

1	GBR	KINDRED, SASCHA	01:22.2	
2	AUS	COCHRANE, BLAKE	01:23.4	
3	**USA**	**GARCIA TOLSON, RUDY**	01:24.0	
4	CHN	LI, PENG	01:24.4	
5	JPN	NAKAMURA, TOMOTARO	01:25.3	
6	CRO	SPANJA, MIHOVIL	01:26.3	
7	GER	MOLL, FLORIAN	01:28.3	
8	GER	BURKARD, CHRISTOPH	01:29.6	

100 M BREASTSTROKE SB8 MEN

1	UKR	KALYNA, ANDRIY	01:07.0	
2	CHN	WANG, XIAOFU	01:12.4	
3	ESP	SANCHEZ, ALEJANDRO	01:13.4	
4	POL	PATERKA, KRZYSZTOF	01:14.2	
5	GBR	HYND, SAM	01:15.3	
6	AUT	ONEA, ANDREAS DANIEL	01:17.7	
7	JPN	YAMADA, TAKURO	01:18.4	
8	**USA**	**PERRY, JARRETT**	01:20.6	

100 M BREASTSTROKE SB9 MEN

1	RSA	PAUL, KEVIN	01:08.6	
2	CHN	LIN, FURONG	01:09.6	
3	RUS	DOROGAEV, DENIS	01:10.2	
4	AUS	PENDLETON, RICK	01:10.9	
5	RUS	POLIN, DMITRY	01:11.7	
6	ESP	CRESPO, JAVIER	01:12.3	
7	FRA	RUPP, VINCENT	01:14.5	
8	BEL	DECAESSTECKER, SVEN	01:15.3	
	USA	**BAILEY, KENDALL**		ELIM1
	USA	**BUREAU, CODY**	DISQ	ELIM1

100 M BUTTERFLY S10 MEN

1	BRA	BRASIL, ANDRE	56.47	
2	ESP	LEVECQ, DAVID JULIAN	58.53	
3	NED	VAN DER ZANDEN, MIKE	59.39	
4	CAN	HUOT, BENOIT	59.68	
5	AUS	BELL, DANIEL	59.85	
6	AUS	PENDLETON, RICK	59.87	
7	GER	LUDWIG, LUCAS	01:00.5	
8	GER	TOBIS, ROY	01:00.7	
	USA	**ZOOK, JUSTIN**		ELIM1

100 M BUTTERFLY S11 MEN

1	ESP	ENHAMED, ENHAMED	01:01.1	
2	UKR	MASHCHENKO, OLEKSANDR	01:04.1	
3	UKR	SMYRNOV, VIKTOR	01:05.8	
3	JPN	KAWAI, JUNICHI	01:05.8	
5	CHN	YANG, BOZUN	01:06.6	
6	JPN	KIMURA, KEIICHI	01:09.4	
7	CAN	TILDESLEY, DONOVAN	01:09.5	
8	**USA**	**SCHOLZ, PHILIP**	01:11.8	

100 M BUTTERFLY S12 MEN

1	BLR	MAKARAU, RAMAN	56.90	
2	BLR	PUNKO, SERGEI	59.72	
3	UKR	STABROVSKYY, ANTON	01:00.5	
4	UKR	KLIPPERT, SERGII	01:00.7	
5	**USA**	**DUPREE, TUCKER**	01:01.5	
6	UKR	DEMCHUK, SERGIY	01:02.3	
7	ESP	OLIVER, ISRAEL	01:03.1	
8	ESP	GELIS, ALBERT	01:03.7	

100 M BUTTERFLY S13 MEN

1	BLR	SALEI, DZMITRY	58.89	
2	GRE	TAIGANIDIS, CHARALAMPOS	59.24	
3	RUS	STROKIN, ANDREY	01:00.8	
4	UKR	CHUFAROV, DANYLO	01:01.0	
5	UKR	FEDYNA, OLEKSII	01:01.5	
6	RSA	BOUWER, CHARL	01:01.7	
7	GER	SIMON, DANIEL	01:02.3	
8	UKR	ALEKSYEYEV, DMYTRO	01:03.3	

100 M BUTTERFLY S8 MEN

1	AUS	LEEK, PETER	01:01.0	
2	CHN	WEI, YANPENG	01:01.5	
3	CHN	WANG, XIAOFU	01:01.7	
4	CHN	WANG, JIACHAO	01:03.0	
5	AUS	AUSTIN, BEN	01:03.5	
6	CAN	CHRISTENSEN, DREW	01:07.7	
7	HUN	CSURI, FERENC	01:08.2	
8	GBR	FRASER, SEAN	01:08.4	
	USA	**GARCIA TOLSON, RUDY**		ELIM1

100 M BUTTERFLY S9 MEN

1	HUN	SORS, TAMAS	59.34	
2	AUS	COWDREY, MATTHEW	59.46	
3	CHN	GUO, ZHI	01:00.1	
4	ESP	COLLADO, JESUS	01:01.3	
5	UKR	KALYNA, ANDRIY	01:02.0	
6	**USA**	**BUREAU, CODY**	01:02.2	
7	AUS	BRAMHAM, SAM	01:02.6	
8	**USA**	**BARR, MARK**	01:03.9	
	USA	**PROUT, MICHAEL**		ELIM1

100 M FREESTYLE S10 MEN

1	BRA	BRASIL, ANDRE	51.38	
2	BRA	RODRIGUES, PHELIPE	54.22	
3	CAN	HUOT, BENOIT	54.26	
4	GBR	WELBOURN, ROBERT	54.40	
5	ESP	LEVECQ, DAVID JULIAN	54.73	
6	GER	TOBIS, ROY	55.07	
7	GBR	EDMUNDS, GRAHAM	55.63	
8	**USA**	**ZOOK, JUSTIN**	55.68	

100 M FREESTYLE S11 MEN

1	ESP	ENHAMED, ENHAMED	57.64	
2	CHN	YANG, BOZUN	59.25	
3	POL	POLKOWSKI, GRZEGORZ	01:00.5	
4	CAN	TILDESLEY, DONOVAN	01:01.9	
5	JPN	KIMURA, KEIICHI	01:02.7	
6	RUS	TYCHKOV, KONSTANTIN	01:02.8	
7	RUS	CHEKUROV, ALEXANDER	01:03.4	
	USA	**SCHOLZ, PHILIP**		ELIM1

100 M FREESTYLE S12 MEN

1	UKR	VERAKSA, MAKSYM	51.93	
2	UKR	KLIPPERT, SERGII	53.81	
3	RUS	NEVOLIN-SVETOV, ALEXANDER	54.58	
4	BLR	MAKARAU, RAMAN	54.77	
5	BLR	PUNKO, SERGEI	54.99	
6	ESP	FONT, OMAR	55.75	
7	**USA**	**DUPREE, TUCKER**	56.16	
8	ESP	GELIS, ALBERT	58.70	

100 M FREESTYLE S13 MEN

1	GRE	TAIGANIDIS, CHARALAMPOS	53.37	
2	UKR	FEDYNA, OLEKSII	54.11	
3	UKR	CHUFAROV, DANYLO	54.26	
4	BLR	SALEI, DZMITRY	54.67	
5	BRA	FARRENBERG, CARLOS	54.70	
6	RSA	BOUWER, CHARL	54.99	
7	RUS	STROKIN, ANDREY	55.19	
8	GER	CLAUSNER, DANIEL	55.54	

100 M FREESTYLE S2 MEN

1	RUS	KOKAREV, DMITRY	02:18.0	
2	GRE	KAPELLAKIS, GEORGIOS	02:23.6	
3	GBR	ANDERSON, JIM	02:24.3	
4	BRA	PEREIRA, ADRIANO	02:32.5	
5	BRA	FEITEN, GABRIEL	02:33.7	
6	**USA**	**LOVEJOY, CURTIS**	02:34.1	
7	UKR	ZHUMELA, DENYS	02:35.9	
8	ISR	SHALABI, IYAD	02:37.7	

100 M FREESTYLE S3 MEN

1	CHN	DU, JIANPING	01:35.2	
2	UKR	VYNOHRADETS, DMYTRO	01:35.6	
3	CHN	LI, HANHUA	01:44.2	
4	GRE	KOSTAKIS, IOANNIS	01:45.7	
5	ESP	MARTINEZ, MIGUEL ANGEL	02:02.3	
6	BRA	ANDRADE, GENEZI	02:06.0	
7	**USA**	**DEMARCO, MICHAEL**	02:07.7	
8	RUS	BAKAEV, ALBERT	02:11.0	

100 M FREESTYLE S4 MEN

1	FRA	SMETANINE, DAVID	01:24.7	
2	ESP	ORIBE, RICARDO	01:26.6	
3	CZE	POVYSIL, JAN	01:26.8	
4	SWE	LINDHE, CHRISTOFFER	01:30.9	
5	ITA	MAZZONE, LUCA	01:31.2	
6	RUS	KHMELNITSKIY, IVAN	01:33.4	
7	**USA**	**MCCARTHY, JOE**	01:34.4	
8	GRE	TSAKONAS, STYLIANOS	01:37.3	

100 M FREESTYLE S5 MEN

1	BRA	DIAS, DANIEL	01:11.1	
2	UKR	KRYZHANOVSKYY, DMYTRO	01:12.7	
3	**USA**	**PERKINS, ROY**	01:15.3	
4	GBR	STEPHENS, ANTHONY	01:16.1	
5	ESP	RODRIGUEZ, SEBASTIAN	01:16.2	
6	BRA	SILVA, CLODOALDO	01:21.1	
7	JPN	SUZUKI, TAKAYUKI	01:25.3	
8	ESP	GORDILLO, JORDI	01:25.9	

100 M FREESTYLE S6 MEN

1	SWE	OLSSON, ANDERS	01:06.0	
2	CHN	TANG, YUAN	01:06.4	
3	CHN	YANG, YUANRUN	01:08.6	
4	ESP	VIDAL, DANIEL	01:10.4	
5	BRA	LIMA, ADRIANO	01:10.9	
6	GBR	WHORWOOD, MATT	01:11.6	
7	JPN	OYAMA, KYOSUKE	01:12.2	
8	GER	MICHAELIS, SWEN	01:12.3	

100 M FREESTYLE S7 MEN

1	GBR	ROBERTS, DAVID	01:00.4	
2	**USA**	**LAMBACK, LANTZ**	01:02.4	
3	GBR	WALKER, MATT	01:04.2	
4	CHN	TIAN, RONG	01:07.6	
5	GBR	FOX, JON	01:07.8	
6	AUS	HADLEY, ALEX	01:07.9	
7	UKR	ANDRIUSHIN, IURII	01:08.8	
8	HUN	BECSEY, JANOS	01:09.2	

100 M FREESTYLE S8 MEN

1	CHN	WANG, XIAOFU	58.84	
2	RUS	LISENKOV, KONSTANTIN	59.01	
3	AUS	LEEK, PETER	59.14	
4	AUS	AUSTIN, BEN	59.78	
5	AUS	MOFFATTI, RICARDO	59.93	
6	GBR	HYND, SAM	01:01.0	
7	GRE	FYKAS, KONSTANTINOS	01:01.4	
8	CHN	TIAN, HENGHENG	01:01.9	

100 M FREESTYLE S9 MEN

1	AUS	COWDREY, MATTHEW	55.30	
2	CHN	GUO, ZHI	56.13	
3	HUN	SORS, TAMAS	56.80	
4	UKR	KALYNA, ANDRIY	57.12	
5	JPN	YAMADA, TAKURO	57.29	
6	POR	GRACHAT, DAVID	57.55	
7	**USA**	**BUREAU, CODY**	58.14	
8	FRA	EL GUEDDARI, SAMI	58.68	
	USA	**PROUT, MICHAEL**		ELIM1
	USA	**BARR, MARK**		ELIM1

150 M INDIVIDUAL MEDLEY SM4 MEN

1	NZL	LESLIE, CAMERON	02:33.6	
2	ESP	TORRES, VICENTE JAVIER	02:40.9	
3	JPN	SUZUKI, TAKAYUKI	02:41.1	
4	ESP	LUQUE, MIGUEL	02:45.7	
5	FRA	SMETANINE, DAVID	02:46.2	
6	ITA	BONACINI, FILIPPO	02:53.5	
7	GRE	TSAKONAS, STYLIANOS	02:58.0	
8	ARG	RAMIREZ, SEBASTIAN	03:01.7	

200 M FREESTYLE S2 MEN

1	RUS	KOKAREV, DMITRY	04:45.4	
2	GBR	ANDERSON, JIM	05:00.0	
3	GRE	KAPELLAKIS, GEORGIOS	05:05.9	
4	UKR	ZHUMELA, DENYS	05:16.3	
5	BRA	PEREIRA, ADRIANO	05:21.3	
6	ISR	SHALABI, IYAD	05:34.5	
7	GER	GOLDBACH, CHRISTIAN	05:37.1	
8	BRA	FEITEN, GABRIEL	05:38.4	
	USA	**LOVEJOY, CURTIS**		ELIM1

200 M FREESTYLE S3 MEN

1	UKR	VYNOHRADETS, DMYTRO	03:23.0	
2	CHN	LI, HANHUA	03:23.4	
3	CHN	DU, JIANPING	03:27.8	
4	GRE	KOSTAKIS, IOANNIS	03:38.4	
5	BRA	ANDRADE, GENEZI	04:15.5	
6	**USA**	**DEMARCO, MICHAEL**	04:39.8	

200 M FREESTYLE S4 MEN

1	ESP	ORIBE, RICARDO	02:55.8	
2	FRA	SMETANINE, DAVID	03:04.5	
3	CZE	POVYSIL, JAN	03:06.7	
4	SWE	LINDHE, CHRISTOFFER	03:11.8	
5	ITA	MAZZONE, LUCA	03:14.8	
6	RUS	KHMELNITSKIY, IVAN	03:15.8	
7	MEX	REYES, JUAN	03:25.6	
8	GRE	TSAKONAS, STYLIANOS	03:40.2	

200 M FREESTYLE S5 MEN

1	BRA	DIAS, DANIEL	02:32.3	
2	ESP	RODRIGUEZ, SEBASTIAN	02:38.9	
3	GBR	STEPHENS, ANTHONY	02:44.7	
4	**USA**	**PERKINS, ROY**	02:46.7	
5	BRA	SILVA, CLODOALDO	02:50.9	
6	NZL	LESLIE, CAMERON	02:57.2	
7	ESP	GORDILLO, JORDI	03:02.3	
8	JPN	SUZUKI, TAKAYUKI	03:02.8	

200 M INDIVIDUAL MEDLEY SM10 MEN

1	AUS	PENDLETON, RICK	02:12.8	
2	BRA	BRASIL, ANDRE	02:14.2	
3	CAN	HUOT, BENOIT	02:15.2	
4	BEL	DECAESSTECKER, SVEN	02:16.2	
5	GER	LUDWIG, LUCAS	02:18.9	

6	AUS	TIDY, JEREMY	02:19.8
7	GBR	WELBOURN, ROBERT	02:19.9
8	CZE	COUFAL, FILIP	02:23.2

200 M INDIVIDUAL MEDLEY SM12 MEN
1	UKR	VERAKSA, MAKSYM	02:12.7
2	RUS	NEVOLIN-SVETOV, ALEXANDER	02:13.9
3	UKR	KLIPPERT, SERGII	02:14.1
4	ESP	FLORIANO, ENRIQUE	02:16.8
5	BLR	MAKARAU, RAMAN	02:18.9
6	USA	DUPREE, TUCKER	02:19.1
7	ESP	GELIS, ALBERT	02:24.8

200 M INDIVIDUAL MEDLEY SM13 MEN
1	UKR	FEDYNA, OLEKSII	02:13.8
2	GRE	TAIGANIDIS, CHARALAMPOS	02:16.9
3	UKR	ALEKSYEYEV, DMYTRO	02:17.1
4	UKR	CHUFAROV, DANYLO	02:18.1
5	GER	CLAUSNER, DANIEL	02:19.0
6	GBR	ELLIS, DAVE	02:21.2
7	GBR	KONURALP, DERVIS	02:23.0
8	NED	TIELBEKE, MICHEL	02:25.4

200 M INDIVIDUAL MEDLEY SM5 MEN
1	BRA	DIAS, DANIEL	02:52.6
2	CHN	HE, JUNQUAN	03:00.9
3	ESP	CIMADEVILA, PABLO	03:01.6
4	HUN	KOVACS, ERVIN	03:12.0
5	USA	PERKINS, ROY	03:23.6
6	BRA	VASCONCELOS, IVANILDO	03:30.6
7	ARG	QUASSI, ARIEL	03:42.9
8	MEX	DOMINGUEZ, VIDAL	03:50.1

200 M INDIVIDUAL MEDLEY SM6 MEN
1	GBR	KINDRED, SASCHA	02:42.2
2	CHN	YANG, YUANRUN	02:43.8
3	CHN	XU, QING	02:48.5
4	GBR	WHORWOOD, MATT	02:55.1
5	CHN	LIU, CE	02:56.9
6	SWE	OLSSON, ANDERS	02:57.3
7	GER	GRIMM, THOMAS	03:08.9

200 M INDIVIDUAL MEDLEY SM7 MEN
1	USA	GARCIA TOLSON, RUDY	02:35.9
2	CHN	TIAN, RONG	02:46.2
3	GBR	WALKER, MATT	02:50.1
4	CHN	GAO, NAN	02:51.5
5	CHN	MA, FEI	02:53.4
6	BEL	LAMBRECHTS, KEVIN	02:55.0
7	JPN	KIMURA, JUMPEI	02:55.0

200 M INDIVIDUAL MEDLEY SM8 MEN
1	AUS	LEEK, PETER	02:20.9
2	CHN	WANG, JIACHAO	02:29.7
3	GBR	HYND, SAM	02:29.9
4	ESP	SANCHEZ, ALEJANDRO	02:36.7
5	CAN	CHRISTENSEN, DREW	02:36.7
6	CRO	SPANJA, MIHOVIL	02:37.8
7	AUS	LEVY, MATT	02:38.3

200 M INDIVIDUAL MEDLEY SM9 MEN
1	AUS	COWDREY, MATTHEW	02:13.6
2	UKR	KALYNA, ANDRIY	02:17.2
3	USA	BUREAU, CODY	02:20.2
4	HUN	SORS, TAMAS	02:21.4
5	JPN	YAMADA, TAKURO	02:24.2
6	USA	PROUT, MICHAEL	02:25.6
7	POR	GRACHAT, DAVID	02:26.1
	USA	PERRY, JARRETT	DISQ

400 M FREESTYLE S10 MEN
1	BRA	BRASIL, ANDRE	04:05.8
2	GBR	WELBOURN, ROBERT	04:07.6
3	CAN	HUOT, BENOIT	04:12.1
4	GER	LUDWIG, LUCAS	04:13.6
5	USA	WISE, JOE	04:15.8
6	BRA	COLLET, MARCELO	04:23.4
7	RSA	PAUL, KEVIN	04:27.7
8	RUS	SAMARIN, EDUARD	04:28.3

400 M FREESTYLE S11 MEN
1	ESP	ENHAMED, ENHAMED	04:38.3
2	CHN	YANG, BOZUN	04:43.3
3	CAN	TILDESLEY, DONOVAN	04:49.5
4	UKR	SMYRNOV, VIKTOR	04:52.3
5	USA	SCHOLZ, PHILIP	04:57.2
6	UKR	MYROSHNYCHENKO, OLEKSANDR	05:05.0
7	ARG	ZAYAS, SERGIO	05:08.1
8	ISL	THRASTARSON, EYTHOR	05:15.6

400 M FREESTYLE S12 MEN
1	BLR	PUNKO, SERGEI	04:08.6
2	ESP	FLORIANO, ENRIQUE	04:15.9
3	UKR	KLIPPERT, SERGII	04:19.5
4	USA	DUPREE, TUCKER	04:24.0
5	ITA	SERPICO, ALESSANDRO	04:32.0
6	ESP	GIL, JUAN DIEGO	04:32.4
7	ESP	FONT, OMAR	04:35.6
8	ARG	GONZALEZ, IGNACIO	04:44.8

400 M FREESTYLE S13 MEN
1	RSA	BOUWER, CHARL	04:14.0
2	UKR	CHUFAROV, DANYLO	04:14.8
3	GRE	TAIGANIDIS, CHARALAMPOS	04:23.6
4	GER	DOERRIES, ROBERT	04:23.9
5	BRA	FARRENBERG, CARLOS	04:27.2
6	UKR	FEDYNA, OLEKSII	04:27.7
7	CAN	GOTELL, DEVIN	04:28.7
8	ESP	MENDEZ, KEVIN	04:33.7

400 M FREESTYLE S6 MEN
1	SWE	OLSSON, ANDERS	04:48.3
2	IRL	MCDONALD, DARRAGH	05:09.7
3	GBR	WHORWOOD, MATT	05:20.5
4	BRA	LIMA, ADRIANO	05:22.9
5	GER	MICHAELIS, SWEN	05:26.2
6	CHN	TANG, YUAN	05:27.2
7	JPN	OYAMA, KYOSUKE	05:28.4
8	NOR	HELGELAND, STIAN	05:32.2

400 M FREESTYLE S7 MEN
1	GBR	ROBERTS, DAVID	04:52.3
2	USA	LAMBACK, LANTZ	04:56.5
3	AUS	DOHNT, JAY	04:59.5
4	USA	DIONNE, ALEX	05:02.6
5	GBR	LINDSAY, ANDREW	05:02.7
6	CHN	TIAN, RONG	05:10.4
7	AUS	HADLEY, ALEX	05:20.8
8	JPN	KIMURA, JUMPEI	05:28.1

400 M FREESTYLE S8 MEN
1	GBR	HYND, SAM	04:26.2
2	AUS	LEEK, PETER	04:31.2
3	CHN	WANG, JIACHAO	04:39.5
4	GER	BURKARD, CHRISTOPH	04:40.6
5	CHN	WANG, XIAOFU	04:50.0
6	GER	WILLIG, NIKOLAI	04:50.4
7	AUS	LEVY, MATT	04:51.8
8	USA	MIAZGA, TOM	05:09.5
	USA	GARCIA TOLSON, RUDY	ELIM1

400 M FREESTYLE S9 MEN
1	ESP	COLLADO, JESUS	04:17.0
2	AUS	COWDREY, MATTHEW	04:17.3
3	HUN	SORS, TAMAS	04:20.3
4	AUS	BRAMHAM, SAM	04:21.3
5	AUS	HALL, BRENDEN	04:22.2
6	JPN	YAMADA, TAKURO	04:25.8
7	USA	PROUT, MICHAEL	04:29.4
8	GER	MOLL, FLORIAN	04:29.7
	USA	BARR, MARK	ELIM1

4X100 M FREESTYLE 34 PTS MEN
1	GBR		03:51.4
2	AUS		03:53.6
3	CHN		03:53.9
4	BRA		03:55.8
5	ESP		03:59.4
6	USA		04:00.0
		BUREAU, CODY	
		LAMBACK, LANTZ	
		BARR, MARK	
		PROUT, MICHAEL	
7	GER		04:04.5
8	RUS		04:10.5

4X100 M MEDLEY 34 PTS MEN
1	AUS		04:11.9
2	CHN		04:12.7
3	UKR		04:19.9
4	ESP		04:21.8
5	GB		04:28.4
6	RUS		04:28.5
7	USA		04:29.4
		BUREAU, CODY	
		ZOOK, JUSTIN	
		LAMBACK, LANTZ	
		GARCIA TOLSON, RUDY	
		PERRY, JARRETT	
		BARR, MARK	
		PROUT, MICHAEL	
8	BRA		04:40.0

4X50 M FREESTYLE 20 PTS MEN
1	CHN		02:18.2
2	ESP		02:18.7
3	BRA		02:30.2
4	GRE		02:58.0
5	MEX		03:02.5
	USA		DISQ
		LAMBACK, LANTZ	
		DENNISTON, DAVE	
		DEMARCO, MICHAEL	
		PERKINS, ROY	

4X50 M MEDLEY 20 PTS MEN
1	CHN		02:33.2
2	BRA		02:39.3
3	ESP		02:40.4
4	USA		02:43.0
		LAMBACK, LANTZ	
		DENNISTON, DAVE	
		PERKINS, ROY	
		MCCARTHY, JOE	
5	UKR		02:45.4
6	THA		02:54.4
7	MEX		03:04.4
8	GRE		03:08.8

50 M BACKSTROKE S1 MEN
1	GRE	TAMPAXIS, CHRISTOS	01:23.2
2	GRE	KATSAROS, ANDREAS	01:44.5
3	POR	MARTINS, JOAO	01:47.8
4	GRE	TAXILDARIS, ALEXANDROS	01:50.5
5	LTU	BICKAUSKAS, ANDRIUS	02:27.7
6	USA	EVANS, GROVER	02:51.2

50 M BACKSTROKE S2 MEN
1	RUS	KOKAREV, DMITRY	01:03.2
2	GBR	ANDERSON, JIM	01:04.3
3	GRE	KAPELLAKIS, GEORGIOS	01:07.3
4	ISR	SHALABI, IYAD	01:10.9
5	BRA	PEREIRA, ADRIANO	01:13.7
6	USA	LOVEJOY, CURTIS	01:14.7
7	UKR	ZHUMELA, DENYS	01:15.4
8	BRA	FEITEN, GABRIEL	01:15.8

50 M BACKSTROKE S3 MEN
1	CHN	DU, JIANPING	44.31
2	KOR	MIN, BYEONG EON	44.80
3	UKR	VYNOHRADETS, DMYTRO	53.37
4	CHN	LI, HANHUA	54.42
5	ESP	MARTINEZ, MIGUEL ANGEL	56.82
6	RUS	BAKAEV, ALBERT	58.31
7	BRA	ANDRADE, GENEZI	59.25
8	USA	DEMARCO, MICHAEL	01:03.0

50 M BACKSTROKE S4 MEN
1	MEX	REYES, JUAN	42.77
2	FRA	SMETANINE, DAVID	48.66
3	CHN	ZENG, HUABIN	49.02
4	CZE	PETRACEK, ARNOST	50.40
5	LTU	SKUCAS, KESTUTIS	50.59
6	GRE	TSAKONAS, STYLIANOS	51.15
7	CZE	POVYSIL, JAN	52.79
8	POR	LOPES, NELSON	53.38
	USA	MCCARTHY, JOE	

50 M BACKSTROKE S5 MEN
1	BRA	DIAS, DANIEL	35.28
2	CHN	HE, JUNQUAN	35.43
3	HUN	VERECZKEI, ZSOLT	38.78
4	HUN	KOVACS, ERVIN	40.61
5	MAS	ABDULLAH, ZUL AMIRUL SIDI	42.94
6	ESP	TEN, RICARDO	45.28
7	BRA	AVELINO, FRANCISCO	47.28
	USA	PERKINS, ROY	ELIM1
	USA	DENNISTON, DAVE	ELIM1

50 M BREASTSTROKE SB3 MEN
1	JPN	SUZUKI, TAKAYUKI	49.06
2	ESP	GIL, VICENTE	49.91
3	ESP	LUQUE, MIGUEL	52.83
4	GRE	KARAOUZAS, KONSTANTINOS	54.47
5	ITA	BONACINI, FILIPPO	55.76
6	GRE	TSAGKARIS, VASILEIOS	55.91
7	CZE	POVYSIL, JAN	57.27
8	BRA	BATISTA, MOISES	01:01.9
	USA	DEMARCO, MICHAEL	ELIM1

50 M BUTTERFLY S5 MEN
1	USA	PERKINS, ROY	35.95
2	BRA	DIAS, DANIEL	36.25
3	CHN	HE, JUNQUAN	37.07
4	HUN	KOVACS, ERVIN	39.33
5	THA	KAEWKHAM, VORAVIT	40.78
6	NZL	LESLIE, CAMERON	44.43
7	MEX	DOMINGUEZ, VIDAL	45.50
8	BRA	SILVA, CLODOALDO	45.74
	USA	DENNISTON, DAVE	ELIM1

50 M BUTTERFLY S6 MEN
1	CHN	XU, QING	30.79
2	JPN	OYAMA, KYOSUKE	31.01
3	GBR	KINDRED, SASCHA	32.49
4	CHN	LI, PENG	32.83
5	ESP	VIDAL, DANIEL	32.97
6	RUS	PLOTNIKOV, IGOR	33.25
7	POL	MICHALSKI, MATEUSZ	35.20
8	BRA	SILVA, LUIS	37.90

50 M BUTTERFLY S7 MEN
1	CHN	TIAN, RONG	30.37
2	GBR	WALKER, MATT	32.24
3	CHN	PEI, MANG	32.47
4	JPN	EJIMA, DAISUKE	33.69
5	BEL	LAMBRECHTS, KEVIN	33.8
6	UKR	ANDRIUSHIN, IURII	34.07
7	RUS	SADVAKASOV, RUSLAN	34.12
8	USA	LAMBACK, LANTZ	34.56

50 M FREESTYLE S10 MEN
1	BRA	BRASIL, ANDRE	23.61
2	BRA	RODRIGUES, PHELIPE	24.64
3	CAN	HUOT, BENOIT	24.65
4	USA	ZOOK, JUSTIN	24.81
5	ESP	LEVECQ, DAVID JULIAN	24.87
6	AUS	ANDERSON, MICHAEL	25.04
7	GER	TOBIS, ROY	25.04
8	GBR	EDMUNDS, GRAHAM	25.11

50 M FREESTYLE S11 MEN
1	ESP	ENHAMED, ENHAMED	25.82
2	JPN	KAWAI, JUNICHI	27.16
3	RUS	CHEKUROV, ALEXANDER	27.26
4	CHN	YANG, BOZUN	27.30
5	UKR	SMYRNOV, VIKTOR	27.74
6	POL	POLKOROWSKI, GRZEGORZ	27.83
7	CAN	TILDESLEY, DONOVAN	28.08
8	UKR	MASHCHENKO, OLEKSANDR	28.44
	USA	SCHOLZ, PHILIP	ELIM1

50 M FREESTYLE S12 MEN
1	UKR	VERAKSA, MAKSYM	23.43

2 RUS NEVOLIN-SVETOV, ALEXANDER 24.73
3 UKR KLIPPERT, SERGII 24.98
4 BLR MAKARAU, RAMAN 25.02
5 ESP FONT, OMAR 25.26
6 **USA DUPREE, TUCKER 25.31**
7 RUS PIKALOV, ALEXANDER 25.92
8 BLR PUNKO, SERGEI 25.97

50 M FREESTYLE S13 MEN
1 UKR FEDYNA, OLEKSII 23.75
2 GRE TAIGANIDIS, CHARALAMPOS 24.19
3 RUS STROKIN, ANDREY 24.55
4 BRA FARRENBERG, CARLOS 24.62
5 BLR SALEI, DZMITRY 24.92
6 UKR ALEKSYEYEV, DMYTRO 25.13
7 GER CLAUSNER, DANIEL 25.39
8 NZL SHARP, DANIEL 25.50

50 M FREESTYLE S2 MEN
1 GRE KAPELLAKIS, GEORGIOS 01:04.9
2 RUS KOKAREV, DMITRY 01:05.2
3 GBR ANDERSON, JIM 01:06.1
4 ISR SHALABI, IYAD 01:10.5
5 UKR ZHUMELA, DENYS 01:12.0
6 **USA LOVEJOY, CURTIS 01:12.6**
7 BRA FEITEN, GABRIEL 01:15.1
8 BRA PEREIRA, ADRIANO 01:15.4

50 M FREESTYLE S3 MEN
1 UKR VYNOHRADETS, DMYTRO 42.60
2 CHN DU, JIANPING 44.19
3 KOR MIN, BYEONG EON 45.75
4 CHN LI, HANHUA 47.15
5 GRE KOSTAKIS, IOANNIS 49.84
6 ESP MARTINEZ, MIGUEL ANGEL 57.11
7 **USA DEMARCO, MICHAEL 01:01.7**
8 RUS BAKAEV, ALBERT 01:04.0

50 M FREESTYLE S4 MEN
1 FRA SMETANINE, DAVID 37.89
2 ESP ORIBE, RICARDO 38.69
3 CZE POVYSIL, JAN 39.35
4 ITA MAZZONE, LUCA 39.60
5 **USA MCCARTHY, JOE 39.95**
6 SWE LINDHE, CHRISTOFFER 42.75
7 MEX REYES, JUAN 43.07
8 RUS KHMELNITSKIY, IVAN 43.93

50 M FREESTYLE S5 MEN
1 UKR KRYZHANOVSKYY, DMYTRO 33.00
2 BRA DIAS, DANIEL 33.56
3 ESP RODRIGUEZ, SEBASTIAN 33.78
4 **USA PERKINS, ROY 34.61**
5 CHN HE, JUNQUAN 34.65
6 GBR STEPHENS, ANTHONY 34.97
7 BRA SILVA, CLODOALDO 35.22
8 ESP GORDILLO, JORDI 36.88

50 M FREESTYLE S6 MEN
1 CHN XU, QING 29.78
2 CHN TANG, YUAN 30.07
3 SWE OLSSON, ANDERS 31.07
4 ESP VIDAL, DANIEL 31.27
5 JPN OYAMA, KYOSUKE 31.37
6 CHN YANG, YUANRUN 31.66
7 GER IWANOW, SEBASTIAN 32.79
8 BRA LIMA, ADRIANO 32.85

50 M FREESTYLE S7 MEN
1 GBR ROBERTS, DAVID 27.95
2 GBR WALKER, MATT 28.60
3 **USA LAMBACK, LANTZ 28.81**
4 AUS HADLEY, ALEX 30.75
5 GRE TSOTRAS, NIKOLAOS 31.01
6 UKR ANDRIUSHIN, IURII 31.12
7 HUN BECSEY, JANOS 31.46
8 GBR FOX, JON 31.53

50 M FREESTYLE S8 MEN
1 CHN WANG, XIAOFU 26.45
2 AUS LEEK, PETER 26.89
3 RUS LISENKOV, KONSTANTIN 27.18
4 CHN GUO, JUN 27.46
5 AUS AUSTIN, BEN 27.82
6 CHN WEI, YANPENG 28.03
7 GER WILLIG, NIKOLAI 28.94
8 AUS LEVY, MATT 29.68

50 M FREESTYLE S9 MEN
1 AUS COWDREY, MATTHEW 25.34
2 CHN GUO, ZHI 25.51
3 CHN XIONG, XIAOMING 25.60
4 CHN WANG, RENJIE 26.03
5 HUN SORS, TAMAS 26.21
6 UKR KALYNA, ANDRIY 26.46
7 FRA EL GUEDDARI, SAMI 26.65
8 ESP MARI, JOSE ANTONIO 26.89
USA BUREAU, CODY ELIM1
USA BARR, MARK ELIM1
USA PROUT, MICHAEL ELIM1

100 M BACKSTROKE S10 WOMEN
1 NZL PASCOE, SOPHIE 01:10.6
1 RSA SAPIRO, SHIREEN 01:10.6
3 ESP MORALES, ESTHER 01:13.8
4 **USA SCOTT, SUSAN BETH 01:14.0**
5 AUS LUCAS, SIAN 01:14.7
6 GBR CATTLE, EMMA 01:14.7
7 AUS MCGAW, TARRYN 01:15.7
8 POL PAWLIK, KATARZYNA 01:20.1

100 M BACKSTROKE S13 WOMEN
1 CAN GOTELL, CHELSEY 01:09.1 WR
2 CAN GRAND MAISON, VALERIE 01:10.4
3 RUS EFIMENKO, ANNA 01:11.0
4 **USA BECHERER, KELLEY 01:11.5**
5 UKR BALASHOVA, IRYNA 01:12.6
6 GBR COUGHLIN, JENNY 01:14.7
7 JPN KASAMOTO, AKARI 01:14.8
8 AUS WATT, PRUE 01:16.1

100 M BACKSTROKE S6 WOMEN
1 NED DE KONING-PEPER, MIRJAM 01:28.3 PR
2 GBR LEWIS, NYREE 01:29.4
3 CHN JIANG, FUYING 01:30.5
4 RUS DIODOROVA, ANASTASIA 01:34.0
5 DEN LAURIDSEN, KARINA 01:34.4
6 MEX GONZALEZ, DORAMITZI 01:36.9
7 GER GOETZE, MARIA 01:39.9
8 **USA UHL, MIRANDA 01:40.4**

100 M BACKSTROKE S7 WOMEN
1 AUS PORTER, KATRINA 01:24.3 WR
2 GER BRUHN, KIRSTEN 01:26.0
3 NED BOONACKER, CHANTAL 01:26.3
4 **USA JORDAN, CORTNEY 01:26.6**
5 AUS ROGERS, SHELLEY 01:30.3
6 CAN NELSON, BRIANNA 01:30.4
7 CAN JENSEN, LAURA 01:31.9
8 KOR KIM, JI EUN 01:34.3

100 M BACKSTROKE S8 WOMEN
1 GBR FREDERIKSEN, HEATHER 01:16.7 WR
2 **USA LONG, JESSICA 01:19.6**
3 NOR VESTBOSTAD, MARIANN 01:20.9
4 ISR LEIBOVITCH, KEREN 01:21.3
5 GBR LATHAM, RACHAEL 01:22.4
6 CHN JIN, XIAOQIN 01:25.5
7 GER WEINBERG, STEFANIE 01:28.0
8 CHN LU, WEIYUAN 01:28.5

100 M BACKSTROKE S9 WOMEN
1 CAN DIXON, STEPHANIE 01:09.3 WR
2 **USA STONE, ELIZABETH 01:11.2**
3 AUS COLE, ELLIE 01:11.9
4 GBR MILLWARD, STEPHANIE 01:14.1
5 GBR SIMPKIN, LIZZIE 01:14.4
6 GBR CASHMORE, CLAIRE 01:14.5
7 CAN SALES, DARDA 01:15.9
8 FRA GRAL, EMILIE 01:16.4

100 M BREASTSTROKE SB12 WOMEN
1 CYP PELENDRITOU, KAROLINA 01:17.6
2 ESP GOMEZ, SANDRA 01:18.1
3 UKR MATLO, YARYNA 01:19.5
4 UKR VOLKOVA, YULIYA 01:19.7
5 ESP FONT, DEBORAH 01:20.4
6 ESP CASALS, CARLA 01:20.7
7 POL MENDAK, JOANNA 01:24.5
8 POL HARAJDA, PATRYCJA 01:28.8

100 M BREASTSTROKE SB4 WOMEN
1 CZE HLAVACKOVA, BELA 01:55.6
2 ISR PEZARO, INBAL 01:57.8
3 ESP PERALES, MARIA TERESA 02:01.3
4 SIN GOH, THERESA 02:02.0
5 JPN KAJIWARA, NORIKO 02:04.2
6 TPE LUO, ALICE HSIAO HUNG 02:04.9
7 HUN ENGELHARDT, KATALIN 02:09.7
8 COL OME, NAIVER 02:28.3

100 M BREASTSTROKE SB5 WOMEN
1 GER BRUHN, KIRSTEN 01:36.9
2 FRA LARDIERE, RACHEL 01:52.3
3 HUN RACZKO, GITTA 01:54.5
4 GBR LEWIS, NYREE 01:56.2
5 FRA LANCIAL, FLORENCE 01:56.7
6 BLR SHAVEL, NATALLIA 01:57.7
7 JPN KITAMURA, YURI 02:03.4
8 HUN ILLES, FANNI 02:07.5

100 M BREASTSTROKE SB6 WOMEN
1 GBR JOHNSON, ELIZABETH 01:41.9
2 AUS BOWEN, SARAH 01:42.4
3 **USA GRUEN, DEBORAH 01:44.0**
4 GBR HENSHAW, CHARLOTTE 01:45.3
5 GER GOETZE, MARIA 01:47.8
6 **USA UHL, MIRANDA 01:48.4**
7 AUS PORTER, KATRINA 01:55.1
8 CAN MCDOUGALL, STEPH 01:57.8
USA JOHNSON, CASEY ELIM1

100 M BREASTSTROKE SB7 WOMEN
1 **USA POPOVICH, ERIN 01:31.6**
2 CHN HUANG, MIN 01:35.5
3 **USA LONG, JESSICA 01:38.6**
4 CHN LU, HONGMEI 01:43.2
5 AUS OLIVER, RHIANNON 01:45.5
6 NED MASSAR, BERNADETTE 01:49.3
7 CAN NELSON, BRIANNA 01:54.4
8 CAN JENSEN, LAURA 01:56.3

100 M BREASTSTROKE SB8 WOMEN
1 RUS VLADYKINA, OLESYA 01:20.6
2 POL WOZNIAK, PAULINA 01:23.9
3 GBR CASHMORE, CLAIRE 01:25.6
4 JPN NOMURA, MANAMI 01:25.9
5 POR CALADO, JOANA 01:28.5
6 IRL KEANE, ELLEN 01:29.7
7 POR MARQUES, LEILA 01:30.1
8 ESP RODRIGUEZ, ESTER 01:34.4

100 M BREASTSTROKE SB9 WOMEN
1 NZL PASCOE, SOPHIE 01:22.6
2 ESP GASCON, SARAI 01:24.5
3 GBR WATKIN, LOUISE 01:26.1
4 CHN QIAN, HUIYU 01:26.3
5 GBR GREY, KATE 01:26.3
6 FRA DIDIER, MAUD 01:26.6
7 ARG GIMENEZ, DANIELA 01:26.8
8 RUS NIKITINA, YULIA 01:27.3

100 M BUTTERFLY S10 WOMEN
1 **USA EAMES, ANNA 01:09.4**
2 NZL PASCOE, SOPHIE 01:10.5
3 CHN WANG, SHUAI 01:11.3
4 FRA LORANDI, ELODIE 01:12.0
5 POL PAWLIK, KATARZYNA 01:13.0
6 **USA SCOTT, SUSAN BETH 01:15.7**
7 RSA SAPIRO, SHIREEN 01:17.1
8 SVK MIKULASIKOVA, VIERA 01:17.1

100 M BUTTERFLY S12 WOMEN
1 POL MENDAK, JOANNA 01:03.3
2 ESP GARCIA-ARCICOLLAR, ANA 01:08.9
3 UKR VOLKOVA, YULIYA 01:10.9
4 ESP CASALS, CARLA 01:11.9
5 VEN MOTA, BELKYS 01:12.5
6 ESP ALONSO, AMAYA 01:15.1
7 POL HARAJDA, PATRYCJA 01:15.2
8 UKR MATLO, YARYNA 01:17.3

100 M BUTTERFLY S13 WOMEN
1 CAN GRAND MAISON, VALERIE 01:06.5
2 CAN COTE, KIRBY 01:06.6
3 CAN GOTELL, CHELSEY 01:06.9
4 AUS WATT, PRUE 01:07.5
5 GBR HENRY, RHIANNON 01:07.5
6 **USA BECHERER, KELLEY 01:08.4**
7 AUS VAN ROOSMALEN, TEIGAN 01:09.5
8 GBR COUGHLIN, JENNY 01:13.0

100 M BUTTERFLY S8 WOMEN
1 **USA LONG, JESSICA 01:12.0**
2 **USA EVERLOVE, AMANDA 01:12.2**
3 CHN JIN, XIAOQIN 01:15.3
4 CHN CHEN, ZHONGLAN 01:15.8
5 CHN LU, WEIYUAN 01:16.7
6 ITA CERASUOLO, IMMACOLATA 01:17.1
7 GBR LATHAM, RACHAEL 01:18.6
8 JPN NOMURA, MANAMI 01:20.6

100 M BUTTERFLY S9 WOMEN
1 RSA DU TOIT, NATALIE 01:06.7
2 AUS COLE, ELLIE 01:10.9
3 AUS WILLIAMS, ANNABELLE 01:11.0
4 CAN DIXON, STEPHANIE 01:11.0
5 ESP GASCON, SARAI 01:11.1
6 GBR SIMPKIN, LIZZIE 01:12.2
7 ITA SECCI, FRANCESCA 01:12.8
8 GBR CASHMORE, CLAIRE 01:13.5
USA STONE, ELIZABETH ELIM1
USA KERLEY, APRIL ELIM1
USA STOCKWELL, MELISSA ELIM1

100 M FREESTYLE S10 WOMEN
1 **USA OWENS, ASHLEY 01:01.6**
2 POL PAWLIK, KATARZYNA 01:01.6
3 **USA EAMES, ANNA 01:01.9**
4 **USA SCOTT, SUSAN BETH 01:02.3**
5 CAN POLINARIO, ANNE 01:04.0
6 ESP MORALES, ESTHER 01:04.2
7 AUS MCGAW, TARRYN 01:04.8
8 AUS GANDOLFO, SAMANTHA 01:05.7

100 M FREESTYLE S11 WOMEN
1 CHN XIE, QING 01:09.0
2 ITA CAMELLINI, CECILIA 01:09.7
3 GER SCHULTE, DANIELA 01:11.1
4 SUI CAVIN, CHANTAL 01:12.2
5 ITA POIANI PANIGATI, MARIA 01:12.7
6 BRA SUGIMORI, FABIANA 01:13.4
7 CAN THOMAS, AMBER 01:14.4
8 CAN TUOMELA, JESS 01:14.8

100 M FREESTYLE S12 WOMEN
1 RUS SAVCHENKO, OXANA 59.47
2 RUS EFIMENKO, ANNA 01:01.2
3 POL MENDAK, JOANNA 01:01.6
4 ESP FONT, DEBORAH 01:02.0
5 ESP GARCIA-ARCICOLLAR, ANA 01:02.4
6 UKR VOLKOVA, YULIYA 01:02.5
7 VEN MOTA, BELKYS 01:07.4
8 ESP ALONSO, AMAYA 01:07.5

100 M FREESTYLE S13 WOMEN
1 CAN GRAND MAISON, VALERIE 58.87
2 CAN GOTELL, CHELSEY 01:00.3
3 **USA BECHERER, KELLEY 01:00.5**
4 CAN COTE, KIRBY 01:01.0
5 UKR BALASHOVA, IRYNA 01:01.6
6 AUS WATT, PRUE 01:01.6

7	GBR	HENRY, RHIANNON	01:01.8
8	GBR	COUGHLIN, JENNY	01:06.9

100 M FREESTYLE S4 WOMEN

1	MEX	MIRANDA, NELY	01:44.1
2	**USA**	**ANGELELLI, CHERYL**	01:50.3
3	**USA**	**BRUDER, AIMEE**	01:55.3
4	BRA	GARCIA, EDENIA	01:58.0
5	POL	HAMER, KAROLINA	01:59.3
6	SWE	EKSTROM, JENNIE	02:00.7
7	MEX	VALLE, PATRICIA	02:02.5
8	GER	CONRADI, ANNKE	02:20.0

100 M FREESTYLE S5 WOMEN

1	ISR	PEZARO, INBAL	01:16.6
2	SIN	GOH, THERESA	01:21.6
3	CZE	HLAVACKOVA, BELA	01:22.2
4	UKR	AKOPYAN, OLENA	01:22.8
5	JPN	NARITA, MAYUMI	01:27.9
6	SIN	GOH, THERESA	01:32.9
7	JPN	KAWAMURA, YUKA	01:35.7
8	JPN	TAKEUCHI, SUGAKO	01:38.2
	USA	**MORRISON, MARIN**	ELIM1

100 M FREESTYLE S6 WOMEN

1	GBR	SIMMONDS, ELEANOR	01:18.7
2	NED	DE KONING-PEPER, MIRJAM	01:19.3
3	MEX	GONZALEZ, DORAMITZI	01:19.4
4	GER	GOETZE, MARIA	01:19.5
5	GBR	JONES, NATALIE	01:21.5
6	JPN	NARA, ERIKA	01:21.8
7	**USA**	**UHL, MIRANDA**	01:22.2
8	**USA**	**JOHNSON, CASEY**	01:26.4

100 M FREESTYLE S7 WOMEN

1	**USA**	**POPOVICH, ERIN**	01:11.8
2	**USA**	**JORDAN, CORTNEY**	01:12.1
3	GER	BRUHN, KIRSTEN	01:12.9
4	NED	BOONACKER, CHANTAL	01:14.6
5	KOR	KIM, JI EUN	01:18.5
6	CAN	JENSEN, LAURA	01:18.7
7	CAN	NELSON, BRIANNA	01:19.1
8	RUS	GUSEVA, OXANA	01:20.7

100 M FREESTYLE S8 WOMEN

1	**USA**	**LONG, JESSICA**	01:06.9
2	GBR	FREDERIKSEN, HEATHER	01:08.5
3	AUS	FRENEY, JACQUELINE	01:08.6
4	**USA**	**EVERLOVE, AMANDA**	01:10.7
5	NOR	NORLAND, CECILIE DRABSCH	01:11.9
6	FRO	ANDREASEN, HEIDI	01:12.0
7	GER	KABUS, JULIA	01:12.7
8	CHN	XU, YANRU	01:13.7

100 M FREESTYLE S9 WOMEN

1	RSA	DU TOIT, NATALIE	01:01.4
2	GBR	WATKIN, LOUISE	01:03.9
3	CAN	DIXON, STEPHANIE	01:03.9
4	AUS	COLE, ELLIE	01:04.2
5	GBR	MILLWARD, STEPHANIE	01:04.5
6	**USA**	**STONE, ELIZABETH**	01:04.9
7	AUS	WILLIAMS, ANNABELLE	01:05.4
8	CAN	SALES, DARDA	01:05.7
	USA	**KERLEY, APRIL**	ELIM1
	USA	**TOCKWELL, MELISSA**	ELIM1

150 M INDIVIDUAL MEDLEY SM4 WOMEN

1	DEN	LAURIDSEN, KARINA	02:47.8
2	AUS	JONKERS, MARAYKE	03:28.9
3	MEX	VALLE, PATRICIA	03:29.4
4	**USA**	**BRUDER, AIMEE**	03:29.8
5	SWE	EKSTROM, JENNIE	03:55.6
6	BRA	FIRMINO, RILDENE	04:05.0

200 M FREESTYLE S5 WOMEN

1	ESP	PERALES, MARIA TERESA	02:47.5
2	ISR	PEZARO, INBAL	02:49.5
3	UKR	AKOPYAN, OLENA	02:52.5
4	SIN	GOH, THERESA	03:14.2
5	NED	TEUNISSEN, LISETTE	03:22.9
6	JPN	KAWAMURA, YUKA	03:24.3
7	MEX	MIRANDA, NELY	03:32.1
8	FRA	PAIROUX-LAGARDERE, GENEVIEVE	03:34.0
	USA	**ANGELELLI, CHERYL**	ELIM1
	USA	**BRUDER, AIMEE**	ELIM1

200 M INDIVIDUAL MEDLEY SM10 WOMEN

1	NZL	PASCOE, SOPHIE	02:35.2
2	FRA	LORANDI, ELODIE	02:39.3
3	POL	PAWLIK, KATARZYNA	02:40.4
4	SVK	MIKULASIKOVA, VIERA	02:40.4
5	**USA**	**EAMES, ANNA**	02:42.5
6	**USA**	**SCOTT, SUSAN BETH**	02:44.0
7	AUS	MCGAW, TARRYN	02:46.6
8	FRA	DIDIER, MAUD	02:47.6

200 M INDIVIDUAL MEDLEY SM12 WOMEN

1	RUS	SAVCHENKO, OXANA	02:30.5
2	POL	MENDAK, JOANNA	02:32.6
3	CYP	PELENDRITOU, KAROLINA	02:35.3
4	ESP	GARCIA-ARCICOLLAR, ANA	02:35.6
5	UKR	VOLKOVA, YULIYA	02:37.4
6	POL	HARAJDA, PATRYCJA	02:40.4
7	ESP	CASALS, CARLA	02:44.7
8	ESP	ALONSO, AMAYA	02:48.7

200 M INDIVIDUAL MEDLEY SM13 WOMEN

1	CAN	GOTELL, CHELSEY	02:28.2
2	CAN	COTE, KIRBY	02:28.6
3	CAN	GRAND MAISON, VALERIE	02:29.3
4	**USA**	**BECHERER, KELLEY**	02:32.2
5	AUS	WATT, PRUE	02:32.9
6	AUS	VAN ROOSMALEN, TEIGAN	02:39.2
7	ESP	BANOS, LIDIA MARTA	02:48.8
8	JPN	KASAMOTO, AKARI	02:55.2

200 M INDIVIDUAL MEDLEY SM6 WOMEN

1	**USA**	**UHL, MIRANDA**	03:13.0
2	GER	GOETZE, MARIA	03:14.6
3	GBR	JONES, NATALIE	03:15.2
4	CHN	JIANG, FUYING	03:15.2
5	GBR	SIMMONDS, ELEANOR	03:18.4
6	GBR	LEWIS, NYREE	03:23.9
7	AUS	ROSE, SARAH	03:29.5
8	RUS	DIODOROVA, ANASTASIA	03:33.2

200 M INDIVIDUAL MEDLEY SM7 WOMEN

1	**USA**	**POPOVICH, ERIN**	02:54.6
2	CHN	HUANG, MIN	03:00.6
3	**USA**	**JORDAN, CORTNEY**	03:08.0
4	AUS	ROGERS, SHELLEY	03:12.7
5	SVK	PROKEINOVA, MARGITA	03:19.0
6	RUS	GUSEVA, OXANA	03:19.5
7	**USA**	**GRUEN, DEBORAH**	03:27.5
8	HUN	RACZKO, GITTA	03:30.4

200 M INDIVIDUAL MEDLEY SM8 WOMEN

1	**USA**	**LONG, JESSICA**	02:41.8
2	**USA**	**EVERLOVE, AMANDA**	02:50.5
3	GBR	FREDERIKSEN, HEATHER	02:53.2
4	RUS	VLADYKINA, OLESYA	02:53.8
5	ITA	CERASUOLO, IMMACOLATA	02:56.2
6	CHN	JIANG, SHENGNAN	02:57.4
7	FRO	ANDREASEN, HEIDI	02:59.0
8	CHN	LU, WEIYUAN	03:00.0

200 M INDIVIDUAL MEDLEY SM9 WOMEN

1	RSA	DU TOIT, NATALIE	02:27.8
2	CAN	DIXON, STEPHANIE	02:37.5
3	GBR	WATKIN, LOUISE	02:40.3
4	GBR	CASHMORE, CLAIRE	02:42.1
5	FRA	GRAL, EMILIE	02:42.5
6	CAN	GRAY, BRITTANY	02:45.5
7	POL	WOZNIAK, PAULINA	02:46.1

400 M FREESTYLE S10 WOMEN

1	POL	PAWLIK, KATARZYNA	04:33.2
2	**USA**	**OWENS, ASHLEY**	04:38.1
3	**USA**	**SCOTT, SUSAN BETH**	04:39.4
4	**USA**	**EAMES, ANNA**	04:44.0
5	AUS	GANDOLFO, SAMANTHA	04:48.0
6	FRA	LORANDI, ELODIE	04:48.5
7	AUS	MCGAW, TARRYN	04:49.8
8	AUS	LUCAS, SIAN	04:50.0

400 M FREESTYLE S13 WOMEN

1	CAN	GRAND MAISON, VALERIE	04:28.6
2	RUS	EFIMENKO, ANNA	04:37.4
3	**USA**	**BECHERER, KELLEY**	04:37.5
3	CAN	GOTELL, CHELSEY	04:37.5
5	GBR	HENRY, RHIANNON	04:41.5
6	AUS	WATT, PRUE	04:46.2
7	GBR	COUGHLIN, JENNY	04:56.8
8	AUS	VAN ROOSMALEN, TEIGAN	05:02.2

400 M FREESTYLE S6 WOMEN

1	GBR	SIMMONDS, ELEANOR	05:41.3
2	NED	DE KONING-PEPER, MIRJAM	05:43.8
3	GER	GOETZE, MARIA	05:49.7
4	**USA**	**UHL, MIRANDA**	05:55.6
5	MEX	GONZALEZ, DORAMITZI	06:06.8
6	GBR	LEWIS, NYREE	06:10.8
7	GBR	LOVE, MHAIRI	06:15.3
8	JPN	NARA, ERIKA	06:26.6
	USA	**JOHNSON, CASEY**	ELIM1

400 M FREESTYLE S7 WOMEN

1	**USA**	**POPOVICH, ERIN**	05:17.4
2	**USA**	**JORDAN, CORTNEY**	05:21.0
3	GER	BRUHN, KIRSTEN	05:28.2
4	NED	BOONACKER, CHANTAL	05:35.3
5	AUS	PORTER, KATRINA	05:44.9
6	RUS	GUSEVA, OXANA	05:46.6
7	KOR	KIM, JI EUN	05:51.5
8	CAN	NELSON, BRIANNA	06:01.0
	USA	**GRUEN, DEBORAH**	ELIM1

400 M FREESTYLE S8 WOMEN

1	**USA**	**LONG, JESSICA**	04:50.2
2	GBR	FREDERIKSEN, HEATHER	04:54.5
3	AUS	FRENEY, JACQUELINE	04:57.2
4	FRO	ANDREASEN, HEIDI	05:20.5
5	GER	KABUS, JULIA	05:22.8
6	CAN	COLE, ANDREA	05:30.0
7	NOR	VESTBOSTAD, MARIANN	05:39.7
8	BRA	LIRA, VALERIA	05:48.9

400 M FREESTYLE S9 WOMEN

1	RSA	DU TOIT, NATALIE	04:23.8
2	CAN	DIXON, STEPHANIE	04:39.7
3	AUS	COLE, ELLIE	04:44.6
4	**USA**	**STONE, ELIZABETH**	04:46.5
5	GBR	WATKIN, LOUISE	04:47.1
6	GER	REPPE, CHRISTIANE	04:51.6
7	CAN	GRAY, BRITTANY	04:58.1
8	AUS	DRENNAN, AMANDA	05:07.2
	USA	**STOCKWELL, MELISSA**	ELIM1

50 M BACKSTROKE S2 WOMEN

1	UKR	IELISAVETSKA, GANNA	01:13.6
2	UKR	SOTSKA, IRYNA	01:15.5
3	ESP	CARRACELAS, SARA	01:16.3
4	UKR	SEMENOVA, NATALIIA	01:23.8
5	GRE	LIASKOU, MARIA	01:24.2
6	GRE	KALPAKIDOU, MARIA	01:25.6
7	GBR	WATTS, DANIELLE	01:27.3
8	ARG	BASUALDO, BETIANA	01:40.1

50 M BACKSTROKE S3 WOMEN

1	SIN	YIP, PIN XIU	58.75
2	GBR	WILLIAMSON, FRAN	01:06.1
3	CHN	XIA, JIANGBO	01:08.0
4	MEX	VALLE, PATRICIA	01:12.9
5	AUS	OVERTON, ESTHER	01:13.3
6	RSA	SHANNON, SARAH	01:13.8
7	GER	CONRADI, ANNKE	01:14.9
8	**USA**	**KOLBE, BETH**	01:18.0

50 M BACKSTROKE S5 WOMEN

1	CZE	HLAVACKOVA, BELA	41.03
2	ESP	PERALES, MARIA TERESA	44.58
3	DEN	LAURIDSEN, KARINA	45.72
4	NED	TEUNISSEN, LISETTE	50.87
5	JPN	NARITA, MAYUMI	51.23
6	HUN	ZAMBO, DIANA	52.04
7	RSA	NOTHLING, BETH	54.29
8	JPN	KAWAMURA, YUKA	55.41
	USA	**MORRISON, MARIN**	DISQ

369

50 M BUTTERFLY S6 WOMEN

1	CHN	JIANG, FUYING	38.44
2	RUS	DIODOROVA, ANASTASIA	39.93
3	UKR	AKOPYAN, OLENA	40.72
4	AUS	ROSE, SARAH	40.95
5	ISR	SHWARTZ, INBAL	41.05
6	**USA**	**JOHNSON, CASEY**	42.35
7	**USA**	**UHL, MIRANDA**	42.5
8	GBR	SIMMONDS, ELEANOR	43.14

50 M BUTTERFLY S7 WOMEN

1	CHN	HUANG, MIN	34.47
2	**USA**	**POPOVICH, ERIN**	37.87
3	BRA	ALMEIDA, VERONICA	38.49
4	SWE	LOUREIRO, LALITA	38.55
5	CHN	YANG, TIANSHU	39.91
6	AUS	ROGERS, SHELLEY	40.02
7	SVK	PROKEINOVA, MARGITA	40.7
8	RUS	GUSEVA, OXANA	41.07
	USA	**JORDAN, CORTNEY**	ELIM1
	USA	**GRUEN, DEBORAH**	ELIM1

50 M FREESTYLE S10 WOMEN

1	CAN	POLINARIO, ANNE	28.51
2	POL	PAWLIK, KATARZYNA	28.92
3	AUS	LEWIS, KATRINA	29.13
4	**USA**	**EAMES, ANNA**	29.17
5	**USA**	**SCOTT, SUSAN BETH**	29.38
6	FRA	LORANDI, ELODIE	29.59
7	ESP	MORALES, ESTHER	29.75
8	SVK	MIKULASIKOVA, VIERA	29.94
	USA	**OWENS, ASHLEY**	ELIM1

50 M FREESTYLE S11 WOMEN

1	ITA	POIANI PANIGATI, MARIA	31.39
2	ITA	CAMELLINI, CECILIA	31.95
3	BRA	SUGIMORI, FABIANA	32.45
4	SUI	CAVIN, CHANTAL	32.58
5	JPN	IKINAGA, NAOMI	32.81
6	GER	SCHULTE, DANIELA	33.05
7	CHN	XIE, QING	33.06
8	JPN	AKIYAMA, RINA	33.88

50 M FREESTYLE S12 WOMEN

1	RUS	SAVCHENKO, OXANA	27.07
2	RUS	EFIMENKO, ANNA	27.82
3	ESP	FONT, DEBORAH	28.23
4	POL	MENDAK, JOANNA	28.34
5	CYP	PELENDRITOU, KAROLINA	28.72
6	UKR	VOLKOVA, YULIYA	28.86
7	ESP	GARCIA-ARCICOLLAR, ANA	28.93
8	VEN	MOTA, BELKYS	30.43

50 M FREESTYLE S13 WOMEN

1	**USA**	**BECHERER, KELLEY**	27.85
2	CAN	GRAND MAISON, VALERIE	27.88
3	UKR	BALASHOVA, IRYNA	28.04
4	CAN	COTE, KIRBY	28.08
5	AUS	WATT, PRUE	28.16
6	CAN	GOTELL, CHELSEY	28.26
7	GBR	HENRY, RHIANNON	28.59
8	AUS	VAN ROOSMALEN, TEIGAN	30.51

50 M FREESTYLE S3 WOMEN

1	MEX	VALLE, PATRICIA	57.05
2	SIN	YIP, PIN XIU	57.43
3	GBR	WILLIAMSON, FRAN	01:04.2
4	CHN	XIA, JIANGBO	01:08.3
5	**USA**	**KOLBE, BETH**	01:10.5
6	AUS	OVERTON, ESTHER	01:12.3
7	RSA	SHANNON, SARAH	01:13.4
8	GER	CONRADI, ANNKE	01:17.9

50 M FREESTYLE S4 WOMEN

1	MEX	MIRANDA, NELY	46.27
2	**USA**	**ANGELELLI, CHERYL**	52.81
3	BRA	GARCIA, EDENIA	53.28
4	SWE	EKSTROM, JENNIE	53.74

SWIMMING RESULTS

5	USA	**BRUDER, AIMEE**	55.04
6	POL	HAMER, KAROLINA	58.46
7	DEN	KRISTIANSEN, CECILIE	01:04.5

50 M FREESTYLE S5 WOMEN

1	ESP	PERALES, MARIA TERESA	35.88
2	CZE	HLAVACKOVA, BELA	37.12
3	UKR	AKOPYAN, OLENA	37.53
4	ISR	PEZARO, INBAL	38.69
5	JPN	NARITA, MAYUMI	39.99
6	JPN	TAKEUCHI, SUGAKO	44.04
7	DEN	LAURIDSEN, KARINA	44.69
8	HUN	ENGELHARDT, KATALIN	45.78
	USA	**MORRISON, MARIN**	*ELIM1*

50 M FREESTYLE S6 WOMEN

1	NED	DE KONING-PEPER, MIRJAM	35.60
2	MEX	GONZALEZ, DORAMITZI	36.52
3	GBR	JONES, NATALIE	37.21
4	GER	GOETZE, MARIA	37.28
5	GBR	SIMMONDS, ELEANOR	37.77
6	JPN	NARA, ERIKA	38.32
7	USA	**UHL, MIRANDA**	39.14
8	GBR	JOHNSON, ELIZABETH	39.41
	USA	**JOHNSON, CASEY**	*ELIM1*

50 M FREESTYLE S7 WOMEN

1	USA	**JORDAN, CORTNEY**	33.84
2	USA	**POPOVICH, ERIN**	33.92
3	GER	BRUHN, KIRSTEN	34.50
4	NED	BOONACKER, CHANTAL	34.54
5	CHN	HUANG, MIN	34.85
6	CAN	JENSEN, LAURA	36.10
7	CAN	NELSON, BRIANNA	37.96

50 M FREESTYLE S8 WOMEN

1	NOR	NORLAND, CECILIE DRABSCH	32.09
2	USA	**EVERLOVE, AMANDA**	32.20
3	AUS	FRENEY, JACQUELINE	32.37
4	CHN	JIANG, SHENGNAN	32.47
5	CHN	XU, YANRU	32.54
6	USA	**LONG, JESSICA**	32.58
7	GBR	FREDERIKSEN, HEATHER	32.59
8	FRO	ANDREASEN, HEIDI	32.66

50 M FREESTYLE S9 WOMEN

1	RSA	DU TOIT, NATALIE	29.20
2	RUS	GRAZHDANOVA, IRINA	29.33
3	GBR	WATKIN, LOUISE	29.80
4	AUS	WILLIAMS, ANNABELLE	29.91
5	USA	**KERLEY, APRIL**	30.20
6	CAN	DIXON, STEPHANIE	30.45
7	GBR	MILLWARD, STEPHANIE	30.45
8	NED	MEENDERINK, MENDY	31.20
	USA	**STONE, ELIZABETH**	*ELIM1*

TABLE TENNIS

Tahl Leibovitz 6/1/1975, Ozone Park, NY
Mitch Seidenfeld 3/18/1963, Lakeville, MN
Noga Nir-Kistler 5/18/1979, Allentown, PA
Andre Scott 6/4/1965, Fort Worth, TX

STAFF

Sean O'neill Head Coach

TABLE TENNIS RESULTS

SINGLES 1 MEN

1	AUT	VEVERA, ANDREAS
2	KOR	CHO, JAE KWAN
3	KOR	LEE, HAE KON
4	FRA	DUCAY, JEAN-FRANCOIS

SINGLES 2 MEN

1	FRA	BOURY, VINCENT
2	FRA	MOLLIENS, STEPHANE
3	KOR	KIM, KYUNG MOOK
4	DEN	HANSEN, LARS

SINGLES 3 MEN

1	CHN	FENG, PANFENG
2	FRA	ROBIN, JEAN-PHILIPPE
3	ESP	PINAS, TOMAS
4	BRA	SILVA, LUIZ ALGACIR

SINGLES 4-5 MEN

1	FRA	DURAND, CHRISTOPHE	
2	KOR	JUNG, EUN CHANG	
3	NOR	URHAUG, TOMMY	
4	EGY	SALEH, SAMEH	
	USA	**SCOTT, ANDRE**	*ELIMP*

SINGLES 6 MEN

1	DEN	ROSENMEIER, PETER
2	GER	ARNOLD, DANIEL
3	NED	BLOK, NICO
4	GER	SCHMIDT, RAINER

SINGLES 7 MEN

1	GER	WOLLMERT, JOCHEN
2	CHN	YE, CHAOQUN
3	ESP	VALERA, ALVARO
4	USA	**SEIDENFELD, MITCHELL**

SINGLES 8 MEN

1	CHN	CHEN, GANG
2	POL	GRUDZIEN, PIOTR
3	SVK	JAMBOR, MIROSLAV
4	CHN	LI, MANZHOU

SINGLES 9-10 MEN

1	CHN	GE, YANG
2	CHN	MA, LIN
3	SWE	ANDERSSON, FREDRIK
4	NED	LAST, GERBEN

TEAMS 1-2 MEN

1	SVK
2	FRA
3	KOR
4	AUT

TEAMS 3 MEN

1	FRA
2	BRA
3	CHN
4	GBR

TEAMS 4-5 MEN

1	KOR
2	CHN
3	FRA
4	NOR

TEAMS 6-8 MEN

1	CHN
2	SVK
3	FRA
4	ISR

TEAMS 9-10 MEN

1	CHN	
2	ESP	
3	FRA	
4	CZE	
	USA	*ELIM1/8*

LEIBOVITZ, TAHL
SEIDENFELD, MITCHELL

TEAMS 1-2 MEN

1	SVK
2	FRA
3	KOR
4	AUT

TEAMS 3 MEN

1	FRA
2	BRA
3	CHN
4	GBR

TEAMS 4-5 MEN

1	KOR
2	CHN
3	FRA
4	NOR

TEAMS 6-8 MEN

1	CHN
2	SVK
3	FRA
4	NOR

TEAMS 9-10 MEN

1	CHN
2	ESP
3	FRA
4	CZE

SINGLES 1-2 WOMEN

1	CHN	LIU, JING
2	ITA	PEZZUTTO, PAMELA
3	ITA	PODDA, CLARA
4	FRA	LAFAYE, ISABELLE

SINGLES 10 WOMEN

1	POL	PARTYKA, NATALIA
2	CHN	FAN, LEI
3	CHN	HOU, CHUNXIAO
4	CZE	LA BOURDONNAYE, MICHALA

SINGLES 3 WOMEN

1	CHN	LI, QIAN
2	SVK	KANOVA, ALENA
3	SLO	PINTAR, MATEJA
4	ITA	BRUNELLI, MICHELA

SINGLES 4 WOMEN

1	CHN	ZHOU, YING
2	SRB	PERIC, BORISLAVA
3	KOR	MOON, SUNG HYE
4	GER	SIKORA WEINMANN, MONIKA

SINGLES 5 WOMEN

1	CHN	REN, GUIXIANG	
2	CHN	GU, GAI	
3	GER	ZIMMERER, ANDREA	
4	JOR	ABUAWAD, KHETAM	
	USA	**NIR KISTLER, NOGA**	*ELIMP*

SINGLES 6-7 WOMEN

1	RUS	MARTYASHEVA, NATALIA
2	RUS	OVSYANNIKOVA, YULIA
3	NED	VAN ZON, KELLY
4	EGY	AFIFY, FAIZA MAHMOUD

SINGLES 8 WOMEN
1	FRA	KAMKASOMPHOU, THU
2	SWE	ABRAHAMSSON, JOSEFIN
3	CHN	ZHANG, XIAOLING
4	FRA	MAIRIE, CLAIRE

SINGLES 9 WOMEN
1	CHN	LEI, LINA
2	CHN	LIU, MEILI
3	TUR	KAVAS, NESLIHAN
4	POL	GRZELAK, MALGORZATA

TEAMS 1-3 WOMEN
1	CHN
2	ITA
3	FRA
4	GBR

TEAMS 4-5 WOMEN
1	CHN
2	GER
3	JOR
4	SRB

TEAMS 6-10 WOMEN
1	CHN
2	POL
3	FRA
4	RUS

Allison Aldrich 1/19/1988, Lincoln, NE
Heather Erickson 5/9/1993, Fayetteville, NC
Alex Gouldie 5/13/1991, St. Paul, NE
Katie Holloway 6/8/1986, Van Nuys, CA

SuGui Kriss 7/6/1987, Ravena, NY
Kendra Lancaster 2/1/1987, W. Lafayette, IN
Hope Lewellen 4/20/1967, Palos Park, IL
Brenda Maymon 6/4/1985, Edmond, OK/Charlestown, IN

Gina McWilliams 7/16/1965, Dallas, TX
Nichole Millage 3/27/1977, Edmond, OK/Champaign, IL
Kari Miller 4/16/1977, Edmond, OK/Washington, D.C.
Lora Webster 8/26/1986, Edmond, OK

STAFF

Mike Hulett Head Coach
Denise Van De Walle Asst Coach

VOLLEYBALL RESULTS

VOLLEYBALL (SITTING) MEN
1	IRI	IRAN
2	BIH	BOSNIA/HERZEGOVINA
3	RUS	RUSSIA
4	EGY	EGYPT
5	CHN	CHINA
6	BRA	BRAZIL
7	IRQ	IRAQ
8	JPN	JAPAN

VOLLEYBALL (SITTING) WOMEN
1	CHN	CHINA
2	**USA**	**TEAM USA**
3	NED	NETHERLANDS
4	SLO	SLOVENIA
5	UKR	UKRAINE
6	LTU	LITHUANIA
7	LAT	LATVIA
8	JPN	JAPAN

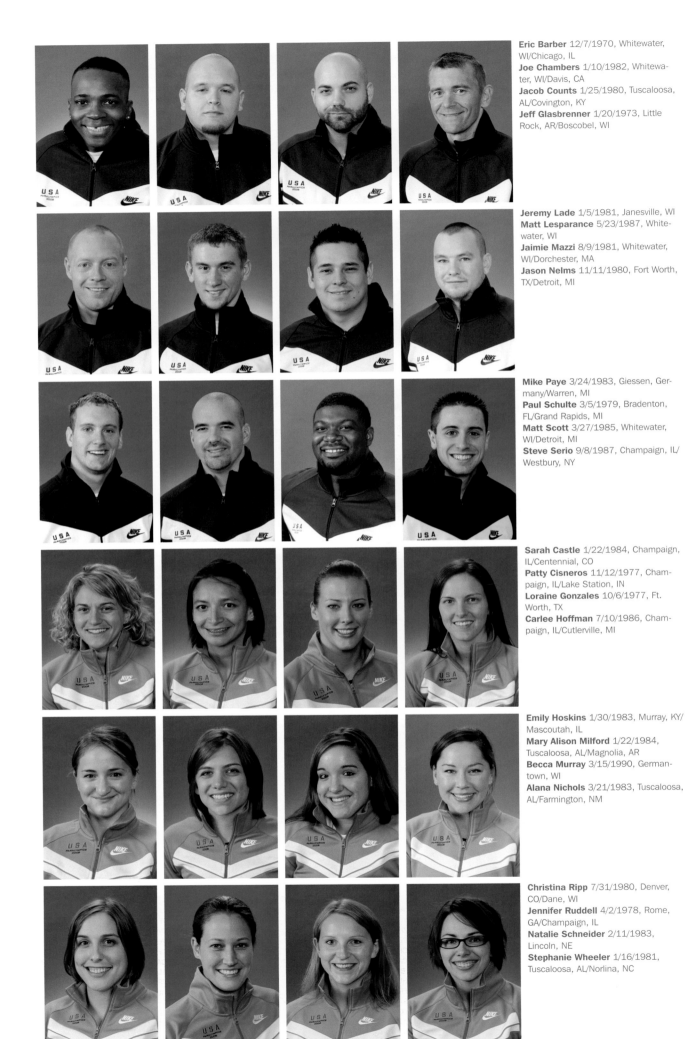

Eric Barber 12/7/1970, Whitewater, WI/Chicago, IL
Joe Chambers 1/10/1982, Whitewater, WI/Davis, CA
Jacob Counts 1/25/1980, Tuscaloosa, AL/Covington, KY
Jeff Glasbrenner 1/20/1973, Little Rock, AR/Boscobel, WI

Jeremy Lade 1/5/1981, Janesville, WI
Matt Lesparance 5/23/1987, Whitewater, WI
Jaimie Mazzi 8/9/1981, Whitewater, WI/Dorchester, MA
Jason Nelms 11/11/1980, Fort Worth, TX/Detroit, MI

Mike Paye 3/24/1983, Giessen, Germany/Warren, MI
Paul Schulte 3/5/1979, Bradenton, FL/Grand Rapids, MI
Matt Scott 3/27/1985, Whitewater, WI/Detroit, MI
Steve Serio 9/8/1987, Champaign, IL/Westbury, NY

Sarah Castle 1/22/1984, Champaign, IL/Centennial, CO
Patty Cisneros 11/12/1977, Champaign, IL/Lake Station, IN
Loraine Gonzales 10/6/1977, Ft. Worth, TX
Carlee Hoffman 7/10/1986, Champaign, IL/Cutlerville, MI

Emily Hoskins 1/30/1983, Murray, KY/Mascoutah, IL
Mary Alison Milford 1/22/1984, Tuscaloosa, AL/Magnolia, AR
Becca Murray 3/15/1990, Germantown, WI
Alana Nichols 3/21/1983, Tuscaloosa, AL/Farmington, NM

Christina Ripp 7/31/1980, Denver, CO/Dane, WI
Jennifer Ruddell 4/2/1978, Rome, GA/Champaign, IL
Natalie Schneider 2/11/1983, Lincoln, NE
Stephanie Wheeler 1/16/1981, Tuscaloosa, AL/Norlina, NC

STAFF

Steve Wilson Head Coach (M)
Tracy Chynoweth Asst Coach (M)
Paul Jackson Asst Coach (M)
Ron Lykins Head Coach (W)

John Sikora Asst Coach (W)
Robb Taylor Asst Coach (W)

WHEELCHAIR BASKETBALL RESULTS

WHEELCHAIR BASKTEBALL MEN

1	AUS	AUSTRALIA
2	CAN	CANADA
3	GBR	GREAT BRITAIN
4	**USA**	**TEAM USA**
5	GER	GERMANY
6	ISR	ISRAEL
7	BRA	BRAZIL
8	RSA	SOUTH AFRICA

WHEELCHAIR BASKTEBALL WOMEN

1	**USA**	**TEAM USA**
2	GER	GERMANY
3	AUS	AUSTRALIA
4	JPN	JA[AN
5	CAN	CANADA
6	NED	NETHERLANDS
7	CHN	CHINA
8	GBR	GREAT BRITAIN

Mark Calhoun 5/17/1983, Bremen, GA
Andrea DeMello 2/26/1969, New York, NY
Gerard Moreno 11/14/1956, Los Angeles, CA
Scott Rodgers 12/25/1971, San Diego, CA

 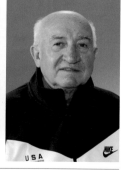

Benjy Williams 1/6/1965, Bethlehem, GA

STAFF

Les Stawicki Head Coach

WHEELCHAIR FENCING RESULTS

EPEE INDIVIDUAL A MEN

1	CHN	TIAN, JIANQUAN	
2	CHN	ZHANG, LEI	
3	POL	STANCZUK, RADOSLAW	
4	FRA	MAILLARD, DAVID	

EPEE INDIVIDUAL B MEN

1	CHN	HU, DAOLIANG	
2	BLR	BEZYAZYCHNY, MIKALAI	
3	UKR	SHENKEVYCH, SERHIY	
4	FRA	CRATERE, MARC-ANDRE	
	USA	**RODGERS, SCOTT**	*ELIM1/4*
	USA	**WILLIAMS, BENJY**	*ELIM1/8*

FOIL INDIVIDUAL A MEN

1	CHN	YE, RUYI	
2	CHN	ZHANG, LEI	
3	POL	PENDER, DARIUSZ	
4	HKG	CHAN, WING KIN	
	USA	**CALHOUN, MARK**	*ELIMP*

FOIL INDIVIDUAL B MEN

1	CHN	HU, DAOLIANG	
2	FRA	FRANCOIS, LAURENT	
3	HUN	SZEKERES, PAL	
4	UKR	KOMAR, ANDRII	
	USA	**RODGERS, SCOTT**	*ELIM1/4*
	USA	**MORENO, GERARD**	*ELIMP*

SABRE INDIVIDUAL A MEN

1	CHN	YE, RUYI	
2	CHN	TIAN, JIANQUAN	
3	ITALY	PELLEGRINI, ALBERTO	
4	HKG	CHAN, WING KIN	
	USA	**CALHOUN, MARK**	*ELIM1/8*

SABRE INDIVIDUAL B MEN

1	FRA	FRANCOIS, LAURENT	
2	HKG	HUI, CHARN HUNG	
3	UKR	SHENKEVYCH, SERHIY	
4	FRA	CRATERE, MARC-ANDRE	
	USA	**WILLIAMS, BENJY**	*ELIMP*
	USA	**MORENO, GERARD**	*ELIMP*

EPEE INDIVIDUAL A WOMEN
1 CHN ZHANG, CHUNCUI
2 HKG YU, CHUI YEE
3 HKG FAN, PUI SHAN
4 HUN KRAJNYAK, ZSUZSANNA

EPEE INDIVIDUAL B WOMEN
1 HKG
2 CHN
3 THA
4 RUS
  USA DEMELLO, ANDREA

FOIL INDIVIDUAL A WOMEN
1 HKG
2 CHN
3 HKG
4 FRA

FOIL INDIVIDUAL B WOMEN
1 HKG
2 CHN
3 CHN
4 THA

Andy Cohn 2/3/1978, San Diego, CA/ Tempe, AZ
Will Groulx 3/11/1974, Portland, OR
Scott Hogsett 10/16/1972, Phoenix, AZ
Bryan Kirkland 8/18/1971, Leeds, AL

Norm Lyduch 7/4/1972, Austin, TX
Seth McBride 2/26/1983, Portland, OR/Juneau, AK
Jason Regier 2/8/1975, Denver, CO
Nick Springer 6/9/1985, St. Petersburg, FL/New York, NY

Chance Sumner 1/20/1977, Denver, CO
Joel Wilmoth 7/31/1989, Hueytown, AL
Mark Zupan 5/20/1975, Austin, TX NC, Tornado

STAFF

James Gumbert Head Coach

Ed Suhr Asst Coach

WHEELCHAIR RUGBY RESULTS

WHEELCHAIR BASKTEBALL MEN
1 USA TEAM USA
2 AUS AUSTRALIA
3 CAN CANADA
4 GER GERMANY

Lee Hinson 7/11/1959, Wallan, Australia/Jacksonville, FL
Paul Moran 12/31/1966, Chicago, IL
Brent Poppen 5/24/1973, Paso Robles, CA
Jon Rydberg 10/7/1977, Oakdale, MN

Nicholas Taylor 11/27/1979, Witchita, KS
David Wagner 3/4/1974, Hillsboro, OR
Stephen Welch 7/28/1972, Bedford, TX
Beth Arnoult 12/1/1965, Paia, HI

Kaitlyn Verfuerth 8/12/1985, Rancho Cucamonga, CA

STAFF

Dan James Head Coach
Jason Harnett Asst Coach

WHEELCHAIR TENNIS RESULTS

DOUBLES MEN
1	FRA	HOUDET, STEPHANE	
2	SWE	WIKSTROM, PETER	
3	JPN	KUNIEDA, SHINGO	
4	NED	SCHEFFERS, MAIKEL	
	USA		*ELIM1/8*
		HINSON, LEE	
		MORAN, PAUL	
	USA		*ELIM1/8*
		WELCH, STEPHEN	
		RYDBERG, JON	

SINGLES MEN
1	JPN	KUNIEDA, SHINGO
2	NED	AMMERLAAN, ROBIN

3	NED	SCHEFFERS, MAIKEL	
4	NED	VINK, RONALD	
	USA	RYDBERG, JON	*ELIM1/8*
	USA	WELCH, STEPHEN	*ELIM1/8*
	USA	MORAN, PAUL	*ELIM1/32*

DOUBLES WOMEN
1	NED	HOMAN, KORIE
2	NED	GRIFFIOEN, JISKE
3	FRA	GRAVELLIER, FLORENCE
4	USA	
		ARNOULT, BETH
		VERFUERTH, KAITLYN

SINGLES WOMEN
1	NED	VERGEER, ESTHER
2	NED	HOMAN, KORIE
3	FRA	GRAVELLIER, FLORENCE

4	NED	GRIFFIOEN, JISKE	
	USA	ARNOULT, BETH	*ELIM1/4*

DOUBLES OPEN
1	USA		
		TAYLOR, NICK	
		WAGNER, DAVID	
2	ISR		
3	GBR		
4	NED		

SINGLES OPEN
1	GBR	NORFOLK, PETER	
2	SWE	ANDERSSON, JOHAN	
3	USA	WAGNER, DAVID	
4	USA	TAYLOR, NICK	
	USA	POPPEN, BRENT	*ELIM1/8*

ALL ABOARD! AFTER AN AMAZING BEIJING GAMES THE USA TEAM CAN NOW SET THEIR SIGHTS ON LONDON | *MICHAEL KAPPELER/AFP/GETTY IMAGES*

AMAZING AWAITS....
LONDON 2012

BRITISH SOCCER PLAYER DAVID BECKHAM HOLDS A BALL TOWARDS THE CROWD DURING THE CLOSING CEREMONY | *GABRIEL BOUYS/AFP/GETTY IMAGES*

TEAM LEADER REPORTS

Welcome to the Team Leader Reports section of the 2008 US Olympic Committee Commemorative Book.

Team leaders are the backbone of team management before, during and after the Olympic and Paralympic Games. Team leaders are liaisons between the USOC, the Olympic Games Organizing Committees, International Federations, and the National Governing Bodies. They are responsible for the planning, preparation, execution and follow-up of all sport-specific team operations and logistics. This job requires an extremely high energy level with the ability to communicate effectively with a wide variety of people. A team leader's primary responsibility is to create the best Games environment possible by minimizing distractions that can interrupt an athlete's ability to compete.

This is not an easy or simple assignment. Team leaders must work closely with USOC staff to make sure everyone in their delegation has appropriate credentials; they must coordinate international travel and local transportation. They are expected to arrive early at team processing and to success-fully steer their team through all processing stations. Through pre-Games visits to the Games sites, they must assess the housing, meals, and facilities that their team will be using. Then, use this information to plan and implement logistics for each athlete's respective needs, as well as those of the team as a whole.

Some team leaders begin their work months, even years, in advance. They are an integral part of an athlete's or a team's training and preparation for the Games, in some cases working with coaches to develop solutions to training and competition barriers. This explains why Bob Largman (fencing) hauled boxes, stocked shoes, and handed out hats to athletes – for 7 days before his team arrived at team processing. It explains why Laura LaCursia (synchronized swimming) arranged for her team to work with acrobatic specialists at the San Francisco Circus School. It also explains why Scott Novak (modern pentathlon) went out of his way to find protective shipping cases so his athletes could be assured of damage-free pistols when traveling.

It is also the team leader's responsibility to plan for the next Games – even as they are executing plans for the current Games. To that end, team leaders are asked to pass on any "lessons learned" to help the next team leader prepare earlier and better. Dean Brenner (sailing) would like to see the Day-Pass credentialing system continued in London; Mary Hodge (Paralympic powerlifting) wants to have body weight classes established early in the quadrennium.

Also included in this section are reports submitted by USOC staff members who, in addition to their regular daily activities, were responsible for key support functions provided by the USOC to the US Olympic Team. The effort given by these individuals continues to be an example of all that is moving and captivating about the Olympic Movement.

The last time team leader & USOC staff reports were included in the commemorative book the US Olympic Team included only 51 women, there were no cell phones, and the team traveled to the Games in a Pan American Airways chartered DC-7C. The year was 1960. As fascinating as the changes in the world and the Olympic Games have been since that time, so too is the way some things remain the same. Team leaders continue to be committed, industrious, creative, and dedi-cated individuals, accomplishing, out of the limelight, feats of organization most know nothing about. We hope you enjoy reading about some of their "behind-the-scenes" efforts.

The team leader reports will be presented in alphabetical order by sport.

USA ARCHERY | *TOM PARRISH – USA TEAM LEADER AND HIGH PERFORMANCE DIRECTOR*

Team selection for the 2008 Olympic Archery Team was a three-stage process, as devised by national head coach Kisik Lee. Prior to the team selection process, the U.S. had secured the maximum three Olympic quota spots for men by finishing in the top eight as a team at the 2007 World Championships in Germany. We also secured one quota spot for women by virtue of the individual performance of Jennifer Nichols.

The first stage of the Olympic team selection process was held in a public park in Conyers, Ga., September 26–30, 2007, hosted by the Georgia State Archery Association. This initial stage was open to anyone and consisted of 66 men and 38 women competitors from across the U.S. The first day was the 144-arrow ranking round at 70M. Those archers making the top 16 in the ranking round (per gender) and possessing the minimum qualifying score (MQS) proceeded to the round-robin match play on days two and three. In the round-robin, each archer shot 15 matches, one against each other archer. Each match was 12 arrows. Ranking and bonus points were assigned to each archer based on the results. The final ranking points from stage one were carried forward to stage two. At the conclusion of stage one, the leaders in the men's category were: 1st—Brady Ellison, 2nd—Vic Wunderle and 3rd—Butch Johnson. The leaders in the women's category were: 1st—Jenny Nichols, 2nd—Khatuna Lorig and 3rd—Karen Scavotto.

Stage two of the selection process was held at the Olympic Training Center (OTC) in Chula Vista, Calif., April 1–6, 2008. An interesting development prior to stage two was that the #16-ranked male, Edwin Eliason, elected to withdraw and was replaced by #17, Jacob Wukie. Also, prior to the second stage, U.S. female athletes competed in the Continental Qualifier in El Salvador, in an attempt to secure two more Olympic quota spots for women. To do so we needed to have two women finish in the top three in El Salvador. We were able to secure only one more spot (Karen Scavotto finished first).

The five days of competition in stage two consisted of a ranking round, round-robin match play involving all 16 archers from each category, a cut to the top eight per category, followed by single-elimination match play and another seven-match round-robin. Once all ranking and bonus points were tallied at the end of stage two, the standings were as follows: for Men: 1st—Brady Ellison, 2nd—Butch Johnson, 3rd—Vic Wunderle and moving all the way up from 16th to 4th—Jacob Wukie; standings for the Women were: 1st—Jenny Nichols, 2nd—Khatuna Lorig, 3rd—Stephanie Miller and 4th—Karen Scavotto.

The third and final stage of the selection process was held on May 1–4, 2008 at the Ben Avery Shooting Range in Phoenix, Ariz., hosted by the Arizona State Archery Association and the Arizona Department of Natural Resources. At this stage, only eight men and eight women remained, and the points earned from this final stage would be added to points earned in stages one and two to provide final ranking points. Stage three consisted of a ranking round, single-elimination match play and a seven-match round-robin. Competition for the third spot on the men's team came down to the final match of the final day. When all was concluded the top finishers and those archers earning positions on the 2008 U.S. Olympic Archery Team were: Men: 1st—Brady Ellison, 2nd—Butch Johnson and 3rd—Vic Wunderle; for the women: 1st—Jenny Nichols and 2nd—Khatuna Lorig. The alternate male was Jacob Wukie and the alternate female was Karen Scavotto. The alternate (replacement) athletes get to compete in the Olympics only in the instance of incapacity of one of the athletes ranked ahead of them.

Failure to secure all of our Olympic quota spots for Beijing was a disappointment for USA Archery; however, the team selection process worked quite well and gave us the best possible athletes for the five Olympic spots that we had secured. Between the conclusion of the selection process and the Olympic Games, our team competed in two World Cup events (Turkey and France) as part of their preparation for the Games. At the event in Turkey, Brady Ellison took the silver medal and won several significant matches against archers from Korea and India. Training camps at the OTC in Chula Vista were also conducted, and we saw steady improvement in performance from all team members, especially in the men's team round.

The 2008 Olympic Archery competition was held in Beijing, China, August 9–15. The team arrived in China on July 27th and trained every day on the ranking round field of the Olympic Archery Venue. Each country was also given a specific time slot on August 7th to familiarize themselves with the competition fields (stadiums A & B). All members of the U.S. Archery Team had competed at this venue previously during the Olympic Test Event in August of 2007.

JENNIFER NICHOLS OF THE UNITED STATES TAKES AIM DURING THE WOMEN'S INDIVIDUAL ARCHERY RANKING ROUND | *PAUL GILHAM/ GETTY IMAGES*

The competition began the day after Opening Ceremonies with a 72-arrow ranking round on August 9. By rule, only 64 competitors are allowed per gender. There were 49 countries represented in archery. The ranking round results for the U.S. men were as follows: 15th—Brady Ellison (664), 40th—Butch Johnson (653) and 41st Vic Wunderle (652). On the women's side Jennifer Nichols was 24th (637) and Khatuna Lorig was 26th (635). The Men's Team was seeded 10th with a score of 1969.

In training sessions in the two weeks leading up to the Olympic competition, the U.S. men's team had averaged 222 and had shot 6 scores of 225 or higher, including two scores of 229. We lost to Chinese Taipei in the first round, 222 to 218. Chinese Taipei shot 211 in their second round.

Following the team round competition on days two and three, the individual competition for women was conducted on day four and day six, while the individual competition for men was conducted on day five and day seven. Khatuna Lorig finished 5th, while Nichols was 26th. Vic Wunderle was the top male U.S. finisher taking fifth, while Ellison and Johnson were 27 and 28, respectively.

Climatic conditions in Beijing were never a problem. The heat and humidity were high at times, but nothing more than we've experienced many times in other locales. The air quality in Beijing was a non-factor. Occasionally the wind was a factor, but never was it strong enough to cause any problem. There were a couple of days when we experienced some rain, heavy at times, but the hard rain did not occur during competition for our athletes. Overall, the conditions were good, especially the conditions inside the competition stadium. The level of competition in archery has increased in the last few years, but no doubt the good conditions also contributed to some very good scores being posted in Beijing.

Also, it is important to note that our travel went smoothly, and housing, meals, daily transportation and other living conditions in Beijing went very well. We owe a great deal of thanks to the capable people at the USOC for their excellent planning and support of Team USA. We also thank the Beijing Organizers (BOCOG) for being great hosts and doing an excellent job of making sure the Games ran smoothly. The Olympic Village was outstanding. The Opening and Closing Ceremonies were spectacular beyond anything previously seen. The Olympic Archery venue and conduct of the competition were both superb.

The 2008 Olympic Games were the most thoroughly covered and most watched of all Olympics. The archery event received more media coverage and attention than ever before, and the spectators and viewing audience were treated to some exciting matches in both the team and individual competitions.

One particular occurrence that caught the eye of spectators was the unexpected appearance of Khatuna Lorig on the field as a coach for Vic Wunderle. Prior to individual match play, Coach Lee asked each archer who they would like to have stand behind them during their matches. Vic requested Khatuna. The staff was perfectly willing to go along with this plan and Khatuna was game for it as well. She was Vic's coach on the field during his first two matches and that went well, so we continued with that arrangement two days later. Vic's win in the second round over Im of Korea was indeed an exciting match and no doubt Khatuna was a good fit as coach for Vic in that situation.

Khatuna's own individual performance in the 2008 Games was also impressive. She competed well as an athlete, finishing fifth; she coached a teammate to a sixth-place finish, she's a four-time Olympian for her third country, a mother, and was dealing with the distraction of events occurring at that time between Russia and her native country of Georgia. She's very proud and appreciative of being an American. When Vic asked her how he could repay her for her help, Khatuna replied, "Just go into the stands and yell 'USA, USA!'" This attitude won

over the athlete delegates for Team USA, and Khatuna was elected to be the U.S. Flag Bearer at the Closing Ceremony. This was the first time an archer carried the flag in the Olympics for the United States.

Budgetarily, we had support through the USOC Performance Pool budget. The support included: Resident Athlete Program support, Elite Athlete Training support and International Competition support, as well as support for our key staff (head coach and High Performance Manager). I drafted our budget request and managed much of how it was used but did not have complete and final authority on budgetary decisions. The decision process included the head coach and executive director. If we had a larger budget to work with, we could have provided more support for our top athletes to travel to events. Our primary budgetary needs are more related to our future, namely, development programs. USA Archery has to develop more depth in our internationally competitive athlete pool and better trained coaches for development programs.

The only structured off-season training we have is with the Resident Athlete Program under the guidance of head coach Kisik Lee. Over the past two years we've managed to mold our Resident Athlete Program into one that is well designed and effective, although we are constantly searching for ways to make it even better. Coach Lee has been in the U.S. for only two and a half years, so we're just now scratching the

VIC WUNDERLE OF THE UNITED STATES TAKES AIM DURING THE MEN'S ARCHERY INDIVIDUAL RANKING ROUND | *PAUL GILHAM/GETTY IMAGES*

surface of success. There are a lot of positive signs for our future if we can continue what we've started. We also have a good junior elite program now that is developing athletes for our future. Another couple of years should bring good dividends from this program as well, although it consists mostly of quarterly camps, including two held during the off-season. All other archers in the U.S. conduct their own training programs, almost completely within the U.S.

Once our Olympic team was finalized, following the final trial, the team traveled to a national event in New Jersey and from there went directly to a World Cup event in Turkey. A few weeks after the Turkey event, we held a team training camp in Chula Vista for several days and then went directly to France for another World Cup event. We held one more short training camp (five days) in Chula Vista before departing for team processing and Beijing.

The Olympic Test Event for archery was in late August 2007 and we attended. All of our Olympic team was present at the test event, as well as all of the staff, except for the assistant coach. This event was very useful in giving us a "dress rehearsal" of the Olympic Games scenario and helped us to be very familiar with the venue. Our men's and women's teams both won bronze medals at the test event.

The facilities for training at the Games were excellent. The official ranking round field, located adjacent to the Olympic Stadium, was the practice venue. We trained there every day from July 28 up to and through the Games competition. We had planned on using the High Performance Training Center (HPTC) at Beijing Normal University (BNU) as a backup training location and shipped equipment over for this purpose. When we arrived in China, we learned that we would not be allowed to shoot arrows at BNU due to the security restrictions. It ended up working out in the end, but this would have been nice to have known before arriving.

As team leader, my Olympic experience was good. There were no major issues or problems and the process went smoothly. Our performance results were disappointing, but we knew it would be tough to medal. There's such a fine line between winning and losing in archery matches, and although our athletes are capable of performing well enough to win, no one from any country shoots their best scores every match. So the outcome of every match depends on who happens to be shooting well at that moment and who can best manage the pressure of the situation. Other than that, the experience for the team members (athletes and staff) was a good one.

Since 2004, we have been trying to change the culture in archery in the U.S. We hired the best archery coach in the world as our national head coach, and we have upgraded our Resident Athlete program and instituted other High Performance Programs to promote a system that will make us more competitive internationally. We knew it would take five or six years to see the results we're looking for and it has only been two and a half years so far.

Although USA Archery did not win a medal in Beijing, we believe each archer gave their best effort, and we're proud of them for representing their country well. It is clear that the level of competition in international archery has risen in recent years. The main lesson learned is that, in order to be competitive on the Olympic stage, we have to train harder (full-time), must be conditioned as athletes, must be mentally prepared and must have shooting technique that holds up well under pressure. No other competition is like the Olympics. The pressure there is real and unavoidable. Those that succeed are those that manage themselves well, mentally and emotionally, in the Olympic environment. By nature of the 12-arrow match play system, there is never any guarantee of success. There's too much parity in the competition for anyone to always win. This is clearly evidenced by the results. Many top-seeded archers finished down the list, and several archers seeded rather low ended up doing quite well.

Every match is determined by who is performing best at that moment in time; however, one can improve one's chances, of course, by being well prepared and well trained. Archery is a highly technical-oriented sport. It requires extreme control, mastery of fine motor movements and consistency of technique. It also requires a high degree of mental and psychological control under pressure. A 12-arrow match does not offer room for any mistakes, and the competitive field is such that almost anyone can win any match at the Olympic level.

The focus going forward for USA Archery is to improve our coach training system and improve our athlete development programs so we create a larger pool of internationally competitive athletes for the future. By doing so, we will raise the bar on performance in the U.S. and improve our chances of future Olympic success.

KHATUNA LORIG OF THE US SHOOTS AN ARROW DURING THE WOMEN'S INDIVIDUAL ARCHERY ELIMINATIONS | *NICOLAS ASFOURI/ AFP/GETTY IMAGES*

USA BADMINTON | *ZI MIN CAI & DAN CLOPPAS*

– USA BADMINTON HEAD COACH AND TEAM LEADER & USA BADMINTON CEO/SECRETARY GENERAL

The 2008 Olympic Games in Beijing, China, was the first Olympic Games to be held in Asia since the inclusion of badminton as an Olympic sport at the 1992 Olympic Games in Barcelona, Spain. With the popularity of the sport in Asia and specifically in China, the 2008 Olympic Games helped to take badminton to another level, particularly with the increased media attention. In 2006, the Badminton World Federation and USA Badminton adopted a new scoring system, the rally point scoring system. The 2008 Olympic Games was the first Olympic Games to utilize the new rally point scoring system. A badminton game consists of 21 points. The team that wins the best two out of three games wins the match. The side that wins a rally adds a point to its score, regardless of whether the team is serving or receiving. If the game is tied at 20, the team which gains a two-point lead first wins the game. If the game continues to 29 all, the side scoring the 30th point wins the game. There is a two-minute interval between each game and a 60-second interval when the leading score reaches 11 points. If there is a third game, players change ends when a side scores 11 points.

For the sport of badminton, qualification for the Olympic Games is based solely on international ranking points within the Badminton World Federation (BWF) events. The qualifying season was from May 1, 2007, through April 30, 2008. When the BWF sent out the first round of invitations for the Olympic Games, the USA was qualified in all five of the Olympic events, with Eva Lee invited to compete in three disciplines: women's singles, women's doubles and mixed doubles. Canada protested that they should have received one of the doubles slots and, despite USA Badminton's best efforts, the BWF ruled in favor of Canada, and the U.S. did not participate in mixed doubles at the 2008 Olympic Games. Even with that disappointment, USA Badminton qualified five athletes for the 2008 Olympic Games, the most athletes USA Badminton has ever qualified for an Olympic Games.

In order to qualify for the Olympic Games, our athletes must travel to a great many tournaments during the qualifying season, which becomes very expensive. The five athletes that qualified for the 2008 Olympic Games were lucky enough to have Don Chew, the owner of the Orange County Badminton Club and K&D Graphics, as a sponsor to help offset their training and travel expenses for the four years leading up to the Games. For badminton to improve in the U.S., though, more funding is desperately needed.

USA Badminton was disappointed when they learned from the USOC that the U.S. Olympic Badminton Team would not be accredited a Team Leader for the 2008 Olympic Games. Instead, the head coach served in dual roles as both head coach and Team Leader. This was the second consecutive Olympic Games that the USA Badminton Team has not received approval and accreditation for a Team Leader, as the 2004 U.S. Olympic Team also functioned with the head coach serving as Team Leader.

Not having a separate Team Leader for the 2008 U.S. Olympic Badminton Team was difficult for the team since it was the largest Olympic Team the United States has fielded for badminton since 1996. Had we had a Team Leader, our coach could have concentrated fully on head coaching responsibilities. It would have helped from a logistical standpoint to have a specific point person take care of the Team Leader duties. It is not fair to the Olympians for a sport to not be treated equally as their fellow Olympic teammates. Badminton was

RAJU RAI OF THE USA PLAYS A SHOT DURING HIS MEN'S SINGLES MATCH | *MICHAEL STEELE/GETTY IMAGES*

the only sport not to have a designated person serving only in the Team Leader role. This reduced the opportunities for the Olympians not only to have a point person for the coach to go to, but the athletes also lost opportunities to attend USOC functions and sponsor-speaking events and to have someone else to give them information about what was going on in village and events. In the end I think this negatively impacted the team's performance. This needs to be rectified before the next Olympics.

Despite not having full support from the USOC regarding the Team Leader situation, our athletes did their best to make the most of the situation. Our Men's Doubles Team of Howard Bach and Khan "Bob" Malaythong made history for the United States at the 2008 Olympic Games in Beijing by becoming the first Americans ever to advance to the quarterfinals in Olympic badminton competition. This was Bach's second Olympic Games, as he also represented the U.S. in the 2004 Olympic Games in Athens, Greece. For Malaythong, this was his first Olympic experience.

For our three remaining athletes, the 2008 Olympic Games was their first Olympic experience. Eva Lee played in both women's singles and women's doubles with Mesinee "May" Mangkalakiri. Raju Rai competed in men's singles. Eva, May and Raju all played hard, but their inexperience showed as they all lost in the first round. We feel that having a Team Leader would have helped tremendously with these three athletes, as a Team Leader could have been a good complement for them from an emotional and motivational standpoint.

We did have trouble with our ticket order through the USOC for the athletes' family and friends. Having a specific Team Leader for our sport would have probably helped resolve several of these issues much easier. Overall, the 2008 Olympic Games was a successful experience for the USA Badminton Team. Our athletes played hard and represented their country well. There are two primary areas to focus on to improve performance in the future. Our athletes have to be better funded throughout the quadrennium and the team desperately needs a specific Team Leader so that the head coach can focus on coaching and not have his attention split with Team Leader responsibilities. If our athletes are better funded over a four-year period and we have a Team Leader and a head coach at the Olympic Games, we will be able to improve our performance.

MALAYTHONG BOB AND BACH HOWARD OF TEAM USA COMPETE DURING THE MEN'S DOUBLES QUARTERFINAL | *INDRANIL MUKHERJEE/AFP/GETTY IMAGES*

USA BASEBALL | ERIC CAMPBELL – GENERAL MANAGER, NATIONAL TEAMS

USA Baseball qualified for the 2008 Beijing Olympic Games after failing to qualify for the 2004 Athens Olympic Games—its only absence from the baseball program dating back to the start of modern baseball, both demonstration and medal, in the Olympic Games (1984).

The International Baseball Federation instituted a new qualification process leading to the 2008 Games, a three-stage (USA qualified during the first two stages) process that saw the USA Baseball teams go a combined 14-1 in two rounds, mixed in with a gold medal performance in the 2007 IBAF World Cup, which served as a final preparation event for all eight teams that would ultimately qualify for the 2008 Games.

Davey Johnson, former Major League Baseball player and manager and a World Series champion as both a player and manager, guided USA Baseball on the field through all steps of qualification, the World Cup victory and led the team in Beijing to a bronze medal finish.

Bob Watson, former Major League Baseball player, coach, general manager and World Series champion as a general manager, guided USA Baseball with all off-field issues in his role as General Manager, Professional Teams, USA Baseball. (Bob served in the same role in the qualification and gold medal victory in the 2000 Sidney Games.)

Paul Seiler, executive director and CEO, USA Baseball, was successful in attaining the continuity in senior leadership from Major League Baseball and with hiring Davey Johnson. Along with Davey, USA Baseball also had the services of Marcel Lachemann, pitching coach; Reggie Smith, hitting coach; Rick Eckstein, third base Coach; and Roly de Armas, bullpen coach. Paul was able to keep the staff in place from the 2006 COPABE qualification event through the World Cup and through the 2008 Games. Staff continuity was a recognized asset to the qualification, preparation and building of the team that earned the bronze in Beijing. (In addition to field staff, USA Baseball was also able to attain continuity with the in-event scouting staff from the MLB Scouting Bureau and the professional scouts on the selection committee. The medical team stayed intact through all levels of competition.)

The 2008 Beijing Olympic Games saw a great baseball competition played on very good facilities with some of the world's most recognized teams and players. In the inaugural 2006 World Baseball Classic, Korea, Japan and Cuba qualified for the final round of play, joined by the Dominican Republic. Japan beat Cuba for the championship. In Beijing, Korea, Japan and Cuba once again qualified for the final round of play. The Dominican Republic did not qualify for the 2008 Games—a sign of world parity in the game of baseball. Essentially, Korea, Japan and Cuba returned the bulk of their World Baseball Classic teams to compete in Beijing. The USA team entered into the final round of play in Beijing and beat a "championship" Japan team 8-5

to earn the bronze medal. After being down 4-1 early in the game, the victory burns bright to this day and is recognized by many baseball leaders in the United States and the world as an overachieving victory for the USA team.

The Beijing Games saw a great baseball tournament played. No one in the baseball industry was shocked to see Korea win a gold medal—they had a great team and baseball in Korea is as strong as anyplace in the world. China, a large underdog to reach the final rounds, played great baseball under the leadership of former Major League Baseball player, coach and manager Jim Lefebvre. As one of the potential legacies of the Games, China beat Chinese Taipei in the new and exciting IBAF tie-breaker format. New to baseball around the world, and possibly serving as a model of tiebreaking moving forward for many baseball events, the IBAF instituted a tiebreaker format that would determine games, starting with preset base runners from any inning after a tied tenth. Even though new, the format proved exciting. (The USA played two of the tiebreaker games, going 1-1.) Not only did China beat Chinese Taipei, they were competitive in all of their pool play games. Pool play was so strong that with the right breaks, any of the eight could have qualified for the final rounds. (After being down 4-0 to Canada, the USA came back to win the game 5-4—changing the fortunes of both federations.)

Excitement for the baseball competition in Beijing was sound. Ticket sales were good, and a good atmosphere surrounded all of the games. Major League Baseball, the International Federation and BOCOG did a very good job coming together to ensure that the facility was as good as it could be. Some questions may remain on whether or not the middle stadium will remain as a baseball facility in Beijing. With the excitement surrounding the 2008 Games and the fact that Major League Baseball played in first-ever games in the complex (Dodgers/

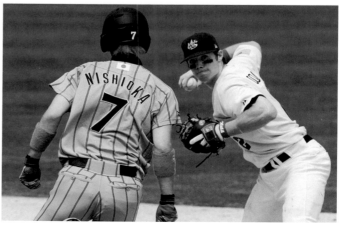

TEAM USA SHORTSTOP JASON DONALD (R) FORCES OUT JAPAN'S TSUY-OSHI NISHIOKA (L) AS HE THROWS TO FIRST TO COMPLETE A DOUBLE PLAY | OMAR TORRES/AFP/GETTY IMAGES

Padres), USA Baseball certainly hopes this facility remains operational and would welcome the day when a national team could return to Beijing for an event in this great new facility. This facility would be a hub of baseball in Beijing and in China.

The current and unavoidable reality of professional baseball in the United States is that younger and less-experienced players are closer to the big leagues than any time in the baseball industry. This fact plays a key role in the selection of any USA Baseball professional team that will be selected for an event that runs concurrent with the Major League Baseball season. USA Baseball is borrowing athletes from one of our most successful, recognizable and important leisure industries. Entering into first rounds of selection committee meetings in February, USA Baseball basically looked at all U.S.-born minor league players (about 3,000) as potential candidates for the 2008 team. Qualified federations selecting (borrowing) players from the 30 MLB teams could view all players not part of a team's 25-man roster as potential candidates. Still, the movement to and from and potentially back to or closely to the 25-man roster creates a unique selection process. To field the best team possible for an Olympic Games, USA Baseball creates many team-building scenarios in the selection process. Add availability issues to the list of injured players, and you have one of the most unique selection vehicles for any sport going to an Olympic Games. The year 2008 was no different for USA Baseball. Team selection, through the great support of the 30 teams and the United States Olympic Committee, came together in late July at the BOCOG deadline.

To punctuate the point about player continuity not being a reliable tool for USA team selection, of the 24 players selected to play on the gold medal 2007 USA Baseball World Cup Team, only three returned to the team that would win bronze in Beijing. The World Cup team was built to win but was also built to have some continuity. Once all the factors surrounding the baseball industry were digested and the final Beijing team was selected, only three players were selected from the gold medal World Cup team. (USA Baseball had projected a 40-50 percent return rate from the World Cup team.) Players move very quickly in the baseball industry and this is an understood, if not easily defined, reality in the selection process that will continue to play a factor in professional team selection.

Still, the 2008 Beijing team was a huge success and fielded great players with great Major League Baseball careers ahead of them. Soon, many members of the team will become household names for the baseball fan. The team did see its ranks diminished by injuries during the Games, which affected the play of the team. Jayson Nix, Matt LaPorta and Mike Hessman lost substantial time from the Team USA batting line-up. Casey Weathers missed the final rounds of competition. A healthier USA team would have been ideal going into the semifinal matchup with Cuba.

More to do with the strength of the game of baseball at the college level versus the state of the game at the professional level, the USA had one lone amateur earn a spot on the team, and he drew a starting pitching matchup versus Cuba. Stephen Strasburg, San Diego State University, pitched a strong performance against the Netherlands in pool play and started against Cuba in the semifinals. This model of selection will be revisited by USA Baseball for future national teams. (Other pitching staff members of the record-setting 24-0 2008 USA Baseball National Team would also have performed well in Beijing.)

It's an honor for all of us at USA Baseball to be able to field teams at all levels. Major League Baseball provides the structure for all of its programs to be able to compete. Baseball is strong in the USA, but it is equally strong throughout the world and continuing to grow in less well-established baseball areas. The World Baseball Classic will once again be very exciting and will continue to draw interest worldwide to this great game.

It's a true honor to take a team to an Olympic Games. From top to bottom, baseball receives great support from the USOC. Beijing Normal University was a great alternate destination for our athletes to train and entertain an alternate food menu from the Village. The team was kept safe by the tireless work of all of the medical teams that were assembled and by the security teams that were in place in Beijing. Baseball has very unique challenges and the support received before, during, and after the Beijing Games by the USOC was tremendous.

BOCOG and the entire county of China should take a bow on the success of these Games. It was truly a historic event. It's a true honor to play a part in one of the great athletic events that world gets to witness every four years.

Baseball also has unique challenges in maintaining its status as an Olympic sport that will be able to compete in future Olympic competitions. While baseball is truly a world game, the IBAF and its many federations are working to put the game on the 2016 Olympic Games program. It will be a truly great day for everybody who works in the baseball industry to once again to see baseball in the Olympic Games.

NATE SCHIERHOLTZ OF TEAM USA SLIDES SAFELY INTO HOME IN THE TOP OF THE ELEVENTH INNING AGAINST CATCHER TOMOYA SATO-ZAKI OF JAPAN | *NICK LAHAM/GETTY IMAGES*

384

USA BASKETBALL – MEN'S | SEAN FORD – *MEN'S NATIONAL TEAM DIRECTOR*

The 2008 Olympic Games will be an Olympics to remember for USA Basketball. Although the history books will list it as the 13th gold medal in the 16 Olympic Games we have participated in, this one was special.

Following a disappointing bronze medal in the 2004 Games, USA Basketball appointed Jerry Colangelo (former owner of the Phoenix Suns and well-respected basketball administrator) as Managing Director of the newly created Men's Senior National Team Program. Through Jerry's leadership, a pool of 33 players made a three-year commitment to the National Team.

Colangelo was also able to assemble a top-level coaching staff that was led by head coach Mike Krzyzewski (Duke University) and assistant coaches Jim Boeheim (Syracuse University), Mike D'Antoni (New York Knicks) and Nate McMillan (Portland Trail Blazers). Additionally, the team staff included athletic trainers Casey Smith (Dallas Mavericks) and Keith Jones (Houston Rockets), as well as team physician Sheldon Burns (Minnesota Timberwolves).

The Olympic Team was selected from the National Team pool of players that had trained together for two summers and competed in the 2006 World Championship (bronze medal) and the 2007 FIBA Americas Championship (gold medal). Once the final list of 12 players was selected in June of 2008, the team training camp and exhibition games were conducted in Las Vegas, NV; Macao, China; and Shanghai, China.

In preparation for the Olympics Games, the USA Basketball staff made a total of nine trips to China. During these trips, we were able to participate in several events coordinated by the USOC, including Key Decision Makers meetings, High Performance Directors summits and the Team Leaders meeting. These events were very helpful in gaining an understanding of the Chinese culture, establishing relationships with our Chinese counterparts and implementing overall logistical plans for the Games.

The Games in China were my fourth Olympic Games, in addition to it being at least the fourth Olympics for four other USA Basketball staff members: Jim Tooley (Executive Director), Carol Callan (Women's Team Leader), Craig Miller (Men's Media Director) and Caroline Williams (Women's Media Director). Having an experienced staff helped greatly with the many challenges that we dealt with in pre-Games planning as well as on a daily basis during the Games.

The overall logistics during the Games went great. We did receive assistance from the USOC with regard to Olympic tickets, parking passes, training time at Beijing Normal University (BNU) and recordings of all the basketball games at the High Performance Training Center for scouting purposes. The demand for basketball tickets was incredible for this Olympic Games and served as our biggest challenge.

From the team perspective, the players and coaches were incredibly focused when we arrived in Beijing. Jerry Colangelo and Mike Krzyzewski were masterful in their leadership of the National Team. They completely changed the culture and perception of the Olympic Team from a disappointment in 2004 to a very popular team in 2008 that was going to make the U.S. proud.

From the moment the team arrived in Beijing, they were on a mission to not only bring home the gold medal but also be ambassadors for the game and for the U.S. The players made their first of many visits to the Olympic Village the night we arrived, seeking out their fellow Olympic teammates and greeting many of the athletes from other countries. This Olympic enthusiasm continued for the entire Olympic Games, with the players attending several different competitions to cheer on their fellow Olympians, including being poolside to witness Michael Phelps wining four of his eight gold medals.

The embracing of the Olympic Games increased the focus of the team. Our first game was a much anticipated matchup against China in what many people consider the most watched basketball game ever—unfortunately there were no worldwide television ratings. United States President George Bush attended the game and visited the team in the locker room prior to the start. The team played a great game and set the stage of dominating the Olympic basketball competition with defense, teamwork and incredibly athletic play. In the process, they became a team that made everyone proud and was followed closely back in the U.S.

This dominance continued through the remaining four preliminary round games, the quarterfinals against Australia and the semifinals against Argentina. In the gold medal game, we faced a Spain team that we had beaten by over 30 points in the preliminary round;

DWIGHT HOWARD, #11 OF THE UNITED STATES, GOES TO THE BASKET AGAINST RUDY FERNANDEZ, #5, AND PAU GASOL, #4, OF SPAIN | *JED JACOBSOHN/GETTY IMAGES*

CARMELO ANTHONY OF TEAM USA TAKES A SHOT NEXT TO AUSTRALIA'S
MATT NIELSEN | *TIMOTHY A. CLARY/AFP/GETTY IMAGES*

however, Spain was the reigning World Champion and had four current NBA players on their roster.

In what will go down as one of the greatest Olympic basketball gold medal games ever, the U.S. was able to defeat Spain by a score of 118-107. It was an incredibly entertaining and competitive game, with Spain pushing the U.S. team to its limits, closing a slim U.S. lead to two points with 8:26 to play in the game. Kobe Bryant (20 points) and Dwayne Wade (27 points) lifted the team to a victory in the end.

The gold medal was celebrated by the players and staff as a great accomplishment and the result of a lot of hard work over the three-year commitment. Each player on the team conducted themselves as a true Olympian by competing at the highest level, in addition to respecting their opponents, their teammates, the host country, and most of all the responsibility they accepted as being Ambassadors of their country.

USA BASKETBALL – WOMEN'S | CAROL CALLAN – WOMEN'S NATIONAL TEAM DIRECTOR

USA Basketball selected its women's Olympic basketball team through a process that spanned three years and resulted in the best team being chosen for these Olympic Games.

This Olympic Team had the best international competition/preparation plan since the inception of USA Basketball's Women's National Team program, which commenced in 1995–1996. The team participated in several training sessions and international competitions against the most competitive women's clubs and national teams. Training occurred as often as possible with the key players and focused on international play, an important ingredient for overall team success.

The team also participated in the Olympic test event as a part of its ongoing international preparation plan. It was helpful to "practice" and prepare in Beijing prior to the Games. The teams participating in the event were competitive.

Team training at the Olympic Games went well after a few initial scheduling conflicts. The team trained at Beijing Normal University (BNU), which was set up by the USOC, and this controlled environment was very effective for the team. Also, the interaction with other U.S. teams was beneficial to a feeling of camaraderie whether between practices or during the scheduling phase.

The U.S. Women's Basketball Team won the gold medal, the fourth consecutive gold medal for the women at an Olympic Games. Given the shortened amount of training immediately preceding the Games, the team's performance and unselfish play were phenomenal and added to the feeling of complete satisfaction. Each of the athletes contributed to the team, with youth and experience meshing well together. Coach Anne Donovan and her staff prepared the team well, using the right amount of video review, strategy and game-day preparation, and gave the appropriate responsibility to the team for its play on the court and its activities off the court.

Women's basketball representatives attended the USOC Team Leadership meetings prior to the Games. The flow of information from the USOC and the collaboration of ideas between NGBs were very valuable components in our preparation. The USOC Key Decision Maker meetings were also valuable, providing great information to assist in the pre-planning process, allowing for everything to run smoothly once the plan was in place.

We were fortunate that our logistical plans all went very smoothly during the Games. It's also important to give credit to our medical staff, which consisted of Ed Ryan and Sheldon Burns, who both are veterans of the Olympic Games. They kept everyone healthy and in a position to perform their best.

Basketball is very popular in China and finding enough tickets for each game was a challenge, but fortunately, all ticket needs were met by going through a variety sources.

As stated above, this was the fourth straight gold medal for the women's team and team preparation has evolved over time. The players have true ownership for a culture that is passed along from Olympics to Olympics, which includes: dedication and devotion to participating on multiple national teams, selfless play on the court, sacrificing individual needs for the compelling goal of a gold medal, and focusing on representing their team in the most positive of ways. The leadership at USA Basketball, the coaches and athletes, have a great respect for the women's basketball programs in other countries and know that the best competition brings out the best performance from themselves.

TEAM USA'S LISA LESLIE AND KOREA'S KWERYONG KIM FIGHT FOR POSITION TO GET A REBOUND | *TIMOTHY A. CLARY/AFP/GETTY IMAGES*

USA BOXING | JEFF STEFFEN & D.K. JOE SMITH
– ASSISTANT DIRECTOR OF EVENTS & TEAM LEADER

Qualifying for the 2008 Olympic Boxing Team was a long and complicated road. Athletes first needed to qualify for the 2007 USA Boxing National Championships by winning a local, regional or specific national qualifying tournament. Once they accomplished that, the top eight finishers from the 2007 USA Boxing National Championship qualified to participate in the 2008 Olympic Trials—Boxing. The Olympic Trials was a double-elimination tournament held in Houston, Texas. The double-elimination format proved to be a good one, as it allowed two athletes to battle back after loses and prove they were the best in the country. However, the process leading to the Olympic Trials was not so forgiving and needs to be adjusted to ensure the best boxers are participating. In the future, I would recommend that the USA Boxing National Championships are not the sole method of entry into the Olympic Trials

After being named to the U.S. Olympic team, the athletes spent a full year in a mandatory resident program at the Olympic Training Center (OTC) in Colorado Springs, Colo. The resident program at the Olympic Training Center was a giant move forward for our sport/team. However, more family and personal coach involvement is just one thing we can do to improve our team for the next Olympics. Throughout that year the athletes attended various international competitions. All boxers participated in the 2007 World Championships, which were held in Chicago, Ill, in late October. This was the first of three qualifiers for the 2008 Olympic Games in the sport of boxing. We qualified five boxers at the tournament, as the remainder went to continental qualifiers held in early 2008. When the qualifying was completed we had qualified nine of the 11 weight classes.

USA Boxing sent a full team to participate in a test event and dual meet held at the Olympic Games venue and Zunyi, China, respectively. Only five boxers participated in the test event, but all 11 participated in the dual event. This was a valuable experience for our team, allowing them a chance to get accustomed to the venue as well as the atmosphere and culture they would soon be experiencing.

Once in Beijing for the Olympic Games, we did all of our training at the USOC High Performance Training Center (HPTC) that had been set up at Beijing Normal University (BNU). The boxing gym set up by USOC staff was amazing! We were able to ship over our own ring and training equipment, which made the transition from the CSOTC to the HPTC seamless. There were no major problems, only a few minor ones, which were quickly and effectively worked out. BNU provided everything we needed and it really felt like home.

We were very excited heading into the Olympic Games. We had a very talented team that had also done well internationally. They were well trained and in excellent condition. However, our team's lack of overall experience (the average age of our team was around 20 years old, while most of the other countries had an average age closer to 27 years old) caught up with us in the end. We lost a lot of very close matches and ended up winning just one medal by Deontay Wilder in the heavyweight division, when he won a bronze.

We had a pretty tight budget to work with for these Games. Most of our expenses were spent on travel and international competition. If we had a larger budget, we would have increased the number of international competitions that we participated in.

The Team Leader meeting in Beijing was a fantastic meeting. Being able to visit Beijing early and become familiar with the city, the surroundings and the venues was invaluable. The information presented by the USOC and the ideas/practices exchanged with other National Governing Body (NGB) leaders was very valuable as well.

Coach Campbell was our representative at the USOC Key Decision-Maker meeting earlier in the year, and he said it was a very valuable experience as well. It proved to be a great opportunity to meet with key

TEAM USA BOXER RAU'SHEE WARREN STANDS BEFORE THE FALLEN SOUTH KOREA'S OKSUNG LEE | *JACQUES DEMARTHON/AFP/GETTY IMAGES*

personnel and make decisions and plans well in advance.

USA Boxing had a great working relationship with the USOC leading up to and during the 2008 Olympic Games. Each member demonstrated constant professionalism and a desire to make sure that the needs of our NGB were met.

We had a minor issue arise with one of our credentials; our technical advisor was issued a transferrable credential, which was not activated until the third day of our competition. This created some logistical problems with regard to our athletes having access to him to critique performances and prepare strategies. Other than this one issue the accreditation process went very smoothly.

USA Boxing worked with the USOC and the United Airlines Olympic desk to book all of our air travel. We had no issues traveling to or from Beijing. As the athletes were eliminated from competition, several chose to go home early; the United representatives did an excellent job of making the arrangements for those athletes. Boxing started competition the first day of the Olympics and went until the last day. We were the first team to arrive in Beijing and were hoping to return the day after competition ended; however, due to the number of teams trying to depart that day we were not able to leave until a day later than requested. The people at United were terrific about changing individual tickets as needed. It was very apparent that all members of the USOC staff worked very hard to make sure that all our needs were met. Being able to work directly with the United desk helped make this a very smooth process.

The Opening Ceremony apparel was very fashionable and attractive. However, it appeared that representatives in charge of this area did not carefully consider the weather and the hot and humid conditions that are often found on August evenings in Beijing, China. By the time our USA delegation marched into the stadium and parked in the infield, the majority had begun to shed coats and ties and many had rolled up sleeves and pant legs. The Opening Ceremony outfitting was too hot for the summer season in Beijing.

During team processing in San Jose, Calif., there was somewhat of a bottleneck with regard to apparel distribution. This was most likely due to several teams arriving at the same time. Also it would have been nice to have known what type of apparel we were going to get so that we could have prepared our athletes better regarding what to pack and what leave at home.

During our stay in Beijing, the only special transportation we required was for the weigh-ins every morning, which were held at the official training venue. We worked closely with the USOC and they were able to provide us with special transportation for this circumstance. Also there must have been a miscommunication regarding airport transportation. We were under the impression that we would have transportation from the airport to BNU; however, it wasn't until the night before we departed that we found out no transportation had been arranged for our arrival. We were able to get it worked out but it was a little stressful. Transportation is very hard, tireless and thankless work, and overall the entire crew did an excellent job.

Everything went well from an information technology standpoint. We had requested an additional phone when we arrived and we received it very quickly with no problems. USA Boxing covered the cost for this additional phone. In the future, it is suggested to have more printers available for team leaders and coaches and to provide more IT support. There were multiple times when a network or a number of connections would go down at once, and there was not enough staff to help accommodate everyone efficiently.

When we first arrived in Beijing, our entire delegation was housed at BNU. We had planned to stay at BNU, as a team, until August 3rd,

when our Olympians and coaches were scheduled to move into the Athlete Village. However, due to security regulations we moved from BNU into the Village several days early. This created some scheduling changes with regard to training, as we had to be transported by bus three times daily from the Village to BNU for training. We realized that this was beyond the control of the USOC; nonetheless, it created some issues for our team.

Our training partners and personal coaches were housed at BNU the entire stay, while our Board members were housed at the Beijing Hilton. We did overestimate the number of Board Members that would attend and we also miscalculated the number of nights guests would need to stay at the Hilton. We worked directly with a member of the USOC team and were able to solve the issues that came up very quickly and effectively. In the end, the BNU group and the Hilton group did a great job in making sure all our housing needs were taken care of.

We had a great medical staff for these Games. Nick Metskas handled all our needs at team processing. He was very knowledgeable about our needs and had worked a lot with each individual while they were residents at the Colorado Springs OTC. Peter Toohey worked with us at the HPTC in Beijing. He was our athletic trainer at the 2007 Pan American Games, so he also knew most of the athletes already. He was terrific and went above and beyond the call of duty. Margie Hunt handled our needs at the Athlete Village. Margie was also very familiar with the athletes from the training center and she was great to work with. Dr. William Kuprevich was our team physician and had also been our physician at the 2007 Pan American Games, so he too was familiar with our sport and athletes. Last but not least, Dan Evans served as our athletic trainer for these Games. This was Dan's first time working with boxers, but he was able to come to an event before the Olympic Games to meet some of the team. His ability to quickly engage and gain the trust of the athletes was invaluable. The willingness of our medical support team to help the athletes was excellent and they were very well prepared with the number and types of support staff onsite.

From my perspective, the responsibilities of the USOC staff at the Olympic Games are enormous. I watched as the USOC staff worked tirelessly to make sure that the needs of every NGB were being met. Anytime we had a request with regard to transportation, lodging, meals or any logistical matter, everyone that was working in the USOC office in the Olympic Village bent over backwards to help with whatever need we had. That staff began their day extremely early in the morning and was available to us until exceptionally late at night. They are to be commended for their outstanding professionalism and kindness to our athletes and staff.

One important lesson that was learned is to make sure that all the *is* are dotted and all the *ts* crossed before arriving at the Games; leave no stone unturned, and then turn it over again, to make sure you didn't just cover something else up. It's also important to make sure that there are strict guidelines and procedures in place for all members of the delegation, making each person accountable for his/her actions.

USA CANOE-KAYAK: SPRINT TEAM | *CLIFF MEIDL – TEAM LEADER*

Olympic Trials were held in Oklahoma City, Okla., and were very successful on many levels. The sponsorship and community hospitality we received from Chesapeake Energy set the stage for a very successful Olympic Team Trails. The venue was organized to be state of the art and very competitive on a global stage. The conditions during the trails created a fair competitive playing field, allowing the athletes to give their utmost. In fact, the results for the men's K1 500 meter event provided another opportunity for two athletes to defend their team positions at the Continental Olympic Qualifier (COQ) event in Montreal, Canada. After providing a great performance at the Olympic Trials, the next big step was to qualify for additional athlete positions for the Olympic Games. This opportunity could be met at the Continental Olympic Qualifier event in Montreal, Canada, and the goal was to send a maximum team size to increase our probabilities for additional qualifications. Prior to the COQ event, USA Flatwater kayak was able to secure two positions for the Olympic Games: men's single 500 meter and women's single 500 meter positions. Unfortunately, the results at the COQ event were not definite and resulted in possible additional qualified positions but were not certain due to vague Olympic qualification interpretations. Weeks later, our hopes for additional athlete qualification fell short, which left us with only two athletes to compete at the Olympic Games.

In order to better acclimatize the athletes for Beijing, we conducted a two-week pre-Olympic training camp in Komatsu, Japan, and everything went exceptionally well. The climate and hospitality provided a great opportunity for Olympic race preparation. Once we arrived in Komatsu, the team was treated like royalty by the local Japanese Canoe Federation, which provided our team with state-of-the-art training facilities and accommodations. In addition to our two Olympic Team athletes, our NGB decided to send a training partner for each athlete; both were alternates to the Olympic Team. This simulated the highest and best possible training environment leading up to the Games.

Traveling to Beijing was a very smooth and positive experience, especially when you consider the uncertainty and distance from Japan to China, as well as our logistical complications. In order to overcome some possible hurdles as we arrived in China and transferred to a hotel near our venue, we prearranged our hotel rooms and confirmed verbally (U.S.-Chinese interpreter) our arrival and our daily itinerary from hotel to venue. To make travel from hotel to venue easier, we purchased bicycles to make the 1000 meter trip; they were more practical than using taxis.

Unfortunately, due to a few shortfalls, the team did not perform as the NGB had hoped. Our two athletes, Carrie Johnson and Rami Zur, both had great chances to medal but were unable to succeed and did not make finals due to illness and extremely difficult semifinals.

In terms of accreditation, all timelines were well laid out in the Games Deliverables document. Our only problem was the lack of athlete quotas, which resulted in a smaller number of credentials. We had to split the credentials between team leaders for flatwater and slalom.

Our air travel went smoothly, with our only concern being the transportation of kayaks back to the United States. We were informed that we would not be able to transport our boats to Europe following the Olympics, as previously planned. This caused extreme anxiety on our part and the USOC assisted with the transport back to the States through one of their containers going back to Colorado.

In regards to apparel, we had some unexpected requests in regards to high-performance racing gear. We would have liked our racing apparel sponsor to have been more responsive to our specific sport needs.

Our requests for ground transportation were taken care of in a very professional and timely manner. The Village to venue daily transport went well, taking an hour each direction. The travel from the Village to venue was a great opportunity to organize needed and useful information from the USOC. The travel time to the venue also allowed for contact with the athletes and coaches regarding the daily schedule. The organizing committee (BOCOG) provided us with an athlete room above the boathouse, which became our venue satellite meeting and rest area.

Beijing Normal University (BNU) provided a great place for the temporary housing of some members of our delegation. During competition, we utilized the taxi service, which worked well. We developed a great relationship with the hotel manager, who assisted with communication barriers. There was an initial transition delay at the hotel as the slalom team checked out and the sprint team checked in, and there were some issues regarding room preparations. The meals and facility were adequate for our needs and the security was good. At the venue, we

CARRIE JOHNSON OF THE UNITED STATES COMPETES IN HER HEAT OF THE FLATWATER WOMEN'S K1 500 M EVENT | *VLADIMIR RYS/GETTY IMAGES*

developed a relationship with a gentleman from the U.S. Department of Defense, providing him with the hotel manifest and introductions to all members. The agency provided exceptional security, comfort and travel arrangements while in Beijing. However, in the future, I would suggest that the athletes and staff be housed at the Olympic Village during competition events. The cost associated with staying at offsite hotels is not necessary and is not indicative of performance.

Our press officer, Bill McMillan, provided great services for media, and we were in direct communication with each other at all times. The media mix zone at the venue provided a smooth transition from racing to interviewing for athletes. Bill was always present to assist with media and athlete interaction. He also assisted in getting the videos from the USOC for our video analysis element. In the future, during regatta, we need to establish better ways to record, download and input video in real time. This would allow coaches quicker evaluation of the athletes. We utilized the BNU services because of the next-day video availability.

I would also recommend that the NGB take advantage of some of the services offered to them through the USOC, like access to an athletic trainer and psychological training prior to the Olympics. This would better prepare our athletes for the Olympics and other international racing events. The USOC provided these services and athletes did not utilize the services to their full potential.

In the future, I think it would be good to provide additional opportunities for racing experience, in addition to the European tours and Nationals leading up to the Olympic Games. For example, the 10K race in Newport Beach in 2008 drew the largest number of international athletes it's had in the past 10 years. There were over five countries and 50 athletes in the K1 race. Perhaps USACK could cosponsor the race in order to provide NAC with further name branding opportunities. In addition, a week prior or after, we could provide athletes an opportunity to race in San Diego at the Olympic Training Center's "Silver Blade" regatta or host an event in conjunction with the San Diego Junior Olympic Program. Long Beach could be another alternative race, in conjunction with the Long Beach Rowing Club. This could be a dual regatta for rowing and sprint. We could obtain a vendor to provide hosting and operational assistance with regattas. We could attract sponsorship for financial and product support and cash prizes.

The intention for promoting these regattas is to provide racing opportunities for athletes and to continue to engage them in world-class international racing. This can add to the international relationships that have been developed by Coach Luce over the past quadrennium. This is an important element for national development for sprint.

Branding these races develops awareness of the sport. Benchmarks for successful regattas include Szeged and the Surf Ski National Championships, held in San Francisco.

We also need to identify our top development programs and regions in the United States. Such programs need additional assistance and guidance in the form of a High Performance Director, coach education, development training, etc. These programs are great examples of our National "pipeline" development programs and they require immediate assistance.

In addition, we currently have a great opportunity with this young but maturing group of athletes in sprint and slalom. These are our "pipeline" athletes and are in need of special attention, as they could be potential medalist in London 2012. On behalf of sprint, we have a great opportunity to continue to develop several team boats (K4 +K2's) and single paddlers that were on the cusp of qualifying for the Beijing Games. Both the men's and women's teams have developed a strong culture of team work, dedication and friendships that have fostered over the past four years with direction from Coach Luce. This is very important in further developing our programs.

BENN FRAKER OF THE UNITED STATES COMPETES IN THE MEN'S CANOE SINGLE HEATS | *LARS BARON/BONGARTS/GETTY IMAGES*

USA CANOE-KAYAK: SLALOM TEAM | ANGELA LOKKEN – TEAM LEADER

Our Olympic team selection worked on a points system. Athletes were awarded points at the 2007 World Championships, 2008 Team Trials and the 2008 World Cup in Augsburg, Germany. The final Olympic team was selected July 7, 2008.

The team participated in two World Cups and had a training camp in western Maryland prior to the Olympic Games. Scott Parsons won a bronze at the Augsburg World Cup, and Benn Fraker made the finals in both the Prague and Augsburg World Cups.

In August 2007, Scott Parsons, Brett Heyl, Jim Wade, Benn Fraker, Jeff Larimer, Tad Dennis, Ashley Nee, Caroline Queen, Austin Crane and Scott McCleskey (2007 National Team members) participated in the Olympic Test Event. Scott Parsons won a medal at the event. It was useful to see how the Chinese Federation put on a major slalom event, and it helped prepare us for what was to come a year later at the Olympic Games.

Our training facilities at the Games were accessible and appropriate for our team. There was no wireless at the venue, and that made it difficult when there was so much downtime for the athletes. We were unable to secure day passes for our non-accredited personnel, which would have been helpful during the training sessions.

During the competition at the Olympic Games, Scott Parson competed for the U.S. in the K1 men's event. Unfortunately, he didn't make it into the semifinals. Benn Fraker competed in the C1 men's event, placing sixth. Heather Corrie placed eighth in the K1 women's event. Rick Powell and Casey Eichfeld competed in the C2 event and placed 11th overall, just missing the semifinals by one place.

Prior to the Olympics, I attended both USOC Team Leadership meetings and found them to be very valuable in getting ready for the Games. I was able to talk with key people in the Games decision-making areas, which was a huge help

The accreditation element was a smooth process. Although we didn't receive the number of credentials that we had requested, we were able to work with the number we did receive.

The team traveled to team processing and the Games with only a few issues. The athletes had an extra expense to transport their boats to team processing. We had planned for this, so it was not a major issue and the athletes were reimbursed by the USOC upon arrival in Beijing. Some of the athletes had their flight canceled at the last minute before traveling to processing. We contacted the USOC and the United Olympic desk, and they assisted them in rebooking another flight.

We didn't have any issues with the apparel. The USOC worked directly with Nike with our color boards, and they made sure we were aware of any changes. In terms of team processing, most of the team was processed at the same time except for one athlete, who went through the day before with the Team Leader. I thought it was a good idea to have the Team Leader go through team processing the day before the team arrived. This allowed me to understand the procedure and answer any questions the next day when the rest of the team arrived for team processing.

The USOC helped us in getting proper security clearance for our two-way radios so we could use them during the events. In addition, the cell phones issued by the USOC were great. We were able to keep in contact with our staff, athletes and the Olympic Village. I appreciated the fact that we had access to the computers and printers in the Village, making our jobs easier.

In terms of ground transportation, we did not order any special vehicles. When we needed to get to our offsite housing, the USOC contacts in the Village went out of their way to help us get cars. If we needed cars, the transportation staff would do everything possible to get a car for us.

We had requested microwave ovens and refrigerators off the rate card but realized that they would not be needed. We were able to return them without any problems, which was very helpful.

The Diplomatic Security Service agents assigned to our event site went out of their way to help our athletes and staff. We were able to call on them at any time for assistance.

Overall, we had a great experience in Beijing. I feel that all the information that was given at the meetings gave me the tools to resolve any problems that arose. The meetings that were held in China gave me knowledge and insight about the city and their customs; they helped me feel very confident as a Team Leader that I would be able to help make the athletes enjoy their Olympic experience in Beijing.

It was a great honor to work with everyone involved in the planning and execution of the Beijing Olympic Games.

USA CYCLING | PAT MCDONOUGH – DIRECTOR OF ATHLETICS

No matter what the sport, the Team Leader at an Olympic Games has to be adept at juggling the many responsibilities he or she has at all times. The sport of cycling at the Olympic Games does have a few unique challenges, though. Olympic Cycling includes four distinct disciplines: Road, Track, Mountain Bike and BMX. These four disciplines all have stand-alone World Championships held annually, yet at the Olympic Games we must oversee team selection, manage team preparation and logistics and of course the competition of all four disciplines. The Olympic Games schedule had cycling competitions planned for 12 days spread across the four different venues. The U.S. Cycling Team was comprised of 23 athletes who had brought more than 60 bicycles, 200 wheels and a plethora of specialized cycling equipment, clothing and training apparatus that were all meant to maximize rider performance.

ADAM CRAIG OF THE UNITED STATES COMPETES IN THE MEN'S CROSS-COUNTRY MOUNTAIN BIKE CYCLING EVENT | *PHIL WALTER/GETTY IMAGES*

The staff of 10 included coaches, mechanics, soigneurs and two Team Leaders, who were all stretched at times to provide the best possible service to this unique group of athletes.

The 2008 U.S. Olympic Cycling Team selection process focused primarily on top-level international competitions dating back one year, as well as international time standards where applicable. The USA Cycling Selection Committee is comprised of former World Champions, Tour de France stage winners and Olympians from all four disciplines. It is this group that makes the final nomination of athletes to the Olympic Team. The final U.S. Olympic Cycling Team that went to Beijing has to be considered one of the most talented we have ever sent. The group included 12 World Championship medal winners representing all four disciplines, four riders who had competed in the Tour de France and the son of two Olympic medal winners from the sport of cycling.

Our team (riders and staff) stayed in the Olympic Village throughout the Games. This decision was made after attending all four "Test Events" leading up to the Games. Our organization is quite capable of organizing all logistical needs for our teams, yet during these test events it became extremely difficult to work independently of the system that BOCOG had set up. We are an equipment-based sport, and as such we have very particular transportation and storage needs. It became apparent that we would need to depend on the systems that BOCOG would set up for the Games. Though we had some "bureaucratic issues" during the Games that many other sports ran into as well, on the whole we found the BOCOG transportation and logistical systems reliable and well organized.

The venues in Beijing were incredible! There was not one training or competition venue we visited that did not have every amenity that one would wish for. I am not sure how any other Games will be able to live up to some of these facilities. The velodrome was beyond state of the art; it is the most impressive cycling facility we had ever seen! The BMX track, which had debuted the year prior, has changed the sport of BMX. We do hope that the facilities survive because for the most part they are one of a kind.

The men's and momen's Road teams were, in a word, "Professional." The teams rode well in the Road races under some very extreme conditions, with the men's Road race held on the hottest day of the Olympic Games and the Women's race held during a torrential downpour. In both races the U.S. Team met their early objectives of putting their earmarked riders into the "finale" (the closing lap of the race), but conditions and mechanical issues took a toll on the team as we finished outside the medals in both road races.

The Time Trial, or "race of truth," is a true strength of the U.S program, as we have become a consistent medal favorite at World Championships and Olympic Games. The challenging course in Beijing was 22km per lap yet provided only one intermediate time check, at the top of the climb, every lap. The men would race two laps and the women only one. The staff and riders felt it would be a great benefit to have an additional time check to provide information and splits for the riders. So the morning of the time trial we dropped off one of the Team Leaders halfway up the climb with a bag that contained 3 stopwatches, 2 cell phones, a handful of sandwiches and bottled water. The highlight of the day came when he got a call during the women's medal ceremony so he could hear the "Star-Spangled Banner" being played in honor of Kristin Armstrong's gold medal performance. (I can tell you it sounds great even over a cell phone!)

The Track cycling team unfortunately was not able to deliver the performances we had hoped for. Sarah Hammer finished fifth in the Pursuit and crashed out in the Points Race, breaking her collarbone. None of us would be surprised to see Sarah, a two-time World Champion, back in top form and ready to compete in London. There was an upside, as 18-year-old Taylor Phinney, the son of Olympic medal winners Connie Carpenter and Davis Phinney, finished seventh in the Men's Pursuit. Taylor only began riding the track nine months prior to the Olympic Games and, as the youngest Olympic cyclist in Beijing, has the potential to be at many more Games.

BMX made its Olympic debut at Beijing and the U.S. Team was the favorite to come home with the most medals. This group came through with flying colors, winning 3 of the 6 medals available. The only U.S. rider not to medal was Kyle Bennett, who dislocated his shoulder in the preliminary rounds. Kyle still qualified for the semifinal and chose to compete anyway. The thought of coming off the ski jump-style start ramp and flying 30 feet through the air side by side with seven other riders is crazy, but to do it with a dislocated shoulder was even more impressive and indicative of the Olympic spirit. There was no quit in any of these BMX riders!

The final competition was the cross-country Mountain Bike race. The heat made a return on this day and was a huge factor in both races. Our women fared well, with both riders finishing in the top 10 with Mary McConneloug taking seventh just ahead of Georgia Gould, who finished eighth. The heat and humidity seemed to get to our men, as they were not able to finish the event.

The U.S. Cycling Team won the most medals since the 1984 Games. We won our sixth and seventh medals in the Road Time Trial since it was added to the Games, the most of any country. We led the medal count in our sports new discipline, BMX. And we saw potential for the future in Taylor.

394

TAYLOR PHINNEY OF THE UNITED STATES COMPETES IN THE CYCLING EVENT | *JED JACOBSOHN/GETTY IMAGES*

USA DIVING | *BOB RYDZE*
– NATIONAL TEAM MANAGING DIRECTOR

As with many of the other sports, there was a pre-Games test event for diving held in Beijing at the Water Cube. USA Diving participated in this event and felt it was very useful. Our athletes and coaches spent two weeks in Beijing getting a feel for the venue as well as the city. Our High Performance Director did not go but would suggest he attend these types of events in the future.

In the middle of June, we had our initial Olympic Trials to pick our first individual athlete in each discipline. Then two weeks later, we conducted a selection camp to pick our second individual and our synchronized diving teams for springboard and platform. As a result, we took the best team available, but in the future, it would be best to hold either a selection camp or an Olympic Trials but not both. Obviously, there are advantages and disadvantages in both processes. For selection for the 2012 team, our new High Performance Director and Competition Committee should keep in mind the deadlines set by the USOC and the OCOG.

Following the trials and selection camp, the divers returned home with their respective coaches to train before departing for Beijing. Some of the divers competed at our U.S. National Diving Championships held at the end of July. All in all the training seemed to go well.

Our training facility in Beijing was the competition pool, and we had great access to the facility. They did a great job on this.

The four synchronized events were held during the first four days of our competition. We were close to medaling in three out of four events. The individual events were held over the next nine days of competition. Seven of our eight individual divers made the finals, and only China did better in that respect. As the pressure mounted to win a medal, our athletes might have tried too hard. There were three out of four individual events in which we had a shot of medaling, but it never materialized. We took a very young team, and although we improved by leaps and bounds from 2004, it was disappointing to walk away with no medals. We hope the experience will be beneficial for the future of the program.

In terms of preparation for the Games, everything ran pretty smoothly. Our accreditation was taken care of in a timely manner with very few problems. I felt we had good support all the way through the accreditation process.

We had no issues with our air travel and we were able to get our tickets booked in a timely fashion. The apparel element went well for us, but we would suggest more attention to the shoes that are issued to athletes and coaches for Opening Ceremony.

The athletes and coaches appreciated the computer labs set up by the USOC but would suggest, given the size of the delegation, to try to provide a few more computers.

We felt that Beijing Normal University was a nice support service for our team. Our athletes and coaches used it as a place to get away and it was a great place for our uncredentialed staff to stay. A few suggestions to improve this in the future would be to have busses to the Village running more often and later in the evening, to accommodate everyone's schedule a little more. Also, the video analysis for diving did not work well because of the time lag between the end of sessions and the time when the DVDs were ready. In the future, we need to get the DVDs much sooner to be useful.

We ended up using the USA House more than I had originally thought we would. It was a great place for athletes to get away and for parents to be able to meet up with their children.

A few other observations that may or may not play into future Games: if the Olympic diving schedule in London is like it was in Beijing, we suggest bringing in the individual divers who are not also diving synchro a little later and to send home the synchro-only divers when their competition is finished. In London, because the time change is not so great, we will not have to arrive as early. But we need to consider the schedule carefully, as this year's schedule was brutal. If it continues like this, then changes need to be made.

We did not lose medals in synchro because of our synchronization scores but because of our execution scores. Execution of the dives needs to become our top priority as we move the program forward. USA divers and coaches need to start with the premise that they are training to win medals, not just on the ideal that they are trying to make the Olympic team. Four years from now, however, we are hopeful the experience from 2008 will pay off.

DAVID BOUDIA OF THE UNITED STATES COMPETES DURING THE MEN'S 10M PLATFORM FINAL| *JAMIE SQUIRE/GETTY IMAGES*

USA EQUESTRIAN | SALLY IKE, GIL MERRICK & SARA IKE

– SHOW JUMPING TEAM LEADER, DRESSAGE TEAM LEADER & EVENTING TEAM LEADER

The local organizing committee (BOCOG) held an Olympic Test Event well in advance of the Games. The United States Equestrian Federation (USEF) sent two Eventing horses and riders to compete in this event. In addition, all team leaders and coaches attended; it was a great way to familiarize ourselves with the venue, and it also gave us a chance to meet with the event organizers, which was very helpful.

Sha Tin was our training and competition venue in Hong Kong. It was a top-notch facility and very accessible. We encountered some stewarding issues and inconsistent enforcement, but we were able to work through them.

Our primary expense is horse transportation. However, if we had a larger budget, we would be able to cover more of the out-of-pocket expenses for horses and riders during the time period before and during the Games. We would provide larger grants to athletes to compete in Europe; the funding we currently provide does not cover riders' expenses.

All three Team Leaders attended both of the USOC Team Leadership meetings and found them very beneficial. It's always valuable to meet with leaders from the other sports and compare notes, but the round-tables are the most valuable for the opportunity to go over the Games Deliverables document face-to-face with USOC staff. All three also attended the USOC Key Decision Maker meetings in 2008 and found it valuable to visit the Equestrian venue in Hong Kong and meet the venue managers. It helped in the preplanning process.

Working through the accreditation process in conjunction with developing the Games Deliverables document gave us sufficient planning time and worked very well. The ability to link the athlete, groom and owners as one group worked extremely well and was very helpful, especially when Eventing had a last-minute replacement.

Initially, there were some problems getting the correct accreditation (full access to all areas of the venue) for our Equestrian Chef de Mission (Jim Wolf). Although this situation was remedied after we arrived, he could potentially have not had access to areas where he needed to be in order to resolve an unexpected medication rule violation case.

Equestrian has a high ratio of support staff to athletes because the equine athletes need as much, if not more, support than the human ones. As a result, if accreditation is limited, the ability to get day passes is essential to enhance the athletes' performance. We had fewer accreditations available to us this year than in 2004, but we met the shortage by working with the organizing committee (BOCOG) to procure day passes. Jim Wolf was very proactive and worked very hard in order to secure day passes for support staff. Although most issues were resolved in a timely manner, one individual had to wait almost one week in Hong Kong and as a result, he was unable to perform physiotherapy on the team horses during that time.

Any questions or issues relating to accreditation had to be routed through the Main Accreditation Center in Beijing and couldn't be resolved by the Center in Hong Kong, causing delays.

Since virtually everything is now done so far in advance, the accreditation process works fairly smoothly. Being able to have accreditation completed at the airport is a huge step forward from the "old days" of lines and lines of people waiting to be photographed.

Air travel for the athletes was coordinated along with the air travel for the horses and we did not require the support of the USOC for these Games. We wish we could make more use of United Airlines for our travel because our experience with them has always been very good. However, given the nature of getting the horses to the host country, we don't have many choices when it comes to air travel. In the future, we would prefer to fly on United Airlines if the logistics of shipping our horses and team members can be accommodated.

When booking our own air travel we were told that it was impossible to book tickets for athletes prior to the team being named. For our sport, this meant we couldn't book tickets until July 15th, which was less than two weeks prior to departure. In the future, we need to find an alternative way of confirming air reservations for our athletes before we know which riders will actually be named to the teams or find a way to book seats with the ability to change names.

We are very appreciative that the USOC allowed our athletes to bypass team processing, which would have been very difficult for them as they were in Europe all summer, and the horses were there as well. For them to have had to go to San Jose, Calif., could have negatively impacted their performance. While we prefer our athletes to go through team processing and apparel distribution, we encourage the USOC to continue to allow us the flexibility to do otherwise if we believe it's in the best interests of the athletes not to do so.

There was an agreement between the USOC and USEF that we would send staff to San Jose to pack for our team. The purpose of doing this was to assist the USOC staff, as we knew they are very busy during this time, and to make sure that the sizes were as correct as possible, since USEF staff would be familiar with who they were packing for. Although we thought that the look and quality of the apparel was exceptionally good, apparel sizing was not consistent between Polo Ralph Lauren and Nike. As a result, many athletes and support staff received clothing that did not fit.

In the future we would like to have the ability to purchase clothing for our alternate athletes, as it always affects team unity and morale when it isn't provided. These athletes are in a difficult position as it is, and not being able to be dressed like their teammates just makes it that much harder.

It was also a huge help that the USOC conducted the Ambassador Program directly to our athletes in Hong Kong.

In terms of ground transportation, we requested three seven-passenger vans, but received only two. We ended up having to rent two more as a result. These extra two vehicles were used by Dressage and Eventing. Jumping used the two vans that we received through our BOCOG request. This caused some unforeseen costs to our budget. However, it was nice to have the ability to rent additional vans when this happened. The USOC was able to assist us in obtaining transportation information from BOCOG. Parking was an issue because we did not receive the correct number of vans and we incurred additional expenses in securing our own parking spots through the Hong Kong Jockey Club.

The daily training/competition schedule prohibited us from making each trip to the venue with the van (due to the cost of having the van available from 8 AM until 11 PM each day) and the actual cost of renting the van was more than expected. Our team traveled by train and taxi for one trip each day to and from the venue to try to keep costs down. On the upside, we received excellent service from Avis and had

the same driver every day.

The cell phones issued by the USOC allowed for very effective communication within the team. Having the pre-loaded phone numbers for all USOC staff was also very helpful. However, the phones we were issued had SIM cards for Beijing and did not work in Hong Kong. Our USOC contact who was with us in Hong Kong bought Hong Kong SIM cards for every phone, and once this was done everything worked well. In addition, we also purchased the radios we needed because it was too complicated to get our own registered.

We shipped some things through the USOC and everything was in the container waiting for us upon our arrival. We were also appreciative of the various food and drinks from the USOC that were sent in our container. Having this food and drink available to us became very important because we weren't able to bring anything into the venue.

We were given the impression that video analysis would be available at the Games, but it wasn't in Hong Kong. Video analysis is important to us, particularly in a remote training situation and we hope this can be worked out in the future.

As for security, the Department of State staff was great to work with. They were attentive, but stayed out of our way. They were self-sufficient and professional.

The presence of the U.S. State Department agents gave the delegation the sense that they were secure. They were very proactive in their communication with us. The agents were extremely personable and professional and made a great contribution to the team spirit.

The logistics involved in competition at these Games were the most challenging we've had yet, largely due to the health requirements imposed by Hong Kong for the horses. The climate and distance involved wasn't so much of an issue, as we'd competed in Kuala Lumpur two years before, which has a similar climate.

USA Equestrian decided to secure outside housing early in the process, and our staff started looking for a location as early as 2004. The hotel that was selected to house our delegation provided us with everything we needed. Because we used outside housing, the management of transportation was more complicated for our team. It was important to be able to stay in the Olympic Village when it was appropriate for performance enhancement. Equestrian will always need to use outside housing due to the age of our athletes and their family situations, which does not lend itself to sharing rooms.

USA Equestrian—Show Jumping

Equestrian has been a part of the Olympic Games since 1912 and is one of only two sports in which one of the athletes is an animal. Consequently, the ability of the horse is as important as the ability of the rider. Medals are won because both athletes have extraordinary talent and are able to work together to achieve clear rounds. If you do, you win a medal; if not, then you don't. It is that simple.

Selection Trials were held in early spring, from which a short list of 10 horse-rider combinations was named. The short list was divided into two groups of five each, each of whom competed in a European tour. Jumping riders compete more than they train, and since the most competitive events are in Europe, it's important to prepare there for the most optimum performance.

Selection was based on European tour performance. The five major European events leading up to the Games were in France, Italy, Switzerland, the Netherlands and Germany. Our athletes performed well, but the primary focus was on performance at the Games, not necessarily winning at these competitions.

WILL SIMPSON OF TEAM USA WAVES WHILE RIDING "CARLSSON VOM DACH" DURING THE EQUESTRIAN JUMPING INDIVIDUAL COMPETITION | *DAVID HECKER/AFP/GETTY IMAGES*

The final team was selected in early July and we felt that the best athletes made the team.

Overall we had a good plan for the 2008 Olympic Games. We executed the plan, and we were very successful—bringing home a team gold medal and an individual bronze medal. I can't emphasize enough the fact that planning all aspects well in advance is key to a successful event.

USA Equestrian—Eventing

Equestrian is a bit unique in that it requires a partnership of top riders and top horses. Eventing requires that the horse-rider combination be proficient in three different disciplines—an "all arounder" rather than a specialist. Cross-country is the defining trait of Eventing and played a major part in the final standings in Hong Kong.

We selected our Olympic team on July 15, 2008. Prior to the team selection, the majority of our riders trained domestically. We would have liked to have more European competition experience to better

prepare, but budget constraints don't allow this yet.

Following the team selection, our riders competed in the Barbury Castle Estate Horse Trials in England and trained in England following the event. We were limited in regards to final competition preparation because of the quarantine requirements placed on the horses for the 2008 Olympic Games.

One of the main lessons learned at these Games is that our team could use more international competition experience and needs more young horses in the pipeline. In the end, we were able to bring home an individual silver medal in Eventing. However, we did this in spite of athlete errors, bad luck and young horses. We had an athlete disqualified due to a new rule regarding overweight boots. We were unaware of the rule, but since the boots were over the weight limit, we did not contest the elimination.

USA Equestrian—Dressage

Dressage is characterized by the combination of a horse that has been developed to the highest level of gymnastic athleticism and a rider who guides the horse through a series of exercises with total harmony, grace and elegance. It is a highly stylized form of competition, with one component of the competition choreographed to music in the same way that Ice Dancing would be, and therefore there is a high degree of subjectivity involved in the judging of the sport. Due to the subjective nature of the judging, an athlete must present the type of horse that the judges want to see competing in the sport in a manner consistent with their expectations. As these expectations can change over time, athletes must be able to modify their performances to suit the changing expectations of the judges. Dressage has been part of the Olympic Games since 1912.

We had a couple of legal issues that arose surrounding these Games. One athlete requested changes to the published selection procedures. USEF was advised that the changes would not be allowed and this was relayed to the athlete. We also had one horse charged with a medical rule violation under very unusual circumstances which resulted in the Dressage Team's fourth-place standing not counting.

398

GINA MILES OF TEAM USA COMPETES DURING THE CROSS-COUNTRY EVENTING COMPETITION | *MIKE CLARKE/AFP/GETTY IMAGES*

U.S. FENCING | *ROBERT LARGMAN* – *TEAM LEADER*

8-8-08 at 8:08pm was the start of the most successful Olympic Games in the history of U.S. Fencing. With the opening of the XXIX Olympiad in Beijing, China, and with billions of people watching and waiting the world over for the drama to unfold, two sports super-powers, USA and China, prepared to duel for Olympic supremacy. Little did we know that that duel would manifest itself in fencing.

At the 2004 Olympic Games in Athens, China won three fencing medals to the United States' two. Building on that rivalry, the first day of the 2008 competition pitted the strongest opportunity for a gold medal for China against the USA's best opportunity for gold—Women's Sabre. In 2004, the U.S. won a gold and bronze medal and China took the silver medal in the first-time Olympic sport of Women's sabre fencing.

On the first day of Olympic competition the world witnessed a U.S. sweep in the Individual Women's Sabre competition:

• Gold—Mariel Zagunis (2004 Olympic Gold Medalist)
• Silver—Sada Jacobson (2004 Olympic Bronze Medalist)
• Bronze—Rebecca Ward (World Champion)

The last time a medal sweep occurred in fencing was 20 years ago at the 1988 Seoul Games, when West Germany's women's foilists won all three medals. With the American women sabreists leading the way, the rest of the U.S. Fencing Team did not waste time following their lead onto the medal podium.

The total Olympic medal tally included:

• Women's Sabre Individual Gold Medal—Mariel Zagunis
• Women's Sabre Individual Silver Medal—Sada Jacobson
• Women's Sabre Individual Bronze Medal—Rebecca Ward
• Women's Sabre Team Bronze Medal—Zagunis, Jacobson, Ward
• Women's Foil Team Silver Medal—Emily Cross, Erinn Smart, Hanna Thompson
• Men's Sabre Team Silver Medal—Tim Morehouse, Jason Rogers, Keeth Smart, James Williams

What took place on August 9, the first day of Olympic competition, in the Fencing Hall of the National Convention Center on the Olympic Green, was historic and just the beginning of a historic Games for U.S. Fencing. U.S. Fencing expectations for medals were three with a stretch for for. The USOC was expecting three medals with a reach goal of five. However, the expectations of the Olympic Fencing Team itself were much higher and they proved their mettle with a haul of six medals (one gold, three silver, two bronze). The U.S.'s medal run in fencing was second only to Italy, who earned their seventh medal on the last day of competition. The next highest country was

France, with four medals. With the results from these Olympic Games, the U.S. moved up on the rungs of fencing powers from an emerging country to an established fencing power. An amazing 77 percent (10 of 13) of our team members returned home with Olympic medals. The next Olympic task will be for U.S. Fencing to find a way to sustain and improve on the 2008 performances.

We knew that Women's Sabre held our best chances for medals going into the Games. With the 2004 performances, expectations were obviously high. However, four medals with an individual medal sweep was beyond dreams.

Our Men's Sabre and Women's Foil squads entered the competition having both qualified as the America's regional champions and representatives. Both squads were outside possibilities to reach the medal round, but with the right seeding, we had chances. Our coaching staff had the teams prepared, as we knew the seeding opportunities well in advance. Having studied tapes and tendencies, strategies and line-ups, our squads fought miraculous bouts to make the medal rounds. Staving off comebacks and creating fantastic points, both squads qualified for the gold medal bout, eventually earning the silver medal.

The Women's Foil Team silver medal is the first ever medal in Women's Foil for the U.S. and the first foil medal for the U.S. since Albie Axelrod won an individual bronze medal in Men's Foil at the 1960 Olympic Games in Rome, Italy.

The final medal that our team won at the 2008 Olympic Games was also one of the most gratifying. The Men's Sabre Team captured the silver medal in the team competition. The extreme gratification came four years after the heartbreaking experience at the 2004 Olympic Games where the same team missed out on two Olympic medals by two touches, losing the semifinal and the bronze medal matches by

A COACH LOOKS ON DURING THE BOUT BETWEEN USA'S KEETH SMART (L) AND RUSSIA'S NIKOLAY KOVALEV DURING THE MEN'S TEAM SABRE SEMIFINAL | *PHILIPPE DESMAZES/AFP/GETTY IMAGES*

one point each. The U.S. Men's Sabre Team entered the competition on a mission to erase the heartache of the 2004 Olympic competition. Kelley Hurley (Women's Epee), Seth Kelsey (Men's Epee) and Gerek Meinhardt (Men's Foil) all competed in incredibly tough draws and fenced well but did not reach the medal rounds. All three are extremely capable and well positioned to continue their Olympic competition in 2012 with even greater opportunities for podium appearances.

U.S. Fencing has finally joined the family of U.S. Olympic medal winning sports.

How did we do this? How did fencing overcome quadrennials of medal opportunities into two consecutive Games of medal hauls? Of course, the obvious answer is years and years of training, coaching, experience and … well … luck. No country or sport could equal the sacrifices, hours and sweat that our athletes, coaches, parents, support staff, NGB staff and extended fencing family poured into this effort. But for the first time, the USFA made the effort to "train" just as hard as our athletes to provide the foundation for Olympic success. We came in with a plan, a timeline, a goal and an objective, and with three years to go until Beijing, we set into play an action plan that would provide our support staff with the knowledge, experience and tools to give our team every opportunity to succeed with the highest level of confidence.

The USFA began its efforts to support the U.S. Olympic Fencing Team on August 23, 2004. This is when we conducted a lessons learned session at the American College of Greece just after the completion of the fencing competition. Conducted with the entire team, including coaches and staff, and then a separate one with just athletes, this session provided the framework, foundation and jumping off points for planning our attack for Beijing.

We started our planning in earnest in 2005 with several planning sessions internal to the USFA with key staff personnel. This quickly was followed by our first visit to Beijing. It is extremely important that the support team has the ability to handle all issues once in-country for the Games. A large part of being able to do that, especially in a country whose customs and culture are very different from our own, is being familiar with the country and how we will operate. The planning team took nine trips to Beijing prior to the Games. These trips were part of competitions, USOC visits, and USFA only. The goal each time was to be better prepared to handle all logistical and operational needs we could envision for the team, coaches, staff, extended team and our friends and family.

Our guiding motto was to be the best prepared support crew in the world. The more situations we were prepared to handle, the better we were able to handle those situations we could not anticipate. You need to be prepared to address everything that comes your way to support the team. The more you can plan for, the more you can do just because you know what to do. That is the main purpose of our advanced trips. This preparation leaves you with the bandwidth to handle those items you didn't plan for. By knowing the lay of the land, by making contacts, by using your ingenuity and familiarity, you can come up with a plan to handle those unforeseen problems. And, if there is one thing you can count on, it's that there will be situations for which you did not prepare.

All of our pre-planning efforts did serve us well, and I believe we were one of the best prepared support teams at the Olympics. To be the best, we need to improve. That improvement comes internally. We needed to communicate better with our extended Olympic Team. That is, our Friends & Family (F&F) program. We had a tremendous F&F presence at the Games, and our plan was to provide a program on which the F&F could rely for housing, transportation, tourism, cultural

and social engagements and much more. While several of our pre-planning trips were primarily dedicated to meet those needs, they never came to fruition. We must do a better job of serving our extended team, as they too impact sustained performance of our Olympic Team. Communications with the USOC, our primary partner in Olympic planning, is another avenue in which we must continue to improve. The primary method of communicating with the USOC was via USOC-sponsored meetings, both domestic and international. A key component at those meetings is the roundtable discussions. In order to be better prepared for the roundtables, the USFA should conduct conference calls to identify issues to address. The roundtable discussions are a good process to relay information and to obtain information. The process was made better this year by the Deliverables Document maintained by the USOC. However, there was too much time spent reviewing what the USOC captured because key information was either left off or noted incorrectly. There should be an online process for the NGB to update and provide comments into the Deliverables Document.

Another area where the USFA has faltered in both 2004 and 2008 is the NGB apparel package for the Olympic Team. In 2000, the USFA was able to work with sponsors to develop a full package of apparel and commemorative items for the team. While seemingly a secondary item for performance, the athletes have all strongly stated that the NGB identification is an important item and goes towards the "look and feel" of the team. Other USA teams have strong NGB identification at the Olympics in supplemental apparel. The USFA is deficient in that category and needs to plan and prepare better for this signature detail for the athletes.

Going forward, I strongly support the continued practice of being in-country three years prior to the Games. A possible schedule might be as outlined here. These planning sessions would be in addition to any trips planned by the USOC, including Team Leader meetings, Key

ERINN SMART (L) OF THE UNITED STATES COMPETES AGAINST VICTORIA NIKICHINA OF RUSSIA IN THE WOMEN'S TEAM FOIL | *CLIVE ROSE/ GETTY IMAGES*

Decision maker meetings, and others.

Three years out	One trip to the Olympic city
	One domestic follow-up meeting
Two years out	Two trips to the Olympic city
	Two domestic follow-up meetings
One year out	Three trips to the Olympic city
	Two domestic follow-up meetings
Olympic Year	One trip to the Olympic city
	One domestic follow-up meeting

In order to be able to provide this support, an Olympic Preparation budget is required. It must cover international and domestic trips, meetings, and planning sessions. For 2008, we did not have an explicit budget, but used pieces of other budgets to do the work that was needed. Our success on the ground is a testament to the value of this activity. In addition to covering these pre-Games planning sessions, the Olympic budget must also cover additional staff people required on the ground at the Games but outside of the Olympic purview. Miscellaneous items such as team celebrations, cultural interaction, competition recordings and the like must be accommodated. It is expensive to train a team for the Games and a budget is required to plan and support that team at the Games. Attention must be paid to this area of Games preparation, for without it performance will be impacted. A short list of line items for an Olympic Preparation budget might include the following. Unfortunately, many of these items were not budgeted in 2008 and caused some deficit spending for the organization.

Olympic planning trips—international

Olympic planning trips—domestic

Secondary Ao room and board

Secondary Ao travel

Secondary Ao apparel

Team/personal coach room and board

Team/personal coach travel

Support personnel room and board

Support personnel travel

Replacement athlete room and board

Replacement athlete travel

Replacement athlete apparel

Training partner room and board

Training partner travel

Team celebrations

Competition recording

USFA apparel package

USFA gifts and commemoratives

Team announcement and celebration

Miscellaneous

Another contributing factor to the success of the planning team was the fact that our Olympic Team was selected early in the second quarter of 2008. This allowed us to provide for many programs with the Olympic Team. We could target our communications better, provide programs such as team building, designate appropriate Olympic staff and cadre, and generally better prepare the Olympic Team for what they would encounter. The more we could make the team familiar with what to expect, the better we would be able to focus on their training and performance. To this end, we also brought in team members to Beijing up to 10 days prior to their competition. This was important for acclimatization to the time, weather, heat, humidity and pollution. But this is also important for getting the "oh gee" factor behind the team.

Equally important is the early selection of key team cadre. Coaches cannot be selected until after the athletes have made the team. However, the Team Leader, Team Armorer, Team Trainer, and Team Captain (if applicable) should be selected as early in the quad as possible. Optimally, the Team Leader should be selected three years before the Games to fully participate in the Games planning. Together, these people and the NGB Executive Director, High Performance Director, and National Team Director will combine to be the Olympic Planning Team.

Credentialing of staff and coaches seemingly brings the same discussions and impossibilities at every Games. It is an issue that never seems to have a resolution. Fencing is not unique in this area, but must continue to fight for an appropriate number of credentials to properly support our Team. The uniqueness of fencing is that it is both a team sport and an individual sport. Traditionally, fencing received six credentials. However, after the Sydney Games, the USOC stopped providing a USOC credential for the Team Armorer. This credential now had to come from the team allotment. Out of a pool of five primary credentials, we now must support a Team Leader (mandatory) and the Team Armorer (a necessity). That leaves three positions for primary team coaches. However, while the USOC has reduced our primary Ao credential allocation by 17 percent, the number of events in fencing has grown by 30 percent, with the inclusion of Women's Team Epee, Women's Individual Sabre, and Women's Team Sabre. These events have all been added since 1996. At the 2008 series of roundtables sponsored by the USOC, this situation was brought to the attention of the USOC and they indicated they would review the credentials awarded to fencing. I propose that U.S. Fencing be allocated six primary Ao credentials and three secondary Ao credentials. I would also suggest that the USOC communicates to the NGBs much earlier about the preliminary allocations for primary and secondary credentials. Realizing that this will change, advanced notice provides the teams with the framework on which they need to identify and select coaches, as well as budget for staff that may not be funded via credentials.

Athlete credentials are not a problem. When an athlete makes the team and is confirmed through the USOC and IOC application process, their Aa credential is secured. The athlete credentialing scenario that is complicated is the "P" credential for the replacement athletes. In Sydney, our replacement athletes did not receive a P credential. The local organizing committee (LOC) had a system worked out for day passes for the practice venue and competition venue. While not optimal, this did work. For Beijing, discussions with the USOC regarding the P credential started early and were taken up at every roundtable meeting and in between. The USOC still held it was the position of the FIE to award the P credential, while the FIE indicated that it was the USOC's responsibility. After several dialogues across the Atlantic Ocean, the FIE provided the USOC with the documentation necessary to show the P credential for fencing is awarded by the NOC, confirming the USFA's original position. The key now will be to "remind" the USOC of this in planning for future Games.

In order to solve the most important issue associated with the P credential, the USFA teamed up with the USOC and has taken full advantage of the USOC's High Performance Training Centers. At the American College of Greece in Athens and at Beijing Normal University in Beijing, the USFA set up training camps and residences. Both of these facilities have proved phenomenal in terms of practicing, housing, dining and "escape" from the Olympic hype. This has been a tremendous program sponsored by the USOC and I strongly recommend continued partnering with the USOC on this front as we look for training and housing facilities for our Team, coaches and staff at the Games.

The USOC apparel package was extensive for the athletes and adequate for the coaches. Polo was a new sponsor and provided many exciting pieces for the athletes. Nike was the other sponsor and while their apparel was useful, many athletes thought their styling was a bit conservative. In the future, it would be helpful if the clothing sponsor(s) could provide sizing charts in advance so that an appropriate number of items at each size can be ordered, as many of the more popular sizes were out of stock. More attention needs to be paid to what coaches and staff will need for the Games. A coach/staff/Team Leader should participate in the apparel selection process so that the Ao Team members are properly outfitted. NGBs count on certain apparel items for their staff as part of their competition uniform.

It should be noted in the Fencing documentation that all Replacement Athletes will be provided with the full Olympic Team apparel package. For each Games, we go through the same discussion about what should happen regarding this item. It should be policy that these athletes will receive the package so that in future Games there is no confusion.

The Opening Ceremony outfit went back to more formal attire from the 2004 casual look. While 2004 may have been too casual, blazers and ties are too formal. The athletes all commented that they would prefer something more casual and more uniquely and distinctively American. A suggestion of incorporating sharp, casual attire that was typically American was … jeans, shirt, blazer (possibly leather), and a baseball hat.

Team Processing is a very organized and well run operation. Minor tweaks may be necessary, but overall, apparel distribution went well. For the 2004 and 2008 Games, the Fencing Team Leader supported Team Processing by working the apparel distribution line for several days in advance of departure for Beijing. This helps the Team Leader be prepared for their team's needs and preparation for their processing. I encourage all Team Leaders to arrive at Team Processing several days earlier to gain this valuable experience.

Partnering with the USOC to create the best possible opportunities for success is not a singular effort from the NGB to the USOC. These efforts must go both ways and the USOC needs to sometimes step out of its processes to best support the NGBs. There were several situations where the USFA could have used USOC support and flexibility rather than USOC guidelines. Some examples included P credentialing and uniform approvals. Regarding the uniform approval issue, the USFA submitted actual uniforms, rather than color boards. A concern was raised regarding the competition apparel and IOC guidelines regarding "logo-ing." Fencing uniforms are required, for control purposes, to in-

clude a mark indicating that it has passed stringent IF rules for safety. These safety tags are sewn onto each item (jacket, knickers, underarm protector, mask). If these safety tags are not in place during submission and inspection of the competition apparel at the Games, then the apparel is not passed and cannot be worn. When submitted for approval to the IOC, via the USOC, we were informed that these safety tags must be removed. This is because the safety tags, by regulation, must also include the name of the manufacturer. Thus, it was ruled that there were too many logos on the apparel. This conflict should be easy to resolve with a little advanced discussion and understanding.

Another area where additional support would be welcomed from the USOC is team celebrations. Despite efforts during the pre-planning visits to Beijing, a suitable location, with "safe" food, was not secured. The USA House was a great alternative and we met with the USA House staff prior to opening. Fortunately, we had many opportunities for celebrations. Unfortunately, there were several occasions when the USA House was full and we could not take advantage of their hospitality. As an alternative, team members went to the Bank of America hospitality center. Unfortunately, not all of the coaches and staff had access to that facility. It would be helpful if the USOC had alternative locations that could be used as spill over … even if it was a special gathering at BNU.

Fencing did not use the two-way radios, but the cell phones provided to the Team were helpful. Pre-populating the phones with all of the numbers was EXCELLENT!!! This should be standard operating procedure going forward. I'm sure it took quite a bit of time, but it was an excellent service. If possible, for future Games, it would be good if the USOC provided text messaging on the Team Leader phones. Many times I would get a text message from an athlete and could not respond via text message.

In the Olympic Village, the wireless signal in the Coaches Lounge was very weak. In the future, consideration should be given to have wireless available throughout the USA Village housing, not just in the lounge areas. There are two drawbacks to this: (1) signal privacy by non-USA Olympians and (2) decreased interaction among all USA Team members. The privacy issue can be addressed through passwords. The social interaction can be addressed by providing very good athlete and coach lounges. However, the advantages of having wireless in all of the housing exceeds any disadvantages.

Perhaps the biggest concern in handling an Olympic Team is the ever-widening gap between Olympic athletes and Olympic coaches. Some examples of where coaches are not treated as equal Olympic Team members include:

- Apparel package
- Access to BOA hospitality
- Sundry bags
- Full payment for the commemorative leather jacket
- Not being allowed to march in Opening Ceremony
- No competition tickets available
- No podium outfit
- Limited access to USA House
- Sparse lounge area
- Access to spectator tickets

Adapting to changes is a key element for successful Olympic planning. As a partner, the USOC could be more informative during planning by providing more data on costs, credentials, travel, estimates and other data points to help the NGBs in their planning exercises. Other areas

MARIEL ZAGUNIS, GOLD MEDALIST OF THE WOMEN'S INDIVIDUAL SABRE, SHAKES HANDS WITH FORMER USA PRESIDENT GEORGE BUSH |
ADRIAN DENNIS/AFP/GETTY IMAGES

where USOC preparation could assist the NGBs include:

• Providing vouchers for excess and/or overweight luggage rather than the reimbursement process

• Online tracking of team movements while at the Games that are accessible by all areas that require that data

Fencing has a standing "special request" for an armory in the Olympic Village. This need should be noted in the USOC Games manual for the Olympic Village for all future Games. Identifying this facility before arrival in Beijing would have allowed us to bring necessary accessories for the armory (e.g., lights, fans, outlets, extension cords). In addition, knowing room assignments and allotments as far ahead as possible would also allow Fencing to accommodate plans and requests. Due to housing restrictions, the original plan for an armory could not be accommodated. However, creative thinking from USOC staff came up with good alternatives.

Medical services support provided to U.S. Fencing was excellent. Doug Rank, our assigned USOC trainer, was available for the team or staff 24/7. Whether support was needed for athletic injuries or medical health reasons, the entire medical staff was superb. Doug had worked with U.S. Fencing at World Championships, domestic events and World Cups. His experience with the sport and sport-related injuries is extensive. Also, his familiarity with the athletes and their needs was crucial. This combination of skills, along with his athletic training skills, made for a tremendous fit for our team needs.

The meals provided at the High Performance Training Center at Beijing Normal University (BNU) were outstanding. Those of us living in the Village were desirous of "night outs" when we could eat at BNU. Fencing's expectations, along with the discussions leading up to the Games, indicated that we would have practice space at BNU similar to a traditional gymnasium. Instead, when we arrived, we were told that we would be practicing in the hallways and foyers of the main gymnasium. There were several problems with this, including:

• Direct sunlight

• Poor artificial lighting

• Poor air-conditioning and lighting

• Subpar floor

• Inadequate room for footwork and general drills and exercises

• Fencing strips split on opposite sides of the building

Despite these drawbacks, the team was able to make use of the space and opportunities presented for successful practices. On a sidenote, once it was determined that we would be practicing in the hallways, more could have been done to create a training venue atmosphere for the athletes with banners, signage, and other "accessories."

U.S. Fencing did request video analysis and feedback/review; however, it did not materialize as expected. We thought that we would be able to download a tape of earlier sessions to review later in the day at the venue. Unfortunately, this was not available to us. For future Games planning, if this opportunity is available, it would be beneficial. Additionally, we requested copies of the competition for archival purposes. Ultimately, this was not available either. In the end, DVDs of the competition were not available to us from BNU, but BOCOG was offering DVDs of the competition at very reasonable prices (10RMB per DVD). Because of the way BOCOG divided the events and camera shots, there were 194 DVDs for complete coverage of the competition. However, this is important data for the evaluation of our performance and for preparation for the upcoming season.

The most important part of Olympic Team support is planning, planning, planning. The better prepared we are to support the Olympic Team, the better we will be able to handle and address the situations not foreseen in a calm and responsive manner. Familiarity with the team, country, facilities and USOC staff all go toward providing the foundation necessary to earn medals. The USFA began its planning with a series of conference calls and used action item registries, agendas, project schedules and many other planning tools to help guide our efforts. Our 2008 Beijing lessons learned session was held on August 19. 2012 planning should begin in earnest.

SADA JACOBSON OF THE UNITED STATES (R) FIGHTS SOFIYA VELIKAYA OF RUSSIA IN THE SABRE SEMIFINALS | *JED JACOBSOHN/GETTY IMAGES*

USA FIELD HOCKEY | *KATE REISINGER* – *NATIONAL TEAMS DIRECTOR*

The year 2008 marked USA Field Hockey's first time at the Olympic Games since 1996, when the USA hosted the Games in Atlanta. 2000 and 2004 saw near misses at Olympic qualifiers, but the ticket finally came through at the 2008 Olympic qualifier in Kazan, Russia.

Although I had been the Team Leader for the Women's National Team on many occasions, including World Cups and Pan Am Games, I had never managed an Olympic Team. While many of the preparations were similar to other events, I was in for a few surprises in Beijing.

The Olympic Team was selected at the National Championships for Women in Virginia Beach in June 2008. After the Team was announced, the entire field hockey community celebrated the Olympic Team at a dinner attended by over two thousand people. It was a perfect send-off for the team.

The team traveled to Germany and the Netherlands in July for its final competition prior to Beijing. Following the tour, the team returned to the Olympic Training Center in Chula Vista, Calif., for the final training phase before leaving for Team Processing on August 1, 2008.

Team Processing was organized perfectly by the USOC to allow our athletes to catch the Olympic "buzz" while gathering Olympic apparel and information about Beijing. The next day, August 2, the team made the final journey from the USA to China. United Airlines staff expertly guided our team through the airport, and the team loaded on the plane for the 12-hour flight to Beijing.

Upon arrival in Beijing, USOC staff met our team and made the arrival process very easy. We loaded into buses and headed to our home for the next three weeks, the Olympic Village. You could feel the team's excitement and anticipation as we entered the Village where, again, we were met by USOC staff who made the entry process effortless for our athletes.

The accommodations in the Village were of a very high standard and extremely comfortable. Once we settled into the Village it was time to remember why we were there—to compete at the Olympic Games. We embarked on a week of training at the Olympic hockey venues.

A few days later we took a short excursion to the Great Wall with a stay at a Chinese resort, Leisure City. There we were able to relax and release the pressures of the Olympic Games with a soak in traditional Chinese spas. This experience was just what the team needed and also allowed us to take in a bit of Chinese culture along the way.

Upon return to the Village, we played a practice match with Korea and finalized our preparations on the field. A few days later it was off to the Opening Ceremony, an event we were all looking forward to. The athletes took this opportunity to meet with other USA athletes and to just enjoy the experience.

August 10th finally arrived and we were ready for the Games to begin with our first match against Pan Am rival Argentina. Games with Japan, Germany, New Zealand, Great Britain and Spain followed, and we finished in eighth place. While the team was disappointed with the result, it was a certain improvement from our seed of 11th.

After taking time to reflect on the Games, I have realized that Olympic experience cannot be replicated. I had traveled to many high-profile field hockey events, but not an Olympics. While I pulled upon my experiences as a manager, nothing could fully prepare me for the Olympic environment. Now that I have experienced what it takes to be a successful Team Leader at the Olympics I can start preparing for London 2012.

EMILY NAYLOR #2 OF NEW ZEALAND AND LAUREN POWLEY #28 OF THE UNITED STATES COMPETE AGAINST EACH OTHER AND THEIR SHADOWS FOR A BALL | *CAMERON SPENCER/GETTY IMAGES*

USA GYMNASTICS – MEN'S | RON BRANT – NATIONAL TEAM COORDINATOR

Our U.S. Olympic Team Trials were held in June 2008, and the results showed the selection process was well thought out. The final team was selected and named following the conclusion of competition at the Olympic Trials.

Following the Trials there was a Senior National Team training camp. This camp was used to simulate the first week at the Olympic Games and included training days, team preliminary events and team final competition days. We hosted an intra-squad meet that was open to the public so fans could watch the Olympic team, and the gym was beyond full. This was also a time for team-building skills and to see how we would function as a team at the Games.

Our training facilities at the Olympics were excellent, and the only thing that changed from the test event was the color of the equipment. The facilities were close to the Athlete Village and provided everything needed to prepare.

The U.S. Men's Team overcame a couple of major obstacles to win the team bronze medal. Prior to the start of the Games, Paul Hamm was injured and dropped out. This was a major blow, as he was the 2004 gold medal winner in the all-around. Then, while in Beijing before competition began, Morgan Hamm, Paul's brother, was injured and had to withdraw. Morgan was an event finalist from the 2004 Olympic Games. Both Paul and Morgan were members of the 2004 silver medal team in Athens.

The team finished fifth in the team preliminary competition and surprised the media, who felt we would not qualify for the team finals. This was a rookie team with no one who had been on an Olympic Team before. No team from any country has ever medaled at the Olympics with a rookie team. With that said, the USA Men's Gymnastics Team won the bronze medal during the team finals and shocked the world and the media. It was a great accomplishment for this team.

With the team finals over, Jon Horton and Alex Artemev qualified for the all-around finals and competed well but unfortunately were unable to pick up any medals.

Alex Artemev qualified for the pommel horse finals and Jon Horton for the high bar finals. Both changed their routines to be more competitive in the finals. Alex missed his routine, but Jon nailed his and captured the silver medal on the high bar. This was only the fourth individual medal won by the USA men since 1984.

Overall the men's team hit 92 percent of their routines over the 10 days of competition and performed beyond expectation, especially after losing Paul and Morgan Hamm to injuries before the Games began. Overall it was a positive experience for the entire team.

JONATHAN HORTON OF TEAM USA COMPETES ON THE FIXED BAR DURING THE MEN'S TEAM FINAL | *KAZUHIRO NOGI/AFP/GETTY IMAGES*

USA GYMNASTICS – WOMEN'S | *KATHY KELLY – TEAM LEADER*

The U.S. Women's Gymnastic Team had their most successful Olympics since 1984, winning a total eight medals. For the first time, the USA won both the gold and silver medals in the all-around, and the team won its second straight team silver medal.

Our team selection process encompasses an Olympic Trials, which determines two athletes from competition results, and a final selection camp to choose the others.

When the Olympic competition got underway, we had two members of our team who were injured, preventing them from competing on all apparatuses. One of the injuries occurred immediately prior to competition in the warm-up gym, so the girls competed four-up, four-count during the qualifying round [eds. note: Normally, in qualifying rounds, a team fields five athletes on each event, but only four scores count. By fielding only four athletes, the pressure and stress on those four is substantially increased]. We had two uncharacteristic falls but still qualified for the team final in second place and had two advance to all-around finals and three athletes qualified for six spots in the Individual Event Finals.

In the team finals competition, the USA finished second to China, who only counted one fall. We competed very well in individual event finals, taking gold and silver medals in the all-around and balance beam, silver and bronze in the floor exercise, and a silver medal, after losing the gold medal tiebreaker with China, on uneven bars. Our only vault participant should have received at least the bronze medal, if not the silver. However, this was not the case due to controversial scoring of the gymnast who fell during finals but was still awarded the bronze. Overall, we are pleased with our medal count of eight—two gold, five silver and one bronze—which topped China's six (two gold and four bronze). Romania was third with two (one gold and one bronze). The only other time the U.S. women have won eight Olympic medals was in 1984.

This was a very cohesive team—both the athletes and the coaches. They dealt with injuries and personal disappointments without letting these affect overall team goals.

BRIDGET SLOAN OF THE UNITED STATES COMPETES IN THE FLOOR EXERCISE DURING THE ARTISTIC GYMNASTICS TEAM EVENT | *AL BELLO/GETTY IMAGES*

UNITED STATES' ALICIA SACRAMONE COMPETES ON THE VAULT DURING THE WOMEN'S TEAM FINAL | *LLUIS GENE/AFP/GETTY IMAGES*

USA GYMNASTICS – TRAMPOLINE | *ANN SIMS* – SR. PROGRAM DIRECTOR

Trampoline is an explosive sport that requires repetition and consistency to be successful. Athletes are bouncing 30 feet in the air to land on a 7' x 14' trampoline bed, so landing in the red box marked in the middle of the trampoline is imperative for optimum performance. This allows the athlete to bounce higher, giving them more time to perform each skill with fewer deductions and to perform the mandatory "kick-out" at 12:00 (highest point of the bounce). Athletes at the Olympic level must perform skills at a high degree of difficulty to be competitive. Athletes perform two 10-skill routines, a compulsory and an optional.

The 2008 USA Trampoline Team was selected using a trial system. There were four competitions (three national and one international) at which athletes earned points based on their final results. Erin Blanchard posted the most points in the women's division, and Chris Estrada was on top of the rankings in the men's.

Both athletes lived and trained at the U.S. Olympic Training Center (USOTC) in Colorado Springs in July. They took a short break following their selection. They had just returned from Switzerland and Japan prior to the final trial. There were no international competitions in July, so their training included competitions with the National Team members at the USOTC.

Chris Estrada finished 15th and Erin Blanchard finished 13th in Beijing. Both athletes said they were nervous and overwhelmed by the size of the audience. Our sport does not normally have large audiences. Both athletes performed their planned routines, but neither of them performed at their highest level. While it wasn't what we hoped for, both athletes placed higher at the Games than they did to qualify.

We received great support from USA Gymnastics and the U.S. Olympic Committee during our preparation for the Games and during the Games themselves.

RUSSIA'S EVGENIYA KANAEVA COMPETES IN THE INDIVIDUAL ALL-AROUND FINAL OF THE RHYTHMIC GYMNASTICS | *FRANCK FIFE/AFP/GETTY IMAGES*

USA JUDO | *LEE WHITE* – *TEAM LEADER*

Judo is an individual sport; it is an extremely physical and combat sport. Because divisions are weight based, athletes need to maintain their weight as well as maintain the requisite high level of physical fitness. Muscle and respiratory endurance are important requisites for success in this sport.

The members of the 2008 Olympic Games judo team were chosen at trials held in June 2008. The top eight competitors in each weight class competed for the single slot available on the team. While I think this process works in terms of selecting the best athletes, I suggest adjusting two parts of the procedure. First, we should hold the trials earlier in the year in order to take advantage of team training time. With the team together longer, we can coordinate more training time overseas where we will face opponents we are likely to see in the Olympic Games. Second, we should reduce the number of athletes competing for the slot to five; eight is too many.

After the trials, the team attended two camps and events in Europe. Unfortunately, the cost of overseas training is quite expensive. If we select our team earlier, some of these costs will be relieved. There was a test event held in Beijing, but we had more pressing budget priorities so did not attend. In the future, if funds are available, I believe attending the test event would be useful in giving us a feel for the venues to be used and the logistics needed to make the Games successful for our athletes.

The 2008 Olympic Games was the stage for some great performances by the U.S. Judo Team. Several athletes continued to be consistent in their ability to be competitive at this highest level. Three athletes placed ninth, narrowly missing medal contention. The matches of Taylor Takata, Travis Stevens and Daniel McCormick were impressive as they fought their way through World Cup medalists and dealt out upsets as they pursued the Olympic podium. We look forward to their continued success in the upcoming years. Other members of the team fought well and competitively but were unsuccessful in their efforts to medal at these Olympic Games. Ronda Rousey, however, was driven and impressive in the 70kg division. Coming in to this event as a silver medalist at the World Championships, Rousey fought confidently and consistently, making her way to the bronze medal stand. She is the third American woman to bring home an Olympic medal in judo.

Accreditation is an ongoing issue at all Olympic Games. We appreciated the effort and communication from USOC staff. Unfortunately, USA Judo was cut on Ao accreditation, which placed extra stress on the staff that did receive accreditation, but this cut was communicated early, so we had time to address it. In the future, we will work with

BRIAN OLSON OF THE USA COMPETES AGAINST DIEGO ROSATI OF ARGENTINA | *MIKE HEWITT/GETTY IMAGES*

USOC to try to credential the judo team as two teams: one male, the other female. This would give us an adequate number of credentials for staff and coaches.

Travel and transportation can be very complicated. We found it very expensive to arrange travel for our athletes' training partners. Ground transportation, once we landed in Beijing, was handled professionally and responsively. The USOC-provided cell phones worked well and were indispensible in helping us stay in touch with our coaches, staff and athletes. It was also very helpful to have workstations with Internet access in the coaches' lounge, although we could have used a few more in order to avoid bottlenecks.

Our medical staff consisted of Dr. Robert Hines, an orthopedic surgeon, and Brent Hamula, an athletic trainer. They are the best in the business and our team was very impressed with their support and their skills.

The biggest challenge that USA Judo faced for these Games was planning a budget to cover all delegation needs appropriately. We would have made different decisions if we had a better idea of the delegation needs as it related to family members, personal coaches, etc.

The USOC support and assistance was invaluable. Obviously everyone on the USOC staff has a tremendous amount of experience and this helped us. On behalf of our board of directors, athletes and membership in general, we thank all of the staff members of the USOC for their guidance and hard work.

HIROAKI HIRAOKA (L) OF JAPAN COMPETES AGAINST TARAJE WILLIAMS-MURRAY OF THE UNITED STATES | *EZRA SHAW/GETTY IMAGES*

USA MODERN PENTATHLON | SCOTT NOVACK – MANAGER OF HIGH PERFORMANCE

The 2008 United States Olympic Team for Modern Pentathlon was represented by two women and two men and saw many "firsts" accomplished. The men competed on August 21 and the women on August 22. Sheila Taormina made Olympic history at the 2008 Olympic Games in Beijing, China, by becoming the first woman ever to compete at the Olympic Games in three different sports (modern pentathlon, triathlon, and swimming). She was joined by 16-year-old Margaux Isaksen on the women's side. Eli Bremer and Sam Sacksen represented the U.S. on the men's side.

Modern Pentathlon is a multi-discipline sport that has many variables. For an athlete to be in a position to qualify for the Olympic Games, they need to be world-class runners and swimmers. To be successful and have a chance of medaling, an athlete needs to use their running and swimming skills to create a strong base score, then have a solid shoot (180 or above) and fence (over 50%). If they do this, they can position themselves to make a run at a medal. The only wild card is the riding portion, which is a random draw of a horse, with only a 20-minute warm-up before the ride.

The following are the disciplines and their specifics: Shooting—air pistol, 20 shots at 10 meters; Fencing—one-touch epee, round-robin format; Swimming—200 meters freestyle; Riding—equestrian show jumping, 12 jumps between three to four feet; and Running—3,000 meters with a staggered start based upon points from the four previous scores. The first athlete to cross the finish line wins the competition.

With this understood, during the two-year lead up we implemented a number of performance enhancement initiatives and accomplished many firsts. The following is a breakdown per discipline:

Shooting—This discipline proved to be the biggest challenge for some athletes. In the spring of 2007, we brought in a shooting specialist to provide a week-long training seminar on shooting systems and approaches to the athletes and the coaches. Additional performance measures that we used included acquiring specialized gun cases to protect the guns during travel. One athlete indicated that he scored low in the World Championships because his sights were out of line due to the lack of a container that provided adequate protection. Working with USA Shooting personnel, we purchased six containers (five small to fit each air pistol and one big for combined shipping). Singapore was identified as being the best training location before the Olympic competition because of the the shooting facilities and logistics of the air pistols made available. Through connections with the Singapore Sports Council and site visits by the Taekwondo Team Leader, Meredith Miller, and Taekwondo Olympic Coach, Jean Lopez,

Singapore was identied as the best staging location. The Singapore Sports Council secured the Singapore Shooting Club for the athletes to train for 10 days before the Olympic competition. This facility consisted of two indoor shooting ranges. Other cities and countries were explored and planned for, but Singapore provided the best overall support and facilities.

Fencing—If an athlete has a strong fencing performance in the Olympic Games, they have the opportunity to place themselves in a position to medal. Therefore, starting in the winter of 2007, fencing footage in the form of video, was taken at different World Cup competitions and World Championships through the 2008 competition season.

The footage was used in two ways: (1) individual athlete video review and (2) scouting analysis. The individual athlete video review consisted of meetings between the athlete and their coach. The athlete would review their own fencing technique from past competitions and discuss this with their coach. The purpose was for the athlete and coach to conduct an analysis and discuss technique and strategy and identify what the athlete needs to work on.

The scouting analysis was a comprehensive scouting process that focused on the athletes and countries qualified and nominated to the 2008 Beijing Olympic Games. The video footage, through the Dartfish system, was broken down by athlete and country and burned to a DVD. Then a three-ring binder was created that had scouting sheets and tabs for each country. The performance goals of this process were to:

—Enable athlete and coach to go through the critical thinking and analysis process with the intent to create a plan for future competitions with strategies and tactics.

—Assist in bridging the communication and understanding gap between the athlete and coaches by sharing their analysis and creating an athlete profile. This way, in competition the communication and understanding of athlete and coach has already been established and can then be implemented to gain touches.

—Be as competitive as possible and gain as many touches in the Olympic fencing competition with the goal of putting each athlete in a position to medal.

—Lastly, from 2007 until the Beijing Olympic Games, athletes from Russia, Egypt, Poland, Germany and other European countries were brought in for camps so that they could train (fence) with the USA athletes. This was due to the lack of fencing training partners at the OTC in Colorado.

Swimming—In the lead up to the games, Sheila Taormina had her own swimming program, as she is an Olympic gold medalist in swimming.

The other USA Olympic female athlete was Margaux Isaksen, age 16, who was still learning swimming technique but is reducing her swim times regularly. She trained with the Olympic head coach Janusz Peciak.

On the men's side, Eli Bremer came from a collegiate swimming background and swam his own program. Sam Sacksen trained under the Olympic head coach, with Margaux. Genadijus Sokolovas, a USA Swimming employee, was contracted to assist with the swimming discipline. He tested the athletes and provided day-to-day training advice for the training sessions.

Riding—The riding discipline is the most unpredictable of the five disciplines. There is a pool of horses, and based upon the athletes' rank in the competition, a random draw is made to select which horse will be ridden by which athlete. The athlete then has a 20-minute warm-up on the horse before riding in competition.

One of the first processes we implemented was to film the Jury Ride that would take place the day before competition. This is where the horses used in competition are tested and approved by the Riding Jury. Early in 2007, we started filming the Jury Ride at each World Cup competition and World Championship. In addition to filming the Jury Ride, the Riding Coach, Michael Cintas, also provided a detailed analysis of each horse. Then on competition day after the draw, the athlete would sit with Michael Cintas, watch the video and review the analysis of that horse.

This process was repeated for two years at each competition, including the 2007 Pan American Games and 2008 World Championships. This process evolved to where the coach would provide a verbal analysis on film during the Jury Ride. So during the Jury Ride competition review the day of competition, the athlete had the option to listen to the analysis with earphones while watching the video footage and having written notes for additional reference.

In regards to budget, our biggest expense was competition expenses. With a larger budget I would fully support the "entire" team (four males and four females) instead of just half (two males and two females). Two of the four Olympic athletes did not have their competition expenses covered during the 2007 and 2008 competition season. A larger budget could have provided full funding for athletes to cover their competition expenses.

I attended all of the Team Leadership meetings going back to June 2005, when I was still working with USA Taekwondo. The roundtables were very valuable, as they provided the one-on-one dialogue with USOC staff that would be responsible during the games. In my opinion, the roundtables should take precedent over other things, like venue tours, when time is a problem.

The only USOC Key Decision Makers meeting that I attended was in the spring of 2006, while I was still working with USA Taekwondo. I was told that the same information would be presented in the spring and fall sessions. However, I found that after each trip to Asia, and specifically Beijing, something new was always gleaned and implemented into planning. So a follow-up trip in the fall of 2006 would have been beneficial, as I did not return to Beijing until the spring of 2007, almost a full year after the first trip. The Olympic Test Event was the 2007 World Cup final, which was held in Beijing in September 2007. This was a successful event, providing details about the venues, horses and transportation. This was the second to last time I was in Beijing prior to the start of the games.

The Modern Pentathlon Olympic selection process was developed and run by the international federation, the Union Internationale Pentathlon Moderne (UIPM). Unfortunately, communication about the Olympic selection process was not as thorough as it should have been and resulted in an American Arbitration Association (AAA) hearing over athlete selection. We had six athletes qualify for four spots, the only country to do so for both genders, and used our criteria to select the top two male and female athletes. For 2012, if the UIPM stays with the same qualification process, only minor terminology changes would be made. If, for 2012, the UIPM changes the selection process, this will require a full understanding of that process and new procedures to reflect the process. This should start earlier rather than later and have complete understanding as to what the UIPM is going to do.

Our team trained year round because of the competition schedule. The Modern Pentathlon Olympic Plan consisted of a riding camp in mid-July 2008, going to Beijing for the Opening Ceremony, then going to a staging

410

camp in Singapore and returning to Beijing six days in advance of our competition. This was considered by the Modern Pentathlon Olympic head coach as the "best" preparation they have ever had for the Olympic Games. Nothing would be changed, as the sequencing of dates and locations was perfect. In Beijing, all of the training, except shooting, was done at Beijing Normal University (BNU). Shooting took place at another venue provided by the organizing committee (BOCOG) and was adequate.

The men's Olympic competition was held on August 21, and Eli Bremer and Sam Sacksen competed. In shooting, Sam was 23rd, shooting a 178, and Eli was 34th with a 165. In fencing, both Sam and Eli fenced just under .500 (50 percent). After shooting and fencing, Sam was in 28th and Eli was 35th place. Eli's goal was to swim below 2:00. He swam a 2:03 and sat in 34th after the swim. Sam had a strong swim but dropped to 30th.

After using the horse scouting analysis and solid coaching in the warm-up, both Sam and Eli had good rides that moved them up the ranking into 15th and 25th, respectively. In the final discipline, the run, Sam finished 18th, dropping three places, and Eli finished 21st, climbing four places. In all, these were strong performances, given the struggles in fencing and shooting.

Sam Sacksen scored 1,112 points in the running portion of modern pentathlon to end with a total of 5,280 points, good for 18th place in the final standings. Eli Bremer was seventh in the run for 1,164 points, giving him 5,204 points and 23rd overall. The gold medal went to Andrey Moiseev of Russia with 5,632 points. The silver was claimed by Edvinas Krungolcas of Lithuania with 5,548, while Andrejus Zadneprovskis of Lithuania won the bronze medal with a score of 5,524.

The women's competition was held the following day on August 22, with Sheila Taormina and Margaux Isaksen competing. In shooting, Sheila shot a 173, which was a good score considering that she is new to the sport. Margaux shot a 171. Despite shooting below 180, both Sheila and Margaux were still in medal contention. It was fencing that knocked them out of contention. Sheila started off with two victories, then went on to lose her next 25 bouts. Sheila finished with four victories and 31 defeats. Margaux, too, started off strong, winning nine in a row, but then dropped 11 in a row. Margaux finished with 15 victories and 20 defeats. After the fence, both USA women were in the lower bottom half of the rankings, with Margaux 28th and Sheila 36th. From there, Sheila went on to swim an Olympic Modern Pentathlon record of 2:08, beating the old record by seven seconds. Margaux did not swim as well, swimming a 2:20.

Due to the riding problems in the men's competition, the UIPM made some minor adjustments to the riding competition for the women. The jumps were lowered and the riding consisted of three rounds instead of two rounds, due to the unavailability of horses that were injured during the men's competition. This meant that there were fewer horses and that a horse would be ridden three times instead of two. Knowing and understanding the struggles from the day before, the USA coaches spent a lot of time with Sheila and Margaux, going through how each horse should be ridden. Margaux rode first and had only a couple of knock-downs. Sheila had one of three perfect rides and had the fastest time; thus, she won the riding portion of the competition. This was also Olympic history for Sheila, as no female athlete had ever before won two disciplines in the same Olympic Games.

In the run, Sheila Taormina picked up 1,220 points and ended the competition with 5,304 points, which placed her 19th. Margaux Isaksen was 21st with 5,292 points, after adding 1,160 in the run. Lena Schoneborn of Germany won Olympic gold in the Women's Modern Pentathlon with 5,792 points. Heather Fell of Britain got the silver after

finishing third in swimming and fifth in running with 5,752 points. The bronze went to Victoria Tereshuk of Ukraine, who was fifth in swimming and fencing and finished strong with a second-place finish in running and 5,672 points.

Our staff used transferrable credentials, which was explained to me in a timely manner so that I could address the situation with our staff. The day of the activation of the credentials, I was provided with detailed instructions and was met at the accreditation center to insure a smooth process. I suggest the USOC continue to "over-communicate" and provide rationalale for decision making in the accreditation process so this can be relayed to team members who are affected by those decisions. This would help with establishing expectations and planning. Lastly, because the credential has to be activated to reside in the Olympic Village, I would suggest that if athletes of that team are staying in the Village, there be at least one staff member activated.

Regarding air travel, we made one change when our riding camp was rescheduled to take place earlier in July 2008 than originally planned. The changes were made, and we were able to conduct the camp and have the team in Beijing for the flag bearer elections. The process to get the air pistols in and out of the country was long but successful.

NIKE provided our competition uniforms for running, swimming and shooting, as well as fencing shoes and riding boots. However for fencing uniforms and riding uniforms we had to outsource. These two pieces were approved based on what the U.S. Equestrian Federation and U.S. Fencing Association had submitted. These were all submitted in a timely manner. The only suggestion I would make is to provide a list of the apparel items and the quantities to Team Leaders so these can be shared with team members. During the roundtables we were shown what we would get, but not quantities and specific types. This helps with packing and what to bring and not to bring. In our case, it would have been nice to know if we would be getting a long-sleeve t-shirt, or a dry fit for the indoor session of shooting where it would be chilly. We did not know and told our guys to bring their own shirts to play it safe.

Our team arrived into Beijing, then left for Singapore and returned to Beijing for competition. Also, our staff was split between BNU and the Village. Everything went smoothly and was arranged and communicated. We did have one athlete return to Beijing from Singpore earlier than expected due to injury.

Cell phones were the best method to communicate, with our staff being split between BNU and the Village. Also, the printer and wireless network met our team needs. We used the printer and wireless network to print the Jury Ride scouting notes that allowed for an easy-to-follow analysis of specific horses.

Shipping was one of the biggest logistical challenges we faced. We had to ship our air pistols, pellets and food items (over 72 items weighing over 500 kg.) to Singapore, then bring the air pistols to Beijing and back to the United States. Additionally, we brought saddles for the riding portion and stored these at BNU. We used Schenker for the shipment to Singapore. In the end the process worked smoothly. Everyone involved in this process did a great job. Once the issues were identified, we strategized to come up with solutions. An example of this was the guns clearing customs. The Singapore Sports Council explained that they could not guarantee the guns would clear customs in the time needed. Thus we issued a letter from the USOC explaining the situation and urgency, and this was accepted. The guns cleared customs and the athletes and coaches were never impacted. This was our most difficult challenge and had the largest ramification if it did not work. In the end, the shipments arrived in Singapore without any issues.

All of our team's needs were met by the services provided at BNU. The training center concept and the use of BNU was a huge benefit and provided the support that made the difference in performance. Please continue to implement this program for future Olympic Games, as this is an area where we have an advantage over other countries.

In the Village, it was good to have the continuity of Village staff from the Pan American Games to the Olympic Games. There were two changes that were approved: (1) our return date from Singapore back into Beijing was moved forward two days, from August 18 to August 16 (the USOC indicated that the Village could accommodate the changes), and (2) we had an injured male athlete who returned from Singapore three days earlier than planned. He was already checked into the Village, but his dates were adjusted and we needed logistical support. The Village staff were accommodating and provided for our needs.

The only thing that I thought would have made things smoother was having at least one staff member staying in the Village with the athletes to serve as the central point of contact with daily issues. As it was, the athletes were in the Village and the staff were at BNU. This caused minor communication issues. In the future the USOC might consider a policy that if any athletes stay in the Village there should be at least one staff member to serve as that point of contact.

Diana Palmer was our assigned athletic trainer. Diana had worked with our team at the 2007 Pan American Games and the 2008 World Championships. She did an outstanding job supporting the team. She was familiar with our athletes, so there was not much of a learning curve.

We did have one issue come up regarding medical support at our training camp in Singapore. We did not have any medical support in Singapore. One athlete was injured during a riding training session. He was diagnosed by Singapore medical officials and told they could not perform aggressive treatment. Margie Hunt, USOC Medical Services

Director, spoke with the Singapore officials and agreed with their assessment. The athlete was sent back to Beijing for further medical treatment by USOC medical staff. The use of the cell phones was very critical. This allowed communication in Singapore back to Beijing and with the Singapore medical officials.

For team processing we had one change that was accepted. We moved our arrival date into team processing by a week. This change then had all but one team member get processed on the same day. Because the athletes needed to attend the Olympic Ambassador Program, all team members departed together, and we arrived in time for the flag bearer meeting. The only suggestion would be to ensure the same message being delivered in the team orientation speech. The first day's presenter gave very detailed and important information, while the presenter on the second day did not relay the same information. If the Team Leader did not catch this, some of the important details could be missed by the athletes. Team processing was very smooth and a great way to start the Olympic trip.

The Olympic plan was deemed a success, even though the performances did not reflect this. The biggest lesson learned was the importance of strong coaching and funding through the entire quad. These are the basis for everything: training programs, team cohesion, respect and professionalism.

SHEILA TAORMINA OF THE UNITED STATES TAKES ON QIAN CHEN OF CHINA IN THE MODERN PENTATHLON | *EZRA SHAW/GETTY IMAGES*

USROWING | ELPI PAGITSAS

– TEAM LEADER & PROGRAMS MANAGER

The rowing competition of the 2008 Olympic Games took place August 9–17 at the Shunyi Olympic Rowing-Canoeing Park in Shunyi, China. USRowing placed seven boats in the A Final, and produced three Olympic medals for Team USA: gold (W8+), silver (W1x) and bronze (M8+), a marked improvement over the 2004 Olympic Games. Several factors and events played key roles in the preparation leading up to the Games and the overall success of the trip.

Prior to the Games, the USOC organized several Team Leadership meetings designed to assist programs' staff in the Olympic planning process. These meetings became more valuable as the Olympic Games and the Olympic Test Event drew nearer. The Olympic Test Event for rowing was the 2007 FISA Junior World Championships. Given that the trip would be strong indicator as to what obstacles may lay ahead at the Olympic Games, I attended the event as Team Leader and made an effort to record team challenges. Attending the Test Event one year before the Games not only helped program staff identify potential obstacles for the Games, but it also gave staff a full year to find solutions to those obstacles.

The 2008 Olympic Team selection procedures consisted of three opportunities for athletes to earn a seat on the Olympic Team. These opportunities consisted of two team trials and a selection camp. The 2008 selection procedure's structure was sound and resulted in the fastest U.S. crews competing at the Olympic Games.

Following the team selection, roughly thirty elite athletes participated internationally in the World Cup circuit, allowing them to compete against those who would be in Beijing a few months later. They were able to gauge their speed and see how they performed against their competition. The second World Cup competition held in Lucerne, Switzerland, proved to be great success for the United States as the competing crews produced six medals, two of which were gold. Based on their performance, the U.S. crews confirmed and validated their speed against the competitors they would meet two months later in Beijing.

Given the climate during the summer months in Princeton, NJ, coaching and program staff chose not to train in an alternate location prior to departure for China. The majority of the team departed Newark International Airport on July 25 and flew directly to San Jose, Calif., for team processing. The USOC worked with the team's travel parameters throughout the entire process, making it easy to organize the trip. As a result, the USOC created an itinerary that not only worked for the athletes but also with the USOC team processing schedule. At team processing, athletes were given their BOCOG accreditation, team gear package and additional information regarding their trip to China. USOC staff arranged for rowers to train on-site in order to maintain their training regimen.

The flight to Beijing was long and keeping the athletes hydrated was a challenge; however, the USOC assisted in providing water to the team at the arrivals hall. Since the Olympic rowing venue was located 45 miles northeast of Beijing and the Athlete Village, USRowing opted to arrange separate outside accommodations through a private vendor in order to minimize athlete transit time to and from the venue. The King and Queen Shunyi Hotel was located just two miles from the rowing venue and proved to be a great investment. Many crews opted to train twice a day, which would have translated into a six-hour daily commute had the team stayed in the Athlete Village. The decision to stay at outside housing minimized the athletes' daily commute to an average of fifteen minutes a day.

Before competition began, the team trained on-site for 12 days, where the main focus was to acclimatize and rest. The United States had the advantage of being one of the only teams on site in Shunyi when the venue opened on July 27, as many other federations opted to train privately in other parts of Asia.

The Opening Ceremony, held on August 8, 2008. marked the official commencement of the Olympic Games, and the rowing team celebrated by watching the ceremonies in their team-issued marching apparel in the private USRowing dining room. Many athletes' first day of competition began the next morning and few made it to the end of the program.

Medical staff consisted of Kristine Karlson and Lisa Hass. Both had previous experience with rowing at an elite level and had a strong understanding of team operation while in competition, which in turn made it easier to address athlete needs in a timely manner.

An area of concern for programs' staff at every international competition is safety, and the Olympic Games are no exception. Despite being an hour's drive from the secure Athlete Village, the USOC was responsive to rowing's security needs and communicated with program staff on a regular basis regarding daily team movements. USOC security staff made it a point to visit the Shunyi Park several times during the competition. Post-competition the rowing team moved to the Athlete Village for the final days of the Olympic Games before returning to the United States.

Through careful long-term planning, the U.S. Olympic Rowing Team had a successful performance at the 2008 Olympic Games. Logistics ran fluidly and many positive relationships developed throughout the entire planning process. Three Olympic medals would not have been obtained without the continued support of the USOC, the USRowing coaching staff and the tenacity of the USRowing athletes.

We have a long history of using a winner-take-all, domestic selection trials. However, over the last two Games, we have realized that our system needs a fresh look, which we are doing now for 2012. Our Olympic Sailing Committee will be making some initial decisions on the 2012 selection in the near future.

We made the decision to hold all of our selection events nearly 10 months prior to the Games, and we believe this was good. We will almost certainly repeat this for 2012. Our athletes commented on the positives of having plenty of time to rest and peak again for the Games.

Our athletes train globally year round. We spent a great deal of time in Qingdao, the site of the 2008 Olympic Games, and in most cases, I felt like we had the right amount of training. In general, however, the performance aspects of our team are managed by our High Performance Director.

We had full teams at both Olympic Test Events. Sailing has two official test events each quad, and these have become major events on our calendar. We treat them as important competitions for our team, for both performance and team-building.

The facilities at these Games were outstanding, and we are unlikely to see anything like this again in the near future. The Chinese outdid themselves from a facility standpoint.

Our team brought back two medals, which we were proud of, but we were not satisfied with our results overall. We had a young team, with 14 of 18 being first-timers and an average age well under 30. We were close to a third medal and could have won a fourth medal. We have outlined our issues in our High Performance Plan and will be looking for solutions to capture more medals over the next few years. We are also looking at the events where we think we can compete in 2012 and are already making significant plans to maximize performances over the next four years.

We have a unique program leadership structure in sailing. Our Olympic Director, our High Performance Director and myself, Chairman of the Sailing Committee, function as a true team, covering all functions of program leadership. We have total trust and open dialogue among the three of us; we make decisions individually when necessary and collectively most of the time. Our Olympic Director managed our Games budget, as well as our overall budget, and I knew my budget limitations in Qingdao as the Team Leader. I was able to make decisions within the framework of our budget, but the three of us discussed any budget items as needed, which was frequently.

We attended both USOC Team Leadership meetings. Our Olympic Director attended the meeting in October and then I attended the one in March. The meeting in October was at just the right time to get issues out on the table. It was after our Test Event, so issues were fresh in our minds, but it was also well enough in advance of the Games that there was time to deal with issues.

Our Olympic Director attended the USOC Key Decision Maker meeting in the spring, but we did not attend the one in the fall since we had a test event and had already seen what we needed to. It was incredibly valuable to have these meetings at the site of the Games. It gave us another opportunity to be on-site at our venues, to meet with key contacts and to learn about the culture. We would recommend maximizing the meeting time within these meetings.

We had a good working relationship with our accreditation contact with the USOC. Sailing was particularly interested in ensuring the USOC fully understood our credential needs for 2008 and didn't just copy what was done in the past. As a result, the USOC really took the time to understand our needs and worked tirelessly to help us get what we needed. It was a huge help to have the credential process somewhat sorted out by January. The earlier the better, and the USOC worked really hard to meet their goal of starting accreditation at the beginning of the year. Even though we knew it wasn't final, it was a huge help to have some idea early. It was critical to have a few extra credentials given since we were at a satellite venue. This will be a key factor again for the 2012 Games.

The day pass process in Qingdao worked extremely well and gave all teams a little extra support without extra full credentials. This was critical, and we ask the USOC to ask the IOC for the same or a similar process for Weymouth. Overall, we thought the credentialing process was 100 times better than the previous quad.

Organizing travel is always a hurdle. Despite our best efforts to get this done early, we didn't quite meet our goal. As soon as we had our plans finalized, the USOC delivered quickly so we could get it checked off

JOHNNY LOVELL (REAR) AND CHARLIE OGLETREE OF THE UNITED STATES OF AMERICA COMPETE IN THE TORNADO CLASS RACE |
CLIVE MASON/GETTY IMAGES

the list. Our travel dates were perfect, exactly what we wanted. When changes were needed, we were almost always able to make them through the USOC. We always have a tremendous amount of baggage, and in most cases, everything arrived safely and was handled perfectly this time around.

We ended up booking the Air China piece to Qingdao through the United Olympic Travel Desk, which made it easier but was very expensive as well. This is a note for 2012 to start planning earlier regarding air travel to keep the cost down. We had lots of travel changes toward the end of the Games, and they were all handled beautifully and easily and for a reasonable fee.

Apparel was an easy process that worked out well for us. This year, we made team processing mandatory for all athletes and optional for paid staff. There were no objections, as we were able to communicate this early enough for athletes to plan accordingly. We scheduled a team send-off party in San Francisco in conjunction with team processing, which was a tremendous success. We will plan to do the same thing for 2012. I felt that holding team processing in the host country worked better than holding it in the U.S. and would recommend that the USOC look for options to repeat that for 2012.

In regards to ground transportation, we initially requested more vehicles through the USOC based on the uncertainty of what would be allocated, but we ended up with the right combination. Our sport required vehicles with trailer hitches, but we understand the limitations in China for this. We had two cars, with drivers available to us nearly at all times, and that was helpful, considering so many of our team members were staying outside the Village. The whole system worked well.

Due to our off-site location, we found the Internet connection to be extremely expensive, so we purchased just one connection. This caused our team to huddle into one room for Internet use. The technology support for video downloading through the USOC was incredibly helpful and successful. If at all possible, we would strongly request something similar for 2012. Our sport, like many sports, is relying more and more on video analysis for coaching.

Sailing had an arbitration hearing for the women's windsurfing discipline. Following Sailing's grievance proceedings, it went to arbitration, where the issue was dismissed before USA Sailing even had a chance to present, based on the merits of the case. However, the legal costs to handle this were outrageous and an unforeseen budget item.

Sailing manages its own logistics regarding the shipping of boats and equipment. We are finding that this element is increasingly more expensive from year to year, so budgeting for all of the logistics needs to increase accordingly. We found it beneficial that the USOC handled food and medical shipments into Beijing and then shuttled them to Qingdao. We would like to repeat this for Weymouth in 2012.

Since the sailing events were not held in Beijing, we did not utilize any of the NGB Outside Housing provided by the USOC but organized our own housing in Qingdao. We had a delegation of over 60 people who traveled to Qingdao to support our athletes. All of the logistics, arrangements, planning and execution were handled by the staff at USA Sailing. We anticipate having to manage this for ourselves again in 2012, unless the USOC is planning something different for Sailing.

We ended up not having enough space in the Qingdao Village to meet all of our needs. There were enough sleeping rooms, but we really needed extra office space. The space that we did have worked, but there was never any privacy, and multiple functions were happening on top of each other. For 2012, we need to ensure LOCOG allocates more space designated as office space.

BENJAMIN BARGER OF THE UNITED STATES OF AMERICA COMPETES IN THE MEN'S RS:X CLASS RACE HELD AT THE QINGDAO OLYMPIC SAILING CENTER | *CLIVE MASON/GETTY IMAGES*

Our medical staff consisted of Scott Weiss and Dr. Amy Myers. Scott joined Sailing as the assigned trainer during the 2003 Pan American Games. Since then, we have brought him into our physical therapists/trainer team, and he has traveled extensively with our team, including two Olympic Games. Having this relationship is key to the success of our team. Dr. Amy Myers was assigned to us by the USOC as we requested a medical doctor for our team in Qingdao. Having a medical doctor provided great peace of mind, and we would love to have her as part of our team again in 2012.

We used a guest pass every day for an additional physical therapist/trainer, Mark Kenna. Having both Mark and Scott there was critical. They have been part of our team for a long time now, they work well together, and having two physical therapists for an 18-person team is important.

The ticketing for these Games was very much a challenge. We were given information quite late in the process, and our ticket allocation, when it finally came, was virtually useless to us, and we couldn't sell the tickets. We had planned to offer tickets to some of our highest donors who had expressed an interest in going to the Games. The allocation we ended up getting was not anything close to what we had requested. Instead of consecutive days of events, we got things all over the place, which was not going to work for the intended recipients. It was a disappointment to our athletes that they were not given two tickets per competition day for their personal use. We ended up working out something on-site that was acceptable to most of the athletes and their families.

This was a great learning experience for me personally, and I believe overall things went well for our team. In my role as Chairman, I worked hard at getting to know our athletes over the last four years, and I think this helped us at the Games. I had strong relationships with many of them, and it allowed me to fit in as a member of the team.

At one point, we considered asking USOC to allow our head coach to also serve as Team Leader. This would have been a mistake. Those two roles should be kept separate. There is too much to do for one person to play both roles.

The Team Leader role is about a lot of things, and one of them is relationships. Knowing whom to call and when is critical to doing the job well. I felt well supported by everyone around me, which allowed me to play an active role with our team. It is also important to know that we divided and conquered some of the Team Leader duties between our Olympic Director, our office staff and myself. Our Olympic Director organized much of the logistical preparation from our office, and this allowed me to play a mentoring, performance-oriented role as Team Leader at the Games. This was a conscious decision on our part, and we think it enhanced the experience for our team.

USA SHOOTING | DWAYNE WEGER

– TEAM LEADER

We selected our Olympic Team six months prior to the Olympic Games. I think our sport has the fairest selection process there is. An athlete must win their way onto the team during the trials. We do not always have exactly who we would like to have on the team, but I can't see a better way of selecting the team.

Following the selection of our team, we went to World Cup and had our National Championships. Our Olympians did well in both. I would not change a thing in this regard.

During the off-season our athletes train in the U.S. I would like to see more camps during this time. Another issue that needs to be evaluated is the fact that our athletes are not always with our Olympic coaches because the athletes are scattered throughout the United States. Having more camps or clinics would allow the coaches more hands-on time with the athletes and also help to promote team unity.

We attended a World Cup in Beijing prior to the Games that served as the Olympic Test Event. The event was very beneficial because our shooters became familiar with the ranges before the Games.

During the Games, rifle and pistol had pre-determined training times, so their training went well. Shotgun had a sign-up sheet that was full before we even arrived. I had a meeting with BOCOG and an ISSF official to voice my concerns about the lack of shotgun training. At the end of the meeting, we were given the training that we needed. Also, the unofficial training was pre-squaded for shotgun from that point forward.

Out of 15 events we won six medals. We won two gold, two silver and two bronze. We had five fourth-place finishes and two fifth-place finishes, doubling our prior record for medal count. Overall we had a tremendous Olympic Games. All of the medalists had outstanding performances. Of particular note was Jason Turner's medal in 10M pistol. Our pistol team was not expected to make the finals in any event, yet we won a bronze and had a fourth-place and fifth-place finish as well. Matt Emmons was disappointed with his performance in 3-position. He had the gold all but sewn up going in to the final shot of the competition. He accidentally discharged his gun before he was ready on the last shot, which moved him down to fourth.

We had an Olympic budget in place and our primary expenses were the pre-Olympic camp in Korea and our additional staff.

Our accreditation process went really smoothly. We very much appreciated the USOC giving us an extra P credential, as that credential was instrumental in our success. Additionally, we had a late Team Leader change, and that was handled well by the USOC.

Air travel worked really well for us and we had no major issues. Having the United representative on-site helped make the system run smoothly. We had two athletes that had to return earlier than expected. Our representative made the changes and worked out all of the details quickly and efficiently.

For the most part, apparel distribution went well, but I felt that the staff clothing was too limited. I don't think the staff should get everything that the athletes do, but they should definitely get more than what was provided. More shorts would have been nice, as it was extremely hot in Beijing. Team processing flowed perfectly, and I felt that those working in this area were true professionals.

Our team did not require any additional ground transportation and just utilized what was already in place.

From an information technology standpoint everything worked pretty well. Having the cell phones was great and having the numbers pre-programmed in the phones was a nice addition. I would suggest that this continue as is. As far as the wireless Internet, I would suggest making it available in the individual Village rooms, if possible.

Our Athlete Village experience was great, and I can't thank the USOC folks enough for their great service. We had a couple of schedule changes, and they made all the necessary changes on the spot to keep everything running smoothly. It was a world-class operation.

Our medical staff consisted of Nicholas Potter, Peter Haberl and Sean McCann. They all did their jobs well and were crucial to our success.

Like many of the other sports, we had a difficult time with tickets, but this was not the USOC's fault. Tickets were not released on schedule, causing a good deal of frustration.

A note for future Team Leaders is that the Team Leader sets the tone for the entire team. If you stay positive and do everything in your power to support your teammates, success will follow. Negativity is cancerous. A negative outlook will cause negative results. If a Team Leader allows themselves, or any other person on the team, to become negative either before or after a performance, it will spread throughout the team and disaster will follow. Our successes came from adequate preparation, positive attitudes and teamwork.

I am the CEO and majority stockholder of a fairly large corporation. I have never had the privilege of doing business with a better run group of people than the USOC staff. The USOC is truly a world-class organization.

WALTON GLENN ELLER (R) OF THE UNITED STATES CELEBRATES WIN-
NING THE GOLD MEDAL | *NICK LAHAM/GETTY IMAGES*

USA SOCCER – MEN'S | *ALFONSO CERDA* – *TEAM COORDINATOR*

The athletes selected for the Olympic Team came out of a player pool that is put together by our National Team coaching staff and scouts. An athlete who has participated in past National Team events is included in the pool, as well as others identified through a variety of programs and tournaments. For the 2008 Olympics, we chose the best athletes available for the team. There was an issue with the 2010 World Cup qualifying process that conflicted with the Olympics, making the decisions and selections more difficult. The final selection of athletes for the team needs to coincide exactly with the selection date from FIFA (Fédération Internationale de Football Association) competitions. By requiring us to select our final roster prior to every other country's selection date, it is fair to say that our team was put at a competitive disadvantage. Oftentimes there were two sets of regulations, the regulations of the Olympic Soccer Tournament and the regulations set by the USOC, which caused some confusion.

Because the deadline for team selection for the Olympic Games is much earlier than is reasonable (considering all of the factors: FIFA deadline being weeks later, player injuries, professional club releases and overall team chemistry), we were unable to meet that deadline, and after being granted one partial extension, we were eventually fined by the USOC.

Following the selection of the team, we participated in the ING Cup in Hong Kong from July 26 through August 3. We tied the first match and lost the second but felt this was a good preparation event for the team.

There was not an Olympic Test Event for soccer as in other sports. However, our facilities seemed to work well, and they were very close to our hotel. We felt very comfortable, as there was very tight security around at all times.

We won our first group match against Japan and then tied the Netherlands in our second match. In our third match, we lost to Nigeria to finish third in our group, eliminating us from the competition.

As a Team Leader there were several moving pieces that had to be coordinated leading up to and during the Olympics. Our group worked well with the USOC accreditation staff, receiving very thorough and timely responses. The majority of our group was taken care of through the official accreditation service, but those who could not get credentialed were taken care of with hotel credentials so that they could stay at the team hotel. The key to making the accreditation process a smooth one is constant communication between the USOC and the NGB. By doing this, you are able to stay ahead of what needs to be turned into the organizing committee and to be assured of meeting deadlines. In the future, we need more staff credentials available to us and a later date for submitting our final team roster, staying consistent with the regulations of the tournament.

MAURICE EDU (R) OF THE US AND VICTOR OBBINA (L) OF NIGERIA FIGHT FOR THE BALL DURING THEIR 2008 BEIJING OLYMPIC GAMES FIRST-ROUND SOCCER MATCH | *PEDRO UGARTE/AFP/GETTY IMAGES*

Trying to coordinate the flight schedule of our staff that was credentialed through the USOC was a challenge. It was confusing because we changed dates of our pre-Olympic camp and thus had to make changes to flights that had already been booked by the USOC (which is why we did not want to book the flights too early in order to avoid changing flights). It would have simplified things to have them all under the U.S. Soccer umbrella instead of splitting them apart. Beyond that, the air travel process was very smooth and information was easily accessible. Since we travel so much internationally, we are used to many of the requirements, especially those regarding excess baggage. Therefore, we didn't have any issues with baggage. I was also pleased with how quickly we were able to get new flights booked after our team lost our final match. The turnaround time on booking these flights was extremely fast.

Team processing went well; however, it was a tight turnaround as we left the next day for the ING Cup. Having the team leader arrive a day before to process was a good move. It allowed time for any last minute questions or changes so that when the team arrives, the processing goes smoothly for them.

The cell phones provided by the USOC to the entire team at processing were a key element, as they helped with communication all the way around. The two-way radio information was unnecessarily confusing to fill out and would suggest in the future just making the two-way radios available to rent at the Olympics.

The office kits we received from the USOC were great. They provided everything we needed in order to perform our normal office functions. Since we were off-site, most of our logistical requests went through the organizing committee instead of the USOC. Having our shipments arrive at outlying hotels make them very difficult to get through security and required a lot of patience and several calls. Some items did not clear customs and were therefore unavailable to the team. There needs to be better coordination to insure all drop-offs go smoothly.

In terms of distributed apparel, we had very few issues. For us it helped that Nike was both the NGB and team supplier. We did have an issue with the color boards, as we were told that we could not have our Federation's crest on our uniforms. This was a big issue because Nike does not make our uniforms without the crest. We eventually had them specially ordered but were unable to get the number we needed for all of our matches and were forced to play in uniforms that had our crests covered with tape in order to be compliant and to avoid another fine. This issue needs to be resolved much sooner in the future, and I'm not sure if that falls to the IOC, USOC, FIFA or U.S. Soccer.

I thought the online registration for apparel worked really well in getting all the sizes to the USOC. In the future a larger percentage of the staff should be able to receive all the apparel instead of just a fraction of it, as we are all one team and do not need to be segregated.

Ground transportation is another key issue for the Olympics. During the entire process we maintained a strong level of communication with the USOC, which helped when there were last minute changes. As a result, any major issues were resolved quickly. We used a bus at the San Francisco Airport to get to processing and back. Our coach decided to add a morning workout on our travel day to Hong Kong, but I worked with the USOC on a transportation solution so that this did not interfere with our team getting checked in at the airport. I felt like the execution of our plan, and the flexibility it allowed, was key to making this part very smooth. In the future, I would suggest more cars at the Village for team use, as we had one occasion where we had a training session and one of our players was drug tested. The athlete and medical staff stayed at the training site but then had to get a taxi back to the Village. An additional car would have helped in this situation.

On housing, we had some very last minute changes, which couldn't have been foreseen. We worked with the USOC, and everything came together well. While we were in Beijing, we decided to have our team stay at the Hilton Hotel, but when we did this, we needed an area set aside for our meals, meeting space and other work rooms. This was a very last minute request, as we moved into the Hilton within 24 hours of deciding the team needed to be at a hotel. The USOC jumped right in and made this change a very smooth one. In the future, I would suggest we begin the outside housing process earlier and carefully consider where it is best to have the team stay. A few things to consider on the housing are the services provided and the convenience

YUTO NAGATOMO OF JAPAN AND MARVELL WYNNE OF USA COMPETE FOR THE BALL DURING MEN'S GROUP B MATCH BETWEEN JAPAN AND USA | *KOJI WATANABE/GETTY IMAGES*

to the training and competition venues. After the team was eliminated we had three staff members move into the Athlete Village for a couple of days, and the USOC contacts were very helpful in providing rooms.

Our medical team consisted of a doctor, a primary trainer and a secondary trainer. The doctor and the primary trainer have been part of the staff with the federation for many years and have traveled with our various teams. Keeping that consistency is crucial to the success of the team.

We didn't use Beijing Normal University as much as the other teams, but we did have a few staff members staying there and they enjoyed it. We attempted to use the soccer field at BNU, but the track team had it reserved at the time we needed it. This was not a problem, as we used the fields FIFA had assigned us. However, in the future that might be a consideration for the USOC to have another field for use by the soccer team. The video analysis we received was very helpful and came in a timely manner, which is crucial.

As with any Games there are never enough tickets, and that was again the case in Beijing. Originally we needed more tickets than we were allotted, but after many calls and emails we were able to secure tickets we were originally told would not be available for a match. Moving forward, I would like to see better cooperation between all involved regarding team ticket needs instead of waiting until the last minute to solve the situation. This would create fewer headaches for everyone.

Through my experience this year, I learned that there are a lot of moving parts at the Olympics. Our team has a hard time fitting into the Olympic mold, as we are at different sites and when we did move to the Village, it was such a different dynamic from the other venues that it was very hard to adjust and get the team focused solely on preparation, which is exactly what the team needed.

We ended up moving off-site in order to give the team the consistency and comfort they were used to from both the tournament and when they play with their professional clubs. More consideration and thought needs to go into planning our accommodations in the future in order to determine how our U.S. Under-23 Men's National Team fits within the normal USOC framework. Hopefully better early planning can allow our team to better enjoy the full experience of being at the Olympic Games.

TAKAYUKI MORIMOTO OF JAPAN (R) AND MICHAEL PARKHURST OF USA COMPETE FOR THE BALL | *KOJI WATANABE/GETTY IMAGES*

USA SOCCER – WOMEN'S | *CHERYL BAILEY* – *NATIONAL TEAM GENERAL MANAGER*

In 2008, the team was selected after a year of tournaments and camps, which included the Olympic Qualifying Tournament in April. Our Swedish coach had been on board just eight months so needed a steep learning curve to identify and select players throughout the U.S. However, our participation in the World Cup in 2007 made identification easier. The selection process will change somewhat with the new league starting up. However, we will continue to identify talent leading up to the World Cup and Olympics and play in tournaments and matches throughout the year both internationally and domestically.

After naming the Olympic Team and before the Games, the women's soccer team played in matches with international teams both in the U.S. and abroad. We participated in the Peace Cup tournament in Korea and then traveled to Norway and Sweden. In addition, we played two matches leading up to the Games against one of the toughest opponents that we anticipated competing against at the Olympics. Going into the Games, we gained a lot of confidence by winning all of our pre-Games matches. I don't anticipate changing this procedure much in the future.

During what is considered the Olympic off-season, we participate in several tournaments internationally as well as several friendly matches in the U.S. The international tournaments and games help us to prepare for the Olympic experience. Since several of our tournaments, as well as the World Cup, were in China we were prepared for the culture and climate issues that were a part of the Olympic Games. I imagine we will play in England at some point leading up to the 2012 Olympics to acclimate to that environment. There will be a women's professional soccer league debuting in 2008/2009 that will provide a new opportunity for Olympic Games preparation.

A test event was held during the draw that the head coach, Team Leader and USOC liaison attended. It was helpful to have a feel for where we would be playing. Most helpful was going to the hotels, training sites and venues that our teams would be using after the draw took place. This allowed us to get a sense of where we would be for the first two rounds.

Beijing Normal University (BNU) was a great training site for us during the Olympic Games. We used the soccer field prior to traveling to our first city and then once again after returning to Beijing. It was great to have our own practice facility and to set our own practice time. The fact that it was so close to the Village was also a great plus. In the other cities, the training facilities were excellent as well. There was a little stress put on us in terms of "exact" practice time since they closed down the streets when our bus was coming and going, but they were generally patient if we went over our scheduled time.

As for the actual competition, our start was certainly not what we had intended, losing to Norway (0-2) in the opening match, but our play improved in each game thereafter. We had lost one of our key players and goal scorers as a result of a broken leg the week before we left for the Olympics. Because of this, we changed our style of play, and it took a little time to adapt to the changes. Fortunately, we had great leadership on the field and, since we had played most of the Olympic teams during the year, we were prepared for their game plans. We also had scouts for each game we played, who proved to be extremely valuable. After losing to Norway, we won the next game against Japan (1-0). We needed a win against New Zealand to advance to the quarterfinals and some help from Japan in order to move out of pool play. We beat New Zealand (4-0), and Japan beat Norway, which was the ticket we needed.

Based on the goal differential, we were first in our pool, so advanced to Shanghai. While in Shanghai, our game against Canada was suspended in the first half for an hour and a half due to a thunder and lightning storm. We had great momentum prior to the game delay but ended up going into overtime. We beat Canada 1-0 as the rain continued throughout the match. With the win we advanced to the semifinal match against Japan, held in Beijing.

One incident that was noteworthy during this match was the decision to resume play. It appeared that FIFA wanted to resume play prior to it being safe to do so and without following any specific protocol. As Team Leader, I consulted with our team doctor, who was in contact with personnel in Beijing. Team USA and Team Canada refused to step onto the field of play until we had followed the protocol set up for

TOBIN HEATH (TOP) OF THE U.S. FALLS ONTO RHIAN WILKINSON OF CANADA DURING THEIR 2008 BEIJING OLYMPIC SOCCER GAME | *LIU JIN/AFP/GETTY IMAGES*

thunder and lightening. This meant delaying the game much longer, but it was the appropriate thing to do.

From Shanghai we traveled to Beijing and defeated Japan(4-2) for the second time, getting goals from three different players. The win moved us into the gold medal match against Brazil. Brazil had beaten us in the World Cup in 2007, making it a very interesting match.

We again went into overtime after a scoreless regulation match. Carli Lloyd scored in the first overtime to put us ahead 1-0. We were able to hang onto the lead throughout the second overtime period with Brazil knocking at the door on several occasions. Winning the gold medal was not expected for this young team that had been challenged with injuries throughout the year, as well as the unexpected loss of Abby Wambach. This made the victory even sweeter and extremely gratifying.

We had a budget in place for the Olympic Games, with our biggest expense coming from the hotel rooms. Because we were off-site so much of the time, we had brought additional people that we would not have brought otherwise. We had a second athletic trainer, massage therapists and an alternate athlete, all of whom traveled with us, so additional hotel rooms and meals were a big part of our expenses, as were flights and train tickets between cities. Additionally, we had some expense with our additional people staying at BNU while we were in Beijing. We also had a very unexpected expense with the high cost of doing laundry at each of the hotels.

Leading up to the Olympics, I attended both USOC Team Leadership meetings. I think it would have been helpful to have those of us who were serving for the first time come in early in order to receive additional background as to what was expected and how it worked. Since several of the people had been Team Leaders in the past or had worked with the USOC in some capacity, they were very comfortable with the process and the personnel, but I was a bit unsure of how it all worked. One suggestion I could offer is to have a sheet of the USOC personnel identified with names and photos, making it easier to put a name and face together. It is also a bit tricky to follow everything presented because soccer does not follow in the same footsteps as most of the other sports. Maybe having someone dedicated to help work with soccer on the differences would be helpful.

I did not attend the USOC Key Decision Maker meetings, as I was not on board in time for these. However, I feel that these meetings would have been beneficial.

We had a few issues arise with the accreditation but were able to work through most of them. We had thought we would receive a second accreditation for the head of the delegation since we had two teams—men and women—but then found out we would receive only one. We made it work with what we had and used FIFA VIP's to get our executive director into better seats during the matches. Like most sports, we would like to have access to a few more credentials.

The other issue we ran into was getting our scouts into the team hotels, even after we followed all of the procedures and submitted all the required paperwork. I worked constantly with the USOC contacts on this issue once the problem arose. Some hotels were cooperative (Shenyang and Shanghai), but others were not—and we were not able to resolve this issue. We had to find alternate hotels on the spot for the scouts.

Air travel went well. We felt it was good to have a specific contact with the USOC to call who was familiar with our group and was able to make the changes we needed. We had an unexpected baggage fee with our excess baggage when we flew from Shenyang to Shanghai, but it all worked out all right.

420

AMY RODRIGUEZ OF UNITED STATES GETS PAST COSTA RENATA (R) OF BRAZIL | *CAMERON SPENCER/GETTY IMAGES*

Regarding apparel, we made a couple of last minute changes and had to add two staff packages to our USOC totals. We were surprised and pleased when we got to team processing and discovered that they had these additional packages already prepared and ready for pickup. In terms of our team's color boards, we had a few issues with the double crest on the uniforms, which was not resolved until the day of the first game. Our team went through team processing as a team, which worked well. It was good to have the team administrator at team processing a day earlier, giving them a chance to go through the process so that they were ready for the team's arrival. I would make sure to do this again in the future.

While in China, we didn't require any additional vehicles.

Having the USOC provide cell phones for the delegation was important. The cell phones weren't always the easiest to use, especially in setting up the voicemail and sending text messages. However, it was great to have them pre-programmed with everyone's name and cell number.

Since we were not in the Athlete Village or at BNU the whole time, we did not have the easiest access to computers or the Internet. It was a bit inconvenient but not sure what we could have done about it given the situation.

Operating out of a hotel for the three weeks during our first four games allowed us to have a floor dedicated to our team. We were able to set up a dedicated meal room and a meeting room, available whenever we needed it. Once we moved into the Village the meeting room set-up was not as easy to access for team scouting meetings and pre-game talks. We ended up having a couple of meetings in our rooms, which was not the best situation. On two different occasions we went to BNU and had our meeting there.

Our medical staff consisted of Grizelle Garcia, our athletic trainer, and Christopher Amann, our team physician. They were both identified early in the process, which gave us the opportunity to work with them during the year, allowing a great deal of mutual comfort.

As stated earlier, we took advantage of BNU when we were in Beijing. The meals at BNU were outstanding. There was a great deal of variety and it was all freshly made, which was a great change from the hotel/ Village food. Additionally, we knew that the nutritional component was spot on. Although we were not in Beijing a great deal, when we were, the training field at BNU was available during the times that we had requested. It was so much nicer to go to BNU at the times that we preferred and use a field that we liked. BNU staff had all the equipment that we had requested ahead of time, including refrigerated drinks. In addition, they were able to provide us with ice baths right on the field, which was great as well.

We had some unique requests regarding video analysis. We needed to get videos of matches played at various venues and in various cities into the hands of our scouts, who were located at still other venues. The logistics of this got very complicated. Our USOC contacts were very helpful in working with us to meet these needs, which sometimes included individuals who hand-carried DVDs to our scouts. This was critical to our preparation for the upcoming matches and was greatly appreciated. We had couriers arriving by planes and trains to get us game film. Getting the videos to analyze will always be a critical component of our preparation, and the extra work that the USOC put in to make sure we received what we needed was very much appreciated. Going forward this will continue to be an important service for soccer.

A lesson learned regarding equipment needs and supplies was that we needed a television so that we could watch the other games being played. Because we were off-site for our preliminary and qualifying

rounds, we found it was too late to request a television once we arrived in the Village. We had not ordered off the rate card because of the minimum 32-day rental.

Security was a bit of a problem in the outlying cities. We worked closely with our USOC liaison and those from the embassy/State Department, but it was still frustrating to deal with so many local security processes and procedures. Each city had its own system and bureaucracy; we had to readjust to a new system every time we moved venues. It caused a great deal of stress for our athletes, their families, and our staff. Once we got to the Olympic Village in Beijing, it was easy to navigate all the security expectations. In the future, it would be good to have contact with the specific local security people so we can learn what to expect.

Tickets seem to always be a problem, and it was no different for us. When we arrived in Beijing for the semifinals, I received information on picking up the 50 additional tickets that were allotted to us by FIFA because we had made the semifinals. As Team Leader, I had picked up the additional tickets we received when we made the quarterfinals, so had no reason to think that I should not be picking up these tickets. However, a misunderstanding between FIFA, the USOC and U.S. Soccer caused confusion over just who was responsible for getting and distributing the tickets. Even though FIFA had communicated with me about these tickets, it turned out that they were actually the USOC's to manage. Fortunately, the USOC turned them over to me, but the confusion was a bit stressful for everyone. In the future, we will "over-communicate" regarding any extra ticket responsibilities.

Soccer rarely seems to fall within the Olympic template. While the USOC is definitely there to support soccer, at times it really doesn't have a lot of experienced personnel who have lived the "soccer at the Olympics life" to understand some of the challenges. Therefore, continual communication is the key to success. I will say having a USOC liaison travel with us was most helpful and should be required for future Games.

I would also recommend that the USOC keep in mind the opportunity to have soccer housed in the USA dorms when they arrive in the Village so that they will feel a part of the delegation and have all the resources at their disposal. I realize this is not always possible, but when it is, it would be very helpful for the athletes and staff.

USA SOFTBALL | RONNIE ISHAM & JULIE BARTEL
– DIRECTOR NATIONAL TEAMS & DIRECTOR OF COMMUNICATIONS

OLYMPIC PLANNING AND PREPARATION

Selecting the 2008 Olympic Softball Team consisted of an ongoing evaluation process to identify top athletes. The process included participating in national and international competitions, as well as National Team camps spread out over a three-year period. Our 2008 Olympic Team was selected in September 2007, and we feel that the process identified the best athletes for the team.

The team participated in the 2008 KFC Bound 4 Beijing Tour, a 42 U.S. city tour that began in February 2008 and ended in July 2008. We also held training camps in January 2008 and again in June 2008. In hindsight, it would have been better to scale back the tour and add a couple more training camps.

The Beijing Organizing Committee for the Olympic Games (BOCOG) held an Olympic Test Event that we attended. It was very useful, as it gave us a chance to familiarize ourselves with the country as well as the venue.

During the Olympic Games, we trained two hours per day at the venue facility. Because it was difficult to get additional training time at the venue due to the policy, we used the training facility at Beijing Normal University (BNU), the USOC's High Performance Training Center, as a secondary option. Individual athletes utilized BNU for extra hitting, cardio, weightlifting, medical and technical needs.

USA Softball had an Olympic Games budget, with our primary expenses being travel and housing. A larger budget would have allowed us to have more technical support for the team and we could have traveled by air more than bus on our U.S. Tour.

I attended the USOC Team Leadership and USOC Key Decision Maker meetings and found them to be very valuable. Receiving the latest and most updated information concerning the Games was a key to a successful plan. Interaction with the other sport Team Leaders and the USOC staff was also helpful. Being able to visit the host country and the Games venue early in the planning process was very beneficial. Also it was great to learn about the country's customs and culture, as well as being able to meet with the Local Organizing Committee.

Although we received the same number of credentials as we did at the 2004 Olympics, the 2005-08 High Performance Plan for USA Softball called for an increase in personnel, specifically for a strength and conditioning coach who we used for all competitions leading up to the Games. Thus, when we lost the one credential, we had to make adjustments in the administration and support staff since eliminating the strength and conditioning coach would impact performance to a greater degree. The impact on the team of losing a female administra-

tor was huge but was overcome. The biggest issue was not having a complete staff as a result of having to cut one and make adjustments. Overall though, the accreditation process worked. As in any organization, one of the most important functions is sound communication between parties, and I believe that was accomplished in this case.

We had a great working relationship with the USOC and United Airlines in terms of our air travel. We had no issue with any of our flights.

The apparel process has been consistent through the years, and this year was no different. The leadership is qualified and performs very professionally. In addition, team processing has always been a great experience for USA Softball athletes and staff. This year was no different.

Communication in regard to ground transportation for the Olympic

CAITLIN LOWE, #26, OF THE UNITED STATES HITS A HOME RUN AGAINST VENEZUELA | *VLADIMIR RYS/BONGARTS/GETTY IMAGES*

Games was outstanding and timely, which helped me with the final decision making in terms of additional requests related to rate card vehicles.

Everything related to information technology worked great at the Games. From the cell phones to the Internet accessibility in the Athlete Village, it was all very much appreciated by all.

We had a minor logistical problem in that four dozen softballs were misplaced between Colorado Springs and Beijing. The USOC staff worked extremely hard to locate replacement balls as a result. I believe the logistical process is sound and will always need to be adjusted according to the standards/procedures in the location of the Games.

The Village staff was outstanding. Every member of the Village staff is to be commended for their professionalism and a "job well done." They were all excellent and willing to assist with any request made by the USA Softball staff and athletes.

Our medical staff consisted of Vinny Comiskey, an athletic trainer from the Olympic Training Center in Chula Vista, Calif., and Kevin Hargrove, USA Softball's doctor and orthopedic surgeon in Oklahoma City, Okla. For USA Softball, it was performance enhancing to have the same staff for the four years leading up to the Games. It definitely contributed to the overall success of the program.

The loss of key USOC personnel prior to the Olympic Games created a tough situation for USA Softball video analysis as far as preparation and training of athletes. The USOC staff, even without the pure softball knowledge, did an outstanding job of working with USA Softball coaches during the Games to provide the live feeds and data preparation for feedback to be used during the pre-game meetings. A lesson learned here is that NGBs should not totally depend on USOC personnel/staff for performance impacting issues/situations like video analysis. The process worked fine after adjustments were made by USA Softball.

The USA House was in a great location and the facility was accommodating for all USA Softball needs. USA Softball staff and athletes really enjoyed the USA House during the 2008 Olympic Games.

Everything that we were confronted with we had either faced or experienced before. The only exception was the constant question and charge from the world media that the reason softball was voted out of the Olympics was due to our team being too good and dominating the sport. In my opinion, the finality that this was the last Olympics for softball and the continued questioning of the dominating success of the USA team being the reason that the sport was voted out had a tremendously negative impact on our team. It took away that little edge and mystique that we seemed to always have, especially on the gold medal day. I have had the honor and privilege of being directly involved with the athletes on the gold medal day in three of the four Olympic Games that softball has participated in. However, August 21, 2008, was a gold medal day that had a totally different feel than the others. Granted, the intensity, confidence, preparation and focus were all there, but I had an uneasy feeling that something was not right.

The USA Softball program has been extremely successful over the last eight years on and off the field, and I feel that all the procedures and processes worked well in 2008. The only changes in the overall process were those that were created by the fact that softball is not on the Olympic program for 2012. We don't anticipate any major changes in the program for 2009 and will wait for the IOC vote on the 2016 Olympic Program before finalizing plans for 2010 and beyond.

My advice to future Team Leaders would be to develop positive relationships with USOC staff and other NGB personnel, ask questions, attend all required meetings, know your sport and organization inside and out,

PITCHER JENNIE FINCH, #27, AND KELLY KRETSCHMAN, #12, OF THE UNITED STATES CELEBRATE AFTER WINNING 9-0 OVER CHINA | *VLADIMIR RYS/BONGARTS/GETTY IMAGES*

be familiar with all your potential athletes and coaches, be flexible and keep an open mind. Don't forget that constant communication is most important and that you need to check your ego at the door.

OLYMPIC RESULTS

USA Softball's 2008 Olympic story wasn't a fairy tale ending, nor did the team close the book with a "happily ever after." But despite the finish, the message in the end wasn't about winning or losing, it was about "hoping for ever after."

In 2005, the IOC made a decision that will forever affect the sport of softball. With the 2008 Games being the final hurrah, the U.S. certainly wanted to complete the "grand slam," coming home with a fourth-consecutive gold medal. Fortunately they came home with a medal, but unfortunately it was not of the golden variety, but silver in nature.

With a 59-1 overall pre-Games tour record, the U.S. was poised, confident and prepared to begin the battle that awaited them in Beijing. Being three-time defending Olympic gold medalists, the target was on their back, with seven other teams waiting in the wings to steal the coveted gold medal.

On August 12, the U.S. met its first opponent in Olympic rookie team Venezuela. Pitcher Jennie Finch opened the Games in successful fashion with a record-setting victory. The U.S. put up 11 runs for an Olympic record for most runs scored in a game, while Finch and Monica Abbott combined for a no-hitter. Olympic rookie Caitlin Lowe led the U.S. effort with a 3-for-4 debut, with one RBI coming on a solo inside-the-park home run.

Game two began the three-game, three-day gauntlet of facing our toughest opponents: Australia, Canada and Japan. On August 13, left-handed pitcher Cat Osterman became just the second U.S. pitcher to ever toss an Olympic complete game no-hitter, with a 3-0 shutout over rival Australia. Osterman was almost perfect in the contest, recording 13 strikeouts and allowing just three runners to reach base via walk.

Next up was northern neighbor Canada, but Mother Nature won out as rain suspended the game in the fourth inning. With the U.S. trailing 1-0, play would resume the next day—after the U.S. captured a win against Japan. The U.S. used a four-run first inning attack en route to victory over Japan. The team connected on eight hits, including a new Olympic record four home runs in a single Games, two of which came from Jessica Mendoza. From the circle, Abbott garnered her first Olympic victory, tossing five complete innings, allowing just one hit and retiring four batters via strikeout.

The Canada game then resumed, and the U.S. battled from behind, coming up with an 8-1 win and improving to 4-0. Capitalizing on

Canadian errors, the U.S. took the lead in the sixth and sealed the win in the seventh, taking the game out of reach for the Canadians. From the circle, Osterman garnered the win. The U.S. would have three games remaining until the playoffs.

Riding an 18-game Olympic win streak dating back to 2000, the U.S. quickly extended the streak to 21 after three consecutive run-ahead rule victories. First was Chinese Taipei, in a 7-0 five-inning triumph that saw Olympic newcomers Vicky Galindo and Lauren Lappin earn their first Olympic career hits, while veteran Finch earned her second win of the Games with a six-strikeout performance.

Then it was the Netherlands, with an 8-0 five-inning victory where Abbott recorded the first perfect game in Olympic history for a USA Softball athlete. She recorded nine strikeouts in the 15-batters faced. The U.S. improved to 6-0 record in Beijing.

Cruising right a long, the U.S. closed round-robin action with a 9-0 win over Olympic host China. Using a first inning nine-run rally, the U.S. secured the number one seed in the playoffs for the second consecutive Olympic Games. Japan finished as the second seed, with Australia and Canada finishing third and fourth, respectively.

With a fourth gold medal just two games away, the U.S. opened playoffs with a heart-pumping 4-1 extra-inning win over Japan. Facing Japanese pitching ace Yukiko Ueno, who had defeated the U.S. on four occasions since the 2004 Games, the game displayed softball at its finest. The pitching of Abbott held off the Japanese through eight innings before the efforts of Lowe and power hitter Crystl Bustos put four runs on the board in the top of the ninth to seal the victory. With the win, the U.S. would move to its fourth consecutive Olympic gold medal game to face Japan—again—who had fought through the bronze medal game. That game was a 12-inning thriller against Australia, who took the bronze as the Japanese advanced to the gold medal game.

Facing Japan for the third time in six days, the game drew a crowd of over 8,000 as history was being made with what could be the final Olympic gold medal game for the sport of softball.

With Osterman in the circle, the U.S. came out strong, holding Japan through the first two innings before Japan struck first with a 1-0 lead in the third. Eri Yamada then drove an Osterman pitch over the fences for a home run and the 2-0 lead. A thirty-minute rain delay then halted play, but the U.S. quickly responded as home run leader Bustos put the game at 2-1. But it just wasn't in the cards for the U.S. as they left six runners stranded in the final innings before Japan added another run for the eventual 3-1 win.

Stunned with disbelief, the U.S. walked away with the silver medal as Japan captured its first Olympic gold. With tears of sadness not only for the outcome but also the sport's sendoff, the medal stand ceremony was very emotional. Laura Berg, Bustos, Kelly Kretschman, Tairia Flowers and Lovieanne Jung all left their cleats at home plate, symbolizing an end to five outstanding USA Softball careers.

As the tears began to dry and hugs contagiously spread, something happened on the field that night that was greater than a victory and more emotional than a defeat. The international softball world sent a message of hope. All three medal winning teams gathered together and spelled out "2016" in softballs just in front of home plate. The enemy lines disappeared and a chant of the words "Back Softball" emerged. Arm in arm, the softball world was uniting in a message to the IOC...and hoping for "happily ever after."

424

MEGU HIROSE, #8, OF JAPAN SLIDES INTO SECOND BASE AS SHORTSTOP NATASHA WATLEY, #28, OF THE UNITED STATES WAITS FOR THE BALL | *JONATHAN FERREY/GETTY IMAGES*

USA SWIMMING | *LINDSAY MINTENKO – NATIONAL TEAM MANAGING DIRECTOR*

Our Olympic Trials were June 29–July 6 in Omaha, Neb. The first-place athlete in each event was selected to the team. In the 100 and 200 freestyle, the top four athletes were selected to the team. If there were enough doubles, then the second-place athletes are added to the team. We also select the fifth- and sixth-place swimmers in the 100 and 200 free if enough spots were left on the team. We were allowed 26 men and 26 women on the team. A suggestion for future teams would be to state in the selection procedures that even though the top four are selected in the 100 and 200 free events, that only the top two swim the individual event.

The team went directly to the training camp from the Olympic Trials. Prior to the Olympic Games, we had an 18-day camp in California and an 8-day camp in Singapore. Both the athletes and coaches have expressed that this camp is way too long to be away from their homes, and they would prefer a shorter camp. However, USA Swimming has done this for the past two Olympic Games and has been very successful. The decision to change this camp will be made only after the Olympic head coaches for 2012 have been selected.

There were Olympic Test Events at both the pool and open water sites before the Games. We did not attend the pool test event but did send staff to observe. We attended the open water test event because it was a way to get an athlete to qualify for the Games.

We took advantage of the USOC's High Performance Center at Beijing Normal University. BNU was extremely helpful for the open water swim team. Our pool team used BNU only once when we did not have competition pool time. It was great to have access to BNU, as our official training site was way outside Beijing. However, our open water team used BNU more often and it was very helpful for them. Without BNU, we would have experienced several problems, especially with open water, since our coaches were not accredited and it would have significantly hurt us to not have our coaches with our athletes.

It was a very successful Olympic Games for swimming. The swim team came away from Beijing with a total of 31 medals: 12 gold, 9 silver and 10 bronze. It was historic as well, with Michael Phelps doing the unimaginable, winning eight gold medals. On the other side of the coin, we also had a few athletes, for whatever reason, not perform well. Our staff and coaches have gone through many discussions on what we need to do better. In open water, our male athlete finished eighth, which was a huge success. More focus will go into open water in the future.

As with any major event, there was a lot of preparation in advance, with the biggest being Olympic accreditation. Due to the timing of our trials and naming of our team we had some tight deadlines, but we worked well with the USOC staff to get all the information submitted and processed. USA Swimming required more accreditation than the USOC was able to give for these Games. In the future, USA Swimming needs to do a better job at making sure to give accreditation to those who will use it the most and get the most out of it. When USA Swimming failed to qualify the maximum number of open water swimmers to the Games, an accreditation was lost. This could have impacted the performance of our open water team, but with the use of BNU, we were able to adapt. In the future, USA Swimming will be requesting more accreditation via our High Performance Plan and evaluate matching accreditations to the appropriate people.

We had a little difficulty with our air travel, mostly in the booking process. We seemed to have trouble getting correct final itineraries, which caused some less than desirable seat assignments, but we made it work. The USOC and United Airlines were extremely helpful in facilitating the transport of our excess team baggage (massage tables, swimsuits, nutritional supplements, technical gear, etc.).

Two things went exceptionally well with our team travel: (1) One year before travel we identified two flights we wanted to take to our training site (Singapore), and the USOC and Olympic Travel Desk were able to block space on those flights, and (2) the USOC developed a check-in system that was extremely efficient.

Given the nature of the system, I think everything went as well as could be expected. We had no real problems, just minor frustrations. The only suggestion for the future would be to assign dedicated agents in pairs so that someone would always be available when questions arise.

The deadlines for Games apparel submissions were a bit tight for us, given our late timing in announcing our athletes and coaches. We had no problems with our competitive apparel supplier meeting the IOC requirements on logo sizes. Receiving the IOC requirements early in

DARA TORRES OF THE UNITED STATES REACTS AFTER WINNING THE
SILVER MEDAL | *ADAM PRETTY/GETTY IMAGES*

the process was a huge advantage. I was able to send it to all our suppliers, and they were able to make adjustments.

We had a great plan to have our men's and women's teams process separately. This worked out very well with the men's team. However, the women's team got behind another team, and the apparel portion of processing took way too long. It is suggested that if there are more than 20 athletes with a team, they should be the only ones processed at that time because otherwise you get too many people and the lines get too long. It should only take a half day with a team of about 25. So for 2012, I would make the request that only one team be allowed to process at a time. Processing in the United States seemed to work better than waiting until you arrive at the Games.

We requested a 15-passenger van with a driver for use while at the Games. This was great to have, although it would have worked just as well with a smaller vehicle. It was good to have a driver and a translator as a part of the package. The only problem we had was that the translator did not have the same accreditation access that the vehicle and the driver did. This made it difficult to get through security at the venue. We often used the vehicle for our coaches' transportation from BNU to the venue.

The USOC provided cell phones for the staff and athletes while in Beijing. The cell phones for the staff were very good. The staff phones were a great way to get in touch with other staff members. Having all the numbers programmed in the phones should remain a requirement. But some athletes were disappointed with the phones they received and consequently did not use them. This made it difficult to communicate with the athletes and staff. This is a concern for us because, in the case of an emergency we need a way to reach our athletes and coaches at all times. This is a policy USA Swimming is looking into and would suggest the USOC doing the same.

We have always had a great relationship with the USOC security team. Because our team is fairly high profile, we had some issues with security throughout the Games. The USOC Chief Security Officer was very helpful with this throughout the competition. I would also like to stress how important it was to have our security officers from the State Department present at the venue.

Our experience in the Athlete Village was very good. The entire Village staff was amazing. They were always enthusiastic and very helpful. If one person could not answer a question, they knew who could. The only real problem we had in the Village was the scheduling of meeting rooms because it was very hard to estimate three days in advance what space we would need. In the future it would be very helpful if the USA delegation had a standard meeting space available at all times and not be required to share the space with the entire village, as was the case in Beijing.

The facilities and the food at BNU were exceptional. The USOC really rose to the occasion and put the needs of the athletes and the NGBs first. Having BNU was very helpful to the entire Olympic Team.

We had one minor issue with the rate card orders causing a few unforeseen budget issues. In the future, a better explanation to NGBs about VIK food would be beneficial as that was a rate card area we would have used more had we known in advance.

One thing we will need to watch more closely in the future is the budget. We went over budget, primarily in expenses for our training camps and for airfare. The rate card was also an expense that we hadn't planned on.

All in all it was a good experience at the 2008 Olympic Games. Having an NGB staff person in the role of Team Leader is a must. I always knew who to contact at the USOC for each question. The USOC conducted two pre-event Team Leader meetings. USA Swimming elected to send two Team Leaders to both, and I think it was a good idea to have both of us attend. It was good for gathering information and making sure all the right questions were asked. One thing I think would be helpful is for the USOC to provide a list of who is in charge of what before we get to the Games. This may have been done, but it seemed that some of the people we met at the Team Leaders meetings were not the same people on the ground in Beijing. It would be helpful to know who would be in charge of what once we are actually in Beijing.

USA Swimming made a decision to send two Team Leaders to the Village three days before the team arrived. I think this was a huge help to all of us. It gave USA Swimming the opportunity to see the Village in full swing and report back what to expect. The logistics of getting such a large USA Team into the Village has to be a nightmare, and the USOC did it very well.

RYAN LOCHTE AND MICHAEL PHELPS OF THE UNITED STATES SHOUT ENCOURAGEMENT TO PETER VANDERKAAY OF THE UNITED STATES|
NICK LAHAM/GETTY IMAGES

USA SYNCHRONIZED SWIMMING | *LAURA LACURSIA* – NATIONAL TEAM DIRECTOR

The core of this team began working together at the beginning of the quad. Starting in the spring of 2006 the entire team started training together and participated in several events including the Swiss Open in July 2006, the FINA World Cup in September 2006, the FINA Trophy Cup in November 2006, the World Championships in March 2007, the Pan American Games in July 2007, and finally the FINA Trophy Cup in October 2007.

The selection process consisted of five phases. The first and second phases centered on the elements portion, phase three was routine, phase four was elements and phase five was routine. The final selection of the Olympic team was in April 2007, prior to the Pan American Games.

In the future, it would be useful to carry more athletes longer and make our final decisions two months prior to the Games rather than 15 months. This would assist with the injury factors, unpredictable situations, and it would help "keep everyone on their toes" longer.

During the 2008 Olympic trials process our coaches were given a prominent role in selecting the athletes. They were able to evaluate the athletes both in and out of competition scenarios. We feel that this definitely contributed to selecting the best athletes.

Following the selection of our Olympic team, our first task was to prepare for the Olympic qualifier, the Pan American Games in July 2007. Our task at this competition was two-fold – qualify for the Olympic Games by securing gold, and position ourselves ahead of Canada. Both tasks were attained.

Following this competition we trained and competed at the FINA Trophy Cup in October of 2007. Traditionally this has proven to be a great competition for the U.S. team to showcase our artistic and choreographic talents. We placed third overall, one place ahead of the year before.

We resumed our training at the beginning of November. With the help of the USOC we developed and implemented a periodization plan dividing the remainder of our Olympic training into three major phases. For the first phase, our focus was on overall fitness and strength, while refining essential synchro skills and choreography. The next two phases followed a natural progression. As our time in the water intensified our training on land decreased proportionally. The coaches and athletes felt this was the smartest we had ever trained.

Another major addition to Olympic year training was a team of consultants from the San Francisco Circus School. This training provided additional flexibility and strength work, but, most importantly, sport-specific acrobatic work. With the help of the Circus School we were able to train our lifts/throw more effectively. That included such activities as putting our flyer in a harness, mimicking the lifts that we do in

the water, and creating original lifts. This training was invaluable and essential to success in our sport.

Our team did not compete from November until the Olympic Games. However, they did perform in six major exhibitions around the United States. In addition to physical preparation, the team spent a considerable amount of time in mental preparation for the competition. Some activities included work on mental imagery, developing a concise pre-competition plan, and creating competition scenarios. However, this team would have benefited from attending an additional competition between November and August and spending less time on choreography. Overall we felt our physical and mental training was effective and well planned out.

Traditionally most of our athletes have come from club programs. However as colleges have become a more popular avenue for the sport, they will play a significant role as we move toward 2012. The final National Championships, for both college and club programs, end in May, which challenges the preparation time for the National Team. Therefore, we have taken the liberty of moving their Championships into the earlier part of the year beginning in 2010 allowing for an earlier start time for the National Team. Our ultimate goal is to develop a year round training program so National Team athletes can receive training and education.

There was an Olympic test event in April 2008. Since the U.S. team had already qualified we were not eligible to participate. We did however conduct a training camp in Beijing to coincide with the test event providing our athletes with the opportunity to see some of their competition, orient themselves to the culture and the Olympic venues/housing location, and experience training in the area. It was extremely valuable for our mental preparation to see how the competition would

CHRISTINA JONES AND ANDREA NOTT OF THE UNITED STATES COMPETE IN THE SYNCHRONISED SWIMMING DUET | *CAMERON SPENCER/ GETTY IMAGES*

be conducted as well as how the areas, such as the warm up pool, the ready room, and the starting platform, would work during the Games. It was also essential for our team to observe where our future competitors stood at that stage of the season.

Training at the Olympic Games proved to be quite troublesome. We had two different pools/venues available each day for practice with music. At least one of the practices each day was scheduled at a venue 40-60 minutes away depending on traffic. Often, upon arrival at our practice venues, we would find that the schedule had been changed without any prior notification. Thankfully many people with the USOC worked very hard to make the Beijing Normal University (BNU) pool available to us. BNU became a key ingredient to our success. Going into the Olympics we had not planned to practice at BNU because the pool was too shallow for our sport. However, because of the training venues provided, it became better to have a shallow pool than uncertain practice conditions. We were also able to have much more practice time available at BNU. It was quiet, private, and easy to focus. In addition the food, staff, camaraderie, and the entire environment at BNU was a great compliment to our Olympic experience. In the future, we would like to make the U.S. High Performance Training Center our primary training venue at an Olympic Games.

Our first Olympic event was the Technical Duet. We felt we had a very solid performance and were mentally prepared.

The next event was the Free Duet preliminaries. We felt we had our best swim to date in this event. Unfortunately, it was not enough to improve our current world ranking. We finished the duet competition with the Duet Free final. While the athletes were well prepared, we did not feel they had their best performance in this event. While parts of the program improved technically between the preliminaries and the finals, we had a few sections that were not as "on" as our preliminary swim.

Next was the Technical Team event. Again we felt we had a very solid performance and were mentally ready. It was our best swim and the potentially risky elements were done well. Having so many Olympic "rookies" on our team, we felt their performance reflected their preparation. We did not feel we were scored high enough for the performance. This was a comment made to us by other countries as well.

Our final performance was the Free Team. One of our most risky components was our lifts which all worked. This was a very huge accomplishment as we had trouble with our lifts in some of the competitions leading up to the Olympic Games. During training, we focused on our lifts and we felt it was obvious we had improved. This was the first time we had competed with this program. After watching the performance, the coaching staff felt we would have been more "competition ready" if we had attended a competition prior to the Olympics. In an effort to keep our choreography "new" we performed at several large exhibitions in the U.S. rather than attending an international competition prior to the Games.

Our primary expenses for this year's Olympic team was the special training events and camps, the training venues, transportation, equipment, operations, performance consultants and the team staffing. We had great financial support from the USOC. The one thing that would make life better is a dedicated outdoor pool that all of our National

428

Teams (Senior, Junior, and now Age Group) could all use for training. The opportunity of having all the teams in one location, the continuity, efficient use of resources, ability to use one trainer instead of three, and immediate access to all coaches, would be an enormous benefit. This is a task for our NGB to consider and decide upon.

We attended the Team Leadership Kickoff meeting in Colorado Springs in October 2007, and appreciated the systematic process that was used. Information was consistent, clear, and concise. We also attended the Team Leadership Countdown meeting in Beijing in March 2008. It was extremely valuable to be able to orient ourselves prior to the Games and have a feel for where our venue was in relation to the Village, and other key locations. We were able to go inside our venue and take video back for the athletes to use in their mental preparation. Unfortunately, we were unable to get down on the competition deck level. That would be something we would recommend for future visits. Our head coach had never traveled to China prior to this meeting and it was very helpful for her to learn about the culture, and participate in the one-on-one meetings in each of the key areas. We would encourage the opportunity for the head coach to travel to the Games locations in the future.

The number of credentials we received worked well but one more would have been ideal. With the access to BNU, we were able to work with our non-credentialed performance consultant while training, which worked out extremely well. The BNU structure with respect to additional non-credentialed staff was key. We also greatly appreciated that the USOC staff was good about making our non-credentialed consultants a priority for entrance into the Village.

We truly appreciated the USOC's and United Airlines' ability to handle all our travel plans. We had several variations on our post Beijing travel itineraries and they were all met with a positive, accommodating, "can do" attitude. We did not have any problems with our travel.

We had one misunderstanding regarding our apparel colorboards and the fact that we thought they were being presented under all aquatic disciplines. However, for some reason they were recognized for swimming only, and not synchronized swimming or diving. We were contacted by the USOC when the problem was discovered, so that we could clear up this matter. Other than that, there were no conflicts with the NGB or team supplier.

In regards to our USOC-issued apparel, we were very fortunate to be able to go through team processing early so there was no waiting, and our athletes had the opportunity for some slight sizing adjustments. During team processing, we made our own arrangements for training, since we had trained in this facility in previous years, and this worked well.

We did not require any ground transportation while in Beijing. We were grateful for the ground transportation that was setup between BNU and the Village. It was consistent, convenient and relieved a great deal of concern for the team.

The cell phones were of great value to the staff members, and met our needs throughout the Games. In addition, the computers and land lines were conveniently located for staff and athletes in the village. The only thing which would have taken it to the next level would have been having wireless in the individual suites in the Village.

We wish to commend the USOC for providing us with the same trainer, Brent Hamula, for the Pan American and Olympic Games. This consistency was extremely valued.

In terms of tickets, not much went well in the ordering or fulfillment process, but was not the fault of the USOC. In the future, anything that can be done to assure that NGB orders result in tickets in a group is

THE UNITED STATES PERFORMS IN THE SYNCHRONISED SWIM TEAM EVENT FREE ROUTINE FINAL HELD AT THE NATIONAL AQUATICS CENTER | *CLIVE ROSE/GETTY IMAGES*

429

encouraged. Many of our tickets were spread across several sections, causing additional problems. We also found that other NGBs received far more favorable ticket locations than the NGB whose athletes were competing (for example, Track & Field had Synchro tickets in rows 1 and 2 of a section, while Synchro received tickets in rows 17-23).

One of the essential lessons we learned was that for this particular team, we needed to attend a major competition during the Olympic year. There is a refined look and confidence that a team exudes when they have competition experience with a particular routine. We made a strong effort to keep our choreography hidden to ensure the "wow" factor. While we did numerous performances domestically, we learned that perhaps there is no substitute for an actual competition.

Also, attending a competition would have given us a chance to promote ourselves, interact with Olympic judges, and receive feedback, all important components of synchronized swimming and a judged sport. Since the United States' strength is choreography, we took it upon ourselves to write several new routines for the Olympic Games. In the future, we will stagger that process so less writing takes place during the Olympic year providing the athletes more time to build confidence with particular routines, more opportunity for feedback, and more actual competition practice.

USA TABLE TENNIS | ROBERT C. FOX – TEAM LEADER

Table Tennis is a centuries old sport played all over the world. It is one of the most participated in sports in the world with a significant television audience as well. Table Tennis requires incredible quickness (both eye-hand and footwork), stamina through long matches and events, amazing agility, and competitive spirit. The ball travels at speeds of nearly 100 miles per hour and the table is 9 feet long. Strokes must be made quickly and with precision (in light of the 4.5 foot landing area). Players begin their careers at a very early age and usually reach peak performance in their 20s. An athlete's training regime is intensive and continuous. Aside from general physical condition, a training regime will concentrate on footwork drills, running, and the development of an incredibly fast reaction time. World class athletes also work on strategy and "gamespersonship".

Team selection is based on a combination of international ranking and Olympic Trials. We secured our first two spots for the women's division by virtue of having two athletes meet the ITTF World Ranking qualification. Then, pursuant to ITTF requirements, we held a US Trials (Philadelphia, January 2008) and selected four players who, in turn, competed against Canadian players at the North American Trials (Vancouver, April 2008). At the North American Trials, we secured another two spots for the women's division: one in singles and another in women's team. We were also able to secure a spot for the men's division in singles. We believe this system works well and would only suggest changing the schedule. If we selected the team earlier, we would have more time for training and preparation for the North American Trials and the Olympic Games.

Once selection, the team began training for the Games. Most training was done individually, with athletes participating in short camps and competing in ITTF Pro Tour Events around the world. This included three events in Asia: Japan, Korea, and Singapore. Our athletes reached the quarterfinals in women's singles in Korea and Singapore. In the future, with additional budget support, we would like to 1) provide a more centralized training program, 2) add one or two more competitions to the schedule, and 3) hold a two-week training camp for all team members.

In Beijing, we had a ten-day training camp at the USOC's High Performance Training Center at Beijing Normal University (BNU), with training partners provided by a local (Beijing) club. USOC staff helped with passes for partners and security issues. BNU was astoundingly helpful for us.

The women's team finished 5th in the women's Team competition (our best ever result), Wang Chen finished in the quarterfinals (top eight; best Olympic result ever) and Gao Jun finished in top 16 in women's singles. The women's team lost its opening match to Singapore, but the women kept their bronze medal hopes alive with wins in the subsequent rounds over Netherlands, Nigeria and Romania. We lost against Korea 3-0, in the semifinal, for the bronze medal and defeated Netherlands in the 5-6th place final, finishing 5th. Over all, this was a fantastic performance for the USA.

In women's singles, Wang Chen made history by finishing in the top 8. She accomplished this by defeating Kristina Toth (HUN) 4-1, and then world and Olympic medalist Kim, Kyung Ah (KOR) 4-3, before losing to Li Jia Wei (SIN). Gao Jun reached the top 16, defeating Eva Odorova (SVK) 4-2, Sayaka Hirano (JPN) 4-2 before losing to Xue Wu (DOM) 4-3. It is worthy of mention that Gao Jun beat Xue Wu in the 2003 and 2007 Pan Am Games finals. Crystal Huang and David Zhuang lost in the opening rounds of women's and men's singles, respectively.

In "real life", I am an attorney and a tenured full professor. I volunteer as co-chair of the USA Table Tennis Elite Athlete Committee and as team leader for national, Pan American Games and Olympic Games teams. I have served as team leader for each Olympic Games since Barcelona 1992.

Beijing was the best Olympic Games ever, in my experience. Everything worked well: team processing was easy, the competition venue was superb, the Olympic Village was excellent, BNU provided incredible support for training and housing and food, transportations was outstanding, USOC support was excellent in all areas. We had time to do more than just put out fires—we could really support the athletes and coaches. Beijing was the best, and it sets a new and high standard for future Games sites and for USOC preparation and team support.

Congratulations to the Beijing Committee and the Chinese people for a phenomenal Games and to the USOC for its incredible support for the Table Tennis Team and its best ever Olympic performance.

MEW CHOO WONG OF THE UNITED STATES COMPETES AGAINST LU LAN OF CHINA | *LARS BARON/BONGARTS/GETTY IMAGES*

USA TAEKWONDO | MEREDITH MILLER – HIGH PERFORMANCE MANAGER

Taekwondo is a combative weight-based sport. In the Olympic Taekwondo competition, each weight category consists of a single elimination tournament with a repechage for the bronze medal contest. The winner of the final contest receives the gold medal and the loser receives the silver medal. Losers to the finalist from all phases will advance to the repechage. In the repechage, the losers of the semifinals during the elimination phase were seeded directly to each of the repechage finals, but on the opposite side of the bracket. Other losers advanced to the repechage unseeded on the same side of the bracket in which they contested during the elimination phase. Two athletes compete against each other in a repechage bracket system. Since its official debut in 2000, and prior to Beijing, the U.S. Taekwondo team had won two gold medals and a silver medal.

Taekwondo is unique in that we go from a full National Team of 16 weight divisions down to an Olympic Team of four weight divisions. A point system was developed to select our weight divisions. From there, athletes could select the division in which they would compete in a multi-step trial process. Athletes winning the first Olympic Trial in August 2007 held in Colorado Springs, Colo., would compete to qualify the country and themselves by name at the World Olympic Qualifier in Manchester, England, in September 2007. Athletes not qualifing (finishing in the top three) at the World Olympic Qualifier would have another opportunity to qualify the country at the Pan American Olympic Qualifier in Cali, Colombia in December 2007. However, this time, they only qualified the division and not themselves by name and were put back into the trials process with athletes who competed in the first Olympic Team Trial. The final trial took place between the winner of the Pan American Olympic Qualifier and the winner of second Olympic Trial, which was held in Colorado Springs, Colo., in January 2008, with an advantage being given to the athlete who qualified the country. This means that the Pan American Olympic Qualifier had to win just once but their opponent had to beat them twice. The final team was named on April 5, 2008, following the Olympic Team Trial in Des Moines, Iowa.

Looking back on the process, we can make some changes to help select a better team in the future. One change that is necessary is having a discretionary process for selecting which weight divisions would be best for the country to compete in. This would keep our best two athletes from fighting each other in one division. Second, we need to develop a procedure that would protect our best athletes in case of an injury. Currently, if a world class star, like Steven Lopez, were to get injured, there is nothing protecting his spot on the team. This is not optimal for medal potential and should be considered when putting together the procedures for the 2012 Games.

Our entire Olympic Team trained together in Houston, Texas, prior to the Olympics. This was the normal training site for all athletes except Charlotte Craig. In addition, we had a total of three training camps between Olympic Trials and the Olympic Games. Two training camps were scheduled at the Olympic Training Center and the third was a staging camp that was held in Singapore for 10 days prior to arriving in Beijing on August 7. The camps were scheduled six weeks apart and allowed us to keep a close watch on all aspects of the athletes training and health. Because the team was training together in Houston, we used the camps in Colorado Springs to focus on things that we couldn't do in Houston. For example, we worked with the Sport Performance division to complete various testing on our athletes and allowed them to take advantage of the sport science facilities at the OTC. I believe the camps were very effective and the time was used wisely.

In February 2008, we attended the Olympic Test Event. This allowed us to not only go through a test competition but our pre-staging training camp as well. Because of our negative experience in Macau prior to the test event we decided to change the location of our camp to Singapore. This was one of the best decisions we could have made. In regards to the test event itself, this was a great exercise for the athletes, coaches and staff. We had no suprises at the Olympics because we attended the test event and the athletes were familiar with the layout of the facility which added comfort to the actual competition day. I would definitely encourage the Taekwondo Team to go to the test event prior to the 2012 Games.

During our time in Beijing, we used Beijing Normal University for all our training needs. BNU proved to be a perfect training site for us and we never even discussed using the organizing committee (BOCOG) facilities. Without the training grounds of BNU, we would have had training

CHARLOTTE CRAIG OF THE UNITED STATES (RED) COMPETES IN THE
WOMEN'S TAEKWONDO | JAMIE SQUIRE/GETTY IMAGES

issues as our training partners did not have access to any Olympic venues.

Charlotte Craig got things started for our team on August 20. She came out strong and won her first match. A format change from the past two Olympics was that after an athlete won their first match there was a two to four hour break before the next session. Charlotte was one of the first women's matches, so she had about four hours between her first two matches. Charlotte lost her second match but learned a lot from the experience. Following her second round loss, the girl that beat her lost before reaching the finals, thus eliminating Charlotte from the bronze medal bracket. A good lesson learned on this day was to keep the athlete engaged in competition mode between matches. Therefore, we decided not to return to BNU for lunch for the next two days of competition.

On the second day of competition, August 21, Mark and Diana Lopez both competed. Both Mark and Diana won their first fights moving on to the second round. Diana lost her second match, however, this time Diana's opponent advanced to the gold medal match putting Diana in the bronze medal bracket. Diana won her final two matches to claim the bronze medal.

Mark won his second round match to advance to the semifinals where he faced Peru. This was a tough match but Mark emerged victorious to face Korea in the gold medal match. After a hard fought match, Korea won 3-2 and Mark won the silver medal.

The final day of competition featured two-time Olympic Gold Medalist Steven Lopez. In his first match, he faced the silver medalist from the 2004 Olympics in Athens. Steven emerged victorious in a hard fought match to face Italy in the second round. In his match with Italy, Steven received a suspect penalty costing him a point prior to the end of regulation. As a result, the match went into sudden death, where Italy scored costing Steven the match. The staff came together immediately and decided to file a protest. Based on the rules, if a referee makes an error in an application of the rule the decision shall be overturned. The protest was dismissed by the arbitration committee without a written response or legitimate reason. The staff, headed by Herb Perez, continued to press the issue with the arbitration board until the competition continued past the point of no return. When Italy advanced to the gold medal match, Steven re-focused and returned to fight and win two matches for the bronze medal.

Steven's winning of the bronze medal marked the most medals ever won by a USA Taekwondo team at the Olympic Games. Steven, his brother Mark and sister Diana, made history by being the first three siblings to medal in the same Olympic Games.

Upon returning home, USA Taekwondo filed an official arbitration with the Court of Arbitration for Sport (CAS). Since filing the arbitration, much progress has been made to revise World Taekwondo Federation (WTF) rules and committees. They have appointed two U.S. officials to important international committees, are revising the protest procedures for competition, as well as the referee selection process, and have admitted, in writing, that a major error was made by the center referee in the Steven Lopez vs. Italy match. The arbitration was withdrawn from CAS based upon USAT's satisfaction with the steps the WTF has made to implement meaningful rule changes.

I had a budget to work from for the Olympic Games and the ability to make financial decisions. Our primary expenses revolved around our training camp in Sinagpore and our training partners (two per athlete). Overall, everything was well budgeted. We did not need to cut corners on any camps or services. If we had a larger budget we would have brought a massage therapist and a nutritionist/chef with us for the entire duration of the pre-staging camp and Olympic Games. I did learn that it would be best to keep some money in the budget for fun activities or team dinners. The Olympic preparation is a long process and everyone needs time away to have fun and avoid "Olympic fever".

I attended both USOC Team Leadership meetings. Both meetings provided good information and opportunities for attendees. In my experience, the round table discussions were most valuable. In addition, scheduled meetings with the venue managers were very helpful in establishing that important relationship which at times helped me get things done when no one else was able to help. For me, the Team Leadership Final Countdown meeting in March was redundant. I was in Beijing two weeks prior for our test event. Because I was local in Colorado Springs, I was not allowed to go through the round table sessions. Not going through round tables in March ultimately caused some confusion for our sport.

Regarding accreditation, the USOC representative took the time to understand why we asked for the amount of credentials that we did and also took the time to understand the role that each staff member would play as it related to our team. We were originally given word that we would receive three primary credentials (team leader, coach, and assistant coach) and one transferable credential (technical specialist). In July we received word that we were going to receive one primary and three transferables. The final allocation, which was changed upon our arrival in the village on August 7, ended up being two primary credentials (team leader and coach) and two transferable credentials (assistant coach and technical specialist).

Dealing with these changes at the last minute caused some issues. We definitely needed four staff credentials to support the entire team and give everyone the best chance to medal. My suggestion to those involved in the allocation process, is to pay close attention to the specifics of each sport and take the time to understand why they are requesting the credentials that they are. Also when estimating what a sport might receive for credentials, I would suggest starting low and then increasing the allocation as it gets closer to the Games. This way teams can plan for the worst knowing their situation may get better. By allocating high and then removing credentials it causes a lot of team leaders, including myself, to make unexpected last minute changes. As it relates to Taekwondo, removing primary credentials from such a small close-knit team caused us some internal problems leading into our time in Beijing.

We had no issues with our air travel and everything went well. Having the United staff onsite helped with the check-in process. Getting the extra baggage fees waived was a huge help for us as well.

The apparel process went smoothly. However, in the future it would be helpful to receive a list of items that will be included in each team processing package prior to arrival. My athletes and coaches were unsure of what to pack.

GOLD MEDALIST SON TAEJIN (RED) OF SOUTH KOREA COMPETES AGAINST MARK LOPEZ (BLUE) OF THE UNITED STATES | *VLADIMIR RYS/BONGARTS/GETTY IMAGES*

We had to change the date for team processing after attending our test event in February. The USOC accommodated our team as requested and everything ran smoothly throughout the day. Everyone processed at one time which worked best for our small team. Our only major problem was that all of our medical paperwork was missing. This did not cause a huge issue, but took longer because everyone had to resubmit their paperwork. We processed on the busiest day but the USOC staff was prepared and worked hard to ensure every team got through in a timely manner.

The transportation team was a huge help in providing us transportation from BNU to the venue on competition days. This allowed us to bring boxed lunches and dinners for all athletes and staff and ultimately helped in our success. The shuttle between BNU and the Olympic Village was great. There was a miscommunication regarding airport transportation for additional staff and training partners living at BNU. I was under the impression that transportation would be provided for these individuals and ended up scrambling at the last minute to get them transportation upon their arrival. Having set transportation for these individuals (at a cost to the NGB) would help greatly.

Having cell phones for all staff was very helpful and important to ensure our team was always on the same page. This was espically important because we had people staying at BNU and the Olympic Village. Regarding computer access, everyone staying at BNU was very happy with the computer setup. I would suggest adding one or two computers to the coaches work area in the Village because during key hours there was often a long wait. Also, I didn't see a printer in the Village or at BNU. When I needed to print something, I emailed the file to someone on the village staff and had them print it for me. This got the job done but was an extra step for me and the village staff. In addition, there was a problem with the approved frequency of our radios. Fortunately, the BOCOG staff was very helpful in getting the problem resolved. After 48 hours we were given a new frequency and the radios were approved.

We had two arbitrations filed within the course of our Olympic selection process and a few additional complaints. Additionally, we filed a formal protest at the Games on behalf of Steven Lopez, which was eventually appealed to CAS. Having the support of the USOC legal department when dealing with Olympic selection is very important. I would encourage keeping them involved in the entire process, start to finish. Despite the efforts of USAT and the team selection working group (TSWG), the Olympic Selection Procedures still had problems. Learning from our mistakes will be key when writing the 2012 procedures.

The overall setup of BNU was great. It gave our team a place to call home and took care of our training partners and additional staff. Finding housing for these additional team members would have been very difficult and expensive without this setup. Day rooms were requested for the Olympians after we learned that they could not live at BNU due to security concerns. The USOC staff provided the rooms at our request. Additionally, a room was provided for Mark Lopez on his weigh-in day. This allowed him to cut weight in a better enviroment and get the proper "re-feed" post weigh-in. Accomodating this request helped Mark be in the best state of mind and body going into competition the following day.

Additionally, having a dedicated training area for our team was ideal. We could change our training times if necessary to accommodate how the athletes needed to train without having to worry about scheduling conflicts. Also the shipping and set-up of the mats was a huge benefit to our team. Being able to train on a taekwondo mat versus a judo mat like they did in 2004 was very beneficial to our team. The food was incredible at BNU and the internet access and the athlete lounge were great as well. Having a High Performance Training Center is an ideal situation for any team at any Olympic Games.

Our medical staff consisted of Jasper Richardson, Chris Schroer and Dr. Larry Nassar. Jasper was our athletic trainer for our staging camp. Jasper had worked with Taekwondo at the Olympics in 2004 and at the Pan American Olympic Qualifier. He understood his role and executed perfectly. Chris was our athletic trainer for the competition. Chris worked with Taekwondo on numerous occasions leading into Beijing. He not only knew the athletes and coaches but had a great working relationship with Jasper which made the transition from Singapore to Beijing seamless. Dr. Larry Nassar hadn't worked with Taekwondo before Beijing but despite his lack of Taekwondo-specific experience, he was a great asset to our team. He took the time to learn the rules specific to medical staff as it relates to our sport and kept an open mind when difficult situations were encoutered. Chris Schroer helped Dr. Nassar deal with the learning curve of Taekwondo. Developing a plan to use Chris and Jasper to fulfill our medical needs was a great idea. They worked well together. Also, because the athletes and coaches were already familiar with both Chris and Jasper there was no learning curve for the medical staff or team at staging camps or the Games. Pre-existing relationships are crucial when it comes to athletic trainers.

The resident security officer at the Taekwondo facility was great. He was helpful yet understood fully when to stay out of the way of our team. In regard to the overall security process, we had no issues.

Making tickets avaliable for USA Taekwondo to order and providing two tickets for each competing athlete was very helpful. The process for ticket distribution was also great. Getting the tickets we ordered well in advance helped us organize everything prior to arriving in Beijing and gave us one less thing to worry about. We were short tickets for family members which in turn added stress for our athletes. In the future, we need to order additional tickets taking into account the families of our athletes. I think this occurred because of the lack of experience of our staff in dealing with the Olympics and budget problems.

Some lessons that I learned in regards to competition is to be prepared with pre-written protests for predicted situations. This will help to avoid any scrambling while at the event. Also, at all times, carry a rule book. In addition, be prepared in 2012 for the long break between the first two fights. We should do more mental training with the athletes to prepare them with ways to get their adrenaline up to ensure they are not caught sleeping in their second match.

In terms of communication, everyone needs cell phones. We provided cell phones for staff but did not have cell phones for training partners. This made it very difficult to keep track of people during down hours and could have caused some problems for us. In the future, I think it would be best, no matter what the cost, for all team members to have cell phone access.

A key component to our success was the number of staff credentials received. Having two coaches was very important, especially the day we had two athletes fighting. As proven by Steven's situation, having a person credentialed for the purpose of filing a protest was very important as well. Finally, having a separate credential for the team leader position was important because it allowed the coaches to focus on coaching without distractions.

In closing, I would suggest to not question what works or make changes to what you've been doing over time just because it is such a high profile event. Stick to what you have been doing and what has gotten you where you are.

USA Track & Field (USATF) selects its team in a head-to-head competition at the Olympic Trials. The 2008 team was selected June 27 – July 6, 2008, in Eugene, Ore. There is some controversy over whether head-to-head competition is the best way to select the track and field team. Most believe it is, with an estimated 95-percent success rate in choosing the best team. USA Track & Field's CEO has formed an audit committee to review the selection process.

Since track and field is not a team sport, each athlete establishes his/her own competition and training schedule with his/her personal coach for the weeks between the Trials and the Games. Many traveled to Europe and Asia to compete against athletes who will also be at the Olympic Games. Olympic team staff track the performances of team members during the days leading up to the Games but have no direct involvement with their training.

USATF hosted a training camp from August 1 – 20, 2008, in Dalian, China. Eighty seven (87) of the 126 athletes and 42 personal coaches attended the training camp. Most athletes felt they had everything they needed to train effectively. Some of the long distance runners were not satisfied with the amount of soft surface training facilities. Strict security policies at training camp caused most of the negative comments. Had we known that the air in Beijing was going to be clean and not an issue we probably would have reduced the number of days at the training camp. Some athletes want a training camp where they can train at any time of the day thus requiring the training facility to be within walking distance of the hotel. This probably isn't feasible considering the type of accommodations athletes expect. Training camp procedures and processes are reviewed after each major event and the athletes' evaluation forms are used to make improvements for the next event.

Leading up to the Olympics, the local organizing committee (BOCOG) hosted an Olympic test event. The U.S. track and field team did not attend. However, staff did attend for the purpose of familiarizing themselves with the facility during competition so that competition timelines could be established. It was very beneficial.

Beijing Normal University (BNU) was an excellent training facility for track & field. The warm-up track at the competition stadium was excellent but only accredited staff could enter so athletes who wanted to train with their personal coaches had to use BNU. The only drawback was the lack of room for long throwers to train at BNU. The long throwers were the most affected by the lack of credentials to get their personal coaches into the official practice facilities. Team coaches worked with the long throwers personal coaches to identify methods of training for those athletes, which allowed their personal coaches involvement when possible.

Track & Field won 23 medals (7 gold, 9 silver and 7 bronze) and finished on top of the medal charts for both total medals and the most gold medals won. . The next-best countries were Russia with 18 medals, six being gold, and Jamaica with 11 medals, six being gold. The 23 medals won by the U.S. team matches the medal tally won in Atlanta in 1996 and exceeds the 17 won in Sydney.

There are those who feel that this was one of our weaker Olympic teams because we won fewer medals than in 2004. I feel very strongly that this was a strong team that had unexpected things happen to it. Had the U.S. won the 4x100m relay, I doubt any of the negative statements about the team would have surfaced. A relay does not define a team. It will be necessary to review our policies to determine if these unexpected happenings could have been avoided.

The women's team was the strongest since 1992, showing the strides that have been made in the development of our female athletes. The U.S. women won nine medals to post their best medal tally since 1992, when they won 10. The U.S. won its first gold medal in the women's discus since 1932. Lolo Jones had the 100m hurdles won but she hit the last hurdle, taking her out of medal contention. Deena Kastor, the bronze medalist in the 2004 Olympic Games marathon, was on pace to capture a medal but had an injury during the race and did not finish.

The three gold medals won by the U.S. women matches their total in 1996 and exceeds 2000 and 2004, when they captured two in each of the two Games. In addition, the nine medals won by the women matches the third-highest Olympic medal total in history for a U.S. women's team. They won 16 in the boycott-affected 1984 Games and 10 in 1992, when Eastern European countries had been weakened by the fall of communism. They also won nine in 1932 and 1988.

The men's team was hampered by injuries. Tyson Gay, Breaux Greer, and Adam Nelson should have medaled had they not had injuries rendering them less than 100-percent. Reese Hoffa had an off day, which came at a very bad time. Inexperience in the men's field events left medals on the table, while two male jumpers, who have consistently medaled at big events, did not make the team. Brad Walker would have medaled in the pole vault had malfunctions in equipment, which delayed the process on his pit during qualifying, not taken the athletes on that pit out of contention. The United States protested this occurrence because the qualifying conditions were not equal. We asked that all entrants be advanced to the final because of the faulty equipment but the protest was denied. The 4x100m relays for both men and women should have medaled and was one of the most disappointing losses of the Games. Had everything come together as planned, the US would have won 28- 30 medals, making this team the best to date.

USATF's Games budget was established in 2006 and, once it was established, the team leader had the authority to make financial decisions, in cooperation with the High Performance Division Executive Committee.

The major expense for the Olympic Games was the training camp. Other expenses included room and board, air travel between Beijing and the training camp in Dalian, ground transportation (including both practice shuttles and rental cars and drivers), security, equipment, hydration supplies, medical, office and lounge workroom rentals, support staff air travel and High Performance filming. The budget for the training camp was affected by the decline in the value of the dollar. If USATF's budget were larger, athletes' request for travel and housing stipends for personal coaches would be at the top of the to-do list.

Prior to the Olympic Games, I attended both Team Leader meetings. They were informative and provided me with the tools needed to begin the planning process. They provided the opportunity for interaction with team leaders from other sports, helping to promote growth through learning from others. Valuable friendships were established that carried over in the trenches in China. It would be helpful if the round table discussions were conducted by the individuals who would be filling that position at the Games.

I also attended the USOC Key Decision Makers meeting. The frame work of the Games Deliverables is an invaluable tool and talking through each item in that document, with the appropriate USOC staff person, provided the necessary guidance to plan efficiently. More time at key stations would be helpful.

Accreditation is a large component of the Olympic Games. For smaller teams and teams that have their Olympic Trials well in advance of the Games, pre-registration (including detailed forms that were required to be mailed or faxed to the USOC by spring of 2008) is a non-issue. However, for track & field, which selected its team in July of 2008, it was a nightmare. Submitting a long list is easy to do but when that long list requires paperwork and photos it becomes almost unmanageable. Track & Field had to take staff from other departments to facilitate this process and even then, we were only about 80-percent compliant. USATF requested and was granted an extension by the USOC.

Originally, USATF requested 18 primary officials credentials, 15 additional officials credentials, and 60 "P" credentials (for personal coaches/medical). Once the USOC had a final determination of the U.S. delegation size, negotiations began to strike a happy medium. Track & Field received 18 primary credentials (with seven being transferable), eight additional officials (all transferable) and 14 "P" credentials. While 14 "P" credentials is not the number needed for a team of 126 athletes, we made it work but not to everyone's satisfaction. USATF did take some backlash on the inability of several personal coaches to get onto the warm-up track. This is a problem that the USOC should consider addressing with the International Olympic Committee (IOC). Medals may well have been left on the table because of a lack of "P" credentials. In order to make best use of the "P" credential, it was decided to give them to the coaches of running event athletes who were projected to medal. As a result, field event athletes lacked the advantage they usually have in international competition because their coach was not with them during their initial warm-up period. Field Event coaches were accommodated with a ticket and a coach's box pass, allowing them some limited communication with their athletes during the competition warm-up. While USATF acknowledges the job that the USOC did in getting 14 "P"'s for track & field, we needed more.

Transferable passes caused track & field some difficulties as well. Track & Field is a sport that needs all of its credentials from beginning to end. It's difficult for the staff to adequately complete their tasks when access is limited due to credential unavailability. The USOC did a great job getting our transferable credentials earlier than projected, but it is still not an efficient policy for track & field. USATF recommends that sports dealing with a large number of athletes be given their full allotment of credentials for the entire period of the Games.

USATF and the USOC need to continue to review their credential procedures. I am not sure anything can be done differently for an Olympic Games because the IOC sets the policies, but I do think that both the USOC and USATF should lobby the IOC and International Association of Athletics Federations (IAAF) to bring about changes to this process. USATF is in the process of reviewing its staff and team selection poli-

JENNIFER STUCZYNSKI COMPETES DURING THE WOMEN'S POLE VAULT FINAL | *GABRIEL BOUYS/AFP/GETTY IMAGES*

cies and practices and this should provide insight into how change can be effected.

Air travel worked great for these Games. The USOC and the United Airlines staff worked with four members of the USA Track and Field staff, which included our travel agent. Because track and field does not travel as a team, our sport presents more problems for a travel agent. USATF staff and the USOC went above and beyond the call of duty to address the individual needs and wishes of approximately 100 of the 126 track and field athletes. The USOC and United Airlines also worked diligently to arrange for athletes desiring to leave Beijing prior to their scheduled departure times. The staff's travel itineraries came a little later than we would have liked but all did get ticketed and received their itinerary just prior to departure.

One thing that worked really well for us was having the United staff at team sign-up at the Olympic Trials. In the future, it is suggested that tickets should actually be booked at the Trials so that athletes leave with their itinerary. Changes made after this time would be made through USATF's travel agent, and at the athletes expense, with revised itineraries sent to the USOC.

Uniforms for a large team is always an issue, however with Nike being a supplier for both USATF and the USOC, we had a good working relationship. Unfortunately, we had a few communication problems when it came to submitting colorboards for IOC approval. USATF thought Nike was handling the approval process and it wasn't until notified by the USOC that our colorboards had not be received that we realized the problem. In the future, we suggest that Nike forward colorboards to USATF and the team leader, who, in turn, will submit to the USOC.

Apparel presented two problems: first, the more fitted styles caused athletes to request the next size up, which caused a shortage in the larger sizes. Second, the choice of two different colors for men and women (in track jackets and award uniforms) meant that some of our female throwers, who require a 4XL size, were outfitted in a different color than their teammates.

We do appreciate Nike's effort to provide a variety of casual wear for the athletes. In spite of the fitting problems, athletes were pleased to have more than just a couple of plain t-shirts. Opening Ceremony outfits needed to be a little more lightweight.

The team processing in San Jose, California, was efficient but the uniform line often got long. This only occurred when large groups were processing at the same time. It was suggested that athletes be broken up into groups with some going to apparel distribution while others went to the briefing.

About 75-percent of the team processed as expected. Track & Field processed in stages. A small number of athletes were allowed to par-

ticipate in a modified processing at the Olympic Trials in order to meet their travel dates for international pre-Games competitions. Overall processing worked well for track & field.

Transportation is key to our success because of the nature of our team. The car that we requested while in Beijing was delivered a few days later than we needed it, however, the USOC shuttle between BNU and the Village worked well and helped meet our team needs until the car arrived. The BNU shuttle operated like clockwork and once athletes found the pick-up location and understood the schedule very few transportation problems occurred. The shuttle from the competition stadium to BNU did not run late enough thus staff often had to find taxis late at night.

Knowing costs for vehicles earlier in the process would have been nice. Not knowing the cost until late in the planning stages caused USATF to drop its order from three vehicles to one van because of the expense. We used public transportation and taxis to supplement our one van.

Also the car and driver that we were assigned had a 14 hour per day limit or we had to pay overtime making the car not available for emergencies late at night. The car set idle during most hours of the day but because we had a need for it each morning to take additional medical supplies and equipment from BNU to the stadium we could not use the driver late at night for after hour drug testing transportation.

In the past, USATF had always had a vehicle that was staged at the competition venue until all athletes had completed the doping control process thus when official transportation stopped before athletes had completed drug testing athletes were stranded with no way back to the Village very late at night (3:00 a.m.) The USOC staff person was awakened several times to send out a pool car that was used for emergencies to pick up the athletes.

Providing NGB's with the ability to rent cars for their use is a good practice and should be continued but cost must be know much earlier in the process.

Communication worked well throughout the Games. The staff cell phones were excellent pieces of equipment. We requested our cell phones be available for pick-up at team processing and they were available to us. We continue to struggle with athletes' phones because of the small amount of prepaid time loaded on them. Once they run out of minutes, athletes do not add any additional time, rendering their phones useless. That meant we could not rely on these phones to reach athletes in an emergency because athletes simply wouldn't carry the phone with them if it is not usable.

The athlete lounge had an adequate amount of computers with internet access; however the coaches/staff area only had two which provided limited access at times. The printer attached to the computers in the coaches' area didn't work for a number of days thus making it hard to print important information.

USATF requested a DSL line for the common area being used as an office; it was operational and connected to four computers by the time we arrived in the Village. Once USATF staff arrived and assessed the overall set up, it was determined that another DSL line was needed in Building 1, so athletes could have access to the internet without having to go to Building C. It took several days for the second line to be installed but it was worth the wait.

The lack of internet access in athlete sleeping rooms caused much frustration. It might be wise to establish a wireless network in all USOC assigned buildings so athletes can use their computers without having to leave their specific building.

Our USOC legal contact, John Ruger, was an excellent support staff to track & field and worked with the Team Leader to resolve several issues with athletes.

We did have an athlete ask for a Court of Arbitration for Sport (CAS) hearing after making the qualifying standard after the established cut off for track & field. USATF felt that since the USOC approved the selection procedures it was an issue for both the USOC and the Federation. The arbitration upheld our selection procedures.

In terms of logistics, the USOC was unable to provide a dedicated space for USATF medical to work in the Village. Not having all of our medical staff in the Village caused athletes to have to plan their medical visits thus making it less user friendly.

In addition, athletes requested the ability to rent TV's for their individual rooms. Neither the USOC, nor USATF, expected the number of request received. As a result, TV's were not readily available and most individual needs could not be met. In the future, USATF and the USOC should order a few extra TV units through the Games Deliverables process so athletes' requests can be accommodated. Athletes were not satisfied with the athlete lounge thus USATF took one of its common areas and added wireless and a TV so that athletes could relax without having to leave their building.

USOC staff was willing to work through problems, finding a satisfactory solution 95-percent of the time. Vaulting poles, which usually are a nightmare to handle, were efficiently moved from BNU to the competition stadium by USOC and USATF staff. Athletes did not have to worry about when or how their poles would be transferred to the competition stadium.

The people the USOC selected for logistical staff were amazing. What they didn't know they found out, what they couldn't do they asked for help with. All egos were left at home.

Outside housing at Beijing Normal University was excellent and met track & field's needs. Having a coaches' room, with internet access, meeting space, and meal service for personal coaches made life easier for both athletes and coaches.

Having USOC nutritionists and chefs prepare meals for athletes training at BNU was a tremendous success. However, the inability of athletes to sleep at BNU created a void when athletes needed to be by themselves, became ill, had a leaky room in the Athlete Village, etc. Had we known from the start that security issues would prohibit the housing of athletes at BNU, we would have booked rooms at a nearby hotel.

Checking in for housing or a credential at BNU was a challenge. It would be best if check-in could be in a non-secured location so that individuals could be processed by English speaking staff. Track & Field had an excellent training facility at BNU. We had exclusive use of the track during the two scheduled track & field practices each day. The team leader worked with the USOC to find a track & field equipment supplier (UCS) to provide the needed equipment at a reasonable cost.

TYSON GAY OF THE US RUNS TO WIN THE MEN'S 100M ROUND 1 HEAT 5
| CHRISTOPHE SIMON/AFP/GETTY IMAGES

Everything athletes needed was available on the track. The weight room was second to none. Everything requested was supplied. The pool provided athletes with a place for water therapy during designated hours each day.

Track & Field made use of the high performance filming equipment and DVD burners. Through the feeds from NBC and USATF's filmers' footage, athletes could review their round of competition or practice session and work on adjusting problem areas before the next round or during the next practice. USATF staff was familiar with most equipment used so little training was needed.

Beijing Normal should become the model for all USOC high performance training centers. It was by far the best track & field has experienced.

In terms of the Athlete Village, it was an amazing venue and the USOC staff was great to work with. Having staff members that were service oriented was the key to success. The check-in procedures set the tone for an athlete's stay in the Village. As athletes arrived, USOC and USATF staff met the athletes making sure their credentials were activated. From there, all luggage was loaded for transport to their apartment and keys were distributed. For a large sport, such as track &field, that has multiple arrival dates and times the check-in/out procedures must be streamlined and extremely organized in order to have an efficient process. The USOC had a plan for this process and it worked well.

Giving the keys to the team leader in advance of the athletes' arrivals was a time saver and allowed the team leader and staff to take a look at the rooms to determine if some were better suited for different types of athletes. In the Village, all rooms are not created equal and being able to evaluate rooms in advance saved USATF staff the headache of having to move larger athletes, who might have been assigned one of the smallest rooms, into rooms that physically accommodated them better.

The USOC office was always staffed, so if you had a problem you could find someone who could place a call or help fix whatever you needed. This was a very helpful situation. The only real problem came from leaks in the rooms. The USOC would ask for repairs but no follow through occurred so several days might pass before and athlete would notify us that the room still was leaking. This problem was primarily one of language barriers and staff and athletes had to work around the leaks until they were fixed.

Guest passes into the Village were a real problem. The USOC had a limited number each day and some were used to bring non-credentialed staff in to work. This will always be the case but the situation of athletes not being able to get their parents in because they needed to sign up days in advance needs to be reviewed. The Athlete Services Coordinators worked extremely hard to make the day passes go around but in the end the U.S. just didn't receive enough passes to meet its needs.

Scheduling medical services for a large sport such as ours is much different than scheduling team sports services. The staff extended hours on a few occasions to meet the athletes' needs.

USATF's medical staff was chosen from our list of approved medical providers and was composed of individuals who had all worked with our athletes at previous competitions. USATF added four individuals to the USOC provided medical staff. They were Benny Vaughn (massage therapist), Randy Ballard and Julie Endreson (athlete trainers) and Glen Lowenburg (chiropractor). The USOC supplied Angie Matsen-Ruffenacht, LaGwyn Durden and Harris Patel (athletic trainers), Monique Burton (physician) and Ross Flowers (psychologist). All athletic trainers approved by USATF must also be licensed massage therapists.

Although planning for medical services for these Games was successfully accomplished at least a year out, we still found that there was not

enough space for all the medical staff supplied by USATF. Because athletes determine early on who they prefer to use for medical services, we believe it is important for the USOC to find a way to provide more work space for all credentialed medical staff.

Out of competition drug testing is always difficult and was no different in China. Drug testing chaperones were not particularly flexible about finding an athlete, showing up at the Village when the athlete was at practice, or vice-versa. Testing during competition, at the stadium, was without issue.

The rate card provides a necessary tool for NGB planning. The process worked well but information was needed at least two years prior, for it to be effective in the budget process for track & field. The timeline in which rates were known was not always conducive to efficient budgeting. Cost of rate card items are needed much earlier than they were available.

In regards to security, the USOC provided assistance to USATF during the planning phase of the training camp in Dalian. They made contacts on our behalf with the State Department and the Embassies in China. They were responsible for the onsite U.S. State Department presence at the training camp thus giving athletes and staff a more secure feeling in a very stressful security setting. Allowing USOC staff to support NGBs outside of USOC events is an added support bonus to NGBs.

Security was a major issue for athletes, staff and family members. Security briefs that can be used for distribution to athletes, staff and family on what to expect and how to act would be helpful.

Tickets for the 2008 Olympic Games were difficult for athletes' families to purchase. USATF and the USOC must take a look at better ways of meeting the needs of athletes' families. While the two free tickets provided by the USOC were greatly appreciated, many athletes struggled to find tickets for their other family members thus causing undue stress before competition. With track & field holding its Trials in July families are not predisposed to purchasing tickets before they know

their athlete has made the team. The ability for an NGB to purchase Olympic Games tickets is always a positive.

However, track & field did not receive all of the tickets they purchased prior to leaving for the Games. The Team Leader picked up the remaining tickets upon arrival in Beijing. This caused stress on the team leader because a staff person had to be reassigned to handle the delivery of the tickets as the individuals arrived in Beijing. In the future, tickets should arrive to the NGB in time for them to be distributed State side.

The Olympic Games is always a learning experience no matter how many staffs you have served on. USATF surveyed athletes prior to their departure from Beijing and the results of the survey indicated that the overall experience was very good.

Some lessons learned this time around were: never expect things to happen quite as planned regardless of the extent of planning; having contingency plans is critical to success; the more you improve your services, the more you are expected to provide and having the right staff in place is absolutely critical to success. Also, we confirmed that some athletes really need their personal coaches, even if just for moral support. The USOC and USATF have to find a way to achieve a better credential plan with the limited credentials provided at an Olympic Games. Policies and procedures for selection of coaches and team members need to be reviewed to determine that we are getting the best possible team and staff.

In closing, the USOC and USATF must continue to build on the strong partnership that was established between staffs leading up to and during these Olympic Games. Having been involved with three different Olympic Games, I still believe in the Olympic Movement and what it brings to the world. Many thanks to all who played even the smallest role in supporting track & field at the 2008 Olympic Games.

USA TRIATHLON | SCOTT SCHNITZSPAHN – SPORT PERFORMANCE DIRECTOR

For triathlon, Olympic performance is fairly well predicted by previous performance on the International Triathlon Union (ITU) World Cup and World Championship events in the two years prior to the Games. As a result of the tactics and high level of fitness required, veteran athletes, with a history of being on the podium at major events, usually perform well and earn medals.

For 2008, USA Triathlon utilized a three race selection procedure for the Olympic Team. The first qualifier earned their spot by being the first U.S. finisher at the Beijing World Cup Olympic Test event in September of 2007, with the second coming from the U.S. Olympic Trials in April of 2008. The third member of the team was selected with a points system that factored in the athlete's best two out of three finishes among the first two selection events and a third at the Des Moines World Cup in June of 2008. These events were chosen for their similarity to the heat, humidity and course profile of the Olympic Games. In the event that the U.S. only qualified two start slots for the Games, the two athletes would be selected based on the Beijing test event in 2007 and the points system.

Ultimately, I believe the system did select the best athletes for the team. However, an argument could be made that the U.S. had four Olympic caliber men and only three could make the team. Which three of the four men were the best for the team depended on their performance on any given day and the best performers made the team in the end.

In hindsight, I would change the procedures to include the events in the process the ITU used to qualify country slots. As it worked out, the U.S. qualified three men and three women, the maximum allowed, but not without some drama and extra effort from the winner of our Olympic Trials, who had to have some great performances to secure his and the United States' third start slot. The Olympic Trials and the Des Moines World Cup were not events that earned ITU Olympic points, and so our Olympic focused athletes skipped important point events to focus on performing well in these events in order to make the team. The location, environment, and timing of the events were our concern in creating the process as we never would have predicted our athletes would not have secured three slots through the ITU's process. In the future, these events must score points in whatever system the ITU will use to qualify country slots. Athletes attempting to make an Olympic team must also be contractually obligated to race these events as well. Additionally, to better peak for the Games, I feel our team should be selected earlier to allow proper training specific to the Games and not the qualifying process. Logistically, the process would be easier for the staff, the USOC, and the athletes and their families if the team is selected earlier.

Our athletes' season is very long and there are usually only a few months, November through February, that might be considered the off-season. Some athletes train at home in the U.S. while others train in Australia or other warm weather locations. For better preparation, we can use more camps and race situations where we mimic the amount of support and logistics that they will experience during the Games. Our athletes have been somewhat independent and self sufficient, but when they have every need taken care of in the week leading up to the Games and travel as a team, it presents a new dynamic. The team atmosphere and support are very good and the athletes reported that when their every need is taken care of, then there are no barriers to performance. This format is out of the ordinary but our athletes should have more experience with this style of team support.

In terms of training following selection of the team, it was different for each athlete depending on when they qualified. For the first qualifiers at the 2007 Beijing World Cup, they could focus their entire season on preparing for one race. The others had to focus on the qualifying events in April and June of 2008. They could not turn their focus to Beijing until they qualified.

The competition schedule varied drastically with each athlete as a result. Laura Bennett raced at an event in Australia in March near her training base to check her fitness and she performed well considering her phase of training. She earned a fourth place finish behind two athletes who would eventually finish in front of her in Beijing. She then struggled in the extreme cold conditions at the World Championships in early June in Vancouver, Canada. She also competed in the World Cup in Des Moines, Iowa, where she finished fourth while suffering from a respiratory infection.

Jarrod Shoemaker, who also qualified in Beijing in 2007, had some promising performances at a World Cup in Japan, where he finished 13th and the Pan American Championships in April, where he finished second. He chose these two events as their heat and humidity would help prepare him for Beijing. He struggled with cramping at the Des Moines World Cup finishing 19th. He finished his preparation with a strong Continental Cup in New York, finishing second.

The qualifiers at the Olympic Trials in April, Julie Ertel and Matt Reed, had very different preparation for Beijing. Julie struggled in the cold and rain of the Madrid World Cup while racing with an illness, then performed well at the Des Moines World Cup in June, finishing seventh. She then won the Continental Cup in July in New York. Her training progressed well through the summer including breakthrough workouts at the Olympic training camp in Korea just before the Games.

Matt Reed, on the other hand, had to race two unplanned World Cups to secure the U.S. men's third Olympic slot: one in South Africa, where he placed second in a sprint finish, and the other in Madrid, Spain, where he finished 10th in horribly cold and wet conditions. He then finished fifth at the World Championships in Vancouver, the best U.S. men's finish. He then struggled at the Des Moines World Cup with an illness and did not finish. After this hectic period of races, his training progressed well through the Korea camp with similar breakthrough workouts to Julie's.

Hunter Kemper and Sarah Haskins focused their training on the trials process. However, while Sarah earned a silver medal at the cold World Championships in Vancouver in June, Hunter stayed home to focus on the final selection event and manage a sports hernia injury that had been plaguing his training through the spring. Both athletes performed well at the Des Moines World Cup, with Sarah finishing sixth and Hunter taking seventh, securing their places on the 2008 team by virtue of consistent top two American performances at the selection events. Both athletes then competed at the LifeTime Fitness Triathlon in July and trained very well up through the Korea camp.

I don't feel any of the athletes' competition and training programs leading up to the Games had a significant impact on performance at the Games one way or the other. I feel they all prepared adequately based on when and how they made the team. While many people feel that Matt Reed's arduous travel and race schedule to secure the third men's slot for the Games and his own place on the team left him flat for the Olympic competition, he had incredible training in the week leading up to the Games and appeared physically ready to race. As stated previously though, I would qualify the team earlier in the future to allow more specific Games preparation over the year leading into the Olympics.

The ITU held World Cup events at the Games site in 2005, 2006, and 2007. All of the team members attended at least two of those events with all of them attending in 2007. The test event was useful in that it allowed the athletes not only to become familiar with the course, but more importantly with the travel, lodging, culture, food, and environmental conditions. The 2007 event also allowed us to rehearse our training camp plans in Korea and work out all of the lodging, food, and travel issues before 2008. Five of the six athletes who made the team attended the 2007 camp in Korea and all six of them stayed at our Games-time hotel during the 2007 test event. This allowed our team to go into familiar surroundings for the Games, having been there under similar conditions in 2007.

Training at the Games provided a number of logistical challenges, beginning at team processing at San Jose State University (SJSU). Due to the hectic schedule to process the team and travel to Opening Ceremony combined with the athletes traveling from three different states, training was individualized to each athlete at SJSU. Matt Reed, Sarah Haskins, Hunter Kemper, and Jarrod Shoemaker arrived one day early to get a full day of training in on the processing day. Julie Ertel and Laura Bennett arrived on the processing day. In the future, I would like to see the entire team have two days at processing to allow for training as this worked well for those who came in early and the pace was less stressful.

Prior to Opening Ceremonies, the team was able to use the USOC High Performance Training Center at Beijing Normal University for one day. This facility allowed the athletes to train in an American-only environment with full support and great facilities. The pool was shorter than optimal at 21 meters, but was effective for the short workout the athletes completed. Cycling was available in the Village with the generous support of USA Cycling who loaned USA Triathlon a stationary trainer and bikes if needed.

Following Opening Ceremonies, we flew to Korea for our Olympic Training. This camp was excellent with the only challenge being locating truly flat roads and softer surfaces for training.

Once back in Beijing at our hotel, training at the official venues was excellent with the 50m pools and the on-course training. The only issues here were communicating some transportation needs and lack of access for personal coaches, training partners and replacement athletes to the venues.

Overall, the team performed well with all three women in the top 20 with our best finish being Laura Bennett in fourth place. Laura was in contention for a silver or bronze medal until the third of four laps on the run when she suffered some cramps, but finished strong. All three women led the group from the swim and rode well in the lead group on the bike as well.

For the men, Hunter Kemper earned our best men's finish ever at an Olympic Games finishing seventh. Jarrod Shoemaker also finished in the top 20, coming in 18th. Matt Reed was in contention until the run where he struggled to finish in the pack in 32nd place. All three men swam well and rode in the large lead pack on the bike, with Matt attempting a breakaway on the bike as well, but not having the energy to sustain it.

USA Triathlon, while disappointed in not earning any medals, was satisfied with the good overall team performance and the individual effort of each team member in the races. They raced well tactically and gave their best efforts on the day. Most importantly they represented the USA and USA Triathlon well throughout the Olympic experience.

USA Triathlon had an Olympic budget with our primary expenses coming from our travel and lodging. If we had a bigger budget we would have been able to pay for the personal coaches expenses.

I was able to attend the USOC Team Leadership meetings and found them very informative. I found the round tables with each area on the deliverables document very helpful. I also attended the USOC Key Decision Maker meetings and found them valuable in regards to the information on how to do business in such a different culture.

We had a few issues arise with our credentials, specifically the transferable credentials. Two of our credentials were transferable, which meant that our coaches had to stay outside the village, at BNU, for the first two nights. This meant they did not travel to and from the airport with the team and were not in the village for some training sessions. It also meant additional cost for USA Triathlon in terms of lodging. However, this was a problem simply because we chose to attend Opening Ceremony. From a performance standpoint, the transferable credentials make perfect sense and are a good way for USOC to support all sports with requested credentials.

We requested, and USOC fought for, credentials for our mechanic, our chiropractor, two coaches, a team leader, and a USOC credentialed trainer. In the end, the ITU had a wrist band system that restricted access to one medical person and three coaching type passes which we used for the two coaches and the team leader. We had to find an alternative plan to get our chiropractor access to the athletes in the hour before the event and our mechanic had very limited access to the field of play.

If ITU is going to control field of play access instead of following the Olympic credential system, then all the work for credentials seems academic. Maybe the IOC and ITU can work together to make the process and access level more clear to the USOC and USA Triathlon next time. Additionally, and even more important, is that the ITU should push the IOC for P credentials for a limited number of personal coaches so that there is access to the training venues for these individuals.

Our air travel went smooth for the most part. We had some bikes at San Jose State University that we were able to send separately with an athlete that went straight to our training camp. We had some additional baggage expense in regards to our training camp because we did not fly United Airlines to Korea and back.

Another issue was in the type of tickets we purchased. We initially requested upgradeable tickets and were told that there was nothing available to upgrade to, so we did not purchase them. As it turned out on every leg there were upgrades available, so we paid to upgrade the ticket. Had we simply purchased upgradeable tickets at the start, we could have saved a significant amount of money and time.

We had trouble getting information from ITU regarding competitive apparel requirements and we had significant delays in getting color boards from our sponsor Speedo for the competition uniforms as well. There were no repercussions other than having to do things last minute.

The team processing, and USOC issued apparel was amazing. However, we weren't sure about where and how to pick up our additional packages for our President and Executive Director, who didn't go through processing. In the end, we found them in Beijing. If possible it would be best to get these packages before leaving home. In addition, I would have liked to have had our chiropractor and mechanic go through processing with us so that they were included in the official team photo. This would also have eliminated the need to pre-pack and ship their gear to them separately.

In terms of our ground transportation the USOC coordinated a truck to take the bikes to the San Francisco airport. Sarah Haskins was flying straight to Korea for the training camp, so the USOC helped her get all the bikes on the flight to Korea with her.

The cell phones provided to us through the USOC were great and the quick reporting of the athlete's numbers was crucial to our communi-

L-R) EMMA MOFFATT OF AUSTRALIA AND LAURA BENNETT OF THE USA COMPETE IN THE RUNNING PORTION OF THE WOMEN'S TRIATHLON FINAL | *ADAM PRETTY/GETTY IMAGES*

cation within our team and with USOC. Having access to the internet was nice but would like to see wireless available in the rooms next time around. We had some issues with our radio frequency registration. Had we been notified that we did not receive our frequency license before we arrived in China, two days before our competition, we could have resolved the issue months prior to the Games. Instead, the issue caused significant stress and multiple trips to the venue with long waits to see the frequency engineers to resolve the issue. In the end, we did get "emergency approval" of a frequency to use for our events.

The only time we dealt with legal was when we almost had to cancel our third selection event due to weather related issues. We altered our criteria in the week before to allow for a backup plan should the event be cancelled. In the end the event took place and there were no issues.

In regards to our medical personnel we may want to travel with our own doctor in the future, especially for remote training camps. We were able to have a nutritionist with us at our training camp that helped educate and facilitate the hydration and acclimation process. His work with us regarding nutrition and helping us secure food from BNU was key in keeping our athletes healthy and ready to compete. Many other countries had significant nutritional illness issues, especially those staying outside of the Village.

In regards to tickets, we did not receive anywhere close to the number of tickets requested, so we had to purchase through our Chinese contacts for staff and additional athlete tickets which involved some processing fees. Many of our athlete's families did not listen to us in passing along the information from the USOC about CoSport and the possible fraudulent ticket sellers. Quite a few families were scammed out of thousands of dollars and arrived in Beijing with no tickets. Luckily, we purchased quite a few extras for the triathlon events through CoSport and local Chinese contacts so that all family members could attend. However, in the future, USA Triathlon and especially the team leader should not get involved in tickets, lodging, or transportation for families.

Overall, our team had an excellent experience at the 2008 Beijing Olympics. Our plan was well thought out, well rehearsed in 2007, and well executed in 2008. With the amazing support of the USOC, our athletes were as prepared as they could be and suffered none of the distractions that are common with Olympic Games.

As a Team Leader, I learned many things that will help in the future. First of all, we need to double check everything with the USOC and Local Organizing Committee - before the Games - to avoid situations like we had with radios not being licensed. Secondly, to ensure our staff can perform well in the Games environment, all primary and replacement staff should attend the test event and any pre-competition camps. Unfortunately, our two coaches did not attend any of the previous Beijing World Cups or the 2007 camp, but they adapted quickly and performed admirably. Third, in countries where we don't speak the language, we should have an interpreter that works for our team instead of relying on the interpretation of a local travel company. Finally,

I also learned the hard way that while USA Triathlon wants to ensure that other staff, board members, family, friends, and supporters of our athletes have a great Games experience, the staff should not have any involvement with their plans for travel, lodging, apparel, or tickets. A volunteer group from USA Triathlon should be set up at least one year out from the Games in the future to deal with family and friends.

I also learned that much of what we did worked. Having a dress rehearsal of any proposed camps and using outside lodging at the test event is crucial in providing familiar surroundings for the Games. Athletes and staff can focus on performance instead of being distracted by their environment or logistical concerns. The Opening Ceremony is also incredibly important to the overall Olympic experience for the athletes and can have a positive impact on performance if managed well. The athletes also need to have the option of not attending if they choose. We managed both situations well for Beijing.

While we always strive for perfection and we can learn from these Games, and while we also would prefer to come home with medals from an Olympic Games, I feel that with the USOC and USA Triathlon support that the athletes had every possible advantage to performing well in their competitions and we should be proud of everyone's performances on and off the field of play.

COMPETITORS DIVE IN FOR THE SWIMMING PORTION OF THE MEN'S TRIATHLON FINAL | *ADAM PRETTY/AFP/GETTY IMAGES*

USA VOLLEYBALL - MENS INDOOR | ROB BROWNING – TEAM LEADER

As a team sport, Volleyball competes together throughout the quad at many high-profile, annual events. As a result, we are quite self-reliant and independent.

Our team selection process is made over the course of months and years leading up to the Olympic Games. The process is highly refined through competition and statistics. Mostly, the process is self-selection – the athlete is either good enough or not. By the time the selection is made there are usually only a few positions where personnel is a question and the head coach, with input from his staff, makes those decisions.

The team participated in the Annual World League with excellent results – winning USA's first ever WL title. This competition prepared the team well for Beijing. The team was fortunate to be able to rest some players before the final weekend of the World League. The travel and late finish of the World League was a risk so close to the Games but it worked out well for our team.

There was an Olympic Test Event held prior to the start of the Olympic Games, but our team did not participate.

Beijing Normal University (BNU) was a perfect training place for us. With the USOC's help and cooperation we were able to work out a good training schedule. We had originally thought we would be sharing with the women's volleyball team but, as it turned out, we shared with them and both the men's and women's basketball teams.

Our team performed brilliantly in spite of the tragedy involving our head coach's in-laws and the resulting fallout. On August 9, our team learned of a terrible incident involving the Bachman family. Hugh McCutcheon's wife, Elisabeth (affectionately known as Wiz) Bachman McCutcheon, a 2004 Olympic volleyball player was with her parents near the Drum Tower in Beijing, when they were attacked. Hugh immediately went to be with them while the assistant coaches and players prepared for their first match against Venezuela.

The day before, during Opening Ceremony, I marched around the track with Hugh and Marv Dunphy. We were soaking it in, enjoying the spectacle and joy of it all. We kept an eye out for Wiz and her parents, looking for a U.S. flag in the lower bowl where Wiz had told Hugh they were seated. Near the end of the lap Hugh spotted them. I'll never forget the image of Wiz jumping up and down, waving the flag with a huge smile on her face, blowing kisses to Hugh. It was a moment of exhilaration she was sharing with Hugh, with her parents by her side.

When we learned of the attack on the Bachman family the next day, the image of Wiz in the stadium wouldn't leave my head. The contrast from one day to the next could not have been greater.

Our team started out well and pretty much controlled the match against Venezuela for two and a half sets. Venezuela hung tough in the third, caught some breaks, and sent us into the fourth set. Venezuela got the momentum they needed in the fourth set to send the match into the fifth set. The fifth set is always a tough set as it can easily go either way. It was close but then our boys made the plays they needed to put it out of reach, winning the match 3-2.

Our next opponent was Italy. In 2004 in Athens, Italy lost the gold medal to Brazil. In 2000 in Sydney they beat Argentina for the bronze medal and in 1996 in Atlanta they lost to Holland in the gold medal match. We had lost to Italy in our group in 2000 and again in 2004, so we were looking for some revenge. We got our revenge beating Italy 3-1 and then defeated Bulgaria 3-1 in our third match. Our next opponent was against host country China.

There were two venues for volleyball. The principal venue was Capital Indoor Gymnasium (CIG) and the secondary venue was the Beijing Institute of Technology (BIT) Gymnasium. BIT is much smaller and cozier than CIG. It played to our advantage when we faced China because the sellout crowd was about 7,000 fewer than it would have been in the main venue. Team USA controlled the match from beginning to end, to defeat China 3-0. Our head coach, Hugh, also returned to the bench for this game and it was great to have him back.

Our next match was against Japan, which was our easiest match; we won 3-0. We then turned in one of the biggest Olympic wins for the USA Men's team since Barcelona in 1992, when we defeated Serbia 3-2. In our semifinal match, we faced off against Russia, defeating them 3-2 to advance to the gold medal match. Our opponent would be Brazil, the defending gold medalists and the No. 1 ranked team in the world. The United States was 4-3 against Brazil since 2004, and we

US PLAYERS WILLIAM PRIDDY (R), DAVID LEE (C) AND CLAYTON STANLEY (L) BLOCK A SPIKE | *MUSTAFA OZER/AFP/GETTY IMAGES*

had defeated the South Americans the last three times we had played. Brazil won the first game 20-25, but the U.S. came back to win the next three games – 25-22, 25-21 and 25-23, defeating Brazil 3-1 for the gold medal. The 2008 U.S. Men's Volleyball Team will be remembered not only for overcoming a tragedy and winning a gold medal, but also for setting aside personal agendas for the good of the team, the sport and the country they love.

I attended the USOC Team Leadership meeting in Beijing. I found it to be very helpful to establish relationships with the USOC staff and the other team leaders. It was very beneficial to see the Athlete Village, the competition venues and have the chance to meet the local organizing committee (BOCOG) staff that we would be working with.

Everything went well from an accreditation standpoint. All our questions were answered and everything was handled in a timely manner. During the Games, we requested an additional credential for Carl McGown in Hugh's absence and the USOC took care of it right away.

444 We had no major issues with air travel. I would suggest that there be some minimum height established so that tall people, especially athletes, are automatically given economy plus if no emergency exit rows or bulk head seats are available.

Everything went well with the apparel and team processing. It was a very smooth procedure for us and I was very impressed considering the complexity and scope of the processing.

The USOC was able to accommodate our team with vehicles during team processing at San Jose State University when we needed them. We also had several requests while at the Games but the USOC was able to accommodate almost every single request.

LIOY BALL, RYAN MILLAR AND GABRIEL GARDNER OF THE US TRY TO BLOCK A SPIKE BY FUKUZAWA TATSUYA DURING THEIR VOLLEYBALL MATCH | *MUSTAFA OZER/AFP/GETTY IMAGESAFP/GETTY IMAGES*

We were very appreciative of the cell phones issued to our staff and athletes while in Beijing as it was a great way to stay in touch. Having access to the internet was very much appreciated.

Perhaps the single most unique experience at an Olympic Games is living in the Olympic Village. It is an amazing mix of people and cultures sharing an extraordinary experience. Neither politicians nor millionaires can lobby or buy their way into the Village—in that sense it is highly exclusive. Yet it is open to anyone who meets the criteria of fast enough, high enough, strong enough—regardless of geography, politics, religion, or economic status.

The Village in Beijing was wonderful. Not that they weren't good in Athens and Sydney (they both had uniquely memorable aspects all their own), but the overall look and accommodations in Beijing surpassed those of recent Olympics. Because of the high-rise style living quarters (apartments), it felt more like an Olympic City than Village.

Our medical staff consisted of Aaron Brock, our full-time trainer, and Chris Kotoures, our regular team physician. They were both great and everything went well for us in this regard.

BNU was an overwhelming success. It was a key to our preparation and training. The staff at BNU was unbelievably helpful. We felt totally supported the entire time. Also, the video analysis procedure worked well for us. We received DVDs of our matches and the USOC also took the time to make a highlight DVD for our team.

With the aftermath of the attack, the USOC security team was there for us, easing our concerns. They were very helpful and supportive to the athletes, the staff and especially toward Hugh and his family.

We learned a lot from previous Olympics and felt that we had enough experience on the team to prepare for all the eventualities and distractions of the Olympics, including the tragedy that occurred. The team was prepared for anything and the staff made sure the team was able to focus on the task at hand, in spite of the grief and distractions following the tragedy. My experience at the previous Olympic Games and my familiarity with the team and staff helped me tremendously.

RYAN MILLAR OF THE UNITED STATES CELEBRATES THEIR WIN OVER SERBIA | *PHIL WALTER/GETTY IMAGES*

USA VOLLEYBALL - WOMENS INDOOR | *JOAN POWELL – TEAM LEADER*

SUPPLEMENTAL INFORMATION PROVIDED BY DIANE FRENCH AND KERRY KLOSTERMAN

Our 2008 Olympic Team was selected from our National Team squad. There are annual open tryouts for the National Team, generally in January or February with broad participation – usually over one hundred athletes from all parts of the country. Our high performance programs for youth and junior players also feed into the National Team program.

During any given competition season, we will have up to 25 athletes in training. From this group we select the 12-player rosters for each event on our schedule. There are major FIVB events in each year of the quadrennial cycle that give us an opportunity to test our players' individual skills and teamwork against high-level competition. We use video and statistical software (Data Volley) to review performance.

We also have a year-round training program for our team. However, there is a different focus at different times of the year. Our competition season runs roughly from late May through November. During this time our National Team is in training at the Olympic Training Center (OTC) in Colorado Springs, Colo. We travel a lot throughout the season, but even when the team is on the road, there is a training group at the training center.

In the winter, most of our veteran players go overseas where they play for professional club teams. During this time, we have a group of younger players at the OTC - usually college-aged players who have finished their eligibility, or have recently graduated. These are players that we hope to integrate into the National Team and we work to bring their skill levels up and teach them the National Team system.

I know that our head coach felt that it was important to keep more of our National Team players together in the U.S. in the off-season prior to the Olympic Games. However, we just cannot compete with the financial offers that they receive overseas. The professional leagues' schedules vary widely, and some of our players are not available to train with us until June. Players arrive at different times and we cannot get our entire team together until shortly before our first event. The training and medical support that they receive from their club teams leave much to be desired and often they return with injuries or in poor condition.

On June 1, 2008, we submitted our top 18 athletes on the nomination form. We then had the following competitions:

• May 30 – June 7: Pan American Cup - because most of our veteran players were just returning from their club teams, we sent younger players who had been training with us through the winter to this event. They finished fifth and qualified the team for the 2009 World Grand Prix. Our veteran players stayed to train together in Colorado Springs in preparation for the following events.

• June 11, 13, and 14: We held Olympic Exhibition matches with Bra-zil in Colorado Springs, Colo. These matches gave us an opportunity to try several different combinations of players against the No. 1-ranked team in the world. We won one match and lost the other two, but it gave some of our newer players valuable experience and helped us evaluate their potential for the Olympic team.

• June 20 – July 13, we competed at the World Grand Prix. This can be a grueling event due to the duration and the travel requirements. Our schedule took us from Japan to Poland to Taiwan then back to Japan for the final round. This was our final evaluation period before naming the 12 members of the Olympic team. The competition was very good as we met several of the opponents that would be in our pool in Beijing. The nature of the event provides a good test of players' attitudes, flexibility, endurance and teamwork, in addition to their on-court skills and competitiveness. The rules of this competition allowed us to make roster changes at the end of each week of competition. This is expensive due to the travel involved, but we felt that it was important to do this year for two reasons. First, it gave the staff an opportunity to evaluate more players before making the final decisions for Beijing, and second, it allowed us to limit the "wear and tear" on some of our veteran players leading up to the Games. We made the final round and finished in fourth place.

Immediately after the conclusion of the World Grand Prix tournament, we submitted our final 12 names for the Olympic Team. Selecting the final 12 is a difficult task, but we believe that the process did result in the best representation in Beijing.

It is hard for us to make too many changes to our procedure because we are constrained by the FIVB event schedule. Teams that qualify for the World Grand Prix are expected to attend with their best players. Some teams will intentionally not qualify for the Grand Prix in an

US PLAYER TAYYIBA HANEEF-PARK (C) SPIKES THE BALL | *ALEXANDER JOE/AFP/GETTY IMAGES*

Olympic year because they are worried about the stress it puts on their team just prior to the Games. In our case, since we had the resources to make some roster changes during the event, it was a good decision for us to participate and we think that the benefits of strong pre-Olympic competition paid off for us.

One thing that we wish we could change has to do with off-season training. We wish that all of our players could arrive together in the spring, in time for a solid training block before we launch into competition. We tried to manage this by keeping our veterans at home during the Pan American Cup, so we at least had a short time together before we left for the Grand Prix.

Leading up to the Games there was an Olympic test event, but it was a Chinese club team tournament, so we did not have a chance to participate.

In regard to training at the Olympic Games, there was one training session provided in each of the competition venues before the first match. Other than those two sessions, we declined all of the training times scheduled by the FIVB/BOCOG for our team and did all of our training at Beijing Normal University (BNU) in a controlled environment. The facilities were excellent, and were really above and beyond our expectations.

Just hours before our first match on August 9, we learned of a terrible incident involving the Bachman family that really impacted our team. Elisabeth "Wiz" Bachman McCutheon, a 2004 Olympic Volleyball player was with her parents near the Drum Tower in Beijing, when they were attacked. Wiz's father was stabbed and killed, while her mother was severely injured. Many of our players knew Wiz, with many of them being former teammates, so it hit the team pretty hard.

In light of that, our team showed incredible strength and mutual support, taking the court against Japan in the 10 p.m. match that day. We won that match, but not without a struggle and it took two more matches for us to settle down and find our rhythm. We lost to Cuba 0-3 in our second match and defeated Venezuela in a performance that was good enough to win, but not up to our standard.

There was a lot of anticipation leading up to our fourth match against China, seen as a "showdown" between our Head Coach Lang Ping and her former countrymen. China was the defending Olympic champions, playing at home in front of 13,000 fans. At this point in the Games, both teams had a loss to Cuba on their records, so this contest had a lot riding on it. It was a battle that lived up to the hype – great volleyball and close competition that went into a tie-break before we won. Certainly that was a highlight and a turning point for our team. The win assured us a spot in the quarterfinals, relieving some pressure and giving us confidence for even bigger matches ahead. We finished pool play beating Poland, a strong team who found themselves in a must-win situation to advance from the preliminaries.

In the draw for the quarterfinals, we were paired with Italy, the second ranked team in the world and a team that we had not beaten in the past four years. We had prepared for the chance of meeting Italy and made our final adjustments in the off-day before the match. We executed the game plan well and had an outstanding performance from Lindsey Berg, coming off the bench, to upset Italy in 5-sets and advance to the semifinals.

In the semifinals, we had a re-match with Cuba and we turned in a convincing 3-0 win. As a result, we knew we would go home with a medal. In the finals, we (appropriately) faced the No. 1 ranked team in the world, Brazil. Brazil had marched through the Olympic tournament without losing a single set. We had a good performance, winning the second set and pushing them to 20-20 in the fourth set. However, Brazil held strong, putting up three big blocks to take the lead and the match. We fought a good fight, but came up just short against a very strong team.

Prior to the Games, I attended the USOC Team Leadership Final Countdown Meeting in March 2007 in Beijing. This meeting was most valuable especially for first time team leaders. The USOC mission was shared, as was an in-depth explanation of the team leader's responsibilities.

The constant and supportive dialogue with the USOC to resolve any issues with accreditation was really a key to a smooth-running process. I would suggest continuing the early planning and meetings with the NGB and the USOC as we prepare for the 2012 Games. It would be helpful if the International Federation and the local organizing committee would provide the appropriate access for the "P" credentials or, at least communicate what sort of access "P" credentials will be allowed earlier in the planning process. This way we can make sure to credential everyone appropriately.

In terms of air travel, I felt that we were kept well informed about the process and that the USOC was very responsive to our needs. There were staff people at the airport to help us through the special check-in and baggage handling procedures. This is obviously a process that has been fine-tuned with experience from previous Games and I thought it worked very well. The USOC also helped us make schedule adjustments as we finalized our plans for our pre-Games training in northern California and in Beijing.

Everything worked really well for us in terms of apparel and team processing in San Jose, Calif. The patient staff at team processing made the long day more bearable and they were very organized, getting everyone through as quickly as they could.

We ended up not needing any additional ground transportation but appreciated the USOC's early dialogue with us, providing constant updates on the status of negotiations and on policies from the organizing committee (BOCOG). This helped in our planning and decision making process regarding our needs while in Beijing.

For our pre-Games training, we had originally planned to stay at outside housing near the Beijing International School and train at their

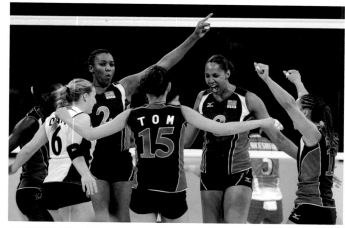

NICOLE DAVIS #6, DANIELLE SCOTT-ARRUDA #2, LOGAN TOM #15, TAYY-IBA HANEEF-PARK #3 AND ROBYN AHMOW-SANTOS #11 OF THE UNITED STATES CELEBRATE | *STREETER LECKA/GETTY IMAGES*

facilities. However, we were told that due to security issues, we could not stay there. The USOC quickly helped us find an alternative and it looked like we were set to stay at Beijing Normal University (BNU) from August 1st until our scheduled move into the Athletes' Village on August 6th. We later were told that we would need to move immediately into the Village. Instead of staying at BNU, we were given access to day rooms from August 2-6, so our players could rest there between training sessions. During that time we were able to train twice a day and had a place for the athletes to rest and shower. The food at BNU was fantastic and very nutritional. We would have preferred to have the day rooms for a longer period of time as it worked really great during the time we had them.

In addition, the High Performance Training Center at BNU gave our athletes a tremendous edge. The facilities and staff were excellent. Having consistent access to that kind of training venue helped us establish a routine surrounded by familiar, friendly faces – from the facilities people to the weightroom staff and the medical staff right there on site. The meeting rooms at BNU were very good and being able to wash the game uniforms in a timely manner was a huge benefit to all of us.

We had a few scheduling issues with our gym at first as we ended up having to share the gym with the men's volleyball team as well as the men's and women's basketball teams. We were able to work everything out but in the future it would be nice to have an additional gym so that these sports can be split up a little more.

During our planning phase, we requested the capability to transmit match video to a server where an analyst in the U.S. could pick it up and help with video breakdown. We asked for this as a contingency plan in case we were unable to cover all of the critical matches with the one technical support person we had on staff. Matches were held in two different venues and sometimes had overlapping match times; we had thought that one technician might have trouble covering this. We did not know for sure if we would need to use this, because the actual pairings were not published until very close to the Games.

A USOC representative worked on setting up the video transfer process for us. I think there were some issues with the size of the video files that we typically use (2GB for each video file and generally three files needed to record an entire match). We did some initial testing of this plan, but it turned out that the schedule allowed our on-site person to cover everything and the file transfer process wasn't needed. So we did not pursue it once we knew that it would not be needed. However, this could be an issue in the future.

Security worked well, especially in light of the incident involving the Bachman family and the high-profile status of our Head Coach Lang

Ping in China. Due to our head coach's prominence in China, we were in need of extra security upon arrival in Beijing, at the competition venues, and during our departure from China. Most of all, we were in need of assistance after defeating China. The four agents assigned to our team were superb and even secured golf carts for our coach and team so we could depart the venue on the BNU bus without much hassle. After the Bachman incident, our agents met with some of our families prior to our first competition to ensure them that the act was random and that there was no reason for them to worry.

Having Peter Haberl, our sports psychologist, in Beijing was very helpful. Our players had met with him on a regular basis during our training in Colorado Springs, so a relationship was already established. The normal pressures of competing at the Games warranted his being there, but we never imagined an incident like the one that affected our team would occur and having him there to help our players through that was a godsend.

The Bank of America Family Center was a great place for our athletes to meet up with their families in a safe, comfortable environment. We hope that center continues for future Games.

Overall everything went smoothly and it was a very successful Olympic Games for our team.

DANIELLE SCOTT-ARRUDA IN ACTION AGAINST CHINA DURING A WOMEN'S PRELIMINARY OLYMPIC VOLLEYBALL POOL B MATCH | *ALEXANDER JOE/AFP/GETTY IMAGES*

USA VOLLEYBALL - BEACH | ALI WOOD LAMBERSON & AL LAU
– DIRECTOR BEACH PROGRAMS & VP AVP PRO BEACH VOLLEYBALL

Beach volleyball is a physically demanding sport and it's a tribute to the skill level of elite players that they make it look easy and graceful. The major differences between beach and indoor volleyball illustrate the key characteristics of the sports: team size (two players vs. six), playing surface (sand vs. hard floor), and playing conditions (players must deal with the elements – wind, rain, and extreme temperatures). Some other differences between the indoor and the beach game include the court size: a beach court measures 8.00 m × 16.00 m, while the indoor court measures 9.00 m × 18.00 m. Another key difference is that there are no substitutions in the beach game, as the two players on a team must compete for the duration of the match.

With these characteristics, the successful, elite beach players must not only be well conditioned athletes, but, as partners, they must have great communication and chemistry.

Beach volleyball at the Olympics is a very unique format. The athletes are accustomed to a two to four day competition format with multiple courts and up to four matches a day, which is used on the AVP and FIVB tours. The Olympic competition lasts 14 days with the athletes playing on one stadium court. Each team plays one match every other day. While this is certainly easier on their bodies, it is mentally very challenging. One unique aspect of our sport is that each athlete has their own personal preferences as it relates to travel, training, etc. This independence is cited by beach athletes as one of the appealing qualities of the sport. In turn, it is a challenge to ensure that Olympic procedure (both prior and at the Games) is followed while respecting the needs and wishes of the athletes.

JAPAN'S KENTARO ASAHI (L) BLOCKS THE BALL FROM SEAN ROSEN-THAL OF THE US | JOE KLAMAR/AFP/GETTY IMAGES

The performance indicators are fairly simple, win/loss record and some basic statistics...blocking, service aces, digs and kills. Any team that betters their seed in the overall competition can be considered successful.

Athletes make the Olympic team based on their best eight finishes on the FIVB World Tour in a 19 month period (January 1, 2007-July 20, 2008.) There is a maximum of two teams per county, with the host country receiving one pre-qualified team. Selections were finalized July 21, 2008. This system needs an overhaul and should be changed dramatically so that athletes are not required to travel to so many events. U.S. athletes should qualify based on a trials system.

Some major issues with the current qualification system include: entry into the main draw of an International Federation (IF) event is based on a point system. This point system favors players who have participated on the IF tour in the years prior to the Olympic qualification period. As a result, a rising star player must rely on a veteran player to get into the main draw of the various events. Also, players can manipulate entry into IF events by blocking main draw access to rising players trying to qualify.

Under the current system, players are required to settle on a partner two years before the Games. This two-year qualification period may allow a team that is performing poorly in the first year to compete in the Games (based on points earned during year one) instead of a team that is performing well during the second year. With only IF events counting for qualifications, U.S. teams must choose between FIVB/AVP events; this places athletes in a difficult position relative to their sponsors and their tour obligations.

A better option would include domestic finishes in determining Olympic qualification. This may range from Olympic qualifying events only in the U.S. or a hybrid system that weighs both domestic and international performances.

Beach volleyball athletes do not train as a team but instead are independent, professional athletes who train primarily in the U.S. with their own private coaches. They compete on the AVP (domestic) and FIVB (international) tours. U.S. athletes exceeded medal expectations in 2008 events and held the top ranking positions in the world. The majority of losses for the U.S. women were to each other. Their training and competition was certainly effective, however, there would certainly be some benefit to playing fewer weekends and traveling less.

In terms of changes, the athletes choose which events they wish to compete in. However, a trials system would cut down on the number of international events that they feel they need to attend, which would have a very positive effect on fatigue and the number of chronic injuries. In addition, to improve the program we should continue the support programs that we have started (sports medicine, videography, other

ELAINE YOUNGS OF THE US DIVES TO RETURN THE BALL TO CHINA'S TEAM IN THEIR WOMEN'S QUARTEFINAL BEACH VOLLEYBALL MATCH|
THOMAS COEX/AFP/GETTY IMAGES

USOC services, etc.) and gradually introduce a system of accountability and a "team" concept for national team athletes and coaches.

Prior to the Olympic Games, there was a test event. However, it was a lower level event and no teams ranked above 24 were allowed to attend, except for the Chinese teams. Therefore, we sent a young unranked team. They took photos, sand samples, wind, temperature, and humidity measurements, and created a directional chart of court orientation, which was all very useful.

Our training facility at the Olympic Games was very accessible and provided a great setup. Whenever we had a scheduling issue, the venue director was very helpful in trying to resolve it. We would have liked better access to the stadium court for training. The times on the stadium court were pre-assigned, and some of our teams were not even in China yet for the times they were assigned. Also, they did not always stick to the rules for practice time assignments, as some teams were allowed to sign up early. A suggested change is to have additional transportation resources as there are four teams competing on various schedules, which makes transport to and from practice challenging.

All our Olympic teams finished their seed or higher. Misty May-Treanor/ Kerri Walsh (seed 2) won the gold medal after going undefeated and turning in flawless performances. This team's ability to focus under intense media scrutiny was remarkable. By winning in Beijing, May-Treanor/Walsh repeated as Olympic champions. No team had ever before done so. And as they did in Athens in 2004, May-Treanor/Walsh not only did not lose a match (match record 14-0 in 2004 and 2008), they did not even drop a single set (set record 28-0 in 2004 and 2008) -- a phenomenal achievement because the caliber of play has improved significantly since 2004. With their Olympic victory, the duo won their 108th straight match, their last loss in an international match came against the silver medal Chinese pair of Tian/Wang, in July 2007.

Todd Rogers/Phil Dalhausser (seed 2) also won the gold medal. They played a very flat opening match after arriving to Beijing later than any other team in the competition. They struggled through a few other matches, but came up big when it counted. Dalhausser's blocking performance in the gold medal match was unparalleled. Dalhausser / Rogers came back from a 9-3 deficit in the first set to defeat the Brazilians 2-1 (23-21, 17-21, 15-4) and claim the gold medal. Dalhausser dominated the deciding third set with four consecutive blocks in their improbable 15-4 victory in Game 3 (he finished with a total of nine blocks in the match — more than twice as many as Brazil's blocker). The U.S. duo showed resiliency and determination during the Games, bouncing back from a loss in their first match at the Olympics to 23rd seeded Latvians and staging an unforgettable comeback from 0-6 in

the third set in the quarterfinals.

Jacob Gibb/Sean Rosenthal (seed 7) finished fifth. Rosenthal was in the zone, playing the best defense of his life when they knocked off the 6th seeded German team. They had a lot of momentum until their final match when they had the unfortunate luck to draw reigning gold medalist Emanuel-Ricardo of Brazil.

Nicole Branagh/Elaine Youngs (seed 5) also finished fifth. This duo beat the teams that they were supposed to beat, but lost to the Chinese team that they have struggled against all year.

We were able to attend the Team Leadership Meeting in Beijing and found it valuable to have a chance to meet key contacts and to get to know the city. It would have been nice if the timeframe had been a little closer to the Games as there were many unknowns on our end and on local organizing committee's (BOCOG) part in March.

In regards to accreditation, since the FIVB did not announce the list of qualified teams until July 21st, it was necessary for USA Volleyball (USAV) to request an extension to the deadline for the athletes and coaches. This new deadline was granted. We requested Ao accreditations for each team's coach (a total of 4). Initially we were granted P accreditations for the coaches. This was the first Games in which P accreditations were allowed for beach volleyball coaches. However, the information was very unclear regarding what access was available for the P accredited coaches. Thus we requested that the coaches receive Ao accreditations instead of P accreditations. This request was granted and the change occurred on July 25.

Since we were able to get the coaches Aos at the last minute, we moved them from Beijing Normal University, the USOC training site in Beijing, to the Athlete Village for the five days preceding the start of competition before moving to the Hilton.

There were several changes made to accreditations last minute without any feedback from the beach department. One very unpopular decision was to pull Al Lau's (our co-team leader) accreditation. This decision was very unpopular with the athletes and put me in an extremely difficult situation. Had I been brought in on the discussion I could have explained that the athletes, who are very loyal to Al, would be extremely upset by this decision, so much so that it would hinder my ability to be successful as a Team Leader. It is very important to keep the Team Leader updated on any changes and involved in decision making process.

Moving forward I would suggest that a better process be established for requesting the number of accreditations without having to specify names for each one. This would have helped with the medical staff. In the end, we ended up getting the credentials we needed and it is suggested that the allocation of credentials that were given in Beijing be the allocation used for future Games. Having this already decided well in advance will prevent unnecessary stress and distraction for the athletes, which unfortunately occurred during the preparations for Beijing. It should be noted that there is talk of increasing the Olympic draw to 32 teams for 2012, which would allow for three USA teams per gender and the possibility of six total medals. If this were to happen a few more credentials would be needed.

Booking our air travel was also a last minute deal as a result of the FIVB's late announcement of the list of qualified teams. As a result the tickets were more expensive than if they would have been booked a month earlier. This added some unforeseen expenses to our budget.

The athletes' competitive apparel and accessories were reclassified as personal performance gear for the first time in 2008. The athletes, through their personal sponsorships, agreed to wear Speedo apparel with each athlete's personal sponsor's manufacturer logo replacing the Speedo logo. The color boards and samples were submitted to the USOC and FIVB. On July 21, I was copied on an email from the FIVB to Speedo informing them that the samples submitted to the FIVB were unacceptable. This dialog went on until the day of the preliminary inquiry in which we were accompanied by the USOC legal team to make sure all rules were followed. The women's suits were ultimately unacceptable to the athletes and to the FIVB. Al Lau was able to negotiate with Nike to provide suits for the female athletes. The men's Speedo uniforms were ultimately approved by the FIVB. The team leaders should have uniform samples well in advance avoid this issue in the future.

In terms of USOC-issued apparel, the only thing we would request is consideration of the athletes comfort level at the Opening Ceremony. It seemed unnecessary to wear uncomfortable, non-supportive shoes, not to mention wool suits in hot, humid weather. We looked great, but were very uncomfortable.

Instead of going through processing and directly to Beijing, the athletes preferred to process a week earlier giving them the flexibility to compete in an AVP event or to rest. The additional costs associated with this were absorbed by USAV.

The cell phones issued by the USOC were very beneficial. However, in the future we would suggest adding a texting plan, as this is a much more efficient way to communicate with multiple people in a team environment. Also having wireless available was a bonus but would be even better if it was placed in all the rooms in the Athlete Village instead of just the lobby areas.

Our medical team this year consisted of Kelly Woods, a physical therapist, who has worked with the athletes on the AVP and FIVB tours for two years. She was the lead medical provider for the U.S. on the FIVB tour in 2008. Ernie Ferrel is a sports chiropractor on the medical board of the AVP and began working FIVB events for USAV in 2008.

Three weeks before the Games one of the athletes requested to be able to bring a personal provider. Although he is the IF provider and is well known to the athletes, the challenge of getting a background and credential check on a foreign national, as well as a Chinese visa, was not easy. With help from the USOC, we were able to get this accomplished in the nick of time.

Beijing Normal University (BNU) was a great place for our athletes to get away from the crowds, have a quiet workout and enjoy a great meal. We also took advantage of the video analysis. Peter Vint was with us the entire time and worked hard to meet the requests of the coaches and athletes. He was excellent and had a major impact on the success of our teams. Ideally, there would be additional video personnel available for the beach teams. With four different competition schedules and matches running daily from 9 am to midnight, the workload for one staff person is exhausting. Also, with late matches and some teams wanting to train after their match, it would be helpful to have late night access to the weight rooms.

The USA House in Beijing was a nice escape sanctuary for the athletes and their families. The athletes and families are grateful to the USOC/USA House staff for the victory celebrations at USA House.

Once we got to Beijing, the experience went quite well. Certainly having two team leaders was beneficial for a variety of reasons. We were able to balance each other's strengths and weaknesses and could provide better service to our eight athletes and staff.

I learned that the athletes need to feel that they are being heard and that their concerns are important, but kneejerk reactions to accommodate every request will lead to bad choices.   .

The changes we would suggest revolve around the planning process. In the future to maximize athlete performance on the court, we need earlier communication between all the stakeholders (e.g., athletes, USOC, USAV, and AVP).

PHILIPPE DALHAUSSER OF THE US JUMPS TO BLOCK A SMASH BY ARGENTINA'S MARIANO BARACETTI
| *THOMAS COEX/AFP/GETTY IMAGES*

USA WATER POLO - MENS
RICK MCKEE – *TEAM LEADER*

In accordance with our athlete selection procedures, we held a series of open tryouts and also invited certain athletes to training sessions for player evaluation. Water Polo is a sport where the cream will rise quickly to the top and it did.

Our training began in January 2008. We did most of our training domestically in Thousand Oaks, Calif. We did take two trips to Europe, one in February 2008 and the other in May 2008. Both trips were highly successful as we were able to train and play games against some of the best teams in the world.

The final player roster was determined and announced on June 26, 2008. The procedure worked all right but I would suggest in the future that we conduct more game-type training sessions to evaluate the athletes. I didn't feel that the weekend open tryout was the most thorough way of evaluating the athletes.

There was a test event in Beijing, before the Olympic Games but we decided not to attend. I was able to attend the USOC Team Leadership meetings and found them to be invaluable for our team's preparation. Having the ability to travel to Beijing and see the venues and the layout of the Athlete Village was extremely helpful in putting a plan together for the Games. It also gave us a chance to build relationships with those from the USOC with whom we would be working. While in Beijing, our training sites were great. We took advantage of the USOC's High Performance Center at Beijing Normal University (BNU). A note for the future would be to have a deeper pool for use by the Water Polo team. BNU's pool was a little too shallow to actually scrimmage, but it still allowed us to swim and do some half court work.

We had a most impressive finish at the 2008 Olympic Games, bringing home the silver medal. The guys really came together and played as a team, which made all the difference in the world. Credit should be given to the coaching staff and their leadership in bringing the team together and getting the best play out of each athlete.

USA Water Polo had a budget to work from with our primary expenses surrounding the training and supplies needed for the team. A larger budget would have allowed us to either travel to play more of the top teams or it would have allowed us to bring them in to train with, and against, our team.

I felt the USOC did a good job in working with us to get all the accreditations submitted properly and on time. The process was easy to follow and understand and we didn't have any issues arise in this respect.

Scheduling our flights to the Olympic Games was a very smooth process with everything coming together and working as we expected.

There was a minor issue with the apparel process in that we had de-

lays in getting the colorboards from Speedo, but thanks to the flexibility of this process, we were able to work through the delay to assure that all was inline before departing for the Olympics.

The USOC was very accessible and responsive to our requests and needs when it came to ground transportation. They were extremely helpful and provided a wealth of information to us.

Being able to connect to the internet both in the Village and at BNU was very helpful. However, it would have been beneficial if we could have been able to connect to the internet from our rooms instead of just the lobby areas. This might be something to consider next time around. Another helpful element was the availability of copy machines and other office equipment. Having the USOC issued cell phones for athletes and staff was very valuable to all.

We ran into a slight road block in terms of housing. We had planned to house the team at (BNU) the week leading up to the Olympics, allowing us to conduct a last minute training camp. We were scheduled to be at BNU starting on July 29. The day we left team processing at San Jose State University in California, we learned that for security reasons, this would not be allowed. The USOC staff began working on this immediately and by the time we arrived in Beijing they had gotten everything worked out so that we could move the team right into the Village. This could have become a real challenge but everyone jumped in and we were able to get through this road block. The Village was very nice and everything went well for us there.

Like many of the other sports, we had some event ticketing issues. Once we got exact ticket numbers, we were able to work through the issues.

The main lesson learned was that teamwork is the key to success. When the NGB and the USOC work together as a team and provide the means for the athlete to do their job, then it all flows seamlessly. If there is a strong framework then even when a problem arises, the team is strong and cohesive enough that it barely misses a beat, allowing for things to keep moving in a positive and productive way.

PETER VARELLAS #2 OF THE UNITED STATES GOES UP FOR A SHOT AGAINST SERBIA | *STREETER LECKA/GETTY IMAGES*

USA WEIGHTLIFTING | FRANK EKSTEN – TEAM LEADER & INTERIM PRESIDENT

USA Weightlifting had four women and two men participate in the competition at the 2008 Olympic Games in Beijing, China. We were pleased that our women's team qualified for a full team of four, but were disappointed to only have two men's slots.

Our selection process consists of an Olympic Trials where athletes compete for a pre-determined qualifying spot in their respective weight classes. We are allotted spots by the International Weightlifting Federation (IWF) based on points our athletes accumulate during various international competitions. This year our team was negatively affected by the positive test of other nations' athletes. This situation required a huge amount of attention and was a major distraction throughout our preparation for, and especially during, Beijing.

Team USA qualified three men for the 2008 Olympic Games based on performances in the past two World Championships, but after many positive doping cases by other countries, the points were redistributed

NATALIE WOOLFOLK OF THE UNITED STATES COMPETES IN THE
WEIGHTLIFTING EVENT | *PAUL GILHAM/GETTY IMAGES*

and we apparently lost out on qualifying for the third spot. We then participated in the Continental Championships in Peru and qualified two men. USA Weightlifting's National Office was notified one week before the Trials that, due to more random doping positives, our men had retained the third slot. Then, after the Trials, we were told that we actually didn't have the third slot. This was frustrating news because we believed that Casey Burgener had earned his spot on our 2008 U.S. Olympic Team at our Olympic Trials.

After much discussion between the USOC and the IWF, the IWF finally agreed to let Casey in, but they only did so two days after the International Olympic Committee (IOC) and the organizing committee's (BOCOG) deadline for entries for the Games. This was a big blow for our sport and our team morale, and especially for Casey. However, throughout this whole process Casey was a real hero. He trained hard every day and encouraged his teammates to do their best. He was our best performer over the past two years in the biggest meets and he really deserved to have his Olympic dream come true. Casey Burgener (along with his coach and father, Mike Burgener) was the only athlete that attended the Olympic Test Event in Beijing in January 2008.

Our Olympic Trials occurred May 16-17, 2008, in Atlanta, Ga. As explained above, we went into the Olympic Trials with the general feelings that we would have three male athletes on the team, although the official word from the IWF was to prepare for two men and two alternates. After the Olympic Trials the word came back from the IWF that we had indeed only qualified two male athletes and continued appeals to the IWF were unsuccessful.

Athletes trained on their own leading up to the Olympic Trials and the Olympic Games. However, there were a lot of reports and much communication between coaches and athletes during this time. Of our six team members, only two trained at the Colorado Springs Olympic Training Center, so this communication was very necessary.

Our training at the Olympic Games was done mostly at the High Performance Training Center (HPTC) at Beijing Normal University (BNU) with a couple of sessions at the official training venue. These sessions helped to familiarize our athletes with the equipment and surroundings. The training at BNU was very good early on as we arrived on July 27. As the facility became more crowded, we had some challenges with providing the right training atmosphere for our athletes. This was resolved by working with the USOC to limit access during our reserved training times and for us to stick to our schedule. Overall I would say the training situation was excellent. We could train at times most appropriate for us and not be constrained by the schedule set up for us by the IWF. We also were then able to utilize the recovery and medical services at BNU which were also excellent.

Overall we had a good showing at the 2008 Olympic Games in Beijing, with two of our four women placing in the top six, and the other two women placing 12th and 14th respectively. One of our men, Kendrick Farris, placed eighth and won the B session, while also setting two American records. He was also only four kilos away from the third highest clean and jerk in his weight class. Our team set three American records and scored five personal bests.

The 2008 Olympic Games was the greatest show on earth. We had an incredible group of athletes, staff and personal coaches attend the event. All of the Team USA weightlifters competed well, with a total of five personal bests and three American records. There were several great performances, led by Kendrick Farris and Melanie Roach, with three American records combined. I can say that the behavior of this team was exceptional. The team unity and support of each other was very inspiring. The team all participated in the Opening Ceremony and had the opportunity to rub elbows with the greatest athletes in the world.

o Melanie Roach has continued to give great results since last year's World Championships and Olympic Trials, and her fantastic lifting continued in Beijing. Melanie went six for six, setting a new American record in the total with 193 kg, scoring three personal best lifts, and placing sixth overall in the 53 kg class. Melanie's coach, John Thrush, prepared her well, and she was in great shape for the Games. John also came to the Games and was at every training session with Melanie at BNU.

o Kendrick Farris was another great performer. He competed in the 85 kg class, winning the B session with a last lift of 202 kg and setting American records in the clean and jerk and total, with 262 kg. Kendrick went five for six in the lifts and finished eighth in the competition. Dr. Kyle Pierce, Kendrick's personal coach, was at all the training sessions at BNU with Kendrick, and prepared him well.

o Cheryl Haworth finished sixth in the 75+ kg class with a six kg improvement in the total from the Olympic Trials. Cheryl prepared for her third Olympic Games in Georgia.

o Natalie Woolfolk and Carissa Gump competed in the 63 kg class and finished 12th and 14th respectively. Both women also attempted American records. Natalie went five for six, trying to snatch 101 kg, but missed. She was able to finish with an improved total of 211 kg from the Olympic Trials. Carissa attempted an American record clean and jerk of 221 kg, but missed the jerk and finished with a 204 kg total.

o Two-time Olympian, Chad Vaughn, made two attempts in the snatch with a very good 147 kg, but failed to make any of his clean and jerks of 182 kg. Chad put out 100 percent effort, but it was just not his day. Dr. William Kuprevich, our assigned physician, made a point of being available at each of our competition sessions and was tremendous. Fortunately we had no catastrophic injuries. Richard Campbell was our athletic trainer and handled a lot of the soft tissue work. Dr. Mike Reed of the USOC staff also handled a lot of the work for us while we were at BNU. The medical support provided to us was great. Having the same staff that we had during the Pan American Games provided good continuity and familiarity for our athletes.

Everything went well in regards to team processing. We had originally planned to process as one group, but changed several months out as the coaches wanted to go in as two groups. This worked well, with no problems for either group.

Our budget was adequate for the expenses of the team. Our primary expense was housing and meals for our personal coaches who were staying at the High Performance Training Center (HPTC) at Beijing Normal University (BNU). Our plans for using the facilities at the Olympic Village and at BNU were in order and worked well.

I attended both Team Leadership meetings. I found both the round-table discussions and the Games Deliverables document to be very valuable in nailing down what we are doing and who and how it was being delivered. I attended the second Key Decision Makers meeting along with our Executive Director at the time, Rodger DeGarmo. This was also important as it allowed us to formulate our plan and see what resources were available.

Overall, we felt the performances of our team and staff went well. Most of our athletes were well prepared and I have mentioned earlier the exceptions and disappointments. A challenge for us continues to be athletes who prepare for the Games away from the OTC. In saying this though, our best prepared athletes for this Games, Kendrick Farris and Melanie Roach, trained and prepared with their personal coaches at their home clubs. So there are no clear cut answers here.

Our training in Beijing, as well as arriving early, served us well. I felt our staff selection was spot on; we all worked very well together. I am certain the best coaches were selected and performed very well. It was a great honor to represent the U.S. Weightlifting Federation in Beijing.

KENDRICK FARRIS OF THE US COMPETES IN THE MEN'S 85 KG GROUP B WEIGHTLIFTING EVENT |
JUNG YEON-JE/AFP/GETTY IMAGES

USA WRESTLING | *MITCH HULL – TEAM LEADER*

The accreditation process went very smoothly for these Games. Our only challenge came when we learned that some of our coaches would not be accredited to stay in the Olympic Village and, instead, had to stay at Beijing Normal University (BNU). This led to a higher-than-expected lodging expense for us. Overall though, preparation was well done in this area and therefore there were no major unforeseen issues.

Our air travel was well planned out in terms of travel days. We met with the USOC several times leading up to the Games to confirm our dates, which helped get our schedules to the USOC as soon as possible after our Olympic Trials. We were surprised to learn that the cost for the airfare was on average about $300 to $400 per ticket more than what had been communicated to us at the team leader meetings. We did have some difficulties reaching our contact at the United Olympic Desk but we don't know if that affected our ticket price or not.

We were very pleased in how the apparel process went. The distribution at team processing was a little slow but everyone involved was helpful and made it as smooth as it could be, especially given the number of those getting processed. I would suggest supplying a warm-up to every member of the delegation, in order to create a unified team look. It is very important that the USOC continue to allow the NGBs to purchase the full apparel package for our additional accredited staff. This is very important to the coaches, allowing them to feel like they are a full part of the Olympic delegation.

During team processing the transportation was well handled and the meals were great. We also took advantage of getting a workout in at 24-Hour Fitness and appreciate the staff's help in making that a possibility.

Leading up to the Games, it was difficult to determine what our transportation needs would be in terms of extra vehicles. When we received the final costs from the organizing committee (BOCOG) we decided to get our own vehicles. This was a little difficult to do because of the process required to get our driver proper accreditation. We were given very little time to submit the information for our driver accreditation, but we managed to get it all done with the USOC's help. The USOC did a great job in keeping us informed as soon as the information was known. The bus service from the village to BNU was very helpful, along with the shuttle service at BNU.

USA Wrestling shipped mats for the High Performance Training Center with the help of the USOC. We also ended up purchasing a sauna in Beijing for use at BNU, which was shipped back afterwards with no major issues. Everything worked well with the shipping logistics because communication was clear during the whole process.

The High Performance Training Center was an outstanding place to train and was a huge benefit for our team as well as the other sports. The USOC staff at BNU was always supportive and worked hard to handle our requests. We did have unexpected costs associated with BNU; the housing and meals costs were more than initially announced and we had to purchase a sauna for our athletes.

Our medical staff included Chad Smidt, Darryl Miller, Chris Schroer and Dr. Hines. Each of these individuals had strong wrestling backgrounds with Chad, Darryl and Dr. Hines working several World Championships for USA Wrestling. All these individuals were recommended by USA Wrestling. Our only issue was Darryl was not able to get into the Village to be with the Freestyle team until the day before the competition. Overall though, allowing USA Wrestling to have strong input into the selection of our medical support was very beneficial to our athletes.

We had our ticket orders in when requested but it became a marathon getting the final ticket allocation. Getting the tickets prior to departure allowed us to get the tickets into everyone's hands prior to Beijing and was very helpful. Having the USOC handle the majority of the ticket issues is a huge benefit for the NGBs and although at times it is confusing, it is still the best route to use.

WOMEN'S FREESTYLE | *STAN ZEAMER - TEAM LEADER*

A wrestling athlete must be disciplined, have his/her life in order, and be able to deal with the key issues of weight management. Elite competitors must be a wrestler full-time or have wrestling as their priority in life. An athlete must be focused to block out distractions. Since this is an individual sport, individual training is important to success and an athlete must realize this.

RADOSLAV VELIKOV (BLUE) OF BULGARIA COMPETES AGAINST HENRY CEJUDO OF THE UNITED STATES | *JED JACOBSOHN/GETTY IMAGES*

RANDI MILLER OF THE UNITED STATES CELEBRATES WINNING
BRONZE MEDAL AFTER THE WOMEN'S FREESTYLE 63 KG BRONZE
MEDAL BOUT | *PHIL WALTER/GETTY IMAGES*

There were excellent training facilities at the Olympic Games. By training at the High Performance Training Center at Beijing Normal Uuniversity (BNU), we were able to keep our training partners very involved in athlete preparation. The food and housing at BNU were outstanding. It would have been ideal to have allowed the training partners to go to the Olympic Village, rather than the other way around, but I understand the credentialing and security issues that were involved, so this was a great remedy.

We were very proud of Randi Miller's bronze medal performance. It was particularly rewarding since we've watched Randi build her confidence and abilities over the last four years. We've seen her increase her intensity and focus, both of which helped her win the bronze. We were disappointed to not win four medals, but we were very close to that, with a bronze and two fifth-place finishes. Those that did not medal did not have problems with attitude or preparation. The coaching was strong and the team was prepared.

In the Olympic Village, the USOC staff was organized and ready for everything. Their people had a strong work ethic and were helpful, positive and available.

Prior to the Games, I attended the team leader meetings and thought they were excellent. I learned that the USOC was looking for excellence in the team leader position, and that there had to be intense focus on the job. The agenda for these meetings addressed, among many topics, culture issues. Having this information in advance helped me feel comfortable and knowledgeable about the Games, which helped me in answering our athletes' questions. The USOC did an excellent job on preparations, leaving no stone unturned. The manual was excellent and the topics, which included transportation and training issues, were very important. They gave examples that we might encounter and the activities were "hands-on." Being with multiple sports gave the meetings the feeling of an Olympic experience. It gave us all a larger picture and clarified its importance. It is hard to find anything I would change.

This is the best sporting event I have ever been involved in. The USOC did an excellent job. The Olympic Village experience was fun, exciting, motivating and inspiring at the highest level. I witnessed the connection with the ancient Games-the drive to excel beyond self. It transcended gender, race and nationality, and we realized that the Olympics are bigger than ourselves. I felt that most in the Village - people were respectful and there for a purpose.

MEN'S FREESTYLE
| STEVE SILVER - *TEAM LEADER*

Everything went great for our athletes and team concerning the training facilities and operations. All of the facilities, the food and the support services were well planned and taken care of at Beijing Normal University (BNU).

We did face some challenges getting our ancillary support people into the training facility at BNU. Because of security issues, some of our people were not allowed into the venue. This impacted our ability to provide adequate preparation for our athletes. Another issue that impacted our preparation was the lack of a sauna, at least initially, at BNU.

I was pleasantly surprised, but also somewhat disappointed, with our final results in Beijing. In regards to Henry Cejudo and his gold medal, Henry had never medaled at a major international event before, and with his amazing effort, became our youngest Olympic champion. That was an exciting surprise to all of us.

I was disappointed that Daniel Cormier, one of our strongest medal contenders, had kidney failure and couldn't compete and couldn't be replaced. I also want to recognize the tremendous teamwork it took to get Mike Zadick added at the last minute in the 60 kg weight class. There was a unified effort between USA Wrestling, the USOC and FILA to get this done. We had worked to train and prepare Mike, not knowing if this opportunity would develop. When Mike was added to the field, it provided an additional chance for us to win a medal.

One lesson learned is that it is a lot tougher process for wrestlers to make weight efficiently at the Olympics than at other major events. I found that even veteran athletes struggled with acclimation, changes in weather and culture and the scope of the Games. Since weight management is so important in this sport, this fact needs to be acknowledged and accounted for in future Games.

MEN'S GRECO-ROMAN
| JOHN BARDIS

Wrestling faces a challenge that most other sports don't – wrestlers must make weight. It must be properly managed to succeed. Each environment is different, and it can be difficult to have access to the resources needed to provide for this.

Olympic Trials and team selection became a major factor in Greco-Roman wrestling. There has to be a fair process which protects the athletes. I believe if an athlete qualifies the United States for the Olympics in a weight class by winning a World medal, he/she should automatically be in the best-of-three series to compete for the Olympic position.

The selection process also includes coaching staff choices, as well as access and credentialing for those coaches. The selection must be based on bringing home medals. At the key times, when medals are

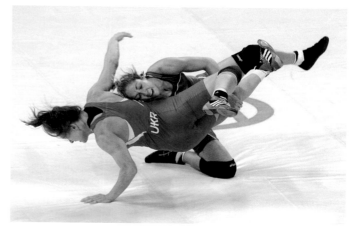

MARCIE VAN DUSEN OF THE UNITED STATES TAKES DOWN NATALIYA
SYNYSHYN OF UKRAINE | *JEFF GROSS/GETTY IMAGES*

determined, the best coaches are essential for competition success.

The training camps, held in Colorado Springs, Colo., prior to the Olympic Games were great. There were good facilities and the format worked well for everyone. This is truly a reflection on our national Greco-Roman coach Steve Fraser. He has created a centralized program, which has been a huge benefit to the program.

Beijing Normal University (BNU) was the finest example of how it can and should be done for a High Performance Training Center at the Olympic Games. It was easy to get to, had a U.S. family environment, the facilities were fantastic and the food was fabulous. There was never a late bus, never a missed practice or meal and numerous facilities were available, even a field for a practice soccer game. It was brilliant. Our only issues were the inability to get people through security on short notice, and the lack of a sauna for our athletes.

In broad terms, the performance in Greco-Roman was disappointing, especially after winning the World Team title in 2007. I was not disappointed in any individual athlete. There were the normal challenges and the close losses which were based upon the quality of the competition. What we lacked was the parallel successes and any surprise performances. The exception to this was the clutch performance by Adam Wheeler in his first senior level competition. He was our top wrestler for the first time and returned home from his first Olympic Games with an Olympic medal. He was one period away from the gold-medal match.

When evaluating performance, you must take into consideration the impact of competition, venue and rules on performance. In Greco-Roman, this is definitely the case, given the results across the board at the 2008 Olympics. There were seven defending World Champions in Beijing, and only one repeated as champion and five did not even win a medal. The format used at the Olympics affected our heavyweight Dremiel Byers, who had no recovery time. He wrestled one extra match than the others, and had three matches in an hour and 45 minutes. Nothing prepares you for that and, as a result, I believe it cost us a medal.

I attended the team leader meetings in Beijing and in Colorado Springs. It was extremely valuable, especially being on site in China before the Games. I was able to understand the flow of the Games, the venue, and the living accommodations. I thought the team leader orientation was first class.

I was impressed by the tremendous hospitality of the Chinese people. They set the gold standard, in regards to performance and operations of a major global event. The venues, event management, spirit and kindness were unprecedented in Olympic history. I was completely impressed with the staff and volunteers of the USOC. They are a world-class organization. They are extraordinary people united by a movement. I was also moved by the respect that every nation has for the United States in the Olympic Village.

MARCIE VAN DUSEN OF THE UNITED STATES COMPETES AGAINST JACKELINE RENTERIA OF COLOMBIA | *JEFF GROSS/GETTY IMAGES*

PARALYMPIC ARCHERY | KIMBERLY CARRICK-BARTKOWSKI — *TEAM LEADER*

Archery competition at the Paralympic Games is different than the competition at World Championships. At World Championships a FITA is shot. A FITA is the combined score of four distances. Each classification has different distances. An example is Men's Open Compound, where the athletes shoot at 90 meters, 70 meters, 50 meters and 30 meters. At the Paralympic Games all athletes shoot only 70 meters. There is a ranking round followed by a single elimination tournament.

The 2008 Paralympic Archery Team had a great Games experience! They tied their total medal count in 2004 but it was with two individual bronze medals. The U.S. did not participate in the Team Competition. The only team events at the Beijing Paralympic Games were Men's or Women's Recurve Team and there were not enough recurve shooters on Team USA to form a team.

The 2008 Paralympic Archery Team was selected from the U.S. Paralympics Selection Ranking List as of March 15, 2008. Medalists from the 2007 IPC Para Archery World Championships were given priority, followed closely by athletes who attained Elite Team standards and then by athletes who attained National Team standards. If slots remained, athletes who shot a minimum qualifying score between January 1, 2007 and March 15, 2008 were selected.

Named to the team were Joe Bailey, Eric Bennett, Lindsey Carmichael, Jeff Fabry, Chuck Lear, Thomas "TJ" Pemberton, Kevin Stone, and Russell Wolfe. Randall "Randi" Smith was the Head Coach and Paul Miller was the Assistant Coach.

There were four camps and competitions to help the Team prepare and bond prior to the Paralympic Games. The first three camps and competitions were all national; the Arizona Cup, the Endeavor Games, and U.S. Archery Nationals.

The last event, the 4th Invitational European Grand Prix, was an international event held in Stoke Mandeville, England. The team did very well. In the Open division qualifying round, Bennett was 5th, Bailey was 9th and Pemberton was 11th. In the W1 division, Fabry was 1st and Lear finished 6th. Carmichael was 7th in the Women's Standing Division. In the Men's W2 Recurve Division Wolfe finished 8th and Stone came in 9th. In the Olympic Round, Fabry won a bronze, Bennett a silver, and Wolfe finished 4th. In the team round, made up of Fabry, Bennett, and Bailey, we dominated and won the gold.

Team Processing was held at the Colorado Springs Olympic Training Center (CSOTC) in Colorado Springs, Colorado. It was an exciting experience for everyone on the team. The athletes loved the apparel! Several comments were made about how wonderful they were treated and how friendly everyone was who helped them. They couldn't believe how generous the sponsors were and they were so appreciative.

We departed the CSOTC for the Denver International Airport (DIA) at 1:00 a.m. on September2, 2008. It was a tough departure time, but the Team was anxious to get going so they didn't complain very much. As the busses pulled up to DIA, Carmichael realized she had left her passport in her old backpack that was being shipped back to her home. Kirk Millburn and the IG staff were heroes and were able to not only find Lindsey's package being shipped back home, but found her passport and had it up to DIA before our flight took off for Beijing! How incredible.

Leslie Gamez and her crew were waiting for us when we arrived in Beijing and we were taken to the Paralympic Athlete Village in no time. We quickly made it through accreditation and started exploring the Village. The rooms were great and the Team settled in with ease.

Opening Ceremonies were fantastic! It finally hit a few of the athletes that they had indeed, made it to the Paralympic Games! All the athletes looked so sharp in the parade-wear. We all enjoyed Opening Ceremonies.

Our training facilities were adjacent to the two areas where the finals would be held. This was very accessible and we had plenty of time to practice. The ranking round was held on the practice field. In retrospect, video analysis of the individual athletes would have been very helpful.

During the ranking round Carmichael finished 13th in the Women's Standing Recurve, Fabry finished second out of 12 in the Men's W1 Compound, while teammate Lear finished last. The Men's Open Compound athletes consisted of Bailey, Pemberton and Bennett. They finished 6th, 14th and 20th respectively. Completing the ranking round in the Men's W2 Recurve was Stone, who finished 10th and Wolfe, who finished 29th.

Following the ranking round came the elimination round. Carmichael surprised everyone with a bronze medal finish in the Women's Standing Recurve. Fabry ended up capturing the bronze in the Men's W1 Compound. Unfortunately in the Men's Open Compound, Pemberton and Bailey faced each other one round sooner than we had hoped and Pemberton eliminated Bailey. Pemberton ended up finishing fourth, while Bailey was fifth. Bennett, who also competed in this discipline, took ninth. Rounding out the competition was Stone and Wolfe in the Men's W2 Recurve. Stone placed 15th, while Wolfe was 29th.

We were disappointed that the only team events were Men's and Women's Recurve. We did not have enough recurve shooters to fill a team.

Closing Ceremonies were as spectacular as Opening Ceremonies. The athletes celebrated with the entire Team USA, as well as all the athletes from around the world. While there were a few disappointments, the overall experience was fantastic!

There were two things particularly that helped make my experience a great success. The first was the USOC Team Leadership meeting that was held in March, 2008. The USOC brought all the Team Leaders and

Coaches to Beijing so that we could orient ourselves, see the village and experience Beijing first hand. That was invaluable.

The second thing that I enjoyed was the camaraderie of the team leaders. This was first noticed in the Paralympic office as we had a total of five team leaders from our staff. We helped each other with deadlines and with finding better ways to get tasks completed. The camaraderie was strengthened at the March Team Leadership meeting when we met all the other team leaders and coaches.

The Paralympic Archery Team had a great Paralympic experience that will always be remembered and cherished.

TJ PEMBERTON OF THE UNITED STATES COMPETES IN THE BRONZE MEDAL MATCH OF THE MEN'S IND. COMPOUND | *ANDREW WONG/GETTY IMAGES*

LEAR CHUCK OF THE UNITED STATES COMPETES IN THE MEN'S INDIVIDUAL-W1 ARCHERY EVENT | *CHINA PHOTOS/GETTY IMAGES*

PARALYMPIC ATHLETICS | TINA KAUFFMAN-CAIN – TEAM LEADER

Overview - Over the last 20 years the number of track and field events on the program of the Paralympic Games has decreased as has the number of participants. Despite this decline the U.S. Paralympic Track and Field Team increased the number of medals brought home from Beijing. The total in 2004 (Athens) was 26; the 2008 Team won 28 medals.

Resident Program - Throughout the quad we focused our time and resources on acquiring expert coaches and increasing the standards for elite level athletes in preparation of the 2008 Paralympic Games. In the fall of 2005, U.S. Paralympics created a track and field resident program at the Olympic Training Center in Chula Vista, CA where athletes live and train full time and are provided with event specific coaching, strength and conditioning coaching, modern training facilities and equipment, sport science and sport medicine support. Ten resident athletes at the direction of Olympian Joaquim Cruz would account for nearly one-third of the team's medals won from World Championships within the first year of the program.

World Championships - Approximately 25% of the slots for the Paralympic Games are obtained through the results/medals won at World Championships. The 2006 IPC World Championships were held in Assen, The Netherlands. Even in the rainy and cold September weather, the U.S. team won 32 medals (16-gold, 12-silver and 4-bronze) and tied with Australia and Germany for second place overall. Of the 35 athletes on this team, only 23 of them would go on to compete at the most prestigious event in amateur sports—the Paralympic Games.

Site Visits - In preparation for the Games, two very beneficial site visits were arranged for team leaders to visit Beijing and get the inside scoop on the developmental planning being done for the Olympic and Paralympic Games. Also, we sent two wheelchair track athletes and the head coach to the National Stadium to participate in the test event. More time and resources should be allocated to get athletes onto the field of play prior to the Games as one of these athletes (Jessie Galli) would go on to become the most decorated track and field athlete of the 2008 Paralympic Games by collecting five medals and attaining a world record in the 400m.

Trials - Arizona Disabled Sports and the City of Mesa won the bid selection for the 2008 U.S. Paralympic Team Trials-Track and Field. Arizona State University hosted the event on their new track built with the same Mondo surface used for the National Stadium. The team selection was announced on June 15, 2008 at the closing banquet based on the results from the previous three days of competition. Men's slots were far more competitive than women's slots as men had to meet or better the elite standard to make the team. (For this reason recruiting women will become a focal point for the future of the sport.) Although the discretionary selection written in the selection procedures should be eliminated/revised for future events, we selected 44 of the best paralympic athletes (27 men and 17 women) in the United States to represent their country as part of Team USA.

Two days after the official final entry forms were submitted to the Beijing Organizing Committee for the Olympic Games (BOCOG), we received the drug test results from Trials. Two athletes named to the team tested positive for a banned substance. Because these athletes were given false information they were reinstated to the team through the arbitration process. Neither athlete made it to the final in their events at the Games.

Let the Games Begin

Team Processing - After Trials, the team would not see each other again until we assembled at the Olympic Training Center (OTC) in Colorado Springs for Team Processing. Once athletes arrived at the OTC they were immediately thrown into two days of chaos. The athletes were outfitted with the same apparel and competition gear as their fellow Olympic athletes received a mere four weeks prior. In addition to receiving thousands of dollars of clothing, they managed to find time for training sessions between two team meetings, alterations, a headshot photo, a team photo, ambassador training, medical review, media training, meals and a few hours of sleep. The OTC staff and volunteers were amazing!

Training Camp - With the support of the United States Department of Defense (DOD), the team was able to travel to Kadena Air Base in Okinawa, Japan in advance of the Games for a training camp. While there is no way for the human body to adjust to pollution, the training camp would allow athletes to train together and adhere to the prescribed amount of time to adjust to the climate and time zone for which they would compete for nine days in Beijing (1-day for each time zone change). Thanks to our friends with the DOD, the swimming and track and field teams were able to fly on a DC-10 chartered plane direct from Colorado Springs Peterson Air Base to Kadena Air Base (the flight would have taken a minimum of three stops and 24 hours of travel if flown commercially). On the return travel (which was on United Airlines commercial flights) the United Olympic Travel Desk and United States Olympic Committee (USOC) representatives did the best they could although the itineraries were late in being developed and some seat requests intended to accommodate athletes' sizes and disability types were not able to be honored, all team members were delivered safely if not totally comfortably.

The officers, volunteers and administration of Kadena Air Base worked tirelessly to provide meals, transportation, housing, entertainment and training facilities for the team. It was like rubbing a lamp and your every wish coming true—they were outstanding. Ten days after arriving at Kadena, the athletes boarded the plane that would take them to the second largest city in China and their one chance to prove that the past four years of training was worth their effort.

Accommodations - The Paralympic Village was a beautiful place; however room assignments were problematic. Many athletes slept in walk-in closets and rooms what would later become a laundry area after the Games renovations. Most beds did not have a mattress and only came with a box spring. The USOC Village staff spent days searching for bed padding which would assist athletes to get proper rest and avoid bed sores for wheelchair athletes.

Our training site in Beijing was assigned two days prior to our arrival. The facility was adequate, but was rarely used due to the long commute. Instead the athletes used the 600m track surface in the Village and the roads throughout the Olympic Green to fine tune their skills prior to competition. It was not uncommon to see drivers dodging athletes in their racing chairs on the bus ride from the village to the National Stadium.

The coaches assigned to the Games team staff all had experience from a previous event and were currently coaching at least one athlete named to the team. The medical staff did a fantastic job and is probably still trying to catch up on sleep.

Competition - Classification took place three days prior to the start of the competition and prohibited one athlete from competing and moved one athlete from a classification in which he held the world record to a class that he could not compete due to the number of entries allowed for each event. Despite the complications and disappointment, these athletes continued to show their support for their teammates. For example, Alex Richter whose amputation through the wrist did not qualify him to compete ran with Josiah Jamison in the 400m as his guide runner.

The athlete performances in Beijing met our goals but left room for improvement. Two very experienced athletes and a relay team did not win their expected medals due to injuries. Paralympian April Holmes saw her world record flash before her as she fell in the last 20 meters of the 200m final. After several stitches in her right eyelid and a bruised hip she would go on to win the gold medal in the 100m and gather her competitors for a parade lap around the track while they waited for the video review. One of the most improved athlete performances came from the youngest member of the team, who qualified to compete in one event at Games by setting a personal record at Trials. In Beijing, Chelsea McClammer beat her personal record by 10 seconds and qualified for the 800m final. The next day she beat her new personal record by another six seconds and finished in the top eight at the Paralympic Games, all at the age of 14!

Four military athletes (Casey Tibbs, Carlos Leon, Scott Winkler and Scot Severn) represented their country on a different battle field and gave quite a show in Beijing. It is estimated that 25% of the 2012 team will be comprised of injured war veterans.

The resident athletes (Jeremy Campbell, Elexis Gillette, April Holmes, Josiah Jamison, Jeff Skiba, Casey Tibbs, and guide runners: Jerome Avery and Wes Williams) would account for 40% of the Beijing track and field medal count.

The U.S. Paralympics track and field team won 28 medals and placed second in the overall team standings behind the host country China who won 77 track and field medals.

From the Great Wall to the Bridge—The Road to London

Quad Plan - We have the potential to win more medals but need to create and implement a thorough plan for identifying and recruiting athletes in the necessary targeted events/classification groups. For example, 25% of the total medals available are in the cerebral palsy (CP) classification events and we had one female athlete (Sabra Hawkes) and not a single male athlete to compete in the Games in these events.

Another issue that impacts our medal count is the number of domestic competitions available for Paralympic track and field athletes. Over the next quad, we plan to establish a domestic 'Grand Prix' series of competitions that will include prize money to both attract quality international competitors to the U.S. (thus decreasing our reliance on international travel) and increase the number of IPC sanctioned events in the U.S.. In addition, these events will also provide more opportunities for us to recruit athletes and to provide media exposure for disabled sports.

We are expanding the Resident Program for the 2009-2012 quad. The Olympic and Paralympic track and field resident programs in Chula Vista were combined in January 2009. The goal is to build a larger athlete base over the next quad which will create a more experienced team for the 2012 Games in London.

International Changes - The International Paralympic Committee (IPC) is making a number of changes to the current classification system which will take effect in January 2009. This will directly affect the eligibility of current national team members who may have to be replaced with athletes who meet the new standards.

The IPC has established a world ranking system over the past quad which has and will continue to increase the professionalism and organization of our sport.

JEFF SKIBA OF THE UNITED STATES COMPETES IN THE MEN'S HIGH JUMP
| *CHRIS HYDE/GETTY IMAGES*

PARALYMPIC BASKETBALL – MEN'S | MIKE BAULER

Athletes who compete in Paralympic wheelchair basketball train primarily in the United States; we do have one athlete who lives and trains in Germany. We do not have a specific off-season training program but our athletes are members of local clubs or train with their college team.

Our Paralympic team was selected in April 2008. With the assistance of a selection committee (our coaching staff and other experts not attending the Games) approximately 30 athletes were nominated to attend the trials in Colorado Springs, Colo. In the end, I believe our process selected the best of the best from the U.S. and I can't think of a better way to select the Paralympic team.

Between the Trials and the Paralympic Games, our team attended training camps twice a month and participated in three international tournaments. The competitions consisted of the Paralympic World Cup in Manchester, England, the World Basketball Challenge in Warm Springs, Ga., and the North American Cup in Birmingham, Ala. The team won all three tournaments where they faced off against teams from Canada, Great Britain, Australia, Sweden, Israel, and Germany, to name a few.

There was a test event at the Paralympic Games site but we were not invited. In terms of training facilities provided by BOCOG, they were all very nice and the volunteers at each venue were amazing. When we had a problem with a broken rim, the gym staff fixed it within minutes!

We entered the Paralympic Games with a lot of momentum, having lost only three games over the past four years. The team received a tough draw for our pool and ended up 4-1 in pool play, which gave us the #2 seed in the playoff tournament. This would be a tough spot for our team because it paired us in the same bracket as the two-time defending Paralympic Champions – Canada. However, we had to get through a very tough Iranian team in the quarterfinals before we played Canada.

Iran was having a great tournament and ended up as the #3 seed in their pool. Unfortunately, we never played them! We were told the team had withdrawn from the Paralympic Games due to a schedule change. Consequently, we had a bye in the quarterfinals, which moved us into the semifinals where we played Canada.

We jumped out to a big lead and controlled the first three quarters of the game. However, in the fourth quarter Canada mounted a comeback and forced the U.S. to make one free throw to advance to the finals. With 30 seconds remaining in the game, we missed both free throws and Canada's star Patrick Anderson drained a three-pointer to send the game into overtime.

In overtime, the same situation came up: we had to make 1 out of 4 free throw attempts to advance to the championship game. We missed all four of them and wound up in double overtime. Unfortunately, by now, three of our five starters had fouled out and we went on to lose the game.

This was a very hard loss for both our athletes and our staff. This feeling of loss is something that our staff and the athletes will never forget because the game was ours to win and was eventually lost on the easiest part of the game…free throws. The letdown was too much for us and we ended up losing to Great Britain in the bronze medal match. We entered the Paralympic Games reaching for gold and came home empty handed.

I was able to attend the USOC Team Leadership Meetings and felt they were important because it gave us a chance to become familiar with USOC staff and the entire Paralympic Games process. The meetings in China were priceless because there is no amount of video or lectures that could have prepared us as well as a personal tour of the Paralympic Village and venues. That was extremely beneficial for me and in turn beneficial for our team.

The USOC does a great job of providing team leaders with the tools and information necessary to complete all paperwork and tasks in a timely manner especially when dealing with accreditation. The pre-set deadlines made it very easy to gauge when individual forms were due to the USOC. The examples provided for accreditation also served as a guide throughout the process.

All of our flights were booked with United through our NGB contact and we were able to meet all of our deadlines. It is great to always be able to use the same contact through United. It makes the job of booking flights much more comfortable when knowing the person you are talking to and feeling that your request will be completed. The relationship with our NGB and the USOC made the job of a team leader and booking flights much easier.

The entire apparel process went well. We had no major issues arise with this. Also team processing was great and everything provided to our team at the Olympic Training Center in Colorado Springs worked perfectly. Getting through all the stations in a timely manner was a bonus for our guys.

The cell phones provided a constant line of communication between USOC staff, our staff, and the athletes. Without the cell phones it would have made our jobs much more difficult. Having the cell phones and everyone's numbers programmed into them was a great resource.

Jill Collins was our athletic trainer and she is a member of the National Athletic Trainer Association. She has eight years of Paralympic experience and serves as the Athletic Director at Lakeshore Foundation. Being able to request a trainer with whom our staff and athletes are familiar made the entire process fantastic.

The USOC video services were very helpful, copies of all of our games were available for the coaches and players to view. .

The biggest thing I learned is that every detail is important. Whether planning flights, getting visas in line, or knocking down a free throw… every detail matters.

PARALYMPIC BASKETBALL – WOMEN'S | *JEFF DOWNES – TEAM LEADER*

The 2008 Paralympic women's wheelchair basketball team was comprised of several athletes in college programs, several athletes playing on women's teams, and one athlete who had just graduated from the junior division. Many of our athletes played with or against each other during the season, which gave our team a solid foundation. We were fortunate that we had several of the players returning from the Athens gold medal team.

Twenty-four athletes were selected by the coaching staff to be invited to our Team Selection camp. These were athletes that have been on previous international teams as well as those that the staff thought showed potential. Over a three-day period we held a variety of drills, scrimmages, and game situation sessions that allowed the staff to see all our athletes perform. The selection staff met each night to review the daily performance of all athletes as we narrowed our selection. I feel that the selection process, discussions and evaluations used to select our final team and our list of alternates worked very well. I do not have any suggestions for changes or improvements.

Following our Trials, our team typically would meet at least once per month prior to the Games for a team training camp. This year, we also had the opportunity to participate in back-to-back international team tournaments hosted in the U.S. Our team won both the Roosevelt Cup in Warm Springs, Ga., and the North America Cup in Birmingham, Ala. These were great opportunities for our team; we improved our skill and gained valuable insight on the teams we expected to see in Beijing. Each athlete maintained a personal workout routine with periodic updates to staff and other teammates. Typically the only challenge the team faced was the ability to get to our training sites; this was primarily due to aircraft limitations using the United Airlines systems. However, we greatly appreciate United's commitment to the USOC.

There was a test tournament in Beijing; however the U.S. was not invited to attend the tournament. I think it would be beneficial for the Team Leader to attend any test event in the future to gain "game experience" regardless if the U.S. team is participating in the test event or not. This experience would provide additional site contacts and firsthand knowledge of successes or challenges at the test event.

Our team was very happy with the training schedule, facilities, and opportunities provided for training prior to the Paralympic Games. In fact, we were pleasantly surprised to find that we had enough time for practices and that appropriate venues were available to us when we landed in Beijing. In the end, we did not experience any significant problems. The volunteers were fantastic and made us feel like "rock stars."

Our performance during the Games can be summed up in two words....GOLD MEDAL! As this team did all along, we stayed focused during the games, played our game, and took the game one possession at a time. This team came from behind many times to go undefeated. We stayed focused on the end result.

The coaching staff developed a great approach to our games using conditioning, speed and line-up management to keep our competition on their heels. Our conditioning proved the difference maker in many of our games. We were able to wear down our competitor's defense while keeping our offense moving and scoring. There was not a single team that could match our combination of speed, endurance, defense and offense.

I attended the team leaders meetings and found these meetings to be extremely valuable. The information that was distributed and the ability to have "on the ground" experience in Beijing allowed me to take a stronger lead in providing information to my team. I greatly appreciate the USOC's commitment to the onsite Team Leader meetings. I feel that seeing the facilities and city/country in advance allows us to address concerns or issues and be better prepared for Paralympic Games situations. I did not attend the key decision makers meeting but feel that team leaders should be given the opportunity to attend all information meetings to ensure we have exposure to as much data as possible.

Overall the accreditation process worked very smoothly. I believe that all deadlines were met in a timely fashion. In the event an extension

EMILY HOSKINS OF THE UNITED STATES SHOOTS DURING THE WOMEN'S GOLD MEDAL WHEELCHAIR BASKETBALL MATCH | *ADAM PRETTY/GETTY IMAGES*

was granted due to a team camp the new deadline was met without any adverse impact to the timeliness of the information. We had a couple of "new requirements" from BOCOG during the process but these were well communicated and typically we had enough response time allowed for any adjustments to be made. I would continue to use email as the primary communication tool for Team Leaders. I would also suggest that a text message tree be developed to alert Team Leaders immediately regarding an "urgent" change or requirement.

The air travel process seemed to go well. I used a spreadsheet to send a listing of preferred flights to the USOC, which they then used to book flights through United. This process eliminated the step of having to check with athletes after a flight was placed on hold. Our USOC contact attempted to eliminate duplication of effort and recommended working specifically with the Team Leader for all Beijing/Games airline tickets. This made the process run much more efficiently.

Regarding apparel and team processing everything went relatively well. Our only issue was the fact that several of our players are very small females and there were some clothing articles that were not available in their sizes. This was disappointing to the athletes. We were able to do some alterations, which were done in an amazingly timely fashion, but it would have been nice to have some smaller sizes. This is just something to keep in mind for the future. Also, I think that the use of "timing" teams through processing helped to keep the amount of people in the processing area controlled. This seemed to work very well to avoid having bottlenecks during the apparel distribution.

463

The USOC-issued cell phones were a useful tool for our team and the preloaded phone numbers and names were very helpful. Also the Village computers and wireless connections that were available were very helpful. However, at times it appeared that the wireless connection had a weak signal. The coaches' room with additional internet cabling was very helpful as was having separate areas for coaches and athletes.

The Paralympic village and staff were amazing. The staff was always there to help. We did have a special request once we arrived as we needed to switch rooms due to an air quality problem. This change was completed in a timely fashion and made very easy by the Village staff.

Ashley White worked as our trainer. Although she was not able to attend many of our training camps, Ashley developed a strong relationship with our athletes and became a valuable member of our staff. I believe that she was well prepared for our team and had a good background to help our athletes. I would continue to use the same staffing matrix for the future.

The USOC did an excellent job in providing us DVD copies for game analysis. We did not have DartFish available which is something that we would like to have available in the future.

The USOC worked very well to keep our Friends & Family in the loop for game changes and did an excellent job in procuring tickets to our games for our Friends & Family group. As a result, we experienced no problems that couldn't be addressed by the USOC staff.

In the future I hope to be involved with the team in the same role as the Team Leader again. I enjoyed the role with all of its challenges. I learned that it is important to be able to adjust to the customs and "way of doing business" based on the host country. I found it important to continually remind my team that our normal way of doing things would likely need to be adjusted to the customs and procedures of the Chinese systems. It is important for the Team Leader to be an ambassador to the host country, not only for their sport but also for the USOC. Simple things such as staying on time, respecting the host country schedules, and providing as much accurate information as possible makes this role easier.

PARALYMPIC BOCCIA | MARK MCMILLAN – *TEAM LEADER*

In preparation for the 2008 Paralympic Games, we concentrated on different strategies to improve our defense maneuvers. We also worked on improving the accuracy of our throws or "shots" on court, placing the ball in strategic locations, "kissing" the target ball, and creating a wall for blocking the opponent.

During the off-season, our one athlete, TJ Hawker, uses the facility at the University of Toledo to practice boccia as his time allows – once or twice a week. TJ was selected to represent the U.S. team as a wild card. He was ranked number 1 in the U.S. ranking system for his class.

After being selected to the team, TJ attended three training camps and competed at Nationals in Warm Springs, Ga. He performed well there and won a gold medal in the individual competition and team competition.

The competition venue in Beijing was very nice and close to the Paralympic Village. However, the transportation only ran every two hours for practice sessions. We tried to hop on other buses that would get us near the venue with no success. Since the venue was close, we chose to walk a few times. During competition, transportation ran every hour.

TJ performed well even though he did not win any of his games. Competition in boccia is very tough for U.S. athletes in international competition.

Our primary expenses were training camps, travel expenses, lodging, competition apparel and equipment.

The accreditation process had several steps and we had some issues leading up to the Games but we got them all worked out and had no issues upon arrival.

In terms of booking our flights, that process went well. We thought we were going to have an issue on our United flight from Chicago to Colorado Springs because it was a smaller aircraft. The United Airlines crew was unsure that they would be able to fit the motorized wheelchair in the belly of the plane. Fortunately it did fit on the plane but this issue would be something to consider on future flights with oversized equipment.

Leading up to the Games, I was kept informed regarding apparel. The only thing I was not aware of was the fact that I could have had the US Paralympics logo embroidered on our competition apparel. As for the team processing element, I liked that it was done in smaller, more manageable groups.

I really appreciated the fact that we had computers with internet access available for us at the Village. It helped us to keep in touch with everyone back home.

We did not require a lot of medical attention but Betsy Nadler was always there and available if we needed her help.

Overall, TJ practiced, trained, and competed very well. He was fo-cused and relaxed before and during his competition matches. I learned that communication is important both verbally and in writing. Everyone was nice and very helpful. The Paralympic Games in Beijing was a wonderful experience.

THE BALL IS PLACED FOR SOUTH KOREA'S PARK KEON-WOO (R) TO TAKE HIS SHOT DURING THE INDIVIDUAL BC3 CATEGORY GOLD MEDAL FINAL | *FREDERIC J. BROWN/AFP/GETTY IMAGES*

PARALYMPIC CYCLING | *JAIME MARTIN – TEAM LEADER*

The 2008 Paralympic Cycling team was very successful at the Paralympic Games in Beijing. The team improved from winning nine medals at the 2004 Paralympic Games in Athens to winning 14 total medals (4 on the track and 10 on the road) in Beijing and finished second in the cycling gold medal count behind Great Britain.

The majority of our team was selected based on performances at the 2007 UCI Paracycling World Championships and 2008 National Championships. We discovered issues with the team selection procedures and had to change them right before our National Championships. Our team size ended up being smaller than originally expected. Instead of receiving 12 total slots we ended up with 10 slots. These two slots were eventually given back to the team when two of our athletes were invited by name. Four of our slots were also ring fenced (by specific classifications), so four of the athletes we brought to Beijing had to be in specific classifications. If we didn't bring athletes in those classifications, we would have lost those slots. Three athletes ended up qualifying from their performances at the 2007 UCI Paracycling World Championships.

The rest of the team (besides the two invited by name) were selected from their performances at the 2008 National Championships which were held in Colorado Springs and Denver, Colorado.

Our team consisted of Alejandro Albor, Barbara Buchan, (Colorado Springs Olympic Training Center resident athlete) Michael Farrell, Allison Jones (Colorado Springs Olympic Training Center resident athlete), David Lee, Greta Neimanas (Colorado Springs Olympic Training Center resident athlete), Jennifer Schuble (military athlete), Oscar "Oz" Sanchez (military athlete), Matthew Updike, Karissa Whitsell (resident athlete) and her pilot Mackenzie Woodring, Ron Williams, and Anthony Zahn. Once formed, the team was honored at a Colorado Rockies game. At the beginning of the game, the entire team was taken onto the baseball diamond and introduced to the crowd..

Between our team selection and departure for Beijing, we had three training camps. The first two camps were for our track cycling athletes. We took them to the ADT Event Center in Carson, California to help them better prepare for track competition in Beijing. We also had a

(L-R) SILVER MEDALIST ALEJANDRO ALBOR OF TEAM USA, GOLD MEDALIST ERNST VAN DYK OF SOUTH AFRICA AND BRONZE MEDALIST OZ SANCHEZ OF TEAM USA CELEBRATE AFTER THE ROAD CYCLING MEN'S ROAD RACE | *FENG LI/GETTY IMAGES*

camp at the Olympic Training Center in Colorado Springs, Colorado right before Team Processing. This was a great opportunity for us to get the entire team together and train as a group.

Team processing went very well for our team. We didn't have any problems outfitting our athletes or getting them through alterations. The athletes and staff were so excited about all of the apparel they received. The USOC and OTC staff did a great job helping our team out.

The trip to Beijing went very smooth besides waking up early in the morning to travel. United Airlines and USOC staff were there each step of the way to make sure we didn't encounter any problems. We traveled to Beijing in two groups. We took those athletes who would be competing in the track competition to Beijing first and then the road specific athletes came a few days later. Traveling in two separate groups made things a lot easier. We found out we needed a few things we didn't bring and were able to ask the second group to bring those items along.

We had four days of track competition. We had five women and two men competing in the Individual Time Trial and Pursuit. We won four medals on the track (two gold, one silver, and one bronze). Jennifer Schuble won one gold and one silver medal, Karissa Whitsell and her pilot, Mackenzie Woodring won one bronze, and Barbara Buchan won a gold.

The team continued to be successful on our first day of road competition. All of our athletes competed in the Time Trial and we won seven medals. Oz Sanchez, Karissa Whitsell and Mackenzie Woodring, and Barbara Buchan all won gold medals. Jennifer Schuble and Allison Jones won silver medals and Alejandro Albor and Anthony Zahn both won a bronze medal. We finished up competition on the road with two days of road races, winning three more medals. Karissa and Mackenzie won a silver medal. Oz and Alejandro's race came down to the final stretch. Alejandro ended up with the silver and Oz ended up with the bronze.

Our goal going into the Games was 10 total medals with two of them being gold. Upon arrival into Beijing our head coach issued a challenge as motivation. If the team won five gold medals, he would shave something into his hair.

After the final day of competition and with our team's five gold medals in hand, we took our coach to get his hair cut in the village. He tried to get out of it and fought us the entire way but, with most of the team watching, he finally let us shave "USA" into the back of his head.

Overall, the entire trip went very well. We had a great staff working with our team. Mark Stovak was our team doctor. He was always willing to help us out especially with making sure the team was taken care of. Our mechanics, Todd Anderson and Chad Contreras, and our soigneurs, Michelle Jacques and Erik Moen, did a fantastic job staying on top of their responsibilities and working together as a team. Our coaches, Craig Griffin and Jim Lehman, did a terrific job as well. They were always willing to help me understand and learn more about cycling.

One of the things that helped make my trip successful was having my team leader support group. Kim Bartkowski, Tina Kauffman, Jimi Flowers, and I all started meeting together before the Games. We helped each other with deadlines, coming up with ideas on how to handle certain situations, and preparing ourselves and our teams for the trip. This continued throughout the Games. I always knew that I had someone I could call whenever I had a problem. We were always there to help each other out.

Our cycling success was a direct result of the USOC staff and all of the divisions, the volunteers, United Airlines, NPC Assistants, our cycling delegation, and everyone else involved in the Paralympic Games working together as a team.

466

BARBARA BUCHAN OF TEAM USA COMPETES IN THE WOMEN'S INDI-VIDUAL PURSUIT | *GUANG NIU/GETTY IMAGES*

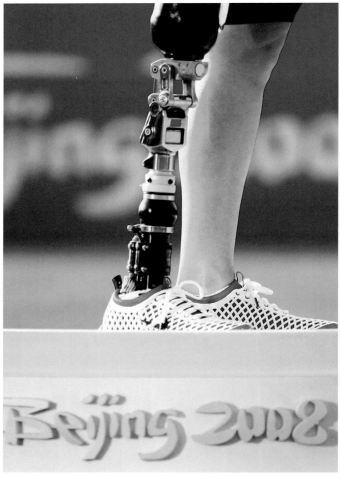

ALLISON JONES OF USA AWAITS HER MEDAL AFTER WINNING SILVER IN THE ROAD CYCLING WOMEN'S TIME TRIAL | *FENG LI/GETTY IMAGES*

PARALYMPIC EQUESTRIAN | PAM LANE – TEAM LEADER

Dressage is characterized by the combination of two elements: one is a horse that has been trained to a high level of gymnastic athleticism; the other is a rider who guides the horse through a set of graceful and elegant exercises. It is a highly stylized form of competition, with one component choreographed to music in the same way that ice dancing is and therefore, there is a high degree of subjectivity involved in the judging of the sport. This subjectivity means that the rider must present both the type of horse that judges want to see and the sort of exercises that judges expect. As these expectations can change over time, athletes must be able to modify their performance to suit the changing expectations of the judges.

Our team was selected June 1. The riders trained in the U.S. with local trainers but it would be advantageous to send rider/horse combinations to Europe for competition experience. This would better prepare them for the level of international competition found at the Paralympic Games. Six weeks before departing for quarantine the riders/horses stayed at the national coach's facility for training. They then trained for two weeks while in Germany for quarantine.

There was a test event held and Eventing sent two riders. Our national coach and I attended as well. This trip allowed us to gain a familiarity with the venue, logistics and other conditions that would impact our team at the Paralympics and proved extremely valuable for our preparation.

During the Paralympic Games, we trained at the Sha Tin Race Course in Hong Kong. In every regard this venue provided the highest quality facility with exceptional management on the part of the host.

Our primary expenses were the shipping of the horses and the quarantine arrangements in Germany. If we had a larger budget we could have scheduled more training sessions and sent rider/horse combinations to Europe to compete.

I attended both team leadership meetings. Networking with other team leaders and learning their best practices, getting to know the USOC Paralympic staff and the roundtables were all very valuable experiences.

Our air travel was a little complicated due to the fact that we had to quarantine the horses in Aachen, Germany, before going to China. However, everyone went out of their way to help us and made it as smooth as they could. In the future, we would like to see assigned seats for athletes on the itinerary, especially those with special needs so that we can avoid any conflicts as we are boarding the plane.

Being able to receive our team apparel in Hong Kong was a great benefit. Unfortunately the sizes were not consistent and many of the athletes and staff received clothing that did not fit. It was also beneficial to the team to be able to schedule the Paralympic Ambassador Program in Gladstone, N.J.

As for transportation having an assigned van and being able to request an accessible van if needed in Hong Kong was very helpful. We found it very helpful to have all the athletes and staff assigned a cell phone. It was much easier to keep in touch as a result.

We greatly appreciated the fact that logistically everything was ready and set-up for us when we arrived on site, as the Olympic horses left only four days before our arrival.

The Paralympic Village in Hong Kong was very well received by athletes and staff. During our stay the Village contracted the Norovirus. This caused some anxiety for the athletes, but was well handled by authorities and communication was excellent.

Our medical staff consisted of Dr. Michelle Look and Debbie Van Horn. Both were excellent and extremely well received by the athletes. I would highly recommend both USOC medical personnel that were provided to us for future Games. They were an excellent addition to our team.

We learned the value of planning 18 months in advance to manage the logistics of the trip. We also learned to have selection procedures that ensure the best qualified horse/rider combinations are selected to the Team. Being staffed completely with volunteers at the Paralympics presented some challenges. One thing I would do for the future would be to expand the allotment of credentials, so that the entire support staff necessary to ensure the highest level of performance for our horses is available at the venue.

LYNN SEIDEMANN OF TEAM USA OMPETES IN THE PARALYMPIC EQUESTRIAN TEAM TEST - GRADE IB | MN CHAN/GETTY IMAGES

PARALYMPIC WHEELCHAIR FENCING | *CHRISTINE STRONG SIMMONS*

– ASSOCIATE EXECUTIVE DIRECTOR

Wheelchair Fencers use a frame to hold the sport wheelchair in place while the athlete attempts to make touches on his opponent while defending his own target. Speed, endurance and tactical ability are all key performance indicators in Wheelchair Fencing.

In a non-Paralympic year, the elite athletes would travel to World Cups from November thru July but train primarily in the U.S. If I could change anything regarding the off-season training, I would better fund our elite athletes to allow them to train more often and to travel to more international competitions, particularly World Cups and World Championships. I would also invest more in our development process in order to expand a shrinking athlete base.

The 2008 Paralympic fencing team was selected based on athlete's international point standings as of February 29, 2008. However, we weren't able to notify the athletes officially until April because there was a delay from the international federation (IF) on posting the final point standings. The point selection process allowed for the best athletes to be on the Team. The thing I would change with this process is a more timely posting of the final point totals, which would in turn allow for more time to work with the team. In addition, two athletes were added to the team in July via the IF and one of the athletes was subsequently pulled as not qualified. This made planning much more difficult and raised the hopes of an athlete that they would be part of the final Team.

Our athletes competed in the World Cups in Germany, Montreal and Warsaw prior to the Games. Scott Rodgers placed in the top three in Germany and in the top 6 and 12 in Montreal. We also held a pre-Beijing training camp in Colorado Springs, Colo., just prior to leaving for the Games. The training and competition was effective but with more athlete funding, they could have devoted more time to training prior to the Games.

The facilities for training in Beijing were appropriate and there were no major problems. Practicing in the same venue as the actual competition is beneficial for future Games.

Scott Rodgers (San Diego, Calif.) advanced to the quarterfinals in both days of his competition in men's foil and epee category B. A three-time Paralympian, ranked fifth in the world, Rodgers won bronze in the epee category B event at the 2004 Paralympics and placed sixth at the 2007 World Cup in Paris. After coming away from a competitive morning preliminary pool with two wins and three losses in foil, Rodgers defeated Athens double medalist Piotr Czop from Poland 15-11 in the Round of 16. Then in the quarterfinals, the U.S. fencer had a four-touch lead, but couldn't maintain the upper body strength to close the door against China's Daoliang Hu.

Rodgers repeated a quarterfinal loss in his bout against Belarus' Mikalai Bezyazychny in epee competition, with a final score of 4-15. Rodgers

and Benjy Williams (Bethlehem, Ga.) both advanced from pool play - Rodgers with wins against Japan (5-1), Spain (5-3), France (5-3), and China (5-4), and Williams with two wins against Kuwait's Alsaedi Abdulwahab (5-4) and Greece's Emmanouil Bogdos (5-4). Then in the un-luck of the draw, the two U.S. fencers were paired together. Rodgers advanced to the quarterfinals with a 15-2 win over Williams.

Also competing in the men's individual foil category B, Gerard Moreno (Los Angeles, Calif.) did not advance from his preliminary pool. The three-time Paralympian and oldest competitor in the field at 51 years old, defeated Korea's Kim Gi-Hong 5-4 in his second bout, but failed to tally enough touches in the other match-ups to secure a spot in the Round of 16.

In men's individual foil category A, Mark Calhoun (Bremen, Ga.) won his first bout in the morning pool 5-4 against Poland's Stefan Ma-

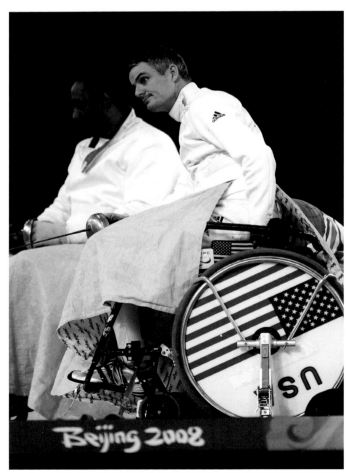

BENJY WILLIAMS OF THE UNITED STATES AND COMPATRIOT SCOTT RODGERS COMPETE IN THE MEN'S IND. EPEE | *ANDREW WONG/GETTY IMAGES*

kowski. He proceeded to lose the next four bouts and did not advance to the rounds. Andrea DeMello (New York, N.Y.), a four-time Paralympian who competed for Brazil in 1996, 2000 and 2004, did not advance out of the preliminary pools of the women's foil or sabre category B events. In epee, DeMello lost 0-5 overall, but managed to score touches in all but one of the bouts. The closest match-up was with Italy's Rosalba Vettraino, who narrowly won the bout 5-4.

Our primary expenses for these Games were clinics and camps for the year, equipment for the team going to Beijing and the travel to the World Cups. If I had a larger budget, I would purchase frames that could be loaned to new programs in the U.S. that would facilitate the development of the sport. I would also hold more camps and clinics around the country to drive interest in this sport.

I attended both team leadership meetings and found the information provided by the USOC/U.S. Paralympic Division to be beneficial for understanding the mission of the Games as well as a tool that assisted with planning for Beijing. As a first time Team Leader, I certainly would have benefited from more time at some of the roundtable discussions.

Regarding credentials, the International Wheelchair and Amputee Sports federation (IWAS) provided two more athlete spots to the US Wheelchair Fencing Team in July. This increased the number of credentials needed for athletes as well as increasing the number of primary (Ao) credentials for our officials. As these changes occurred, the Games Deliverables Document was updated and the number of accreditations increased accordingly. Adding both athletes and an official in July was a challenge. The main lesson learned here is that viewing the Deliverables Document as a work in progress is essential. Providing quick turnaround time on changes to this document and to the accreditation section in particular, allows the Team Leader to focus on the other details that require their attention.

As for air travel, working with one primary United Olympic Desk representative was very helpful. However, the United Olympic Desk was very busy prior to and during the Olympic Games. Therefore, itinerary changes during this time took longer than expected. In addition, there was no aisle chair on the flight to Beijing and this meant that our wheelchair athletes could not use the restroom unless assisted.

Our sponsors provided uniforms and equipment for the Olympic Team but not necessarily the Paralympic Team. So, US Fencing purchased fencing bags, gloves, uniforms and other equipment items to outfit the team. Adding two more athletes and another official was unexpected but this was dealt with in a timely manner so that apparel was taken care of.

Team processing was seamless and well thought out and our team had plenty of time to get through processing. The staff was helpful, energetic and genuinely committed to making this experience special for the entire team. My only suggestion would be to add more space to try on the clothing especially for the wheelchair athletes.

Transporting equipment, sports chairs and athletes via the bus was difficult. When transporting sports chairs, equipment and athletes to the practice venue, we could not use the Village transportation but had to carry all of this to the bus depot and then into the practice hall. We then had to follow the same process to transport the chairs, equipment and athletes from the practice hall to the Fencing Hall for competition. It was a challenge to use the bus system for this transport. It would have been beneficial if there had been information on companies (and their rates) that provide ground transportation for wheelchair users. Also, it would have been helpful to know if there were transport services in the Village to get equipment to the various venues.

The cell phones were a great tool but we had some difficulty getting voice mail set-up and retrieving messages. However, this didn't re-

469

BENJY WILLIAMS OF THE UNITED STATES AND COMPATRIOT SCOTT RODGERS COMPETE IN THE MEN'S IND. EPEE | *ANDREW WONG/GETTY IMAGES*

ally have that big of an impact on our communication. The athletes enjoyed and appreciated the USOC Athlete Lounge set up with email and internet access. It was a good place for them to talk with other athletes and to decompress. My only suggestion would be to add more computers and have a larger work area for the future.

We ended up using some outside housing at the beginning of the Games for two of our officials. The USOC worked with me prior to arriving in Beijing to ensure that our officials had a hotel and that they knew which hotel it would be. When the time came to move them into the Village, the USOC walked them through this process. Transportation from the hotel to the Village and to the practice venue was difficult for these two officials. In the future it would be nice if a daily transport system was established from the main hotel to the Village and venues.

During the Games, we had various medical staff that was assigned to our athletes but all of them were very responsive to our athletes needs. They were always available to our team.

The information about tickets for the athletes was straightforward and easily understood. However, tickets for friends and family were not easy to purchase and very limited. Also, the athletes were allowed to watch other events but the coaches and staff were told that they had to purchase a ticket. I don't know if this was specific to Beijing but I was informed that at previous Games, the coaches were allowed to attend these other sporting events to cheer for the U.S. delegation.

Something to consider in the future is the fact that the athletes trained in Colorado Springs and again in Beijing for two weeks. We scaled back on the training sessions, as we got closer to the competition, but may have over-trained for the Games. Less time training just prior to the competition may have helped to boost our results. Moreover, we arrived on September 4 and fencing competition did not begin until September 14. For future Games, perhaps the team should arrive closer to the actual competition days.

PARALYMPIC GOALBALL – MEN'S | JOHN POTTS – TEAM LEADER

Goalball is a team sport designed for blind athletes. It was devised by Hanz Lorenzen and Sep Reindle in 1946 as a rehabilitation activity for blind and visually impaired World War II veterans. Goalball evolved from a rehabilitation activity into a highly competitive sport over the next few decades. It became a demonstration event at the 1976 Summer Paralympic Games and has been contested as a medal event since 1980.

Participants compete in teams of three and play on a court measuring 9 x 18 meters. The object of the sport is to roll the ball into the opponent's goal while opposing players try to block the ball approaching them with their bodies. Sounds made by bells inside the ball indicate the direction of the on-coming ball. Goalball players must use the sound of the bell to judge the position and movement of the ball. Therefore, while play is in progress, complete silence is required in the venue to allow the players to concentrate and react instantly to the ball. All players wear blackout goggles which provide all athletes, regardless of vision status, equal competitive opportunity. String embedded under the taped court lines provides orientation. Games consist of two 10 minute halves.

Goalball is unique as a Paralympic sport because it is the only sport that is not an adaptation of an able-bodied counterpart. It is also one of the most popular Paralympic sports and is played in more than 112 countries around the world.

The international competitive season is in the summer months. The USA competitive season is January – June, which meant our athletes compete January through September. During the international "off season" athletes competed and trained with their home clubs. Athletes also developed individual performance plans and provided periodic progress reports to the coaching staff. Most off-season training activities were conducted in the USA although some athletes played with their club teams in Canadian tournaments.

The trials process consisted of three trials camps and observation of athletes participating with their home clubs in U.S. Association for Blind Athletes (USABA) regional tournaments. During these camps, athletes were evaluated on their technical, tactical and mental skills, physical conditioning and ability to play within the coaching staff's playing system. Additionally they were evaluated on non-skill related attributes such as teamwork, enthusiasm, versatility, leadership, competitive spirit and work ethic.

The first trials camp was held Nov. 1-5, 2007 at the Lake Placid Olympic Training Center. The second camp was Feb. 13-17, 2008, also in Lake Placid, N.Y. Ten athletes were invited to this camp. At the conclusion of this camp, the athlete roster was narrowed to eight names. These final eight athletes were invited to the final trials camp that was held April 17-21, 2008, at the Lakeshore Foundation Training Site. The outcome would determine which six athletes would be nominated to the U.S. Olympic Committee as the 2008 Goalball Paralympic team. The remaining two would serve as team alternates.

In addition to the camps, any interested athletes were also observed as they played for club teams at three USABA regional goalball tournaments held in Kalamazoo, Mich., Westmont, N.J., and Colorado Springs, CO

The final team consisted of Stephen Denuyl, Christopher Dodds, Donte' Mickens, Tyler Merren, Edward Munro, Daryl Walker, Timothy Dornbrock (alternate) and Andrew Jenks (alternate). The following individuals were the staff that reviewed and made selection recommendations: Tom Parrigin – Head Coach, Michael Lege' – Assistant Coach, John Potts – Team Leader and Dustin Williams - athletic trainer.

Between naming the team and the actual Games, athletes engaged in a number of training activities as individual athletes, as members of their club teams and as members of the USA National Team.

During this period, all athletes continued to train according to their individual performance plans. Each athlete submitted periodic workout reports to the coaching staff and they reviewed the workout reports with each athlete to assess progress towards individual training goals. Modifications were made as needed to ensure continued progress.

Athletes also continued to train and compete with their home clubs which added team playing experience between national team camps and competitions. All athletes competed with their home clubs during the 2008 USABA Goalball National Championships, held in Salt Lake City, Utah, June 19-21. The 2008 National Championship team, Northeast Florida, included 2008 Paralympic Team members Donte' Mickens, Edward Munro and Daryl Walker. Paralympic team alternate, Timothy Dornbrock also competed with the Northeast Florida team.

In June 2008, the team traveled to Vilnius, Lithuania, where they competed in the Vytaus the Great Lion's Cup Tournament. This tournament included a number of top teams, including Lithuania, China, Sweden, Belgium and Finland. We competed against many of these same teams during the September 2007 Paralympic test event, so this competition gave us the opportunity to observe any roster and tactical changes the teams had made since that time. Because he was recuperating from a muscle pull that affected his throwing, we did not bring Donte' Mickens to the Great Lion's Cup Tournament. He was replaced by alternate, Timothy Dornbrock. Although defense was very strong (Tyler Merren placed third in tournament scoring), Mickens' absence prevented us from attaining an optimal offensive outcome. We noted the Chinese team improved at a rate far greater than we observed from any other Paralympic qualifier team. It was apparent to us that the Chinese ability to train on a daily basis as a team was paying them dividends and that if they continued to improve at the same pace as we had observed in the past, they would finish strong at the Paralympic Games. Lithuania looked very strong during this tournament as they continued to play a very quick and fundamentally sound game. The U.S. team would finish this tournament behind teams from China and Lithuania.

The team's "dry run" tournament prior to the Paralympic Games was the Men's Malmo Intercup, held in Malmo, Sweden, July 30 through August 4, 2008. All teams invited to this tournament (China, Sweden, Denmark, Spain, Iran, Belgium, Finland and USA) were teams that would compete in the 2008 Paralympic Games. China was a last-minute withdrawal from the tournament, so we weren't able to observe any changes they may have made after the Lithuania tournament. Donte' Mickens had recovered from his injury and competed at this tournament. At tournament end, Sweden and the USA had similar win-loss records and the U.S. beat Sweden in head-to-head play. However, Sweden's overall point differential against all opponents was two points higher than USA's, giving the USA a second place finish.

In addition to all of this, two training camps were conducted. The first was held at the Lake Placid Olympic Training Center, July 10-14, 2008. The final training camp was held immediately prior to team processing (August 27-31) at the Colorado Springs Olympic Training Center.

A major training hurdle for this team was the fact that the athletes were located across the country which posed a logistical challenge when planning training opportunities. Fortunately, we were provided ample funding and access to quality training facilities. Although we did not attain the outcome we had targeted to achieve at the Paralympic Games, we believe the number and variety of training and competition activities were effective.

As mentioned earlier, a test event was conducted for men's goalball, the Good Luck Beijing – 2007 Invitational Goalball Tournament. This was the only Paralympic test event held by the 2008 Beijing Organizing Committee.

The top six finishers from the 2006 World Goalball Championships and two additional teams were invited to participate in the test event. USA competed against teams from China, Lithuania, Canada, Denmark, Sweden, Japan and Finland. Participation afforded the opportunity to capture video footage and conduct assessments of each competitor during game play on the actual Paralympic competition floor. The rosters of most teams had changed significantly since we competed in the 2006 International Blind Sports Federation (IBSA) World Goalball Championships (the first Paralympic qualification event). We were able to compete against many of these teams earlier in 2007 and we were able to use those experiences to develop strategies tailored against each team that we were able to implement/assess during this event.

The information gained from this competition provided tremendous exposure to some top Paralympic competition as Team USA continued to prepare for the Paralympic Games. Additionally, the athletes found the ability to play in the actual competition venue and on the actual competition floor beneficial as it allowed them to judge their ability to throw on the resilient flooring surface used specifically for the Paralympic Games. It also permitted them to also experience the venue's acoustics, which is important for a sport like goalball where auditory skills are necessary to be able to effectively track the ball.

Training facilities at the Games were provided at two venues: The Olympic Sports Center Gymnasium was available to all teams during the period August 30 – September 14, 2008. All teams had equal court time (90 minute sessions) during the period August 30 - Sep-

tember 6. Additionally, practice time could also be scheduled after competition began. This venue had two practice courts. The flooring surface, nets, etc., were identical to what was provided at the competition site. This facility provided changing rooms, medical services (we brought our own athletic trainer to all practice sessions), and an athlete's lounge that offered light refreshments. This venue was located 3km from the Paralympic Village. Scheduled dedicated shuttle buses were provided by the organizer. Busses were on time, remained at the venue during the practice session, and provided prompt return to the Village at the end of all practice sessions.

The second training facility was at the Beijing Institute of Technology Gymnasium, which was the competition site but was scheduled for all teams during the period August 30 – September 5 for training. It provided three courts, with two courts being used as warm-up session courts during the Paralympic tournament. The third court was the actual court used for Paralympic competition.

To ensure fair time on the competition floor, each team was provided one session on the actual competition floor. The flooring surface, nets, etc., on the practice courts were identical to the competition floor. This facility also provided changing rooms, medical services, and an athletes' lounge. The venue was located 19km from the Paralympic Village with scheduled, dedicated shuttle buses provided by the organizer.

The only training difficulty we encountered was that our training session to practice on the competition floor was scheduled for a time prior to our arrival in China. Recognizing the fact we had not received the practice schedule prior to departure from the USA, the competition manager agreed to our request to provide us another practice session.

The men's goalball competition was a 12-team tournament. Competing teams were selected through three different methods: The six finishers from the 2006 IBSA World Goalball Championships conducted in Spartanburg, S.C. (Lithuania, Sweden, USA, Slovenia, Canada, Denmark), the top five teams that competed during the 2007 IBSA World Championships and Games, held in Sao Paulo, Brazil (Spain, Brazil, Iran, Finland, Belgium) and the remaining team was the host nation, China.

The competition progressed through a preliminary round (pool play), quarter-finals, semifinals and finals. There was also a classification round to determine fifth through 12th places.

The U.S. was placed in Pool B for the preliminary rounds with the teams from Brazil, Canada, China, Iran and Sweden. Our first game was against host country China supported by a very lively home crowd. China jumped out to a quick early lead, and the USA was quick to respond with three unanswered goals. Not eager to concede defeat, China rebounded with 11 unanswered goals bringing the final score to China 13 – USA 3.

Our second game was against Canada, which has been a long-time rival of Team USA. Canada was eager for a win after their last Paralympic encounter where Team USA rallied from behind to take the Bronze medal. Canada jumped out to an early lead in response to a long ball penalty committed by Tyler Merren. Team USA rebounded a little over a minute later with a goal scored by Donte' Mickens. Although Team USA scored one more time, penalties haunted them as the Canadian team was able to ultimately score several times on penalty throws. In the end, Team USA didn't generate the offense to come back. The game ended with Canada on top winning 8-2.

Looking to turn the tide in our third game, we faced Brazil. This was the first encounter for these teams since 2005. Donte' Mickens started the game with a score, followed by two more scores from teammate Tyler Merren, giving Team USA a 3-0 lead at the end of the first half. Although Team USA allowed four goals in the second half, Mickens and Merren would contribute three more goals giving Team USA a much needed first win. The final score was USA 6 – Brazil 4.

Team USA was looking for a second win as they entered the fourth game against Iran. They were also looking to keep their hopes of making the quarter-finals alive. After a hard fought 4-3 win over a very competitive Iranian team, Team USA moved to fourth place in pool play and into contention for advancement to the quarter-final competition round.

After two consecutive wins, Team USA faced the 2004 Paralympic Silver medalist team from Sweden. Unfortunately, Sweden scored on their first throw and did not look back. Team USA, plagued with penalties provided Sweden with multiple opportunities to add to their early lead. This game ended with the USA losing to Sweden 9-1. This was the last game of pool play and Team USA would finish with a 2-3 record, fourth in their pool. Their next game matched them against the Pool A first place and only undefeated team, Slovenia.

Team USA entered the game against Slovenia needing a win to stay in the medal hunt. In a change of strategy, Team USA started Edward Munro in the right wing position. This change produced a more settled team that jumped ahead 2-0, after goals from Tyler Merren and Munro. Slovenia's Ivan Vinkler closed the gap by one goal just before halftime. Just after halftime, Slovenia's Dejan Pirc, equalized the score. Just when it appeared Team USA's positive momentum may have slipped, Team USA's Tyler Merren scored almost immediately after Pirc's goal to retake the lead. Edward Munro added to that lead with a successful penalty shot, clinching a penalty-free 4-2 win that knocked Slovenia out of medal contention and moved Team USA into the semifinal competition. In addition to the victory, the win assured Team USA a berth in the 2010 IBSA World Goalball Championships in Sheffield, England, the first qualification event for the 2012 Paralympic Games.

In the semifinals, Team USA would face China for the second time in the Games. After the successful outcome against Slovenia, Team USA again started Edward Munro in the right wing position. Although this lineup again prevented Team USA from making any costly penalties, the very unique bouncing ball perfected by the Chinese proved to be too much for Team USA. Using this bouncing ball technique, China scored four unanswered goals against Team USA. China advanced to the gold medal game against Lithuania, while Team USA competed against Sweden for the bronze medal.

In this final game, Team USA was eager for a win and the opportunity to repeat as Paralympic bronze medalists. Less than a minute into the game, Team USA's Edward Munro posted the game's first goal. Although both teams played solid games, Sweden managed to successfully penetrate Team USA's defense five consecutive times. With less than a minute left in the game, Tyler Merren scored Team USA's second goal. Unfortunately, it was too little, too late for Team USA. Sweden would take the 2008 Paralympic bronze medal with a 5-2 win over Team USA. China won the gold medal and Lithuania took the silver.

I had a budget to work with and was empowered to make financial decisions. Because the team was geographically dispersed, the largest expense was travel to camps and competitions. I believe the budget we were provided was sufficient to meet all training and competitive activities approved under our high performance plan.

I was able to attend the USOC team leadership meetings and thought the format for both meetings encouraged interaction between team leader and USOC counterpart, as well as among team leaders of other teams. The deliverables document was a great concept as it provided a point of contact.

The Men's Goalball team didn't have any accreditation problems and I believe that having the advance meetings, the team leader guide and the deliverables document insured all the information was available to allow me to accomplish all accreditation-related matters in a timely fashion. So overall, everything worked well with this process and the USOC folks listened to our needs.

Much like our accreditation, our team's air travel was smooth and problem-free. I felt that if we had issues they would have been taken care of without any problems whatsoever. Also, sending out the team in smaller groups versus a large group in a charter plane really seemed to decrease the amount of waiting time. It all worked great.

We couldn't have asked for better apparel support. Although we had minimal needs, we knew who we needed to contact if we did and we knew that if we needed support it was certainly there. All of our needs for team processing were anticipated and the athletes (especially the first-timers) felt this was an extremely memorable experience for them.

We were processed as a group. We are a small group and all members were ambulatory. Having the processing at the Olympic Training Center provided the right environment for the athletes and made them feel that they were embarking on one of the most significant experiences of their lives. The entire staff pulled out all the stops to ensure everything made this a special event. Every member of the USOC should be commended for the entire team processing experience smooth, problem free and memorable.

We didn't have any ground transportation needs at the Games, however, we did have a training camp at Colorado Springs OTC prior to team processing and departure that required some ground transportation support. All contacts were easy to reach and ensured we had what we needed to accommodate the camp and team processing.

Also, the transportation that got us and our luggage from the OTC to the airport, from the Beijing airport to the village and from the Village back home was outstanding. I don't think things could have gone any smoother from getting our luggage checked and on to planes, as well as getting us back and forth from airports. It really made the trip relaxing for us and we had no travel-related issues.

We did not request 2-way radios but the cell phones worked well. I received a lot of positive feedback from athletes who had competed in Athens saying the provided cell phone service provided them and the VOIP service provided in the lounges was a huge improvement over the Athens games.

It would have been nice if there could have been a couple of more computers in the coaches' lounge because a lot of coaches and staff were waiting to use the two available computers. I brought my own laptop and it worked great with the wireless service. Feedback from athletes who brought their own computers was positive as well.

The Paralympic Village was made particularly nice by US Paralympics staff who really took the time and effort to anticipate our needs. Consequently, we didn't have any issues that required timeline extensions or special requests and, for me, it doesn't get any better than that.

Our medical staff consisted of Katherine Dec, our team physician, and Dustin Williams, our athletic trainer. We also had others who came out for games which demonstrated to us their interest in goalball athletes. We couldn't have asked for better support. I believe all members of the medical staff really cared about their roles in the delegation, anticipated needs and provided outstanding support during the Games.

During the Games, we requested video support and were provided cameras/tripods, and our tapes were converted to DVD format very quickly, which was greatly appreciated.

From a team leader perspective, I liked being out of the ticket business and I also liked the fact that the tickets were centrally managed. I really believe a lot of tickets from other sports that may have otherwise gone unused did wind up in spectator hands. It also made it easier for us to get tickets to other sports to cheer on teammates.

Although we did not have the competitive outcome we wanted from Beijing we did find several targets of opportunity that we can work towards as we prepare for the 2010 IBSA World Goalball Championships. For example:

• The bouncing ball perfected and used effectively by the Chinese gave them a distinct advantage over other teams. This ball works best on the resilient (taraflex) flooring surface.

– China was the only country that had regular access to taraflex flooring which enhanced their unique ability to practice throwing and defending this type of ball

o In order to create tactics to defend this type of ball a team must also develop the throw; the ball sounds, bounces and tracks differently on this type of floor surface which makes it difficult to replicate on a normal wood floor

– Conversations with other teams indicate they are in the process of acquiring a taraflex surface or finding training facilities that have a taraflex floor.

• In order to keep up with the changing nature of sport, we will need to acquire more practice time on a taraflex surface similar to the type used for World Championships and Paralympic Games

• Despite the numerous opportunities to train and compete, the fact that our athletes are located across the country will continue to chal-lenge us as we select and train teams for future competitions. Presently, the bulk of our training is conducted at the Lake Placid Olympic Training Center. This is a wonderful facility as it is extremely accessible for blind and visually impaired athletes, plus we have an outstanding working relationship with the staff. Unfortunately, this center is not located near a major airport. Getting everyone to a camp requires one travel day each way; with airlines cutting back on flights, it has become even more difficult to manage travel in and out of Lake Placid. Further, bad winter weather has resulted in a number of flight cancellations or people stuck in airports. Also, this is a small sport in terms of the total number of participants. Those who have the talent and motivation to train and compete at the elite level further limits our ability to build quality teams

–Most athletes are introduced to goalball at state schools or agencies serving the blind; we need to continue to partner with these agencies to continue to identify and develop future goalball athletes while they are in an environment where they can train, develop skills and compete at a young age

–We must also continue to look for a training area or areas that minimize the logistical challenges we face when conducting trials or training activities.

473

EDWARD MUNRO SHOUTS AFTER A SUCCESSFUL PLAY AS HE COMPETES IN A GOALBALL MATCH | *NATALIE BEHRING/GETTY IMAGES*

PARALYMPIC GOALBALL – WOMEN'S | *LOU THOMSON* – TEAM LEADER

The athletes of the 2008 Paralympic Women's Goalball team were chosen by the coach in early February 2008. We were fortunate to have several talented young players who should be considered for the 2012 Team as well. Our athletes trained individually and at training camps at the Lakeshore Foundation and the Olympic Training Center in Colorado Springs.

In the Paralympic Games tournament, we faced strong competition from several countries, including Japan, Brazil, Germany, Canada and Sweden. We were matched against Denmark in the semifinals

MILLER ASYA OF THE UNITED STATES COMPETES IN THE WOMEN'S PRELIMINARIES GOALBALL MATCH | *CHINA PHOTOS/GETTY IMAGES*

and managed to win the double overtime game with a 4-3 score. In what was a very intense game, our team beat China for the gold medal; the score was 6-5. This was the second time we faced China in the tournament; we lost the first games 4-0. There were 7,000 people in the stands, with standing room only. We were very pleased with our team's on-court abilities and with the cohesion and team-spirit they displayed throughout the tournament. We were also very proud to have Jenny Armbruster chosen by the entire Paralympic Team to carry the U.S. flag and lead the delegation in the Parade of Nations during Opening Ceremony.

I attended the team leadership and key decision-maker meetings and found them to be very valuable. I really enjoyed the trip to Beijing in March as it gave us a chance to get to know the culture and some firsthand knowledge of the city. This proved to be very useful during the Games.

I was very pleased with the USOC's attentiveness to the team and the help that employees were willing to give during the accreditation process as well as everything else. We had to add a credential for the trainer because the head coach believed that if this particular trainer was not credentialed, it would negatively impact the performance of the team. With the help of the USOC, we were able to get this done. Overall, the process ran smoothly.

The apparel distribution process at team processing was fantastic and time saving. They moved the athletes in and out with no major delays. The whole process was very well organized. We had some sizing issues with some of the apparel items but the alterations staff worked with us to adjust what they could.

Everyone appreciated the cell phones given to the athletes and staff. It made keeping in touch with everyone so much easier.

The Paralympic Village was great and I really appreciated the fact that our USOC contact was in such close proximity to the athletes and staff and was available 24/7.

Gwen Short served as our athletic trainer for these Games. Gwen has been our trainer for the women's goalball team for several years now and we requested her for the Beijing Games.

I definitely learned many things during the Games. I believe if I had the opportunity to be a team leader again, I would have a better understanding of the things that I needed to do, now that I have served in this role. I have to admit that the paper work required by the organizing committee was a bit much at times. I also learned that no matter how many times team members have been to an international competition they still have numerous questions that they would like answered, so knowing who to contact to get the information for them is essential.

Athletes wanting to qualify for the 2008 U.S. Paralympic judo team started by competing in the International Blind Sports Federation (IBSA) World Judo Championships in 2006. They then competed in the two final qualifying tournaments: the 2007 IBSA World Games and the International Paralympics Committee (IPC) Parapan American Games. Based on successful participation in these three events, IBSA awarded points qualifying weight categories for each country. As the host country to the Beijing Games, China was awarded a slot in each of the available 13 weight categories. Furthermore, IBSA limited participation in each weight category to the top 12 male and top eight female athletes in each weight division. The ultimate outcome of the selection criteria resulted in 84 men from 25 countries contesting seven weight categories including: 60, 66, 73, 81, 90, 100 and +100 kilos; and 48 women from 20 countries contesting six weight categories including: 48, 52, 57, 63, 70 and +70 kilos.

The United States qualified four men and one woman in the +100, 100, 90, 81 and 70 kilo weight categories, respectively. The United States Association of Blind Athletes (USABA) coordinated a final team trials tournament for athletes wanting to compete in the available weight categories. These trials were conducted in conjunction with the Northglenn Judo Championships on Saturday, April 26, 2008. The only contested weight category was the female 70 kg. division. This contest was between Jordan Mouton, of Houston, Texas and Lisa-maria Martinez, of San Francisco, Calif., with Mouton winning the best out of three matches. The final team of athletes included Greg DeWall in the 100+kg, Myles Porter in the 100kg, Andre Watson in the 90kg, Scott Jones in the 81kg and Mouton in the women's 70kg.

The coaching and team leader positions were named in early March 2008. Raul Tamayo, Jr., Stanford University Judo Club and Scott Moore, Denver Judo Club, were named as coaches. Marc Vink, Liberty Bell Judo Club was named as team leader. Tamayo served as the Assistant Coach at the 2004 Olympic Games in Athens and Moore had won gold and bronze medals in three previous Paralympics Games. Vink had held the Head and Assistant Coaching positions to all qualifying competitions leading to the Beijing Games. All staff had coached and traveled with the athletes over the course of the previous three-years and were familiar with each athlete.

U.S. Paralympics assigned John Nyland, Certified Athletic Trainer as the team trainer. John was instrumental in keeping the athletes free of injury. He was appropriately briefed for his role with the judo team. He was exceptionally attentive to individual team members. His presence had a meaningful impact on team performance. Based on experience with previous IPC events, the USOC appears to recruit high level and responsive professionals. In all cases of previous IPC events, these individuals have been exceptional.

The coaching staff monitored each athlete's weekly training schedule via telephone and email communications to both athletes and their personal coaches. The weekly training schedule typically included a minimum of three days of technical practice supplemented with two to three days of weight training. Athletes were required to submit monthly update reports to the coaching staff.

Athletes competed in several regional and national competitions during the year leading up to the Beijing Games. Additionally, the coaching staff conducted three, five-day training camps conducted at the Olympic Training Center in Colorado Springs, Colo., in April, June and August. Also, several athletes attended both national and overseas elite training programs with able bodied judoka.

Upon arrival in China the team trained each day at the Capital Institute of Physical Education Training Hall.

The competition venue was the Beijing Workers' Gymnasium, which had approximately 13,000 seats. The facility had excellent spectator seating overlooking the two mat areas of play. The three days of competition started at noon on Sunday, September 7 and continued for three consecutive days. Two supersized close circuit screens provided instant playback allowing fans to see the action in slow motion. A 300 meter warm-up area, athlete and team official lounge, change and shower facilities were also provided.

The Chinese audience was knowledgeable, well organized and extremely vocal in cheering their athletes. Since the United States did not qualify any of the lower weight categories in either the men or women categories, no team members competed on the first day of competition.

Scott Jones (81kb) fought his first round match against Kanji Oga (JPN) on September 8, 2008. Scott was thrown early in the match with an inner thigh throw (uchimata). He was thrown a second time with the same throw which ended the match at 4:57 minutes with a full point (ippon). The Japanese contestant went on to lose his next match to a Cuban fighter and thus Scott was eliminated from further competition.

Andre Watson (90kg) received a bye for the first round of matches. As his opening match, Andre fought Nine Messaoud (ALG) the 2004 Paralympic Games gold medalist. Andre had fought and thrown Nine at last year's World Games. He knew the Algerian's style and had trained hard to beat him. This match went scoreless for almost four and a half minutes when suddenly Nine appeared seriously injured with what was believed to be several broken ribs. With less than 30-seconds left in the match and knowing that it was unlikely that Nine could continue to fight another five minutes in an over-time (golden score), Andre received a non-combatively penalty (shido) from the referee which cost him the match. In repechage, (loser's pool for the bronze) Andre faced Anatoliy Shevchenko (UKR). The Ukrainian was first to attack with a running lift throw that ended the match with a full point at 0.36 seconds. The Ukrainian contestant went on to lose his next match to a French fighter which eliminated Andre from further competition.

Jordan Mouton (70kg) fought a first round match against Maria Del Carman Herrera (ESP), the 2004 Paralympics gold medalist and current World Champion. After several good exchanges, Herrera attacked with an inner thigh throw (uchimata) resulting in a full point. In repechage Jordan faced Szabo (HUN). Using her high school wrestling experience, Jordan fought well. However, she was finally caught with a hand throw (te guruma) that ended the match in ippon.

At 22 years of age, Myles Porter (100kg) was the youngest athlete in this weight division. He received a bye for the first round of matches. For his first match, Myles fought Antonio Silva (BRA), the 2004 Paralympic Games gold medalist. He had fought Silva on two previous occasions and was eager to even the score. After 3:13 minutes of excellent back and forth attacks and down by a penalty, Silva threw him with a shoulder throw that ended the match in a full point (ippon). In repechage, Myles faced Hamzeh Nadri (IRI) and secured a cross arm bar (juji gatame) bar to end the match in 2.05 minutes. He next faced Bill Morgan (CAN) whom he had also competed against in two previous qualifying tournaments. Myles got off to a quick lead by scoring a half- point (waza ari) with a dropping shoulder throw (seoi nage) and followed-up with the same throw to end the match in 1.05 minutes. This win placed him in the bronze medal round.

To secure the bronze medal, Myles had to beat Juan Carlos Cortada (CUB). He had fought Cortada in the 2007 Parapan American Games for the silver medal and believed that he had won that match with an arm bar despite the judge's decision. Cortada came out strong and countered Myles' hand wheel (teguruma) attempt with an inner thigh throw (uchimata) in 0.51 seconds to take the bronze medal. As a result, Myles had to settle for fifth place.

At slightly heavier than 110 Kilos, Greg Dewall (110+kg) was clearly the lightest athlete in the division. He fought his first round match against former world champion Yargaliny Jimenez (CUB). Greg had lost a gold medal match against Jimenez in the 2007 Para Pan American Games and was eager to start his day with a win. He did not disappoint and took early control of the match by holding the Cuban in a strong mat hold for a full point (ippon), which ended the match at 0.41 seconds. Greg next faced Wang (CHN) in front of Wang's home crowd. Wang was able to score a wazar-ari, yuko and koka to reach a judges' decision in the 5:00 match. In repechage, Greg faced Alexander Parasyuk (RUS) and won the match with another strong mat hold for a full point (ippon) in 1:40 minutes. This win placed him in the bronze medal round.

To secure the bronze medal, Greg had to beat Jung-Min Park (KOR). The Korean dominated most of the match but had developed a serious head gash that would not stop bleeding. After three separate attempts to stop the Korean's head bleeding, the judges awarded the decision to Greg as required under Article 29 of the International Judo Federation rules (kiken-gachi). Greg's win makes him only the eighth U.S. player to ever win a Paralympics judo medal.

As the judo competition came to a close, the USOC honored Raul Tamayo, Jr. with The Order of Ikkos. The medal was presented by Laura Ryan, Associate Director, Sports Programs, U.S. Paralympics. Coach

Tamayo is the first Paralympic team coach to receive the medal. The medal represents excellence in coaching. The Order is named after Ikkos of Tarentum who was the first recorded Olympic Coach in ancient Greece. Ikkos won the pentathlon at the 84th Olympiad in 444 B.C. and later became known for his remarkable coaching ability.

The importance of a good draw became a significant variable to Myles Porter, Andre Watson and Jordan Mouton who all drew defending Paralympic gold medalists for their opening matches. The five athletes making up the 2008 U. S. Paralympic Judo Team was the smallest delegation ever sent to a Paralympic Games. The team was also the youngest with the least amount of experience. Each of the athletes had less than four years of judo experience and faced athletes with ten to 15 years of experience.

Thirty-three countries qualified weight division slots for the 2008 Beijing Paralympic Games. Of these, 19 countries won medals and 13 countries won no medals. The clear dominant country was China with seven total medals including four gold medals within the female weight divisions. While Russia captured six total medals, five of these were bronze all coming from within the female weight divisions. Brazil captured five total medals, two silver and two bronze coming from within the female weight divisions. While the United States competed for two bronze medals, we only secured one. We tied with five other countries capturing one bronze medal.

Eight countries within the Pan American Union qualified weight division slots for the Beijing Paralympics Games. The United States ranked sixth within the Pan American Union for total medals won. Only Canada and Uruguay won no medals.

Prior to the Games, I was able to attend both USOC team leadership meetings in Colorado Springs, Colo., and in Beijing. I felt both were very beneficial.

Regarding accreditation for these Games, the eight credentials requested were not in line with the selection procedures. The team consisted of five athletes. We were allowed one coach and we requested an additional assistant coach based on the visual limitations of the athletes. Ultimately, we were granted an additional Assistant Coach with the understanding that Paralympic Village space was tight and that immediately after competition, both coaches would leave the Village. The two coaches left the day after competition and stayed in a nearby hotel. U.S. Paralympics paid for the first night of hotel stay, and the two coaches paid for the remainder of their stay as agreed to before we left for China.

Overall though, we had no major problems with this process because of clear and frequent communication with USABA, U. S. Paralympics and others. The clear and frequent communications between interested parties is vital. Additionally, we had ample preparation and lead response timeAs for air travel, travel dates specified for the athletes, two coaches and the Team Leader were met in the scheduled time. The team met the Head Coach in San Francisco and from there flew directly to China. U.S. Paralympics provided boxes and shipping, so that some athletes and staff could mail home unneeded clothing following team processing. Several athletes packed and shipped boxes home, which simplified baggage issues. Overall this process was seamless and went very well. I would not change any areas.

All of our initial deadlines for apparel were met but I did find that manufacturer's apparel interpretation issues were frustrating. Extensions were provided that did not cause repercussions. My estimates for the number of staff apparel packages were accurate. I was made aware of the costs of additional packages but this did not impact my activities or final plans. I submitted my teams' colorboards and Apparel & Equipment Forms. To the best of my knowledge there were no conflicts between the sport suppliers and the team suppliers. The judo gi is ubiquitous within the International Judo Federation and its associated international bodies, including the International Blind Sports Federation. Photographing the gi top, pants and belt for display was not necessary.

Generally, all apparel fit. We did have a few athletes that received apparel that didn't fit. I tried to replace this apparel with the appropriate size without success. The entire team was processed at one time. This seemed to work great for our team. We requested training facilities and/or equipment which were available and adequate. Overall, this process was smooth and well rehearsed.

Our need for vehicles was under estimated. However, when we needed vehicles, our USOC contact provided them with little difficulty. Overall, the process used worked well. The cell phones we were issued for the Games met our requirements.

Computer and internet connections were available and accessible when needed and connection speed met our expectation.

We had two coaches that needed outside housing for three days after competition. We were able to contact the USOC for the needed housing and they responded timely and appropriately. We accurately estimated the delegation and staff housing requirements. We also accurately estimated the scheduling of delegation and staff members arrival and departure. We did not experience any unexpected requests or issues with regard to this.

We changed the departure dates for five individuals but the changes were handled with minimal effort. We wanted three athletes and two coaches to travel back to the United States on the first Saturday after competition. Once we made our wishes known, tickets were provided. The request did not impact budget/cost.

The training venues were accessible when we needed them. Unfortunately, we did not have some of the technological equipment we requested. For instance, we requested the use of video equipment but never received it. I resolved this issue by inadvertently wandering into the media center, live feed recording room, and requested if I could have a copy of all judo matches. This request was honored and we now have several weight categories to study for future events.

Positive outcomes from these Paralympic Games include the experience gained for our young athletes. The challenge will now be to retain this group as a core unit to advance our future competitive opportunities.

PARALYMPIC POWERLIFTING | MARY HODGE – TEAM LEADER

In March 2008, the U.S. was awarded two wild card spots in Paralympic Powerlifting for the Paralympic Games. We selected two athletes based on rankings. It was unfortunate that we were limited to two spots because one of our most promising athletes has not yet competed enough to be ranked high enough to be included on the team.

Generally, our athletes train on their own with their individual coaches. However, we do conduct one or two small camps where our athletes are able to train as a team. For the 2012 Paralympic Games, I suggest we place our hopefuls into a specific body weight category by 2010. With athletes maintaining a set body weight, we can design and implement more effective training programs.

Following team selection, we held two camps and a national competition. We also maintained weekly (sometimes more) contact with the personal coaches. I sought nutritional support through US Paralympics; the assistance they provided was terrific. Our athletes performed well during this time, but two months prior to the Paralympic Games one of our athletes was clearly hurt. There were several discussions with US Paralympics and we decided if he hit a certain performance marker, he should be kept on the team. Fortunately, he was able to hit the mark!

Our training facilities at the Paralympic Games were terrific. There were plenty of weights and benches. In fact, it was one of the nicest venues and training areas we've seen.

As for the competition at the Paralympic Games, both of our athletes suffered from injuries sustained prior to the Paralympic Games. Our female athlete, Mary Stack, was diagnosed with a muscle tear. This was very disappointing because she was considered a contender in her weight class. Unfortunately, Anderson Wise's injury also kept him from competing at his best.

We had no issues with our accreditation, as I was kept in the loop throughout the whole process. The meeting and overview newsletter was great for the athletes and helped answer their questions.

In regards to air travel, I thought the spreadsheet procedure was very helpful and made it easy to get all the information needed to the USOC on a timely manner. Plus if we had any changes it was easy to make them and kept everyone on the same page. I also thought that everyone was extremely helpful at the airport and it was obvious that everyone was very prepared for our group.

The deadlines for competition apparel submission were hard to comply with. We have a hard time finding a vendor in the United States for our competition uniform which uses only 20% lycra and may not have any manufacturer logos on them. The deadline was in February and we still had a lot of unanswered questions, including who would be on the team.

Team processing went very smoothly and it was very well organized. The schedule was timed well with not too much to overload the athletes. Our athletes were pleased with the great information they received during the review sessions. They also felt the sessions weren't too long like many of those sessions can be.

The staff and athletes really appreciated the computer and wireless set-up in the Village as they were able to keep in touch with friends and family. They also appreciated the televisions provided in the Village.

The Paralympic Village staff was great. One of our athletes needed the bed raised and it was done by the end of the day. We did have to request an egg crate to make the beds a little softer as the mattresses were pretty hard. Overall though, the Village staff was very accommodating and all the athletes' needs ere taken care of.

Our medical staff consisted of Betsy Nadler from the USOC and an assigned athletic trainer. Everyone had sports training and knew the injuries associated with our sport. We had a very well educated medical staff and they worked well with the athletes.

I had requested videos of the competition but because our sport was not aired, we did not receive any. These videos are very useful for future training, so we need to solve this problem before London 2012.

Some comments for going forward would be that body weight classes need to be established within the first two years of the quad. We also need to establish internal checks on body weight with personal coaches as well as better communication prior to the Paralympic Games between athletes, personal coaches, and national team coaches.

The 2008 Beijing Paralympic Games marked the first year that rowing was included on the program. We had an outstanding performance for the debut of rowing in the Paralympic Games. Three out of four boats made it to the "A" final, and two of those boats medaled. Laura Schwanger, rowing in the AW1x, came back from sixth place in the first half of her race to take the bronze medal. Ron Harvey, in the AM1x, raced a very competitive final but came up just short of the bronze and finished fifth. In the LTA4+, Simona Chin, Jamie Dean, Jesse Karmazin, Tracy Tackett, and Emma Preuschl, also made a strong comeback in their final to fight off powerhouse Great Britain to win the silver medal. Scott Brown and Angela Madsen, rowing the TA2x, won the "B" final to give them a seventh place overall finish.

There was a lot of preparation leading up to the Paralympic Games. In 2007, I attended the Junior World Championships, which were held at the Olympic and Paralympic rowing venue in Beijing. It was very useful for us to get an idea of how operations were run at the venue, what the water and wind conditions were like, and a general idea of the air quality. This trip also allowed us to experience the travel time between downtown and our venue, as it was about an hour outside of the city. I also attended both of the team leader meetings hosted by the USOC.

In the summer leading up to the Games the athletes had the opportunity to be selected for the team in two manners. The LTA4+ was chosen at a selection camp held at the beginning of June 2008. The athletes invited to the camp were raced to find the fastest possible combination. The AM1x, and the TA2x were selected at an open trials event held in late June 2008.

Between Trials and the Paralympic Games our team competed in the Canadian Royal Henley Regatta where they raced the Canadian adaptive team, among others. This was very helpful because it gave us a preview of the competition we would be facing in Beijing. In the LTA4+ we edged out Canada by one tenth of a second, which set the stage for a very intense rematch in September. During the summer we also had two training camps that brought all the athletes and both coaches together in one location. This time training together had a strong positive impact on the results in Beijing.

Team Processing at the Olympic Training Center in Colorado Springs went smoothly and prepared us well for arrival in Beijing. I met with our medical staff, Cindy Trowbridge and Dr. Catherine Dec, and briefed them on our team's needs so that care could begin immediately upon arrival in China. Both Cindy and Dr. Dec made themselves available to the athletes at all hours of the day and really went above and beyond their duties to make sure that everyone was well taken care of. Once we were on the ground in Beijing, the only major problem we encoun-

tered related to training was our oars getting damaged in the shipping container so that when we arrived several of them were not usable. It's important that all the equipment in the containers be checked upon arrival so that any problems can be noted early.

The biggest lesson I took away from this experience was that no amount of advance preparation can prevent certain things from going wrong during an event. Many times we rely on work done ahead of time to guarantee our success, but sometimes elements are out of our control. You have to be prepared to react quickly and know who around you can help you solve certain situations. That was one of the strengths of the USOC in Beijing; they made it easy for team leaders to get in touch with them to solve whatever difficulties crossed our paths. You don't have to do everything alone; there is always someone who can help you.

LAURA SCHWANGER OF THE USA COMPETES IN THE WOMEN'S SINGLE SCULLS -A ROWING EVENT | *NATALIE BEHRING/GETTY IMAGES*

PARALYMPIC RUGBY | *PATTY CORNELIUS* – TEAM LEADER

Wheelchair Rugby is played by persons with impairment in at least three limbs. The majority of participants are incomplete quadriplegics. Although other disabilities are seen at the club level, the elite level participants are usually quadriplegics or amputees. Athletes are classified based on the level of their disability from 0.5 to 3.5. A 0.5 is the most disabled and a 3.5 is the least disabled. Although women play the sport, it is primarily played by men. The 2008 Paralympic Games was the first time that the International Paralympic Committee (IPC) allowed teams to have a 12-person roster if the team included a female player. Otherwise, the roster was limited to 11. Even with this mandate, only half of the teams that participated in Beijing had a female on their roster. However, more women have become part of developmental programs; future Paralympic Games will probably reflect this.

All of our team members play in the United States Quad Rugby Association (USQRA) club program and have played for at least 3 – 5 years, if not more. Most of the more advanced players play for teams coached by current or past USA players or coaches on fairly successful teams within the USQRA. Several of the athletes have played on national championship teams.

Most of our athletes are sponsored by or affiliated with two of the top wheelchair rugby chair manufacturers in the U.S. (Eagle Sportschairs and Vesco Metal Products) and have custom-made rugby chairs.

Most of our athletes train 5 – 6 days a week for most of the year and have worked with some type of trainer or strength & conditioning specialist to develop a workout program. These athletes have also been using Dartfish technology to analyze their competitors as well as their own performance. A few are regularly utilizing sport psychology services.

Although only compensated through a minimal stipend, our head coach worked full-time for USA Rugby. He was dedicated to our national program, spending 5 – 7 days a week in preparation for the Beijing Games. Additionally, he worked to create and run a developmental pipeline program to identify future athletes. As the team leader/national program manager of the USA Wheelchair Rugby program, my employer (Lakeshore Foundation Olympic and Paralympic Training Site) has allowed me to dedicate 50-percent of my time toward USA Wheelchair Rugby since 2005.

Twenty-four athletes were invited to participate in a tryout camp in December 2007. These athletes were invited after observation during the 2006 – 2007 national team and USQRA seasons and at USQRA developmental camps. Athletes participated in a three-day tryout camp where they were tested in a variety of standard rugby skills and participated in a variety of drills and scrimmages under observation of a selection committee. At the end of the weekend, athletes were ranked by classification and selected based on skills, effectiveness in potential lineups, past experience, future potential and selection committee consensus. A total of 12 athletes (and four alternates) were selected to train and compete with the team until June 2008 when the final 11 were selected. We felt that the best athletes in the United States were selected. Almost all of these same athletes were part of the 2006 World Championship team, which won gold.

I believe we have a good selection process. Improvements could include: 1) start the observation process at the beginning of the USQRA season the year before (September – April); 2) develop and finalize written procedures by September for a December selection camp; and 3) focus on a developmental program that creates a pipeline for a stronger athlete pool.

Following the selection camp, the team trained in February, April, May, June, July and August. All were three-day weekend camps, except one in August which was a 10-day residential camp. We participated in the North American Cup and Canada Cup in June. Both of these events were pre-Paralympic tournaments in which the U.S. took first place. Both tournaments included competitors that were going to be in Beijing. We felt the schedule was effective, however the coach would have liked to train every month leading up to the Games and would have liked to add an earlier international competition. We did request to participate in Lakeshore Foundation's Demolition Derby in January 2008 where there would be international competition, but US Paralympics felt the tournament was going to be a developmental tournament. We felt that participation in at least one international tournament during the winter/off season and January and March would have been beneficial.

There was no test event leading up to the Games that we were aware of. The training facilities were provided by the International Wheelchair Rugby Federation in Beijing. The site was appropriate, however the day we were scheduled to participate in a training session at the competition venue, we were not allowed on the competition floor because basketball was using the court. We trained on the warm up court, which defeated the whole purpose of going to that venue to train. The only problem we had with the training was that we had to transport our equipment back and forth from the village and training venue several times leading up to the Games.

The team went undefeated throughout the entire competition in Beijing and took home the gold medal. Although we were anticipating playing Canada in the finals, they were beaten in the crossover and we played Australia. Out of all the teams in the tournament, Australia was the one team we hadn't played in the two years leading up to

Beijing. This win allowed us to be able to say that we had finally faced every strong competitor in the world and won.

Our budget was made up of cash and "value-in-kind" (VIK). Since, I am the National Program Manager, I had the discretion to make all financial decisions. I consulted with US Paralympics before making any unbudgeted large purchases. Our primary expenses were training camps and two international competitions leading up to Beijing. Our coach would always prefer to have more camps and more early competition, but I feel the budget we had provided us with the necessary training time and competitions. Although we kept a close eye on our VIK and extra baggage costs, in the end we had enough in our budget to cover everything we needed.

I attended both team leadership meetings. It was good to be with all the other team leaders and coaches to hear/learn the information together. It was an opportunity to discuss issues together and hear issues I may not have thought of. It was also good having all of our contacts in one place. The round table discussions at the end of the Colorado Springs meeting felt rushed and some of the people we met with were not the actual contacts we would have later. The meeting in Beijing was a great opportunity to see the actual venues and meet with the organizing committee (BOCOG). I especially enjoyed the Amazing Race/scavenger hunt experience around Beijing.

In terms of accreditation, we had an athlete that was not able to get classified until after the final deadline for the submission of athlete names. Until he was classified, we were not going to know if he would be able to participate in the Games, as a higher classification would have classed him out of the sport. We discussed this with the USOC at the first team leadership meeting and we were granted the extension. We were able to give the final list to the USOC by the end of June and there were no issues. In addition, there were some questions by the USOC about the number of staff we requested. They were not able to tell us whether all seven of our staff members would be allowed to attend the Games until July. They were not sure of the number of credentials available until that time.

Overall, I would say that the open communication lines were the best part of the accreditation process. The potential problems were discussed many times prior to deadlines and all parties were well aware of the late submission. Having the first team leader meeting in November and then the final meeting in March provided two well spaced out opportunities to discuss any potential issues. Also the background check process was very smooth and easy for staff to complete in a short amount of time. There was some initial confusion with the photo request that had some Olympic deadlines included, but it was good to see the time that went into making sure only Paralympic information was sent to Paralympic folks. The changes that BOCOG made with the Sport Entry forms at the last minute with fairly quick turnaround deadlines was time consuming and repetitive at a time when we were very busy with final competitions, but I understood that the USOC had little control over this.

We finalized our airline ticket requests toward the end of the deadline period and had quite a few detailed requests pertaining to after-competition travel, but everything was submitted in time. The process of getting the team out of Denver following team processing in Colorado Springs, Colo., was exceptional. Having the private gate with our own agents was so smooth. The process home was a little slower, but we had a lot more people on the flight. Although this process took a little longer, it was still smooth and all baggage needs were handled without incident. In addition, the preparation of the gate agents for the isle chair needs was excellent when leaving Beijing. All athletes were loaded quickly since they had several isle chairs and the agents to assist with transfers.

For the most part all went well with the apparel. One comment I would make regarding this year's apparel distribution would be that staff receives very little recognition for the time and effort they put in toward working with teams. This year the apparel offered to staff was not similar in quantity as that offered to athletes; in addition, the medical staff commemorative ring was a different style than the one offered to athletes, coaches, and other staff. Staff should receive apparel and other commemoratives that represent the level of dedication and commitment they give to the team.

As for team processing, I thought it was well organized and smooth. During my team leader walk-through, I noticed that the changing rooms didn't have an area for my athletes to lie down and change. This was brought up to the USOC and they arranged for mats to be brought in. From the time our team arrived for processing all we did was follow the schedule. Transportation and the daily schedule were well organized and detailed and helped everything run smoothly. The Ambassador Program was a lot of information and a pretty long session. It was a good idea, but a little too long. Overall the USOC group did a great job with coordinating the apparel portion. It was good having our team be one of the only groups there during our session. This allowed for the additional time we needed. A suggestion would be to have a larger space to allow for more room for all of the chairs and larger changing rooms.

We did not have any ground transportation needs prior to arriving in Beijing, except to get equipment to the Denver airport after processing. This was a coordinated effort and we had no issues.

We appreciated the USOC-issued cell phones even though they were a little confusing to use. It was a great way to communicate with everyone. In terms of the wireless set-up in our buildings in the Paralympic Village, we had a very weak signal in our building. There was a modem set up on the second floor, but, since it was in such a small room and in the common area where people were staying, all residents were forced to sit in the stairwell to get a signal. According to the USOC, they could have set-up another modem that was found on the first floor, but they didn't have all of the necessary equipment. All buildings should have had access as we were only in a few buildings. The staff and athletes' lounges were much smaller than Athens, so additional wireless should have been set-up. I suggest that the USOC continue to offer Skpe technology in future Games.

Logistically everything worked well in getting things shipped to China. We were pushed to get things to the warehouse earlier than the announced deadline but we made it work. All equipment was easy to identify and was undamaged when we arrived in Beijing.

Prior to competition, we had to move our rugby equipment to/from the Village several times. The USOC assisted with helping to physically move the equipment each time. We also requested special transportation for meetings, early game preparation and a special team outing. The USOC was very accommodating, even when a couple of the requests were at the last minute.

As for the Village, we had several players complain about how hard the beds were and the medical problems that they were experiencing because of this. After explaining that this was a medical issue, the USOC stepped up and said there would be no charge to the athletes and mattress pads were delivered the next day. The team uniform laundry set-up was very helpful and worked well with our game schedule. As with most of the other topics, open communication, pre-planning to the best of our ability and flexibility for the unforeseen issues that came up was a key aspect in a successful Village stay. I was very impressed with the organization and professionalism demonstrated by the USOC staff. Although two of the staff members were from the Olympic side, they demonstrated a passion for what they were doing and showed the upmost respect for the Paralympic athletes.

Our medical staff consisted of Jim Murdock, our athletic trainer, and Yanni Zinis, our team doctor. Jim has been with the rugby program since 2004. Dr. Zinis is one of the physicians for the Colorado Avalanche Ice Hockey Team. Jim briefed him on the needs of our team and they worked well together. Overall, the fact that we were able to secure the athletic trainer that had been working with the team since 2004 was extremely helpful. Betsy Nadler was very helpful with answering all of our WADA, USADA and TUE questions. Dr. Zinis immediately clicked with the team and quickly fell in love with our sport.

We made a request for video analysis both at the team leadership meetings in Colorado and again in Beijing. The tech had never seen Rugby before and wasn't sure she could do what was asked. We had our Dartfish tech from Lakeshore email the boards that would assist the Beijing tech. We just needed her to attend the games to video tape, as the video produced by BOCOG could not be used for analysis. Since there was only one tech in Beijing, she was never able to make it to any of our games, so we were unable to use the Dartfish system. However, we were able to get copies of all of our competitions, as the tech recorded and burned all games from the BOCOG live feed. As was the issue in Athens, we again only had one Dartfish tech assigned to the Paralympic Games. More and more teams are using Dartfish technology and have come to rely on its benefits. Therefore, we need more techs to be assigned to the Paralympic Games.

We received initial information about tickets and the Friends and Family program at the team leadership meetings. We were told this was going to be a great program. We received several updates from the USOC and CoSport(the only official ticket sales agent in the U.S.), however many families reported quite a bit of confusion leading up to the Games in trying to place ticket orders. The program was a good idea, but never really developed into what was promised. We did appreciate the USOC and US Paralympics help in getting last minute Opening and Closing Ceremony tickets for several of our athletes in Beijing.

One thing I learned was that the Village was well equipped to provide for a number of services that we just assumed we could only get from US Paralympics. In the future, I would suggest utilizing those services, as that is what they are there for. I didn't know to look to the Village for some of this support in Athens. Examples would be meeting room space, A/V equipment and computer/Skype service.

As I had learned in Athens, it is very important to communicate with your Sports Desk early and on a regular basis to work out all potential problems. I did this in Beijing and we had no problems with training or transportation.

The use of Dartfish was very beneficial to our team during the two years leading up to the Games. For the second time in as many Games in which I have participated, only one technician was provided for the entire U.S. delegation. I would suggest that teams push harder for a stronger level of support during the team leader meetings. Teams should provide specific details for what they anticipate they will need so that the USOC can be better prepared. Otherwise, the 2008 Paralympic Games went well.

JOEL WILMOTH OF THE USA SINGS THE NATIONAL ANTHEM WITH BRYAN KIRKLAND (CENTRE R) AND TEAM MATES AFTER DEFEATING AUSTRALIA | *JAMIE MCDONALD/GETTY IMAGES*

PARALYMPIC SAILING | *SARAH HAWKINS – TEAM LEADER*

Sailing competition is based the cumulative scores earned in a series of races that are held over a period of several days to a week. A typical regatta is five to eleven races in a series. The sport is heavily reliant on travel and logistics. We do not train out of a national or regional training facility since our athletes are located throughout the country. We typically run training camps in seasonal locations. All of this requires coaches and athletes to travel to and from events. Our equipment is large and heavy, and subsequently, very expensive to transport. This holds true for coaching equipment such as coach boats.

The Olympic Sailing Committee of US Sailing spent a lot of time thinking about the Trials system used to select teams to go to the Olympic and Paralympic Games in China. All of the trial events for the Olympic and the Paralympic disciplines were held simultaneously, with the exception of one Olympic discipline. There were positives and negatives to this system, which we will evaluate for team selection for London 2012. The greatest positive was holding the trials far enough in advance to enable teams to plan, prepare, fundraise, and travel to the venue prior to competition. The greatest negative was perhaps not including any sort of international competition as part of the Trials.

Sailing does not really have an "off-season" as we move training and competition to warmer climates during the northern winter months. The quietest time is October -December. However, from November through March, our athletes continue to compete in events in Florida which are preceded by 1-2 days of practice followed by 3-6 days of competition. This schedule may change with the addition of World Cup events.

Our Paralympic Sonar and SKUD teams trained almost entirely within the U.S., with the exception of the Paralympic Test Event in Qingdao. The Paralympic 2.4mR team traveled and competed in Europe about 25% of the year. In the future, working with our Performance Enhancement Team (PET), I would like to increase our team's international exposure through travel abroad. I would also like to have the team compete in the Paralympic sailing venue prior to the Games.

Training after the trials and before Games was based on competition schedule and in the SKUD team's case, physical capacity for travel and training. The 2.4mR trained monthly for 7-10 days in addition to attending eight events both abroad and domestically. Performance at events showed marked improvement from Trials to Games, especially against international competitors. This was all done with a selected "team" coach who worked solely and consistently with the athletes. This was complemented by physical training in the gym and work in nutrition and sports psychology. Their training plan was effective.

The training for our SKUD 18 athlete included competing in three events which they won decisively. The crew participated in a fourth competition to hone boat handling skills just prior to Games. Our athlete was not physically capable of traveling much post-trials so all training camps were transferred to the West Coast and were held monthly (5 day camps) from April through August. Training partners were brought in for competitive training, as were able-bodied athletes. This program was sufficient for this discipline, but would not be ideal for the next quad moving forward. Instead, we will follow something similar to the above 2.4mR program.

For the Sonar 6 training, our athletes competed in major events plus weekend club racing from June- August. Half of the events were preceded by training sessions. From the latter half of May through August, the weekend racing was supplemented by an intense training day just prior to the race. Physical training (in the gym) complemented this program, but more work with sport psychology and other PET areas needed to be done. More international competition should have been in the plan, as well. The lack of international training directly impacted this teams' performance and adjustments to that effect should be made moving forward.

There was a test event in May 2008. It was highly productive since we were able to stay in the Paralympic Village in Qingdao and train/ race out of the venue that would later host the Olympics and Paralympics. The majority of our Paralympic athletes, medical staff and regular staff attended this and that was a huge benefit. Two athletes were unable to attend due to health concerns but overall it was a very beneficial trip.

Our training facilities were accessible and appropriate in China. We had no major problems. Our one issue was the fact that it was a large venue which mandated much movement of heavy equipment. This put a large burden on the coaching staff as 5 of the 6 athletes were in chairs. It was very helpful to have had some prior experience with the venue in May. That test event experience gave our sailors and staff a degree of comfort and familiarity with the facility and conditions. More time there would have been helpful especially related to testing the winds and tide.

Our SKUD 18 duo lived up to our expectations. They were gold medal favorites going into the event, and they did not disappoint. John Ruf in the 2.4mR rose to the occasion. Staff knew he had the potential to medal, but he was more of a wild card going into the Games. His performance at the Games can be attributed to intensive training sessions with a dedicated coach with whom he related well. He was relaxed and focused. Consistency, especially in speed and set-up, was particularly important to his performance. His bronze medal was unexpected but not a surprise. He was underestimated by his competition throughout the event.

The Sonar team's performance was a bit disappointing at the Games. After winning the 2007 World Championship in September and the trials in October, the on-water performance suffered slightly leading up to the Games. The team had consistent coaching from both staff and private coaches and had the ability to post strong results at the Games as evidenced by their win in race one and top 4 finishes in 5 of the 11 races. Five races in the bottom of the fleet cost them any chance at a medal.

We had a budget for these Games and it was part of our overall Olympic/Paralympic program budget. Over the course of the 4 years, US Sailing was able to subsidize critical portions of the Paralympic Sailing Program that were not funded by US Paralympics. Winning two out of three medals under the current funding structure is a tremendous accomplishment, but we can do better with a larger budget and better funding choices. If we had a larger budget we would spend more on coaching, athlete grant support and sports medicine. More funding in the coaching category would enable us to host more clinics for our athletes, which in turn would allow them to train more. More funding for the athletes would enable the athletes to attend more international events which would give them more experience racing against their competition in foreign waters. And finally, if we had a larger budget we would like to give our athletes more exposure to sports medicine resources. Ideally the athletes could forge a relationship with a sports psychologist, trainer, etc. early in the quad.

I attended both team leader meetings in October and March. I think our meeting in October was valuable for getting our needs on the table and to submit our requests. The trip to Beijing in March was valuable for executing those plans. It was also nice to get familiar with Beijing. Sailing flew to Qingdao for a day for a site visit with a couple of USOC representatives which was highly valuable.

Accreditation went well. In the future, we would like to bring a boatwright to help with boat repairs, boat preparation on a daily basis, etc. This was taxing for the coaches. We had six athletes in Qingdao and five of them were in wheelchairs, so were unable to do anything related to their equipment. The coaches needed to focus on the task of coaching. Therefore, we would need to increase our credential numbers. In addition, this year credential numbers were announced in early spring of the Paralympic year which was excellent for staff planning. As always, knowing this information early was beneficial.

Our airline tickets were issued at the very last minute. We understand the Department of Defense was paying and there were several issues with the tickets. A better process for tickets needs to be established for next time. Many of our athletes wanted to upgrade their tickets, and it was difficult to do at the 11th hour. At the very least, more communication on the process is needed for next time. In addition, sailing has lots of excess baggage and we greatly appreciate the USOC and United's baggage allowance. We flew United to Beijing like the rest of the U.S. delegation, but since Sailing was based in Qingdao and United does not fly there, we had to fly on Air China. There were some hiccups with the Olympic Team's Air China tickets and we were able to learn from their mistakes for the Paralympic tickets. However, it was not perfect. We had a few staff and athletes who arrived at the Air China ticket counter and the ticket agent could not find record of their travel. This was stressful to the athletes, and ultimately the staff. Sailing will have similar logistical needs in 2012 when we are at a satellite venue again. Solving the hurdle of how to get to Weymouth early in the quad will be key to alleviate stress, so we can all focus on more important tasks.

Our group went through team processing as a team in Colorado Springs. The athletes enjoyed being able to see the Olympic Training Center, however, those in wheelchairs found it difficult to get to Colorado Springs. There were several plane transfers and busing involved making the travel not as easy as it could have been if team processing was at a direct flight location.

Our team left for San Francisco two days after team processing, allowing us to break up the long trip. This was a good decision, especially for the wheelchair athletes.

While in China, the organizing committee (BOCOG) provided two cars for our use during the Paralympics, but neither car was handicap accessible. I would recommend at least one accessible car during the Paralympics next time.

We were given the cell phones that the Olympic sailing team had used and for the most part they worked alright. Some of the phones were a bit old but we had some spare ones when the phones failed. It was a good idea to just use the Olympic phones but if I was not in Beijing when our Sailing Olympic team flew home I am not sure how we would have obtained the phones for the Paralympic Team. I purchased SIM cards for the Paralympic team in Qingdao and the USOC reimbursed me. It was easier for us to buy Qingdao SIM cards, rather than Beijing SIM cards. I would encourage a similar process for London since Sailing will be in Weymouth. As for computers, BOCOG had made some computers available to athletes, but our athletes didn't take advantage of this. Most brought their own computers or didn't want to get on a computer while in Qingdao. In addition, BOCOG had a business center in Qingdao that had a black and white printer, which was helpful.

In the Paralympic Village, we mixed athletes and staff together to make our number of males, females and room numbers work. We only had one room for our medical staff and we had a female doctor and male trainer. We mixed our group so it would work out, but if we were not able to mix we would have had to put a male and female staff together which we do not feel is appropriate.

Our medical staff consisted of Dr. Anne Allen and David Ray, our athletic trainer. Perhaps due to Qingdao being a remote venue, we had trouble with the schedules for our medical staff. My recommendation is for the USOC to set a schedule for the medical staff and let the team leader execute the details and coordination. In addition, we had a small problem when we needed to ship medical supplies back to Beijing after the Paralympic Games. Eventually, the USOC arranged for Schenker to come and pick up the supplies but it was done just before we left. I recommend this be planned in advance to avoid last minute stress.

Regarding ticket availability, we need to work closer with the USOC and the organizing committee to ensure that our Friends and Family group receive the same amenities that are available to those at the main Games site. We did not receive the allotment of tickets were had been promised, a major disappointment for the friends and family members who attended the Games. We were able to purchase tickets from other sources but it was a stressful situation for our entire group.

Overall Sailing's experience in Qingdao was positive. We came away with two medals in three classes so we were all extremely happy with our athletes' performances. I think that pre-Games site visits are incredibly important for the team leader and our head coach. These two roles – team leader and head coach - are expected to be the information center to the team, and the more site visits that can happen, within reason, the better.

PARALYMPIC SHOOTING | *DAN DURBEN – TEAM LEADER*

Team slots for participation at the Paralympic Games were determined through a formula established by the International Shooting Committee for the Disabled (ISCD), based primarily on the number of athletes who obtained a Minimum Qualifying Score (MQS) in a designated international competition during the quadrennium, through 2007. The USA had four athletes shoot at least two MQS's, resulting in one Team slot being awarded to the USA through the ISCD formula. According to ISCD rules, only athletes who fired two MQS's were eligible to fill awarded Team slots. The USA Team slot was filled by Danielle Fong who placed highest in the USA Paralympic Team Trials, which were based on performances in ISCD sanctioned competitions. The USA gained one more additional slot through an IPC bipartite invitation to Mike Dickey. I would recommend more funding for athletes capable of shooting an MQS (but not capable of obtaining US Paralympics performance standard scores) and sending them to ISCD competitions in order to increase the number of Team slots awarded through the ISCD formula.

One issue with the ISCD selection rules for this quadrennium was that athletes had to shoot their first MQS no later than July, 2007, in order to be eligible for the Paralympic Games. This eliminated from consideration any fast-rising athletes who may have been competitive at the Games, but were not ready over one year out. The USA had one athlete who began winning international medals during the Paralympic year but was not eligible for the Games because he did not have the scores for US Paralympics funding, or the personal resources, for international competition over one year earlier. I would recommend the ISCD allow countries to fill awarded Team slots with athletes who shoot MQS's during the Paralympic year, up through the date that names must be submitted to the IPC.

Training prior to the final team selection focused primarily on group training sessions, building training plans, and competing in domestic competitions. I would recommend adding training sessions in Europe and/or Asia with some of the top teams and adding more international competitions, which were not feasible this quadrennium due to budget constraints.

Training after final team selection included a training camp after the trials, a training camp before departure for Beijing, and USA Shooting (USAS) competitions, including the USAS Nationals. These activities were good preparation for the Games, ensuring that athletes were on track with their training plans, that their equipment was optimized, and that any other issues that could affect performance were addressed. I would recommend keeping this training schedule.

The USA athletes did not medal at these Games but both competed in a mature and professional manner and represented the USA well both on and off the field of play. Danielle Fong had a personal best performance in the Women's 3x20 Smallbore event and one of her best personal performances in the Women's Air Rifle event. In both events she followed her competition plan and did an excellent job dealing with competition issues as they arose. Michael Dickey's performances in Men's 3x40 Smallbore and Air Rifle Prone events may have been adversely affected by a medical condition, but he performed to the best of his abilities in both events.

The USOC/USP Team Leadership meetings in Colorado Springs and Beijing were valuable. The opportunity to ensure that all aspects of the Games Deliverables Document were in order well in advance of the Games helped provide for a smooth Games experience for the Team. It was also helpful to travel to Beijing in order to address any local issues that might have impacted athlete performance. I recommend continued participation in USOC/USP Team Leadership activities.

DANIELLE FONG OF THE UNITED STATES COMPETES IN THE WOMEN'S R2-10M AIR RIFLE STANDING SH1 | *ANDREW WONG/GETTY IMAGES*

One potential travel issue with the Shooting Team is traveling to the Games with firearms and ammunition. Thanks to pre-planning and timely submission of forms, the process ran smoothly on the inbound trip. On the outbound trip for those with an early departure from the Games there was some confusion over where to find the firearms at the airport (it ended up that they were late arriving to the airport as the organizers used old departure information rather than the correct departure information that was given to them in Beijing). Also, the United Airlines agents were insisting on charging the athlete for excess bags (another agent eventually sorted this out). There were no USOC staff members at the Beijing airport to help with these issues. I would recommend that the USOC have a staff member on site at the departure airport to assist all athletes with an early departure, especially when athletes are traveling with firearms.

Team processing in Colorado Springs was very well organized and an excellent experience for the athletes. Having processing occur at the Olympic Training Center allowed the Team to participate in a very good pre-Games training camp utilizing the Olympic Complex facilities and resources. The USOC should continue to subsidize the shipping of at least one box home during team processing, especially for those athletes who will be on site, with extra clothing and equipment, for an extended period of time.

The arrangements for the Team inside the Paralympic Village were generally conducive to good performances. The USA location in the Village was convenient to the dining facilities and the transportation mall. The layout of a central area for athletes, for coaches, and for USP offices made it easy for everyone to stay informed. The USOC-issued cell phones were essential for keeping in touch with the Team while in Beijing. Having computers and internet access available in the USA section of the Village was quite nice, although more computers were needed in the coaches' area. Several athletes did have problems with the very hard mattresses in the rooms. It took a few days, but this was eventually remedied by USP purchasing foam pads for the beds.

Ticketing worked well for event days. However, parents could have used more help in obtaining Opening Ceremony tickets. There was also no way for parents to obtain tickets and attend official training sessions that occurred before events started.

USA Shooting will become the National Governing Body for Paralympic Shooting in January, 2009. USAS will hire a full-time coach, implement programs for grassroots development and for emerging athletes, and develop and fund training and competition opportunities for elite athletes. These changes should lead to improved Team performances in 2012.

VALERIY PONOMARENKO OF RUSSIA COMPETES IN THE MIXED P4-50M FREE PISTOL-SH1 | *CHINA PHOTOS/GETTY IMAGES*

PARALYMPIC SWIMMING | JAMES FLOWERS – TEAM LEADER

History of Paralympic Swimming–Swimming for men and women has been a part of the Paralympic program since the first Games in 1960 in Rome, Italy. Today, the races are highly competitive and among the largest and most popular events in the Paralympic Games. Paralympic swimming competitions occur in 50-meter pools and, while competing, no prostheses or assistive devices may be worn.

Paralympic swimming competition is open to male and female athletes with physical disabilities such as dwarfism, amputation/limb loss, blindness/visual impairment, spinal cord injury/wheelchair-users, cerebral palsy/brain injury/stroke and Les Autres.

2008 Paralympic Swim Team Journey–Following a fifth place finish with 35 medals (16 gold, 4 silver, 15 bronze) at the Athens 2004 Paralympic Games and after finishing #1 in the world at the 2006 IPC World Championships, the focus shifted toward the 2008 Paralympics Games in Beijing, China.

It all started in March with the Team Leadership meeting in Beijing. There we were able to gather much information, ask questions and visit the Paralympic Village and the Water Cube. Following the meeting, we were prepared and ready to select the 2008 Paralympic Swim Team.

The 2008 US Paralympic Swimming Trials were held April 3-5, 2008 in Minneapolis, Minnesota; the US Team would consist of 18 women and 20 men. At the trials the women's team was led by 7-time gold medalist Erin Popovich and Cheryl Angelelli, both named Team captains along with 5-time Paralympian Aimee Bruder. For the first time an injured military athlete, Melissa Stockwell, not only participated, but set an American record and earned a spot on the team. The men were led by 2004 Paralympians Justin Zook, Jarrett Perry, Rudy Garcia-Tolson, Curtis Lovejoy and 5-time Paralympian Aaron Paulson. The day after the Trials, the team was honored on the field at a Minnesota Twins baseball game.

The team assembled for the first time at the Olympic Training Center in June. At the camp the team not only trained, but had informational meetings to prepare them for upcoming events such as team processing, training camp in Okinawa, Japan, Kadena AFB, the Water Cube, the Paralympic Village and, of course, the city of Beijing. Many team activities were performed, goals were set and the team was ready.

Assembling once again in Victoria, Canada for the final competition before the Paralympic Games, the team swam in their last tune-up competition before departing for Japan then China. At that competition we saw Jessica Long break her world record in the 100 fly. The majority of the team swam best times or came very close to the times they would need to get on the podium in Beijing. The stage was set – On to Beijing!

Team processing took place at the Olympic Training Center in Colorado Springs, Colorado. This was an exciting time and the entire US Paralympic Team were all treated first class by the OTC and IG staff. The most exciting time, of course, was when the team received their Paralympic uniform. Apparel distribution is where they actually take a shopping cart and fill it with everything they need for the Games. Once everyone received apparel, we assembled for the Ambassador program. The athletes and staff were briefed on security measures, media training, Chinese culture as well as other items that were important during their stay. Once they completed this program the team once again had the excitement of taking their official headshot, measuring for their rings, getting sized for their leather jacket and signing many posters for USOC sponsors. Swim practice and training took place at the USOC Aquatics Center where the team once again received first class treatment from staff at the pool.

On August 23rd, the US Paralympic Swimming and Track & Field teams took off from Colorado Springs bound for Okinawa, Japan and Kadena AFB on a private charter plane provided by the Department of Defense. Everyone on the plane had their own row or at least plenty of room and, once again, received first class treatment.

With a short stop in Anchorage to refuel, the plane landed on the airstrip of Kadena, AFB, Okinawa Japan where we were greeted by many of the best servicemen in the US military. Each athlete had their own sponsor to take care of them during our 9-day stay. The athletes and staff each had their own suite and were provided breakfast and lunch by the staff at Kadena. This was assisted by our own USOC Dining Services.

Our swim practice and training took place at Foster Marine Base, a short bus ride away. We had the privilege of hearing our National Anthem every morning at 8am when the colors were presented, just before we began our workout. During our training we had exclusive use of the pool and, once again, the staff was outstanding. The training and living environment at Kadena, AFB, as well as that at Foster Marine Base, provided the best possible pre-Games scenario for us. The last evening in Okinawa the Kadena AFB personnel honored both teams, as well as those who served us during our stay, in a moving and fun ceremony which included local cultural performers. After nine days of excellent training and team bonding, it was time to head to Beijing.

We arrived in Beijing, China on September 2, 2008. The USOC and IG staff met us at the airport and transported the team to the Paralympic Village, where we validated our credentials. We then headed toward the building where TEAM USA was being housed. The athletes settled into the roomy apartments in which they would live for the next

16 days. The dining service was the first place they visited and they enjoyed the array of food that was delicious and nutritionally sound.

After a short rest, the excited team headed to the Water Cube. Everyone was anticipating seeing what they had watched on TV during the Olympic Games. Once they were actually inside - the look on their faces was priceless. They realized this was going to be a special and great Paralympic Games for TEAM USA.

Opening Ceremonies took place on September 6th. Just assembling outside National Stadium was enough to give everyone goosebumps but when the team came out of the tunnel into a stadium with 91,000 cheering fans, well, every athlete was speechless: another priceless look on their faces! The ceremony and pageantry were the best we have seen. Watching Hou Bin, the Chinese wheelchair athlete, pull himself up a rope to light the Paralympic cauldron was an emotional but perfect ending.

The next day, September 7th, was our first day of competition. The swimming competition took place September 7th – 15th. With 17 gold medals, the team won the gold medal standings. We also took 14 silver & 13 bronze for a total of 44 medals. The team also had seventeen 4th place finishes and over 85% of our athletes posted personal best times. Erin Popovich added to her medal count with 6 more medals (4 gold, 2 silvers); Jessica Long also won 6 medals (4 gold, 1 silver, 1 bronze). Newcomer Cortney Jordan proved she will be a contender in 2012 by winning 4 medals (1 gold, 2 silvers, 1 bronze), as will be Amanda Everlove who won 3 silver medals. On the men's side, Lantz Lamback earned 4 medals, Roy Perkins and Rudy Garcia Tolson both earned two medals, respectively.

When the final race was over, and the last person had touched the wall, the 2008 Paralympic Swim Team walked out of the Water Cube for the last time, having accomplished their goal of being the best in the world. We won the gold medal standing with 17 golds and came in second in the overall medal ranking with 44 total medals. The day following the competition the team enjoyed Beijing by visiting the Great Wall of China as well as the famous Silk Market.

September 17th, Closing Ceremonies. The entire team enjoyed the festivities and watched as their teammate, Melissa Stockwell, with great pride and a greater smile, carried the American flag into the stadium.

Along with all the people of China, we watched as the Paralympic Flame was extinguished. Our team left Beijing full of pride and feeling honored to have represented their sport and, more importantly, their country.

488

JESSICA LONG OF THE U.S.A COMPETES IN THE WOMEN'S 50M FREE-STYLE | *CHINA PHOTOS/GETTY IMAGES*

PARALYMPIC TABLE TENNIS | LARRY ROSE – TEAM LEADER

Competitive Table Tennis is a very technical discipline, requiring thousands of hours of training. Athletes must deal with ball speeds in excess of 50 miles per hour and large amounts/varieties of spin, with their opponent only 10 feet away. Opponent's playing styles vary widely, requiring mastery of varying tactics to win. Top Paralympic table tennis players are adept at attacking their opponent's weaknesses, while covering their own.

Off-season training is done primarily in the United States. In fact, three out of our four athletes trained exclusively in the U.S., while the fourth athlete spent some time in Europe at two separate training camps in Germany and Slovakia. Table Tennis is primarily a year round sport. One change to improve athlete's performance might be to require players to take off 6-8 weeks during the year to encourage full physical and mental recovery.

Athletes were selected to the team based on their individual world rankings and through the regional qualifiers, the ParaPan American Games in Rio de Janeiro, Brazil, in August 2007. The IPTTC's Bipartite Committee selected wildcards of up to 3 players per class. Once players qualified for singles play, doubles teams were created based on similar classes or on wheelchair or standing divisions.

The selection procedure was controlled by the International Federation with the USOC submitting three players for potential wild cards. One wild card (Andre Scott) from the U.S. was selected. Our most competitive players were selected through the world ranking and regional qualifiers.

There are no real changes to be made to this system that are within our control, but we can encourage our players to participate in more international events to improve their world rankings under the present system.

Following team selection, the team participated as a group at a training camp in San Diego, Calif., in May; in the German Open in June; and in the US Open in July. Each player followed his/her own training program with their personal coach at their local club.

International results were mixed with Tahl Leibovitz winning his class at the German Open, while Mitch Seidenfeld, Noga Nir-Kistler, and Andre Scott failed to medal at the same event. The US Open was primarily an able-bodied championship event with a domestic-only Paralympic event. Mitch and Tahl played in one additional tournament in Maryland two weeks before team processing. I recommend that we conduct two to three training camps specifically to allow the athletes more chances to work with the Paralympic coaching staff.

Once in Beijing, most of the athletes were able to set-up training times based on their own personal needs. Our event started the day after the Opening Ceremony. Athletes trained one day at an auxiliary training center. Having various levels of play between wheelchair and standing players required a little coordination to make sure everyone got the time and practice they needed. Coach and Team Manager acted as practice partners to maximize training times. Once, when additional tables were available, our athletes practiced with players from other countries who they would not be facing in the competition in the early rounds.

Mitch Seidenfeld started Team USA's efforts with a painful round robin loss (1-3) to the group's #2 seed Adam Jurasz of Poland. In a four player round robin with only one advancing, this placed Mitch in a very precarious position. He would need Jurasz to lose while he steamrolled the rest of the competition. His match with overall #4 seed Stephane Messi of France was great one. Mitch was focused on going out and playing his best and not getting too wrapped up with the "what ifs." That strategy, along with excellent decision making and shot selection, placed Mitch into a "zone" as he proceeded to take out the defending class 7 gold medalist 3-0.

Now, Mitch really needed Messi (whom he just knocked out of the competition) to come through with a win over Jurasz in order to guarantee Mitch's advancement (assuming a victory over Johan DuPlooy [RSA]). Mitch won his match, 3-0. At the same time, at the other end of the tables, Messi pulled a major league comeback (down 9-3) against Jurasz. After blowing such a big lead in the first game it was evident that Jurasz had nothing left in his tank. Mitch would be playing for hardware in stage two of the Class 7 singles.

Mitch faced China's Chaoqun Ye in the semifinals of Class 7 singles. As we had seen throughout the tournament, the first game in the best of five really set the rhythm for the match. It was additionally critical to help take the crowd out of the match. Both players tried to force their game on the other with Mitch going up 9-7, but unable to close the door. Game two was all Ye, confident of his powerful forehand loop and backhand punch; he won 11-4. Mitch turned things around in game three with a 10-6 offensive swing of his own, only to be denied again, losing 15-13.

In the Paralympics, just as in the Olympics, the unhappy semifinalist must shake off their losses and get ready to battle for bronze, their last chance to make it to the podium. In the bronze medal match, Mitch would face top seeded Alvaro Valera of Spain who was upset in the semis by eventual champion Jochen Wollmert of Germany. Although Mitch and Alvaro had never played before, Mitch had watched Alvaro at the German Open and studied his matches on tape beforehand.

In the first game, Mitch established his backhand as a weapon and built a 9-8 lead, only to succumb 13-11 after a number of strong combinations by the Spaniard. Tied at 6 in the second, Mitch lost 4 in a row, but then won 4 in a row to force a second deuce game.

Down 0-2, but not out of the match, Mitch kept his hopes alive with a solid 11-7 victory in game 3. Unfortunately, Valera regained his initial momentum to win the bronze medal.

Noga Nir-Kistler followed with an extremely close 3-1 loss to Japan's Kimie Bessho after coming back to win the first game in dramatic fashion. As if a strong opponent wasn't enough, Noga had to make a major adjustment the day before the competition when her Globe 999 rubber failed to pass the International Table Tennis Federation (ITTF) reflection test due to being too shiny. Always the competitor, Noga affixed legal rubber supplied by teammate Andre Scott and went out to battle, but Bessho was up for the challenge and had strong leads in each game. Noga's second match was against Maria Nardelli of Italy and while Noga again started slow, she mounted a nice comeback to get back into the match. Streaky play occurred on both sides of the table in the first two games which went to the Italian. In game three there was never more than a two point margin and Noga took charge by winning in deuce. Noga lost her momentum in game four while Nardelli found hers, winning the match at 3-1. Noga's final match was with the top player in her group Khetam Abuawad of Jordan. Due to Abuawad's initial victory over Nardelli (ITA) and her colossal comeback, trailing 2-1 in games and 10-5 in the third against Bessho (JPN), she would be advancing regardless of the outcome. One could see in the match the difference in the amount of international and wheelchair-to-wheelchair experience between the two as Abuawad often set up angles that Noga had no way to cover. The final score was 3-0 in Abuawad's favor.

Andre Scott took to the TV court table against Germany's Dietmar Kober and provided a major kick-start to the team's momentum. Andre dominated both with consistency and shot-making and left the German players and coaches scratching their heads. Game, set and match to USA with a 3-1 victory. As the #3 seed in a three player round robin, taking out the top seed put Andre in the driver's seat. Andre's second and final round robin match was against Scottie Robertson of Great Britain. Due to Andre's upset of top seeded Kober of Germany, Scottie knew he could not afford to drop a game in this match. Scottie became the aggressor throughout the contest to preserve a 3-0 victory. Since Kober took one game from Andre and Scottie won in straights, Andre would have no chance to advance. In the group's final match, Kober returned to his top seeded form and beat Scottie 3-0, advancing to single elimination play.

Tahl Leibovitz concluded the first day's competition with a controlled straight games victory over the always fiery Tonnie Heijnen of The Netherlands. Tahl found an extra 10% to come back and steal the final game after trailing 10-8. Tahl's match against Esa Miettinen of Finland was, in essence, a round of 16 match as both of them were undefeated going into their final round robin match. These players had battled twice before, at the German Open, with Tahl coming out on top both times. Miettinen is known for his fight and determination with wins over many of the top class 9 players in the world. All four games were decided by two points and Tahl had a sizable lead of 7-4 or 9-5 in each, but the pressure from the spinning Finn was just too much to overcome. The match went to Miettinen 3-1.

After the singles there was a one day break and then the team event started. Based on our singles entries, the U.S. only qualified one team and it was in the least disabled event - the Men's 9-10 combined class. Tahl and Mitch almost made the quarters at the World Championships in Monteux, so the field wasn't entirely foreign to them.

After an initial error, the draws were redone to match international rules and the U.S. faced the Ukraine first. In two German Opens, Tahl had faced both Ukrainian players and was undefeated, while Mitch had lost to one of them.

Mitch drew Kubov first and battled to a 3-1 loss after coming back to deuce in the first game after trailing 10-7. Tahl evened up the contest with a see-saw 5-gamer over Shchepanskyy. The doubles didn't go as expected with the righty-lefty pair from the Ukraine jumping out to leads and holding them comfortably taking the match 3-0. Tahl dodged a major bullet trailing 2-1 in games and 9-6 to keep his singles streak alive against Kubov with another teeter-tottering win in 5.

In the fifth and final match of the contest, Mitch and Yuriy Shchepanskyy competed with the score reaching 5-5 in the first game. Yuriy kept his unforced errors to a minimum in the second half of the game, winning 11-6. Game 2 was quite similar with Mitch making a valiant late game surge from 5-10 to only lose 11-8. Up 4-0 in game three, but down 10-6, Mitch had given it everything his body and mind could muster and the Ukrainian team sealed the deal and match with 3-2 victory to send them to the final 8 in the team event.

The level of top Paralympic table tennis players continues to improve, making it more difficult to reach the medal stand.

Prior to the Games, I attend the USOC team leadership meetings and found them very valuable. It was a great way to get to know the USOC staff and the other sport staff members.

The accreditation process went really smoothly for us. I feel that the process worked well as we had great communication with the USOC and US Paralympics throughout the whole ordeal.

In addition, our air travel worked well. We had two athletes leave Beijing early but all the coordination with United Airlines personnel was smooth and efficient.

In terms of apparel USA Table Tennis handled all the colorboards for the competition apparel as we used the same type uniforms as the able bodied competitors. However, IPC's requirements for athlete names on clothing came very late in the process. This did not affect the USOC apparel but our competition apparel did not match IPC's requirements. In the end, we didn't run into any problems at the venue but want to be sure to deal with this far in advance of London 2012.

The other apparel issue to deal with in advance is sizing. We need to work with our competition apparel supplier and the USOC to ensure that the sizing issues faced by many Paralympic athletes are addressed.

Craig Elder served as our athletic trainer during the Games. Craig had previously supported the team at the 2006 Worlds in Montreux, Switzerland and the Parapan American Games in Rio De Janeiro, Brazil. He was familiar with the athletes and their medical issues. He was kept up-to-date on current conditions of the athletes. We also had Dr. Chang as our Chief Medical Officer. All went well and we had great support from both.

Overall, I learned that mental preparation of the players is critical and that both the players and staff need to improve their methods in this area. I believe that all players should have spent more pre-event time with sports psychologist, Dr. Hillyer, so it wasn't a new skill at the time of the games.

In addition, players and coaches should have been more aware of all equipment testing procedures that would be taking place – witness the problem that Noga Nir-Kistler had when her racket was deemed illegal due to the shiny rubber. The testing technique for glossy rubber is not common in U.S. tournaments, although the reflectivity rule has been in place for many years, so this is something to consider for future Games.

PARALYMPIC TENNIS | DAVID SCHOBEL – TEAM LEADER

Wheelchair tennis athletes play tennis by the same rules as able-bodied athletes with one exception – the ball is allowed to bounce twice if necessary. It follows that stroke technique would be different when done from a wheelchair but the game is basically the same.

The team for the 2008 Paralympic tennis team was selected in the middle of May 2008. Team selection is completely based on world rankings as established at a predetermined date by the International Tennis Federation (ITF). The process provided us the best athletes for this team. In the future, we would like to receive a wildcard position for another player.

Our athletes train year-round. They have the opportunity to have a hometown visit from either our national coach or our assistant national coach. In addition, we send at least one of these coaches to major competitions so that they can available to the athletes competing. Each athlete works with these coaches to create and implement an annual training schedule. Between team selection and the Games, we held one training camp. Our athletes also participated in World Team Cup. We believe the training and competition schedule followed this year was very effective.

Our team brought home a gold medal in the quad doubles and a bronze medal in the quad singles. We had hopes for a gold or silver in the quad singles but David Wagner faced an unknown opponent; his loss meant that only Wagner would be on the medal stand. Although she did not medal, Beth Arnoult had a great tournament, defeating the world's sixth ranked athlete in women's singles.

Although our budget was adequate for these Games, we could use additional funding to create more opportunities for our athletes to gain international competitive experiences and to provide them with more in-depth and personal training. We would like to offer more financial support to our athlete as well.

I was only able to attend one of the USOC Team Leadership meetings but it was the one in Beijing, which was very helpful. The interaction with the other sports was very helpful and by having the meeting in Beijing we were able to learn a little more about the city, the culture and the individuals with whom we would be working when at the Games. I also thought the scavenger hunt was a very good way of seeing what the city and its challenges held for our athletes.

For the most part accreditation went well. However, for some reason our coaches and I received different credentials than anticipated and had to have them revised upon arrival in China.

The United Airlines Olympic desk was very helpful in getting our airline tickets booked. I was also very impressed with the United Airlines personnel at the Denver Airport during our outbound flight following team processing. They did a fantastic job and everything worked like clockwork.

Team processing went very smoothly. I thought the USOC staff and volunteers did an outstanding job with keeping things rolling and they had things very well scheduled. Having the tailors right on site was a bonus and really helped the athletes in getting their apparel to fit properly. Like many sports, we name our team close to or after the deadline for submitting team sizes; we'd like to have the deadline more in line with team selection calendars. We'd also like to see coaches and staff receive the same clothing that athletes receive.

The cell phones, computers and wireless connections in the Paralympic Village worked great, as did everything else in the Village. We had a terrific medical staff that was always available for any athlete's needs. The major issue we faced was with tickets for the games. I realize that this is complicated issue involving several organizations but it is a process that needs a major overhaul before London.

Generally, we have a good system and excellent coaches. However, we can not compete with other tennis world powers without better financial support for our athletes. We need to create a player development system and to provide administrative support for our national team coach.

DAVID WAGNER OF THE UNITED STATES CELEBRATES AFTER WINNING THE MEN'S MIXED SINGLES-QUAD BRONZE MEDAL MATCH |
CHRIS HYDE/GETTY IMAGES

PARALYMPIC VOLLEYBALL – WOMEN'S | ROGER NEPPL – TEAM LEADER

The 2008 Paralympic women's volleyball team was selected through a trials process. I believe this process was reasonable and resulted in the best athletes being identified for the team and therefore would not make any changes to this process.

Prior to the trials, our athletes trained by attending short camps and by competing in select international competitions. They trained primarily in the U.S. however in the future more international experience would be of great benefit to their competitive growth.

Following the team Trials, the team participated in the World Cup and performed well. However, this was not enough international competition to prepare them as a team for the Paralympic Games. Preparation for London 2012 should include more post-trials international level competitions. In the end, we had a successful Games bringing home the silver medal.

I attended both of the USOC Team Leadership meetings and found them valuable in identifying the key logistical support areas and related personnel.

The accreditation process was smooth and painless. I felt we had great support from the USOC throughout the entire process. In ad-dition, our team travel went well with the key being great communication between all entities throughout the process. As a result, the booking and actual travel was well organized professionally managed.

Team processing was very well organized and issues such as sizing we addressed and resolved in very well managed process. Having team processing take place on the Olympic Training Center helped to inspire and motivate our athletes.

Individual communications was supplemented by USOC provided cell phones and this was considered a great benefit. Also having the computer and internet connections set-up in the Village was a huge benefit for the athletes, coaches and staff.

The Paralympic Village staff did a great job and were readily available to assist in the resolution of any need or issue.

Our medical staff consisted of our athletic trainer George Davies, who has over 30 years experience as a physical therapist; he provided great care to all athletes. Mark Stovak served as our team doctor and he had vast experience in the area of sports medicine and provided care as needed to our athletes.

LORA WEBSTER (C) AND TEAM USA CELEBRATE DURING THE SITTING VOLLEYBALL MATCH | *ADAM PRETTY/GETTY IMAGES*

ACCREDITATION | REBECCA CRAWFORD – DIRECTOR, GAMES OPERATIONS

Definition of Accreditation and International Olympic Committee (IOC) Accreditation Quota

Accreditation refers to the identification worn by every official U.S. delegation member competing or working at the Olympic Games. The IOC issues a formula which allocates a specific number of accreditations to each National Olympic Committee based on the total number of athletes qualified and entered in the Games, i.e., the larger our total USA team size (athletes), the more accreditations we receive. The United States qualified and entered 598 athletes in the 2008 Olympic Games in Beijing, China. Based on 598 athletes, the USOC was awarded a quota of approximately 412 accreditations, of which approximately 200 were transferable and able to be used by a second person, depending on training and competition schedules.

USOC Accreditation Strategy

The USOC mission drives our Olympic Games accreditation strategy – to maximize opportunities to win medals by identifying the appropriate number of qualified staff needed to serve U.S. athletes/teams.

All accreditation allocations to NGBs were customized to meet individual sport/discipline needs and followed a specific process and timeline:

1. NGB submission of staff selection procedures – the actual job descriptions, qualifications and process by which NGBs selected their performance staff.

2. Review and approval of NGB staff selection procedures by the USOC Team Selection Working Group (TSWG) – a sport performance working group comprised of USOC staff members from Sport Partnerships, International Games, Legal and U.S. Paralympics.

3. Ongoing engagement of NGBs in discussions to ensure maximum impact on sport performance.

4. NGB nominated Olympic staff completed/passed mandated criminal background search.

5. Medical candidates completed medical training as required by the USOC and completed/passed a medical credential review in addition to the criminal background search.

6. NGB nominations of the individuals selected to perform the specific job requirements at the Olympic Games.

7. USOC approval of NGB Olympic staff nominations.

Accreditation Types and Allocations

Although there are numerous types of accredtiation for an Olympic Games, there are three (3) primary types of accreditation that the USOC allocates: "A (Aa, Ao, Ac)," "P" and "NOC (NOC, GT)." Listed below is a summary of the three (3) primary types of accreditations that the USOC allocated for the 2008 Olympic Games in Beijing:

598   Aa = Athletes

412   Ao = Team Officials – coaches, team leaders, performance support, medical, media, Village

4 Ac = Chef de Mission, Deputy Chef de Missions, Attache

27 P = Personal coaches, training partners, IF allowed additional athletes

4 NOC = USOC President and Guest; USOC Secretary General and Guest

24 NOC = Horse Owners (2/per horse)

58 NOC (Guests) = USOC Board of Directors, NGB Executive Directors/Presidents, Sponsors, Donors

1127 TOTAL Accredited USA Delegation

Accreditation Process and Relationship with Beijing Olympic Organizing Committee (BOCOG)

Deadlines for submission of accreditation documentation from the NGBs to the USOC were driven by BOCOG. All Olympic Team nominations were due to the USOC by July 1, 2008 and to BOCOG (from the USOC) by July 23, 2008. The USOC granted several extensions to NGBs for the selection of athletes to the Olympic Team to ensure the fairest, best and most timely selection process with the greatest potential for winning medals.

The USOC's relationship with our BOCOG NOC liaisons was very strong. Our primary liasons were LiJia (NOC Services), Song Lijuan and Zhenhang Zhou (Accreditation) and Gao Haozhe (Sport Entries). All four were very accessible and responsive prior to the commencement of the Games, and even more responsive during the Games. The language barrier was minimal, as all were extremely fluent in both Mandarin and English. Troubleshooting was ongoing, but was 100% anticipated. All issues were addressed qjuickly and professionally – although BOCOG rarely allowed for or exhibited flexibility. Ongoing relationship building was critical to mutual understanding, respect and timely problem solving at the Games.

Accreditation Challenges and Solutions at the Games

Without a doubt, the biggest challenge facing us during Games time was related to entry/exit visas and any changes or mistakes that occurred with regard to delegation members' passports (e.g., names, numbers, new passports) between the time that pre-valid cards (PVCs) were issued and arrival at the Games. Because the PVCs served as multiple entry visas to enter and exit China, changes made after they were issued (approximately 3 months prior to the Games) initially caused delays in immigration upon arrival in Beijing. However, once we understood the Visa Hotline process, we were able to manage all PVC/

passport/visa issues in an immediate and effective manner.

On a couple of occasions, the transferable accreditation plan was not clearly communicated to NGB Olympic Games staff in advance, causing confusion and disappointment. On these occasions, USOC and NGB staff worked together to manage staff expectations and provide timely solutions.

Learnings from Beijing / Recommendations for Future Games

Going forward, I recommend building on/enhancing the accreditation strategy and process to ensure the most strategic, performance enhancing process by eliminating non-performance, time consuming, duplicative inititatives. The following five (5) accreditation activities and processes worked well for Beijing and I would suggest enhancing them for Vancouver 2010, London 2012 and beyond:

1. Ongoing regular communication prior to and during the Games with NGBs/Team Leaders to finalize accreditation plans – especially transferables. The primary method for tracking this information was the NGB Deliverables document, a joint services/resource agreement between the USOC and the NGBs used to capture changes/updates to NGB high performance plans.

2. Meeting with/updating targeted USOC divisions (media, medical) and the USOC Chief of Sport Performance on accreditation plan and finalizing same for NOC accreditation (guest, Board of Directors, candidate city, government officials).

3. Allocating accreditaitons to NGBs earlier in the quad, primarily according to medal potential by including accreditation in overall sport performance resource allocation and requiring NGBs to make it part of their high performance plans.

4. Linking sport entries and accreditation people/processes and Games plans – the two are inseparable from the Organizing Committee standpoint.

5. Developing a more effiicient Games accreditation document that tracks transferable accreditations and daily "usage" for the entire U.S. delegation.

In addition, I suggest implementing four (4) strategies that I believe would enhance the USOC accreditation process working with NGBs and select USOC divisions:

1.Through the Team Selection Working Group (TSWG) – the USOC group that reviews and approves all NGB athlete and staff Games selection procedures and nominations, require the NGBs to nominate their staff prior to or no later than when athletes are nominated. Historically, there has been no deadline for NGBs to nominate staff, causing issues with background checks and meeting deadlines;

2.Earlier and more thorough review of Games competition schedules and the appropriate number of USOC and NGB staff needed (especially media and medical) to ensure coverage that will have the greatest impact on performance;

3.Individual meetings with USOC divisions and NGBs/Team Leaders prior to the scheduled Team Leadership meetings to discuss sport specific accreditation plans;

4.Developing the transferable accreditation plan earlier in the overall process. It takes at least one Olympic Games to fully understand the accreditation process. To make the job more efficient, I would:

a. Implement the four strategies outlined above;

b. Continue to enhance the allocation of Games accreditation through the Sport Performance resource allocation process; and

c. Allocate human resources within IG more effectively, i.e, ensure that the structure of IG allows for more than one person (current practice) to understand and assist with the accreditation process from start to finish.

AIR TRAVEL | *NANCY GONSALVES*
— DIRECTOR, GAMES OPERATIONS

Managing the air travel needs of over 2000 individuals, all coming from different locations but all headed to the same destination, is a complicated, detail-oriented, at times chaotic, process. The USOC coordinates air travel for athletes, coaches, administrators, staff, and other delegation members. We are lucky to have an excellent sponsor in United Airlines; working with them makes this job possible.

The process starts at least one year out from the start of the Olympic Games. We meet with our United Olympic Desk liaisons to identify and reserve blocks of seats on certain flights. For these Games, San Francisco International (SFO) was our launching point, although we certainly took advantage of Chicago O'Hare (ORD) and Washington Dulles (IAD) for return trips home. We know that there will be a number of changes in the coming year but this method gives us the best price possible. When we were able to use these reserved seats, our average per ticket cost was about $1700.

Booking air travel is like a slow dance – a lot of back and forth! The first step was deciding on dates of travel and setting aside a specific number for each sport team. Then as plans solidified, requests for changes were made and accommodated if at all possible (most were). Then once the team was named, actual itineraries were created, agreed upon and ticketed. Since many team trials are very late [in relation to the start of the Games], we were issuing tickets from mid-April (USOC staff and some NGB team staff) all the way until August 7th!

Some teams are more organized and structured than others, making ticketing easier and quicker. We developed a template to assist Team Leaders with the process and those that used the template found ticketing to be much simpler than it was in previous Games.

I had very little interaction with the organizing committee (BOCOG) except to provide them with arrival and departure information to support their ground transport movements. Like all other organizing committees, their timeline and forms were much too restrictive for a National Olympic Committee (NOC) that had about 2,000 people to consider. However, they were very appreciative of our spreadsheet format and the detailed content I provided. For the Paralympics Games, I also provided our master manifest which helped, especially with regards to wheelchair passengers arriving and departing.

I worked extremely close with United Airlines. All the agents on the United Desk were assigned specific sports so I spoke to all of them almost daily. I also worked with their supervisors on the seat block. Even though I was very involved, I think there is still a lot that goes on that I will never know - like the supervisors sending itineraries to the rate desk to be fared at a lower cost, or pulling seats that aren't available and giving them to the USOC. United really puts the USOC and our athletes first! From May 2007 through Opening Ceremony, there were perhaps 80 or so revisions to the seat block request. Most often, I needed to request more seats but as we approached opening day, I was able to release excess inventory back to United to sell.

In addition to the United Desk, we met several times with the United Airport personnel at SFO. Kirk Milburn, Team Process transport manager, was point for actual operations and met with the airport staff numerous times to learn the space, flow, and lay-out of the facility. He also met often with Denver International Airport (DEN) airport staff to review operations in preparation for Paralympic athlete travel. Because of the personal relationships and numerous site visits, operations went very smooth. A benefit of this relationship is that check-in time for our Olympic and Paralympic athletes was kept to an average of 30 seconds! Since we were based stateside, we did not have as much involvement in the Beijing airport operations, although on site visits we met with the key people and laid the groundwork. We used email to communicate with United staff based in Hong Kong, so operations were also very smooth for our equestrian teams.

In the future, if time permits, I would recommend a trip to Detroit to meet face-to-face with our United Desk agents. The agents were great to work with via phone and email but dedicated meeting time would have been more efficient and helpful.

There were two things that worked particularly well and that I would recommend be continued in the future: ticketing at trials and using a template. We traveled to the USA Track & Field Olympic Trials in Oregon in July. It gave us an invaluable jump start on ticketing over 140 athletes and staff. We created a sport-specific template for each NGB to assist them in making itineraries for their athletes and staff. About half of the NGBs used it, making for a much smoother and coordinated process.

A YOUNG FAN TAKES A PHOTO IN THE NATIONAL STADIUM ON DAY 9 OF THE BEIJING 2008 OLYMPIC GAMES | STU FORSTER/GETTY IMAGES

OLYMPIC GAMES APPAREL | NANCY GONSALVES – DIRECTOR, GAMES PREPARATION

Work on procuring apparel for the Olympic Games ideally begins 18 months prior to the Games. This timeline is impacted by the status of the apparel sponsor secured for the Games, quad (4 year period) or multi-quad period. It is also dependent on whether we chose a domestic or Games site location for distribution as the shipping times and customs have to increase by approximately 6 months. For the 2008 Beijing Olympic and Paralympic Games, Nike was the apparel sponsor for Podium and Village wear and Polo Ralph Lauren was the apparel provider for the Opening and Closing parade. Competitive attire is left to each National Governing Body to secure and provide.

The 2008 Games were Nike's second Games as the official USOC sponsor so we had the benefit of a lot of lessons learned from the previous 2006 Winter Games in Torino; we were familiar with each other and the process. We also learned a few more lessons in Beijing that will directly impact the Vancouver Games apparel plan. Having a sponsor for an 8-year commitment has been wonderful. Polo Ralph Lauren was a new provider in 2008. They were secured to fill a recent void, giving us just 6 months from design to delivery. It was incredibly rushed and stressful for both them and the USOC. Due to the fact that we were conducting Olympic and Paralympic team processing in the United States (San Jose, California and Colorado Springs, respectively) and therefore did not have to ship product to China, we were able to outfit all delegation members as scheduled.

The first steps taken in the process are twofold. One is to estimate the total number of people that require outfitting, including athletes, team staff, medical staff, press officers and general support. Groups are divided into categories and packages created for each category depending on their specific functional needs, with the athletes receiving the most items that are created especially for them. Because the order is placed so far out from the Games, the numbers have to include the potential maximum team size which often times ends up being more than actually qualify to participate. Conversely, due to a relatively new accreditation policy that allows for transferring Games accreditations, we now have to assume a greater number of support staff will require outfitting as well.

Second, we need to initially decide what types of items (i.e. how many shorts, t-shirts, hats, etc) we are interested in supplying to our team. Since our sponsors have their own specific objectives relative to brand development and retail applications, they are given a lot of lattitude in the design process. In fact, the USOC has become more of a review and approving body. For the Games, our constituents are divided into 3 categories: athletes (1), accredited team staff, USOC medical personnel, and USOC Board of Directors (2) and all other general USOC support staff (3). The products offered by the apparel companies are then assigned to each category and packages are created. For the Beijing Games our category 3 individuals, who are also referred to as the "non-marching" delegation members, were not supplied with Parade apparel; instead they were given a variety of shirts from both manufacturers. Then, each work day during the Games period, we assigned a specific color to be worn so that our working delegation looked unified and was easy to identify. An added benefit this year was that since staff received separate and unique items, we were able to distribute this to the staff a month prior to their departure to Beijing which was really appreciated by all.

For the Beijing Games, Nike provided the athletes with 26-29 different items for Podium, Leisurewear and training. Item sizing was gender specific which is much preferred and much appreciated by all. The men and women athletes may have had similar items but color and fit were tailored specific to each gender. Polo Ralph Lauren provided an additional 30 items to make up the Opening Ceremony, Closing Ceremony and village wear package. All in all the athletes left processing with two pieces of luggage packed to overflowing! The approximate retail value of the athlete package was $3,000.

The actual placing of the order with each manufacturer is another time consuming and stressful process! The manufacturers provide a range of sizes for each item, from XXS to 4XL tall. In some cases, one item may have 38 different sizes offered, including men's and women's. Since the actual naming of each delegation member will not be know for another year, the quantities ordered per size is based on some historical data and recent styling trends, as well as how the apparel piece is supposed to fit (loose, form fitting, etc.). It is easy to assume the body type of say a gymnast or basketball player, but teams such as sailing and shooting have no "standard" body type. So in order to be able to (hopefully) outfit everyone appropriately, we place a 15% overage per piece. As another safeguard, alterations personnel are provided at the team processing site and each athlete is fitted, with emphasis on the Podium and Parade pieces. In Beijing, since the chosen Parade outfit was tailored trousers and a blazer, every single person had to have something altered. It took a team of 5 people plus volunteers working well into the night to have athlete's clothes ready for them when they departed the next day for China. For the Paralympic athletes, many of the other items provided in leisure wear also had to be altered to accommodate prosthesis, dwarfs and wheelchair athletes.

After the order is placed with the manufacturer and accounting purchase orders submitted to support the order, we start receiving product within 6 months. Ideally the apparel comes boxed and on pallets according to how the order was placed but that is not often the case. The manufacturer's factory sends the product as they receive it. A team of USOC warehouse staff have to open each and every box and perform a piece count, as well as an inspection to ensure the correct logo has been used and the inventory is verified. The items are then re-boxed according to how and when the planned distribution will take place and the boxed is labeled accordingly. Because of the manpower needed, we ask for shipments to be received 4-6 months prior to the Games. For Beijing, because of the very late Polo Ralph Lauren deal, we were receiving product daily and up to the day our six container trucks departed for Olympic team processing in San Jose California. And because we had to skip the counting and inspection process for many late arriving items, we found we had brought some of the Paralympic inventory to San Jose instead of Olympic product and had to utilize overnight shipping almost daily to correct the error.

It took five days to unload the six containers in San Jose and set-up the apparel distribution room at San Jose State University. One container alone held nothing but luggage and we parked that at the facility to restock as needed. While we had the use of a large ballroom, we were still cramped for space and had to utilize two nearby meeting rooms for extra product storage. Items were grouped by category and gender. To make the distribution process smooth, at least one size of everything has to be displayed for try-on, which took a lot of physical space. Tables were stacked two high and the floor and both table tops were all crammed with boxes in size order. We also provided dressing rooms for men and women. In order to expedite the process, which can take about 2 hours, we encouraged people to come dressed in swimsuits so they could avoid the dressing rooms. It makes team processing apparel distribution a fun and interesting place to work!

The first stop for a delegation member is at apparel check-in. Here they are greeted by the apparel manager who has a distribution sheet prepared for them. Every item they are eligible to receive is listed so that the 30-45 volunteers and staff working distribution know what to give that person based on their function (athlete, doctor, coach, etc). Included on that distribution sheet is the size they indicated they wanted when they registered on-line for the Games months before. Those sizes are used as a starting point for distribution and become very important if a delegation member is unable to go through processing and the apparel has to be packed for them by a teammate or staff member. Because the athletes are given a generous amount of clothing options, many want to pick some of the items for spouses, friends or family members. While it is an understandable request, we can not honor it because we have to ensure that the last delegation member who goes through in two weeks time still has apparel appropriate for them! We encourage people to trade with their teammates after they have been given all apparel in their own size and gender. It is very stressful until that last person is outfitted and until then, you hope and pray that your crystal ball was working one year before with the order! For Beijing, we did an okay job but there were definitely some disappointed people who simply could not fit in the apparel sizes that were left. Most were understanding and took pieces for friends and for those items that were essential or a favorite, we offered additional alteration services.

As mentioned above, the USOC does not procure or distribute the competitive attire for each team. The National Governing Body (NGB) has their own sponsors and some individual athletes do as well. However, the IOC has very strict rules on what the field-of-play apparel looks like and the USOC works to ensure that the NGB's are compliant. For Beijing, the IOC created an on-line tool called Rule 51, which refers specifically to the size and placement of the manufacturers trademarks allowed on the clothes. There is also a restriction on national federation logos or graphics appearing on the apparel. The USOC apparel manager requests from each NGB a detailed description and line-art on all the items to be worn and then submits on their behalf to the IOC. The IOC then signs off with their approval or justification for refusal. It is then the NGB's responsibility to wear the clothing that had been approved. As we look to future Games, there needs to be continued improvement in NGB timely submission to the USOC and the IOC enforcement of the rule during the Games.

In addition to apparel, several commemorative items are also provided for delegation members. O.C. Tanner supplied a base ring free of charge to all delegation members with any associated upgrade costs (gold count, diamond embellishments) at the expense of each individual. They staffed a station at team processing where they took orders and offered sizing and the opportunity to view samples. The rings were mailed to individuals post Games. A commemorative watch was also provided and sent to each eligible delegation member along with copies of team photos, White House photos, and any other memorabilia received which has included certificates of participation and medals from the organizing committee, athlete pins from the IOC and DVDs of Games highlights, to name a few.

HIGH PERFORMANCE TRAINING CENTER | DOUG INGRAM
– MANAGING DIRECTOR, PERFORMANCE SERVICES

The USOC Sport Performance Division has setup a High Peformance Training Center (HPTC) for our Olympic Team at each Olympic Games since 2000 in Sydney, Australia. The HPTC was created to give our athletes training opportunities that they would normally be difficult to arrange during the Games. We provide basic training facilities, nutritionally balanced meals, video feedback technology, and room and board for key support staff (personal coaches, training partners, scientists, medical staff, etc.).

Although language was not an issue in our relationship with the organizing committee (BOCOG), we found challenges in dealing with BOCOG staff with little or no previous Games experiences and with adjusting to the cultural differences in conducting business. Fortunately, we had two outstanding BOCOG individuals working with us: Laszlo Vajda, our primary contact, and Gary Yi, our broadcast technology contact. Once we started working directly with Laszlo and Gary, our relationship with BOCOG improved.

The HPTC was located on the campus of Beijing Normal University (BNU), providing us with a secure environment to set up housing, venue rental, and science and medical support. Although the bureaucracy of working with BNU administrators was challenging, we were helped immensely by the 20-plus U.S. college students assisting us. All spoke Mandarin, making the language barrier almost disappear. We also worked closely with the Yumadun restaurant on the BNU campus, which we rented to serve over 17,000 meals.

We had excellent relationships with our USOC sponsors who supported our efforts at the HPTC. They were:

> United Airlines (primary contact: Stephanie Walker) – monitored airport arrivals and departures and handled air travel changes, as well as excess luggage issues.
>
> 24Hour Fitness (primary contact - Elizabeth Gentry) – equiped a state-of-the-art strength and conditioning facility and provided the personnel to keep the facility ready at all times.
>
> Tyson foods (primary contact - Alicia Mosley) – provided US meat products for over 17,000 meals and included the necessary storage and refrigeration.
>
> Coke (primary contact - Jenny Whitaker) – provided a variety of beverages for the cafeteria, dorms, medical, and training venues and included the necessary coolers to house the beverages.
>
> Panasonic (primary contact - Jon Holvey) – provided the technical equipment to support out video capture, analysis, and review system.
>
> McDonald's Beijing (primary contact - William Wong) – provided food and paper goods supporting our Americana-themed food service.

Overall the High Performance Training Center (HPTC) was a magnificent success from accreditation to training to technology to housing to food to transportation, etc. We had outstanding teamwork. There was a great camaraderie among the HPTC team and the outstanding effort was completely performance oriented. No one worried about who got credit, they just pitched in as necessary! This was due to an excellent staff selection process, plus outstanding leadership and "followership"! The careful selection of the USOC staff based on a combination of their skill sets and ability to function in a Games environment was critically important; as was the willingness of staff and leadership to "coach" fellow staff when changes or improvements were needed on site. In the long run the personal characteristics and willingness to integrate into an effective team may actually be more important in the selection process than actual technical competence.

The screening/interview process used to select our key volunteers was also a critical element in assuring we got the best and the brightest. The standards used for determination were: first, their Mandarin/English language skill (must have been a 4.5 or better on a 5 point scale). If they passed that test, then I wanted someone with a true elite sport background (bare minimum - coaching/playing at the Div I national championship level with international experience preferred). Finally, if they progressed this far, then at least one of their references must have been known to us. This was an admittedly rigid standard but it paid off immensely in the contributions of these individuals to the mission! In addition, we had two Colorado College interns (also rigidly screened) and up to 20 (at any particular point in time) additional Mandarin-speaking college students, primarily from Dartmouth, as part of their summer abroad programs, all assisting in translation in the various areas of the HPTC. These were the true unsung heroes of the Games!!!

We began the search for a HPTC site almost five years prior to the Games. We visited many sites, eventually narrowing it down to a handful, of which BNU was selected about two years out from the Games. We entered into a prolonged negotiation process that continued into the summer of 2008. In addition, we formed a steering committee of four USOC Sport Performance staff and held weekly planning meetings beginning 11 months before the Games. Then, on-site at the Games, we held daily all-staff meetings at the HPTC for the first month; we then reduced them to only the function area personnel for the last two weeks.

Looking ahead, we need to consider the following issues:

> 1. we had to restrict our hours of operations to 12 hours per day, which included limited access to the venues. This was primarily due to unanticipated security costs;

2. the USOC IT function was understaffed, causing some delays in responding to requests for assistance;

3. the ability to electronically access the Deliverables Document on-site at the Games would be extremely useful. In fact having one data-base that captures all of housing, transport, accreditation, etc, should continue to be explored. In addition, just as the NGB Executive Director signs off on the Deliverables Document, have the NGB Team Leader do so as well, since they are our main Games contact. Finally, have the NGB Team Leader's sign an "agreement" on their actual Job Description to ensure clarity.

4 we need a better system for insuring the background checks are in proper order. An earlier deadline should be in place. I recommend a working group be put in place to determine a better system and to implement it before Vancouver.

5 if venues are separate from the housing, dining, office areas – as it appears will be the case in London - better connectivity (computers, fax machines, fixed lines, even TV with live feed) than just cell phones needs to be in place.

6 finally, we should have planned better on the little things needed for supplies and equipment. Far too much time, energy and resources were spent on last minute shopping trips in Beijing. In addition, everything that is shipped should be fully tested beforehand, especially equipment that has been warehoused for an extended period of time.

The development and use of the Deliverables Document as the basis for our planning with NGBs was key to our success. And the development of a relationship with Team Leaders and coaches, based on the meetings and site visits before the Games, was key as well. I can safely say the HPTC met or exceeded expectations on absolutely every "deliverable" identified for the 22 sports that used our facilities and a number that did not actually use the physical facilities. This is only possible by multiple meetings with NGBs, discussing their "Games" plans and clearly articulating what we will and will not be able to deliver within the context of a HPTC.

Transportation was another area where we exceeded expectations. The shuttle system between the Village and BNU supported the train-ing athletes well. The internal shuttle system was efficient and provided great support for coaches, training partners and staff. Additionally, our staff was able to provide special transportation assistance for a lot of projects that silently contributed to our success – for example, hauling 500 lbs. of ice out to the Rowing hotel every morning.

The food service created by Frambois catering and the USOC personnel was nothing short of spectacular. It created a "home away from home" with American food served in a restaurant style. As noted previously, we served over 17,000 meals during our month of operation. The popularity of this service was evidenced by the number of teams that choose to extend their time beyond their training at BNU to include one or more meals per day and some teams that may have trained elsewhere but still came to the HPTC for meals. A tremendous side benefit of the dining experience being so good was the Team USA atmosphere that was created among the normally disparate teams.

The dorms utilized at BNU were as good as any American university. That plus the superlative work that our housing personnel did managing the rooms made for a positive environment. We peaked at 561 beds occupied (training partners; personal coaches, food service personnel, USOC/NGB, media staff, etc)!!

Our Performance Technology Team met all the needs of our NGBs and then some. True to their title they enhanced our Olympic team's performance through cutting edge technology. The decision upfront to only provide real-time performance enhancing technology vs archival (which the sports could order from the local organizing committee) proved to be a great decision. And, as we fine-tune our process in educating coaches and team leaders about technology, we will see a expansion of this service at future Games. In addition, the wireless set-up that USOC IT personnel created for us in the housing/office area made our daily work exceedingly effective.

In spite of the hurdles presented and the endless negotiations required to gain approval, the HPTC team can be very proud of quality and availability of the training venues made available to the teams.

OLYMPIC MASCOTS ARE SEEN IN THE POOL AT THE NATIONAL AQUATICS CENTER | *JAMIE SQUIRE/GETTY IMAGES*

MEDIA SERVICES | BOB CONDRON – DIRECTOR OF MEDIA SERVICES

USOC Media Services is responsible for the planning, staffing, and implementation of media and communication areas for the USA Team and delegation. This includes assigning press officers for sport support and Village duty, overseeing credential allotment for press officers, creating and maintaining the USOC office in the Main Press Center, planning and hosting the US Olympic Team Media Summit, and establishing relationships with BOCOG staff.

The Beijing Olympic Games was one of our most successful Games. There are a number of procedures and activities that contributed to this success, including:

•High Performance Training Center at Beijing Normal University. An excellent setup, concept and staff. In addition to the obvious advantages for athletes and coaches, it provided us with an outstanding media operation to cover these athletes and teams. The access was controlled and overseen, interview opportunities were comfortable and informal and this concept was one of the bright spots of the Games. The housing and dining for the media staff was good and the transportation system to the MPC and the Village worked well. The work area on the second floor was very good and was used extensively by the Associated Press and Yahoo.

•Transportation. USOC transportation from the HPTC to the MPC was effective and timely. The best improvement involving transportation was the addition of drivers. This is one aspect that needs to be included in future Olympic Games. One drawback was the loss of the VAPP Parking which included all venues and was a cornerstone of our Managing Victory program. Parking at the MPC was good, but not what we had planned for. BOCOG's transportation was on time, efficient and worked. A host on every media bus was very nice. The host made it his or her business to make sure the bus was on time and everything was in order.

•Breaking News Bureau. Our Breaking News Bureau was outstanding in keeping media and Olympic Family up to date on breaking U.S. Olympic Team News. We oversaw a direct e-mail Breaking News service to more than 800 journalists and Olympic Family members and were able to keep everyone up to the moment on U.S. performances during the Games. In the past we've posted Breaking News on our media site www.usocpressbox.org, but with the e-mail addition, we improved our service ten-fold

•USA Daily. The delegation newsletter was outstanding. Kodak printed the newsletter on four-color glossy paper, Getty Images supplied the photos. Lisa Ramsperger oversaw the publication and served as editor. The publication was a preview issue in order for media and Olympic Family to be able to plan their day and see what's coming up for U.S. teams and athletes.

•U.S. Media Credentials. The credential process for United States media was directed by the U.S. Olympic Committee. The IOC allotted 530 media credentials for U.S. media and the USOC devised a process for allocating these credentials. Working with a sub-committee representing the Associated Press Sports Editors the USOC coordinated this two-year process to complete success for U.S. media. This process was fair and equitable. The APSE liaison to the USOC was Roy Hewitt, managing editor for sports for the Cleveland Plain Dealer.

A PHOTOGRAPHER WALKS IN THE RAINY PITCH AS THE MATCH IS DELAYED DUE TO THE THUNDERSHOWERS | LIU JIN/AFP/GETTY IMAGES

• The USOC's "Managing Victory" plan went well in Beijing, and was enlarged to include many more NBC stops in the operation. The Plan is a follow-up to a medal performance and involved stops at the Main Press Center, the International Broadcast Center, various NBC shows, NBCOlympics.com and the NBC affiliate stations. Other stops included USA House, Bank of America's Hometown Hopefuls and ESPN and CNN studios. The most difficult aspect of this program is the non rights-holding broadcasters because it usually involves taking an athlete out of security. The Main Press Center is the optimal spot for Managing Victory because it is easily accessible for the media, including the non rights-holders and is well run and managed. It was also located across the street from the International Broadcast Center which reduced the need for travel.

• U.S. Embassy. The U.S. Consulate provided staff members to be part of the USOC Media Services staff. These staff members performed a variety of tasks, including: providing our staff each day with a capsule of Chinese news coverage of U.S. Teams and athletes by noon each day; helping get our messages and information out to the Chinese media each day; alerting Chinese media about our athlete press conferences or availabilities; distributing U.S. athletes comments that were complimentary to China and the Olympic Games; providing council to our staff concerning Chinese media and serving as a tremendous resource for special needs that arose at the Games.

A few things that we need to review before the next Games are listed below. Not all of these are within our control but our input should be forwarded to those who do make the decisions.

• The Mixed Zone. The broadcast part of the mixed zone seemed to have more problems at these games than ever before. Athletes were held up waiting for commercials to air, there was too much chit-chat after and before interviews were done, there were athletes stacked up waiting to speak with one broadcaster when other broadcasters could have been taken care of with a quick question or two while waiting. One of the problems in the mixed zone area was the Medal Ceremonies. The MC staff was relentless in their zeal to get the athletes to the waiting area. This meant a total of about 7 minutes in the mixed zone at most. At least 5-6 were taken in the broadcast area, leaving 1-2 for both agencies and the rest of the print media. A few more minutes would have helped take care of the media requests without adversely affecting the medal ceremonies. Organizing committees should consider incorporating a "common room" in the mixed zone. This area would serve as a mixed zone for high profile athletes. It would contain a riser, a speaker, a backdrop, possible mult boxes. In the written area of the mixed zone it would be a one-stop spot for athletes and would not take any more of the athletes' time. However, it would be in a more media and athlete-friendly area and be better adapted to deal with the Michael Phelps-type quick quotes. Not all athletes would be directed into this area. The others would proceed through the "normal" mixed zone but selected athletes would be directed into the "common room."

• There needs to be more training for press officers for the Olympic Games. With the cancellation of the Olympic PR Association's annual workshop the past two years, the preparation and knowledge level of the press officers for the individual sports has suffered. We need to have an Olympic preparation workshop before each Games. Budget cuts did not allow us to conduct the workshop this year.

500

MEDICAL SERVICES | MARGARET HUNT – *HEAD, ATHLETIC TRAINER*

The USOC's Medical Services Team provides complete medical services for our athletes, coaches, and other delegation members. The Team is composed of medical doctors, chiropractors, athletic trainers, massage therapists, physical therapists and a pharmacist. Over the course of the Games, we completed over 8,700 treatments, including 1,310 tapings, 4,600 massages, and over 600 injury assessments.

We had a good working relationship with the organizing committee (BOCOG) through our primary contact, Dr. Dai, Chief Medical Officer for BOCOG. He and his assistants were proactive, responsive and reliable. For future Games, I recommend that the USOC Medical Director meet early and often with the organizing committee's chief medical staff; establishing this relationship is a key component to quick responses and good planning. In particular, the relationship could help make the process of submitting supply formularies easier. This is a challenging process because the formularies have to be submitted 8-10 months in advance of the Games, which is difficult to do given budget allocation issues, in-house supply inventory shortages, and sponsor relationships.

Early on, we established a new, strong, professional relationship with Beijing United Family Hospital. We had three main contacts at the hospital, the President, the Chief of Marketing, and the Chief of Hospital Services. Each of them worked diligently with us to ensure that all of our needs would be met. This proved beneficial as we needed their facility and services for quick, seamless care for our non-accredited delegation members, as well as ancillary services for our accredited delegation members. As this was a western medicine hospital, all of the contacts there were English speakers, so there was no issue with language.

We had two primary sponsors, Johnson & Johnson, and GE Healthcare. We worked with multiple individuals to ensure the delivery of purchased J&J products, as well as coordinated training on the GE Healthcare Diagnostic MuskuloSkeletal Ultrasound and EKG equipment. All of this occurred in the 2-4 years prior to the Olympic/Paralympic Games, with a big push in the last 12 months. This last year was also when we were diligently focusing on athlete care, NGB support and event logistics. Ideally, we should coordinate our needs and training early in the quad. Outlining agreed upon goals earlier in the quad may help to alleviate some of the red tape and hold-ups that were experienced by many parties. The year prior to the Games was a very challenging one and I'm pleased to say that our sponsors rose to the occasion by supporting athlete care first.

We also had some key medical supply vendors that supported us with loaner products and special purchasing rates. These companies were, Chattanooga, Inc., US Foam, BioCare Systems, Inc. Ferris Mfg. Corp., and New Options. While these companies are not USOC sponsors, we appreciate their support and could not have provided our standard high-level quality of care without them. Our medical inventory, including equipment, supplies and pharmaceuticals for all three villages (Beijing, Qingdao and Hong Kong) and our high performance center at BNU, filled 12 pallets. These supplies not only supported the Olympics, but also stayed for our Paralympic delegation and medical staff needs.

We did have some challenges with medical staff that did not have as much international multi-sport games experiences as we would have preferred. In some cases, they were not prepared for the long hours or the intense stress of working at the Games. I recommend that the USOC continue to pursue the goal of having each medical staff member progress through every step of the USOC volunteer program and not skip any of the key learning and exposure opportunities.

I would also recommend being more proactive in communicating with the organizing committee to clearly identify and understand the licensing/practicing requirements of their country, as well as the emergency, environmental, and customs logistics involved. Once all this is determined, focus and attention can be given to effective planning and communication with the NGBs and assigned medical staff.

With the Beijing medical staff, we implemented a communication strategy that relied on electronic newsletters and emails. I suggest that we also convene a meeting, approximately 2 months prior to the Games, with assigned medical staff to review all expectations and logistics. We have held such meetings with NGB executives, team leaders, and coaches and have found them to be very beneficial. We should expand that positive approach to the medical staff training.

Several processes and decisions worked well and should be kept for the next Games. These include:

•Place an experienced USOC medical staff employee at Team Processing. This person can deliver critical doping control information/requirements to athletes and coaches and proactively deal with athlete medical issues prior to athletes' final departure, and effectively communicate issues/needs with the medical director.

•Place a Family Practice physician in our delegation's headquarters hotel to assist with any executive team and support staff medical needs. This physician can also serve as a liaison with the extended delegation families in the event of an emergency. This allows the accredited medical staff to remain focused on athlete medical needs.

•Continue to assign medical staff to teams based on size of the team, medical risks of the sport, and the performance needs of the athletes. Selecting staff from a pool of volunteer candidates who have demonstrated that they can meet the challenges of working at a huge international, multi-sport event continues to work well.

•Continue to support our volunteer medical staff with good communication tools. Cell phones were our best and most effective means of communication. Our volunteers were particularly pleased to have wireless internet access in the medical clinic as it allowed them to maintain communication with family at home and co-workers at the office. Since many of these volunteers donate the 3-7 weeks of their time, this convenience is a small payback.

ATHLETE VILLAGE | KELLY SKINNER
— DIRECTOR, SPORT PARTNERSHIPS

The Athlete Village is the home for the athlete during the Games. The Village is created and maintained by the organizing committee (in this case that was BOCOG). The US Olympic Committee is responsible for daily operations of the US section, setup and teardown of equipment and supplies, and providing servicing for U.S. Team members.

We had a good working relationship with BOCOG through their liaisons, Lazlo and Lilly. Lazlo, in particular, helped us with almost any questions or issue that came up but he was especially responsive to anything regarding our team. At one point, BOCOG decided that NOC Assistants could not enter the sport information center without a team leader. This decision would have impaired our teams ability to work effectively. Lazlo stepped in to help and was able to change the decision so we could continue.

We also had good working relationship with our primary vendors: Coca-Cola, Schenker, and the Village Logistics team. Our liaisons with these companies were responsive to any ideas or concerns we had. They made every effort to put the athletes' needs first.

Looking ahead to London, there are a few things we need to consider:

•Village staff scheduling – we need to identify key staff and have them in the Village at least 2-3 days before the first team arrives. This will give them time to review processes and procedures and get to know the general layout of the Village.

•Athlete Services Coordinators (ASC) – these individuals continue to be very helpful but the USOC needs to review the timing of naming ASCs so that they can participate in pre-Games meetings and planning.

•Day Pass – the procedure by which day passes are distributed needs to be reviewed for consistency and fairness. Visits to the Village should be encouraged and supported but need to better planned so that staff and athletes can be prepared to appropriately welcome the group.

•Village Director – the Village Director needs to be determined as early as possible and then needs to be involved in all village planning meetings. The more the Director knows about organizing committee restrictions, logistics, staffing, and supplies, the better the Village can be run.

By far, the best aspect of the Village at these Games was the staff. An absolutely fantastic staff was built for these Games. There is no doubt that the same people can't keep doing the same thing every Games – it is important that we prepare others for these roles – but the staff in Beijing was amazing and would be a great team to reassemble for any future Games.

SECURITY | *LARRY BUENDORF*
— CHIEF SECURITY OFFICER

The USOC Security Team's mission was to ensure a safe and secure environment for the U.S. delegation through strong liaison work with the U.S. Diplomatic Security and the Chinese authorities. In order to fulfill this mission, the Security Team did the following:

• Briefed all athletes upon their arrival in the Athlete Village. Provided the latest information available on activities, processes, and procedures used throughout the Games area.

• Worked with the organizing committee (BOCOG) regarding their unanticipated decision to add an extra layer of security at our High Performance Training Center at Beijing Normal University.

• Met with and shared information with other NOC security liaisons, especially those from Canada and Great Britain. These relationships will be beneficial in future Games.

In considering future Games, it is recommended that the security team continue to be included in the earliest planning in order to ensure that all aspects of the US effort is covered by security planning. This includes the High Performance Training Center, the Athlete Village, the USA House, and the Media Center.

RAIN FALLS WHILE FANS ARRIVE AT THE MEN'S TRAP QUALIFICATION
SHOOTING EVENT | *JAMIE SQUIRE/GETTY IMAGES*

TEAM PROCESSING | *NANCY GONSALVES* — *DIRECTOR, GAMES OPERATIONS*

Team Processing (TP) is the process by which the USOC gathers and/or distributes pre-Games apparel, information, commemorative items, airline tickets, and team photographs. All athletes and delegation members are strongly urged to come through the centralized location. For those team members unable to do so (due to extraordinary circumstanced), TP staff creates "pre-packs" of apparel and other items and ship them to the team's location.

TP is most often located in, or near to, the city that is hosting the Games. However, in 2008, it was decided to hold TP in the U.S.; the facilities at San Jose State University were deemed excellent and most team were U.S. based prior to the Games. The first athletes arrived in San Jose on July 17, but TP staff was on the ground 6 days earlier in order to setup the stations each athlete would visit. Stations were: apparel distribution, commemorative Olympic rings, commemorative leather jackets, medical information and review, official photographs, travel allowance distribution, Chicago 2016 support, and United Airlines Desk.

Athletes and delegation members used the new SJSU dormitories, with meals overseen by USOC food services staff and coordinated by USOC nutritionists. Practice facilities on the campus and in the community were scheduled upon request.

San Jose State University was an almost ideal location to conduct team processing (only negative was its location one hour from SFO airport). The campus was laid out well, we were treated as "VIPS" by the administration, the weather was consistently perfect (no rain, not too hot) and all the amenities we needed were on campus or close by. Accommodations were comfortable and although it is an open campus, we felt secure and protected by the campus police force. Over the course of two years, I made 4-5 site visits to campus, contributing to the good working relationship we had with the entire campus leadership. The Student Union held all stations, including apparel distribution, as well as the main office and transport office. We were centrally located and easily found. We ordered street pole banners for the main promenade on campus, which stretched from the dorms to the Student Union. They looked great and really gave an Olympic feel to the site.

We had almost the right number of staff, although the transport team was burning the candle at both ends – departures (over 210 trips to the airport, with equipment and luggage) starting at 4:00 am and often continuing through 11:00 pm. We could have used two more people in transport. The San Jose Sports Authority did a great job recruiting and managing volunteers. We conducted an orientation and had many serve every day in core roles. We had quality people who we could count on! We also utilized their summer interns daily to provide administrative assistance, data entry, and to assist at the various stations. They were invaluable!

We planned our schedule well (July 12-August 11). It took 6 days to really make sure we were fully set up and ready for the first team. There was A LOT of apparel to distribute and store! For the most part the flow worked out well but our biggest days were too big (80+) and out slow days too small (5). Based on the competition schedule and the travel desires of the NGB's for peak performance, we were opened longer than normal but that allowed us to accommodate training, training camps, and arrival times in to Beijing. If we were on-site at the Games (i.e. in London), then we could shorten our processing time by about 5 days. It took 3 days to pack up and return the space to the condition in which we found it.

The team briefing format was changed a bit and focused on bigger picture topics versus the minutiae such as laundry hours in the Village. Jeff Howard, USOC Media operations, oversaw the presentation and scheduling; he also oversaw the Olympic Ambassador Program. All in all it was well received; we kept discussions to just an hour and spoke on leadership, expectations, Opening Ceremony and Podium apparel and behavior and then finished with an inspiring "amazing awaits" video.

I consider this one of the best team processing staffs and sites ever. Everyone got along for 30 days and really looked after each other. Looking ahead, I would suggest the following:

•Try to find and use a college campus – living on campus, even in a dorm, for 30+ days was preferable to a hotel.

•Consider using the team processing environment as part of sponsor activation. There are opportunities to have athletes sign banners and other items that could be used as thank-you gifts or sold as fundraisers for USOC programs. We did have visitors from Nike, Bank of America and AT&T but could accommodate more visitors and events.

•Evaluate what team is processing when, and with what other team. How the teams mix is critical to their overall experience and the daily flow. Having men's basketball come through by themselves on a Saturday was a great outcome. They were not rushed and there was minimal outside interference.

503

AN OLYMPIC VOLUNTEER LOOKS AT THE NATIONAL FLAGS OF SOME OF THE PARTICIPATING OLYMJPIC COUNTRIES | *MICHAEL KAPPELER/AFP/GETTY IMAGES*

USA BUSINESS & HOSPITALITY CENTER | JERRI FOEHRKOLB
– MANAGING DIRECTOR, MEETINGS & EVENTS SERVICES

The USA House Business and Hospitality Center (aka USA House) serves as an integrated hospitality program for our key constituents; sponsors, suppliers, licensees, donors, National Governing Bodies, International Relations & Chicago 2016, Olympians and U.S. Olympic Team Members. The House includes such services for our guests as: live Olympic Games feed, internet café, business center, concierge desk, private meeting space, press conference area, retail store with U.S. Olympic Team merchandise and food & beverage service throughout the day.

The USA House provides a platform for our partners to showcase their products & services, conduct business meetings and/or press conferences, host special events as well as interact with Olympians and the U.S Olympic Team Members.

At past summer games the USOC's hospitality plan has consisted of two locations. The OCOG (with the IOC approval) has invited the USOC to purchase into the sponsor hospitality village which we did in Sydney and Athens. In Beijing, we made the decision to not participate in the village at the Olympic Green due to the physical location of the space within the Green, costs, limited accessibility by the guests. This was due to the policies and procedures set by BOCOG for the venue.

Once the USA House location was finalized (Jasmine Restaurant & Lounge) and our program outlined the USA House staff worked with the NGB Team Leaders at each of the Team Leader meetings to discuss their needs to host meetings and events at the USA House beyond their normal access provided by the USOC. Based on those discussions, we incorporated their requests for special events, VIP visits, and administrative functions into our master calendar for the House. Correspondence is sent out to the rest of our partners as well and similar meetings and scheduling takes place with them to help meet their needs at the Games; especially our U.S. Olympic Team sponsors and suppliers.

Jasmine Restaurant and Lounge was chosen as our USA House Business and Hospitality location in Beijing because of its location (proximity to the Beijing Hilton, the USOC Headquarters, the HPC, the Olympic Village and the Beijing City Center), square footage and general layout to meet all of our needs. We had a very strong relationship with Jasmine Restaurant ownership, which helped us coordinate other vendors providing needed services for the House. The USOC brought in our own catering service from the U.S., Framboise Catering. Jasmine Restaurant acted as a liaison with local companies providing cleaning, security, painting, electrical work and other services. Although we were able to effectively communicate with Jasmine Restaurant staff when meeting face-to-face, we found that long-distance communication suffered from some language barrier and they were more inclined to get projects moving and completed when we were there in person.

We also had very strong relationships with many of our U.S. Olympic Team partners, particularly those that extended their marketing platforms within the USA House. These included AT&T, Hilton, J&J (Splenda), Anheuser-Busch, and Lenovo. A number of partners hosted special events at the USA House; Kleenex, McDonalds and Hilton to name a few.

This year's USA House was the most successful to date. We had over 16,000 guests utilize the facility including the likes of Former President Bush, Tom Brokaw, Dick Ebersol, Henry Kissinger, Vince Vaughn, David Schwimmer, Janet Evans and Bob Beamon.

When managing a 42,000 square foot facility and putting over 1,000 people through the House on certain days there are bound to be situations that arise so troubleshooting is a given in such a complex and busy environment. We prepare for it as best we can by reviewing previous USA House experiences and by working closely with our primary vendors. This year we dealt with leaky roofs due to heavy rains, late deliveries, language and cultural barriers with staff, etc. Our staff has to think on their feet, not get overwhelmed and make the best decisions they can under the circumstances.

In planning for future USA House implementation, we need to work with IT to develop a better calendar/event tracking system so that we do not over extend ourselves. In addition, we need to develop a more structured but fluid transition between our morning and evening staff shifts. We will look to institute a brief but effective meeting between key staff members on each shift in order to transfer important information from one to the other so our operation is as seamless as possible